Complete Course

South-Western

College Keyboarding Enhanced

Charles H. Duncan, Ed.D.
Eastern Michigan University

Susie H. VanHuss, Ph.D.
University of South Carolina

S. ElVon Warner, Ed.D.
S. E. Warner Software, Inc.
Salt Lake City, Utah

Contributing Authors:

Connie Forde, Ph.D.
Mississippi State University

Donna L. Woo
Cypress College, California

JOIN US ON THE INTERNET
WWW: http://www.thomson.com
EMAIL: findit@kiosk.thomson.com A service of I(T)P®

South-Western Educational Publishing
an International Thomson Publishing company I(T)P®

Cincinnati • Albany, NY • Belmont, CA • Bonn • Boston • Detroit • Johannesburg • London • Madrid
Melbourne • Mexico City • New York • Paris • Singapore • Tokyo • Toronto • Washington

Managing Editor: Karen Schmohe
Project Manager—Keyboarding: Jane Phelan
Production Services: CompuText Productions, Inc.
Production Coordinator: Jane Congdon
Manufacturing Coordinator: Carol Chase
Marketing Coordinator: Tim Gleim
Photo Editor: Alix Parson
Design Coordinator: Michelle Kunkler

Photo Credits:
Cover ©Walter Wick Photography
Level openers: Location courtesy of Northwestern Mutual Life, 312 Walnut Street, Cincinnati, Ohio
p. xvi: Greg Grosse
pp. 18, 49, 51, 65, 84, 147, 149, 169, 173, 197, 238 (a), 252, 253, 265, 275, 290, 335, 368, 369 (a), 374: © 1995, PhotoDisc Inc.
p. 16: Courtesy of International Business Machines Corporation
p. 105, 306: Herman Miller, Inc.
p. 133: Michael Philip Manheim/Photo Network
p. 155, 220, 350: Reprinted with permission of Compaq Computer Corporation. All rights reserved.
p. 202: Scanned photo provided by Eastman Kodak Company
p. 203, 239 (b), 353: Photo courtesy of Hewlett-Packard Company
p. 236: Alan Brown/Photonics
p. 238 (b): © Jeff Greenberg
p. 250: Tiffany Office Furniture
p. 257: Courtesy of Videotowne, Cincinnati, Ohio
p. 288: Courtesy of Sayett Technology
p. 328: Courtesy of AT&T
p. 338: Dictaphone Corp.
p. 369 (b): Good Samaritan Hospital
p. 386: Photonics Graphics

I(T)P®
International Thomson Publishing

South-Western Educational Publishing is a division of International Thomson Publishing Inc. The ITP logo is a registered trademark used herein under license by South-Western Educational Publishing.

ISBN: 0-538-71538-3
1 2 3 4 5 6 7 8 9 H 03 02 01 00 99 98 97

Printed in the United States of America

Preface

Keyboarding is the foundation skill for today's workers. It is a skill needed for success in virtually every career. The keyboard, once used primarily by secretaries and clerks, is now a tool used extensively by managers, scientists, engineers, and a host of other workers. Attached to a powerful computer, the keyboard provides access to information worldwide.

Keyboarding is a skill. As with any skill, you will be successful if you apply proper techniques and meaningful practice in each session.

COLLEGE KEYBOARDING, Complete Course, is designed to help you achieve the following goals:

- Key the alphabetic and numeric keys by touch using proper techniques.
- Format letters, memoranda, reports, tables, and administrative documents properly.
- Produce documents efficiently.
- Apply decision making to language arts, formatting, and document handling.

Many subskills—such as the ability to use language effectively and to evaluate the quality of your work—are embodied in these goals. Emphasis is placed on applying these skills so that you can use the keyboard to facilitate communication.

What's New in the Enhanced Version?

Thirty-two new pages and several new features have been added to the Complete Course to address word processing and ensure mastery of formatting skills.

Welcome to Windows. A three-page introduction to *Windows 3.1*/*Windows 95* has been added to the Appendix to get you up and running.

Word Processing Workshop. An 11-page workshop presents a brief overview and activities for learning the basic functions for creating, editing, and formatting documents using the popular *Windows*-based programs. These functions can also be applied to Projects 1 and 2, which follow the workshop.

Selkirk Communications—Project 1. This in-depth project gives you a chance to work independently and apply the keyboarding, formatting, and word processing skills you have learned in Lessons 1-60. Options are included for extending your skills using features such as Copy, Paste, and Bullets.

Pommery Air Service, Inc., Business Plan—
...ject 2. This project applies many of the report skills
...essons 61-120. Additional word processing fea-
...he workshop can be integrated.

File Management Workshop. The exercises apply basic file operations for *Windows 3.1* and *Windows 95.*

New Topics. A special segment called News and Views highlights issues or topics of current interest. Exercises to prevent repetitive stress injury are included.

Software Support

- *Alphanumeric* keyboarding software will help you learn the keys by touch and build a strong foundation skill. Numeric keypad is included. This software correlates to Lessons 1-30.
- *MicroPace Pro* (for *Windows*) or *MicroPace Plus* (for DOS) are timed writing and skill-building software. Error diagnostics is an option. Timings available for measurement are labeled with an icon.
- Word processing functions that may be applied within various documents are identified with a word processing icon.

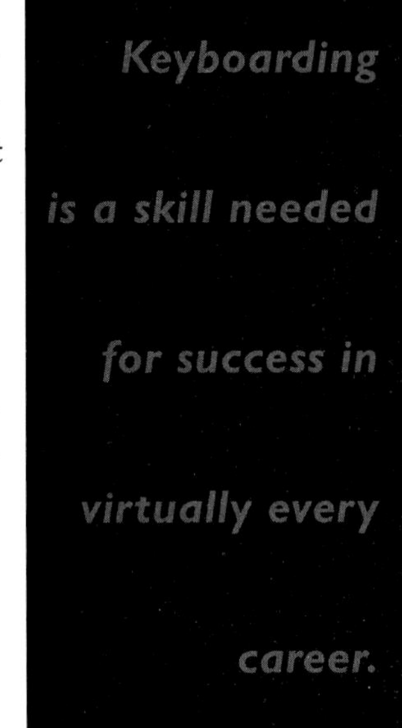
Keyboarding
is a skill needed
for success in
virtually every
career.

Icons

Additional icons appear throughout this textbook; each conveys a specific message:

OS Appearing in Lessons 19-30, this formatting exercise may be completed in the open screen of *Alphanumeric* software. You also have the option of using word processing software.

This icon indicates that a timed writing is available on the diskette labeled Timed Writings Selected from *College Keyboarding*, 13th edition. This disk may be used with either *MicroPace Plus* or *MicroPace Pro* (for *Windows*).

LA The letter(s) in the icon indicates the level of difficulty of timed writings: Lessons 1-30 are labeled E (easy); Lessons 31-45, LA (low average); and Lessons 46-60, A (average).

The authors gratefully acknowledge the contributions made by instructors and students who have used prior editions of this textbook.

Table of Contents

Level 3 Formatting Business Correspondence, Lessons 61-90

Level 4 Formatting Reports, Tables, and Administrative Documents, Lessons 91-120

Know Your Computer

Computers consist of these essential parts:

1. **Central processing unit:** The internal operating unit, including the processing unit, memory chips, disk drives, etc.
2. **Disk drive:** A unit that reads and writes onto disks.
3. **Monitor:** A screen that displays information as it is keyed and messages from the computer called *prompts*.
4. **Mouse:** Input device. *Windows* software is designed to be used with a mouse.
5. **Keyboard:** Input device for entering alphabetic and numeric data and symbols as well as special keys for entering commands.

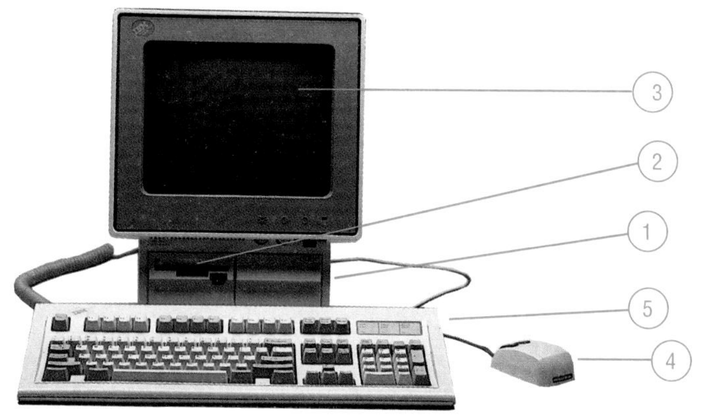

Monitor

The monitor, or screen, displays information as it is keyed and messages from the computer called **prompts**. Most monitors have a separate on/off switch.

Adjustments for brightness and contrast can be made on most monitors. Monitors are either monochrome or color. A monochrome monitor displays in one color and a color monitor displays many colors.

The System Unit (CPU)

The system unit is the box that houses the Central Processing Unit (CPU), memory chips, disk drives, and the on/off switch.

The on/off switch may be located on the right side of the system unit or on the front side, depending on the model of computer you are using. The computer is turned on by moving the switch to the on position.

The CPU, or "brain" of the computer, is a processor chip that controls the keyboard, mouse, monitor, and printer and performs all of the computing instructions.

The CPU also includes memory. Random Access Memory (RAM) stores data while it is being processed. Programs, such as word processing, are loaded or read into RAM. The amount of RAM determines the programs that can be run.

Disk Drives

Disk drives enable the user to save data entered in the computer's memory onto a disk and to read information from the disk drives into the memory of the computer for processing.

A computer must have at least one disk drive. If it has only one drive, it is designated as drive A. If the computer contains two disk drives, the drive on top is designated drive A and the one on the bottom drive B. If the two drives are side by side, the drive on the left is drive A and the one on the right is drive B. Computers today generally contain hard disks, which are completely enclosed in the system unit. Hard disks are referred to as drive C. More elaborate computers contain built-in zip drives, usually designated drive D.

Printers

A printer provides a paper printout of the copy keyed. A variety of printers are found in schools, such as dot matrix, ink-jet, daisy wheel, and laser. The quality of print that is produced by each of these printers differs considerably. Consult your instructor about the location and operation of the printer you will be using.

Keyboard Arrangement

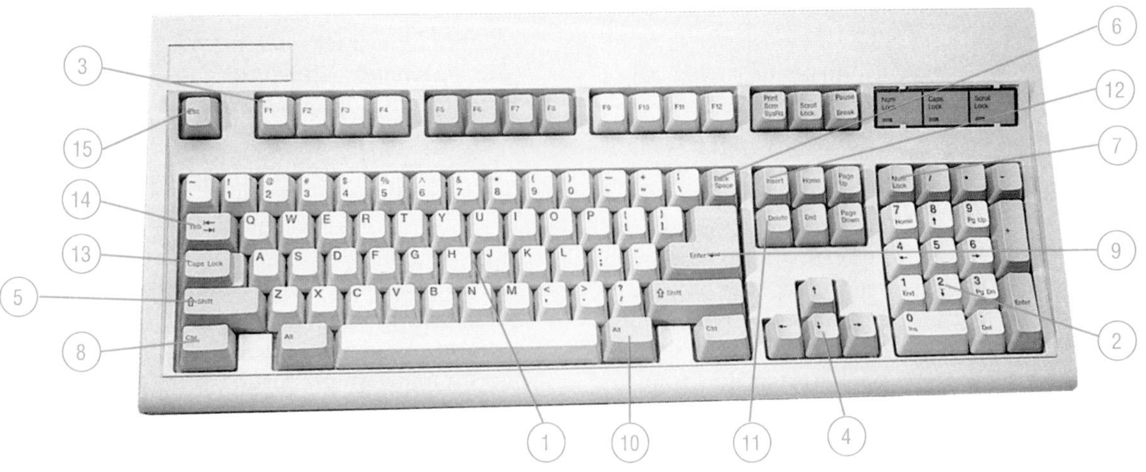

1. **Alphanumeric keys:** Center portion of the keyboard.
2. **Numeric keypad:** Calculator-type keys used for entering statistical data. To turn on the keypad, press the NUM LOCK key.
3. **Function keys:** Perform a software function; used by themselves or with other keys.
4. **Arrow keys:** Move the insertion point.
5. **SHIFT:** Makes lowercase letters uppercase.
6. **BACKSPACE:** Deletes the character to the left of the insertion point.
7. **NUM LOCK:** Switches the numeric keypad between numeric and editing.
8. **CTRL:** Expands the use of function keys.
9. **ENTER:** Advances the insertion point to the next line. ENTER is often used to execute a command.
10. **ALT (Alternate):** Used with another key to execute a function.
11. **DELETE:** Erases text to the right of the insertion point.
12. **INSERT:** Toggles the software between insert mode and typeover/overstrike mode.
13. **CAPS LOCK:** Capitalizes all alphabetic characters.
14. **TAB:** Moves the cursor to a preset position.
15. **ESC (Escape):** Exits a menu or dialog box in word processing software.

Keyboard

The keyboard is used to enter instructions and text into the CPU. Most keyboards resemble the keyboard shown above.

Alphanumeric keys. The center portion of the keyboard contains the alphanumeric keys. The symbols may vary slightly in location, but the letter and number keys are in the same location as those of a typewriter.

Numeric keypad. The numeric keypad, with keys arranged similar to those of a calculator, is used for entering statistical data or doing arithmetic calculations. To activate the keypad, press the NUM LOCK key.

Function keys. Function keys are located across the top of the keyboard or along the left. They help you perform specific functions depending upon the software. Function keys will not place numbers or letters on the screen.

Cursor movement. The cursor is a symbol on the screen, such as a block or underline, that indicates where the next character will be displayed. The cursor usually flashes so that it can be identified easily. The cursor moves one space to the right as text is entered.

Software

The computer cannot function by itself; it needs a set of instructions to direct it. Such instructions are called software. Software comes in two forms: operating systems software and applications software.

Operating systems software. The operating systems software directs the operations of the computer, such as the input, printing, and storing of data.

Applications software. Applications software enables the computer to perform specific functions or applications. Word processing software such as *WordPerfect* and *College Keyboarding Alphanumeric* software are examples of applications software.

Disks

Disks store information entered into the computer. Storage disks are available in various sizes. The most prevalent sizes are 5.25 inches and 3.5 inches. The 3.5-inch disks hold twice as much data as the 5.25-inch disks.

Disks are coated with a magnetic substance; therefore, they must be handled carefully.

- Do not touch exposed areas of the disk.
- Keep 5.25" disk in a protective paper jacket when not in use.
- Use a felt-tip pen to write on the disk label.
- Keep disk away from magnetized objects, heat, and liquids.

Know Your Software: Alphanumeric

With the full-featured *College Keyboarding Alphanumeric* software, you can use the power of your IBM-compatible computer to learn alphabetic and numeric keyboarding. The 30 software lessons correlate to the first 30 lessons in the *College Keyboarding* textbook.

The lessons contain a variety of activities, including practice drills, textbook keying, and timings. Many lessons introduce new keys—letters, punctuation, numbers, and symbols—while others review what you have learned. Some lessons include document formatting exercises performed in the Open Screen, a simple word processor. Others contain a challenging keyboarding game.

You will key from the screen and from the textbook, with software prompts to guide you. The software tracks your performance and provides feedback. You can display or print daily your cumulative progress reports.

Loading the Alphanumeric Software

Follow these steps to load the software:

1. To save your data to disk, have a formatted disk ready. If you plan to save on a hard drive, create a directory or subdirectory for data storage. You will enter the name of this directory or subdirectory as the pathname in the configuration options.
2. If the software is installed on a hard drive, change to the directory where the program is stored and key **control** at the C> prompt. If you are running the software from the program disk, key **control** at the A> prompt.

Setting the Configuration Options

Press ENTER to move through the opening screens until you see the Drive and Pathname screen (Figure 1). Fill in drive and path [drive (a); path (\)] and strike F1. Follow instructions until you reach Create New Records File. Fill in appropriate information and strike F1. The first time you use the program, you will set the configuration options. Later, you can press ESC at the opening screen to go directly to the Main menu. Insert your program disk and strike ENTER. The next screen is the Main menu.

Main Menu

You can access any feature of the *College Keyboarding Alphanumeric* software from the Main menu through the pull-down menus at the top—File, Lessons, and Open Screen. Choose one of these by using the left and right arrow keys and ENTER to select, or by striking the appropriate character. Striking ESC closes the pull-down menu and returns you to the Main menu.

Helpful instructions on how to use the software appear at the bottom of the screen. Notice that some of the configuration options you set are shown in the *Current* status line.

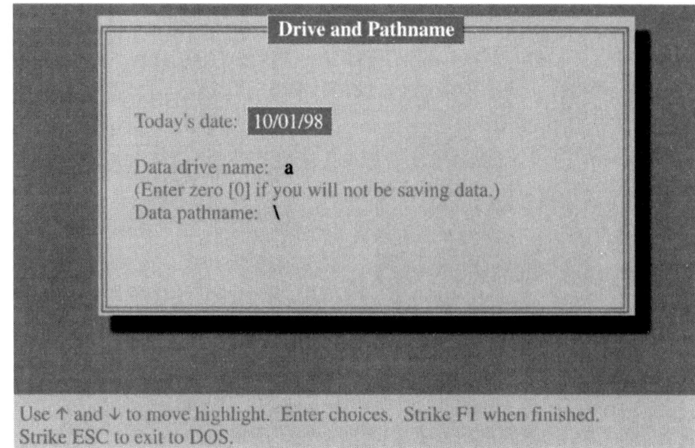

Figure 1: Drive and Pathname Screen

File Menu

The File menu lets you manage information. To save and print data, you must have selected these options on the Configuration Screen. An asterisk (*) beside an option indicates that it is available. Strike ESC to close the File menu.

Save records. Saves records to your data disk, including the exercises you have completed, your speed scores, and the drill lines keyed.

Print lesson report. Prints a report of your performance on a specific lesson and lets you print the drill lines keyed.

Display summary report. Shows which lesson parts you have completed and, for timed writings, your average keying speeds.

Print summary report. Prints the summary report and gives you an option to print the drill lines.

Print open screens. Prints files saved in the Open Screen.

Delete open screens. Deletes files saved in the Open Screen.

Change configuration. Lets you change the configuration options you set.

Quit. Ends the program, performs an automatic save of your records, and takes you to the DOS prompt.

Lesson Menu

All 30 lessons on the software are listed in the Lesson pull-down menu. Scroll down to the bottom of the box to see more lessons. An asterisk (*) beside a lesson indicates that you have completed it. Strike ESC at any time to close the Lesson menu.

When you choose a lesson, the menu for this lesson appears beside the Lessons menu, as shown in Figure 2. After you complete an exercise, the program automatically advances to the next one. You can strike ESC at any time to return to the menu, but if you quit in the middle of an exercise, no score is retained.

The exercises differ from lesson to lesson, providing a variety of activities for skill building. Each type of exercise is explained below.

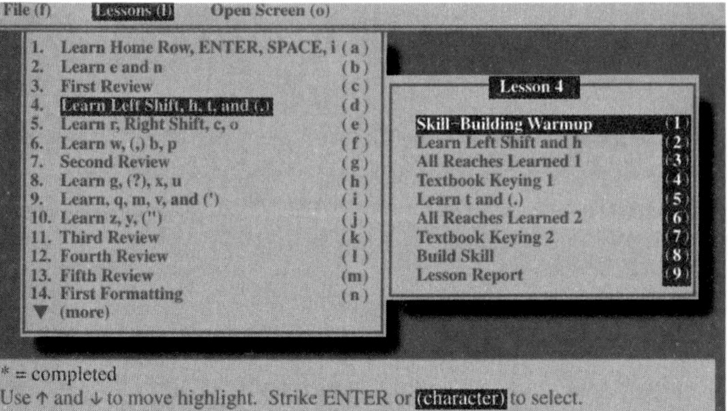

Figure 2: Lessons Menu

Skill-Building Warmup. The warmup (Figure 3) reinforces the learned keystrokes. Screen cues give instructions, remind you to use good techniques, and tell you how fast you are keying.

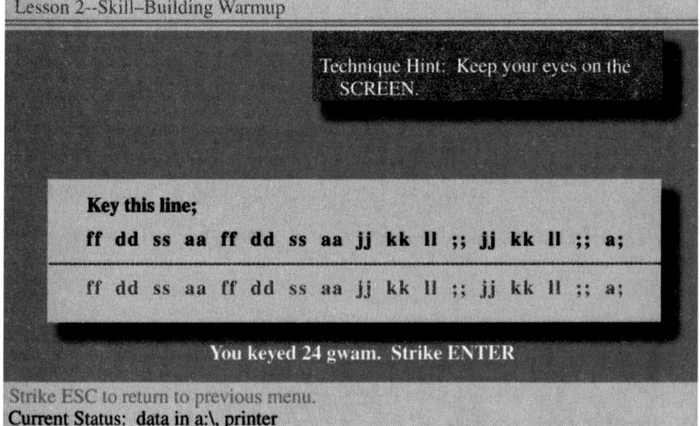

Figure 3: Skill-Building Warmup

Learn New Keys. On-screen graphics demonstrate the keyreach. Drill lines appear on screen.

All Reaches Learned. On-screen prompts remind you how to make the keyreaches, with drill lines for quick review.

Improve Keystroking. Drills emphasize specific keys and good techniques. The software provides technique hints, instructions, and feedback. You will have three opportunities to key a word correctly.

Textbook Keying. The software directs you to key an exercise from the textbook. There is space to key 12 lines. Availability of the backspace key depends on the configuration options. You can print or repeat the exercise.

Build Skill. The software times you and reports results as you key drills from the screen. Technique hints appear, along with a speed goal in gross words a minute *(gwam)*.

Game. The game challenges you to meet a speed goal as you key drill lines from the screen. A measurement bar and screen prompts show your progress.

Lesson Report. After the last exercise in a lesson, a lesson report appears showing which exercises were completed and, if applicable, your speed scores. The software then asks if you wish to go on to the next lesson.

The Open Screen

The Open Screen (Figure 4) is a simple word processor available from the Main menu. An icon (shown above) in the textbook identifies timed writings and formatting exercises to be completed in the Open Screen. The software will tell you when to complete these exercises. Use **Timed keyboarding** for taking timed writings and **Keyboarding practice** for entering any type of document. Documents entered in the Open Screen may be retrieved, edited, and printed. Instructions are available on-screen.

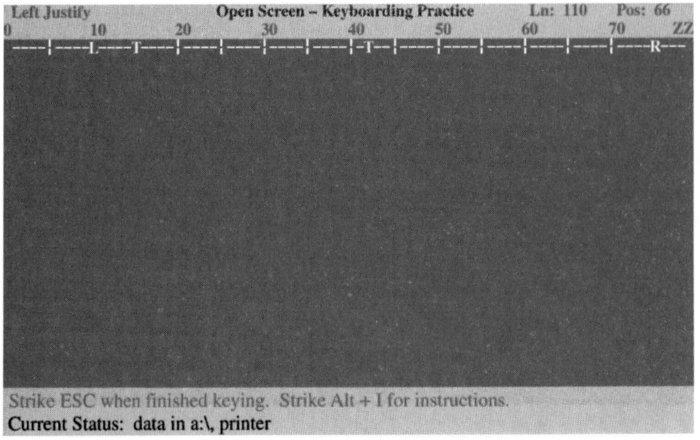

Figure 4: Open Screen

The Open Screen has line and position indicators in the upper right corner to assist you in formatting documents. The editing and formatting features include the following:

Backspace key. Deletes the character to the left of the cursor.

Cursor. Arrow keys and Page Up/Page Down move the cursor.

Wordwrap. Text automatically moves to the next line.

Centering. Press **Alt + C** to center left-justified text.

Formatting (margins and tabs). Press **Alt + F** to use the ruler at the top of the screen to set margins and tabs. Default margins are set at 10 and 75. Position the cursor and strike the letters **L** and **R** to set left and right margins. Press the TAB key to set or clear a tab. Default tabs are set at 15 and 42 (center).

Strike ESC when you are finished keying a document in the Open Screen. You may then print or save a document, or clear the screen and start again. Note that you can also print a saved Open Screen document from the File menu.

Quitting the Alphanumeric Software

Use the Quit option under the File menu to exit. If you have been saving data, the Quit option automatically saves your records.

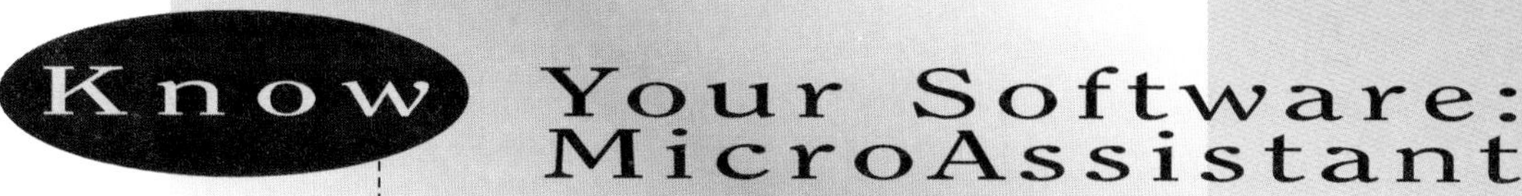

Know Your Software: MicroAssistant

Introduction to MicroAssistant Software

MicroAssistant is production software that will enable you to key and format any exercise in this text. It has features for timing, checking, as well as recording your progress on drills, timed writings, production exercises, and tests. You will receive immediate feedback on your progress while you develop keyboarding and formatting skills.

To use MicroAssistant, you will need the following:

1. A program disk.
2. A template disk.
3. A formatted storage disk for saving activities.

The program disk and template may be loaded on a hard drive or network; additionally, documents may be saved to a hard drive or network—check with your instructor.

Loading MicroAssistant

1. Format a disk for storing your work. If you plan to save your work on the hard drive, your instructor will need to identify the subdirectory that has been set up for this purpose. (You will enter the name of the subdirectory as the *pathname.*)
2. If the software is loaded on a hard drive or network, change to the directory where the program is stored and key **control**. If you are running the program from the program disk, key **control** at the A>.

Configuration Menu

Your instructor will prepare a Class Options File prior to your using MicroAssistant. If the program cannot find this file, it will terminate. The first time you use MicroAssistant, you will need to create a student record. Check with your instructor to determine if an ID code has been assigned to you. Follow these steps to configure your system:

1. Enter a three-digit ID code. Remember your ID code; you will need to enter this code each time you use the program.
2. Enter your name. Once accepted as correct, your name will be permanently written to your student record. All your work will be identified by your name and ID code.
3. Follow the prompts on the screen. You can change the options if your instructor has given you this right (F1).
4. Enter your ID code when prompted and strike ENTER.
5. Review the preliminary information screens and strike ENTER. You may press F1 to bypass these screens the next time you use the software. The Main menu is now displayed.

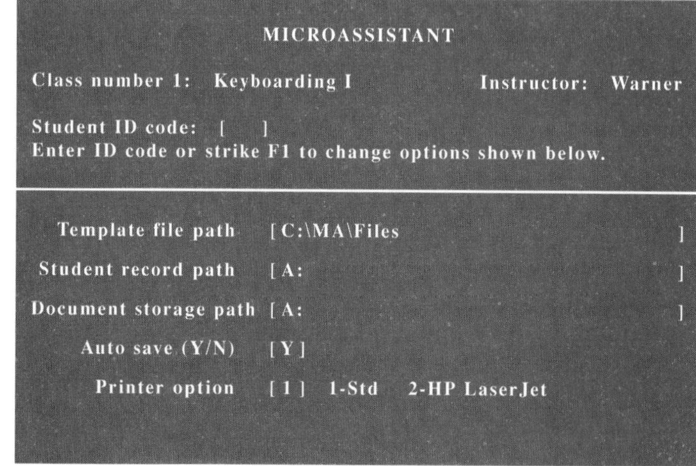

Figure 1: Configuration Menu

Main Menu

From the Main menu you can select a lesson, enter the Open Screen, display or print your performance record, or quit the program. See Figure 2 on p. xii.

To select a lesson, key the number of the lesson and strike ENTER. If the activities are found in a workshop, the Laboratory Materials, or an Achievement Test, enter the letter and number of the workshop/activity. Examples are shown below.

S1	Skill-Building Workshop 1
C1	Communication Workshop 1
F1	Formatting Workshop 1
E1	Enrichment Activity 1 (from Laboratory Materials)
A1	Achievement Test 1

```
MICROASSISTANT

Entry lesson number: 31          (Alt-C=Clean field.)
or enter one of the following codes:

O - Open screen
D - Display student performance record
P - Print student performance record
U - Print a saved document
V - Delete a saved document
W - Prepare a backup file of saved documents

Q - Quit

If the exercise is found in a nonnumbered lesson, enter the letter
and number of the activity (for example, C1=Communication Workshop 1):
A=Achievement     E=Enrichment     S=Skill building
C=Communication  F=Formatting
```

Figure 2: Main Menu

Lesson Menu

After you select a lesson, the Lesson menu will display. The subparts of the menu correspond directly with the lesson exercises in the text. Should an exercise contain more than one drill/document, they will be listed on another submenu.

You may return to the Main menu or quit the program from the Lesson menu.

```
LESSON NO: 31

A  Skill-building warmup
B  Straight copy skill building [OTM]
C  Compose at the keyboard
D  Business letters in block format
P  Print all parts of this lesson
U  Print a single lesson part
V  Delete a saved document
W  Prepare a backup of saved file
X  Exit this lesson

Enter Letter:
```

Figure 3: Lesson Menu

Entering a Lesson

Figure 4 displays the work screen. While creating or editing a document, you can use special function keys to format it. These keys are described briefly below.

F1 = Setup	Displays the default options for this exercise. The ability to change these defaults depends upon how your instructor has set the Class Options File.
F2 = Set Tab/Mar	Sets tabs and margins.
F3 = Help	Accesses all commands.
F5 = File	Loads, deletes, prints, or prepares a backup file. Displays or prints performance record (not available while keying an exercise).
F6 = Count-down timer	Sets the length of your timing (e.g., 3 minutes).
Alt + B = Bold	Turns bold on or off.
Alt + D = Delete line	Deletes a complete line of text.
Alt + I = Temporary left margin (indent)	Sets a temporary left margin 5 spaces from the left margin. Alt turns the function on and off.
Alt + U = Underline	Turns underline on or off.

When you have completed an exercise, MicroAssistant will automatically check and save the document. Both keyboarding and formatting errors may be displayed.

```
Page: 1   Line: 4   Space: 10   Spacing: SS
F6: Set count-down timer option

....|....▯....|....2....|....3....|....4....|....5....|....6....|....7....|....8
         L                                                         R

F1=Setup  F2=Tab/Mar  F3=Help  F5=File Menu  F7=Exit
Lesson 31  Part C  Page 70                              Insert
```

Figure 4: Work Screen

Handling Documents

Once a document is keyed, you can print it and save it to a formatted disk. It can then be retrieved, edited, saved, and printed again. An entire lesson may be printed from the Lesson menu or individual exercises may be printed using the File option (F5).

Documents may be printed with or without error identification. The document is printed with a three-line header, including the following information and more: your name, date, class; the status of various options, such as correction and the number of times the error checker was run; your GWPM and errors (keying and formatting).

Production Tests

Documents can be combined and graded as one production test. This option is available on the Lesson menu of lessons that contain measurement. You will need to set the timer for the appropriate time.

Student Performance Record

While you use MicroAssistant, a record of your work is maintained, including:

- Five best straight-copy official timed writings (labeled OFT on the Lesson menu).
- Five best rough-draft, script, or statistical timed writings.
- The number of attempts at each lesson part.
- Results (errors, words, percent complete) for each production job.

Your student performance record may be displayed or printed from the Main menu.

Your Electronic Typewriter

The parts of an electronic typewriter are illustrated at the right. Because all typewriters have similar parts, you probably will be able to identify the parts on your equipment from this illustration; but if you have the manufacturer's booklet for your typewriter, use it to locate each machine part identified.

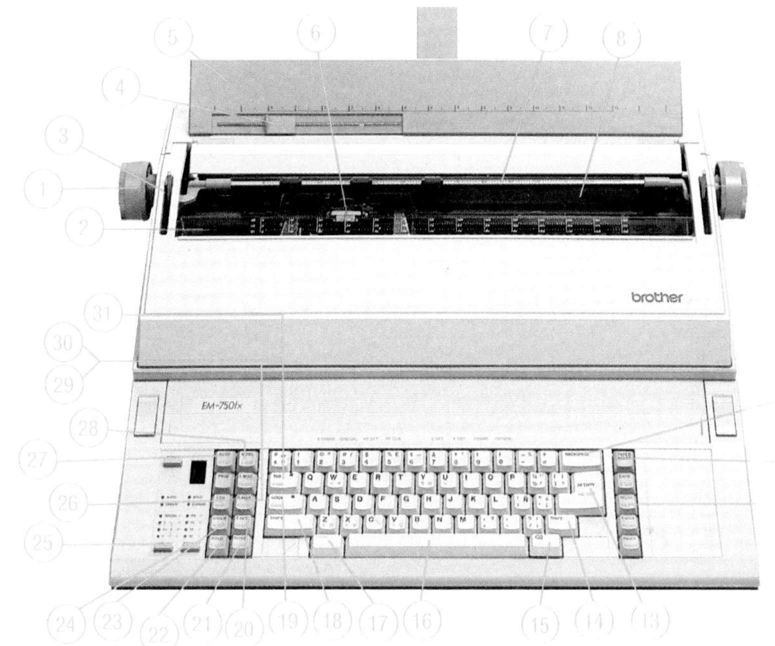

1. **Left platen knob**—used to turn platen manually (not on some models).
2. **Line-of-writing (margin) scale**—indicates pitch scales (10, 12, and 15); may indicate margin positions and the printing point.
3. **Paper-bail release lever**—used to pull paper bail away from platen.
4. **Paper guide**—used to position paper for insertion.
5. **Paper support**— supports paper when it is in the machine.
6. **Print carrier**—includes ribbon cassette, correction tape, carrier adjust lever, and printing mechanism.
7. **Paper bail and rollers**—used to hold paper against platen.
8. **Platen (cylinder)**—provides a hard surface against which the print mechanism strikes.
9. **Paper release lever**—used to adjust position of paper.
10. **Backspace**—used to move printing point to left one space.
11. **Paper insert**—used to feed paper to specified loading position.
12. **Relocate (RELOC)**—used to return printing point to previous position after corrections are made.
13. **Return**—used to return printing point to left margin and to move paper up.
14. **Right shift**—used with keys controlled by the left hand to key capitals or symbols.
15. **Correction**—used to erase a character.
16. **Space bar**—used to move printing point to the right one space at a time.
17. **Code**—used simultaneously with another key to cause that key to perform a special function.
18. **Left shift**—used with keys controlled by the right hand to key capitals or symbols.
19. **Caps Lock**—used to key text in ALL CAPS (capital letters).
20. **Tab set**—used to set tabulator stops (tabs); tab clear may be same key on some models.
21. **Repeat**—used to repeat a previously struck key or function.
22. **Bold**—used to print boldface characters.
23. **Underline (UNDLN)**—used to print underlined characters.
24. **Pitch select**—used to set type size (10-, 12-, or 15-pitch) to correspond to the printing device being used.
25. **Line-space selector**—sets machine to advance the paper 1, 1.5, 2, or 3 lines when return key is used.
26. **Centering**—used to center text automatically between the left and right margins.
27. **Auto**—set to return the printing point automatically to the left margin, next line when it reaches the right margin.
28. **Margin release**—used to move printing point beyond the margin settings.
29. **Left margin (L MAR)**—used to set left margin.
30. **Right margin (R MAR)**—used to set right margin.
31. **Tabulator (Tab)**—used to move printing point to tab locations.

Know Repetitive Stress Injury

Repetitive stress injury (RSI) is a result of repeated movement of a particular part of the body. A familiar example is "tennis elbow." Of more concern to keyboard users is the form of RSI called **carpal tunnel syndrome (CTS)**.

CTS is an inflammatory disease that develops gradually and affects the wrist, hands, and forearms. Blood vessels, tendons, and nerves pass into the hand through the carpal tunnel (see illustration below). If any of these structures enlarge or if the walls of the tunnel narrow, the median nerve is pinched, and CTS symptoms may result.

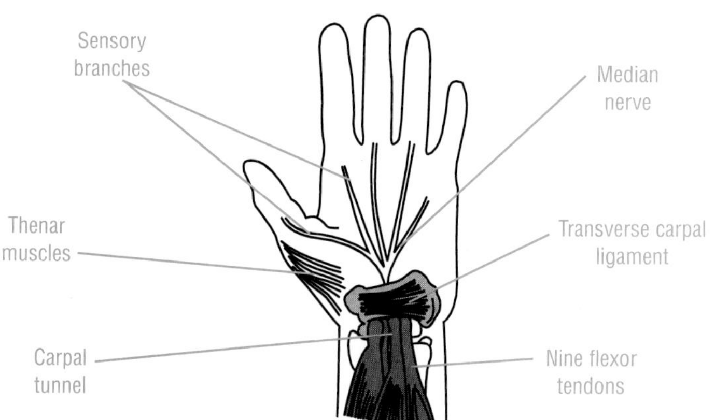

Palm view of left hand

Symptoms of RSI/CTS

CTS symptoms include numbness in the hand; tingling or burning in the hand, wrist, or elbow; severe pain in the forearm, elbow, or shoulder; and difficulty in gripping objects. Symptoms usually appear during sleeping hours, probably because many people sleep with their wrists flexed.

If not properly treated, the pressure on the median nerve, which controls the thumb, forefinger, middle finger, and half the ring finger (see top right), causes severe pain. The pain can radiate into the forearm, elbow, or shoulder and can require surgery or result in permanent damage or paralysis.

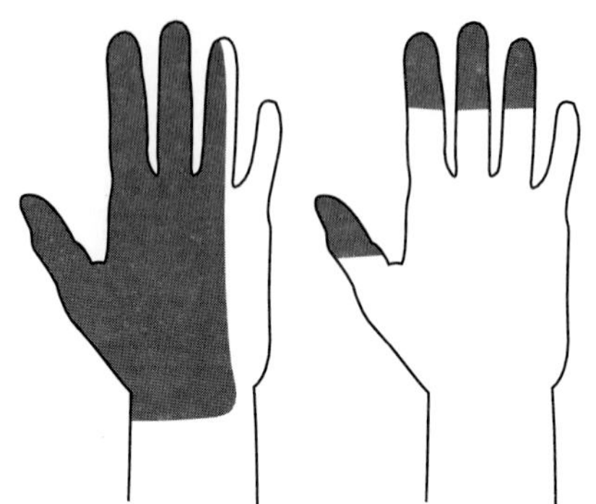

Areas affected by carpal tunnel syndrome

Causes of RSI/CTS

RSI/CTS often develops in workers whose physical routine is unvaried. Common occupational factors include: (1) using awkward posture, (2) using poor techniques, (3) performing tasks with wrists bent (see below), (4) using improper equipment, (5) working at a rapid pace, (6) not taking rest breaks, and (7) not doing exercises that promote graceful motion and good techniques.

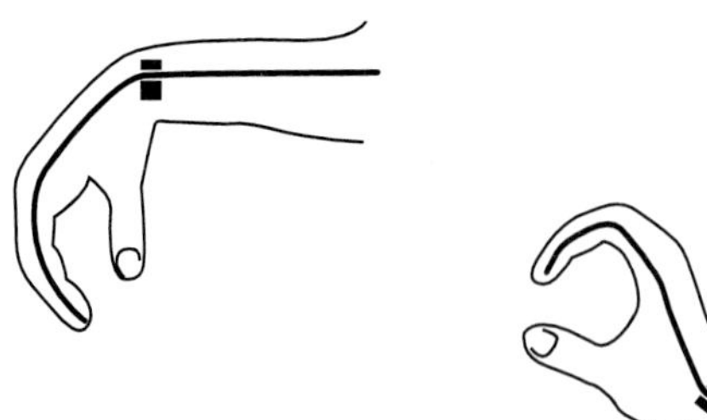

Improper wrist positions for keystroking

Other factors associated with CTS include a person's genetic makeup; the aging process; hormonal influences; obesity; chronic diseases such as rheumatoid arthritis and gout; misaligned fractures; and hobbies such as gardening, knitting, and woodworking that require the same motion over and over. CTS affects over three times more women than men, with 60 percent of the affected persons between the ages of 30 and 60.

Reducing the Risk of RSI/CTS

Carpal tunnel syndrome is frequently a health concern for workers who use a computer keyboard or mouse. The risk of developing CTS is less for computer keyboard operators who use proper furniture or equipment, keyboarding techniques, posture, and/or muscle-stretching exercises than for those who do not.

Keyboard users can reduce the risk of developing RSI/CTS by taking these precautions:

1. Arrange the workstation correctly:
   a. Position the keyboard directly in front of the chair.
   b. Keep the front edge of the keyboard even with the edge of the desk or table so that the wrist movement will not be restricted while you are keying.
   c. Position the keyboard at elbow height.
   d. Position the monitor about 18 to 24 inches from your eyes with the top edge of the display screen at eye level.
   e. Position the mouse next to and at the same height as the computer keyboard and as close to the body as possible.
2. Use a proper chair and sit correctly:
   a. Use a straight-backed chair, or adjust your chair so that it will not yield when you lean back.
   b. Use a seat that allows you to keep your feet flat on the floor while you are keying. Use a footrest if your feet cannot rest flat on the floor.
   c. Sit erect and as far back in the seat as possible.
3. Use correct arm and wrist positions and movement:
   a. Keep your forearms parallel to the floor and level with the keyboard so that your wrists will be in a flat, neutral position rather than flexed upward or downward.
   b. Keep arms near the side of your body in a relaxed position.
4. Use proper keyboarding techniques:
   a. Keep your fingers curved and upright over the home keys.
   b. Keep wrists and forearms from touching or resting on any surface while keying.
   c. Strike each key lightly using the fingertip. Do not use too much pressure or hold the keys down.
5. When using a keyboard or mouse, take short breaks. A rest of one to two minutes every hour is appropriate. Natural breaks in keyboarding action of several seconds' duration also help.
6. Exercise the neck, shoulder, arm, wrist, and fingers before beginning to key each day and often during the workday (see Precaution 5). Suggested exercises for keyboard users are described below. You can do all the exercises while sitting at your workstation.

Exercises for Keyboard Users

1. **Strengthen finger muscles.** (See Drill 1 on p. xvi.) Open your hands, extend your fingers wide, and hold with muscles tense for two or three seconds; close the fingers into a tight fist with thumb on top, holding for two or three seconds; relax the fingers as you straighten them. Repeat 10 times. Additional finger drills are shown on p. xvi.
2. **Strengthen the muscles in the carpal tunnel area.** While sitting with your arms comfortably at your side and hands in a fist, rotate your hands inward from the wrist. Repeat this motion 10 to 15 times; then rotate outward from the wrist 10 to 15 times. Extend your fingers and repeat the movements for the same number of times.
3. **Loosen forearms.** With both wrists held in a neutral position (not bent) and the upper arm hanging vertically from the shoulder, rotate both forearms in 15 clockwise circles about the elbow. Repeat, making counterclockwise circles.
4. **Stretch the arms.** Interlace the fingers of both hands; with the palms facing forward, stretch your arms in front of you and hold for ten seconds. Repeat at least once. Next, with your fingers still interlaced, stretch your arms over your head and hold for ten seconds. Repeat at least once.
5. **Loosen elbows.** Place your hands on your shoulders with elbows facing forward; slowly move your arms in increasingly larger circles in front of you 10 to 15 times.
6. **Relieve shoulder tension.** Interlace the fingers of both hands behind your head and slowly move the elbows back, pressing the shoulder blades together; hold for ten seconds. Repeat at least once.

Finger Gymnastics

Brief daily practice of finger gymnastics will strengthen your finger muscles and increase the ease with which you key. Begin each keying period with this conditioning exercise. Choose two or more drills for this practice.

DRILL 1. Hands open, fingers wide, muscles tense. Close the fingers into a tight "fist," with thumb on top. Relax the fingers as you straighten them; repeat 10 times.

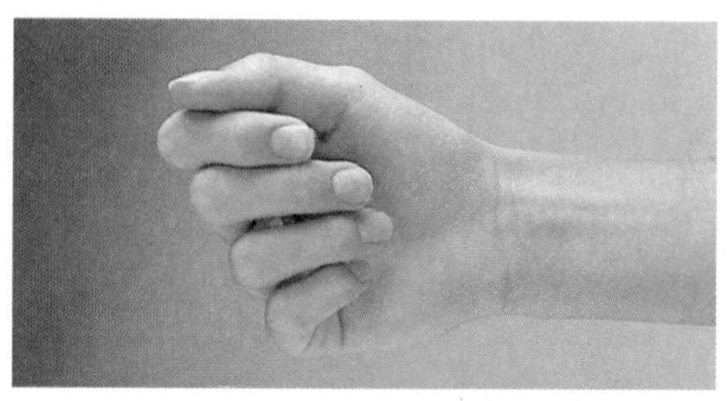

DRILL 2. Clench the fingers as shown. Hold the fingers in this position for a brief time; then extend the fingers, relaxing the muscles of fingers and hand. Repeat the movements slowly several times. Exercise both hands at the same time.

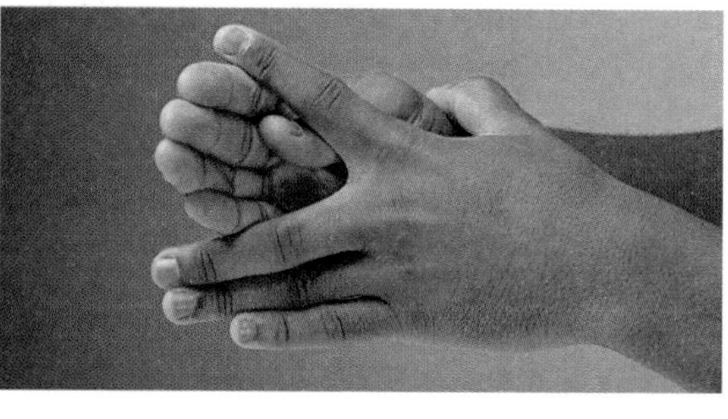

DRILL 3. Place the fingers and the thumb of one hand between two fingers of the other hand, and spread the fingers as much as possible. Spread all fingers of both hands.

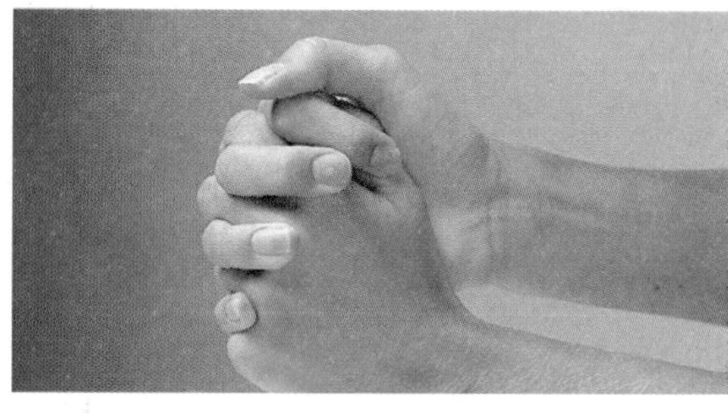

DRILL 4. Interlace the fingers of the two hands and wring the hands, rubbing the heel of the palms vigorously.

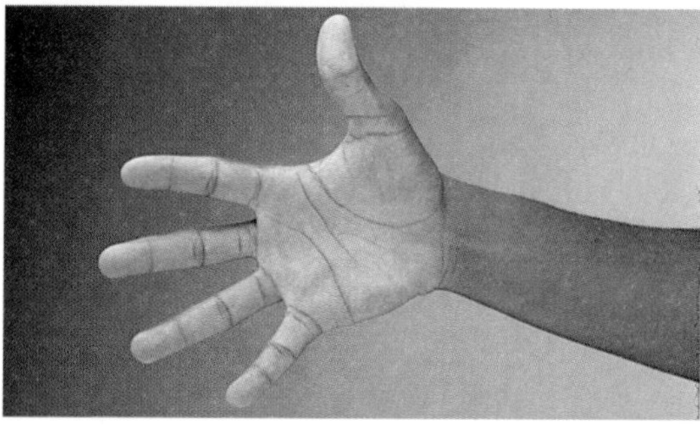

DRILL 5. Spread the fingers as much as possible, holding the position for a moment or two; then relax the fingers and lightly fold them into the palm of the hand. Repeat the movements slowly several times. Exercise both hands at the same time.

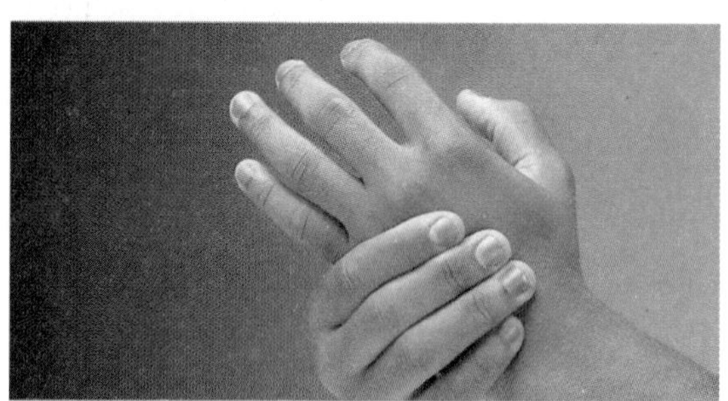

DRILL 6. Rub the hands vigorously. Let the thumb rub the palm of the hand. Rub the fingers, the back of the hand, and the wrist.

DRILL 7. Hold both hands in front of you, fingers together. Hold the last three fingers still and move the first finger as far to the side as possible. Return the first finger; then move the first and second fingers together; finally move the little finger as far to the side as possible.

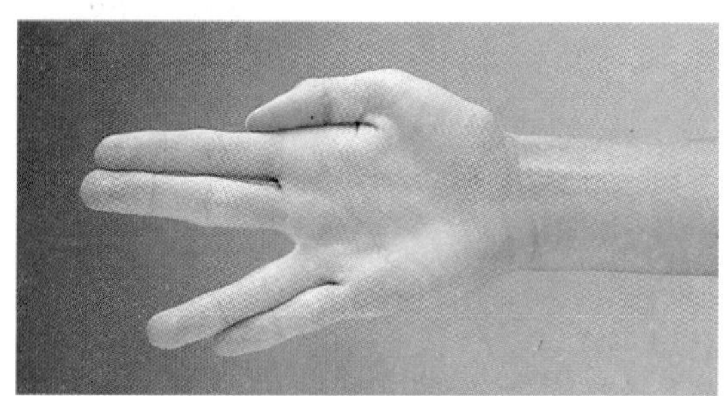

Level One Learning to Operate the Keyboard

OBJECTIVES

KEYBOARDING

To key the alphabetic and numeric keys "by touch" using the proper techniques.

FORMATTING SKILLS

To set margins and tabs, and center text horizontally.

COMMUNICATION SKILLS

To apply proofreaders' marks and revise text.

Drill 12

A all letters

gwam 1'

People may debate that quality is better than quanity. 13
They also may argue that poor work can't be justified by merely 26
increasing a workers' out put. However, if a minimum quanity 38
can't be paroduced, the standard of quality may bot be signifi- 54
cant in the market. The best view perhaps is one thatexpects 67
high quality yet recognizes a need for a minimum out put. 79

Writing 30

 all letters

gwam 1' | 3'

Most need to feel satisfied that our employer is looking 13 | 4
for our wel fare. Our wel fare is made up of such items as job 25 | 9
secutiry, frint benefits and retirement. Dozens of other items 39 | 13
also could be listed under our welfare, but we can handle those 53 | 18
items if the basic 3 are covered. For most of us, our wel fare 67 | 23
means more than having the basics of life, which are food, 79 | 26
clothing, and shelter; we also want to feel secure and to have 94 | 31
a few extras. 97 | 32

Job secutiry is perseived usually as their most critical 12 | 37
item on the list. If you do not possess good job security, 24 | 41
adaquate fringe benegits or sufficient retirement will be of 39 | 45
little use to you. If you are like most, you also expect your 52 | 50
job to be pleasant and to pay well as well; in fact, a work 67 | 55
place will probably be more important than wages. Your whole 81 | 59
look on life can be better when you feel there is much more 91 | 63
security in your job. 95 | 64

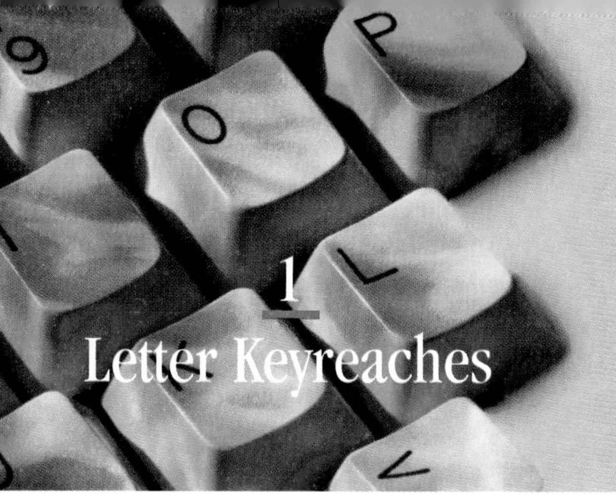

Learning goals:
1 To master alphabetic reaches.
2 To key "by touch"–without looking at fingers or keyboard.
3 To key easy paragraph copy smoothly and fluently.
4 To key at a rate of 14 or more gross words a minute (*gwam*).

Formatting guides:
1 Default margins or 50-space line.
2 Single-space drills; double-space between groups.

1a

Get ready to key

1 Read "Get ready to key."
2 Prepare equipment for keying.

Get ready to key

Prepare your work station

- Elevate the textbook.
- Clear unneeded books and clothing from work area.

Prepare your equipment

Typewriters

- Set paper guide so that the left edge of your paper will be at 0 on the line-of-writing scale.
- Set left margin for a 50-space line (pica, 17 and 67; elite, 26 and 76; set right margin at end of line-of-writing scale).
- Set line-spacing for single spacing (1).
- Turn on machine; insert paper.

Computers

- Turn power switch to "on."
- Turn monitor on if it has a separate switch.
- Use the default (preset) margins.
- Refer to *Know Your Software: Alphanumeric* for directions for using the keyboarding software.

Take proper position

- Sit back in chair, body erect.
- Place both feet on floor to maintain proper position.
- Let your hands hang at your sides. Notice that your fingers relax in a curved position. This relaxed, curved position is the one always used for keying. Repeat this step each day before you begin to key.

Drill 11

A all letters

	gwam 1'
Are you quite troubled and confused about the technical	11
definitions of data and information? Data are unorganized	23
facts, concepts, or ideas; whereas information is data that	35
have been linked in some order that has meaning and is	46
helpful to a user. For example, a ten-digit number might	57
be just data to someone; yet this same number may	67
be information to you -- your phone number.	77

Writing 29

A all letters

	gwam 1'	3'
The shift toward computerization of office tasks has	11	4
caused quite a bit of confusion about the differences between	23	8
data and information. Some people say that data and	34	11
information are one and the same; they are just	43	14
different terms to denote the same thing. Others say	54	18
that vast differences exist between the two terms.	64	21
For people with the latter point of view, it makes	75	25
sense to use information as an umbrella term -- a	84	28
category, so to speak, in which to fit all words, figures,	96	32
voices, and pictures that convey meaning.	104	35
Data, those people would say, are the "bits and	10	38
pieces" that on their own convey little or no meaning.	21	42
Thus, the function of so-called "information processing"	32	46
is to transform data -- individual words, numbers, sounds,	43	49
and images -- into something meaningful to	52	52
decision makers. Therefore, before a person collects any	63	56
data of any kind, he or she must consider how the pieces	74	60
of data will be combined to make a point or shed light	85	63
on a subject. Are data and information one and the	96	67
same? Are sugar, flour, eggs, etc., the same as a	106	70
chocolate cake?	109	71

1b

Locate home keys, space bar, and return

Find the keys **a s d f** and **j k l ;** . Practice several times the steps at the right for placing fingers in home row position and for reaching to the Return key and Space bar.

1 Drop hands to side allowing fingers to curve naturally.

2 Lightly place the left fingertips over **a s d f** .

3 Lightly place right fingertips over **j k l ;** .

4 Repeat.

Return: Reach with the 4th (little) finger of the right hand to the **return/ enter** key and tap it. Quickly return the finger to its home position (over ;).

Space bar: Strike the **space bar** with a down-and-in motion of the right thumb.

1c

Learn home keys

Key each line twice single spaced (SS); strike the return key twice to double-space (DS) between 2-line groups. Do not key the numbers.

Note: Even if your equipment has word wrap, use the Return key here.

1 ff jj ff jj fj fj fj dd kk dd kk dk dk dk **Return**
2 ff jj ff jj fj fj fj dd kk dd kk dk dk dk
Strike Return twice to double-space (DS)

3 ss ll ss ll sl sl sl aa ;; aa ;; a; a; a;
4 ss ll ss ll sl sl sl aa ;; aa ;; a; a; a;
(DS)

5 fj fj dk dk sl sl a; a; fjdksla; jfkdls;a
6 fj fj dk dk sl sl a; a; fjdksla; jfkdls;a
(DS)

1d

Practice return

Key each line once; double-space (DS) between lines.

7 f j d k s l a ; **Return twice**

8 ff jj dd kk ss ll aa ;;

9 fff jjj ddd kkk sss lll aaa ;;;

10 ff jj dd kk ss ll aa ;; fjdksla; fjdksla;

Drill 10

all letters and figures

Statistics make the point that unfortunately a sizable number of the young people in our nation (25 to 30 percent) do not exhibit even the most basic abilities in simple math. About 26 to 30 percent of all 13-year-old children cannot work just basic math problems presented in the elementary grades (3, 4, and 5); and 45 to 50 percent of the 17-year-old youths cannot do the math required in Grades 7, 8, and 9.

Writing 28

all letters and figures — *gwam* 3' | 5'

Simple arithmetic problems include addition of two 2-digit 4 | 2 | 53
numbers, such as 45 and 18, and two 3-digit numbers, such as 8 | 5 | 55
407 and 698. Also, a part of basic math is subtraction of two 12 | 7 | 58
numbers, such as 26 from 65 or 710 from 938, and division of a 16 | 10 | 60
2-digit number by a 1-digit number, such as 40 divided by 5. 21 | 12 | 63
Finding monetary values also is a basic arithmetic application. 25 | 15 | 65
For example, if 50 cents is needed to take the trolley, should 29 | 17 | 68
you give the driver 10 pennies and 8 nickels or 2 quarters? 33 | 20 | 70
If you begin with 97 cents and purchase 1/4 pound of bananas at 37 | 22 | 73
36 cents per pound and 3 tangerines at 25 cents each, can you 41 | 25 | 75
still buy 1/2 pound of potatoes at 28 cents per pound? 45 | 27 | 78

Many other math operations create major problems for 55 to 49 | 29 | 80
60 percent of the general public. Working with zeros, such as 53 | 32 | 83
dividing 970 by 30.4, and computing percentages, such as finding 58 | 35 | 85
61 percent of 80, frequently are hard tasks for a lot of people. 62 | 37 | 88
Also, when multiplying numbers, such as 407 by 20.09, some have 66 | 40 | 90
difficulty with how to do the problems as well as where to put 71 | 42 | 93
the decimals in the final answers. If "back-to-basics" and 75 | 45 | 95
problem solving approaches are used in the next 13 to 15 years, 79 | 47 | 98
the math skill reports of the future should be much more posi- 83 | 50 | 100
tive than this one. 84 | 51 | 101

gwam 3' | 1 | 2 | 3 | 4 | 5
5' | 1 | 2 | 3

1e

Practice home row

Key each line twice (SS); (DS) between 2-line groups.

Note: Even if your machine has an automatic return or word wrap, use the Return key here.

```
11 a; sl a;sl dk fj dkfj a;sl dkfj a;sldk a;sldkfj a;
12 a; sl a;sl dk fj dkfj a;sl dkfj a;sldk a;sldkfj a;
```

Strike return twice to double-space (DS)

```
13 as as ask ad ad jak lad all fall add lass all fall
14 as as ask ad ad jak lad all fall add lass all fall
```

(DS)

```
15 a lass; ask dad; a lad asks dad; ask all; jak fall
16 a lass; ask dad; a lad asks dad; ask all; jak fall
```

1f

Learn i

1 Find **i** on the illustrated keyboard; then find it on your keyboard.

2 Study "Reach technique for i."

3 Watch your finger make the reach to **i** and back to **k** a few times without striking the keys. Keep fingers curved and wrists low.

4 Key each line twice; DS between groups. Try to keep your eyes on the copy as you key.

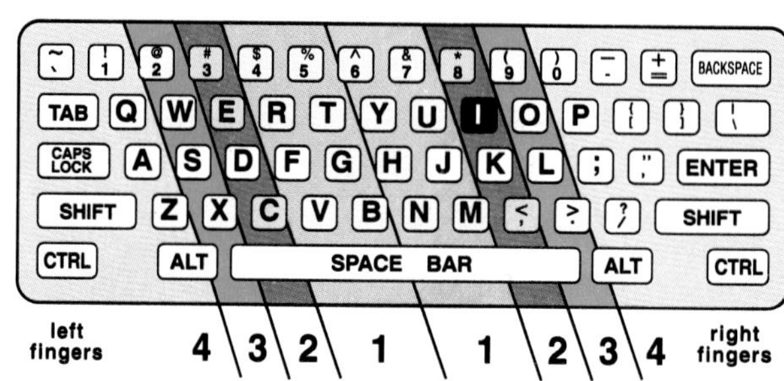


```
17 i ik ik ik is is id id if if il il ail did kid lid
18 i ik aid ail did kid lid lids kids ill aid did ilk

19 id aid aids laid said ids lids kids kiss disk dial
20 id aid ail fail sail jail ails slid dill sill fill

21 fill a sail; aid a lad; is silk; if a dial; a jail
22 is a disk; dads said; did fall ill; if a lass did;
```

1g

End the lesson

(standard procedures for all lessons)

Electronic typewriters

1 Press Eject key to remove the paper.
2 Turn off the power.

Computers

1 Exit the software.
2 Remove disk from drive and store it.
3 Turn off power if directed to do so.
4 Turn off monitor if it has a separate switch.

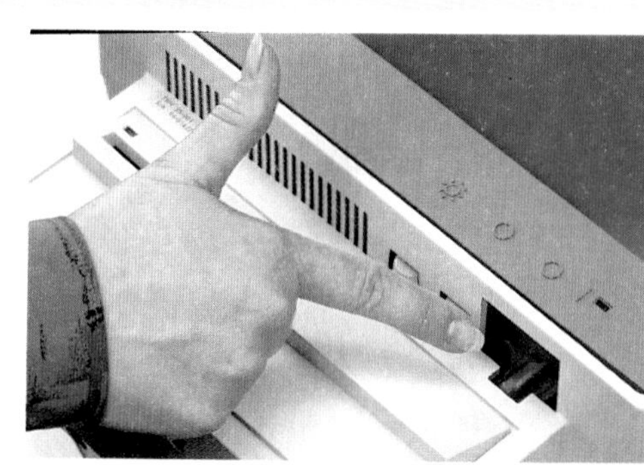

Writing 26

all letters gwam 3' | 5'

School records are important to an employer who is re- 4 | 2 | 47
cruiting a new employee. In addition to a student's academic 8 | 5 | 50
record, an employer is interested in the type of work habits the 12 | 7 | 53
student had while in school. Many employers are very concerned 16 | 10 | 55
when they see a candidate with a poor school attendance record. 21 | 12 | 58
They know that the habits a student forms while in school more 25 | 15 | 60
than likely will be those carried over to the job. For this rea- 29 | 18 | 63
son, an employer probably will seek references from a teacher or 34 | 20 | 65
from someone who knows the type of work habits the candidate has. 38 | 23 | 68

A student's school habits often reveal much more than is 42 | 25 | 70
realized about the way a person may perform on the job. This 46 | 28 | 73
fact has led many employers to be very interested in how the 50 | 30 | 75
prospective employee was perceived in school. Employers want to 54 | 33 | 78
know how dependable the person was in school as well as how suc- 59 | 35 | 80
cessful at managing time, organizing work, and caring for school 63 | 38 | 83
property. An employer wants to know how cooperative the student 67 | 40 | 86
was and how well he or she was able to get along with others. 72 | 43 | 88
Obviously, these factors are quite important to job success. 75 | 45 | 91

Writing 27

all letters gwam 3' | 5'

Writing good letters comes with practice and by applying a 4 | 2 | 47
few basic rules. Because you want the reader to be interested 8 | 5 | 50
in what you are saying, you want the reader to see the advan- 12 | 7 | 52
tages of your message. Creating a letter of this type doesn't 16 | 10 | 55
need to be a difficult task if you plan what you are going to 21 | 12 | 57
say prior to keying your thoughts onto the paper. Strive to 25 | 15 | 60
convey correct information in a clear, concise manner and to 29 | 17 | 62
provide the appropriate facts. Providing complete information 33 | 20 | 65
that is organized in a logical way also is essential to good 37 | 22 | 67
writing. 38 | 23 | 68

When you analyze a well-written letter, you will find a 41 | 25 | 70
natural flow of thought throughout the communication. You can 46 | 27 | 72
achieve this flow by using transitions from one sentence to an- 50 | 30 | 75
other. As you tie each thought to the next one, also vary the 54 | 32 | 77
structure of the sentences. For example, use a mix of simple 58 | 35 | 80
and compound as well as short, medium, and long sentences. An- 62 | 37 | 82
other excellent rule to follow is to use only one main idea in a 67 | 40 | 85
paragraph. Short, to-the-point paragraphs that do not jump from 71 | 43 | 88
one main idea to another create the reader interest required. 75 | 45 | 90

gwam 3' | 1 | 2 | 3 | 4 | 5 |
5' | 1 | 2 | 3 |

2 E and N

Skill-Building Warmup

2a

each line twice SS; DS between 2-line groups

- ✓ **Eyes** on copy
- ✓ **Fingers** curved
- ✓ **Wrists** low
- ✓ **Elbows** hanging loose

```
home row      1 ff dd ss aa ff dd ss aa jj kk ll ;; jj kk ll ;; a;
i             2 i i ill ilk did kid lid aid ail kid kids lids slid
all reaches   3 if a lad; as a jail; is silk; fill a dais; did aid
easy          4 jak aid did flak laid said is id if dial disk jaks
```

2b

Learn e and n

Read carefully the "Standard procedure" at the right. Use it to learn new keyreaches in this lesson and in lessons that follow.

Standard procedure for learning new keyreaches

1 Find the new key on the illustrated keyboard; then find it on your keyboard.

2 Study the illustrated keyreach.

3 Watch your finger make the reach to the new key a few times. Keep other fingers curved in home position. For an upward reach, straighten the finger slightly; for a downward reach, curve it a bit more.

4 Key each line twice (slowly, then faster); DS between 2-line groups.

5 Repeat if time permits. Work to eliminate pauses.

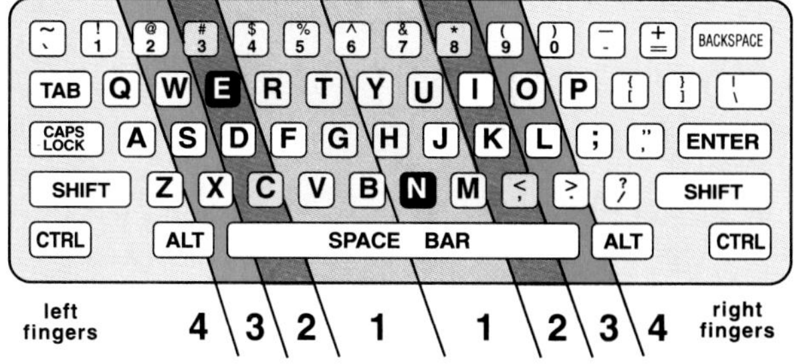

Reach *up* with *left second* finger.

e

```
 5 e ed ed led led lea lea ale ale elf elf eke eke ed
 6 e el el eel els elk elk lea leak ale kale led jell
 7 e ale kale lea leak fee feel lea lead elf self eke
```

n

```
 8 n nj nj an an and and fan fan and kin din fin land
 9 n an fan in fin and land sand din fans sank an sin
10 n in ink sink inn kin skin an and land in din dink
```

Reach *down* with *right first* finger.

all reaches learned

```
11 den end fen ken dean dens ales fend fens keen knee
12 if in need; feel ill; as an end; a lad and a lass;
13 and sand; a keen idea; as a sail sank; is in jail;
```

Drill 9

Dressing well does not mean you must select only the most expensive high-quality clothing. Many experts say you should favor styles that not only make you feel good when wearing them but also flatter your figure. Selecting clothes by these standards usually will produce a desirable result. Follow your instincts, but be aware there are rules just as there are for most areas of life.

Writing 25

  **all letters**

	gwam 3'	5'	
Creating a wardrobe of high fashion can be achieved if	4	2	69
you plan and buy carefully. For some people this means buying at	8	5	71
the beginning of the season when there is a good selection of	12	7	74
styles and sizes. Buying once or twice a year does have its	16	10	76
drawbacks, however. For example, you probably will not be able	21	12	79
to take advantage of the majority of sales that usually take	25	15	81
place in the clothing industry throughout the year. Also, having	29	17	84
to pay regular price or more than you feel you should for your	33	20	86
clothes may force you to purchase fewer outfits. For most	37	22	89
people, buying only a limited amount of clothing each year re-	41	25	91
quires a great deal of planning and coordination. Quality be-	45	27	94
comes a primary factor in the selection process, and shopping	50	30	96
during the year usually will center on buying accessories to	54	32	98
change the look of your basic wardrobe.	57	34	100
Because even many best dressed people limit how much they	60	36	103
spend on their wardrobes, more and more people have turned to	65	39	105
tailors to have their garments made. Custom clothing can offer	69	41	108
many advantages. For some it is the uniqueness of having outfits	73	44	110
that will never be seen on anyone else. For others it is the ex-	78	47	113
citing challenge of creating a completely new design. But for	82	49	115
most people, having clothes custom made ensures that a garment	86	52	118
will fit, no matter what the size. A quality tailor will be	90	54	121
able to cover any body imperfections as well as enhance the good	94	57	123
qualities by merely taking a tuck here and placing an accent	98	59	125
there. However, whether you buy ready-made clothing or have your	103	62	128
clothes made by a tailor, the total effect should be to look your	107	64	131
best, to give you confidence, and to feel relaxed.	111	66	133

gwam 3' | 1 | 2 | 3 | 4 | 5 |
5' | 1 | 2 | 3 |

2c

Practice keying techniques

each line twice SS; DS between 2-line groups

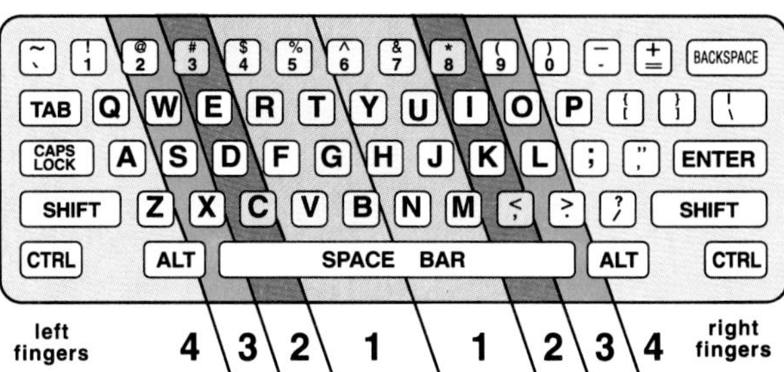

home row

14 a fad dad all fall as ad ask lass sad lad fad jaks

e

15 el see ale eke ade eel eld fed fee kea led lea sea

i

16 is id ill dill if aid ail fail did kid ski lid ilk

n

17 an fan and land fans flan sans sand sank flak dank

all reaches

18 ade alas dike else fife ken; jell ink jak inns if;

2d

Practice keying words and phrases

each line at least twice SS; DS between groups

Use correct technique

- ✓ Fingers curved and upright
- ✓ Wrists low but not touching machine
- ✓ Forearms parallel to keyboard
- ✓ Eyes on copy
- ✓ Elbows hanging loosely
- ✓ Body erect; feet flat on floor

all reaches learned

19 a an ale an and as ask fa fan la lad el elk inn if

20 ad ale an and did end a is elf els fie jak ken lei

21 alas a dial el elan elf kale la lake an lane is if

22 add a line; and safe; asks a lass; sail in a lake;

23 dine in an inn; fake jade; lend fans; as sand sank

24 and nine less; sad lads; adds line nine; dank lane

2e

End the lesson

(use standard procedures)

Turn off power; clear work area.

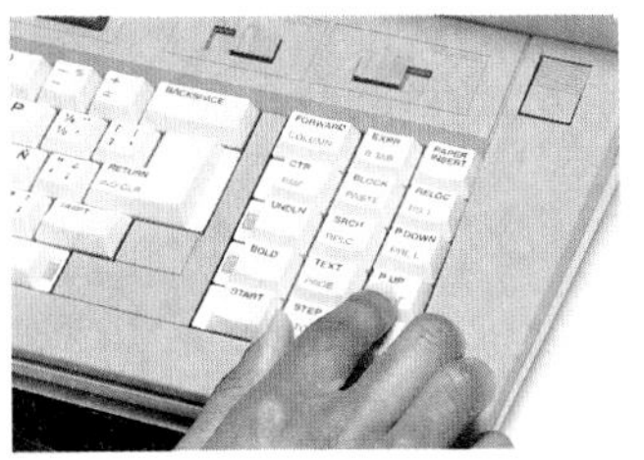

Exit software.

Drill 8

Fluency and technique improvement

Key each fluency line twice to increase speed.

Key the techniques lines each once; work for control.

Fluency

1 The official amendment may be a problem for their firm to handle.
2 The sigh of this man was audible as the big dog got on the boxes.
3 When Susie got a penalty, she did lament she was haughty to them.
4 Sheila did go down to their island to see fish and to eat papaya.
5 I may visit the ancient ivory chapels when I roam the papal town.

Techniques

6 Zola's optional plans of using buzz saws and axes were plausible.
7 Brazil has various exotic cocoa, coconut, and banana concoctions.
8 Jackie, Clyde, Isaac, and Ross may go to South Nepal and Algiers.
9 Her report said the open reservoir spoiled their leasing options.
10 I met Janet at noon to discuss all the errors Lynn has committed.

| 1 | 2 | 3 | 4 | 5 | 6 | 7 | 8 | 9 | 10 | 11 | 12 | 13 |

Writing 24

  **all letters**

	gwam 3'	5'	
Critical thinking is associated with knowing how to ana-	4	2	66
lyze a situation and how to use good judgment to weigh facts and	8	5	69
take correct action. To employ this process, a person may need	12	7	72
to develop a broad factual base about a situation. Once that	17	10	74
person has enough information to make a sound decision, he or she	21	13	77
must know how to sort out and prioritize the essential facts that	25	15	79
will lead to a good decision. The process involves quite a few	30	18	82
steps and may require a person to evaluate frequently, to change	34	20	84
directions, and even to collect more facts.	37	22	86
Analytical thinking skills, which some refer to as higher	41	24	89
level thinking skills, are learned in a gradual process. As	45	27	91
people build up a good store of facts and gain expertise at deci-	49	30	94
sion making and problem solving, they are able to make better de-	54	32	96
cisions and to solve harder types of problems. Most people find	58	35	99
their abilities to think critically can be improved with prac-	62	37	101
tice, just as skills are honed with use. It has been shown that	66	40	104
there are a great number of benefits in other areas, such as	70	42	106
speaking and writing, when thinking skills are improved.	74	45	109
A good critical thinker acts in a precise, exact, and highly	78	47	111
organized way to cause appropriate actions to be taken in any	82	49	114
situation. Simply stated, this probably means that the right	87	52	116
thing is done in the right place and at the right time. A person	91	55	119
who always takes appropriate action regardless of the complexity	95	57	121
of the circumstances is someone who will have a clear advantage	100	60	124
over the competition. It should be quite obvious that this type	104	62	126
of person is a valuable asset to a business.	107	64	128

gwam 3' | 1 | 2 | 3 | 4 | 5 |
5' | 1 | 2 | 3 |

Remember: Practice should be purposefully done, not just copied. Simply swinging at a golf ball does not create a better golfer; skill growth requires purposeful practice.

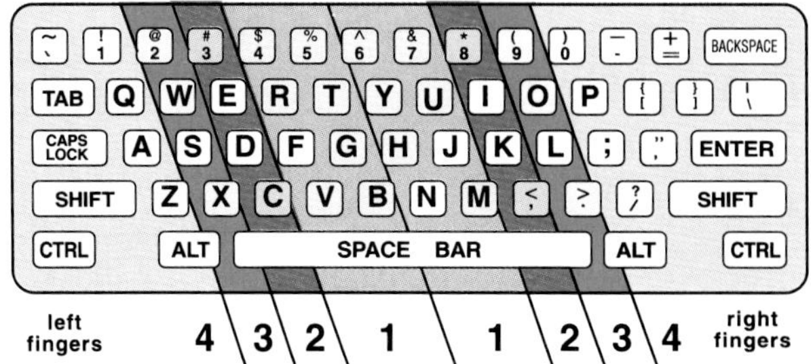

3 Review

Skill-Building Warmup

3a

each line twice SS (slowly, then faster); DS between 2-line groups

```
home keys    1 a s d f j k l ; as df jk l; asdf jkl; a; sl dk fj;
home row     2 ad ads lad fad dad as ask fa la lass jak jaks alas
i/e/n        3 fan fin an eel el nine in life if kiss is idea did
all reaches  4 a jak and a land and an elf and a dial and a lens;
```

3b

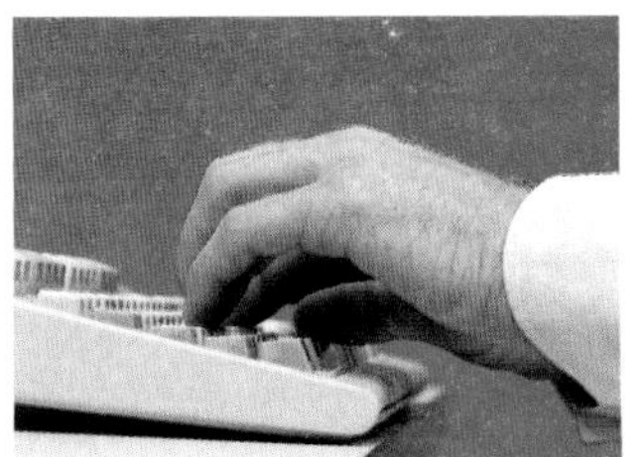

Strike the space bar with a quick down-and-in motion. Do not pause before or after striking the space bar.

Reach to the Enter key, strike the key, and release it quickly.

Practice keying phrases

lines 5-12 once as shown; keep eyes on copy

Note: Do not key the vertical rules separating phrases.

```
   home row
 5 as a jak;|as a lass|ask dad|as a lad;|as a fall ad
 6 ask a lass;|as a dad|a fall fad|as all ask;|sad ad

   i
 7 if as is;|is a disk|aid all kids|did ski|is a silk
 8 skis skid|is a kid|aid did fail|if a dial|laid lid

   e
 9 as kale|sees a lake|elf fled|as a deal|sell a sled
10 sell a lead|seal a deal|feel a leaf|as a jade sale

   n
11 in an inn|sank in sand|nine fans|in a land|and end
12 line is in ink | send in a fan | line nine | a fine land
```

Drill 7

Tab and numbers

Key each line once; operate tab with left little finger without pausing. Set 4-space intercolumn tabs.

1	route	497	savor	2149	incur	8637	flute	4975	motor	7959
2	taken	518	under	7633	piano	0816	juror	7749	marks	7148
3	vigor	485	zebra	1354	cover	3943	value	4197	amend	1736
4	ozone	919	yacht	6136	fixed	4823	havoc	6149	ninth	6865
5	kudos	873	banjo	5167	urban	7451	wrote	2495	jeans	7316
6	scuba	237	timer	5873	cough	3975	total	5951	while	2689

Writing 23

all letters

	gwam 3'	5'	
The kinds of leisure activities you choose constitute	4	2	62
your life style and, to a great extent, reflect your personality.	8	5	65
For example, if your daily activities are people oriented, you	12	7	67
may balance this by spending your free time alone. On the other	17	10	70
hand, if you would rather be with people most of the time, your	21	13	72
socialization needs may be very high. At the other end of the	25	15	75
scale are people who are engaged in machine-oriented work and	29	18	77
also enjoy spending leisure time alone. These people tend to be	33	20	80
rather quiet and reserved.	35	21	81
Every individual needs a certain amount of relaxation to	39	23	83
remain physically and mentally alert. However, what one person	43	26	86
finds relaxing may be just the opposite for another person. For	48	29	89
example, one person may like to read a good book; another may	52	31	91
find that reading causes nervousness and fatigue. The same holds	56	34	94
true for the person who enjoys sports. Studies have shown that	61	36	96
jogging may be quite good for a person who enjoys it but may be	65	39	99
detrimental to another person who does not enjoy it.	69	41	101
Experts have noted that the proper balance of leisure,	72	43	103
relaxation, and recreation is almost essential for individuals	76	46	106
who live and work in a highly automated world. This balance is	81	48	108
necessary if each person is to be productive in handling the	85	51	111
everyday pressure and stress of life. Because every person has	89	53	113
unique needs that are met in a variety of ways, one must properly	93	56	116
assess all of the day's activities if the maximum benefit is to	98	59	118
be gained from each day of life.	100	60	120

gwam 3' | 1 | 2 | 3 | 4 | 5 |
5' | 1 | 2 | 3 |

3c

Practice common reaches

each line twice SS; DS between 2-line groups

Goals:

- ✓ Strike keys quickly.
- ✓ Strike space bar with down-and-in motions.
- ✓ Return with a quick flick of the little finger.

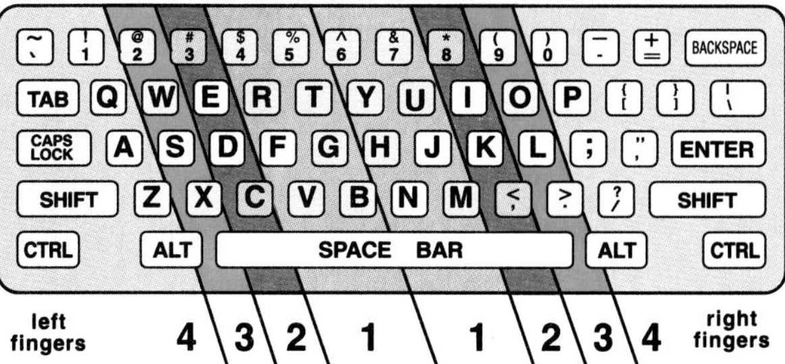

ea

13 ea sea lea seas deal leaf leak lead leas flea keas

as

14 as ask lass ease as asks ask ask sass as alas seas

sa

15 sa sad sane sake sail sale sans safe sad said sand

le

16 le sled lead flee fled ale flea lei dale kale leaf

el

17 el eel eld elf sell self el dell fell elk els jell

ad

18 ad add ads ade jade lad lads fad lead dad fade sad

an

19 an and fan dean elan flan land lane lean sand sane

in

20 in fin inn inks dine sink fine fins kind kine lain

3d

Practice special stroking techniques

each 2-line group twice SS

home row: fingers curved and upright

21 jak lad as lass dad sad lads fad fall la ask ad as

22 asks add jaks dads a alas ads flak adds sad as lad

upward reaches: straighten fingers slightly; return quickly to home position

23 fed die led ail kea lei lea did ale fife silk leak

24 sea lid deal sine desk lie ale like life idea jail

double letters: don't hurry when stroking double letters

25 fee jell less add inn seek fall alee lass keel all

26 dill dell see fell eel less all add kiss seen sell

Drill 6
Number reaches

Key each line at a comfortable rate; practice difficult lines.

1 My staff of 11 worked 11 hours a day from May 11 to June 11.
2 Her flight, PW 222, lands at 2:22 p.m. on Thursday, June 22.
3 We 3, part of the 333rd Corps, marched 33 miles on August 3.
4 Car 444 took Route 4 east to Route 44, then 4 miles to Aden.
5 The 55 wagons traveled 555 miles in '55; only 5 had trouble.
6 Put 6 beside 6; result 66. Then, add one more 6 to get 666.
7 They sold 7,777 copies of Record 77, Shubert's 7th Symphony.
8 In '88, it took 8 men and 8 women 8 days to travel 88 miles.
9 The 9 teams, 9 girls and 9 boys, depart on Bus 999 at 9 a.m.
10 Million has six zeros; as, 000,000. Ten has but one; as, 0.

Writing 22

  all letters

	gwam 3'	5'	
Planning, organizing, and controlling are three of the	4	2	65
functions that are familiar to all sorts of firms. Because these	8	5	68
functions are basic to the managerial practices of a business,	12	7	71
they form the very core of its daily operations. Good managerial	17	10	73
procedures, of course, do not just occur by accident. They must	21	13	76
be set into motion by people. Thus, a person who plans to enter	25	15	78
the job market, especially in an office position, should study	30	18	81
all of the elements of good management in order to apply those	34	20	83
principles to her or his work.	36	22	85
Leadership is another very important skill for a person	40	24	87
to develop. Leaders are needed at all levels in a business to	44	26	89
plan, organize, and control the operations of a firm. A person	48	29	92
who is in a key position of leadership usually is expected to ini-	52	31	95
tiate ideas as well as to carry out the goals of a business.	57	34	97
Office workers who have developed the qualities of leadership are	61	37	100
more apt to be promoted than those without such skills. While	65	39	102
leadership may come naturally for some people, it can be learned	70	42	105
as well as be improved with practice.	72	43	106
Attitude is an extremely important personality trait that	76	46	109
is a big contributor to success in one's day-to-day activities.	80	48	111
Usually a person with a good attitude is open-minded to the ideas	85	51	114
of others and is able to relate with others because he or she has	89	53	117
an interest in people. Thus, one's attitude on the job often	93	56	119
makes a great difference in whether work gets done and done	97	58	122
right. Because teamwork is a part of many jobs, developing a	101	61	124
good attitude toward work, people, and life seems logical.	105	63	126

gwam 3' | 1 | 2 | 3 | 4 | 5 |
5' | 1 | 2 | 3 |

4 Left Shift, H, T, Period

Skill-Building Warmup

4a

each line twice SS; DS between 2-line groups; keep eyes on copy

home row 1 al as ads lad dad fad jak fall lass asks fads all;
e/i/n 2 ed ik jn in knee end nine line sine lien dies leis
all reaches 3 see a ski; add ink; fed a jak; is an inn; as a lad
easy 4 an dial id is an la lake did el ale fake is land a

4b

Learn left shift and h

each line twice SS; DS between 2-line groups

Follow the "Standard procedures for learning new keyreaches" on page 5 for all remaining reaches.

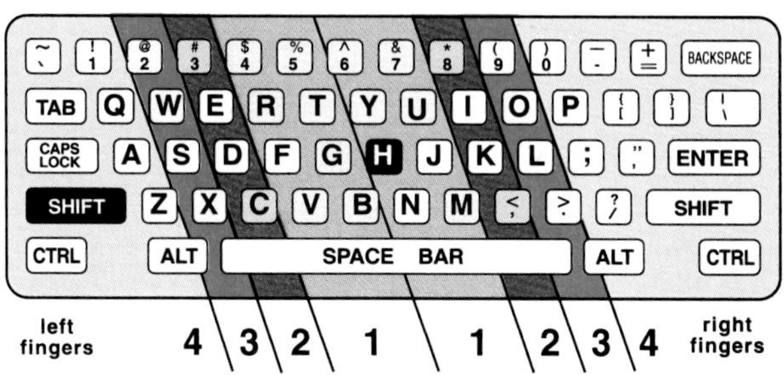

Reach *down* with *left little* finger.

Reach to *left* with *right first* finger.

left shift

5 J Ja Ja Jan Jan Jane Jana Ken Kass Lee Len Nan Ned
6 and Ken and Lena and Jake and Lida and Nan and Ida
7 Ina Kale; Jill Lask; Nels Insa; Ken Jalk; Lin Nial

h

8 h hj hj he he she she hen aha ash had has hid shed
9 h hj ha hie his half hand hike dash head sash shad
10 aha hi hash heal hill hind lash hash hake dish ash

all reaches learned

11 Nels Kane and Jake Jenn; she asked Hi and Ina Linn
12 Lend Lana and Jed a dish; I fed Lane and Jess Kane
13 I see Jake Kish and Lash Hess; Isla and Helen hike

4c

Practice return

Key the drill once; DS and repeat. Use fluid, unhurried movements.

return: return without looking up

14 Nan had a sale;
15 He did see Hal;
16 Lee has a desk;
17 Ina hid a dish;

Drill 5

Double letters and space bar

Key each group twice; keep thumb curved and close to the space bar.

Double letters

1 Anne Sneed was keen at assessing the needs of our swimming class.
2 Three raccoons, mammals with ringed tails, scurry under the tree.
3 We will attach Emma's current address to the anniversary balloon.
4 Kenny called Anne as soon as the ballots arrived from Cincinnati.

Space bar

5 Did the six men bid for the car? Les and I saw Ken put in a bid.
6 If it is time to pay Jen for the oak hen, then let Jason pay Jen.
7 Did Pam say she may copy the forms in a day or two for all of us?
8 Who won the match? I nominated two: Mr. Fuji Kitts and E. Chaz.

| 1 | 2 | 3 | 4 | 5 | 6 | 7 | 8 | 9 | 10 | 11 | 12 | 13 |

Writing 21

 **all letters**

	gwam 3'	5'	
Many people find that creative thinking can be nurtured	4	2	66
with effort. One way to do this is to find multiple solutions to	8	5	68
a problem. Alternatives to a problem should be sought out when	12	7	71
there seems to be only one possible solution as well as when a	17	10	73
solution has already been found. The more ideas generated, the	21	13	76
more options there may be. If a person can identify the options	25	15	79
that are available and experiment with them, then possibly he or	30	18	81
she can come up with several other options. This approach	33	20	84
fosters new ideas and stimulates the creative thinking process.	38	23	86
Another way to be creative is to try to relate present	41	25	88
events to past events and define common elements that can be ap-	46	27	91
plied to a current problem. This method of relating a past expe-	50	30	93
rience to a current event, even though the situations may be very	54	33	96
different, helps a person find a connecting link between things	59	35	99
or concepts. The point is to find the similarities between what	63	38	101
has happened previously and what is taking place at the present	67	40	104
time. By finding a connection between the elements, a person may	72	43	106
discover new ways to analyze and solve problems.	75	45	108
A creative individual does not just give up if a problem	79	47	111
seems too difficult to solve. A person who sticks to a problem	83	50	113
also is more likely to succeed in solving it than the individual	87	52	116
who gives up and goes on to other things. Brainstorming may also	92	55	119
be constructive in finding alternatives. All in all, being cre-	96	58	121
ative doesn't mean you have to solve a problem by yourself, that	100	60	124
the solution must be found immediately, or that unique solutions	105	63	126
must be found.	106	63	127

gwam 3' | 1 | 2 | 3 | 4 | 5 |
5' | 1 | 2 | 3 |

4d

Learn t and . (period)

each line twice SS; DS between 2-line groups

Period: Space once after a period that follows an initial or an abbreviation; space twice after a period that ends a sentence. Do not, of course, space after a period at the end of a line.

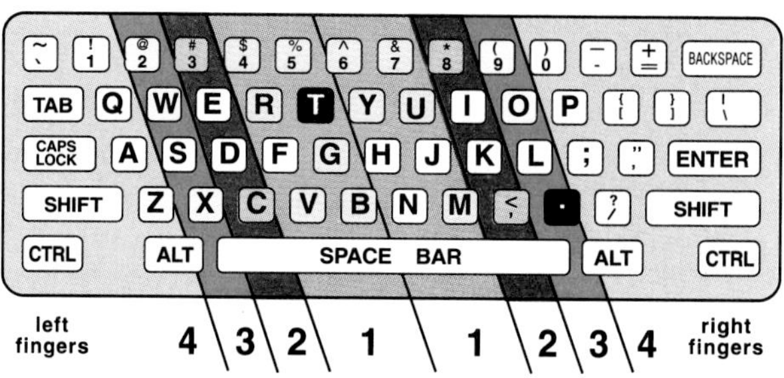

Reach *up* with *left first* finger.

Reach *down* with *right third* finger.

t

18 t tf tf aft aft left fit fat fete tiff tie the tin
19 tf at at aft lit hit tide tilt tint sits skit this
20 hat kit let lit ate sit flat tilt thin tale tan at

. (period)

21 .l .l l.l fl. fl. L. L. Neal and J. N. List hiked.
22 Hand J. H. Kass a fan. Jess did. I need an idea.
23 Jane said she has a tan dish; Jae and Lee need it.

all reaches learned

24 I did tell J. K. that Lt. Li had left. He is ill.
25 Lee and Ken left at ten; the jet had left at nine.
26 I see Lila and Ilene at tea. Jae Kane ate at ten.

4e

Key words and phrases

1 Key each line once at an easy, continuous pace, keeping fingers curved and upright as illustrated.

2 Key each line again at a slightly faster pace.

eyes on copy

27 ah an la el ha if is id it aid aha all and did die
28 id end she elf els fit jak ken lei the tie hen sit
29 alas dish disks elan fish flan half halt hand jell
30 kale laid lake land lane leis lend lens than title
31 Ina lies in the sand at ten; she needs a fast tan.
32 Jan asks if I had all the tea that Len said I had.

Drill 4

Adjacent keys and direct reaches

Key each group twice.

Tip: Keep fingers upright (not slanted) over the keys.

Direct reaches

1 Barb saw hybrids at the fairgrounds--hydrangea, hyacinth, grapes.
2 Unless I get two discounts, any price for brass is not a bargain.
3 Volumes of excellent municipal records were a target for thieves.
4 The brilliant young graduate counted a hundred brochures for Jim.

Adjacent reaches

5 Opal went to Salem to buy Ervan a poster and play her new guitar.
6 San Diego was a possible site for opening a pony and saddle shop.
7 The poinsettia was a popular potted flower at the yuletide sales.
8 Ty transferred to a guidance position to join Wendy in the Yukon.

| 1 | 2 | 3 | 4 | 5 | 6 | 7 | 8 | 9 | 10 | 11 | 12 | 13 |

Writing 20

 **all letters**

	gwam 3'	5'	
An essential part of analyzing a career option is to de-	4	2	65
termine the type and extent of education that is required for a	8	5	67
selected career. A main factor to consider about an education is	12	7	70
how long it will take to get the skills that are needed to com-	17	10	73
pete successfully for a job. This factor includes any other	21	12	75
training that may be essential at the outset of employment. Be-	25	15	78
cause jobs change, also assess how an educational program is	29	17	80
structured to meet work changes.	31	19	81
Many people choose a career without considering how well	35	21	84
they may be suited for it. For example, a person who is outgoing	39	24	86
and enjoys being around people probably should not select a	43	26	89
career that requires spending long hours working alone. A job	48	29	91
that requires quick, forceful action to be taken probably should	52	31	94
not be pursued by a person who is shy and contemplative. Just	56	34	96
because one has an aptitude for a specific job does not mean he	60	36	99
or she will be successful in that job. Thus, be sure to weigh	65	39	101
individual personality traits before making a final career	69	41	104
choice.	69	42	104
Money and inner satisfaction are the two leading reasons	73	44	106
why most people work. For most persons, the need for money	77	46	109
translates into food, shelter, and clothing. Once the basic	81	49	111
needs of a person are met, satisfaction is the greatest motivator	85	51	114
for working. To the average person, a job is satisfying if he or	90	54	117
she enjoys the work, likes the people associated with the work,	94	56	119
and feels a sense of pride in a job well done. Because you may	98	59	122
not be the average person, analyze yourself to discover what will	103	62	124
provide job satisfaction.	104	63	125

gwam 3' | 1 | 2 | 3 | 4 | 5 |
5' | 1 | 2 | 3 |

5 R, Right Shift, C, O

Skill-Building Warmup

5a

each line twice SS; DS between 2-line groups; keep eyes on copy

home keys 1 a; ad add al all lad fad jak ask lass fall jak lad
t/h/i/n 2 the hit tin nit then this kith dint tine hint thin
left shift/. 3 I need ink. Li has an idea. Hit it. I see Kate.
all reaches 4 Jeff ate at ten; he left a salad dish in the sink.

5b

Learn r and right shift

each line twice SS; DS between 2-line groups

r

5 r rf rf riff riff fir fir rid ire jar air sir lair
6 rf rid ark ran rat are hare art rant tire dirt jar
7 rare dirk ajar lark rain kirk share hart rail tart

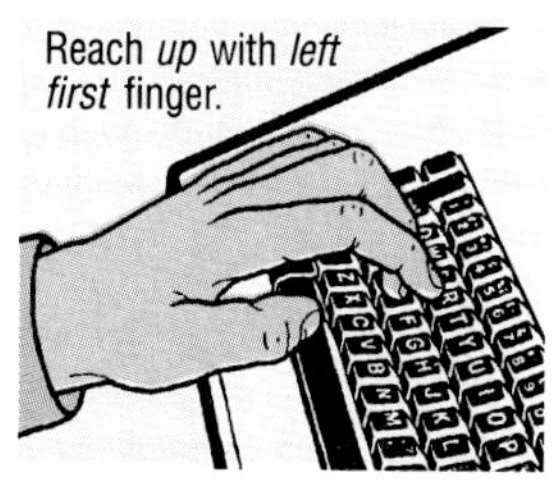
Reach *up* with *left first* finger.

right shift

8 D D Dan Dan Dale Ti Sal Ted Ann Ed Alf Ada Sid Fan
9 and Sid and Dina and Allen and Eli and Dean and Ed
10 Ed Dana; Dee Falk; Tina Finn; Sal Alan; Anna Deeds

Reach *down* with *right little* finger.

all reaches learned

11 Jake and Ann hiked in the sand; Asa set the tents.
12 Fred Derr and Rae Tira dined at the Tree Art Fair.
13 Alan asked Dina if Neil and Reed had left at nine.

5c

Practice techniques

each line once, striving for the goals listed below:
Lines 14-15: Smoothly, without pauses.
Lines 16-17: Without looking at hands or keyboard.
Lines 18-20: Without pausing or looking up from the copy.

14 Kent said that half the field is idle in the fall.
15 Lana said she did sail her skiff in the dark lake.

16 All is still as Sarah and I fish here in the rain.
17 I still see a red ash tree that fell in the field.

18 I had a kale salad;
19 Elia ate his steak;
20 and Dina drank tea.

Drill 3
Specific fingers

Key each group of lines twice; rekey troublesome lines.

1/2 fingers

1 Bedlam erupted when young Jarv kicked the beanbag into the china.
2 Joyce sketched beautiful magpies for my next needlepoint pattern.
3 Ten yellow jackets buzzed around the honeysuckle in the sunlight.
4 Cut the johnnycake Gib made from cornmeal, flour, eggs, and milk.

2/3 fingers

5 The district legislators were seeking more knowledge of the area.
6 Roxie lost her locket leaning from windows at the Edgewood plant.
7 Eddie exceeded his goal this week and sold six windows with trim.
8 The wooden oar, a well-waxed keepsake, hangs on our kitchen wall.

3/4 fingers

9 Six poodles squealed as they spotted two dozing foxes and a lion.
10 A papoose squealed when he spotted the lizard basking in the sun.
11 Lex was too lazy to study for his quizzes and exams in pathology.
12 Alexis was equipped to propose a law to protect the ozone layers.

| 1 | 2 | 3 | 4 | 5 | 6 | 7 | 8 | 9 | 10 | 11 | 12 | 13 |

Writing 19

  **all letters**

	gwam 3'	5'	
At no other time in history than the present day has there	4	2	61
been such a great concern for eye care. This increased in-	8	5	63
terest in vision and the need for good eye care has resulted, in	12	7	66
part, from the wide use of computers. With such a variety of	16	10	68
uses for computers, vast numbers of people are using visual dis-	21	12	71
play terminals on a daily basis. Each year finds more and more	25	15	73
people using the technology mainly because it makes work easier	29	17	76
and enhances leisure activities.	31	19	77
If you spend long hours using a computer, you should un-	35	21	80
derstand some of the problems involved in using the display ter-	39	24	82
minal. If some of these problems are recognized, good judgment	44	26	85
in utilizing display terminals can be applied. For example, com-	48	29	87
fort in front of the screen is important to avoid fatigue. A	52	31	90
screen should be at eye level, about the same distance from you	56	34	92
as you would hold a book. Reference material should be as close	61	36	95
to the screen as possible to minimize head and eye movements.	65	39	97
Of equal importance to you as a computer user is screen	69	41	100
light intensity, which should be three to four times greater than	73	44	102
room lighting. Also, never place your screen toward a window or	77	46	105
a bright light where glare forces you to strain your eyes. A	82	49	107
general rule to follow when using computers is to take a short	86	51	110
break every hour, even if only for five minutes. Adhering to	90	54	112
this very sensible practice on a regular basis will be beneficial	94	57	115
to your eyes and will add to your productivity.	97	58	117

gwam 3' | 1 | 2 | 3 | 4 | 5 |
5' | 1 | 2 | 3 |

5d

Learn c and o

each line twice SS; DS between 2-line groups

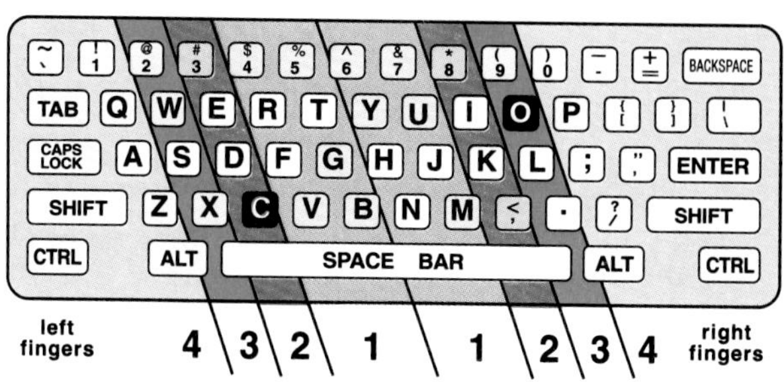

Reach *down* with *left second* finger.

Reach *up* with *right third finger.*

c

21 c c cd cd cad cad can can tic ice sac cake cat sic

22 clad chic cite cheek clef sick lick kick dice rice

23 call acid hack jack lack lick cask crack clan cane

o

24 o ol ol old old of off odd ode or ore oar soar one

25 ol sol sold told dole do doe lo doll sol solo odor

26 onto door toil lotto soak fort hods foal roan load

all reaches learned

27 Carlo Rand can call Rocco; Cole can call Doc Cost.

28 Trina can ask Dina if Nick Corl has left; Joe did.

29 Case sent Carole a nice skirt; it fits Lorna Rich.

5e

Key words and phrases

each line once DS; maintain good body position

e / n

30 end need lend lean ken lend fen keen nee dens send

i / t

31 tail lit tiff tilt fit kit lit kits slit silt flit

c / h

32 cash chat chalk hack char hick chic each arch chit

r / o

33 or for lord soar door oar rods roll fork ford oral

all letters learned

34 Jack and Rona did frost nine of the cakes at last.

35 Jo can ice her drink if Tess can find her a flask.

36 Ask Jean to call Fisk at noon; he needs her notes.

Drill 2
Specific rows

Key each set twice.

Tip: Reach to the first and third rows with a minimum of hand movement; keep hands quiet.

Third row

1 We refused to support your ideas to greet the trio of protesters.
2 Peter tested his theory of selling quality ideas to his superior.
3 We were to report at a ferry to people who had written the story.

4 If you type too quickly, you will probably make lots of mistakes.
5 Your pewter is too twisted to put out for your top people to use.
6 Tip is our top reporter for writing up the story of the oil pipe.

First row

7 Mendez came in a cab for a minimum of six dozen zinnias and mums.
8 My bunny munched five dozen boxes of beans and a bin of cabbages.
9 Boxing can be viewed at varied time zones on Mayfoxx Cablevision.

10 Numerous local zip codes were available for box-address mailings.
11 Much to the concern of Vivian, boxcars occupy the condemned zone.
12 Zeb made the extra van into a taxicab. Can civic members wax it?

1 2 3 4 5 6 7 8 9 10 11 12 13

Writing 18

all letters

gwam 3' 5'

Telephone conference calls have been used for years. Today, 4 2 47
graphic data can also be conveyed over telephone lines to enhance 8 5 50
the calls. Two types of devices are used to send the data. The 13 8 52
first type is an electronic blackboard. The terminal, although 17 10 55
it does look like a blackboard, is really used to send written 21 13 57
material over telephone lines to a screen. The second type is a 26 15 60
digitized graphics tablet. The graphics tablet looks very much 30 18 63
like a tablet of art paper. An image is formed on a pressure- 34 20 65
sensitive surface, and the data is entered into the computer. 38 23 68

Conference calls may not be as effective as face-to-face 42 25 70
meetings, but they are far less expensive than the travel 47 28 73
required for many face-to-face meetings. The time workers spend 51 31 75
away from the office while they are traveling is also costly. 55 33 78
The key to success in using conference calls is to select 59 35 80
carefully the type of meeting to be conducted by a call. The 63 38 83
primary objectives of many types of meetings can be attained 67 40 85
through conference calls, especially if the calls are enhanced by 72 43 88
utilizing terminals to transmit graphic data. 75 45 89

gwam 3' 1 2 3 4 5
5' 1 2 3

6 W, Comma, B, P

Skill-Building Warmup

6a 8'

each line twice SS; DS between 2-line groups; avoid pauses

Note suggested minutes for practice shown in heading.

home row 1 a ad as lad las fad sad; jak flask fall jaks salad

n/i/t 2 in tin nit nil its tan din tie ten tine fins stein

c/h/r/o 3 code herd rode cold hock hark roll rock ache chore

all reaches 4 Holt can see Dane at ten; Jill sees Frank at nine.

1 | 2 | 3 | 4 | 5 | 6 | 7 | 8 | 9 | 10

6b 12'

Learn w and , (comma)

each line twice SS; DS between 2-line groups

Comma: Space once after a comma.

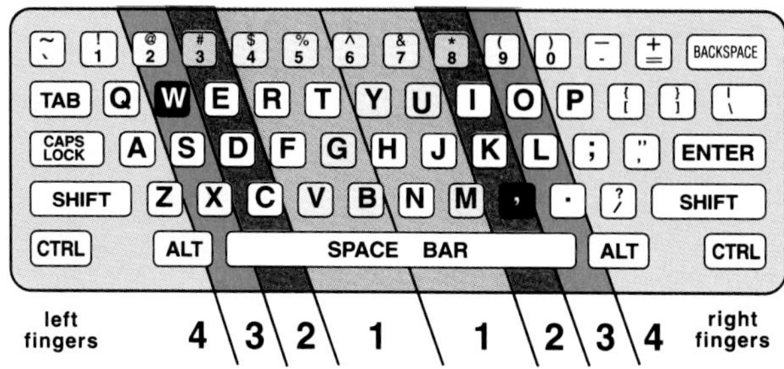

Reach *up* with *left third* finger.

Reach *down* with *right second* finger.

w

5 w ws ws was was wan wit low win jaw wilt wink wolf

6 ow wow how owl howl owe owed row cow cowl new knew

7 wide sown wild town went jowl wait white down walk

, (comma)

8 k, k, k, irk, ilk, ask, oak, ark, lark, jak, rock,

9 skis, a dock, a fork, a lock, a fee, a tie, a fan,

10 Jan, Lee, Ed, and Dan saw Nan, Kate, Len, and Ted.

all reaches learned

11 Win, Lew, Drew, and Walt will walk to West Willow.

12 Ask Ho, Al, and Jared to read the code; it is new.

13 The window, we think, was closed; we felt no wind.

6c 8'

Improve techniques

each line twice

shift keys: shift; strike key; release both quickly

14 Fiji, Don, Cara, and Ron will see East Creek soon.

15 Kane Losh and Janet Hart will join Nan in Rio Ono.

double letters

16 Renee took a class at noon; call her at Lann Hall.

17 Ed and Anne saw three deer flee across Wood Creek.

Skill-Building Workshop 4

1" margins or 65-space line

MicroAssistant: From the Main Menu, key **S4** to access Skill-Building Workshop 4.

Drill 1
Variable rhythm patterns

Key each line twice SS; DS between 2-line groups; rekey difficult lines.

Fluency (key phrases and words, not letter by letter)

1 When Bo's dog bit a neighbor, he rushed the cur to a city kennel.
2 When the alto is on key, she will enrich the chant of the ritual.
3 She will visit the island town with eight men from the coal firm.

Control (key at a steady but not fast pace)

4 My crew in the reserve regattas exceeded the minimum set by Dave.
5 Ed darted to the bazaar to get poppy seeds for the zebras to eat.
6 We reversed the monopoly opinion after Polly presented the facts.

Variable rhythm (vary pace with difficulty of words)

7 Faster signals are needed to decrease the problems for Cave City.
8 All cabbage crates were stored for Ellen after she agreed to pay.
9 Jo fears the amendment statement signals a penalty for the union.

| 1 | 2 | 3 | 4 | 5 | 6 | 7 | 8 | 9 | 10 | 11 | 12 | 13 |

Writing 17

To access these writings on MicroPace Plus software, key **W** and the writing number. For example, key **W17** for Writing 17.

A all letters

	gwam 3'	5'	
Much of the cost of hiring a new employee is clear:	3	2	40
Recruiting trips, placement fees, and advertising expenses are	8	5	43
much higher than ever before. Recruiting, even when successful	12	7	46
and free of problems, accounts for only part of the cost. The	16	10	48
lower productivity rate of a new employee while she or he is	20	12	51
being trained is a hidden cost factor. The time lag between when	25	15	53
a person is hired and when that person actually becomes produc-	29	17	56
tive may frequently extend from six to ten months.	32	19	58
As expensive as the cost of recruiting and training is,	36	22	60
the investment is very worthwhile if an employee is kept produc-	40	24	63
tive and remains with the company. A large number of poor em-	44	27	65
ployees who stay on the job become uninspired about their jobs.	49	29	68
Such people are retirees in residence. The workers who may feel	53	32	70
that their expectations have not been realized begin to do just	57	34	73
enough to get by and find the greatest challenge and fulfillment	62	37	75
in finding new ways to avoid work.	64	38	77

gwam 3' | 1 | 2 | 3 | 4 | 5 |
5' | 1 | 2 | 3 |

6d 12'

Learn b and p

each line twice; DS between 2-line groups

Reach *down* with *left first* finger.

Reach *up* with *right little finger.*

b

18 b bf bf biff boff bit bid bib bird boa ban bon bow
19 be rib fib sob dob cob bob crib lab slab fobs blob
20 born oboe blab bribe able bode belt bath bide both

p

21 p p; p; pa pa; pal pal pan pad par pen pep pap per
22 pa pa; lap lap; nap nap; hep ape spa asp leap clap
23 span park paper pelt tips soap pane pops rope ripe

all reaches learned

24 Barb and Bob wrapped a pepper in paper and ribbon.
25 Rip, Joann, and Dick were all closer to the flash.
26 Bo will be pleased to see Japan; he works in Oslo.

6e 10'

Determine gross words a minute

1 Key line 27 for 30". Try to finish the line as time is called (12 *gwam*).

2 Key line 28 for 1'. Try to finish the line as time is called (10 *gwam*).

3 Repeat for paired lines 29-34.

all letters learned

27 Dick owns a dock at this lake.
28 Dick owns a dock at this lake; he paid Ken for it.

29 Jane also kept a pair of owls.
30 Jane also kept a pair of owls, a hen, and a snake.

31 I blend the cocoa in the bowl.
32 I blend the cocoa in the bowl when I work for Leo.

33 Blair soaks a bit of the corn.
34 Blair soaks a bit of the corn, as he did in Japan.

| 1 | 2 | 3 | 4 | 5 | 6 | 7 | 8 | 9 | 10 |

To determine gross words a minute:

1 Note the figure beneath your last completed line (6 words for each odd-numbered sentence and 10 words for each even-numbered sentence).

2 For a partial line, note the figure beneath the last word keyed.

3 Add these two figures. The total is gross words a minute (*gwam*) for a 1' writing. (To figure *gwam* for a 30" writing, multiply the total by 2.)

Document 1 (continued)

words

Serif. A serif is defined as a line crossing the main 282
strokes of a character or small cross strokes at the edges of 294
letters. Examples of typefaces with serifs include Times 306
Roman, New Century Schoolbook, and Palatino. Seriftype is 318
reccomended for body text. 323

Script. the script typeface looks like handwriting and 392
is often used for wedding or other invitations, awards, amd 404
certificates. A example of a script typeface is the ITC Zapf 417
chancery. 419

San serif. The word san serif means with out serifs; 336
thus, no extensions or small cross strokes are found at the 348
edges of letters. Examples of san serif typefaces include 360
Helvetica and ITC Avant Garde Gothic Book. San serif type- 372
faces are reccomended for headlines. 380

Selecting the appropraite typeface is a very important 430
beginning for the new desktop publisher. To master this 441
skill, they read current literature on page design layout. 452
But, more importantly, experimenting with the different type- 463
faces will provide hands-on experience that will reap satisfy- 474
ing results. 477

______________ 480

Document 2
Unbound report
Prepare the report SS in unbound format.

Document 3
Title page
Prepare a title page for the report in Document 1 using the information below:

Sarah A. Striplin, Manager
Information Support Services

April 28, 19--

(Total words: 21)

REFERENCES 482

Typography Brief: The Changed Face of Type. Economist, Vol. 497
319, No. 7708 (May 25, 1991). 503

Will-Harris, Daniel. WordPerfect: Desktop Publishing in 523
Style. 2d ed. Berkley: Peachpit Press, 1990. 534

Parker, Roger C. Looking Good in Print. Chape Hill: Ventana 551
Press, 1988. 553

7 Review

Skill-Building Warmup

7a 8'

each line twice SS; DS between 2-line groups; begin new lines promptly

home row 1 fa la la; a sad lad; jaks fall; a lass had a salad

1st row 2 Ann Bascan and Cabal Naban nabbed a cab in Canada.

3d row 3 Rip went to a water show with either Pippa or Pia.

all letters 4 Dick will see Job at nine if Rach sees Pat at one.

| 1 | 2 | 3 | 4 | 5 | 6 | 7 | 8 | 9 | 10 |

7b 14'

Check keyreach technique

lines 5-13 SS as shown; DS between 3-line groups

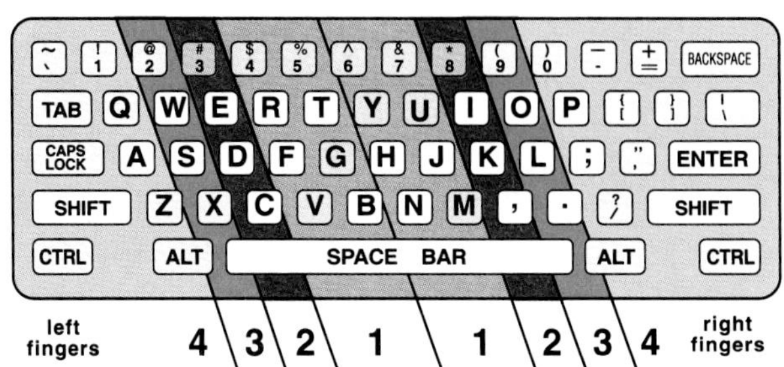

concentrate on words

5 a an pan so sot la lap ah aha do doe el elf to tot

6 bow bowl pin pint for fork forks hen hens jak jaks

7 chap chaps flak flake flakes prow prowl work works

concentrate on phrases

8 is in a|as it is|or if|as a|is on a|to do it|is so

9 is for|did it|is the|we did a|and so|to see|or not

10 as for the|as for the|and to the|to see it|and did

concentrate on words and phrases

11 Jess ate all of the peas in the salad in the bowl.

12 I hid the ace in a jar as a joke; I do not see it.

13 As far as I know, he did not read all of the book.

| 1 | 2 | 3 | 4 | 5 | 6 | 7 | 8 | 9 | 10 |

How to set a goal: Use this formula to determine writing time to reach a goal:

$$\frac{\text{words in line being keyed}}{\text{your } gwam \text{ goal}} \times 60'' = \text{seconds to key writing}$$

Example: $\frac{10 \text{ words}}{15\ gwam} \times 60'' = 40''$

180a-b 15'

Skill-building warmup

Use Skill-building warmup and read "Production measurement procedures" on page 390.

180c 35'

FORMATTING

Production measurement

Document 1
Leftbound report

DS the leftbound report. Add bold to the heading:

TYPEFACES: SELECT THE RIGHT ONE

words

words in heading 6

Within the past six years, the business of making text 17
presentable has become everybodys concern (Economist, 1991, 32
94). More and more businesses have realized the benefits of 45
inhouse desktop publishing and have purchased the necessary 55
desktop publishing software and laser printer to produce 67
professional-looking documents. 73

These new desktop publishers must not only master the 92
desktop publishing software, but they must also acquire basic 104
principals of page design and lay out. One important element 117
of good page design is the selection of an appropriate 128
typeface(s). Typeface refers to the style--or shape--of the 140
letters and numbers (Parker). Times Roman and Helvetica are 154
commonly used typeface. At least 10000 typefaces are in 167
existance today. However, no more than a few hundred are used 181
with any frequency (Economist, 1991, 94). 191

Typefaces should match the message the writer wants to 207
get across (Will-Harris, 1990, 164). A sign warning trespass- 218
ers printed in script, a very formal typeface reserved for 229
wedding invitations, would not inhibit anyone (Economist, 243
1991, 94). 245

Typefaces are classified as (1) serif, (2) san serif, 265
and script. 268

7c 12'

Check spacing/shifting technique

each set of lines twice SS; DS between 3-line groups

▼ Space once after a period following an abbreviation.

spacing

```
14 ad la as in if it lo no of oh he or so ok pi be we
15 an ace ads ale aha a fit oil a jak nor a bit a pew
16 ice ades born is fake to jail than it and the cows
```

spacing/shifting

```
17 Ask Jed.  Dr. Han left at ten; Dr. Crowe, at nine.
18 I asked Jin if she had ice in a bowl; it can help.
19 Freda, not Jack, went to Spain.  Joan likes Spain.
```

| 1 | 2 | 3 | 4 | 5 | 6 | 7 | 8 | 9 | 10 |

7d 16'

Build staying power

1 Key line 20.

2 DS; key lines 20 and 21 SS; do not pause at the end of line 20.

3 DS; key lines 20, 21, and 22 SS. Key fluidly; eyes on copy.

4 Key all 4 lines SS. Work for steady, unhurried key flow.

5 Take two 1' writings on all 4 lines. Calculate *gwam.*

Goal: at least 10 *gwam*

```
20 Jake held a bit of cocoa and an apricot for Diane.

21 Jan is to chant in the still air in an idle field.

22 Dick and I fish for cod on the docks at Fish Lake.

23 Kent still held the dish and the cork in his hand.
```

| 1 | 2 | 3 | 4 | 5 | 6 | 7 | 8 | 9 | 10 |

NEWS *on. . .* Netiquette

With the growth of the Internet, it is becoming increasingly important for people to be aware of good online etiquette. Netiquette (Net etiquette) is the unwritten code of behavior for the Net, news groups, chat rooms, the World Wide Web, e-mail, and other networks. The basic premise of netiquette is to treat people with courtesy and consideration. Apply these basic rules of netiquette:

Stick to the subject, whether chatting in a theme room, posting to a news group, or answering e-mail. Posting an irrelevant message is considered rude and exposes you to being "flamed" or electronically abused by others. Also, don't send irrelevant e-mail messages; people don't have time for frivolous mail.

Use shortcuts with care. Emoticons such as :- (sad, :-) happy, ;-) a wink for a joke or sarcasm are sometimes fun to use. Some people believe, however, emoticons are becoming obsolete. Acronyms such as IMO (in my opinion) are effective only if both parties know the meaning.

Write clearly and concisely. State exactly what you mean to reduce time and need for clarification. And, remember to use proper grammar. Avoid using ALL CAPS for emphasis, particularly in a chat room or news group; it is considered SHOUTING.

As the Internet evolves so will its protocols, including netiquette. So stay "plugged in."

Document 3
Block letter with variable information
(LM p. S127)
Use standard margins and block format; insert the following variables where indicated:

V1— **Mr. Thomas B. Harris**
P.O. Box 233
Conway, AR 72032-8264
V2— **Mr. Harris**
V3— **April 20-21**
V4— **254**
V5— **April 20**

words

April 2, 19-- 3

(V1) 14

Dear **(V2)** 17

I am delighted that you will be attending the Desktop Publish- 30
ing Principles and Application Workshop on **(V3)** at McCoy Col- 44
lege. The workshop will begin at 8 a.m. on both days. Please 56
come to Room **(V4)** of the Harper-Kock Union Building. 67

The first segment of the workshop will be spent learning prin- 79
ciples of desktop publishing and applying these principles in 92
isolated exercises. After appropriate reinforcement, you will 104
create several impressive desktop publishing documents. Imag- 117
ine the comments you will receive from your colleagues when 129
they see your professional brochures, flyers, pamphlets, 140
transparencies, announcements, and newsletters. 150

Directions to Hathorn Hall, the residence hall designated for 162
summer workshop participants, are enclosed. You may check in 175
at Hathorn from 8 a.m. to 10 p.m. Housing payment can be made 187
at the residence hall. 192

(V2), I look forward to seeing you on **(V5)**. 203

Sincerely | Jane D. Gunter | Workshop Coordinator | xx | Enclosure 215

Document 4
Topic outline
Use 2" top margin and apply correct capitalization. Add the following heading in bold:
THREE QUALITIES OF GOOD WRITING

words in heading 6

I. INTRODUCTION 9
II. POSITIVE TONE 13
A. Use Positive Tone. 27
(1. Pleasure 2. Quality 3. Satisfied 4. Service)
B. Avoid Negative Words. 40
(1. Cannot 2. Deny 3. Impossible 4. Refuse)
CONCICE NESS (S) 42
Use Short Words⊙ 46
Edit ~~out~~ unnecessary Words. 62
(1. If (in the event of) 2. During (during the course of))
COURTESY 64
Gain Reader's Attention. 69
Maintain Reader's Interest⊙ 74
1. Incorporate "you" attitude. 81
2. Appeal to reader's needs. 87
C. Create Reader's Desire (to Act). 94
D. Request Reader's Action. 99
SUMMARY 101

8 G, Question Mark, X, U

Skill-Building Warmup

8a 8'

each line twice SS; DS between 2-line groups; eyes on copy

all letters 1 We often can take the older jet to Paris and back.

w/b 2 As the wind blew, Bob Webber saw the window break.

p/, 3 Pat, Pippa, or Cap has prepared the proper papers.

all reaches 4 Bo, Jose, and Will fed Lin; Jack had not paid her.

| 1 | 2 | 3 | 4 | 5 | 6 | 7 | 8 | 9 | 10

8b 6'

Reach for new goals

two 30" writings on each line

Goal: complete each line—12 *gwam*

5 Blake owns a pen for the foal.

6 Jan lent the bowl to the pros.

7 He fit the panel to the shelf.

8 This rock is half of the pair.

9 I held the title for the land.

| 1 | 2 | 3 | 4 | 5 | 6 |

8c 12'

Learn g and ?

each line twice SS; DS between 2-line groups; eyes on copy

Question mark: The question mark is usually followed by two spaces.

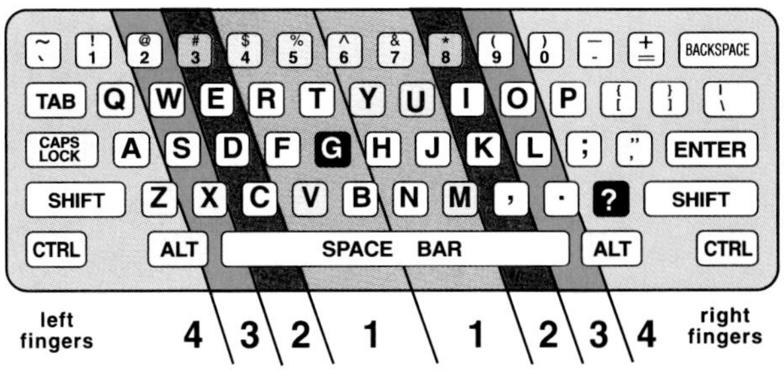

Reach to *right* with *left first* finger.

Left shift; reach *down* with *right little finger.*

g

10 g g gf gaff gag grog fog frog drag cog dig fig gig

11 gf go gall flag gels slag gala gale glad glee gals

12 golf flog gorge glen high logs gore ogle page grow

?

13 ? ?; ?; ? ? Who? When? Where? Who is? Who was?

14 Who is here? Was it he? Was it she? Did she go?

15 Did Geena? Did he? What is that? Was Jose here?

all reaches learned

16 Has Ginger lost her job? Was her April bill here?

17 Phil did not want the boats to get here this soon.

18 Loris Shin has been ill; Frank, a doctor, saw her.

179a-b 15'

Skill-building warmup

Use Skill-building warmup and read "Production measurement procedures" on page 390.

179c 35'

FORMATTING

Production measurement

Document 1
Modified block letter

(LM p. S123)

Use standard margins and the information below to prepare the letter in modified block format with mixed punctuation.

Date: **March 26, 19--**

Address:

Mr. Kelly Stinson
Computer Corporation, Inc.
3211 Cresswell Street
Cincinnati, OH 45236-6543

Re: Account No. 6120-122-2330

Closing: **Sincerely**

Sender: **Frank Lawrence, Manager**

Document 2
Simplified block letter

(LM p. S125)

Use standard margins and simplified block format.

Date: **March 26, 19--**

Address:

Ms. Kathryn T. Kirby
Software Analyst
Technologies, Ltd.
P.O. Drawer 20383
Dallas, TX 78403-7654

Sender: **P. Susan Osaka, Systems Analyst**

Document 1

words

words in heading 30

immediate 40

Please send replacement of forty InterLan N16510 TelMark 43

boot proms. 45

During the time that pucrhase orders were issued for 56

these boot proms, we uncovered a problem that caused unneces- 68

e

sary network traffic betwen the booting PC and the TelMark/ 80

MSD server. Our agreement was that wewould receive the 92

i

neccesary upgrade at no additonal cost when we received the 104

e

boot proms. To expidite matters please ship the replacement 116

proms by overnight mail. We would appreciate your immediate 129

so that we can meet our system deadlines.

attention to this matter. 142

words in closing 149

Document 2

words in heading 23

ICC Software Information 28

In response to your request for information regarding 39

ICC software, our records indicate that we have purchased 50

and installed 107 licenses for the product through 61

with

January 31, 19--. This includes 7 licenses bought on a 73

purchase order dated 1/23/--. In addition, we have 85

either purchased or have purchase orders pending for 96

28 more licenses which will bring our total to 105

unprotected

135 through March of this year. 112

Our standing arrangement with ICC is that we 123

recieve a single copy of the software, which we 133

reinstall whenever new licenses are purchased. 143

We are presently using version 1.30 U/3.60--the first 153

version free of problems we reported during our 163

lengthy verification/debugging process. 171

Ms. Kirby, if I can provide additional information, 181

please let me know. 185

words in closing 192

8d 12'

Learn x and u

each line twice SS; DS between 2-line groups

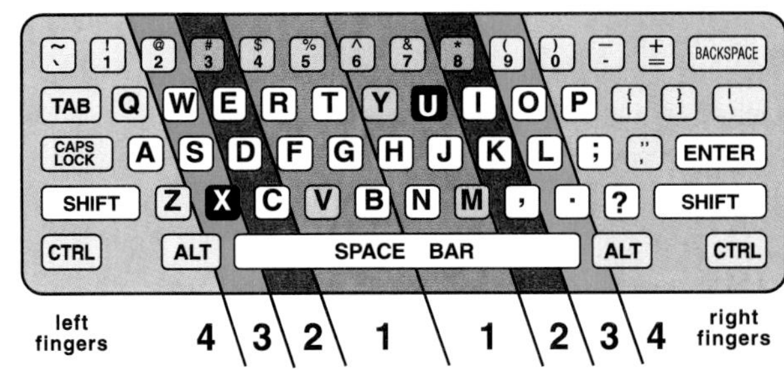

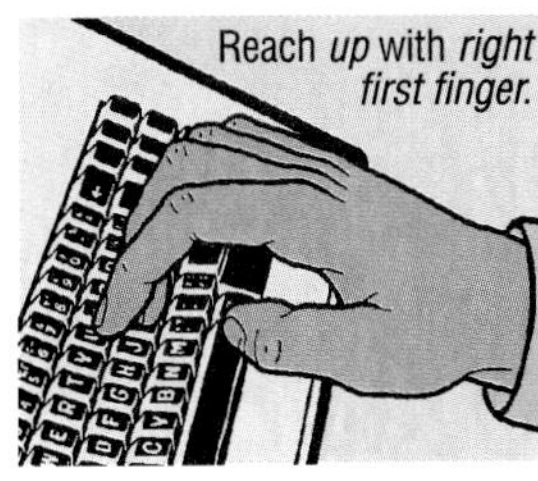

x

19 x x xs xs ox ox lox sox fox box ex hex lax hex fax

20 sx six sax sox ax fix cox wax hex box pox sex text

21 flax next flex axel pixel exit oxen taxi axis next

u

22 u uj uj jug jut just dust dud due sue use due duel

23 uj us cud but bun out sun nut gun hut hue put fuel

24 dual laud dusk suds fuss full tuna tutus duds full

all reaches learned

25 Paige Power liked the book; Josh can read it next.

26 Next we picked a bag for Jan; then she, Jan, left.

27 Is her June account due? Has Lou ruined her unit?

8e 12'

Build staying power

1 Key Paragraph 1 (¶1) twice.

2 DS and key ¶2 twice.

3 Work to avoid pauses, not for speed.

Optional

1 Take a 1' writing on each ¶.

2 Find *gwam* using the dots and figures above the lines (a dot equals 2 words).

Goal: 12 *gwam*

OS If you are using the Alphanumeric software, complete this exercise in the open screen using the timing option.

E all letters learned

. 4 . 8 .
How a finished job will look often depends on how
12 . 16 . 20
we feel about our work as we do it. Attitude has
. 24 . 28 .
a definite effect on the end result of work we do.

. 4 . 8 .
When we are eager to begin a job, we relax and do
12 . 16 . 20
better work than if we start the job with an idea
. 24 . 28 .
that there is just nothing we can do to escape it.

Document 2
Standard memo

Send the memo to **Computing Center Staff** from **William Thorne, Manager, Systems & Network Programming**; date **March 25, 19--**. Add an appropriate subject line. A copy will be sent to **Richard McDaniel**.

words

words in heading 27

PC/TCP, a very powerful set of PC network utilities is 38
now operational on every PC in the Computing Center. PC/TCP 51
was installed in conjunction with the ICC/ALDSTATION software 63
that provides UTS terminal emulation across the network into 75
the ALD80 mainframe. Training will be provided concerning the 90
major capabilities of PC/TCP. ~~By providing additional train-~~ 98
~~ing in these areas, we hope~~ to gain the productivity promised 105
by vendors of PC/TCP. 110

PC disk back up is the first capability of PC/TCP to be 121
~~discussed~~. Disk back up is an important chore that most of us 133
ignore because of the tedium involved in handling dozens of 145
floppy disks needed to hold a 20 or 40 megabyte back up. By 157
using a 1/4 cartridge tape that can hold up to 150 megabyes of 176
data, users can solve this problem. The attached document out 188
lines procedures for using PC/TCP to back up the PC hard disk 202
across the network to a tape drive on the Computing Center 214
network server. If you have questions about the PC disk 226
back up ~~after studying the report~~, please call any member of 232
the Systems & Network Programing group at 5523. 242

words in closing 248

Document 3
Three-column table with blocked column heads

Center the table horizontally and vertically; block column headings. Add bold to all headings; main and secondary headings are:

CONTRACT AWARDS
April 1, 19--

words in heading 7

Contract	Award Amount	Project Director	
Greyson Production	$74,550	Molly Tomlinson	31
M & K Industries	59,800	William Mott	38
L. P. Yachts, Inc.	38,900	Jake Letterman	47
Prince, Watts, & Overbee	25,675	Maurine Gilbert	56
Sieverston, Ltd.	17,250	Mike Arroyo	63
Mellon and Mellon	6,910	Kathryn LeGrande	71

Document 4
Simplified memo

Prepare the memo in Document 2 in simplified format. Omit ¶3.

9 Q, M, V, Apostrophe

Skill-Building Warmup

9a 8'

lines 1 and 2 twice SS; DS between 2-line groups; try to key lines 3 and 4 in 40" (15 *gwam*), or set your own goal

all letters 1 Lex gripes about cold weather; Fred is not joking.
space bar 2 Is it Di, Jo, or Al? Ask Lt. Coe, Bill; he knows.
easy 3 I did rush a bushel of cut corn to the sick ducks.
easy 4 He is to go to the Tudor Isle of England on a bus.

1 | 2 | 3 | 4 | 5 | 6 | 7 | 8 | 9 | 10

9b 12'

Learn q and m

each line twice SS; DS between 2-line groups

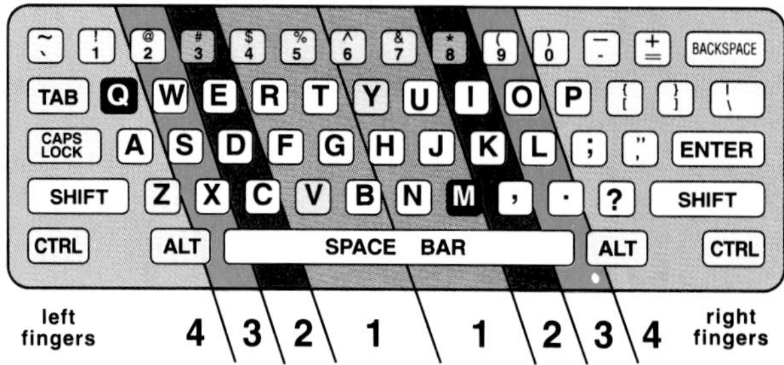

Reach *up* with *left little* finger.

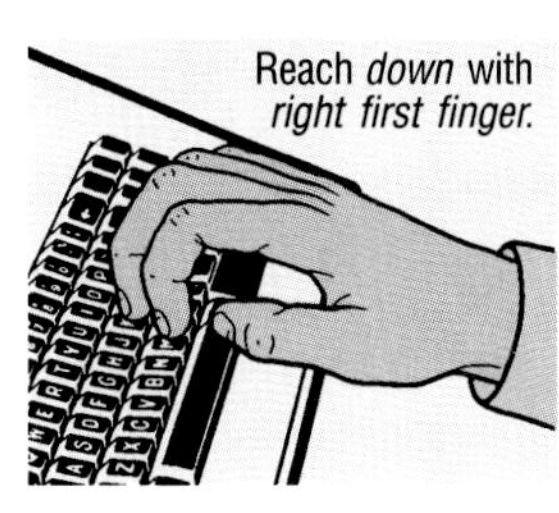
Reach *down* with *right first finger.*

q

5 q qa qa quad quad quaff quant queen quo quit quick
6 qa qu qa quo quit quod quid quip quads quote quiet
7 quite quilts quart quill quakes quail quack quaint

m

8 m mj mj jam man malt mar mar maw me mew men hem me
9 m mj ma am make male mane melt meat mist amen lame
10 malt meld hemp mimic tomb foam rams mama mire mind

all reaches learned

11 Quin had some quiet qualms about taming a macaque.
12 Jake Coxe had questions about a new floor program.
13 Max was quick to join the big reception for Lidia.

9c 8'

Practice downward reaches

each line twice; repeat lines where you sensed a loss of continuity

x
14 Max Exan, their expert, next exposed six wax oxen.
c
15 Chuck can check their inaccurate accident account.
b
16 Robb won; he lobbed the basketball behind Barbara.
m
17 Emma hummed as she aimed her small camera at Mame.
n
18 Ann is not running in the Ninth Annual Nantes Run.

35 Production Measurement

Measurement goal:
To measure speed and accuracy of document production.

Machine adjustments:
Margins and spacing: as appropriate for documents.

178a 5'

Skill-building warmup

Use this drill to prepare for each lesson in Section 35.

alphabet 1 Kim Gaby, a rap fan, was quite perplexed to have won a jazz disc.
fig/sym 2 I used $176,345.90 as my total to figure increases of 8% and 12%.
direct reach 3 Muttering angrily under her breath, the ecologist left the spill.
fluency 4 To make the problem right turn visible, I cut a bush by the lane.
| 1 | 2 | 3 | 4 | 5 | 6 | 7 | 8 | 9 | 10 | 11 | 12 | 13 |

178b 10'

FORMATTING

Production measurement

Follow the procedures at right for Lessons 178-180.

Time Schedule
Assemble materials .... 3'
Timed production .... 35'
Final check;
compute *n-pram* .... 7'

1 Arrange stationery from the Laboratory Materials, plain paper, and reference sources.
2 Proofread and correct errors before going to the next document. Proofread carefully; some documents contain unmarked errors. Supply enclosure and attachment notations as required. Start over with Document 1 if you finish before time is called.
3 Proofread and circle all errors in the document that you are completing when time is called.
4 Compute *n-pram* (net production rate a minute): Total words keyed – penalty* = *n-pram.*
*Penalty is 15 words for each uncorrected error.

178c 35'

FORMATTING

Production measurement

Document 1
Simplified memo

Date the memo **March 25, 19--**. Send it to **Ginger Tate, Public Relations Department**. The subject is **NETWORKED ELECTRONIC MAIL**. The memo is from **William Thorne, Manager, Systems & Network Programming**. Format the items in ¶2 as a two-column table; total the column.

words

words in heading 12

A configuration for a Torres computer system that will allow 24
your office to participate in the networked electronic mail environment 39
presently being used by top management is summarized below: 51
Torres II / si (2 MB memory, 40 MB hard drive), $2,450; 62
Keyboard, $160; Full-page portrait monitor, $780; 4 MB memory 74
upgrade, $140*; Nubus adapter card, $175; Techtalk card, $425; 87
Technet transceiver, $160*; Technet transceiver cable, $65*; Saga 102
E-mail software, $80; Saga Word w/p software, $100; Saga Compute 113
spreadsheet software, $189; Lasertech II NT Personal Printer, 125
$2,175 126
As the prices listed above are only estimates, you must obtain 139
exact prices before issuing a requisition. All items except those 152
marked with an asterisk can be purchased from the Computing 164
Center. If you need reccomendations for vendors for the other items, 178
please call me at 5532. 183

words in closing 194

9d 12'

Learn v and ' (apostrophe)

each line twice SS (slowly, then faster); DS between 2-line groups

Apostrophe: The apostrophe shows (1) omission (as Rob't for Robert or it's for it is) or (2) possession when used with nouns (as Joe's hat).

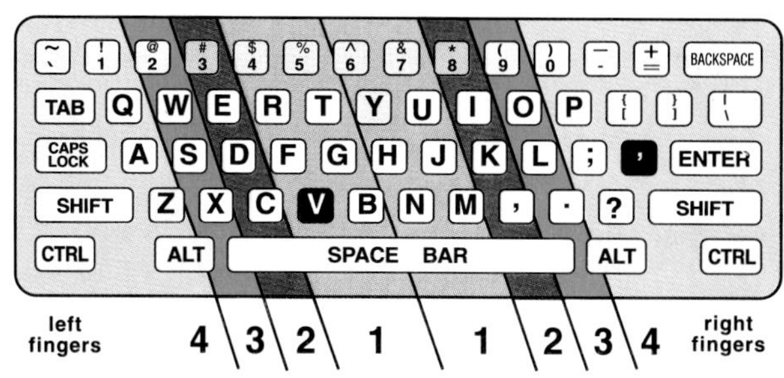

Reach *down* with *left first* finger.

Reach to ' with right *little* finger.

v

19 v vf vf vie vie via via vim vat vow vile vale vote
20 vf vf ave vet ova eve vie dive five live have lave
21 cove dove over aver vivas hive volt five java jive

' (apostrophe)

22 '; '; it's it's Rod's; it's Bo's hat; we'll do it.
23 We don't know if it's Lee's pen or Norma's pencil.
24 It's ten o'clock; I won't tell him that he's late.

all reaches learned

25 It's Viv's turn to drive Iva's van to Ava's house.
26 Qua, not Vi, took the jet; so did Cal. Didn't he?
27 Wasn't Fae Baxter a judge at the post garden show?

9e 10'

Practice returning and spacing

each group once as shown; DS and repeat as time permits

return: reach for the enter key without pausing or looking up

28 Keep fingers in home position;
29 reach little finger to return;
30 flick; return to home position
31 at once. Do not glance up; do
32 not break the flow of the work.

space bar: do not pause before or after striking the space bar

33 we or be up ah go ox it an la ok if ad is he as no
34 When did R. J. Coe go? Lt. Bem ordered her to go.

| 1 | 2 | 3 | 4 | 5 | 6 | 7 | 8 | 9 | 10 |

Document 8
Interview follow-up letter

After submitting a resume and completed employment application form to St. Louis Memorial Hospital (Document 2), you were invited to the company for a job interview. Yesterday you were interviewed by Mr. Jeffrey A. Abraham, Director of Human Resources. Prepare the follow-up letter drafted at the right. Proofread carefully for errors in keying and grammatical and punctuation errors—it is essential that you send an error-free letter.

Thank you for taking the time yesterday to talk with me about working for ~~your company~~ St. Louis Memorial Hospital. Thank you, too, for the tour of your office and facilities; both are impressive.

Your discussion of your companys need for a health fitness program use thesaurus for word ______ me. As I mentioned, the "Health Kick" program that I organized in my hometown was well recieved and successful. ~~Possibly~~ Perhaps this program could be adapted for your company.

Mr. Abraham, please consider this experience in adition to my other qualifications when ~~making your decision,~~ selecting an assistant office manager.

Document 9
Job offer acceptance letter

Within a week after sending a letter to Mr. Abraham (Document 8), you received a telephone call from him. He offered you the assistant office manager position.

You have considered the job offer and have drafted the acceptance letter at right. Prepare the letter to Mr. Abraham. Add your own personal letterhead.

Thank you for your confidence in my ability to sewe St. Louis Memorial Hospital as assistant office manager. yes, I accept your offer of the position.

As we agreed in our telephone conversation, I will report to work at 8 a.m. on Monday, October 3. I understand that the first six months will be a probationary period. After successfully completing this trial period, I will be designated as a permanent employee. Future performance reviews will be regularly administered in January.

Thank you, Mr. Abraham, for this opportunity. I look foward to working with your company.

10 Z, Y, Quotation Mark

Skill-Building Warmup

10a 8'

each line twice SS; DS between 2-line groups; line 4 as 40" writings (15 *gwam*)

Goal: 15 *gwam*

```
all letters  1 Quill owed those back taxes after moving to Japan.
    spacing  2 Didn't Vi, Sue, and Paul go?  Someone did; I know.
      q/v/m  3 Marv was quite quick to remove that mauve lacquer.
       easy  4 Lana is a neighbor; she owns a lake and an island.
               | 1 | 2 | 3 | 4 | 5 | 6 | 7 | 8 | 9 | 10 |
```

10b 12'

Learn z and y

each line twice SS; DS between 2-line groups

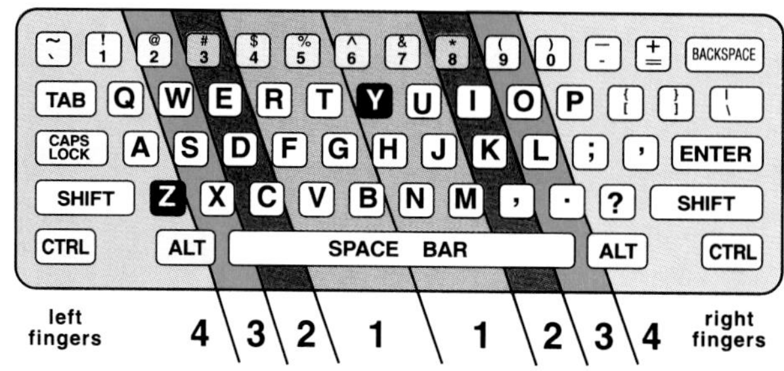

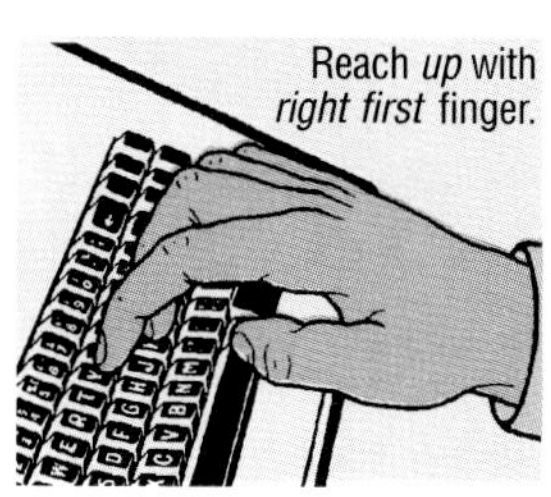

Reach *down* with *left little* finger.
Reach *up* with *right first* finger.


```
z
 5 za za zap zap zing zig zag zoo zed zip zap zig zed
 6 doze zeal zero haze jazz zone zinc zing size ozone
 7 ooze maze doze zoom zarf zebus daze gaze faze adze

y
 8 y yj yj jay jay hay hay lay nay say days eyes ayes
 9 yj ye yet yen yes cry dry you rye sty your fry wry
10 ye yen bye yea coy yew dye yaw lye yap yak yon any

all reaches learned
11 Did you say Liz saw any yaks or zebus at your zoo?
12 Relax; Jake wouldn't acquire any favorable rights.
13 Has Mazie departed?  Tex, Lu, and I will go alone.
```

10c 10'

Practice specific keyreaches

each line twice SS; DS between 2-line groups; repeat troublesome lines

```
g
14 Is Gregg urging Gage to ship eggs to Ragged Gorge?
x
15 Dixi expects Bix to fix her tax bill on the sixth.
u
16 It is unusual to house unused units in the bunker.
b
17 Barb Robbes is the barber who bobbed her own hair.
p
18 Pepe prepared a pepper salad for a special supper.
```

Document 7
Functional-style resume

The resume at right was prepared by Karen Witzig to emphasize the skills she has acquired. Note she has had little or no related job experience. Using the example as your guide, prepare a resume of your qualifications for one of the positions at the right.

wp Vary typefaces and point sizes. Use graphic lines to separate parts of the resume.

Legal Assistant
Requires ability to keyboard, format precise legal documents ... excellent proofreading skills ... legal terminology helpful. Send inquires to:
Jacobus, Pentyala, and Associates
112 County Line Road
Jackson, MS 39206-0112

Project Secretary
Must have excellent interpersonal and communication skills ... must key from rough draft, proofread. Write:
Beckett-Yeatman Engineering Company
932 West Second Street
Phoenix, AZ 85007-3219

Medical Assistant
Keyboarding ... medical forms, correspondence ... light bookkeeping ... knowledge of medical terms a plus. Write to:
Family Medical Center, Inc.
Medical Arts Complex
9932 Hanover Street
Seattle, WA 98102-0302

Resume is attractive, functional, and reflects creativity.

Objective reflects current and long-term goals.

Experience and education are combined to reflect applicant's achievements.

KAREN E. WITZIG
16203 Dunworth Boulevard
Warm Springs, GA 31830-9871
(404) 555-3796

OBJECTIVE

Seeking a word processing position with training for supervisory position.

QUALIFICATIONS

Organized	Headed Sigma Gamma Beta's "Wall of Fame" planning committee. Assisted in organizing Senior Career Day with 22 local businesses participating; engaged speakers, reserved meeting rooms, drafted meeting schedule. Served on committee for library expansion project.
Dependable	Attended all but two classes last year; always on time for classes and work. Awarded "Employee of the Month" for outstanding attendance and service of part-time workers at fast-food chain. (Maintained a 20-hour-week schedule for 18 months while attending school.) Met all biweekly deadlines as contributor to school newspaper.
Leadership Ability	Chaired the student council in high school. Led campaign to bring a Business Professionals of America chapter to school; served as first president.
Knowledgeable	Graduated this spring with an A.A.S. degree with major in Office Administration. Proficient in word processing, database, spreadsheet, and desktop publishing software. Worked part-time while attending college; received scholarship from Southern Life Insurance Co.
References	Will be furnished upon request.

10d 8'

Learn " (quotation mark)

each line once; repeat lines 21-24

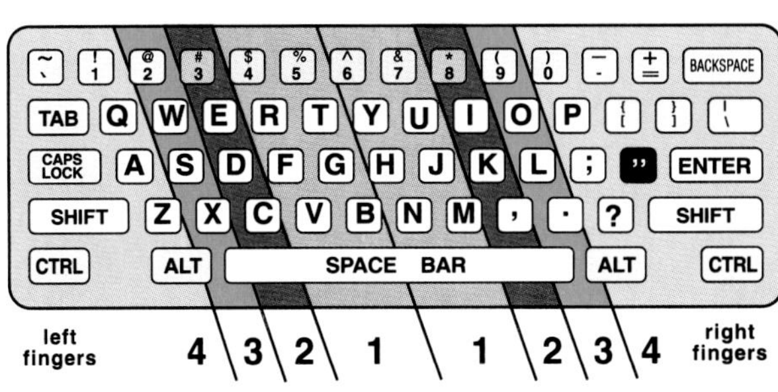

Shift; then reach to " with *right little* finger.

" (quotation mark)

19 "; "; " " "lingo" "bugs" "tennies" I like "malts."
20 "I am not," she said, "going." I just said, "Oh?"

all letters learned

21 The expression, "I give you my word," or as it is
22 put quite often, "Take my word for it," is just a
23 way I say, "I prize my name; it clearly stands in
24 back of my words." I offer "honor" as collateral.

10e 12'

Build staying power

1 Key both ¶s once SS line for line; DS between ¶s. Work for smooth, continuous stroking (not speed) without looking up, especially at the ends of lines.

2 Take two 1' writings on each ¶; determine *gwam*.

Suggested goal: 15 *gwam*

OS Users of Alphanumeric software should complete this exercise in the open screen using the timing option.

E all letters

All of us work for progress, but it is not always
easy to analyze "progress." We work hard for it;
but, in spite of some really good efforts, we may
fail to receive just exactly the response we want.

When this happens, as it does to all of us, it is
time to cease whatever we are doing, have a quiet
talk with ourselves, and face up to the questions
about our limited progress. How can we do better?

Document 5
Compose a list of references

Joseph Brennan prepared the reference list at right to leave with the interviewer. The references were prepared on stationery of the same color, texture, and weight as used for the resume.

Using the guide (at right), prepare the list of references you will take to your next interview. For each reference, include a courtesy title (Mr., Dr.), full name of person, company name, position title, address, and phone number for working hours. Select references who can provide an objective summary of your qualifications. Do not use friends, relatives, or clergy as references.

wp Vary typeface and point size for heading and body; the font selected should compliment the resume. Try using a graphic line for interest.

REFERENCES FOR JOSEPH A. BRENNAN

1771 Russell Boulevard
St. Louis, MO 63104-3883
(314) 555-1456

Mr. William W. Turner, President
Maddox National Bank
P.O. Box 322
St. Louis, MO 63104-0322
(314) 555-0982

Dr. Diahn Osaka, Professor
Department of Office Systems
St. Louis University
P.O. Drawer 1122
St. Louis, MO 63104-1122
(314) 555-3627

Dr. Julia Hedrick, Adviser
SLU Business Association
St. Louis University
Department of Management
P.O. Drawer 3003
St. Louis, MO 63104-3003
(314) 555-7788

Document 6
Interview questions and suggested answers

Key the list of interview questions (at right). Below each question, key your answer. Use current articles to write effective answers.

INTERVIEW QUESTIONS AND SUGGESTED ANSWERS

1. What are your career plans (long-term and short-term)?
2. What are some of the factors that led you to choose your college major? your college/university?
3. What courses did you like least? best? Explain.
4. What do you know about our company?
5. Why do you want to work for us?
6. Why should we hire you? What qualifications do you have that make you believe you should be hired over others?
7. What do you think determines a person's progress in an organization?
8. Describe a time when you have worked well under pressure.
9. Describe something you have done that shows initiative and willingness to work.
10. What are your salary expectations?

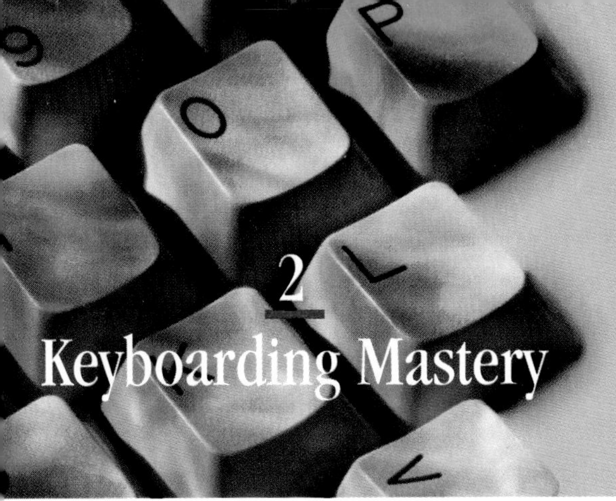

2 Keyboarding Mastery

Learning goals:

1. To achieve smoother stroking.
2. To improve use of service keys.
3. To develop a relaxed, confident attitude.
4. To increase stroking speed to at least 15 *gwam.*

Formatting guides:

1. Default margins or 50-space line.
2. Single-space drills; double-space between exercises.

11a 8'

Skill-building warmup

each line twice SS (slowly, then faster); DS between 2-line groups

alphabet 1 Max Jewel picked up five history quizzes to begin.
" (quote) 2 Can you spell "chaos," "bias," "bye," and "their"?
y 3 Ty Clay may envy you for any zany plays you write.
easy 4 She kept the fox, owls, and fowl down by the lake.

| 1 | 2 | 3 | 4 | 5 | 6 | 7 | 8 | 9 | 10 |

11b 8'

Improve keying techniques

each line once

first row: keep hand movement to a minimum; pull fingers under

5 Can my cook, Mrs. Zackman, carve the big ox roast?
6 Did Cam, the cabby, have extra puzzles? Yes, one.

home row: use fingertips; keep fingers curved

7 Jack was sad; he had just lost his gold golf ball.
8 Sal was glad she had a flashlight; Al was as glad.

third row: straighten fingers slightly; do not move hands forward

9 Did Troy write to Terry Reppe? Did he quote Ruth?
10 Powers quit their outfit to try out for our troop.

| 1 | 2 | 3 | 4 | 5 | 6 | 7 | 8 | 9 | 10 |

11c 8'

Practice newer keyreaches

1 Key each line once; checkmark any line that you do not key fluently.

2 Repeat each checked line. Work for smoothness, not for speed.

y
11 Why did you not play any really happy songs today?
'
12 I'll see if Lenny can't use Ray's book; it's here.
z
13 Liz Zahl saw Zoe feed the zebra in an Arizona zoo.
m
14 A drummer drummed for a moment, and Mimi came out.
v
15 Have Vivian, Eva, or Vi visited Vista Valley Farm?
q
16 Did Enrique quietly but quickly quell the quarrel?

A well-developed resume that works well with the letter of application (cover letter) is an indispensible tool for securing a job interview. The content of a resume will vary from person to person and from job to job, though the kindes of information provided may be similar. A reverse-chronological-style resume focus on a applicant's education and work experience and includes identification; references; and, often, a career objective and personal information. A functional style resume focuses on an applicant's job skills and characteristics, such as analytical ability, creativity, leadership, and organiztion and planning skills, and incl8udes brief evidence of those competencies and traits.

For resumes, no format is regarded as "standard." However, a wise job applicant keeps the following guidelines in mind:

1. Headings an other items stand out when underlines, ALL CAPS, indenting, hyphens, dashed and/or asterisks are used.
2. Even spacing between groups of information contribut5te to readability of a resume; even-width margins contribute to a favorable impression.
3. Headings of one or two words or a short phrase may be center centered or blocked at the left.
4. Meticulous proofreading by the applicant and another person to detect typographical, grammatical, punctuation, spelling, and capitalization errors is worth the time and trouble.

Preparing an error-free letter of application and resume that "work" together are a job applicants' investments in themselves. These employemnt documents are tickets--winning tickets--to the applicant's future.

Document 4
Employment application
(LM pp. S119-S121)
Complete the employment application form that you obtained from St. Louis Memorial Hospital (in response to your application letter in Document 2) to apply for the assistant office manager position. Enter accurate information in *every* section of the form. Indicate "None" or "Not Applicable" where appropriate. Sign and date the form with a black pen.

11d 12'

Control service keys

each line once

return: key smoothly without looking at fingers

17 Make the return snappily
18 and with assurance; keep
19 your eyes on your source
20 data; maintain a smooth,
21 constant pace as you key.

space bar: use down-and-in motion

22 us me it of he an by do go to us if or so am ah el
23 Have you a pen? If so, print "Free to any guest."

shift keys: use smooth shift-key-release motions

24 Juan Colon will see Lyle Branch in Oak Creek Park.
25 Mo, Lucy, and Sky left for New Orleans, Louisiana.

11e 14'

Reach for new goals

1 Key ¶1 line for line; then take two 1' writings on the ¶. DS between ¶s.

2 Repeat Step 1 for ¶s 2 and 3. Key all ¶s. DS between ¶s. Goal: **16 *gwam***

OS If using the Alphanumeric software, complete this exercise in the open screen using the timer. This instruction will not be repeated.

all letters

Have we thought of communication as a kind of war that we wage through each day?

When we think of it that way, good language would seem to become our major line of attack.

Words become muscle; in a normal exchange or in a quarrel, we do well to realize the power of words.

VIEWS *on*. . . One Space or Two?

Traditionally, two spaces follow end-of-sentence punctuation in documents. In desktop publishing, one space generally follows end-of-sentence punctuation. As a result of desktop publishing and the proportional fonts of today's word processing programs, some users have suggested change.

With proportional fonts, characters use a varied amount of space depending upon their width. Monospace fonts such as Courier (also used by typewriters) use the same amount of space for each character; thus two spaces are required after end-of-sentence punctuation for readability.

We believe the critical factors are readability and ease of retention, and not all fonts provide a distinct end-of-sentence look. End-of-sentence punctuation decisions will continue to be reevaluated with changing technologies. In this textbook, you will use two spaces after end-of-sentence punctuation for typical document production. In the Word Processing Workshop, however, you may use one.

Document 3
Report

Your counselor asked you to summarize the main points you have picked up at Job Seekers. You planned and edited the report. Prepare an error-free report (unbound, DS) from the rough draft at the right and on page 386. Use the main heading **THE WINNING TICKETS TO YOUR CAREER** and the secondary heading **Letters and Resumes That Win Job Interviews.** Insert the following side headings between ¶s 1 and 2 and ¶s 5 and 6, respectively:

Letter of Application

Resume

Use the hanging indent format for enumerations. The report will be distributed to future clients for inclusion in their employment files.

Review the resume and letter of application that you prepared (Documents 1 and 2). Note on them any changes that need to be made.

A first impression is a lasting impression. No one needs to keep this idea ~~concept~~ in mind more than a job applicant. While a job interview will usually determine wheter ~~or not~~ an applicant will be hired, a well-written application letter and neatly organized resume determines whether an interview will take plaze.

A letter of application is a job applicant's introduction to a prospective employer. The application letter should "sell" the applicants qualifications to the reder of the letter. Like all business letters, it should be clear complete, concise, correct, and considerate of the reader.

The applicant should make every effort to determine the anme of a particular individual to whom to send the letter. ~~but~~ if a person cannot be identified, then the letter may be sent to the Director of Human Resources ~~Personnel~~ and either "Ladies and Gentlemen" ~~"Dear Sir or Madam"~~ or "Dear Director" may be used as the salutation.

in providing detalis about her or his qualifications, an applicant shoul consider the prospective employer's viewpoint. The application letter should be tailored ~~written~~ for a particular position or type of job in the employer's organization. In addoition, the letter from beginning to end shoul involve a "you" approach (what applicant can do for employer), rather than an "I" approach (what applicant wants).

Any of the standard letter formats--block, modified block, of simplified block--may be used for a letter of application. The letter should be confined to one page and should be prepared on high-quality plan paper of personal stationery.

12 Review

Skill-Building Warmup

12a 8'

each line twice SS (slowly, then faster); DS between 2-line groups

```
alphabet 1 Which big market for quality jazz has Vi expanded?
       q 2 Quin Racq quickly and quietly quelled the quarrel.
       z 3 Zaret zipped along sizzling, zigzag Arizona roads.
    easy 4 Can they handle the auditory problems of the city?
             1 | 2 | 3 | 4 | 5 | 6 | 7 | 8 | 9 | 10
```

12b 9'

Practice newer keyreaches

1 Key each line once; work for smoothness, not for speed.

2 Repeat lines you do not key fluently.

```
   m / b
 5 Bob may remember he was a member of my brass band.
   z / '
 6 Inez isn't fazed by Zeno's use of Al's jazz music.
   w / ,
 7 I asked Wendy, Lew, and Walt to walk my dog, Paws.
   p / "
 8 "Oh," gasped Pan, "someone put pepper in my soup."
   q / ?
 9 Where is Quito? Qatar? Boqueirao? Quebec? Birqash?
   h / .
10 Mr. H. H. Hannah asked Dr. Heath to help him push.
```

12c 10'

Control service keys

each line once

```
   return: do not pause or look up to return
11 Successful keying is not just
12 a matter of speed; rather, it
13 is a combination of rapid and
14 slow, but constant, movements.

   space bar: use correct spacing after each punctuation mark
15 Was it here?  I saw it; Jan saw it, too.  We did.

   shift keys: depress shift key firmly; avoid pauses
16 Pam was in Spain in May; Bo Roy met her in Madrid.
   | 1 | 2 | 3 | 4 | 5 | 6 | 7 | 8 | 9 | 10 |
```

Document 2
Application letter

1 Study the application letter, noting the purpose of each paragraph. The letter correlates with the sample resume on page 383.

2 Compose a letter of application in response to the ad in Document 1. Use Mr. Brennan's letter as a guide, but substitute information from the ad and your resume (Document 1). Supply fictitious information if necessary to complete the letter.

Use personal/business letter format or personal/business stationery.

1771 Russell Boulevard
St. Louis, MO 63104-3883
April 30, 19--

Address letter to proper person. →

Ms. Beverly C. Garick
Freeman National Bank
P.O. Drawer 601
St. Louis, MO 63166-0601

Dear Ms. Garick

Opening indicates the position for which one is applying and that one's qualifications match the position requirements. →

Your advertisement in today's <u>St. Louis Gazette</u> has prompted me to apply for the position of office manager. Major qualifications I could bring to your organization are my skills and experience from my previous employment in a bank and my college training in office systems.

Qualifications relate directly to the position. Experience is emphasized. →

Software courses provided the theory and practice needed to become proficient in word processing, database management, spreadsheets, and graphics. In addition to my training, I gained work experience in a bank and in a university department. After working only six months at Maddox National Bank, I was promoted to a shared salaried position. As the afternoon assistant to the president and vice president, I prepared all appointments with the computerized calendaring system, planned all travel, and maintained the financial records for these offices.

Reference to resume is made. →

As you will read in my enclosed resume, I have held a leadership role in my professional association and have earned recognition through scholarship awards and competitive events.

Job interview is requested. →

May I have an interview at your convenience to tell you more about the contributions I could make to Freeman National Bank? Please call me at (314) 555-1456. I look forward to hearing from you.

Sincerely

Joseph A. Brennan

Enclosure

12d 9'

Improve keying technique

1 Key each line once; work for smooth, unhurried keying.

2 Repeat lines you did not key fluently.

adjacent reaches

17 Bert read where she could stop to buy gas and oil.
18 We three are a trio to join the Yun Oil operation.

direct reaches

19 Grace Nurva hunted my canyon for unique specimens.
20 My uncle and my brother have run many great races.

double reaches

21 Jeanne took a day off to see a book show in Hobbs.
22 Will Anne and Betty take three books to the troop?

| 1 | 2 | 3 | 4 | 5 | 6 | 7 | 8 | 9 | 10 |

12e 14'

Build staying power

1 Key each ¶ SS; DS between ¶s.

2 Key each ¶ for two 1' writings.

3 Key both ¶s for 2'.

Goal: 16 *gwam*

To determine gross words-a-minute rate for 2':

1 Note the figure at the end of the last line completed.

2 For a partial line, note the figure on the scale directly below the point at which you stopped keying.

3 Add these two figures to determine the total gross words a minute (*gwam*) you keyed.

all letters *gwam* 2'

. 4 . 8 .
There should be no questions, no doubt, about the 5
12 . 16 . 20
value of being able to key; it's just a matter of 10
. 24 . 28 .
common sense that today a pencil is much too slow. 15

. 4 . 8 .
Let me explain. Work is done on a keyboard three 5
12 . 16 . 20
to six times faster than other writing and with a 10
. 24 . 28 .
product that is a prize to read. Don't you agree? 15

gwam 2' | 1 | 2 | 3 | 4 | 5 |

Document 1
Reverse chronological resume

1 Read "Resume Format Review"; study the format and organization of the resume below.

2 Prepare a one-page resume of your qualifications for the position of assistant office manager. Include college courses related to your job objective such as keyboarding, word processing, computer applications, and communication management.

Resume Format Review

1 Use 1" side margins and a top margin appropriate to the length of your resume.
2 Use all capital letters, bold, and asterisks (*) or bullets (·) to display and emphasize information.

3 Keep the resume to one page if possible.

4 Proofread and edit carefully. *No errors are permissible.*

wp If your software will allow you to vary typefaces and sizes, experiment with the following features:

- Vary typefaces and point size, giving emphasis to the title and headings.
- Use graphic lines or borders for emphasis.
- Use italics, underline, or bullets to add interest and emphasis.

ASSISTANT OFFICE MANAGER

Local firm seeking assistant office manager:

- high school diploma;
- 3 years administrative support experience or related college courses; good organization and communication skills;
- 65 gwam;
- proficient with word processing, database, and spreadsheet software.

Send resume to Jeffrey A. Abraham, Director of Human Resources, St. Louis Memorial Hospital, (*Your city, state, ZIP Code*). No calls.

This resume is prepared in reverse chronological style, listing the most recent data about one's education and experience first.

The opening is complete and balanced.

JOSEPH A. BRENNAN

1771 Russell Boulevard
St. Louis, MO 63104-3883
(314) 555-1456

Career objective reflects short- and long-term goals.

CAREER OBJECTIVE

To obtain an administrative support position with opportunities for advancement.

Competencies that relate directly to the job are emphasized.

COMPUTER COMPETENCIES

Computer Systems: MS-DOS and Unix

Application Software: WordPerfect, Excel, and CorelDraw

Work experience emphasizes both duties and achievements. Job title, organization, and dates of employment are included.

WORK EXPERIENCE

Administrative Assistant. Maddox National Bank, St. Louis, Missouri, September 1991 to May 1993. (Worked 20 hours per week.)
- Promoted to assistant to the president after six months (shared salaried position with morning assistant).
- Maintained electronic calendar and completed travel arrangements for president and vice president.

Student Assistant. Department of Office Systems, St. Louis University, St. Louis, Missouri, September 1990 to September 1991. (Worked 15 hours per week.)
- Monitored computer laboratories and assisted students as needed.
- Selected as the Outstanding Student Assistant, 1993.

Educational degree earned, dates, and special honors are included. GPA (if at least 3.0) and seminars and/or workshops that relate to job objective may be included.

EDUCATION

B.S. degree, Office Systems Administration, St. Louis University, May 1993. Cum Laude. President's and Dean's Scholar.

Honors and activities that show creativity, initiative, leadership, and teamwork may be included.

HONORS AND ACTIVITIES

Recipient, 1991 J. L. Matthews Scholarship of Merit
President, SLU Business Association

First place, Information Management, 1992 Business Merit Conference

Indicate how to obtain references.

REFERENCES

Available upon request.

13 Review

Skill-Building Warmup

13a 8'

each line twice SS (slowly, then faster); DS between 2-line groups; use line 4 as 1' writings as time permits

alphabet 1 Bev quickly hid two Japanese frogs in Mitzi's box.
shift 2 Jay Nadler, a Rotary Club member, wrote Mr. Coles.
comma 3 Jay, Ed, and I paid for plates, knives, and forks.
easy 4 Did the amendment name a city auditor to the firm?

1 | 2 | 3 | 4 | 5 | 6 | 7 | 8 | 9 | 10

13b 12'

Practice response patterns

each line once as shown SS; DS between 3-line groups

word level response : key short, familiar words as units

5 is to for do an may work so it but an with them am
6 Did they mend the torn right half of their ensign?
7 Hand me the ivory tusk on the mantle by the bugle.

letter level response: key more difficult words letter by letter

8 only state jolly zest oil verve join rate mop card
9 After defeat, look up; gaze in joy at a few stars.
10 We gazed at a plump beaver as it waded in my pool.

combination response : use variable speed; your fingers will let you feel the difference

11 it up so at for you may was but him work were they
12 It is up to you to get the best rate; do it right.
13 This is Lyn's only date to visit their great city.

| 1 | 2 | 3 | 4 | 5 | 6 | 7 | 8 | 9 | 10 |

13c 5'

Practice keyreaches

each line once; fingers well curved, wrists low; avoid punching keys with 3d and 4th fingers

left 1st

14 Trevor forgot to drive through the covered bridge.

right 1st

15 Johnny says you jammed your knuckle on this trunk.

left 3d/4th

16 A sad Sam Essex was assessed a tax on his savings.

right 3d/4th

17 Polly L. Apollo polled the populace on Proposal L.

| 1 | 2 | 3 | 4 | 5 | 6 | 7 | 8 | 9 | 10 |

34

Job Seekers

Job Placement Office

(Lessons 173-177)

Learning goals:

1 To analyze and compose letters of application in response to job ads.

2 To study and develop a reverse chronological resume and a functional resume.

3 To complete an employment application form.

4 To format error-free documents from script and rough draft.

Office job simulation

Information about your work assignment appears on this page. Study the information carefully.

Daily plan

Skill-building workshop 4 .... 5'-15'
Simulation .... 35'
OR
Simulation .... 50'

Work assignment

Job Seekers is a small career counseling service in your area. The firm counsels individuals and groups on the subjects of professional image, self-assessment, employment opportunities, employment communications, and job interview techniques.

In Section 34, you are a *client* of Job Seekers and are ready to begin your job search. Consultants at Job Seekers are very knowledgeable of the "fine points" of preparing winning resumes and in writing letters of application.

The Job Seekers' consultant who works with you believes firmly that the best way to learn to write employment communications is by writing them. "Practice" is the byword at Job Seekers. Therefore, in Lessons 173-177, you will practice preparing two types of resumes, a reverse chronological style and a functional style; a letter of application; a list of references; an employment application form; and interview follow-up and job acceptance letters. Follow the instructions below to produce the documents:

1 Prepare all application correspondence on plain bond stationery.

2 Use the personal business letter format, keying your return address immediately above the date, or create your own letterhead using bold and centered copy.

3 Use 1" or default margins.

4 Use the current date for all letters.

5 Correct any errors you find in rough-draft copy.

6 Proofread each document several times to ensure that it is error-free. Follow these proofreading procedures:

a Read the copy on the screen display or before removing it from the typewriter. Compare the copy to the original copy word for word. Check that words, sentences, or lines have not been omitted.

b Read from left to right to locate content, grammatical, and punctuation errors (incorrect word choice, incomplete sentences, incorrect date, etc.).

c Read the copy from right to left to identify keying, capitalization, and spelling errors. If spelling verification software is available, use it to check spelling.

7 If possible, make a photocopy of all documents and keep them in a file labeled "Employment Documents." Refer to this file whenever you apply for employment.

WP Use special features such as varying typefaces and size of type, bold, underline, bullets, graphic lines, and boxes to emphasize key information and to add interest. By including these features, you are showing prospective employers your software expertise and your commitment to producing attractive documents.

13d 13'

Practice stroking techniques

1 Key each line once.

2 Check each line that you could not key smoothly.

✓ fingers curved and upright

p
18 Pat appears happy to pay for any supper I prepare.

x
19 Knox can relax; Alex gets a box of flax next week.

v
20 Vi, Ava, and Viv move ivy vines, leaves, or stems.

'
21 It's a question of whether they can't or won't go.

?
22 Did Jan go? Did she see Ray? Who paid? Did she?

.
23 Ms. E. K. Nu and Lt. B. A. Walz had the a.m. duty.

"
24 "Who are you?" he asked. "I am," I said, "Marie."

;
25 Find a car; try it; like it; work a price; buy it.

| 1 | 2 | 3 | 4 | 5 | 6 | 7 | 8 | 9 | 10 |

13e 12'

Build staying power

1 Key each ¶ for two 1' writings.

2 Key both ¶s for two 2' writings.

Goal: 17 *gwam*

E all letters

	gwam 2'
The questions of time use are vital ones; we miss	5
so much just because we don't plan.	9
When we organize our days, we save time for those	14
extra premium things we long to do.	17

gwam 2' | 1 | 2 | 3 | 4 | 5 |

Document 11
Unbound report

Prepare the guidelines clients are to follow when making a deposition. Key the firm's name, address, and telephone number (601-555-3833) in the upper right corner on line 10.

Document 12
Letter composition

(LM p. S117)
Write a letter to Ms. Estavan; include the following information:

- Accident deposition is scheduled for (next Friday's date), 10 a.m., at our office.
- Review enclosed guidelines for preparing responses for deposition.
- If client has questions, call (give office number).

ESTAVAN, MITZI
322 CHEROKEE ROAD
JACKSON, MS 39206-0322
(601) 555-7720

ACCIDENT DEPOSITION: GUIDELINES FOR WITNESSES

A deposition is a statement made under oath by a witness in response to questions asked by an attorney. ~~When-ever you are deposed~~ [stet] [stet], an attorney from our office will be present. Your attorney will not answer questions for you; therefore, please review the following suggestions [for responding at the deposition]:

[Indent and SS enumerated items.] [1.] Listen carefully to each question. [2.] Answer honestly and completely, but do not supply information that is not requested. [3.] Speak clearly and loudly so that your words may be recorded.

Be prepared to answer questions about the following:

[list in outline form]
1. Accident--[1.1] When, [1.2] Where, [1.3] Who, [1.4] How
2. Injuries--[2.1] Symptoms at time of accident ~~and~~ [2.2] subsequent symptoms
3. Loss of Income--[3.1] Amount lost since accident, [3.2] Past three tax returns, [3.3] Medical and other related expenses

Document 13
Simplified memo

Warren Pentyala, office manager, sends you the following voice mail message:

I need the memo about the WP demo to go out this afternoon. Remember to use my title. You will very likely find errors in my handwritten notes—I drafted them very quickly while at the courthouse this a.m.

To Support Staff

Plan to attend a demonstration of to leading word processing software package on Wednesday, (next Wednesday's date), at 1 p.m. in Suite 430.

Following the demonstration, you will complete a rating sheet for each package. The rating sheets are enclosed for your review before Wednesday afternoon. A software decision will be made on Monday. Thanks for your assistants.

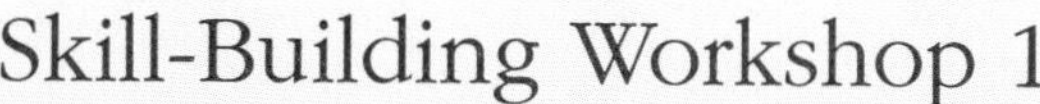

Skill-Building Workshop 1

OS Use the open screen of Alphanumeric software for Workshop 1.

Default margins or 50-space line

Drill 1
Goal: reinforce key locations

Key each line at a comfortable, constant rate; check lines that need more practice; repeat those lines.

Keep
- your eyes on source copy
- your fingers curved, upright
- your wrists low, but not touching
- your elbows hanging loosely
- your feet flat on the floor

```
A        We saw that Alan had an alabaster vase in Alabama.
B        My rubber boat bobbed about in the bubbling brook.
C        Ceci gave cups of cold cocoa to Rebecca and Rocco.
D        Don's dad added a second deck to his old building.
E        Even as Ellen edited her document, she ate dinner.
F        Our firm in Buffalo has a staff of forty or fifty.
G        Ginger is giving Greg the eggs she got from Helga.
H        Hugh has eighty high, harsh lights he might flash.
I        Irik's lack of initiative is irritating his coach.
J        Judge J. J. Jore rejected Jeane and Jack's jargon.
K        As a lark, Kirk kicked back a rock at Kim's kayak.
L        Lucille is silly; she still likes lemon lollipops.
M        Milt Mumm hammered a homer in the Miami home game.
N        Ken Linn has gone hunting; Stan can begin canning.
O        Jon Soto rode off to Otsego in an old Morgan auto.
P        Philip helped pay the prize as my puppy hopped up.
Q        Quade quit squirting Quarla after quite a quarrel.
R        As Mrs. Kerr's motor roared, her red horse reared.
S        Sissie lives in Mississippi; Lissa lives in Tulsa.
T        Nat told Betty not to tattle on her little sister.
U        It is unusual to have an unused unit in the union.
V        Eva visited every vivid event for twelve evenings.
W        We walked to the window to watch as the wind blew.
X        Tex Cox waxed the next box for Xenia and Rex Knox.
Y        Ty says you may stay with Fay for only sixty days.
Z        Hazel is puzzled about the azure haze; Zack dozes.
alphabet Jacky and Max quickly fought over a sizable prawn.
alphabet Just by maximizing liquids, Chick Prew avoids flu.
         |  1  |  2  |  3  |  4  |  5  |  6  |  7  |  8  |  9  |  10  |
```

Prepare divorce decrees (Documents 9 and 10) using the form at the right and the sets of variable information below.

wp Key the divorce decree with stop codes. Then prepare the documents.

Document 9

Divorce decree
(LM pp. S105-S109)

(1) 83733
(2) 6
(3) LATONYA T. KEELEY
(4) NATHAN J. KEELEY
(5) 1st
(6) (you supply next month)
(7) Kaplan, Riggan, and Riggan
(8) irreconcilable differences
(9) MELINDA JEAN and WILLIAM CLAY

Refer to the divorce decree illustrated on page 375 and key the closing lines that include signature lines for the Judge and for the defense attorney. In the line reading *Attorney for . . .* include the defendant's name.

Document 10

(LM pp. S111-S115)

For the Scoggins decree, variables 2, 5, 6, and 8 are the same as for the Keeley decree; other information follows:

(1) 83740
(3) CHRISTOPHER MICHAEL SCOGGINS
(4) LEIGH ANNE SCOGGINS
(7) Sellers and Schoenrock
(9) CHRISTOPHER MICHAEL, JR., CAROLE ANNE, and DEAN ERIC

IN THE DISTRICT COURT IN AND FOR THE CITY OF

JACKSON AND STATE OF MISSISSIPPI

CIVIL ACTION NO.__(1)__, DIV.__(2)__

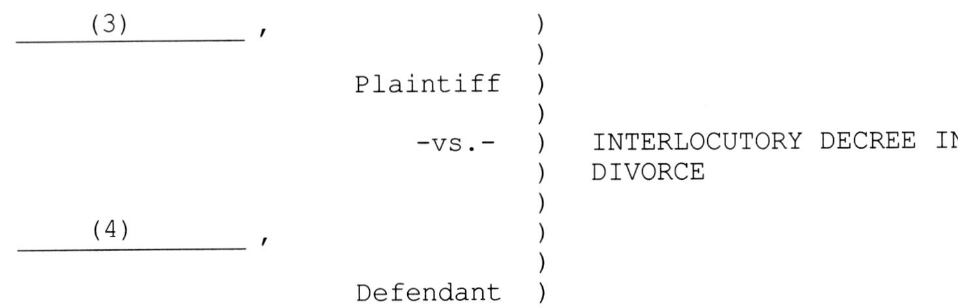

__(3)__,)
)
Plaintiff)
)
-vs.-) INTERLOCUTORY DECREE IN
) DIVORCE
)
__(4)__,)
)
Defendant)

THIS CAUSE, coming to be heard on this _(5)_ day of _(6)_, 19___, upon its merits, the plaintiff being represented by Jacobus, Pentyala, and Associates, attorneys of record, and the defendant appearing by _(7)_, attorneys of record, and the Court having examined the full record herein, finds that it has jurisdiction herein; and having heard the evidence and the statements of counsel, the Court now being fully advised

DOTH FIND that a divorce should be granted to the plaintiff herein upon the statutory grounds of _(8)_.

IT IS ORDERED, ADJUDGED AND DECREED by the Court, that an absolute divorce should be granted to the plaintiff, and an Interlocutory Decree of Divorce is hereby entered, dissolving the marriage of plaintiff and defendant six months after the date of this Interlocutory Decree.

IT IS EXPRESSLY DECREED by the Court that during such six months period after the signing of this Interlocutory Decree that parties hereto shall not be divorced, shall still be husband and wife, and neither party shall be competent to contract another marriage anywhere during such period, and the Court during all of said period does hereby retain jurisdiction of the parties and the subject matter of this cause and upon motion of either party, or upon its motion, for good cause shown, after a hearing, may set aside this Interlocutory Decree.

IT IS FURTHER ORDERED, ADJUDGED AND DECREED by the Court that the sole care, custody and control of the minor children, _(9)_, is hereby awarded to the plaintiff as a suitable person to have such care and custody until further order of the Court with the defendant to have reasonable visitation rights.

THE COURT FURTHER DECREES that after six months from the date hereof this Interlocutory Decree shall become a Final Decree of Divorce and the parties shall then be divorced, unless this Interlocutory Decree shall have been set aside, or an appeal has been taken, or a writ of error has been issued.

Done in open Court this _(5)_ day of _(6)_, 19___.

Drill 2

Goal: strengthen up and down reaches

Keep hands and wrists quiet; fingers well curved in home position; stretch fingers up from home or pull them palmward as needed.

home position

1 Hall left for Dallas; he is glad Jake fed his dog.
2 Gladys had a flask of milk; Hal had a jello salad.
3 Jack Hask had a sale; Gala shall add half a glass.

down reaches

4 Did my banker, Mr. Mavann, analyze my tax account?
5 Do they, Mr. Zack, expect a number of brave women?
6 Zach, check the menu; next, beckon the lazy valet.

up reaches

7 Prue truly lost the quote we wrote for our report.
8 Teresa quietly put her whole heart into her words.
9 There were two hilarious jokes in your quiet talk.

Drill 3

Goal: strengthen individual finger reaches

Rekey troublesome lines.

first finger

1 Bob Mugho hunted for five minutes for your number.
2 Juan hit the bright green turf with his five iron.
3 The frigates and gunboats fought mightily in Java.

second finger

4 Dick said the ice on the creek had surely cracked.
5 Even as we picnicked, I decided we needed to diet.
6 Kim, not Mickey, had rice with chicken for dinner.

third/fourth finger

7 Pam saw Roz wax an aqua auto as Lex sipped a cola.
8 Wally will quickly spell Zeus, Apollo, and Xerxes.
9 Who saw Polly? Zoe Pax saw her; she is quiet now.

Drill 4

Goal: strengthen special reaches

Emphasize smooth stroking. Avoid pauses, but do not reach for speed.

adjacent reaches

1 Falk knew well that her opinions of art were good.
2 Theresa answered her question; order was restored.
3 We join there and walk north to the western point.

direct reaches

4 Barb Nunn must hunt for my checks; she is in debt.
5 In June and December, Irvin hunts in Bryce Canyon.
6 We decided to carve a number of funny human faces.

double letters

7 Anne stopped off at school to see Bill Wiggs cook.
8 Edd has planned a small cookout for all the troop.
9 Keep adding to my assets all fees that will apply.

| 1 | 2 | 3 | 4 | 5 | 6 | 7 | 8 | 9 | 10 |

Document 5 (continued)

and report of *sale* thereof; that the ward has been served with notice of the hearing on the petition and report as provided by the order of this Court and that this Court has jurisdiction to appoint a guardian ad litem for the ward; and that a competent attorney at law should be appointed as such guardian ad litem in this case to represent the ward at the hearing and in all related matters subsequent thereto.

Now, therefore, it is ordered, adjudged, and decreed by the Court that *RUBEN D. JACOBUS*, a competent attorney at law, of Jackson, Mississippi, be and hereby is appointed guardian ad litem to represent the ward, *LISA DAWN ALEXANDER*, at the hearing on the conservator's petition for authority to *sell the ward's interest in the real estate* and report *of sale thereof on (next Monday's date, 19--) at 10:00 a.m.* in the courtroom in the county courthouse in Jackson, Hinds County, Mississippi, or at the continuation or adjournment thereof, and in all matters pertaining to the petition *and sale* subsequent thereto.

Document 6
Settlement statement
(LM p. S101)
Prepare the settlement statement for the Peterson residence. Compute the totals for last column. Omit underlines except where needed. Key the date in the lower left corner (mm/dd/yy).

wp Use the math feature to compute totals.

Document 6

SELLER'S SETTLEMENT STATEMENT

Mr. and Mrs. Lamar Peterson
83 West Leflore Street
Jackson, MS 39207-0083

Gross amount due to seller:		
Contract sales price	$ *115,000.00*	
Down payment	*40,000.00*	
Balance due on contract		$ ______
Reduction in amount due seller:		
Real estate commission	$ *8,050.00*	
Abstracting fee	*230.00*	
Attorney's fees	*100.00*	
Recording release	*7.50*	
Revenue stamps	*126.30*	
Proration of real estate taxes	*2,000.00*	
Mortgage payoff	*5,750.00*	
Total reductions		______
Amount due seller at closing		$ ______

Document 7
Letter composition
Compose a **form letter** for transmitting settlement statements (Document 6). Include the following variables: closing day and date, time and place of closing, and amount due at closing. Key a description of the variables in parentheses (*day and date of closing*). Key the document name in the lower left corner. Remember to include a subject line.

Document 8
Letter
(LM p. S103)
Prepare a letter for Mr. and Mrs. Peterson (Document 6). Closing date is two weeks from today at 10 a.m. in our office.

Drill 5

Goal: improve troublesome pairs

Use a controlled rate without pauses.

d / k

1 Dirk asked Dick to kid Drake about the baked duck.

e / i

2 Abie had neither ice cream nor fried rice in Erie.

b / v

3 Did Harv key jibe or jive, TV or TB, robe or rove?

t / r

4 In Toronto, Ruth told the truth about her artwork.

u / y

5 Judye usually does not buy your Yukon art in July.

Drill 6

Goal: build speed

Key each sentence for 1'. Try to complete each sentence twice (20 *gwam* or more). Ignore errors for now.

1 Dian may make cocoa for the girls when they visit.

2 Focus the lens for the right angle; fix the prism.

3 She may suspend work when she signs the torn form.

4 Augment their auto fuel in the keg by the autobus.

5 As usual, their robot did half turns to the right.

6 Pamela laughs as she signals to the big hairy dog.

7 Pay Vivian to fix the island for the eighty ducks.

| 1 | 2 | 3 | 4 | 5 | 6 | 7 | 8 | 9 | 10 |

Drill 7

Goal: build speed

Take 30" writings on selected sentences. From the columns at the right, choose a *gwam* goal that is 2-3 words higher than your best rate. Try to reach your goal.

		words 1'	30"	20"
1	Did she make this turkey dish?	6	12	18
2	Blake and Laurie may go to Dubuque.	7	14	21
3	Signal for the oak sleigh to turn right.	8	16	24
4	I blame Susie; did she quench the only flame?	9	18	27
5	She turns the panel dials to make this robot work.	10	20	30

| 1 | 2 | 3 | 4 | 5 | 6 | 7 | 8 | 9 | 10 |

Document 3 (continued)

Article II. I give and devise my condominium located in Destin, Florida, to my daughter JENNIFER LYNNE and her heirs and assigns forever.
Article III. I give and bequeath to my daughter CARRIE ELIZABETH five hundred (500) shares of common stock of Merikas, Inc.
Article IV. I give and bequeath the following sums of money to the following, to wit:
(a) The sum of Five Hundred and Sifty Dollars ($560) to SUMO TONAKA of San Francisco, California.
(b) The sum of Ten Thousand Dollars ($10,000) to the Education Endowment Fund of Coleson University, located in Jackson, Mississippi.
Article V. I give and bequeath the remainder of my property and possessions to my wife LYNNE. In the event she precedes me in death, my property shall be divided equally between my daughter JENNIFER LYNNE and my daughter CARRIE ELIZABETH and their heirs and assigns forever.
Article VI. I hereby name my wife LYNNE as executrix of my estate.

Document 5
Court order (appointing guardian)
(LM pp. S97-S99)

Prepare the court order shown below; Judge McCormick will sign it tomorrow (supply date). Refer to the illustration on page 375; use the information below.

Headings:

IN THE MISSISSIPPI DISTRICT COURT FOR HINDS COUNTY

IN THE MATTER OF THE CONSERVATORSHIP OF LISA DAWN ALEXANDER

PROBATE NO. 329
ORDER APPOINTING GUARDIAN AD LITEM

Closing:

BY THE COURT

____

Judge of the First Judicial District of Mississippi

Use a graphic line for drawing lines and a footer for numbering pages.

Document 5

Now on this _______ day of ______________, 19___, this matter comes on for hearing on the application of the conservator for the appointment of a guardian ad litem to represent the ward, LISA DAWN ALEXANDER, in connecton with the conservator's petition for authority to

sell the ward's interest in realestate described as:
Lot No. 621, Meeks, Porter, and McNutt Addition,
Jackson, Mississippi

Drill 8
Goal: build staying power

each ¶ SS line for line for a 1' timing; then a 2' timing on both ¶s; DS between ¶s

 all letters

Writing 1: **18 *gwam***

gwam 2'

Why spend weeks with some problem when just a few 5
quiet minutes can help us to resolve it. 9

If we don't take time to think through a problem, 15
it will swiftly begin to expand in size. 18

Writing 2: **20 *gwam***

We push very hard in our quest for growth, and we 5
all think that only excellent growth will pay off. 10

Believe it or not, one can actually work much too 15
hard, be much too zealous, and just miss the mark. 20

Writing 3: **22 *gwam***

A business friend once explained to me why he was 5
often quite eager to be given some new project to 10
work with. 11

My friend said that each new project means he has 16
to organize and use the best of his knowledge and 21
his skill. 22

Writing 4: **24 *gwam***

Don't let new words get away from you. Learn how 5
to spell and pronounce new words and when and how 10
finally to use them. 12

A new word is a friend, but frequently more. New 17
words must be used lavishly to extend the size of 22
your own word power. 24

gwam 2' | 1 | 2 | 3 | 4 | 5 |

Document 3
Last will and testament
(LM pp. S89-S93)

Prepare the Merikas will. The keyed paragraphs are standard to all wills, while the handwritten paragraphs (page 378) represent variable information.

Provide signature lines for three witnesses (see illustration on page 375). Choose "her" or "his" when referring to the testator. Use next Friday's date as the date for signing the will.

wp Use a graphic line for drawing lines and use a footer for numbering pages.

THE LAST WILL AND TESTAMENT OF

FRANKLIN MERIKAS

I, FRANKLIN MERIKAS, of Jackson, Hinds County, State of Mississippi, being of sound mind and disposing memory, do make, publish and declare this to be my Last Will and Testament, and hereby revoke any and all former wills and codicils by me made.

ARTICLE I

I hereby direct my executors hereinafter named, to pay all my just debts and funeral expenses as soon after my demise as possible.

Insert Articles 2-6

ARTICLE VII

IN WITNESS WHEREOF, I have signed my name at the foot and end of this my Last Will and Testament and affixed by seal this ____________ day of __________, 19__.

____
~~NAME~~ FRANKLIN MERIKAS

The foregoing instrument, consisting of _____ pages, including this page, each page being printed only on one side, was at the date thereof by the said ________________ signed, sealed; published and declared to be his/her Last Will and Testament in the presence of us, who, at her/his request, in her/his presence and in the presence of each other, have subscribed our names as attesting witnesses thereto.

Executed the ______day of __________, 19___.

Document 4
Letter composition
(LM p. S95)

Prepare a letter to Mr. Merikas informing him of the following information:

- Will is ready to sign.
- Appointment (for signing):

Date--next Friday's date

Time--2 p.m.

Place--Ruben D. Jacobus's office

- May bring witnesses or use our staff as witnesses.
- Call before noon Wednesday to change appointment.

Include a confidential notation and subject line. Key your name and office title, **Legal Assistant**, in the closing lines.

MERIKAS, FRANKLIN
1733 HUNTCLIFF DRIVE
JACKSON, MS 39206-1733
(601) 555-1353

Writing 5: **26 *gwam*** *gwam 2'*

We usually get best results when we know where we 5
are going. Just setting a few goals will help us 10
quietly see what we are doing. 13

Goals can help measure whether we are moving at a 18
good rate or dozing along. You can expect a goal 23
to help you find good results. 26

Writing 6: **28 *gwam***

To win whatever prizes we want from life, we must 5
plan to move carefully from this goal to the next 10
to get the maximum result from our work. 14

If we really want to become skilled in keying, we 19
must come to see that this desire will require of 24
us just a little patience and hard work. 28

Writing 7: **30 *gwam***

Am I an individual person? I'm sure I am; still, 5
in a much, much bigger sense, other people have a 10
major voice in thoughts I think and action I take. 15

Although we are each a unique person, we all work 20
and play in organized groups of people who do not 25
expect us to dismiss their rules of law and order. 30

gwam 2' | 1 | 2 | 3 | 4 | 5 |

Document 1
Legal terms

Prepare a glossary of legal terms from the list you have begun. Key the terms in the first column and tips for handling them in the second column. Boldface the terms and alphabetize.

wp Use the table and sort features. Store the file so that additional terms can be added.

LEGAL TERMS

Beneficiary The person named to receive the proceeds ^or benefits^ of an estate.

Testament A legal declaration of a person's mind as to the disposition of his/her property ^or real estate^ after death.

Admissible When writing about admissible evidence, the word ends in -ible, not -able.

Defendant The person being sued; the word ends in -ant.

Plaintiff A party who files a lawsuit.

Guardian A person legally responsible for the care of ~~a~~ the person and/or affairs of another.

Judgment A judicial decision; drop the e from the word judge.

Causal If something is related to the cause, the word is causal--not casual

Liable The responsibility to pay civil damages--not libel

Libel Written or printed defamation--not liable

Personalty Refers to personal property.

Separation--As in separation agreement; the vowel second in separation is an a, not an e.

Allege--To assert to be true; there is no d in allege

Document 2
Acknowledgment of signature by notary public

(LM p. S87)
John Kelly Carskadon will be in today to sign a complaint (legal document) and an acknowledgment attesting that the facts stated in the complaint are correct. (Use today's date.)

Prepare the acknowledgment page for signature by Mr. Carskadon. Refer to the format illustrated on page 375 and key the closing lines.

wp Key document using stop codes for variables. Then prepare the document.

STATE OF MISSISSIPPI

COUNTY OF HINDS

Personally appeared before me, the undersigned authority in and for the jurisdiction aforesaid, the within named (INSERT CLIENT'S NAME), who being by me first duly sworn, states on (insert pronoun) oath that all facts and matters contained in the above complaint are true and correct as therein stated and that the complaint is not filed by collusion with the defendant.

Witness my signature this the xx day of xx, 19--.

____
(INSERT NAME OF CLIENT)

SWORN TO and subscribed before me on this the xx day of xx, 19--.

____
NOTARY PUBLIC

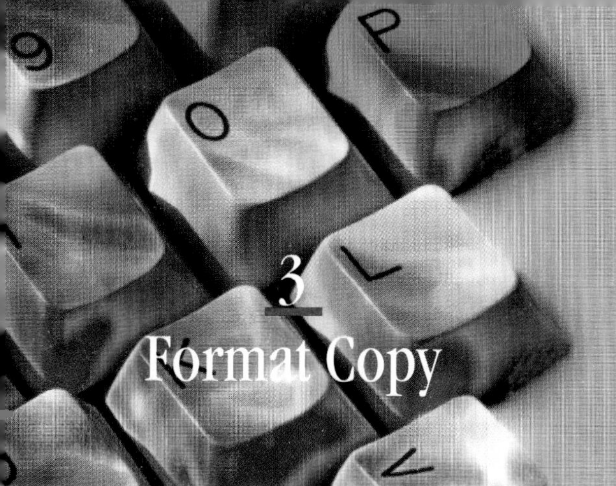

3 Format Copy

Learning goals:
1. To set side and top margins.
2. To clear and set tabs.
3. To center copy horizontally.
4. To change line spacing.

Formatting guides:
1. Default margins or 50-space line.
2. Single-space drills; double-space paragraphs.

14a 7'

Skill-building warmup

each line twice SS; DS between 2-line groups

```
alphabet 1 Fave Maxwelt quickly jeopardized his buying power.
       q 2 Quenched in quandary, he quickly acquitted Quincy.
 shift/? 3 Did you ask Paul?  Would Ivan, Jon, or Carol know?
    easy 4 Ken may wish to pay big bucks for the giant rifle.
           | 1 | 2 | 3 | 4 | 5 | 6 | 7 | 8 | 9 | 10 |
```

14b 7'

SKILL BUILDING

Improve keystroking

Key each line once SS; DS between 2-line groups.

```
de / ed
 5 ed fed led deed dell dead deal sled desk need seed
 6 Dell dealt with the deed before the dire deadline.
lo / ol
 7 old tolls doll solo look sole lost love cold stole
 8 Old Ole looked for the long lost olive oil lotion.
as / sa
 9 as say sad ask pass lass case said vase past salsa
10 Ask the lass to pass the glass, saucers, and vase.
op / po
11 pop top post rope pout port stop opal opera report
12 Stop to read the top opera opinion report to Opal.
   | 1 | 2 | 3 | 4 | 5 | 6 | 7 | 8 | 9 | 10 |
```

14c 6'

FORMATTING

Pitch/typeface

1 Read the copy at the right.
2 Determine the pitch of your machine by comparing your type to the copy at the right.

Pitch / typeface

Most keyboarding systems have at least two type sizes or pitches: 10-pitch (pica) and 12-pitch (elite). Pitch refers to the number of keystrokes in one horizontal inch.

```
10 pitch   1234567890
12 pitch   123456789012
```

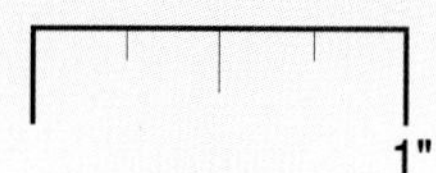

A standard sheet of paper, 8.5 inches wide, has 85 ten-pitch keystrokes (8.5" x 10) or 102 twelve-pitch keystrokes (8.5" x 12).

wp The default *typeface* for many word processing programs (and typewriters) is 10-pitch Courier. Prestige elite is also common. Size is measured in width or *characters per inch (cpi).*

```
Courier 10 cpi
Prestige elite 12 cpi
```

Alternate typefaces, such as Helvetica and Times Roman, may be available and in different point sizes. Point size refers to the height of a letter. The larger the point size, the larger the print.

Times Roman 12 pt. Helvetica 8 pt.

2"

IN THE MISSISSIPPI DISTRICT COURT FOR HINDS COUNTY

QS

IN THE MATTER OF THE	)	PROBATE NO. 110
CONSERVATORSHIP OF	)	ORDER APPOINTING
LYLE GAFFORD	)	GUARDIAN AD LITEM

QS

1.5" →

Now on this 21st day of May, 1993, this matter comes on for hearing on the application of the conservator for the appointment of a guardian ad litem to represent the ward, Lyle Gafford, in connection with the conservator's petition for authority to sell the ward's interest in real estate described as:

Lot No. 63, Addison, Greene, and McMannis Addition, Jackson, Mississippi

and report of sale thereof; that the ward has been served with notice of the hearing on the petition and report as provided by the order of this Court and that this Court has jurisdiction to appoint a guardian ad litem for the ward; and that a competent attorney at law should be appointed as such guardian ad litem in this case to represent the ward at the hearing

thereof, and in all matters pertaining to the petition and sale subsequent thereto.

BY THE COURT

QS

____

Judge of the First Judicial
District of Mississippi

↑
Center Point

Court Order

2"

STATE OF MISSISSIPPI

COUNTY OF HINDS

DS

Personally appeared before me, the undersigned authority in and for the jurisdiction aforesaid, the within named ALIDIA J. JABRI, who being by me first duly sworn, states on her oath that all facts and matters contained in the above complaint are true and correct as therein stated and that the complaint is not filed by collusion with the defendant.

Witness my signature this the first day of May, 1993.

QS

____

ALIDIA J. JABRI

SWORN TO and subscribed before me on this the first day of May, 1993.

QS

____

NOTARY PUBLIC

MY COMMISSION EXPIRES:

QS

____

(SEAL)

Acknowledgment—Signature by Notary Public

2"

THE LAST WILL AND TESTAMENT OF

KARENSA T. PEAVEY

QS

I, KARENSA T. PEAVEY, of Jackson, Hinds County, State of Mississippi, being of sound mind and disposing memory, do make, publish, and declare this to be my Last Will and Testament, and hereby revoke any and all former wills and codicils by me made.

ARTICLE I

I hereby direct my executors, hereinafter named, to pay all my just debts and funeral expenses as soon after my demise as possible.

IN WITNESS WHEREOF, I have signed my name at the foot and end of this my Last Will and Testament and affixed my seal this 12th day of December, 1993.

QS

____

KARENSA T. PEAVEY

The foregoing instrument, consisting of three pages, including this page, each page being printed only on one side, was at the date thereof by the said KARENSA T. PEAVEY signed, sealed, and published and declared to be her Last Will and Testament in the presence of us, who, at her request, in her presence and in the presence of each other, have subscribed our names as attesting witnesses thereto.

Executed the _____ day of __________________, 1993.

__________________________ residing at ________________________

__________________________ residing at ________________________

__________________________ residing at ________________________

Page 3 of 3

____

Will

2"

IN THE DISTRICT COURT IN AND FOR THE CITY OF

JACKSON AND STATE OF MISSISSIPPI

CIVIL ACTION NO. 89342, DIV. 7

QS

LISA JANE PATTERSON,	)	
	)	
Plaintiff	)	
	)	
-vs.-	)	INTERLOCUTORY DECREE IN DIVORCE
	)	
PAUL ALLEN PATTERSON,	)	
	)	
Defendant	)	

THIS CAUSE, coming to be heard on this 10th day of August, 1993, upon its merits, the plaintiff being represented by Jacobus, Pentyala, and Associates, attorneys of record, and the Court having examined the full record herein, finds that it has jurisdiction herein; and having heard the evidence and the statements of counsel, the Court now being full advised

DOTH FIND that a divorce should be granted to the plaintiff herein upon the statutory grounds of irreconcilable differences.

Done in open Court this 10th day of August, 1993.

BY THE COURT

QS

____

Judge

APPROVED AS TO FORM:

QS

____

Attorneys for Paul Allen Patterson

Divorce Degree

14d 30'

FORMATTING

Margins

Read the information at the right; then do Drills 1 and 2 below.

Determining margin settings

Side margins are the distance between the edge of the paper and the print. Up to this point, you have been using preset or **default** margins.

To achieve an attractive page layout, set the margins an equal distance from both edges of the paper. Documents are often formatted with 1", 1.5", or 2" side margins. The *line of writing* is the space available for keying. It is determined by subtracting the side margins from the width of the paper, 8.5".

Side margins may be expressed in spaces. When spaces are used, the settings will differ depending upon the pitch (pica or elite) used.

In this course, margins will be expressed in inches; it is assumed that the defaults will be 10 pitch (pica) and 1" margins (65-space line).

Inches	1"	1.5"	2"
Line of writing	6.5"	5.5"	4.5"
10 pitch (pica)			
Left	10	15	20
Right	75	70	65
12 pitch (elite)			
Left	12	18	24
Right	90	84	78

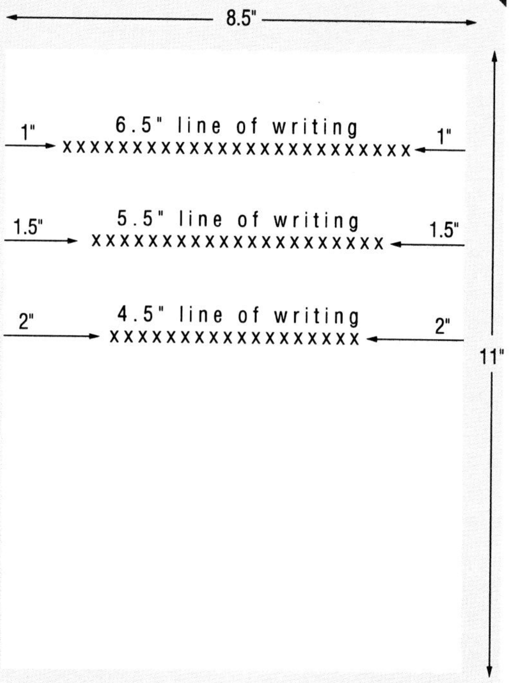

8.5"

1" 6.5" line of writing 1"
xxxxxxxxxxxxxxxxxxxxxxxxxx

1.5" 5.5" line of writing 1.5"
xxxxxxxxxxxxxxxxxxxxxx

2" 4.5" line of writing 2"
xxxxxxxxxxxxxxxxxxx

11"

Setting side margins

Typewriters: Be sure the paper has been inserted with the edge at 0. Move the desired number of spaces from the left and right edge of the paper and set margins.

Keyboarding software: Set margins in the open screen by accessing the format line **(Alt + F)**. Then position the cursor and press either **L** or **R**. Exit the format line **(Alt + F)**.

Drill 1

Set 1.5" left and right margins. You should be able to key the copy line for line as printed.

Note: A warning may sound as you approach the end of each line; listen for it.

Copy that is arranged attractively on the page appeals
to the reader. An attractive document shows respect
for the reader.

Drill 2

Format the ¶s using 2" side margins.

Documents are more attractive when the margins are set an equal distance from the left and right edges of the paper. This gives the document the appearance of being balanced. How the copy looks is just as important as what you key.

33

Jacobus, Pentyala, and Associates

Legal Office
(Lessons 168-172)

Learning goals:

1 To adapt formatting skills to legal documents.

2 To produce documents by using information obtained from several sources.

3 To compose routine legal office correspondence.

Office job simulation

Information about your work assignment in a legal office appears on this page and page 375. Note especially the procedures that will help you become more productive in completing the simulation.

Daily plan

Skill-building workshop 4 .... 5'-15'
Simulation .... 35'-45'
OR
Simulation .... 50'

Work assignment

Mr. Ruben D. Jacobus is a senior partner in the law firm of Jacobus, Pentyala, and Associates. You are a legal assistant to Mr. Jacobus in the small firm located at 112 County Line Road, Jackson, MS 39206-0112.

Your primary responsibility is to produce legal documents for Mr. Jacobus, who handles most of the firm's divorce, real estate, and testamentary (will) cases. Mr. Jacobus is concerned about maximizing productivity with the firm's new computer system. With your excellent background in computer applications, Mr. Jacobus has asked you to note areas where technology can be effectively utilized. You will initiate the use of a form letter file for correspondence that occurs frequently.

You, of course, are expected to use the reference manual, dictionary, etc., on which you have relied in your previous work assignments. Also, you will refer often to the guidelines and illustrations in the "Procedures Manual for Legal Assistants." Excerpts from the manual follow.

wp To increase efficiency, use features such as spell check, math, sort, stop codes, and merge for form letters.

Procedures Manual for Legal Assistants

Proofreading/error correction: All documents should be error-free, but names and numbers in legal documents must be free of error. The error-free rule applies to money amounts—expressed in numbers *and* words. Key the sentences in the documents as you see them—do not correct the word order or punctuation in legal language, even though it may seem irregular to you.

Stationery: Legal documents should be prepared on 8½" X 11" legal paper or on plain paper of the same size. Letters must be on the firm's letterhead; memos, rarely used in this small office, may be prepared on plain paper. As a general rule, settlement statements are prepared on letterhead stationery.

Formatting guides for legal documents: (*See the illustrations on page 375.*) Each page should have a left margin of 1.5", a top margin of 2" (for binding at the top), and a bottom margin of 1" to 2". At least two lines of the body of a document must appear on the same page as the signatures of the maker(s) and witness(es), if any.

The right parenthesis **)** is used to divide parts of certain documents as shown on page 375.

Paragraphs are indented 10 spaces. Generally, the body of a document is double-spaced (the "witness section" of a will is an exception). Quoted material of four or more lines and all land descriptions are single-spaced, and the entire quote or description is blocked 10 spaces from the left margin.

Page numbers for second and succeeding pages are centered at the bottom of each page a double space below the last line of text and are preceded and followed by a hyphen (e.g., -3-). When the last page is a partial page, key the number at the bottom of the page.

Page numbers for wills vary because of the need for maximum security. On the first page of a five-page will, key Page 1 of 5 at the left margin at the bottom of the page. The second page is numbered Page 2 of 5. Then at the right edge, key a 5-space line (maker will initial each page on this line).

Lines for signatures are 3". Double-space between the lines when more than one signer is involved.

Letters: Prepare letters in block format; use variable placement. Include a reference line and/or subject line. On letters to be signed by an attorney, include the firm name in the closing lines. Follow the attorney's name with the title Attorney at Law.

15 Tabs

Skill-Building Warmup

15a 7'

Note: Line 3 has two ALL-CAP items. To key them, depress the Caps Lock (21) with the left little finger; key the item; release the lock by striking Caps Lock again.

alphabet 1 My fine axe just zipped through the black wood quite evenly.
' / " 2 I said, "Yes, Jan, I know. It's like stepping into a book."
shift/lock 3 ADIEU ANGELINA is a song on the NANA MOUSKOURI French album.
easy 4 Sit here; she may fix a big dish of papaya and mango for us.

| 1 | 2 | 3 | 4 | 5 | 6 | 7 | 8 | 9 | 10 | 11 | 12 |

15b 12'

SKILL BUILDING

Improve techniques

1 Key the lines once SS; DS between 3-line groups. Key each phrase (marked by a vertical line) without pauses between words.

2 Repeat drill at a faster pace.

easy words

5 am it go bus dye jam irk six sod tic yam ugh spa vow aid dug
6 he or by air big elf dog end fit and lay sue toe wit own got
7 six foe pen firm also body auto form down city kept make fog

easy phrases

8 it is | if the | and also | to me | the end | to us | if it | it is | to the
9 if it is | to the end | do you wish | to go to | for the end | to make
10 lay down | he or she | make me | by air | end of | by me | kept it | of me

15c 8'

OS

FORMATTING

Tab key

Learn to set tabs on your equipment; then complete the drill below.

Typewriters

1 Clear all tabs: Press the Tab Clear and repeat keys.

2 Clear single tabs: Press the Tab key to move carrier to the tab that is to be cleared. Press Tab Clear key.

3 Set tabs: Strike the space bar to move the carrier to desired tab position. Press Tab Set key.

4 Tabulate (tab): Press Tab with the closest little finger; release it quickly and return to home row position.

wp **Default tabs.** Tabs are preset by the word processing software. Default tabs are usually set every 5 spaces.

Keyboarding software: Tabs can be set or cleared in the open screen by pressing **Alt + F**, positioning the cursor and pressing **Tab**.

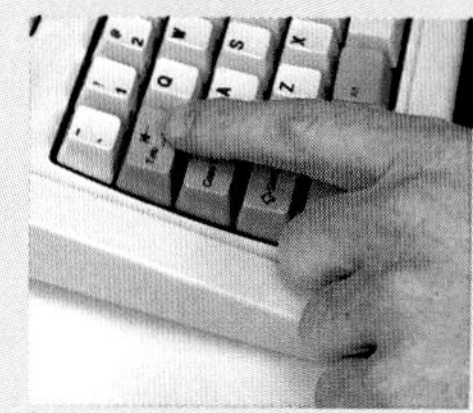

Drill

1 Set 1" left and right margins. On typewriters, clear all preset tabs.

2 Set tabs 5, 10, and 15 spaces from the left margin.

3 Key each line once. Begin the first line at left margin; tab once for line 2; twice for line 3; three times for line 4.

Format the text by determining the position of tab settings.
tab once → Erase all preexisting tabs using the tab clear feature.
tab twice → Set the tab to move quickly to the various points.
tab three times → Use your fourth finger to strike the tab key.

Document 8
Form letter

(LM p. S85)

Use the information on the Form Letter Variables Sheet at the right to compose a return-to-work **form** letter. Address the letter: TO THE EMPLOYER OF (Patient's Name). Omit a letter address since the patient will deliver the letter. Indicate variables by placing a description in parentheses. For example, (Patient's Name).

wp Place stop codes in the form letter where variables are to to be inserted. If a scanner is available, scan Dr. Mitchell's signature and store in the form letter.

Document 9
Appointment schedule

Key Dr. Mitchell's appointment schedule for tomorrow from the appointment book shown at right. Center each line of the three-line heading in bold:

APPOINTMENT/SURGERY SCHEDULE

Dr. Carla B. Mitchell

Day and Current date

Omit unscheduled times. Use the hanging indent style in items that exceed one line. SS items; DS between items. Key abbreviations as shown. Add a **7 p.m. meeting of the Seattle Symphony Executive Committee, Room 2339, First Bank Building.**

RETURN-TO-WORK FORM LETTER VARIABLES SHEET

Document Name: WORK

Patient: Brad Kruiger

Office visit: Tuesday of last week

Treated for: Chronic fatigue syndrome

Return to work: 6 wks from office visit

	Time		Time	
...)	8 00	HGH, SR1, C. Sanchez (appendectomy)	8 00	HGH, SR...
	15		15	
	30		30	
	45		45	HGH, ro...
	9 00	HGH, rounds	9 00	
	15		15	
	30		30	
	45		45	
	10 00		10 00	
	15		15	
	30	HGH, Conf. Rm A Consult Drs.	30	S. Garret...
	45	Bryant + Hargrave RE: F. Wilson	45	G. Suar...
	11 00		11 00	↓
	15	M. Johnson (back pain)	15	
	30	C. K. McIlwain (ankle)	30	P. Moore...
	45		45	B. Wang...
	12 00		12 00	
	15		15	office
	30		30	confer...
	45		45	
	1 00		1 00	
	15		15	
...up)	30	T. Travis (physical)	30	
	45	new (555-4989)	45	
...ain)	2 00	O. Fulton (allergy follow-up)	2 00	
	15	J. Presley (vomiting, weakness)	15	
	30		30	
	45	S Davidson (stomach cramps, headache)	45	
	3 00	T. Simms (broken wrist follow-up)	3 00	
	15		15	
...w up)	30	H. Tschritter (stubbed toes)	30	
	45	D Mansing (rash, itching on hands)	45	
	4 00		4 00	
...hroat	15	V. Denton (neck pain)	15	
	30	M. Ford (fever, headache)	30	
	45		45	
	00		00	

15d 8'

FORMATTING

Indented paragraphs

Set 1.5" side margins and set a tab for a 5-space ¶ indention. SS ¶s; DS between ¶s. Repeat.

Ending lines

The **word wrap** feature automatically returns the cursor to the next line as you key. Copy too long to fit on one line moves automatically to the next line.

Electronic typewriters (ET): Most ETs have an automatic return option. The carrier returns automatically if the operator strikes the space bar or hyphen within the "Line-ending zone" (about 5 spaces).

Typewriters: A warning sounds from 6 to 10 spaces before the margin stops. When the warning sounds, 1) finish keying the word, 2) key the next word if it is short or strike Return if the next word is long. (In Lesson 25, you will learn to divide words.)

The topic of stress has received considerable attention over the past few years. Everyone has experienced some form of stress during his or her lifetime.

People are affected by stress in many different ways. A situation that causes stress may upset some people but may not have an effect on others. Coping with stress and knowing the difference between productive and nonproductive stress will help you to live a full and happy life style.

15e 15'

FORMATTING

Top margin

Read "Top margin"; key the ¶s below following the instructions for Drills 1 and 2.

Top margin

One vertical inch contains 6 lines. A standard sheet of paper is 11" long; therefore, it contains 66 vertical lines (11 x 6).

Top margins are usually specified as 1", 1.5", or 2". The default top margin in word processing software is often 1", with the first line printing on line 7.

Top Margin	Begin Keying
1"	line 7
1.5"	line 10
2"	line 13

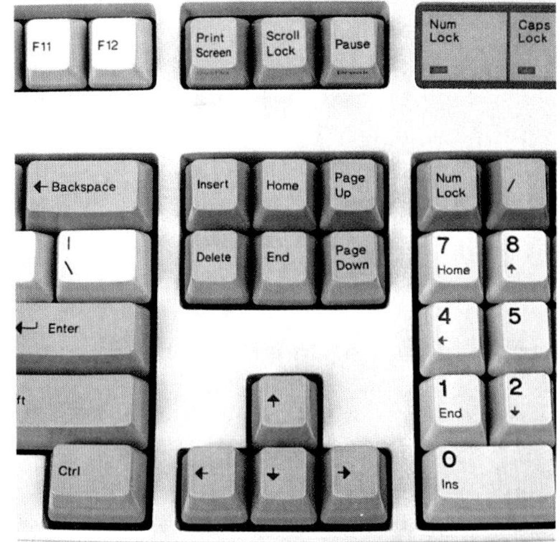

Drill 1

Set 1" side margins, 2" top margin, and a tab for a 5-space ¶ indention.

Drill 2

Set 1.5" side margins, 1.5" top margin, and a tab for a 5-space ¶ indention.

Drill 3 (optional)

Rekey 14d, Drill 1, page 35. Set 1.5" side margins, 1" top margin, and a tab for a 5-space ¶ indention.

Keyboarding is an important skill that everyone needs to survive. Regardless of whether you learn to key on a typewriter or on a computer, the alphanumeric keys are in the same location.

Computer keyboards have additional keys that are not found on typewriters. These keys are function keys, cursor movement keys, and a numeric keypad.

Document 6
Discharge summary

Dr. Mitchell has dictated the discharge summaries (Documents 6 and 7). Special instructions are shown in parentheses. Ms. Lawrence is 17; determine her year of birth; she was discharged yesterday.

Document 7
Discharge summary

J. H. Willcutt, a cataract surgery patient, was admitted ten days ago and discharged yesterday. Mr. Willcutt is 72 years in the current year; determine the correct year for DOB.

wp Prepare a macro with pauses and use for both discharge summaries.

Discharge summary

A Discharge Summary reviews the patient's care while in the hospital. Such a document is often dictated for processing.

1 Use plain paper.
2 Display all headings in bold (see example).
3 Key ¶ heads in ALL CAPS and bold.
4 Add punctuation as needed.
5 Below the summary, key the doctor's name, reference initials, and current date.

HERITAGE GENERAL HOSPITAL
Discharge Summary

PATIENT'S NAME:
DOB:
REF:
ADMISSION DATE:
DISCHARGE DATE:
(Key summary here single-spaced.)
Carla B. Mitchell, M.D.
xx
8-15-94

Document 6

patient is claire lawrence; date of birth is January 14, 19--; reference is 286488; admitted Monday of this week; (¶ HEAD) operation (COLON) open extraction of two impacted fourth molars (OPEN PAREN) douglas laughlin (l-a-u-g-h-l-i-n COMMA) D (PERIOD) D (PERIOD) S (PERIOD, CLOSE PAREN, PERIOD) (¶ HEAD) course in hospital (COLON) claire lawrence (COMMA) a 17 year old female (COMMA) was admitted on (SUPPLY THE DATE) for open extraction of two impacted fourth molars (DASH) one upper and one lower bilaterally (PERIOD) no difficulty in anesthesia administration and no abnormal hemorrhaging were noted (PERIOD) response of patient was excellent (PERIOD) (¶ HEAD) condition on discharge (COLON) slight swelling and inflammation of gums (OPEN PAREN INITIAL CAP) lingual side (CLOSE PAREN) was present at discharge on (SUPPLY DATE OF DISCHARGE) (PERIOD)

Document 7

patient is jh willcutt; DOB September 23, 19--; REF 230375; (¶ HEAD) operation (COLON) right cataract removed (OPEN PAREN) dr nicolis (n-i-c-o-l-i-s) estava (e-s-t-a-v-a CLOSE PAREN, PERIOD) (¶ HEAD) infection (COLON) recurrent urinary tract infection (PERIOD) (¶ HEAD) course in hospital (COLON) jh willcutt (COMMA) a 72 year old male (COMMA) was treated upon admission with ampicillin because a preliminary bacterial count exceeded one hundred thousand per milliliter (USE THE ABBREVIATION ml) (PERIOD) the organism later was identified as (CAPITAL) e (PERIOD, SPACE, LOWERCASE) coli (SEMICOLON) streptomycin tested as most effective (PERIOD) ampicillin therapy was continued however because of impaired kidney function (PERIOD) he received fluids and other supportive measures (PERIOD) 3 days after cataract surgery (OPEN PAREN) performed without significant benefit (CLOSE PAREN) the patients urinary tract infection had subsided (PERIOD) prognosis is only moderate because of his weakened condition (COMMA) depression (COMMA) and history of infection (PERIOD) (¶ HEAD) condition on discharge (COLON) patient went home (COMMA) to be seen in the office in 7 days (PERIOD)

16 Spacing and Horizontal Centering

Skill-Building Warmup

16a 7'

each line twice SS; DS between 2-line groups

Line 4: Set first tab 5 spaces from left margin. Then set 5 more tabs 10 spaces apart.

alphabet 1 The five proposed jurors were quickly examined by Eliza Wig.
’ apostrophe 2 It’s time to clean Luke’s and Coral’s rooms; they’re a mess.
shift/lock 3 The IRS cooperated with the CIA and the FBI at their behest.
tab review 4 tab right tab ivory tab laugh tab fight tab chaos tab blame

16b 18'

FORMATTING

Set line spacing

Read “Line spacing.”

Line spacing
Single-spaced text is keyed on each line. Double-spaced text has one blank line between lines of type.

this is single spacing	this is double spacing

Typewriters: Double spacing can be achieved by striking return twice at the end of each line or by changing the line space selector to **2.**

wp **Line spacing:** The default for line spacing is single spacing.

16c 10'

SKILL BUILDING

Build staying power

DS ¶s; 5-space ¶ indention

1 Key the ¶s as shown once for orientation.

2 Take two 1' timings on each ¶.

3 Take a 3' timing on all ¶s. Determine *gwam*.

Goal: 17 *gwam*

gwam 3'

Most people will agree that we owe it to our children 4
to pass the planet on to them in better condition than we 7
found it. We must take extra steps just to make the quality 12
of living better. 13

If we do not change our ways quickly and stop damaging 16
our world, it will not be a good place to live. We can save 21
the ozone and wildlife and stop polluting the air and water. 25

gwam 3' | 1 | 2 | 3 | 4 |

16d 15'

FORMATTING

Center horizontally

Read the information at the right and the information at the top of page 39 appropriate for your equipment. Then key Drills 1-3 on page 39.

Center point
The horizontal center point of a line of writing is determined by adding the numbers on the line-of-writing scale at the left and right edges of the paper and dividing by 2. If the paper guide (left edge) is at 0, the center point for 10-pitch is 42; for 12-pitch, 51.

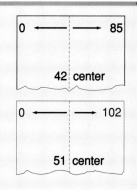

0 ← → 85
42 center

0 ← → 102
51 center

wp **Center.** This feature centers text horizontally between the left and right margins. Generally, the center command is entered before text is keyed.

Document 4
Form letter

(LM pp. S79-S83)

1 Prepare a form letter request for each overdue account listed on the spreadsheet; the letter is addressed to the guarantor (person responsible for payment).

a Remove the form letter requests from the supplies.

b Use the table produced in Document 3 to determine the variables. Write the variables on the form letter requests. The first request has been completed.

2 Key the letters using the form letter requests. Mr. Hunter will sign the letters. Include Melissa Bryan's initials (caps) as the originator with your reference initials **(MB:xx)**.

Use merge.

Dear __________

Your unpaid balance of _____ is now past due. We have requested payment from you on three occasions; however, we have received neither payment nor an explanation as to why payment has not been made.

The staff here at the Family Medical Center are very concerned. Further charges cannot be made until your account is up to date. Therefore, medical services can be provided to you and your family on a cash basis only.

Although we have no desire to cancel your credit privileges, we are forced to disallow any increase to your balance until payment of the past-due amount is paid. Please call me at (206) 555-3322 and make arrangements for paying your overdue account.

If we do not hear from you regarding a revised payment schedule, please pay $____, a minimum payment. This payment must be received by (supply date ten days from today).

Accounts Payable Spreadsheet
Current Date

Name	Balance	Days Past Due	Minimum Payment
Brown, Holly	$120	120	$25
Iannone, George	$400	120	$75
Haug, Cliff	$253	120	$50

Document 5
Table

Arrange the list of frequently called numbers by common categories such as **Hospitals** and **Referring Physicians**. Use **Other** category for names you cannot classify in the common categories. Arrange categories in alphabetical order; indent items under category headings; SS items, DS between categories. Include a note explaining how to use a speed number.

Note: To use speed dialing, just press the * button and the two numbers that follow.

LIST OF FREQUENTLY CALLED NUMBERS

Place/Doctor	Speed #	Number
Children's Hospital	*08	555-3822
Davidson Pharmacy	*07	555-~~1111~~ 7763
Health Department	*13	555-9874
Heritage General Hospital	*10	555-1283
Northside Drive Pharmacy	*12	555-3682
Police Department	*00	555-~~0087~~ 0891
Westland Circle Pharmacy	*01	555-8267
Referring Physicians		
Kozuma, Sam	*02	555-2145
Sandhu, Al	*03	555-5765
Nichols, Tom	*14	555-9321
Rivera, Karen	*15	555-0428

Electric typewriters:

1 Set one tab at center.

2 From center, strike the backspace key once for each two letters, spaces, or punctuation marks in the line to be centered. Do not backspace for a leftover stroke at the end of a line.

3 Key the line of text, beginning where you completed the backspacing; return.

Example:

1 2 3 4 5 6 7 8 9 10
BA CK SP AC Espace FR OM spaceC EN TE R

Electronic typewriters:

1 Insert paper with left edge at 0.

2 Strike return; then press the Center key.

3 Key the first line. The characters will not print as you key the line.

4 Strike return; the line will print.

Keyboarding software: Text can be centered in the open screen. Strike **Alt + C** to turn centering on and off.

Drill 1

3" top margin (begin on line 19); center each line; space as shown; the highlighted letter *i* in each line will align when the text is centered properly

AUTOMATIC CENTER**I**NG FEATURE

DS

Eliminates Tedious Count**i**ng and Backspacing
Expedites Center**i**ng Duties
Featured on Electron**i**c Typewriters

Drill 2

2" top margin (begin on line 13); center each line; space as shown

TENTH ANNUAL OFFICE AUTOMATION CONVENTION

DS

Demonstrating the Latest Technologies
Telecommunications
Voice Activated Systems
Laser Optical Discs
FREE ADMISSION

Drill 3

1 Set 2" top margin,1.5" side margins, DS, 5-space ¶ indention.

2 Center heading. Indent ¶ and end lines properly.

3 Center each of the last 4 lines; change line spacing to SS after keying **MUTUAL FUNDS**.

MAKE THE MOST OF YOUR MONEY

Robert Gronin, a leading Texas economist and financial adviser, will be the guest speaker at the September meeting of the Business Club. The following topics will be included in his speech:

MUTUAL FUNDS
LIMITED PARTNERSHIPS
REAL ESTATE
STOCKS AND BONDS

Document 3
Table

Drew Hunter, office manager, has given you the following handwritten list of past-due accounts. Prepare a centered four-column table in landscape orientation (width of paper is 11"). Arrange in alphabetical order by guarantor.

Main heading:

Past Due Accounts

Secondary heading:

Current Date

Column headings:

Patient, **Address**, **Guarantor**, and **Date of Last Payment**.

wp Use the table feature to create the table. Use the sort feature to arrange names in alphabetical order.

Add a fourth column for date of last payment

Patient	Address	Guarantor
Jay Brown 3/30	242 St. Helen Street Tacoma, WA 98402-0242	Holly Brown
George Iannone 3/31	P.O. Box 2999 Olympia, WA 98507-2999	George Iannone
Cliff Haug 4/2	Route 1, Box 388 Everett, WA 98205-0388	Cliff Haug
Vicki Wefford 4/4	1196 45th Avenue Seattle, WA 98105-1196	V. C. Wefford
Lucinda Ryals 3/30	One Concord Drive Seattle, WA 98101-0001	Daniel Sanders
Kathryn Essig 4/3	Route 2, Box 82 Olympia, WA 98507-0082	Susan Essig
Jon Rodriques 3/28	P.O. Box 1311-B Tacoma, WA 98402-1311	J.C. Rodriques
Hui Ling 4/2	32 Chad Court Seattle, WA 98105-0032	Hui Ling

17 Review

Skill-Building Warmup

17a 6'

each line twice SS (slowly, then faster); DS between 2-line groups

alphabet 1 Mandif expects to solve my big jigsaw puzzle rather quickly.

" (quotation) 2 She sang the songs "Life Is Eternal" and "Fisherman's Song."

space bar 3 Fill the box with dirt and moss to keep the ivy plant moist.

easy 4 Jane Burien may wish to work downtown for a giant auto firm.

| 1 | 2 | 3 | 4 | 5 | 6 | 7 | 8 | 9 | 10 | 11 | 12 |

17b 7'

SKILL BUILDING

Finger reaches

Key each set of lines SS; DS between each group; fingers curved, hands quiet.

first finger

5 by bar get fun van for inn art from gray hymn July true verb
6 brag human bring unfold hominy mighty report verify puny joy
7 You are brave to try bringing home the van in the bad storm.

second finger

8 ace ink did kid cad keyed deep seed kind Dick died kink like
9 cease decease decades kick secret check decide kidney evaded
10 Dedre likes the idea of ending dinner with cake for dessert.

third finger

11 oil sow six vex wax axe low old lox pool west loss wool slow
12 swallow swamp saw sew wood sax sexes loom stew excess school
13 Wes waxes floors and washes windows at low costs to schools.

fourth finger

14 zap zip craze pop pup pan daze quote queen quiz pizza puzzle
15 zoo graze zipper panzer zebra quip partizan patronize appear
16 Czar Zane appears to be dazzled by the apple pizza and jazz.

17c 7'

SKILL BUILDING

Response patterns

Key lines SS; DS between groups.

words: think and key words

17 may big end pay and bid six fit own bus sit air due map lays
18 also firm they work make lend disk when rush held name spend
19 city busy visit both town title usual half fight blame audit

phrases: think and key phrases

20 is the | to do | it is | but so | she did | own me | may go | by the | or me
21 it may | he did | but if | to end | she may | do so | it is | to do | is the
22 the firm | all six | they paid | held tight | bid with | and for | do it

easy sentences

23 Did the chap work to mend the torn right half of the ensign?
24 Blame me for their penchant for the antique chair and panel.
25 She bid by proxy for eighty bushels of a corn and rye blend.

| 1 | 2 | 3 | 4 | 5 | 6 | 7 | 8 | 9 | 10 | 11 | 12 |

Document 2
Patient record

Key a continuation sheet **(Page 2)** for **Ky Chen** (reference number **549318**), born 18 days ago. Dr. Mitchell has dictated the information for the patient record. You must provide correct capitalization, punctuation, grammar, and number expression. Key EEG in ALL CAPS. Other special instructions are shown in parentheses.

Continuation sheets

The first page of a Patient Record is keyed on a preprinted form. All subsequent pages, called Continuation Sheets, are keyed on plain paper.

1 Margins 1"; center **CONTINUATION SHEET**

2 Key at left margin the **PATIENT'S NAME**, date of birth **DOB**, reference number **REF**, the physician's name, and the page number. Use bold as shown.

3 Key ¶ heads in ALL CAPS and bold.

4 Key your reference initials below body and then, below them, key the current date.

5 Each additional entry must be dated.

CONTINUATION SHEET

PATIENT'S NAME: Jacquelyn Forbes
DOB: January 14, 1955
REF: 328311
Carla B. Mitchell, M.D.
Page 2
(Text keyed here is single-spaced.)
xx
4-12-94

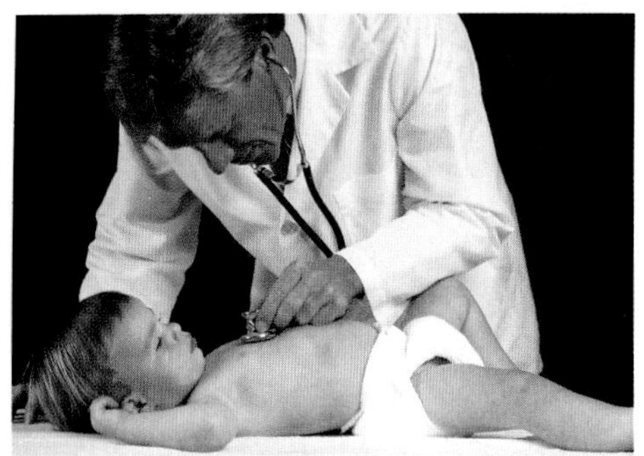

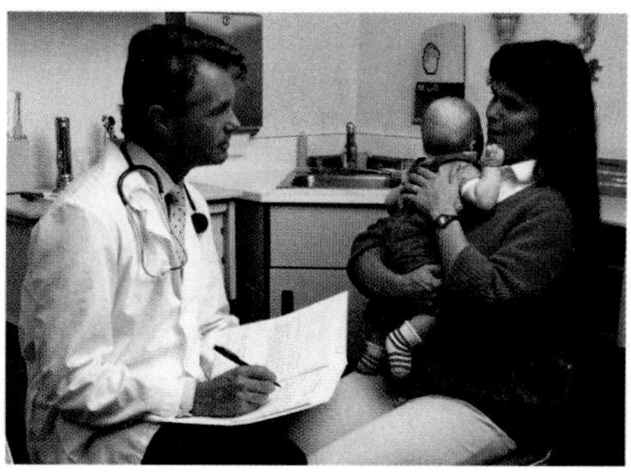

an eeg was ordered for suspected seizure activity on this three week old male patient (PERIOD) (¶ HEAD) eeg (COLON) the eeg results indicate a nearly continuous record of activity (PERIOD) an occassional bicentral sharp wave was present (PERIOD) brief attenuation of electrical activity (OPEN PAREN) up to six seconds duration (CLOSE PAREN) increases slightly during sleep (PERIOD) no seizure activity noted during eeg (PERIOD ¶) central delta waves show frequencies of point 4 to point 9 cycles per second (PERIOD) bilateral beta waves are present as are bilateral theta waves in the temporal leads (PERIOD) (¶ HEAD) impression (COLON) for gestational age (OPEN PAREN) 32 weeks (CLOSE PAREN) (COMMA) eeg appeared to be within normal range (PERIOD) apparent episodes of apnea seem to be central in origin (PERIOD) (¶ HEAD) recommendation (COLON) monitor activity (SEMICOLON) order another eeg in 2 weeks (PERIOD)

17d 10'

SKILL BUILDING

Measure skill growth

DS ¶s; 5-space ¶ indention

1 Key the ¶s once.

2 Take 1' timings on each ¶ and a 3' writing on all ¶s. Determine *gwam*.

Goal: 18 *gwam*

all letters — *gwam* 3'

A wise man once said that we have two ears and one 3
tongue so that we may hear more and talk less. Therefore, 7
we should be prepared to talk less quickly and exert more 11
effort to listen carefully to what others have to offer. 15

Most people do not realize that when we listen, we use 19
not just our ears, but our eyes and mind as well. To form 23
the art of listening well, show interest in what is said, 27
pay attention, ask questions, and keep an open mind. 30

gwam 3' | 1 | 2 | 3 | 4 |

17e 20'

FORMATTING

Review formatting

Drill 1

1 Set 1.5" top margin, 1.5" side margins, and DS. Center heading and key first ¶. Line endings will be different than shown here.

2 Center the longest line in the listing; set a tab at that point. Begin all other lines at the tab; SS list.

THRIVING IN A MULTICULTURAL WORK PLACE

To avoid conflict and misunderstanding in the work place, we must be aware of the cultural differences that exist among peoples from other cultures. Become more sophisticated in your relationships by knowing some American customs that often prove confusing to persons from other countries.

Love of individualism
Informality of workers
longest line → Hierarchy and protocol
Directness

Drill 2 (optional)

1 Set 1.5" top margin and 1.5" side margins; DS; 5-space ¶ indention.

2 Center heading. Do not add extra space between ¶s.

THE VALUE OF AN EDUCATION

Who are happier, people with much education or those who have little? Education is no magic elixir.

Education is only a tool that can help us to know how to win out over problems. The answer lies in how we use our education.

We can use what we learn, through experience as well as through school, to recognize those values that have great significance to us. We can use those values to help us find the satisfaction in life we all seek.

Document 1
Patient referral letter
(LM p. S77)

Dr. Mitchell asks you to key the patient referral letter keyed earlier for Janna Lomenick; supply necessary letter parts.

Ann Herring, M.D.
La Galerie Bone and Joint Clinic
900 First Avenue
Seattle, WA 98104-0900

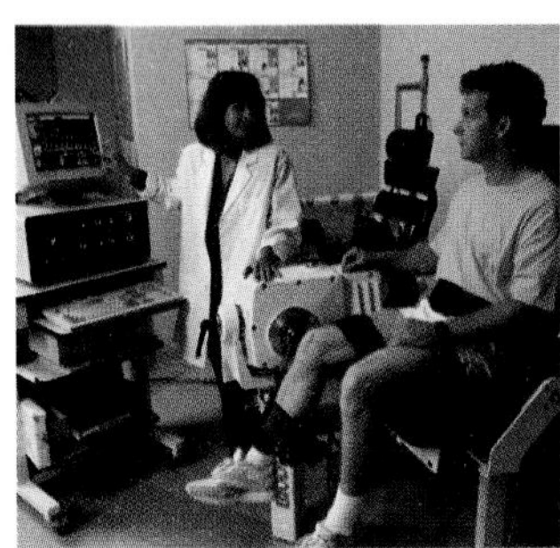

RE: JANNA LOMENICK

This letter confirms our conversation this morning concerning my referral of Janna Lomenick; Her history is as follows:

Janna is of slight build, a 13-year-old female, has had normal childhood diseases with no history of illness. She had her appendix removed at age 6. She is active in sports and is energetic.

September 23, 19--: Janna incured minor bruises on her face and upper right arm from falling on the sidewalk while carrying tools. She experienced pain in the left knee; but no redness appeared to be present.

September 25, 19--: Janna was examined by me after complaining of pain and stiffness when walking and extending her left leg. A moderate eusion of the knee joint was found; know ligamentous instability was present. Pain was experienced from forced extension. Tenderness was found in both medial joint space and posterior region. No abnormalities were found in x-rays of lateral projections of the knee (x-rays examined by Dr. G. Hong and me). An arthrogram revealed a capsular tear in the posterior horn of the medial meniscus. The tear extended down to about 1/3 of the thickness of the meniscus.

Diagnosis: Peripheral capsular tear at posterior part of the medial meniscus of the left knee. Recommendation: Reduced activity for three weeks; no sports for six to eight weeks.

October 19, 19--: Upon examination, Janna was found to have good range of movement. However, a ligamentous laxity in the posterior capusle of the left knee joint is present. Note that Janna admitted to playing volley ball twice in the past two weeks.

Recommendation: Guarded activity; surgery may be a possibility; see again in 6 months.

Impression: Ligamentous leaxity of left knee joint. Your impression of Janna Lomenick's condition will be appreciated. Mrs. Carol Lomenick will call for an appointment.

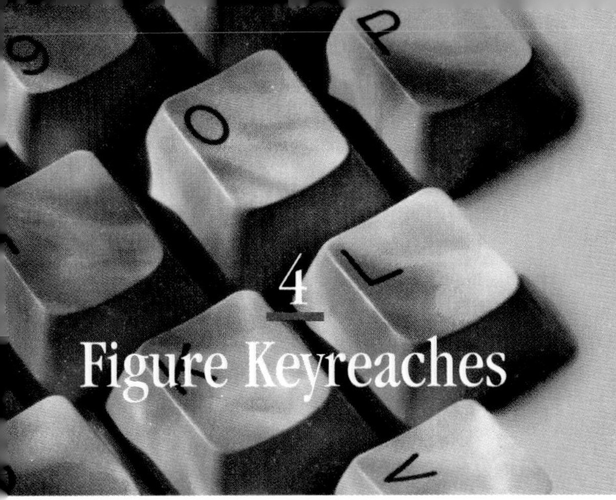

4 Figure Keyreaches

Learning goals:
1. To master selected symbol (top-row) keyreaches.
2. To edit (proofread) and revise copy.
3. To key from statistical copy.
4. To key from script copy.
5. To improve staying power.

Formatting guides:
1. Default margins or 60-space line.
2. Single-space drills; double-space paragraphs.

18a 7'

Skill-building warmup

each line twice SS; DS between 2-line groups

Note: Margins for a 60-space line are pica, 12-72; elite, 21-81.

alphabet 1 Jessie Quick believed the campaign frenzy would be exciting.
shift keys 2 L. K. Coe, M.D., hopes Dr. Lopez can leave for Maine in May.
third row 3 We were quietly prepped to write two letters to Portia York.
easy 4 Kale's neighbor works with a tutor when they visit downtown.

| 1 | 2 | 3 | 4 | 5 | 6 | 7 | 8 | 9 | 10 | 11 | 12 |

18b 14'

Learn 1 and 8

each line twice SS; DS between 2-line groups

Note: The digit "1" and the letter "l" have separate values on a computer keyboard. Do not interchange these characters.

Abbreviations: Do not space after a period within an abbreviation, as in Ph.D., U.S., C.O.D., a.m.

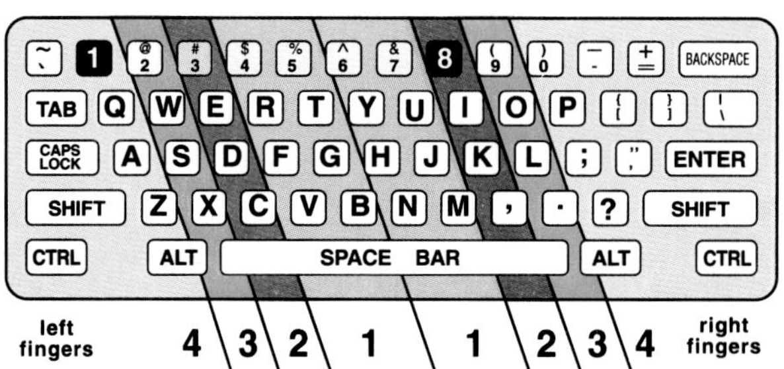

1 Reach *up* with *left little* finger.

5 1 1a a1 1 1; 1 and a 1; 1 add 1; 1 aunt; 1 ace; 1 arm; 1 aye
6 1 and 11 and 111; 11 eggs; 11 vats; Set 11A; May 11; Item 11
7 The 11 aces of the 111th Corps each rated a salute at 1 p.m.

8 Reach *up* with *right second* finger.

8 8 8k k8 8 8; 8 kits; ask 8; 8 kites; kick 8; 8 keys; spark 8
9 OK 88; 8 bags; 8 or 88; the 88th; 88 kegs; ask 88; order 888
10 Eight of the 88 cars score 8 or better on our Form 8 rating.

all figures learned

11 She did live at 818 Park, not 181 Park; or was it 181 Clark?
12 Put 1 with 8 to form 18; put 8 with 1 to form 81. Use 1881.
13 On May 1 at 8 a.m., 18 men and 18 women left Gate 8 for Rio.

32

Family Medical Center, Inc.

Medical Office

(Lessons 163-167)

Learning goals:

1 To prepare documents containing medical terminology.

2 To format the kinds of documents used frequently in medical offices.

3 To apply basic communication and document production skills to medical office tasks.

Office job simulation

Read "Work assignment" at right carefully. Make notes of procedures that will save time as you complete the projects in this medical office simulation.

Daily plan

Skill-building workshop 4 .... 5'-15'
Simulation .... 35'-45'
OR
Simulation .... 50'

Work assignment

You have recently accepted a position as medical administrative assistant in the professional corporation Family Medical Center, Inc. The staff consists of five physicians (three in family practice, one in pediatrics, and one in dentistry).

Family Medical Center, Inc., organized two years ago, is located at 9932 Hanover Street on the fourth floor of the Medical Arts Complex. Patients may schedule appointments from 10 a.m. until 5 p.m. weekdays. A very valuable service offered by this group is an after hours and weekend clinic, designed primarily for emergency cases.

You are currently working for **Carla B. Mitchell, M.D.**, one of the family physicians. Because Dr. Mitchell has a heavy case load at the office and at Heritage General Hospital, you must work with little supervision. Therefore, you frequently must use your judgment in completing tasks. Refer to this reference manual, your electronic and manual dictionaries, and a current office procedures reference manual.

Dr. Mitchell carries a portable dictation machine with her and dictates many of the documents you will prepare. You must provide correct spelling, capitalization, punctuation, grammar, and number expression. Proofread carefully.

Note Dr. Mitchell's preferences for preparing the following documents:

Correspondence: Letters are keyed in block format and printed on letterhead stationery. When addressing a letter to a doctor, include a professional title such as M.D. after the name in the letter address and omit Dr. Standard placement is used for all letters.

When appropriate, a patient's name is used as a reference line (**RE:** PATIENT'S NAME). **Sincerely** and **Carla B. Mitchell, M.D.** are used in the closing.

Reports: The preferred report format features single-spaced, blocked paragraphs. Exceptions and special features are brought to your attention by the doctor.

Tables: Tables are centered horizontally and vertically. Column headings are blocked. Use bold in headings.

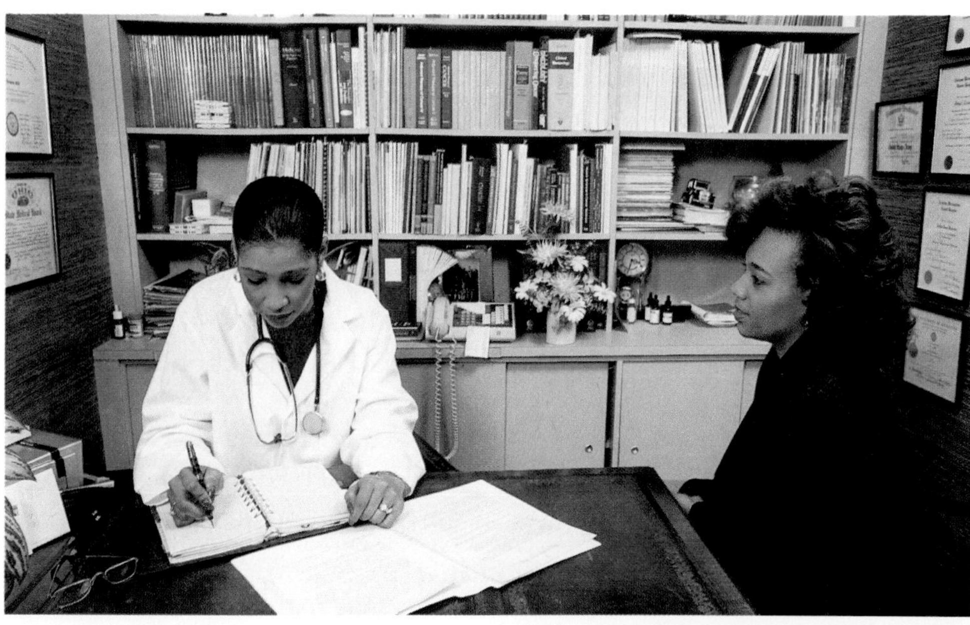

18c 8'

SKILL BUILDING

Improve figure keyreaches

Control your reading speed; read only slightly ahead of what you are keying. Key each line once DS; repeat lines 15, 17, and 19.

14 The 8 men in 8 boats left Dock 1 at 1 p.m. June 1.

15 *On August 1, I saw 8 mares and 8 foals in Field 1.*

16 The 81 boxes on Pier 18 left at 8 p.m. on March 1.

17 *Jan is 18 and Sean is 18; their grandfather is 81.*

18 Our 18 trucks moved 188 tons on May 18 and June 1.

19 *Send Mary 18 No. 1 panes for her home at 8118 Oak.*

18d 13'

SKILL BUILDING

Reach for new goals

Key each sentence twice as "Return" is called every 30".

Goal: To reach the end of each line as "Return" is called.

Goals for 1'

14-15 *gwam*, acceptable
16-17 *gwam*, good
18-20 *gwam*, very good
22+ *gwam*, excellent

	gwam 1'	30"
20 I paid for six bushels of rye.	6	12
21 Risk a penalty; this is a big down.	7	14
22 Did their form entitle them to the land?	8	16
23 Did the men in the field signal for us to go?	9	18
24 I may pay for the antique bowls when I go to town.	10	20
25 The auditor did the work right, so he risks no penalty.	11	22
26 The man by the big bush did signal us to turn down the lane.	12	24

18e 8'

SKILL BUILDING

Improve keying techniques

each line twice; DS between 2-line groups

first row
27 Can Max Babbs, my zany cousin, raze Ms. Mann's vacant manor?

home row
28 Sada and Jake had a dish of salad; Gail had a glass of soda.

third row
29 At our party, Roy quietly poured tea for our worried guests.

top row
30 In July, 81 men visited 8 cities and 18 towns on 11 islands.

| 1 | 2 | 3 | 4 | 5 | 6 | 7 | 8 | 9 | 10 | 11 | 12 |

Document 9
Letter
(LM p. S75)
Prepare the letter to the hotel in Mexico, reserving the hotel rooms and meeting space and placing equipment and catering orders. Send the letter by **facsimile** mail to:

Sr. Rafael Lopez
Hotel Manager
Hotel del Desierto
Avenida Primera No. 1000
Juarez, MEXICO

Use the salutation **Senor Lopez**. Include Mr. McKibben's courtesy title in the closing.

set up as a table

Please make the following room reservations for January 10 and 11, 19--: 1 double, Carlos Petrillo and Coty Schrock; 1 double, Sarah Webber and Lisa York; 1 king, Francis McKibben; 1 single, Walter Winfield.

In addition, please reserve a small conference room on Wednesday, January 11, from 7 a.m. until 3 p.m. Room setup should include 3 round tables with a sketch pad and easel at the front of the room. Equipment requests are itemized on the enclosed equipment request form. Please have your catering department fill the following refreshment order for a party of 6:

7:30 a.m. Breakfast rolls, juice, coffee
10:15 a.m. Coffee and soft drinks

Please send all room confirmations directly to me as well as copies of the catering and equipment orders. We look forward to our visit to the Hotel del Desierto.

Enclosure: Equipment Request Form

Document 10
Promotional insert
A new promotional package is being prepared for distribution to prospective clients. Use your creativity to prepare an attractive one-page insert on service rates.

wp Use the table feature and shade the column headings. Vary point size as follows:
Main heading: large
Column headings: medium, bold
Body: medium
Footnotes: small

CELLULAR CONNECTION
Service Rates

Monthly Service Plans	Monthly Service Charge	Peak Airtime Rate*	Off Peak Airtime Rate**	Free Airtime Included
Economy Service	$ 6.95	.70/min.	.25/min.	NA
Basic Service	~~1~~ 9 5.95	.35/min.	.25/min.	NA
Frequent Caller	39.95	.~~6~~ 3 0/min.	.25/min.	100 min.
Super Saver	85.95	.~~4~~ 2 5/min.	.25/min.	350 min.

*Peak airtime is 7a.m. to 7p.m., Monday through Friday.
**Off peak airtime is all other times and special holidays.

19 5 and 0

Skill-Building Warmup

19a 7'

each line twice; DS between 2-line groups

alphabet 1 John Quigley packed the zinnias in twelve large, firm boxes.
figures 2 Idle Motor 18 at 8 mph and Motor 81 at 8 mph; avoid Motor 1.
shift/lock 3 Lily read BLITHE SPIRIT by Noel Coward. I read VANITY FAIR.
easy 4 Did they fix the problem of the torn panel and worn element?

| 1 | 2 | 3 | 4 | 5 | 6 | 7 | 8 | 9 | 10 | 11 | 12

19b 9'

SKILL BUILDING

Improve response patterns

each line once SS; DS between 2-line groups

word response: read word by word

5 el id la or by doe so am is go us it an me ox he of to if ah
6 Did the air corps hang a map of the glens on the big island?

stroke response: read stroke by stroke

7 up you be was in at on as oh are no ad pop fad pun cad hi ax
8 Face bare facts, we beg you; read a free tract on star wars.

combination response: vary speed but maintain rhythm

9 be a duty | as junk | to form | at rest | of corn | do work | he read it
10 Doria paid the taxes on six acres of rich lake land in Ohio.

| 1 | 2 | 3 | 4 | 5 | 6 | 7 | 8 | 9 | 10 | 11 | 12 |

19c 14'

Learn 5 and 0

each line twice SS; DS between 3-line groups

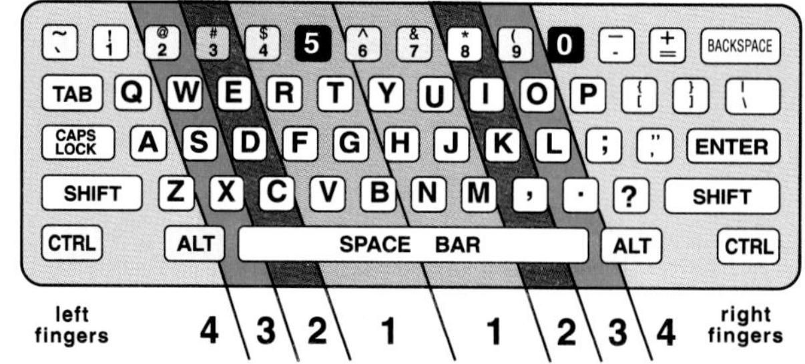

5 Reach *up* with *left first* finger.

11 5 5f f5 5 5; 5 fans; 5 feet; 5 figs; 5 fobs; 5 furs; 5 flaws
12 5 o'clock; 5 a.m.; 5 p.m.; is 55 or less; buy 55; 5 and 5 is
13 Call Line 555 if 5 fans or 5 bins arrive at Pier 5 by 5 p.m.

0 Reach *up* with *right little* finger.

14 0 0; ;0 0 0; skip 0; plan 0; left 0; is below 0; I scored 0;
15 0 degrees; key 0 and 0; write 00 here; the total is 0 or 00;
16 She laughed at their 0 to 0 score; but ours was 0 to 0 also.

all figures learned

17 I keyed 550 pages for Invoice 05, or 50 more than we needed.
18 Pages 15 and 18 of the program listed 150, not 180, members.
19 On May 10, Rick drove 500 miles to New Mexico in car No. 08.

Document 5 (continued)

(A)

<u>Personalismo</u>. Mexicans take great pride in personal uniqueness and require considerable supportive praise. In fact, Mexico is often called the "Nation of Personal Islands." If treated as a part of a group and not as an individual, a Mexican may appear arrogant or become insulted. Children are taught from birth to respect dominant men in their lives.

<u>Machismo</u>. Mexicans demonstrate virility, zest for action, caring and competitiveness, and the will to conquer.

<u>Kinship ties</u>. Family ties are deep and strong. Obligations to family come first over job, community, etc. The quality of daily life ranks high.

Document 6
Appendix

Prepare the appendix page for the Mexico report. Remember to prepare a half title page.

Reference: page 358

Document 7
Title Page

Prepare a title page for the Mexico report; indicate that it was prepared by Carlos Petrillo.

Use graphic lines.

Document 8
Table of contents

Prepare a table of contents for the Mexico report. Include all side and paragraph headings and the appendix.

Use leaders and key the page numbers flush right.

Use table of contents feature.

ARRIVAL/SURVIVAL LANGUAGE

(Prepare as the appendix)

Do you speak English?	Habla usted ingles?
Good morning... afternoon... evening	Buenos dias... Buenos tardes... Buenos noches
Hello	Hola ("ola")
Goodbye	adios or hasta luego
How are you?	Como esta usted?
Fine, very good.	Bien, muy bien.
Where is...?	Donde esta ...?
Glad to meet you.	Mucho gusto en conocerle.
The pleasure is mine.	El gusto es mio.
I like it very much.	Me gusta mucho.
I don't like it.	No me gusta.
I do not understand.	No entiendo.
Please	Por favor
Yes	Si
No	No
Thank you very much.	Muchas gracias.
You are welcome.	De nada.
I am very sorry.	Lo siento mucho.

19d 8'

SKILL BUILDING

Improve figure keyreaches

Work to avoid pauses; each line once DS; repeat 21, 23, and 25.

20 After May 18, French 050 meets in Room 185 at 10 a.m. daily.
21 *Read pages 5 and 8; duplicate page 18; omit pages 50 and 51.*
22 We have Model 80 with 10 meters or Model 180 with 15 meters.
23 *Between 8 and 10 that night, 5 of us drove to 580 Park Lane.*
24 Flight 508 left Reno at 1 on May 10; it landed in Lima at 8.
25 *They need to use Rooms 10 and 11; lock Rooms 50, 80, and 85.*

19e 12'

SKILL BUILDING

Improve speed

Follow the procedures at the right.

Guided writing procedures

1 Take a 1' writing on ¶1. Determine *gwam*.

2 Add 4 words to your 1' *gwam* to determine your goal rate.

3 From the table at the right, select from Column 4 the speed nearest your goal rate.

Note the ¼' points at the left of that speed.

4 Take two 1' writings on each ¶ at your goal rate guided by the quarter-minute calls (15", 30", 45", and 1').

5 Take a 2' and 3' timing without the guide.

gwam ¼'	½'	¾'	1'
4	8	12	16
5	10	15	20
6	12	18	24
7	14	21	28
8	16	24	32
9	18	27	36
10	20	30	40

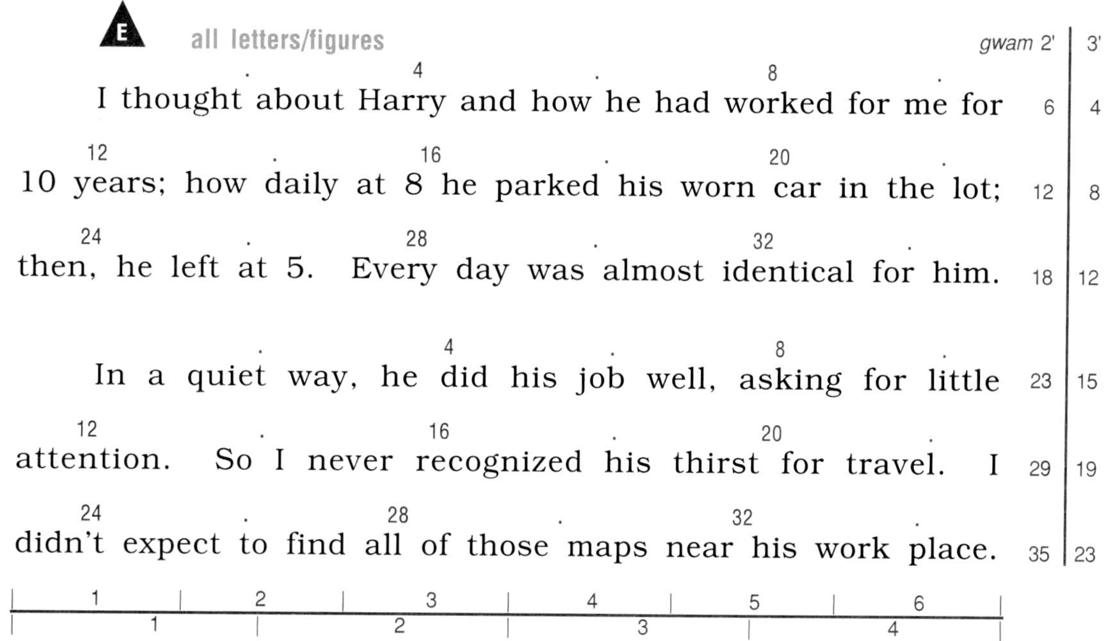

E all letters/figures

	gwam 2'	3'
I thought about Harry and how he had worked for me for	6	4
10 years; how daily at 8 he parked his worn car in the lot;	12	8
then, he left at 5. Every day was almost identical for him.	18	12
In a quiet way, he did his job well, asking for little	23	15
attention. So I never recognized his thirst for travel. I	29	19
didn't expect to find all of those maps near his work place.	35	23

gwam 2' | 1 | 2 | 3 | 4 | 5 | 6 |
3' | 1 | 2 | 3 | 4 |

Document 5 (continued)

1. Shake hands. The general hello and goodbye to a large group is not adequate. Speak individually to every person in the room. Look the person in the eye, call him or her by name, and offer a pleasant comment. Taking the extra moment to shake hands at every meeting and again on departure will reap benefits.

2.________________. Being a friend is important first; conducting business is secondary. Establish a friendship; show interest in the individual and the family. Learn peoples names and pronounce them correctly in conversation. People are more important than business deals. Praise frequently. Avoid direct negatives or criticism.

3.________________. Mexicans place more importance on family, personal, and church-related activities than on business activities. Accordingly, they have longer lunches and more holidays. Therefore, they place less importance on adherence to schedules and appointment times than Americans do.

4.________________. Protocol with reguard to who takes precedence is important i.e seating at meetings, speaking, and walking through doorways. Do not interrupt anyone.

5.________________. Americans consider 18 inches a comfortable distance between people; however, Mexicans prefer much less. Adjust to their space preferences. Do not move away, back up, or put up a barrier such as standing behind a desk.

6.________________. Mexicans are generous with hospitality and expect the same in return. For example, when hosting a party, prepare a generous menu.

7.________________. Although the business meeting may be conducted in English, speak Spanish in social parts of conservation. This courteous effort will be noted. Refer to the appendix, page , for a list of arrival/survival language.

Summary

To be successful in business relationships with Mexicans, remember to take time for courtesies, to establish friendships, and show respect for the Mexican culture and system.

20 2 and 7

Skill-Building Warmup

20a 7'

each line once; then take two 1' writings on line 4; determine *gwam*

alphabet 1 Perry might know I feel jinxed because I have missed a quiz.
figures 2 Channels 5 and 8, on from 10 to 11, said Luisa's IQ was 150.
shift/lock 3 Ella Hill will see Chekhov's THE CHERRY ORCHARD on Czech TV.
easy 4 The big dog by the bush kept the ducks and hen in the field.

1 | 2 | 3 | 4 | 5 | 6 | 7 | 8 | 9 | 10 | 11 | 12

20b 14'

Learn 2 and 7

each line twice SS; DS between 2-line groups

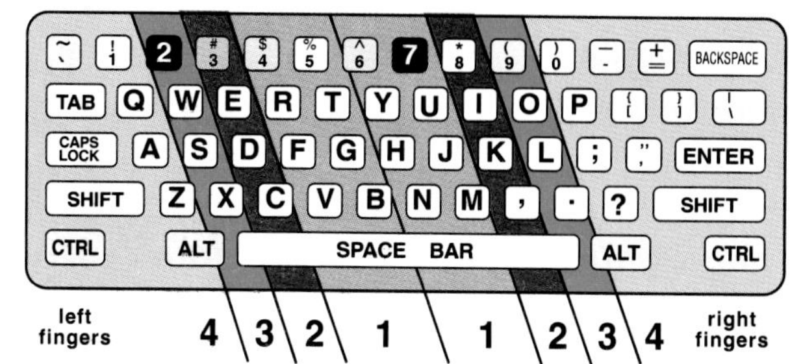

2 Reach *up* with *left third* finger.

5 2 2s s2 2 2; has 2 sons; is 2 sizes; was 2 sites; has 2 skis
6 add 2 and 2; 2 sets of 2; catch 22; as 2 of the 22; 222 Main
7 Exactly at 2 on August 22, the 22d Company left from Pier 2.

7 Reach *up* with *right first* finger.

8 7 7j j7 7 7; 7 jets; 7 jeans; 7 jays; 7 jobs; 7 jars; 7 jaws
9 ask for 7; buy 7; 77 years; June 7; take any 7; deny 77 boys
10 From May 7 on, all 77 men will live at 777 East 77th Street.

all figures learned

11 I read 2 of the 72 books, Ellis read 7, and Han read all 72.
12 Tract 27 cites the date as 1850; Tract 170 says it was 1852.
13 You can take Flight 850 on January 12; I'll take Flight 705.

20c 10'

SKILL BUILDING

Improve keying techniques

fingers curved, wrists low; each line twice SS; DS between 2-line groups; repeat as time permits

shift/lock
14 Our OPERATOR'S HANDBOOK says to use either AC or DC current.
adjacent reaches
15 He said that poised talk has triumphed over violent actions.
direct reaches
16 Murvyn must not make any decisions until Brad has his lunch.
double letters
17 He will tell all three cooks to add a little whipped butter.
combination
18 Kris started to blend a cocoa beverage for a shaken cowhand.

Document 5
Report

Carlos Petrillo asks you to prepare the report on Mexico that is to be distributed with the memo from Francis McKibben.

1 Use large fonts for the headings if available. If not, use bold for the main headings and bold underline for side and paragraph headings.

2 In your revision:

- Italicize foreign words, (underline if italics are not available).
- Proofread carefully for undetected errors.

WP Use a large font for the main and side headings and a medium font for paragraph headings.

Mexican

~~SOUTH AMERICAN~~ **CULTURE AND CUSTOMS** DS

Estados Unidos Mexicanos (United Mexican States), located immediately South of the United States, is a federal republic. Descended from the Spanish and Indians, Mexicans speak spanish, the official language of Mexico; thier religion is predominately Roman Catholic.

Juarez, the largest of the Mexican cities along the U.S. border, has a population of ~~approximately~~ about one-half million. Located in an arid desert area surrounded by treeless mountains, Juarez is an oasis filled with parks, lawns, and tree-lined streets. High winds make lined coats, hats, and gloves comfortable there. Juarez is in the mountain time zone.

The peso is the Mexican currency. ~~A peso is divided into 100 centavos with denominations of 1, 5, 10, 20, and 50. The expression $2.50 in Mexico means two pesos and 50 centavos~~. Currently $1 in United States money is equivalent to 3,034 pesos. Traveler's checks and are accepted in most businesses in Mexico; however, no personal checks are accepted. Some major credit cards ~~are accepted.~~

Mexican Culture

Historical events in Mexiço that assist in understanding its society and its personalities includes (1) the early Indian influence, (2) the conquest of Mexico by Cortez in 1521, (3) the fuedal control of the Spaniards, and (4) the independence of Mexico in 1821. Thus, (3) central factors have evolved from this historical influence and account for the present day society ~~in~~ Mexican. These factors are machismo, personalismo, ~~hierarchy and rank,~~ and kinship ties.

Customs and Practices Insert A

Because the United States is a major trading partner in Mexico, North American business executives must acquire a knowledge of customs and practices of their new business partners. The following suggestions provide an important bridge for conducting business with Mexicans:

20d 9'

SKILL BUILDING

Compare skill sentences

1 Take a 1' writing on line 19.

2 Take 1' writings on lines 20 and 21; try to match the number of lines completed with line 19.

3 Repeat Steps 1 and 2 with lines 22-24.

19 Both towns bid for six bushels of produce down by the docks.

20 *The cowl of the formal gown is held down by a bow.*

21 I work 18 visual signals with 2 turns of the lens.

22 Did he fix the shape of the hand and elbow of the clay form?

23 *The ivy bowl is a memento of their visit to Japan.*

24 Did 7 of them fix the signals for the 50 bicycles?

| 1 | 2 | 3 | 4 | 5 | 6 | 7 | 8 | 9 | 10 | 11 | 12 |

20e (Optional)

SKILL BUILDING

Reach for new goals

Key each line once as "Return" is called every 30".

Goal: To reach the end of the line just as "Return" is called.

	30"	20"
25 Pam visited the island in May.	12	18
26 The auditor may handle the problem.	14	21
27 He bid by proxy for the bushels of corn.	16	24
28 Did a man by a bush signal Ken to turn right?	18	27
29 If they wish, she may make the form for the disks.	20	30
30 Did the chap focus the lens on the airy downtown signs?	22	33
31 The formal gowns worn by the girls hang in the civic chapel.	24	36
32 Di paid us to go to town to bid for an authentic enamel owl.	26	39
33 Busy firms burn coal; odor is a key problem in the city air.	28	42

20f 10'

FORMATTING

Review centering

full sheet; 2" top margin; DS; center each line horizontally

The Surprise of 1870

Sadie's 25 Days in London

WHY THE 75 FROGS LEFT FOR POUGHKEEPSIE

1207 Rue Martinique

88 Keys and Me

BETTY KEYES' 85 LOW-CALORIE LUNCHES

Document 4
Itinerary

1 Prepare the itinerary for the Mexico site visit. (Use the airline schedule notes to fill in travel arrangements.)

Heading:

ITINERARY FOR MEXICO SITE VISIT

January 10-12, 19--

2 Adjust the vertical spacing or top margin so that the document will fit on one page.

3 Prepare copies (or originals) for each employee and attach to his/her memo (Document 3).

- On Carlos Petrillo's copy, highlight all meetings except with the controller.
- Highlight Schrock's responsibilities on his copy.

Tuesday, January 10, 19-- Colorado Springs to Juarez, Mexico

8:30 a.m. Briefing in Room 323.

Please add details of airline schedule

4:00 p.m. Arrive Juarez, Mexico. Drive to Hotel del Desierto, Avenida Primera No. 1000. (Hotel confirmations are attached.)

Wednesday, January 11, 19-- Juarez

7:30 a.m. Breakfast with Armando Cruz, President (lc) of Voz del Cielo, at Restaurante del Mundo. (McKibben and Petrillo)

9:30 a.m. Initial tour of facilities by Tito Gonzales, vice president of production. (all)

2:00 p.m. Meeting with Armando Cruz, Tito Gonzales, and Reuben Puente. (McKibben, Petrillo, York, and Webber)

2:15 p.m. Meeting with Felipe Gomez, controller. (Schrock)

~~7:00~~ 8:30 p.m. Dinner at Los Hermanos with top management. (all)

Thursday, January 12, 19-- Juarez to Colorado Springs

~~7:30~~ 8:00 a.m. Meeting at Hotel del Desierto. (Continental breakfast will be provided.)

1:00 p.m. Write report in hotel conference room.

4:15 p.m. Leave Juarez, Mexico.

Please add airline schedule for return.

1/10/--

11a. Leave Col. Springs, Hooper Flight 3832 (direct flight, stop in Dallas; lunch).

3:20p. Arrive in El Paso. Rent cars at Econo Car Rental in airport. (Reservations made and confirmations attached.)

1/12/--

5:30p. Leave El Paso, Hooper Flight 2393 (direct flight, stop in Dallas; dinner).

9:30p. Arrive Col. Springs.

21 4 and 9

Skill-Building Warmup

21a 7'

each line twice; DS between 2-line groups; 1' writings on line 4 as time permits

alphabet 1 Bob realized very quickly that jumping was excellent for us.
figures 2 Has each of the 18 clerks now corrected Item 501 on page 27?
space bar 3 Was it Mary? Helen? Pam? It was a woman; I saw one of them.
easy 4 The men paid their own firms for the eight big enamel signs.

| 1 | 2 | 3 | 4 | 5 | 6 | 7 | 8 | 9 | 10 | 11 | 12 |

21b 14'

Learn 4 and 9

each line twice SS; DS between 2-line groups

4 Reach *up* with *left first* finger.

5 4 4f f4 4 4 4; if 4 furs; off 4 floors; gaff 4 fish; 4 flags
6 44th floor; half of 44; 4 walked 44 flights; 4 girls; 4 boys
7 I order exactly 44 bagels, 4 cakes, and 4 pies before 4 a.m.

9 Reach *up* with *right third* finger.

8 9 91 19 9 9 9; fill 9 lugs; call 9 lads; Bill 9 lost; dial 9
9 also 9 oaks; roll 9 loaves; 9.9 degrees; sell 9 oaks; Hall 9
10 Just 9 couples, 9 men and 9 women, left at 9 on our Tour 99.

all figures learned

11 Memo 94 says 9 pads, 4 pens, and 4 ribbons were sent July 9.
12 Study Item 17 and Item 28 on page 40 and Item 59 on page 49.
13 Within 17 months he drove 85 miles, walked 29, and flew 490.

21c 9'

SKILL BUILDING

Improve figure keyreaches

each line twice; DS between 2-line groups

14 My staff of 18 worked 11 hours a day from May 27 to June 12.
15 There were 5 items tested by Inspector 7 at 4 p.m. on May 8.
16 Please send her File 10 today at 8; her access number is 97.
17 Car 47 had its trial run. The qualifying speed was 198 mph.
18 The estimated score? 485. Actual? 190. Difference? 295.

Document 3
Two-page memo with Distribution list
(LM p. S73)

Cellular Connection will be purchasing a foreign plant for production of parts.

1 Prepare the memo, outlining the details of the first site visit to Juarez, Mexico. Address the memo to **Distribution List**; include the employees highlighted in the Directory of Employees in the distribution list. For a subject line, use **Site Visit to Voz del Cielo--Juarez, Mexico**.

2 Follow the procedures in the Cellular Connection Procedures Manual for formatting a distribution list and preparing copies for distribution.

3 Add a postscript to the memo sent to Carlos Petrillo indicating that, because of his fluency in the Spanish language, he is to attend all sessions (except with the controller).

4 Hold the memos until Document 4; you will need them.

WP Use bullets for highlighting list. Use em-dash for dash in subject line. Key title of book in italics.

DIRECTORY OF EMPLOYEES

Name	Ext.
Adams, Victor	363
Baeuerlin, Scott	338
Bouchillon, Curtis	214
McKibben, Francis	333
Petrillo, Carlos	311
Reid, Craig	199
Pogue, Helen	302
Reno, Carol	227
Schrock, Coty	332
Webber, Sarah	386
Winfield, Walter	388
Wyckoff, Teresa	245
York, Lisa	309
Ziomek, Brian	376

Final approval for plant expansion to a foriegn country has been received. The ~~decision was reached that~~ purchase of an already existing plant was decided to be ~~would be the~~ most cost effective. The sites being considered are ~~as follows~~: Japan, Mexico, and France. ← alphabetize

Visits will be scheduled for each of the three proposed sites. The first visit will be on January 10-12, 19--, to Voz del Cielo in Juarez, Mexico. An itinerary is enclosed for your planning purposes. ~~Note~~ your highlighted reponsibilities have been

Overview

The small cellular phone production plant is located in Juarez, Mexico, about (10) sp miles south of El Paso, Texas. Juarez has a population of supply no. from report people. The physical plant covers approximately 20,000 square feet and houses approximately (100) sp employees. ¶ The following management team will ~~has~~ be ~~agreed to~~ meeting with us: Armando Cruz, President; Tito Gonzales, Vice President of Production; and Reuben Puente, Vice president of Marketing.

Immediate Attention

Two factors we must consider when preparing for this meeting are ~~as follows~~: ~~(1)~~ bullet • Our counterparts are Mexican with a different ~~ing~~ culture and customs. ~~and (2)~~ • The meeting is in Mexico, a foriegn country to most of us. Please begin preparing for this meeting by completing the following items:

~~1.~~ • Study the cutlure and customs of Mexico.

~~2.~~ • Study the book *An Easy Guide to Conversant Spanish*. Being famil ar with the language will assist us in our negotations.

~~3.~~ • Secure copy of birth certificate. This official record will be required when we enter Mexico.

Use the enclosed report prepared by Carlos Petrillo as a point of departure.

21d 8'

SKILL BUILDING

Improve keying techniques

key smoothly; repeat 20, 22, and 24

1st finger

19 Hagen, after her July triumph at tennis, may try volleyball.
20 Verna urges us to buy yet another of her beautiful rag rugs.

2d finger

21 Did Dick ask Cecelia, his sister, if she decided to like me?
22 Suddenly, Micki's bike skidded on the Cedar Street ice rink.

3d/4th finger

23 Paula has always allowed us to relax at La Paz and at Quito.
24 Please ask Zale to explain who explores most aquatic slopes.

| 1 | 2 | 3 | 4 | 5 | 6 | 7 | 8 | 9 | 10 | 11 | 12 |

21e 12'

SKILL BUILDING

Reach for new goals

1 Key each ¶ for a 1' writing. Compute *gwam*.

2 Take two 2' writings on all ¶s. Reach for a speed within two words of 1' *gwam*.

3 Take a 3' writing on all ¶s. Compute *gwam*. Reach for a speed within four words of 1' *gwam*.

E all letters

	gwam 2'	3'
We consider nature to be limited to those things, such	6	4
as air or trees, that we humans do not or cannot make.	11	7
For most of us, nature just exists, just is. We don't	17	11
question it or, perhaps, realize how vital it is to us.	22	15
Do I need nature, and does nature need me? I'm really	28	19
part of nature; thus, what happens to it happens to me.	33	22

gwam 2' | 1 | 2 | 3 | 4 | 5 | 6 |
3' | 1 | 2 | 3 | 4 |

Document 1 (continued)

■ Side heading

"Cellular DT-3200 helps me stay ahead of my competition because I'm always in touch with my customers," states Jennifer Warner. "My clients can literally reach me 24 hours a day. When I leave the car, I place the Mini-Cell in my coat pocket. You'll often find me in a restaurant making or receiving a call. My real estate sales have shown a 30 percent increase since purchasing a cellular phone."

Insert A

Cellular Connection is dedicated to providing the best service to our clients and to ~~make~~ making people aware of the benefits of cellular phone ownership. For more information about cellular phones and a demonstration, call one of our sales representatives at 555-6106. With a Cellular DT-3200, ~~begin~~ you can ~~making~~ make more effective use of your time, feel a increased sense of safety, ~~and~~ maintain closer contacts with clients, and

Document 2
Mailing List
(LM pp. S65-S71)

Prepare the form letter (Document 1) for each newcomer with children. Use the computer printout provided by the Colorado Springs Chamber of Commerce.

- Identify the newcomers who have children.
- Prepare a list of variables for each newcomer identified.
- Prepare the letters to newcomers.

wp Save the variables as **PROMOTE1.LST**. Merge the form letter **PROMOTE1.LET** with the list of variables.

CS509 NEWCOMERS REPORT
COLORADO SPRINGS CHAMBER OF COMMERCE
December 15, 19--

NAME	ADDRESS	ZIP	TEL. NO.	CHILD.	OCCUPATION
Caldwell, John & Paula	2000 Meadowlark Ln.	80931	555-0188	Y	M.D./Homemaker
Chang, Tao Chou	110 Park Lane Rd.	80933	555-4689	N	Student
Gordon, Ronald	Route 2, Box 92	80935	555-2238	N	Student
Luhanga, Lena	609 Seville Place	80934	555-0997	N	Retired
Maeda, Koji	40 Holtsinger Av.	80914	555-2506	N	USAF cadet
Nolen, Chris & Barbara	606 Lincoln St.	80931	555-8662	N	D.D.S./Anesthetist
Peay, Eric	66 East Lee Blvd.	80913	555-6307	N	Rabbi
Rekhi, Sanjay	18 Northside Dr.	80934	555-1471	N	Student
Respess, David & Deborah	470 Whispering Ln.	80913	555-3776	Y	Engineer/Lawyer
Samaniuk, Theresa	312 Russell St.	80934	555-1325	Y	Nurse
Schofield, Howard & Lisa	1000 Gillespie St.	80934	555-1169	N	Faculty/Faculty
Simpson, Jason	102 South Circle	80914	555-9327	N	USAF Captain
Tenhet, Kerry	509 San Marcos Dr.	80914	555-1621	N	USAF Cadet
Umbdenstock, Jeff	804 Highland Av.	80914	555-5434	N	USAF Cadet
Vinson, G. T. & Marilyn	2710 Hillside Dr.	80914	555-6232	N	USAF Captain/Homemaker
Wehr, Ervin	108 Chestnut Ln.	80914	555-4635	Y	USAF Lieutenant
Wittmayer, Bobby	719 Sycamore St.	80914	555-0087	N	USAF Cadet

22 3 and 6

Skill-Building Warmup

22a 7'

each line twice SS; DS between 2-line groups

alphabet 1 Jim Kable won a second prize for his very quixotic drawings.
figures 2 If 57 of the 105 boys go on July 29, 48 of them will remain.
shift/lock 3 Captain Jay took HMS James and HMS Down on a Pacific cruise.
easy 4 With the usual bid, I paid for a quantity of big world maps.

| 1 | 2 | 3 | 4 | 5 | 6 | 7 | 8 | 9 | 10 | 11 | 12 |

22b 14'

Learn 3 and 6

each line twice SS; DS between 2-line groups

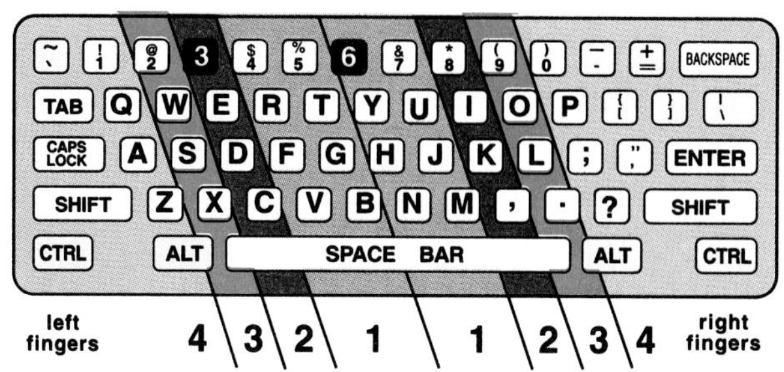

3 Reach *up* with *left second* finger.

5 3 3d d3 3 3; had 3 days; did 3 dives; led 3 dogs; add 3 dips
6 we 3 ride 3 cars; take 33 dials; read 3 copies; save 33 days
7 On July 3, 33 lights lit 33 stands holding 33 prize winners.

6 Reach *up* with *right first* finger.

8 6 6j 6j 6 6; 6 jays; 6 jams; 6 jigs; 6 jibs; 6 jots; 6 jokes
9 only 6 high; on 66 units; reach 66 numbers; 6 yams or 6 jams
10 On May 6, Car 66 delivered 66 tons of No. 6 shale to Pier 6.

all figures learned

11 At 6 p.m., Channel 3 reported the August 6 score was 6 to 3.
12 Jean, do Items 28 and 6; Mika, 59 and 10; Kyle, 3, 4, and 7.
13 Cars 56 and 34 used Aisle 9; Cars 2 and 87 can use Aisle 10.

22c 10'

SKILL BUILDING

Improve keying techniques

each line twice; do not pause at the end of lines; DS between 2-line groups

shift/lock
14 The USS San Simon sent an SOS; the USS McVey heard it early.
adjacent reaches
15 Ersa Polk sang three hymns before we lads could talk to her.
direct reaches
16 Brace Oxware hunted for a number of marble pieces in Greece.
double letters
17 Tell the cook to add eggs and cheese to Ann's dinner entree.
one hand
18 Jimmy's drab garage crew tests gears fastest, in my opinion.

Document 1
Two-page
form letter

Mr. McKibben has given to you a draft of a form letter to be mailed to newcomers to Colorado Springs. Proofread for errors that may have been overlooked.

Identify the name, letter address, and the salutation on the first page of the letter and the name in the second-page heading as variables.

Compose a side heading to introduce each of the reasons for purchasing a cellular phone. For emphasis, indent the text below the headings .5" from both margins; display the side headings in bold and precede them with the letter **o** or a graphic bullet ■.

Reference: pages 247, 316

WP Insert the appropriate codes for the variables. Print a graphic bullet ■ before the side headings. Save the document as **PROMOTE1. LET.**

Cellular Connection is very pleased that you have chosen Colorado springs as your new home. To ease your move to our fine city, we are happy to give you the enclosed cards with emergency listings and frequently used numbers. Just attach one of these handy reference cards to phones in your kitchen, bedroom, office, car, boat . . .

Boat? Car? Seem surprised? Yes, many people today are enjoying the many benifits of cellular phones. National telecommunication experts predict that use of cellular phone will increase to 8 out of 10 people in the next five years. Why? Read the following reasons given by cellular phone owners.

■ Side heading

Robert Ball, a corporate president, was often detained at the office waiting for an important call or frequently missed a timely call because he was en route to a meeting. "I needed a solution to this time waster. Cellular Connection solved the problem. With the Cellular DT-3200--in my opinion a time management gem--I can communicate anytime and anywhere."

■ Side heading

Sally Jones, a 19-year old student, commutes 45 miles to college every day. Often her schedule demands she travel during late hours and through remote areas. Her parents explain, "Knowing that Sally has the Cellular DT-3200 with her gives us such a feeling of security and relieves our tension about her safety. She can reach us immediately if necessary. In case of an emergency, she can call 911 without leaving the safety of her car." (A)

Insert on next page

22d 10'

SKILL BUILDING

Improve response patterns

each line once SS; DS between 2-line groups; repeat

word response: think and key words

19 he el id is go us it an me of he of to if ah or bye do so am
20 Did she enamel emblems on a big panel for the downtown sign?

stroke response: think and key each stroke

21 kin are hip read lymph was pop saw ink art oil gas up as mop
22 Barbara started the union wage earners tax in Texas in July.

combination response: vary speed but maintain rhythm

23 upon than eve lion when burley with they only them loin were
24 It was the opinion of my neighbor that we may work as usual.

| 1 | 2 | 3 | 4 | 5 | 6 | 7 | 8 | 9 | 10 | 11 | 12 |

22e 9'

SKILL BUILDING

Build staying power

Work for good rhythm; key two 1' writings, then a 2' writing and a 3' writing.

Goals:

1', 17-23 *gwam*
2', 15-21 *gwam*
3', 14-20 *gwam*

all letters

	gwam 2'	3'
I am something quite precious. Though millions of	5	3
people in other countries might not have me, you likely do.	11	7
I have a lot of power. For it is I who names a new	16	11
president every four years. It is I who decides if a tax	22	15
shall be levied. I even decide questions of war or peace.	28	19
I was acquired at a great cost; however, I am free to all	34	23
citizens. And yet, sadly, I am often ignored; or, still	40	27
worse, I am just taken for granted. I can be lost, and in	46	30
certain circumstances I can even be taken away. What, you	52	34
may ask, am I? I am your right to vote. Don't take me	57	38
lightly.	58	39

gwam 2' | 1 | 2 | 3 | 4 | 5 | 6 | 7 |
3' | 1 | 2 | 3 | 4 | 5 |

Cellular Connection

Communications Office

(Lessons 156-162)

Learning goals:

1 To format realistic communications.

2 To apply communication skills in document production.

3 To pull data from several sources in preparing documents.

Office job simulation

Information about your work assignment appears on this page. Study the information carefully.

Daily plan

Skill-building workshop 4 .... 5'-15'

Simulation .... 35'-45'

OR

Simulation .... 50'

Work assignment

You are now employed as a word processing specialist at Cellular Connection, a young, progressive company in Colorado Springs, Colorado, that manufactures and markets cellular telephones. The president, **Francis McKibben**, is your supervisor.

A very exciting development at Cellular Connection is the recent approval to purchase a plant in a foreign country for production of cellular parts. Countries being considered are France, Japan, and Mexico. A site visit will be scheduled for each prospective plant. You will be working on the site visit to Juarez, Mexico. Your knowledge of Spanish will be very helpful in completing these assignments.

Cellular Connection Reference Manual

Letters: Letters are prepared in modified block format, mixed punctuation, on Cellular Connection letterhead. Use standard margins of 1" and a second-page header for multiple-page letters. **Sincerely yours** is used for the closing.

Memos: Memos are prepared in the standard format on memo stationery. When memos are sent to multiple persons, they are addressed to Distribution List. A distribution listing is included at the end of the memo following the reference initials; names are listed in alphabetical order. Copies are prepared for each person on the list. Highlight or checkmark a different name on each copy to indicate how copies should be distributed.

Distribution List:
- Victor Adams
- Helen Pogue
- Sarah Webber
- Bram Ziomek

Reports: Reports are double-spaced in leftbound format. A title page and table of contents are required for most reports. A half title page is used to divide sections of reports. This page is numbered, although a number is not keyed on the page. A heading such as the one that follows is centered vertically on the page:

APPENDIX

NEWS *on*. . . Accent Marks

Some foreign words are used frequently in the English language. Word processing software today allows you to include the diacritical marks required in these words. Two common accent marks are acute and grave accents. Use the Help feature for more information on other accented characters.

- **Acute accent** over the letter e (é) means (1) the letter is to be pronounced "ay" as in may and (2) the letter é is a separate syllable. Hold the CTRL key, key an apostrophe, and then key the letter e.

  Examples: French: attaché, café, cliché, fiancé, fiancée, protégé, résumé, Jeré. Spanish: José, Jiménez, inglés, francés, and aléman.

- **Grave accent.** Hold the CTRL key, key grave accent (lowercase of tilde key), then key letter.

  Examples: à la carte, à la mode, and vis-à-vis Some words may require both accents: déjà vu.

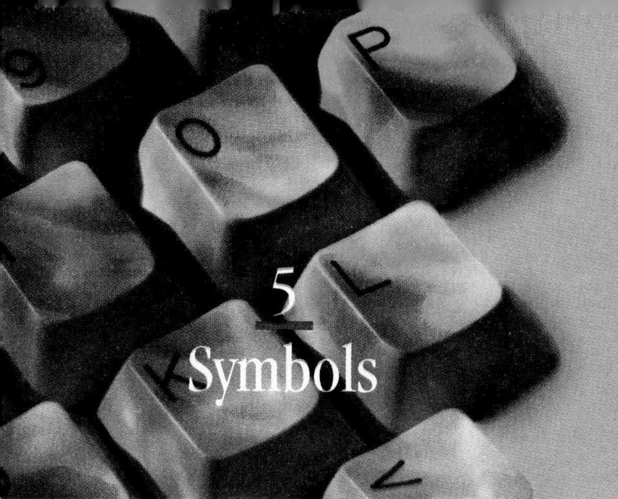

5 Symbols

Learning goals:
1 To master figure reaches.
2 To edit (proofread) and revise copy.
3 To key from statistical and script copy.
4 To improve staying power.

Formatting guides:
1 Default margins or 60-space line.
2 Single-space drills; double-space paragraphs.

23a 7'

Skill-building warmup

each line twice SS (slowly, then faster); DS between 2-line groups

alphabet 1 Why did the judge quiz poor Victor about his blank tax form?
figures 2 J. Boyd, Ph.D., changed Items 10, 57, 36, and 48 on page 92.
third row 3 To try the tea, we hope to tour the port prior to the party.
easy 4 Did he signal the authentic robot to do a turn to the right?

| 1 | 2 | 3 | 4 | 5 | 6 | 7 | 8 | 9 | 10 | 11 | 12 |

23b 14'

Learn $ and - (hyphen)

each line twice SS; DS between 2-line groups

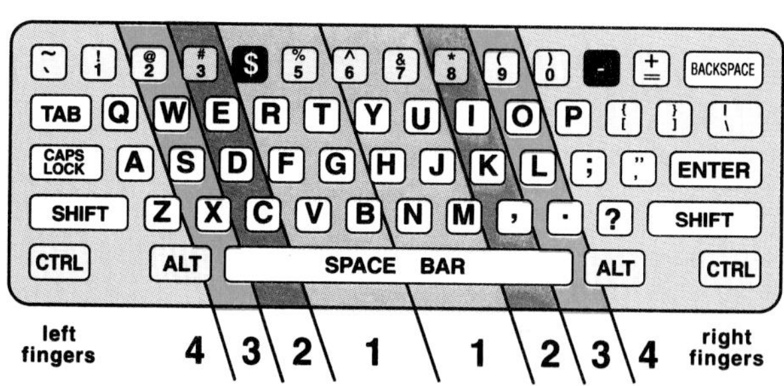

$ Shift; then reach *up* with *left first* finger.

5 $ $f f$ $ $; if $4; half $4; off $4; of $4; $4 fur; $4 flats
6 for $8; cost $9; log $3; grab $10; give Rolf $2; give Viv $4
7 Since she paid $45 for the item priced at $54, she saved $9.

- (hyphen) Reach *up* with *right little* finger.

8 - -; ;- - - -; up-to-date; co-op; father-in-law; four-square
9 pop-up foul; big-time job; snap-on bit; one- or two-hour ski
10 My sister-in-law paid a top-rate fee for a first-class trip.

all symbols learned

11 I paid $10 for the low-cost disk; high-priced ones cost $40.
12 Le-An spent $20 for travel, $95 for books, and $38 for food.
13 Mr. Loft-Smit sold his boat for $467; he bought it for $176.

Document 10
Transmittal

Complete the transmittal (Document 8) to accompany the blueprints you are sending Mr. Mercier.

Project Manager: William T. Thornton

3 sets	28391-D2	Plumbing (Areas 18, 21)	1
2 sets	28373-K2	Electrical (Panels A-1, A-6, B-3, C-2)	2

Document 11
Table of contents

Ms. Hill gives you the following instructions:

On this morning's flight from Los Angeles, I was able to draft the entire Claremont field report (had my laptop computer on this trip). All I need to finish the report (leftbound) is this table of contents.

The correct page numbers are indicated in parentheses. Use spaced leaders between columns for easier reading and a 1.5" top margin. Refer to your procedures manual for correct capitalization. Check my spelling.

 Use leader tab and flush right.

Table of Contents

Page

23c 9'

COMMUNICATION

Edit as you key

Read carefully; each line contains two errors, but only one is circled. Correct both errors as you key.

14 i asked Ty for a loan of $40; his interest rate is two high.

15 Please advise me how I can spent $18 for a second-hand book?

16 I'm sorry I lost you first-balcony tickers for the concert.

17 Lynda saws 3659 Riley rode is her daughter-in-law's address.

18 She can key 100 storkes a mintue at a 20-word-a-minute rate.

23d 20'

COMMUNICATION

Learn number-usage rules

Study the rules at right, then key the sample sentences below.

Numbers expressed as words

Good writers know how to use numbers in their writing. The following rules illustrate when numbers should be expressed as words. Key as words:

- a number that begins a sentence.
- numbers ten and lower, unless they are part of a series of numbers any of which is over ten.
- the smaller of two adjacent numbers.
- isolated fractions and approximate numbers.
- round numbers that can be expressed as one or two words.
- numbers that precede "o'clock."

Note: Hyphenate spelled-out numbers between 21 and 99 inclusive. Also, hyphenate fractions expressed as words.

19 **Six** or **seven** older players were cut from the **37**-member team.

20 I have **2** of **14** coins I need to start my set. Elia has **nine**.

21 Of **nine** **24**-ton engines ordered, we shipped **six** last Tuesday.

22 Shelly has read just **one-half** of about **forty-five** documents.

23 The **six** boys sent well over **two hundred** printed invitations.

24 **One** or **two** of us will be on duty from **two** until **six** o'clock.

23e (Optional)

COMMUNICATION

Revise as you key

Change figures to words as needed.

25 The meeting begins promptly at 9. We plan 4 sessions.

26 The 3-person crew cleaned 6 stands, 12 tables, and 13 desks.

27 The 3d meeting is at 3 o'clock on Friday, September 2.

28 6 members, half of the team, were early for the 10 a.m. game.

Document 8
Transmittal form
(LM p. S63)

Ms. Hill left the following instructions in your electronic mailbox.

F1 Help F8 Options

To: Project Assistant
From: Hill
Subject: Transmitting Blueprints
Date: 07--08-- **Time:** 10:15a

Please design a form for transmitting blueprints titled **TRANSMITTAL FORM.** At the left margin, key **To:** and provide 5 lines for the address. In an adjacent column, key **Date:** and provide a line. Below the last address line, key the headings **Project:**, **Project No.:**, and **Project Manager:** and provide lines for information that will be filled in.

Bold all callouts or headings.

Below this information, set up a four-column table with the headings
No. of Sets **Item No.** **Description** **Revision No.**

(The Description column should be about double the width of the other columns.) Set the column headings off with a single rule above and below them.

Leave about 20 blank lines below the last rule. Then provide three lines for **Comments:** and one line for **Approved by.**

View Message

Document 9
Itinerary

I will be traveling to Las Vegas, Nevada, to visit the Claremont Hotels project. Here is a draft of my itinerary. Refer to the airline schedule below to insert travel information. Supply the correct dates for Monday through Wednesday of next week. Please include a reminder that the hotel confirmation is attached.

The heading should include ITINERARY FOR (MY NAME), Project and No., Destination City, and Inclusive dates of travel.

Monday, (date) **Phoenix to Las Vegas**

2:00 p.m. Tour (CH) [sp] project cite; meet Stacy Hinton in hotel lobby.
7:30 p.m. Meet Stephen C. Wood of Claremont Hotels in hotel lobby for dinner show. (Wood purchasing tickets.)

Tuesday, (date) **Las Vegas**

8:00 a.m. Work at Claremont Hotels project cite.
7:30 p.m. Dinner with David Pacer, contractor.

Wednesday, (date) **Las Vegas to Phoenix**

7:30 a.m. Breakfast meeting, Brent Walker and Karen Okhuysen. Meet at Courtyard Cafe.
Return to office to file field report.

Mon.-
9:15 - Leave Raggs Airfield - co. plane.
11:23 - Arr. LV Airport; take shuttle to LV Resort

Wed.-
11 - Leave LV from Suns Aviation Terminal
1:15 pm - Arr. Phoenix

24 # and /, Number Expression

Skill-Building Warmup

24a 7'

each line twice SS; DS between 2-line groups

alphabet 1 Freda Jencks will have money to buy six quite large topazes.

symbols 2 I bought 10 ribbons and 45 disks from Cable-Han Co. for $78.

home row 3 Dallas sold jade flasks; Sal has a glass flask full of salt.

easy 4 He may cycle down to the field by the giant oak and cut hay.

| 1 | 2 | 3 | 4 | 5 | 6 | 7 | 8 | 9 | 10 | 11 | 12 |

24b 14'

Learn # and /

each line twice SS; DS between 2-line groups

Note:
= number sign, pounds
/ = diagonal, slash

\# Shift; then reach *up* with *left second* finger.

5 # #e e# # # #; had #3 dial; did #3 drop; set #3 down; Bid #3

6 leave #82; sold #20; Lyric #16; bale #34; load #53; Optic #7

7 Notice #333 says to load Car #33 with 33# of #3 grade shale.

/ Reach *down* with *right little* finger.

8 / /; ;/ / / /; 1/2; 1/3; Mr./Mrs.; 1/5/94; 22 11/12; and/or;

9 to/from; /s/ William Smith; 2/10/n,30; his/her towels; 6 1/2

10 The numerals 1 5/8, 3 1/4, and 60 7/9 are "mixed fractions."

all symbols learned

11 Invoice #737 cites 15 2/3# of rye was shipped C.O.D. 4/6/95.

12 B-O-A Company's Check #50/5 for $87 paid for 15# of #3 wire.

13 Our Co-op List #20 states $40 for 16 1/2 crates of tomatoes.

24c 7'

SKILL BUILDING

Reach for new goals

Key 30" writings on both lines of a pair. Try to key as many words on the second line of each pair. Work to avoid pauses.

gwam 30"

14 She did the key work at the height of the problem. 20
15 Form #726 is the title to the island; she owns it. 20

16 The rock is a form of fuel; he did enrich it with coal. 22
17 The corn-and-turkey dish is a blend of turkey and corn. 22

18 It is right to work to end the social problems of the world. 24
19 If I sign it on 3/19, the form can aid us to pay the 40 men. 24

Document 7
Letter

(LM p. S61)

The Public Works Department has denied Ms. Hill's request for a permit to construct a Claremont Hotels property in Las Vegas.

Here is a draft of a letter to the building inspector about the permit rejection on the Claremont Hotels property in Las Vegas. The draft needs much improvement if we are to get approval. Please rewrite my draft using the following outline and check for errors.

¶1 Eliminate wordiness by combining sentences and deleting information that the reader knows. Number the three issues that were raised at the March 5 meeting. You may wish to enumerate.

¶2 Add a statement to introduce the actions taken to modify and/or clarify concerns. Follow statement with a colon. Emphasize the three areas of concern by indenting them 5 spaces from the left margin and underlining paragraph heads.

¶3 State that the revised blueprints are being sent by special delivery. Request that the inspector review the blueprints and approve the new building permit request form that is enclosed. Give telephone number should questions arise.

Mr. Patrick T. Mercier
Building Inspector
Public Works Department
2011 Aladdin Boulevard
Las Vegas, NV 89101-3427

This letter is a reply to your concerns about our building permit for the Claremont Hotels property at 232 Spruill Avenue. You raised three specific issues that I wish to address; namely, the adequacy of the number and type of drains; the wiring specifications for selected panels in A, B, and C; and the practicality of a helistop. My response is based on my meeting with you on March 5.

Plumbing: Three drains for the Data Analysis Lab (Area 18), with requirments for trap priming, have been added to the new blueprints. The single drain in the records area (Area 21) have been deleted from the new plans.

Electrical: Requirements for load and primary wiring for Panels A-6 and B-3 have been revised and are included in the new blueprints. Note the overcurrent protection for Panels A-1 and C-2 in the new plans.

Helistop: The helistop has been in existence over 3 years and is under a 10-year limited-use permit. Helistop permit agreement is enclosed.

I certainly appreciate your time in going over these items to clarify concerns related to a permit on this project. Thank you for reviewing the permit request and outlining your concerns. The new set of blueprints will be sent to you. Call me if you have any questions about them. Another Building Permit Request Form is enclosed, also.

24d 8'

COMMUNICATION

Review number usage

DS; decide whether the circled numbers should be keyed as figures or as words and make needed changes. Check your finished work with 23d, page 53.

20 Six or 7 older players were cut from the 37-member team.

21 I have 2 of 14 coins needed to start my set. Elia has 9.

22 Of 9 24-ton engines ordered, we shipped 6 last Tuesday.

23 Shelly has read just 1 half of about 45 documents.

24 The 6 boys sent well over 200 printed invitations.

25 1 or 2 of us will be on duty from 2 until 6 o'clock.

24e 14'

SKILL BUILDING

Improve speed

1 Take 1' guided writings (see page 45 for guided writing procedures).

2 Take a 2' and 3' timing.

¼'	½'	¾'	1'
4	8	12	16
5	10	15	20
6	12	18	24
7	14	21	28
8	16	24	32
9	18	27	36
10	20	30	40

gwam

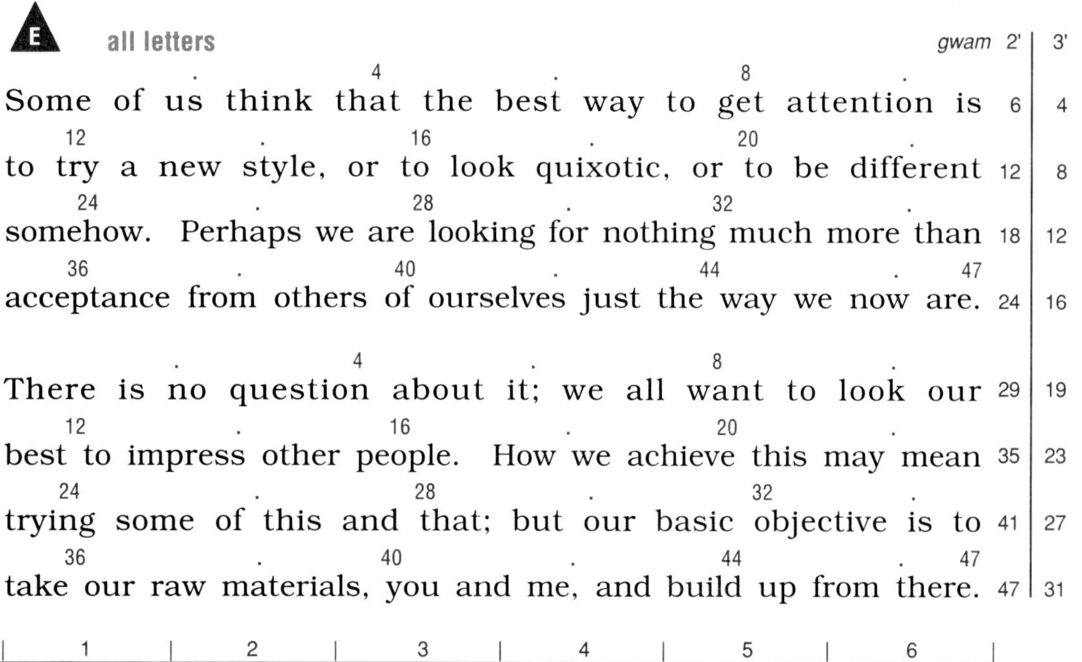

E **all letters**

	gwam 2'	3'
Some of us think that the best way to get attention is	6	4
to try a new style, or to look quixotic, or to be different	12	8
somehow. Perhaps we are looking for nothing much more than	18	12
acceptance from others of ourselves just the way we now are.	24	16
There is no question about it; we all want to look our	29	19
best to impress other people. How we achieve this may mean	35	23
trying some of this and that; but our basic objective is to	41	27
take our raw materials, you and me, and build up from there.	47	31

gwam 2' | 1 | 2 | 3 | 4 | 5 | 6 |

3' | 1 | 2 | 3 | 4 |

Document 5
Letter
(LM p. S59)
Arrange the table in descending numerical order according to cost of project. Center the table horizontally and please include a total for the cost column. You may use Mr. Inmon's first name in the salutation. Prepare copies for Charles Cade and Kari Crenshaw.

Mr. Todd Inmon
Project Manager
J. K. Mayfield & Associates
12733 Van Buren Street
Phoenix, AZ 85001-6732

wp Prepare a macro for the closing lines; then use it to prepare this letter. Use the sort feature to place numbers in descending order. Use the math feature to compute total cost.

The changes you requested on the structural drawings that we transmitted to you on September 4 have been evaluated, and new costs have been figured. We have based cost estimates on the unit price schedule in Exhibit C of the original contract, No. AT-129. The cost quotations are as follows:

Work Order No.	Engineer Specs.	Cost
AT-PP-3	703-1437	$ 6,114
AT-RQ-21	83-730	58,832
AT-W-11	3382-82	8,266
AT-MJ-07	7739-9	3,053
AT-SM-5	4983-03	63,283

If you wish to discuss the items in this quotation, call me. I will be out of the office Tuesday through Thursday next week; however, Charles Cade, associate project manager, will be available in my absence to provide details or answer questions about the quotation.

Document 6
Table
Ms. Hill hands you this memo with the following instructions:

We need to prepare an announcement about the Autocad seminars for display on the staff bulletin board. Format as a table; include main heading, date, time, and location of each workshop.

wp Place a border around the announcement.

Beckett-Yeatman Engineering Company
Interoffice Memorandum

TO: Senior Engineers

FROM: Helen S. Hill, Senior Engineer

DATE: September 9, 19--

SUBJECT: Autocad Workshops Scheduled

The installation of Autocad has been completed by M-Tech Corporation. This innovative software will provide the technological assistance we need in preparing accurate blueprints. Jim Pruett of M-Tech will teach the following Autocad seminars for our staff: 10:15 a.m., Friday, September 15, Conference B; 9:15 a.m., Monday, September 18, Room 329; 3:30 p.m., Wednesday, September 20, Conference A; 1 p.m., Monday, September 25, Room 123; and 2 p.m., Tuesday, October 3, Conference B.

25 % and --, Word Division

Skill-Building Warmup

25a 7'

each line twice SS; DS between 2-line groups; take 1' writings on line 4 if time permits

alphabet 1 Merry will have picked out a dozen quarts of jam for boxing.
symbols 2 Jane-Ann bought 16 7/8 yards of #249 cotton at $3.59 a yard.
first row 3 Can't brave, zany Cave Club men/women next climb Mt. Zamban?
easy 4 Did she rush to cut six bushels of corn for the civic corps?

1 | 2 | 3 | 4 | 5 | 6 | 7 | 8 | 9 | 10 | 11 | 12

25b 14'

Learn % and -- (dash)

each line twice SS; DS between 2-line groups

Note:
% = percent sign
Use % with business forms or where space is restricted; otherwise, use the word "percent."
-- = dash
No space precedes or follows the dash.

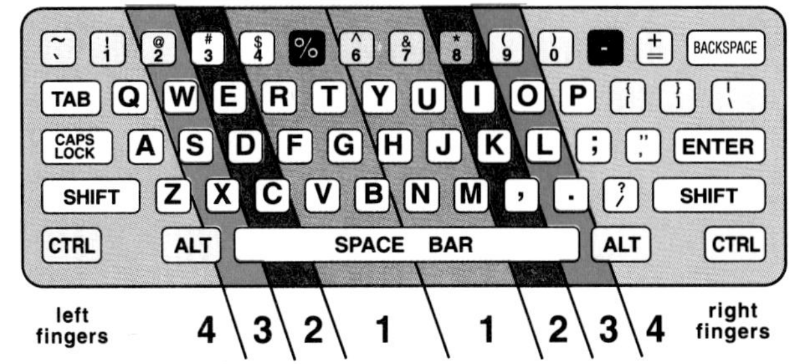

% Shift; then reach up with *left first* finger.

5 % %f f% % %; off 5%; if 5%; of 5% fund; half 5%; taxes of 5%
6 7% rent; 3% tariff; 9% F.O.B.; 15% greater; 28% base; up 46%
7 Give discounts of 5% on rods, 50% on lures, and 75% on line.

-- Reach *up* with *right little* finger.

8 -- --; ;-- --; one--not all--of us; Hap--our brother--drives
9 look--really look--and; why--and, indeed, why not--deny that
10 We--I mean the entire group--saw the movie--and we liked it.

all symbols learned

11 The total class--by "total" I mean 95% to 100%--voted to go.
12 Invoice #20--it was dated 3/4--billed $17, less 5% discount.
13 I did my CPR cases--1-6 yesterday, 7-9 today--and rated 89%.

25c 4'

SKILL BUILDING

Practice speed runs with numbers

Take 1' writings; the last number you key when you stop is your approximate *gwam*.

1 and 2 and 3 and 4 and 5 and 6 and 7 and 8 and 9 and 10 and

11 and 12 and 13 and 14 and 15 and 16 and 17 and 18 and 19

and 20 and 21 and 22 and 23 and 24 and 25 and 26 and 27 and

Document 4
Action minutes

Ms. Hill keyed a rough draft of minutes of a recent meeting of engineers, contractors, and inspectors. Align company names as shown.

Please prepare the final copy of the minutes of the meeting about the Cachet Designs building (K2774). Prepare a copy for each person named in the minutes.

CACHET DESIGNS/#
September 5, 19--

Action Minutes QS

Facilitator: HSH

Participants: Beckett-Yeatman (HSH, Richard Quarles, Lisa Romero)
Oswalt Contractors (Marion Farron, A.T. Allstat)
Hilbun & Synnott (Perry Synnott, David Ulmer)

Capacity testing on the Cachet Designs building, ~~located at~~ 901 Rosewood Drive, will be for a minimum of 200 hours, beginning ~~at~~ 9 a.m. on Sept. 10. Duration beyond 200 hours will be approved by mutual agreement of all parties (contacts: Quarles, Allstat, Ulmer) and will be monitored by the lead operator. Consensus to continue beyond 200 hours must be reached by 5 p.m. on Sept. 16; otherwise, testing will conclude at 5 p.m. on Sept. 18.

A log of processing time and unscheduled shutdown time will be kept by the lead operator. Shutdown time will not be scheduled but will be determined at the discretion of the lead operator and documented by her or him. A maximum of nine hours ~~of unscheduled shutdown time will be allowed.~~

A ~~maximum~~ minimum of 2,500 tons of MSW is to be processed during testing. No changes in capacity testing procedures will be made without prior approval of all parties (contacts: Romero, Farron, Ulmer).

25d 10'

SKILL BUILDING

Improve speed

1 Take 1' guided writings.

2 Take a 2' writing; try to maintain 1' rate.

3 Key one 3' writing.

Goals: 2', 15-22 *gwam*
3', 14-20 *gwam*

1/4'	1/2'	3/4'	1' *gwam*	1/4'	1/2'	3/4'	1' *gwam*
4	8	12	16	8	16	24	32
5	10	15	20	9	18	27	36
6	12	18	24	10	20	30	40
7	14	21	28				

all letters

	gwam 2'	3'	
As a member of Group #1 in my car club, I get $1--or	6	4	19
10%--off on each $10 I spend at top-quality motels/inns as	12	8	23
I travel; I expect, too, my card will soon be recognized by	18	12	27
most major city department stores. The cost is only $45.	24	16	31

gwam 2' | 1 | 2 | 3 | 4 | 5 | 6 |
3' | 1 | 2 | 3 | 4 |

25e 15'

FORMATTING

Learn to divide words

Study "Word division guides" at the right; then key the problem below.

1 Set 1" side margins and 1" top margin; DS.

2 Clear tabs; set three new tabs 15 spaces apart. Center WORD DIVISION PRACTICE.

3 Key the first line, striking the tab key to move to the second, third, and fourth columns.

4 Key the words in Columns 2 and 4 with a hyphen to indicate the first correct division.

Word division guides

To achieve a more even right margin, long words (over five letters) must occasionally be divided. Follow these rules when dividing words:

1 Divide between syllables. One-syllable words cannot be divided. Consult a dictionary when in doubt.

cor- rect   weighed   planned

2 Key at least two strokes on the first line and carry at least three strokes to the next line.

ex- plain   enough   crafty

3 Divide between double consonants except when dividing a syllable from a root word that ends in double consonants.

chal- lenge   enroll- ment   set- tled

4 Divide after a single-letter syllable within a word; divide between consecutive one-letter syllables.

resi- dent   situ- ation   usa- ble

5 Divide compound words with a hyphen after the hyphen. Compound words without a hyphen are best divided between the word elements.

son- in-law   dead- lines   self- help

6 Do not divide a contraction, abbreviation, or most numbers.

wouldn't   NAACP   1,680,900

7 Avoid dividing nouns that should be read as a group such as proper nouns, dates, or places. When a division must be made, divide at a logical break.

Mr. John / Langford   July 27, / 1997
Austin, / Texas   1539 Madison / Avenue

WORD DIVISION PRACTICE

DS

telescope tab	tele-scope tab	catalog tab	cata-log
deposit		first-class	
situation		spelling	
through		987,900	
membership		swimming	
pica margin 10	tab 25	tab 40	tab 55
elite margin 12	tab 27	tab 42	tab 69

Document 3
Memo
(LM p. S57)

Ms. Hill returns to you a memo you keyed as a rough draft for her this morning. Her instructions dictated on your transcribing machine are as follows:

Just minor changes are needed to the memo you drafted for me this morning. Please spell out abbreviated terms, except BTU. Send a copy to Scott Hamilton at Fulgham Nursery and Landscape.

Terms

lb.—pound
TPD—tons per day
kw—kilowatt
lb./hr.—pounds per hour

wp Key the memo heading as a macro inserting pauses after **TO**, **FROM**, **DATE**, and **SUBJECT**. When you retrieve the macro, the heading will automatically print, and the pause will allow you to insert the variable information in the heading. Then use the macro to prepare this memo.

TO: Kevin Casey, Los Angeles Office

FROM: Helen S. Hill, Phoenix Office

DATE: Current date

SUBJECT: Acceptance Testing for FN&L Facility (Insert Project #)

The report from the independent firm of Skinner & Webb to estimate the expected power generation ath the Fulgham Nursery and landscape facility has been was recieved yesterday. Skinner and Webb's report (dated 09/01) indicate s that the design acceptance test is based upon calculations of incinerator/ boiler performance using under the following conditions:

Heating value: 4,000 BTU/lb.

Charge rate: 101 TPD/unit

Preheated comubustion air: maximum 300°F

Processing 325 TPD at 4,500 BTU/lb. is possible with a generator rated at 9,4500 kw, 89,980 lb./hr. throttle steam flow, and zeor extraction. Generator capacity for processing waste of 4,500 BTU/lb. is was satisfactory. Evidence indicates that as long as the ajustment value of the gross heating power is directly proportional to the waste value, the generator is capable of handling sucessfully the generation of steam.

¶ (The preheated combustion air was achieved through the hearth cooling system and steam emission--a standard heat recovery method.)

26 (and)

Skill-Building Warmup

26a 7'

each line twice SS; DS between 2-line groups; take 1' writings on line 4; try for 18 *gwam*

alphabet 1 Avoid lazy punches; expert fighters jab with a quick motion.
symbols 2 Be-Low's Bill #483/7 was $96.90, not $102--they took 5% off.
shift/lock 3 Report titles may be shown in ALL CAPS; as, BOLD WORD POWER.
easy 4 Do they blame me for their dismal social and civic problems?

1 | 2 | 3 | 4 | 5 | 6 | 7 | 8 | 9 | 10 | 11 | 12

26b 14'

Learn (and) (parentheses)

each line twice SS; DS between 2-line groups

Note:
( ) = parentheses
Parentheses indicate offhand, aside, or explanatory messages.

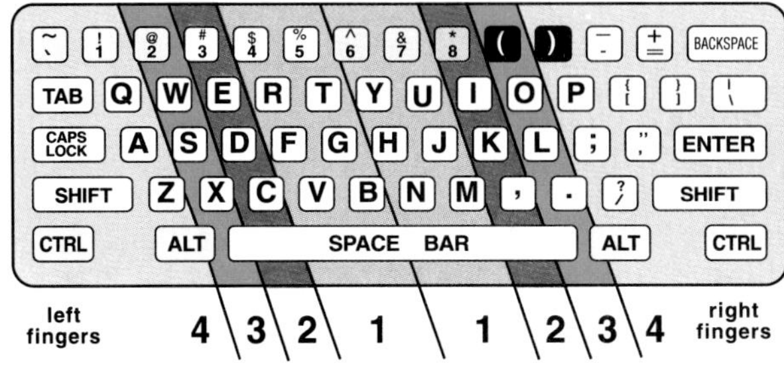

5 ((l l(((; Reach from l for the left parenthesis; as, (((.
6)); ;))); Reach from ; for the right parenthesis; as,)).

( )

7 Learn to use parentheses (plural) or parenthesis (singular).
8 The red (No. 34) and blue (No. 78) cars both won here (Rio).
9 We (Galen and I) dined (bagels) in our penthouse (the dorm).

all symbols learned

10 The jacket was $35 (thirty-five dollars)--the tie was extra.
11 Starting 10/29, you can sell Model #49 at a discount of 25%.
12 My size 8 1/2 shoe--a blue pump--was soiled (but not badly).

26c 6'

SKILL BUILDING

Review numbers and symbols

Key each line twice, keeping eyes on copy. DS between pairs.

13 Jana has one hard-to-get copy of her hot-off-the-press book.
14 The invoice read: "We give discounts of 10%, 5%, and 3.5%."
15 The company paid Bill 3/18 on 5/2/95 and Bill 3/1 on 3/6/95.
16 The catalog lists as out of stock Items #230, #710, and #13.
17 Elyn had $8; Sean, $9; and Cal, $7. The cash total was $24.

Document 1
Travel expense form
(LM p. S53)
Ms. Hill returned today from a field consultation at Emergency Medical Service. Use her travel expense log to prepare the travel expense form. Double-check all computations.

TRAVEL EXPENSE LOG FOR Helen S. Hill

Authorization No. 18369 Advance: $ 250.00

Project/Account No. D2890

Destination Jackson, MS From 9/1/-- To 9/3/--

Purpose of Travel Field consultation

Round Trip Miles 268 @ .29 per mile = $ ______

MEALS

Day	Monday	Day	Tuesday
B	—	B	6.21
L	5.26	L	8.40
D	12.94	D	15.28

Day	Wednesday	Day	
B	5.92	B	
L	7.02	L	
D	—	D	

HOTEL:

2 nights @ $ 99 = $ ______

OTHER: Itemize below and attach receipts

Client entertainment $65.25 - 9/1/--
Transportation 38.86 - 9/1/--
Transportation 38.86 - 9/3/--

Document 2
Letter
(LM p. S55)
Ms. Hill left this handwritten draft of a letter to Kathleen Pfaus (address below) about the Apple Tree project.
Compose a sentence and insert it at the end of the first paragraph to explain that the numbers in parentheses refer to the structural plans.

Ms. Kathleen T. Pfaus
Structural Consultant
1021 North 12th Street
Phoenix, AZ 85001-6728

Your recent letter expresses ~~questions~~ concerns about the heating, ventilation, and air conditioning ^(HVAC) on the Apple Tree project. As we discussed yesterday on the telephone, the following are explanations of the ^specific items.

1. No structural above-ceiling air returns are required through new corridor walls (34). 2. No ^fire dampers are required on rated wall penetrations (16). 3. ~~Harrison~~ Pyne, Inc., will estimate the cost of changes and additions to the HVAC system.

Call me if ~~you have~~ other questions ^arise. Your careful attention to the details of this project is appreciated.

26d 14'

COMMUNICATION

Learn number-usage rules

Study the rules at the right; then key lines 18-23.

Numbers expressed as figures

In most business communications, some numbers are expressed in figures, while others are expressed in words. The following guidelines indicate instances when writing numbers as figures is preferred practice. Key as figures:

- numbers coupled with nouns.
- house numbers (except house number One) and street names (except ten and under); if street name is a number, separate it from the house number with a dash (--).
- time when expressed with a.m. or p.m.
- a date following a month; a date preceding the month (or standing alone) is expressed in figures followed by "d" or "th".
- money amounts and percents, even when approximate, are written as figures (use the $ symbol and/or the words "cents" or "percent").
- round numbers in the millions or higher with their word modifiers (with or without a dollar sign).

Note: When speaking or writing numbers (as in writing numbers on a check), the word "and" should be used only to signify a decimal point. Thus, 850 is spoken or written as "eight hundred fifty," not "eight hundred and fifty."

18 Ask **Group 1** to read **Chapter 6** of **Book 11 (Shelf 19, Room 5)**.

19 All **six** of us live at **One Bay Road**, not at **126--56th Street**.

20 At **9 a.m.** the owners decided to close from **12 noon** to **1 p.m.**

21 Ms. Vik leaves **June 9**; she returns the **14th or 15th of July**.

22 The **16 percent** discount saves **$115**. A stamp costs **35 cents**.

23 Elin gave **$3 million** to charity; our gift was only **75 cents**.

26e 9'

FORMATTING

Paragraph review

1 Set 1.5" side margins and a 2" top margin; DS.

2 Key ¶ once; your lines will not match those in the text.

3 Divide words appropriately.

KEYBOARD--TOOL OR TOY?

Like most other mechanical devices, a keyboard is nothing more than a tool; and, like most other tools, the skill with which it is used defines the caliber of what is accomplished with it. The wise student, therefore, works to gain fast, accurate skill combined with knowledge of how, when, and where to use that skill.

Beckett-Yeatman Engineering Company

General Office
(Lessons 151-155)

Learning goals:

1 To format administrative communications, action minutes, itinerary, and table of contents.

2 To prepare and design forms.

3 To apply communication skills to document production.

4 To pull data from several sources while preparing documents.

Office job simulation

Read "Work assignment" at right carefully in preparation for the jobs in Section 30.

Daily plan

Skill-building workshop 4 .... 5'-15'
Simulation .... 35'-45'
OR
Simulation .... 50'

Work assignment

Beckett-Yeatman Engineering Company is a large firm headquartered in Phoenix, Arizona. You have been assigned as project assistant to Ms. Helen S. Hill, senior engineer. Ms. Hill will supervise your work on six major engineering projects.

Much of Ms. Hill's time is spent out of the office visiting the six project sites. Often, she gives you oral instructions or dictates them (shown in colored type). Thus, you will be required to use your judgment as well as the Beckett-Yeatman Reference Manual, a desk reference manual, dictionary, and your list of team projects and project numbers.

Accuracy is very important. Proofread each document once for content errors and a second time for keying and grammatical errors. Technical terms, numbers, and mathematical computations should be verified.

wp If available, utilize time-saving features of your software that will increase your productivity and accuracy such as macro, math, and sort.

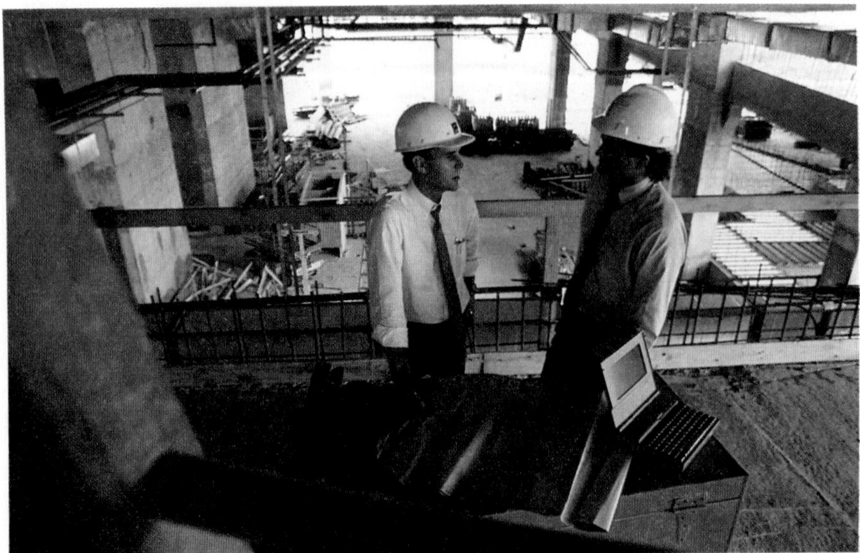

Beckett-Yeatman Reference Manual

Letters: Prepare letters in block format on letterhead stationery using standard 1" margins. Include a reference line positioned a double space below the letter address. The reference line indicates the project number referred to in the letter (e.g., Project No. D2890). The project number can be located in the PROJECT NOS. list shown below:

PROJECT NOS.

Emergency Medical Service	D2890
Cachet Designs	K2774
J. K. Mayfield & Associates	A4193
Fulgham Nursery and Landscape	W6065
Apple Tree, Inc.	P5479
Claremont Hotels	N9732

Use **Sincerely** for the closing, followed by the sender's name, and on a separate line, position title. Enclosures are listed following the enclosure notation.

Memos: Prepare memos in the traditional memo format on memohead stationery. On memos sent outside the Phoenix office, be sure to key the location (e.g., Los Angeles Office) of the recipient and the sender.

Tables: Center tables vertically and center column heads. Bold is used within headings except when tables occur in letters.

Minutes and itineraries: Use plain sheets, 2" top and 1" side and bottom margins. Use bold for emphasis.

General:

- Use hanging indent format for enumerations.
- The mailroom staff prepares address labels for sending blueprints, etc.
- If possible, prepare the number of photocopies indicated.
- Ms. Hill's ID number is 3218933.
- Use the current date on all documents.

27 & and :, Proofreaders' Marks

Skill-Building Warmup

27a 7'

each line twice SS; DS between 2-line groups

alphabet 1 Roxy waved as she did quick flying jumps on the trapeze bar.
symbols 2 Ryan's--with an A-1 rating--sold Item #146 (for $10) on 2/7.
space bar 3 Mr. Fyn may go to Cape Cod on the bus, or he may go by auto.
easy 4 Susie is busy; may she halt the social work for the auditor?

| 1 | 2 | 3 | 4 | 5 | 6 | 7 | 8 | 9 | 10 | 11 | 12 |

27b 14'

Learn & and : (colon)

each line twice SS; DS between 2-line groups

Note:
& = ampersand, "and" sign
The & is used only as part of company names.

: = colon
Space twice after a colon.

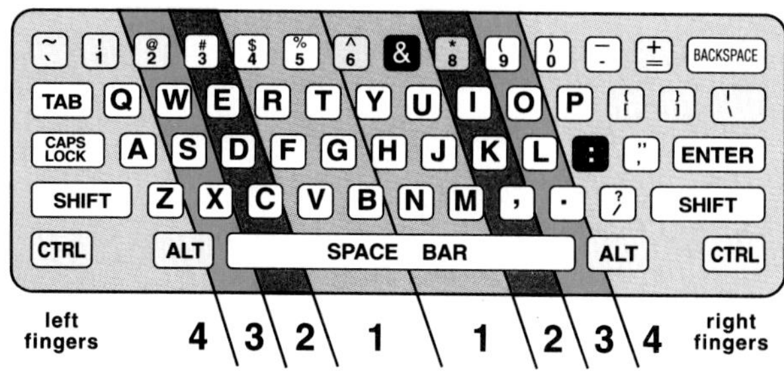

& (ampersand) Shift, then reach *up* with *right first* finger.

5 & &j j& & & &; J & J; Haraj & Jay; Moroj & Jax; Torj & Jones
6 Nehru & Unger; Mumm & Just; Mann & Hart; Arch & Jones; M & J
7 Rhye & Knox represent us; Steb & Doy, Firm A; R & J, Firm B.

: (colon) Left shift; strike key.

8 : :; ;: : : :; as: for example: notice: To: From: Date:
9 in stock: 8:30; 7:45; Age: Experience: Read: Send: See:
10 Space twice after a colon, thus: To: No.: Time: Carload:

all symbols learned

11 Consider these companies: J & R, Brand & Kay, Uper & Davis.
12 Memo #88-899 read as follows: "Deduct 15% of $300, or $45."
13 Bill 32(5)--it got here quite late--from M & N was paid 7/3.

27c 9'

SKILL BUILDING

Improve response patterns

1 Key each line once; check difficult lines.

2 Key again each line checked.

3 Take a 1' writing on line 16; then on line 19. Determine *gwam* on each writing.

word response

14 Did the busy girl also fix the torn cowl of the formal gown?
15 Clement works with proficiency to make the worn bicycle run.
16 They may pay the auditor the duty on eighty bushels of corn.

stroke response

17 Lou served a sweet dessert after a caterer carved oily beef.
18 After noon, a battered red streetcar veers up a graded hill.
19 Jim gave up a great seat; give him a few cases of free soap.

| 1 | 2 | 3 | 4 | 5 | 6 | 7 | 8 | 9 | 10 | 11 | 12 |

Level Six
Advanced Office Simulations

OBJECTIVES

FORMATTING SKILLS

To produce error-free documents using proper formats and decision-making skills.

COMMUNICATION SKILLS

To locate and correct errors and apply language arts skills to document processing.

KEYBOARDING SKILLS

To key approximately 60 wam with good accuracy.

27d 8'

COMMUNICATION

Edit as you key

each drill line once DS; repeat if time permits

Errors are often circled in copy that is to be rekeyed. More frequently, perhaps, the copy is marked with special symbols called "proofreaders' marks" that indicate desired changes.

Some commonly used proofreaders' marks are shown below. Study them. Read carefully. Concentrate on content of the copy as you key.

Symbol	Meaning	Symbol	Meaning
Cap or ≡	Capitalize	#	Add horizontal space
^	Insert	/ or *lc*	Lowercase letters
(delete mark)	Delete (remove)	(close-up mark)	Close up space
[	Move to left	(transpose mark)	Transpose
]	Move to right	*stet*	Leave as originally written
		¶	Paragraph

20 We miss 50% in life's rowards by refusingto new try things.

21 do it now--today--then tomorrow's load will be 100%% lighter.

22 Satisfying work--whether it pays $40 or $400--is the pay off.

23 Avoid mistakes: confusing a #3 has cost thousands.

24 Pleased most with a first-rate job is the person who did it.

25 My wife and/or me mother will except the certifi cate for me.

26 When changes for success are 1 in 10, try a new approach.

27e 12'

SKILL BUILDING

Build staying power

Key two 1' writings on each ¶; then two 3' writings on both ¶s; compute *gwams*.

Goals: 1', 20-27 *gwam*
3', 17-24 *gwam*

 all letters

gwam 3'

Is how you judge my work important? It is, of course; I hope you recognize some basic merit in it. We all expect to get credit for good work that we conclude.

I want approval for stands I take, things I write, and work I complete. My efforts, by my work, show a picture of me; thus, through my work, I am my own unique creation.

	gwam 3'	
Is how you judge my work important? It is, of course;	4	26
I hope you recognize some basic merit in it. We all expect	8	30
to get credit for good work that we conclude.	11	33
I want approval for stands I take, things I write, and	14	37
work I complete. My efforts, by my work, show a picture of	18	41
me; thus, through my work, I am my own unique creation.	22	44

gwam 3' | 1 | 2 | 3 | 4 |

Tabs

Word processing software has default tabs set every 0.5". These preset tabs may be cleared and custom tabs set. Tabs can be set on the ruler using the mouse or from the Tab dialog box.

The numbers on the ruler indicate the distance in inches from the left margin *(Word)* or from the edge of the paper *(WordPerfect)*. Generally four tab types are available:

Tab	Symbol	Result
Left	└	Aligns text to the right of the tab. Default tab setting.
Center	┴	Centers text at tab.
Right	┘	Aligns text to the left of the tab.
Decimal	┴.	Aligns numbers at the decimal.

To set a tab on the ruler, click the desired position on the ruler.

To delete a tab, point to the tab, hold down the left mouse button, and drag the tab into the document area.

To move a tab, press the left mouse button and drag the tab to the new location.

Document 11
Set tabs on the ruler

1. From the View menu, display the ruler.
2. *WordPerfect:* Click the right mouse button and choose *Clear All Tabs.*
3. Set the tabs from the left margin as marked in the document below.
4. Key the drill; save and print. Do not close the document.
5. Move the insertion point to the beginning of the document. Move the decimal tab, the center tab, and the right tab 0.5" to the right. (*Word:* Select each column before moving the tab.)

Left 0.5"	Right 2.5"	Center 3.5"	Decimal 5.0"
Chester	Northwest	Baltimore	400.00
Cambridge	Midwest	Chicago	20.20
Langfield	Southeast	Tucson	1,000.00

Flush Right

Flush Right is a *WordPerfect* feature that aligns text even with the right margin. Flush Right is turned on by pressing ALT + **F7** or by choosing **Line** from the Format menu and then *Flush Right.* If you press ALT + **F7** twice, leaders will connect Column 1 to Column 2.

Word does not have a Flush Right command. Text is aligned with leaders by setting a right leader tab. Set a right leader tab in the Tab dialog box (choose **Format** menu, **Tab**), key the tab position, and then click to select a leader type under Leader.

Writing 43 all letters

	gwam 3'	5'	
Small business has grown in the past decade because compe-	4	2	70
tition has forced our nation to rely on small business as the	8	5	72
primary source of new jobs. The risk, however, in starting any	12	7	75
new business may be quite high for the new business owner who	16	10	77
makes a substantial investment of money and security in the hope	21	12	80
of making a profit. Statistics show that large numbers of busi-	25	15	82
nesses fail within the first year, and more than half of all new	29	18	85
firms will not be in operation ten years later. Entrepreneurs	34	20	87
who survive these high odds definitely should be applauded.	38	23	90
Today, the biggest risk facing a small business is how to	42	25	92
get an unknown firm to compete in a market of large, well-	45	27	94
established companies. For the young entrepreneur, a myriad of	50	30	97
problems may come with starting a new business. First, he or	54	32	100
she needs to have a keen perspective of the mechanics of opening	58	35	103
up and operating a new firm. Also, it will be very useful to	62	37	105
have managerial expertise, an ability to sell or market products	67	40	107
or services, and an understanding of how contingencies can be	71	42	110
used to combat all the obstacles that face a new business owner.	75	45	112
Some people start their own businesses after finding their	79	47	115
career objectives blocked in the firms where they work. How-	83	50	117
ever, before making such a decision and leaving a job, a pros-	87	52	120
pective business owner has to realize that working extended hours	92	55	122
and dealing with problems of every magnitude and type are almost	96	58	125
always the norm. Also, to be a successful entrepreneur, a person	100	60	127
must have good business ethics as well as know some techniques	105	63	130
for coping with stress. To own a firm may seem at first look to	109	65	133
be attractive, but it is not free of irritants.	112	67	134

gwam 3' | 1 | 2 | 3 | 4 | 5 |
5' | 1 | 2 | 3 |

Indent

Indent moves the current paragraph to the first tab position. Hanging Indent places the first line of a paragraph at the left margin and indents remaining lines to the first tab. Hanging Indent is commonly used in bibliographic entries, glossaries, and bulleted and enumerated items. Indent is available by choosing *Paragraph* from the Format menu. In *Word*, you choose the type of indention from the Indents and Spacing tab.

Document 9
Apply Indent

1. Key the following text, using Indent or Hanging Indent as shown.
2. Check the spelling and proofread.
3. Save as **Doc9** and print.

Cheating has become a more wide-spread problem in colleges and universities than was originally thought.

Indent →

> In a poll of 15,000 juniors and seniors at 31 universities, more than 87 percent of business majors admitted to cheating at least once in college, the largest such percentage.

The same poll showed that less cheating took place among Engineering and Humanities students.

Hanging Indent →

Holtinger, Richard C. "Suggestions on Referencing Using MLA Style." *National Education Journal,* February 1997, pp. 36-40.

Publication Manual of the American Psychological Association. 4th ed. Washington, D.C.: American Psychological Association, 1994.

Document 10
Indent

Word: Key the entire document, pressing TAB after the headings Presiding and Participants. Allow the names in the second line to wrap to the left margin.

- Position the insertion point at the beginning of the first name "Lanete Garriga." Drag the bottom marker on the ruler to align with "Cynthia Housely" in the heading above.

WordPerfect: After keying "Participants," press Indent (**F7**) to indent the runover lines.

```
SYSTEMS FOR EMPLOYMENT TRAINING
March 1, 19--      -DS
Action Minutes
```

Bold and center

```
Presiding:   Cynthia Housely  DS
Participants:   Lanete Garriga, Diane Rodgers, Cary Tabb,
Nancy Riser, Ricky Boler, W. C. Wax, Jr., and Anne Stokes

     Cynthia Housely welcome the group and announced that
SystemsTraining, Inc. was the host for the meeting.  In
addition Systems invited the group to serve as consultants
in the development of computer-based training systems.
```

Writing 44 all letters

	gwam 3'	5'	
To ensure that you are getting the nutrients you need every	4	2	69
day, meal planning should take into consideration choosing food	8	5	71
from the four food groups. The suggested daily plan is to eat	12	7	74
at least four servings each from the bread and cereal group and	17	10	76
from the fruit and vegetable group. Two servings every day from	21	13	79
the milk and cheese group and from the meat and eggs group are	25	15	82
suggested. From this last group, it is important to include	29	18	84
seafood in your diet at least once a week. Because the body	33	20	86
needs calories or energy-burning food, it also is necessary that	38	23	89
you include some fat and sugar in your diet. Without a certain	42	25	92
amount of fat and sugar, your body does not benefit fully from	46	28	94
the other foods you eat. Good nutrition will take place when	50	30	97
proper eating habits are continuously reinforced by being fol-	54	33	99
lowed daily.	55	33	100
Presenting food in an interesting manner is equally impor-	59	36	102
tant as choosing from the four food groups. In particular, this	64	38	104
means that food should appear appetizing and have variety. These	68	41	107
features are achieved by combining various foods that make a	72	43	110
meal. For example, not everything on the table should be the	76	46	112
same color. Varying the form and texture of foods served at the	80	48	115
same time should be an additional detail to consider. A com-	85	51	117
bination of soft and crispy foods is a good idea as well as	89	53	119
serving some that are bland and tangy. Similarly, it is a good	93	56	122
idea to have both hot and cold foods in one meal just as you	97	58	124
would vary the flavors of the food served. Spices and garnishes	101	61	127
can add a lot to the flavor of food. Certainly they are espe-	105	63	130
cially good for altering recipes and in dressing up food for	109	66	132
special occasions.	111	66	133

gwam 3' | 1 | 2 | 3 | 4 | 5 |
5' | 1 | 2 | 3 |

Editing a Document

You have learned to modify text that has already been keyed. Other common edits include copying and moving text, changing text from all caps to lowercase or vice versa, and finding text and replacing it with other text.

Cut — Deletes blocks of text. Select the text and click the **Cut** button.

Paste — Paste is often used with Cut to move blocks of text. First, cut the block; then move the insertion point to the new location and click the **Paste** button. The text has now moved to the new location. Text can be cut and pasted between documents.

Copy — When you need another copy of text, select the text and click **Copy.** The text is copied to the clipboard. Position the insertion point where the copy is needed and paste the text. Text can be copied between documents.

New — Takes you to a fresh, new document. If two documents are open, click the name of the other document from the *Window's* menu.

Change Case — Changes text keyed in all capital letters to lowercase or to initial caps or title case. This option is available from a menu. (*Word:* Format menu, Change Case; *WordPerfect:* Edit menu, Convert Case.)

Hard Page Break — Hold down the Control key and strike ENTER to move text to the next page.

Spell Check — The Spell Check command looks for misspelled words in your document.

Document 8
Change Case

1. Key the lines shown.
2. Save the document as **Doc8**.
3. Copy the entire document to a new screen. Save as **Doc8b**.

1. Add the side heading facilities and equipment.
2. Cindy Sturzenberger is chairman and ceo.
3. Britt Burge, president, ASSOCIATED TRAVEL SERVICES
4. DM POMMERT, ASSOCIATES
5. ms. margarita valadez
   1130 confederation dr.
   saskatoon sk s71 4k5

4. Edit **Doc8b** as shown at the right.

1. Add the side heading facilities and equipment.
2. Cindy Sturzenberger is chairman and ceo. person
3. Britt Burge, president, ASSOCIATED TRAVEL SERVICES
4. DM POMMERT, ASSOCIATES
5. ms. margarita valadez
   1130 confederation dr.
   saskatoon sk s71 4k5

initial Caps

Writing 45

all letters

	gwam 3'	5'	
What would happen if a company lost all of its important	4	3	39
records in a disaster? Most companies could not continue and	8	5	41
would just go out of business. Records kept on paper as well as	12	7	44
records stored in a computer must be protected. Paper records	16	10	46
are often copied and stored at a separate site, and duplicates	21	12	49
are placed on microfilm to reduce the amount of storage space	25	15	51
needed. Backup copies are usually made of records stored on	29	17	54
magnetic media.	30	18	54
The cost of duplicating records is sizable, but it is an	34	20	57
excellent investment. The consequences of not protecting vital	38	23	59
records are far too great to risk. A natural disaster is not	42	25	62
the only hazard a business may face. An upset worker may do	46	28	64
just as much damage as a fire or flood. It is hard to believe	50	30	67
that workers on your payroll may sabotage your records, but it	55	33	69
does happen. Trusting workers is important; protecting your	59	35	72
records is also important.	61	36	73

Writing 46

all letters

	gwam 3'	5'	
Most people are afraid to stand up and speak before a group.	4	2	39
The ability to make presentations is a skill that is required for	9	5	41
success in business. The job is easy if you do your homework	13	8	44
and if you develop confidence in yourself. Always plan a presen-	17	10	46
tation carefully; organize your material, and then rehearse the	21	13	49
speech several times. The first time you get up is the hardest;	26	15	51
it gets easier each time. Experience helps to make you feel	30	18	54
more comfortable.	31	19	55
A quality presentation can be made even better with the use	35	21	57
of visuals to enhance the spoken word. Neat, well-prepared	39	24	60
visuals that are used in an effective manner help the audience	43	26	62
to focus attention on the important points you want to communi-	48	29	65
cate. They can also serve as cues to the next point you wish to	52	31	67
present; these cues make you less dependent on your notes. Good	56	34	70
visuals are uncluttered, attractive, and easy to read.	60	36	72

Document 5
Use Align

1. Select **Left align**; key ¶ 1.
2. Select **Center align**; key ¶ 2.
3. Select **Right align**; key ¶ 3.
4. Save as **Doc5**.

Text is traditionally keyed ***left-aligned***. The first letter of each line begins at the left margin, making an even left margin and a ragged right margin. Left-aligned text is easy to read.

Center Align

Center align automatically centers
each line between the left and right margins.
Center align is often used in keying announcements.

Right Align

All text lines up with the right margin.
This produces a ragged left margin.

Document 6
Review formats

1. Set the line spacing to **2** or **DS.**
2. Key the title. Select it and apply 14-point size.
3. Key the ¶s using word-wrap. Correct errors.
4. Single-space and italicize the last two lines.

NEW MISSION FOR EDUCATION ← 14 pt.

In a time of increasing emphasis on diversity, schools must find a way to focus on conveying common human and democratic values and to validate their expressions in a multicultural context.

As reflected in our mission statement, the fundamental expectations of our schools are to develop:

Well-Informed Citizens

A Professional, Adaptive, World-Class Workforce

Document 7
Add Bullets and Numbers

1. Format the list using the Numbers feature. DS between items.
2. Save and print. Then select the numbers and change them to bullets.
3. Use the Spelling feature, proofread, and print.

Recording an appropriate voice mail greeting is very important as we provide our clients with excellent and friendly service. Please study the following essential parts of an effective voice mail greeting.

1. State your name.
2. Include the day and date you are recording the greeting.
3. Describe why you are not available to take the call.
4. Request caller to leave a message or directions for obtaining personal assistance.
5. Provide an approximate time when the call will be returned.

gwam 1'

Writing 47

Can you visualize an area of 29 square miles? Can you ap- 12 91
preciate the size of an area approximately 495 centimeters wide 24 103
and 7 meters long? Some people easily remember that 3 feet is 36 38 117
inches long, that 16 ounces make a pound, that 4 quarts (16 cups) 51 130
equal a gallon, and that a mile is 5,280 feet or 1,760 yards 63 142
long. For others, the metric system, based on units of 10, is a 76 155
major advantage. 79 158

all letters and figures

gwam 3' 5'

Writing 48

A conversion table is a real convenience for making changes 4 2 54
between a U.S. and a metric weight or measure. To determine the 8 5 57
metric value of 6,783 feet, 129 miles, or some similar measure, 13 8 59
simply multiply feet by 30, yards by 0.9, and miles by 1.6 to 17 10 62
get centimeters, meters, and kilometers. Use the same procedure 21 13 64
if you know the metric value; that is, just multiply meters by 25 15 67
1.1 to get yards, by 3.3 to get feet, or by 0.6 to get miles. 29 18 69
Volume changes are made by multiplying the number of cups by 34 20 72
0.24, pints by 0.47, quarts by 0.95, and gallons by 3.8 to 37 22 74
determine liters. Or, multiply the number of liters by 3.1, 42 25 77
1.06, or 0.26 to determine the quantity of pints, quarts, or 46 27 79
gallons. 46 28 80

Conversions of area (size) and weight are easily determined 50 30 82
by the same process. For making changes in area, multiply square 55 33 84
centimeters by 0.16 to get square inches. Square meters are 59 35 87
changed to square yards if they are multiplied by 1.2, and square 63 38 90
kilometers become square miles if multiplied by 0.4. If you want 68 41 92
to obtain square meters, multiply square feet by 0.09 and square 72 43 95
yards by 0.8. The same rules apply to obtain a weight value; 76 46 97
that is, approximately 0.035 ounce is the same as one gram 80 48 100
(28 grams in an ounce), and about 2.2 pounds make a kilogram 84 50 102
(or 0.45 kilogram makes a pound). 86 52 103

gwam 3' | 1 | 2 | 3 | 4 | 5 |
5' | 1 | 2 | 3 |

Document 3
Edit text

1. Open the file **Doc2** that you keyed earlier.
2. Make corrections to the text as marked. Save as **Doc3**. Print.
3. Undo the last edit. Print.
4. Redo the last edit.

Writing ~~concise~~ responses, formulating ~~competitive~~ bids, creating ~~effective~~ business plans, answering ~~customer~~ feedback, composing messages ~~and letters~~ to clients, responding to customers and staff, maintaining relations with coworkers and supervisors, interpreting messages, and persuading customer these are just a few examples of written and oral communication that ~~is~~ handled ~~by~~ everyday by competent business people. ~~Communicating skills and a keen knowledge of business are valuable assets for anyone seeking success in business.~~

Formatting a Document

Formats such as line spacing, bold, italic, font styles and sizes, and alignment enhance the appearance of a document and provide emphasis. Many of these formats are available as buttons on the toolbar. If an arrow appears on the button, click the arrow to see other options. Other font options, such as font color or SMALL CAPS, are available by choosing *Fonts* from the Format menu.

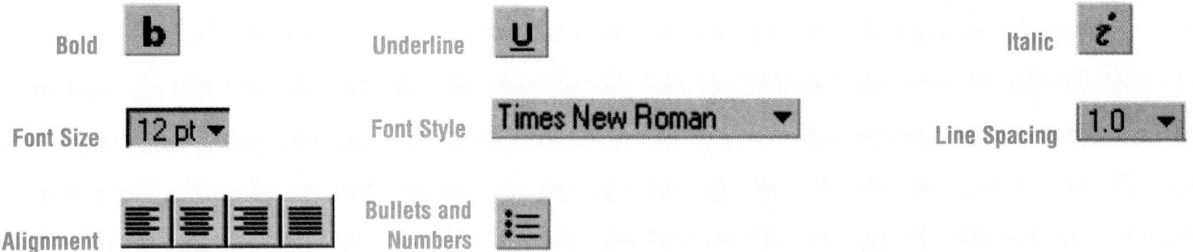

Formats can be applied as you key or after the text is keyed.

- *To apply formats as you key*, click the appropriate button and key the text. The function will stay on until you click the button to turn it off.
- *To apply formats to text that has already been keyed*, select the text and then click the format button.

Numbers and bullets emphasize listed information. Use numbered items if the list requires sequential order. Use bullets or symbols for unordered items. Bullets and numbers may be added as text is keyed or after. Bullets and numbers are available on the toolbar or from a menu such as the Insert menu or Format menu.

Document 4
Apply formats

1. Open the file **Doc4** that you keyed earlier.
2. Key the title PLAY IT SAFE. Select the title and apply 14-point size.
3. Edit the text as marked.
4. With the insertion point in the paragraph, apply a different font.

italic

Accidents on the job can often be avoided if each employee is aware of the hazards involved in his or her duties. Employees should be informed of things that they may inadvertently do or leave undone that may jeopardize others.

It is always better to play it safe when working with others. Remember, accidents don't just happen; they are caused.

Writing 49

all letters and figures

gwam 3'

Will you order a book on travel (#478XZ) from the red cata- 4 | 36
log on my desk. The book costs $25, or $20 when 4 or more books 8 | 41
are ordered at a time--this can save us 20%. I am sure you will 13 | 45
like the chapter "On the Road"; it is quite good! 16 | 48

Do write on the form the full name and order number of each 20 | 52
book we wish to order, and send an extra $1.25 with the order-- 24 | 56
this is used to pay for shipping the books. A bill is now sub- 28 | 61
ject to 6/10, net 30. Can't we order 4 books by 9/30? 32 | 65

gwam 3' | 1 | 2 | 3 | 4 | 5 |

all letters and figures

gwam 3' | 5'

Writing 50

This profile of our company may be useful to you in decid- 4 | 2 | 43
ing to buy stock. We have been in existence since 1968. In 8 | 5 | 46
1973, the focus of the 12 restaurants was shifted from quick 12 | 7 | 48
service to superior food served home style. The results have 16 | 10 | 51
been just amazing. Currently, we have 75 restaurants run by us 20 | 12 | 53
and 40 franchised restaurants. Within the next 12 to 14 months, 25 | 15 | 56
we will have 10 facilities in new locations. Our 4,983 full-time 29 | 17 | 58
workers and 1,298 part-time workers are located in 27 states. 33 | 20 | 61

Sales this year were $186,379,204, a 35 percent gain over 37 | 22 | 63
last year. The revised price scheme was a key factor in the 41 | 25 | 66
increase in revenues. Our net earnings were $17,986,340, a 46 45 | 28 | 68
percent gain over last year. Our general and administrative 49 | 30 | 71
expenses were 4.5 percent of total revenues this year. Last year 54 | 32 | 73
the expenses were 5.3 percent of total revenues. We are very 58 | 35 | 76
satisfied with the cost-cutting measures that have been in- 62 | 37 | 78
stalled. This year has been a profitable one, and the outlook 66 | 40 | 81
for next year is even better. 68 | 41 | 82

gwam 3' | 1 | 2 | 3 | 4 | 5 |
5' | 1 | 2 | 3 |

Creating a New Document

As you key a new document, wordwrap automatically moves text to the next line. Strike the ENTER key only between paragraphs. Wavy red lines may appear on the screen as you key, indicating that an error has been keyed. The red lines will not print if you do not correct the error. If you make a mistake, use the Insert or Delete functions.

Insert Position the insertion point where the new text should appear and key. If text is replaced as you key, press the Insert key to turn on Insert mode.

Delete Erases text to the right of the insertion point. To delete text to the left of the insertion point, strike the BACKSPACE key.

Undo Reverses the last change made. Certain commands such as Save cannot be undone. You can click on the down arrow next to Undo (or Redo) to view previous actions or select a specific action.

Redo Reverses the last Undo.

Save As Select the appropriate folder and then key the file name. Click the **Save** button to save an existing document.

Print When you click the Print button, a dialog box may display. Options are available for choosing pages that you print, number of copies, etc. Click **Print** from the dialog box.

Select Identifies text that has been keyed so that it can be changed. Selected text appears black on the screen. Select text using the mouse. Cancel Select by clicking the mouse button again.

To select:	Microsoft	WordPerfect
a word	Double-click	Double-click
a paragraph	Triple-click	Quadruple-click
several lines	Click the mouse and drag through the lines.	

Document 2
Create and save document

1. Key ¶ 1.
2. Apply wordwrap as you key; do not strike ENTER within the paragraph.
3. Save as **Doc2**.
4. Key ¶ 2 following Step 2 above. Save as **Doc4**.

Writing concise responses, formulating competitive bids, creating effective business plans, answering customer feedback, composing messages and letters to clients, responding to customers and staff, maintaining relations with coworkers and supervisors, interpreting messages, and persuading customer—these are just a few examples of written and oral communication that is handled by everyday by competent business people. Communicating skills and a keen knowledge of business are valuable assets for anyone seeking success in business.

Accidents on the job can often be avoided if each employee is aware of the hazards involved in his or her duties. Employees should be informed of things that they may inadvertently do or leave undone that may jeopardize others. It is always better to play it safe when working with others. Remember, accidents don't just happen; they are caused.

APPENDIX

NUMERIC KEYPAD

INTRODUCTION

Most computer keyboards contain a numeric keypad separate from the alphanumeric keys. When you are keying a large amount of numeric input, such as spreadsheets or data entry, you will find keying numbers with the keypad much more efficient than using the numbers above the alphabetic keys.

The numeric keypad is generally located to the right of the alphanumeric keys. It is often referred to as the ten-key keypad because the numbers are arranged in the same format as a standard calculator. The skills you learn in this unit can be transferred to any electronic calculator.

College Keyboarding Numeric Keypad Software

Keypad instruction is available on *College Keyboarding Numeric Keypad* software. If you are using a 3 1/2" disk, the keypad software is on the same disk as *College Keyboarding Alphanumeric.*

Loading the Keypad Software

1. If you are running the software from the program disk, key **keypad** at the A>prompt. If you are running the program from the hard drive, change to the directory where the program is stored and key **keypad** at the C> prompt.
2. Select the keypad that most clearly resembles the one on your computer.

Main Menu

You can select any part of *College Keyboarding Numeric Keypad* software from the Main menu by using the pull-down menus at the top—File, Lessons, Data Sets, and Open Screen. Select an option by using the left and right arrow keys and striking ENTER.

File. The File option lets you manage the information keyed. Use the arrow keys and ENTER to select; strike ESC to return to the Main menu.

Lessons. The Lessons option presents the figures 1-9, zero, decimal point, and the ENTER key in four lessons. Activities include the following: Warmup, Learn New Keys, Improve Keystroking, Build Skill, and Lesson Report, which show the exercises you completed and the scores achieved.

Data Sets. These on-screen exercises are designed to improve speed, accuracy, and facility of keypad operation. They emphasize various rows and types of data.

Open Screen. The Open Screen is designed for reinforcing the numeric keypad using the drill material on the next four pages. Exercises must be keyed from the text.

In the Open Screen, as well as in the tutorial, the computer will align the numbers at the display and display the total after the last number in a set has been entered.

Using the Open Screen

1. Key the drills on pages A53-A56 in Open Screen, keeping your eyes on the copy.
2. Strike the keypad ENTER key after each number.
3. To obtain a total, strike ENTER twice after the last number in a group.
4. Key each problem until the same answer is obtained twice; by doing this, you can be reasonably sure that you have the correct answer.

APPENDIX

WORD PROCESSING WORKSHOP

Getting Familiar with the Work Screen

When you open word processing software, the screen contains a blank document just waiting to be created. The work screen shown is *Microsoft Word* 7. Your work screen may vary, but all *Windows*-based word processing programs are similar.

Menu bar: Click to access any feature of the software.

Toolbar: Click for quick access to common commands. The name of the button displays when you point to it.

Insertion point: The blinking insertion point shows where the text you key will appear. The insertion point moves to the right as you key.

Ruler: Change tabs, margins, and indents on the ruler. Default tabs are set every half inch.

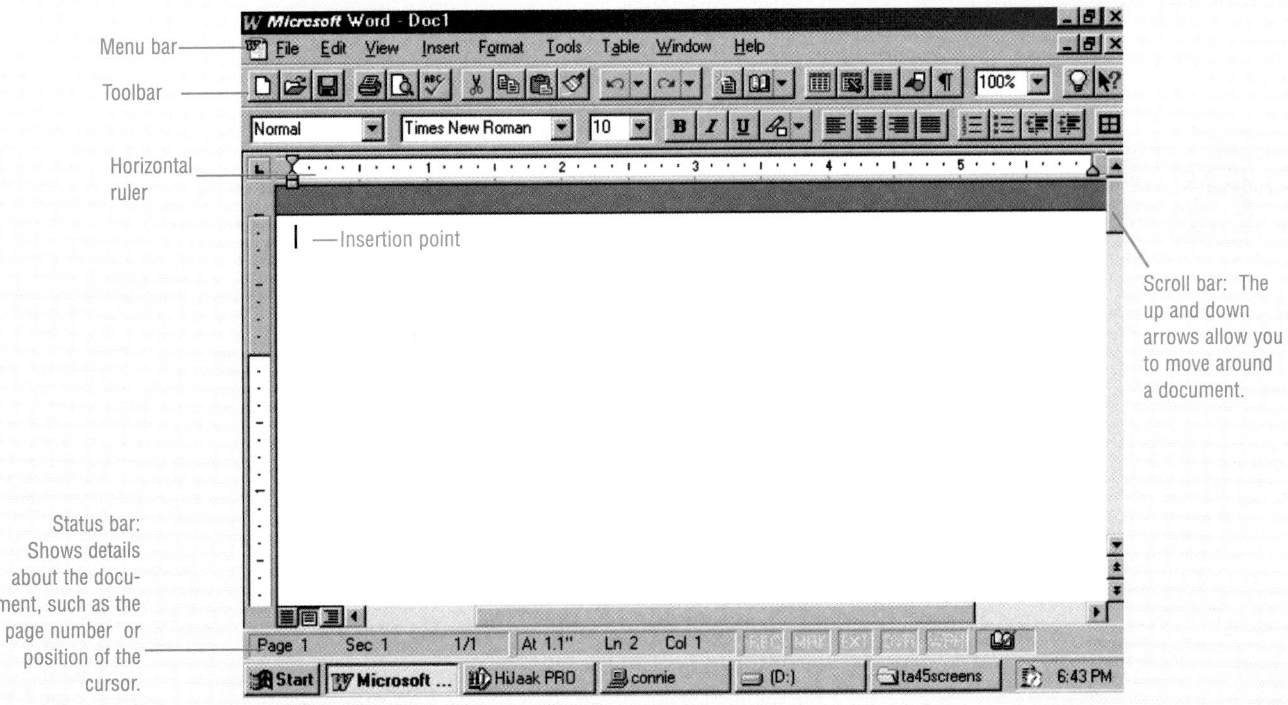

Document 1
Use menus

1. Click **File** on the Menu bar. Observe the items in the File menu.
2. Click **Open** to display the Open dialog box. An ellipsis (...) following a command indicates that a dialog box will display. If a command is not available, it appears dimmed. From the Open dialog box, click **Cancel** to close the dialog box.
3. Click all other menus to view the items on them.
4. Move the mouse over the buttons. *Windows 95* software displays their names.

KEYPAD DRILLS 1, 2, 3

Follow the directions on p. A52.

Practice 1. Reach down with the first finger to strike the **1** key.

Practice 2. Reach down with the second finger to strike the **2** key.

Practice 3. Reach down with the third finger to strike the **3** key.

Technique tip

Keep fingers curved and upright over home keys. Keep right thumb tucked under palm.

Num Lock / * −
7 Home 8 ↑ 9 PgUp +
4 ← 5 6 →
1 End 2 ↓ 3 PgDn Enter
0 Ins . Del

1 | 2 | 3 | 4

Drill 1

a	b	c	d	e	f
11	22	33	14	15	16
41	52	63	36	34	35
24	26	25	22	42	62
27	18	39	30	20	10
30	30	10	19	61	43
32	31	21	53	83	71

Drill 2

414	141	525	252	636	363
141	111	252	222	363	333
111	414	222	525	333	636

Drill 3

111	141	222	252	366	336
152	342	624	141	243	121
330	502	331	302	110	432
913	823	721	633	523	511
702	612	513	712	802	823
213	293	821	813	422	722

Drill 4

24	36	15	12	32	34
115	334	226	254	346	246
20	140	300	240	105	304
187	278	347	159	357	158
852	741	963	654	321	987
303	505	819	37	92	10

Drill 5

28	91	37	22	13	23
524	631	423	821	922	733
15	221	209	371	300	25
823	421	24	31	19	107
652	813	211	354	231	187
50	31	352	16	210	30

Windows 95

The opening screen of *Windows 95* simulates a *desktop* working environment. The icons displayed on the screen are symbols of items on your desk. Your screen may have additional icons besides those listed below.

My Computer displays the disk drives, CD-ROM, and printers that are attached to the computer.

Network Neighborhood allows you to view the available resources if you are connected to a network environment.

Recycle Bin stores documents that have been deleted from the hard drive. Documents deleted in error can be retrieved and returned to their folders. When the recycle bin is emptied, however, the files are gone.

Start displays the Start menu. From the Start menu, you can open a program, open Help, change system settings, close and exit *Windows 95*, and more.

The Start button is located on the *taskbar* at the bottom of the desktop (Figure 2). It is always visible when *Windows 95* is running. When you click Start, a menu displays with the commands for using *Windows 95* (Figure 3). Each time you open a program, a button with the name of the program displays on the taskbar. The taskbar in Figure 2 shows that *Microsoft Word* is open.

Figure 2: *Windows 95* Opening Screen

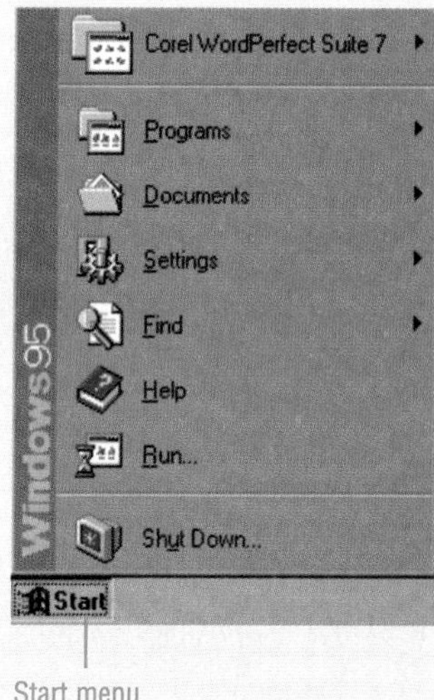

Figure 3: Start Menu

Exercise 1
Open *Windows 95*

1. Turn on the computer and monitor.
2. Welcome to *Windows 95* screen displays with a tip. Read the screen as it offers helpful tips, then click the **Close** button.
3. Click the **Start** button to display the Start menu. (Your Start menu may not look exactly like the illustration.)
4. Point to the Programs menu; a submenu displays to the right listing all software programs loaded on your system.

KEYPAD DRILLS 7, 8, 9

Key the drills at the right following the directions p. A52.

Practice 7. Reach up with the right first finger to strike the **7** key; return to the home keys. Keep the fingers in home position.

Practice 8. Reach up with the right second finger to strike the **8** key; return to the home keys. Keep the second finger in home position. You may raise the first finger slightly, but keep it close to the 4 key.

Practice 9. Reach up with the right third finger to strike the **9** key; return to the home keys. Keep the first finger in home position and the second finger close to the 5 key.

Technique tip

Keep fingers curved and upright over home keys.

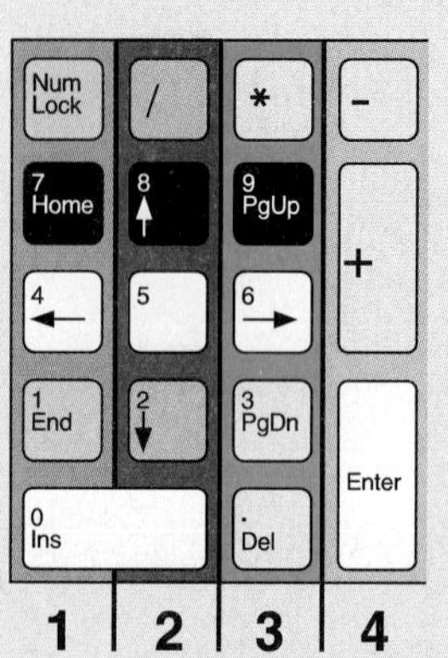

Drill 1

a	b	c	d	e	f
74	85	96	70	80	90
47	58	96	87	78	98
90	70	80	90	90	70
89	98	78	89	77	87
86	67	57	48	68	57
59	47	48	67	58	69

Drill 2

470	580	690	770	707	407
999	969	888	858	474	777
777	474	888	585	999	696

Drill 3

858	969	747	770	880	990
757	858	959	857	747	678
579	849	879	697	854	796
857	967	864	749	864	795
609	507	607	889	990	448
597	847	449	457	684	599

Drill 4

85	74	96	98	78	88
957	478	857	994	677	579
657	947	479	76	94	795
887	965	789	577	649	849
90	80	70	806	709	407
407	567	494	97	80	70

Drill 5

50	790	807	90	75	968
408	97	66	480	857	57
87	479	567	947	808	970
690	85	798	587	907	89
94	754	879	67	594	847
489	880	97	907	69	579

Windows 3.1

Program Manager: The name of the program that is currently running appears on the top line of the window, called the title bar.

Group icons: Each software program installed on the computer should be identified with a group icon. For instance, the group icon for *Word* will either be *Microsoft Word for Windows* or *Microsoft Office*. *Microsoft Office* includes *Word, Excel, PowerPoint,* and *Scheduler*.

Control Menu bar: Click on this bar to display a menu allowing you to manipulate the windows.

Minimize and Maximize buttons: The Minimize button reduces a window, and the Maximize button expands a window.

Scroll bars: Move the window display in the direction of the arrow.

Menu bar: Click any item on the Menu bar to display a pull-down menu.

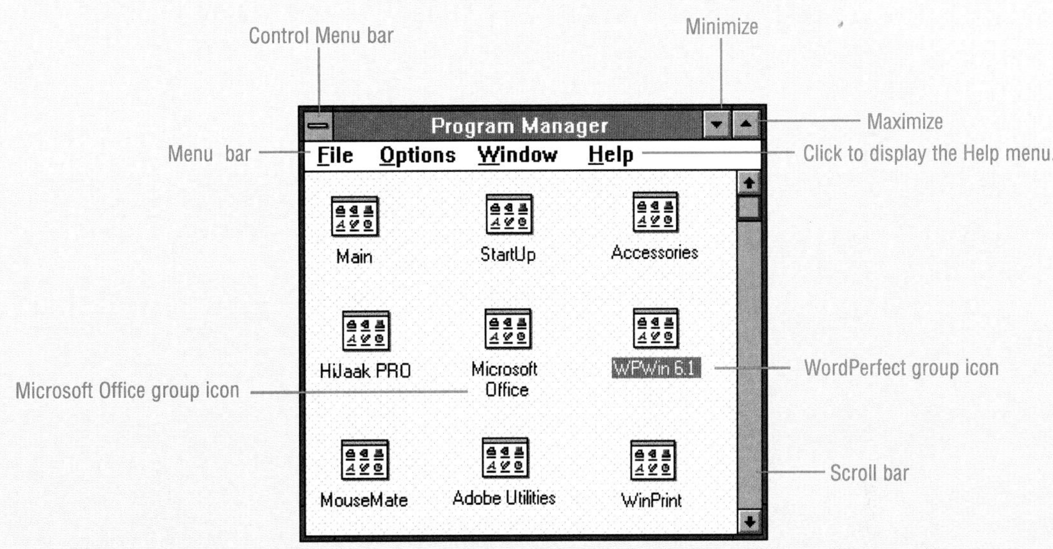

Figure 1: *Windows 3.1* Program Manager

Starting *Windows 3.1*

1. Turn on the computer and monitor.
2. Open *Windows*:
   - If your screen resembles Figure 1, you are already in *Windows*.
   - If only the Program Manager icon is displayed at the bottom left of the screen, double-click on the icon.
   - If the DOS prompt C> is displayed on your screen, key **win** and press ENTER.

Windows 3.1 Tutorial

If you are not familiar with *Windows*, complete the *Windows* Tutorial.

1. Click **Help** in the Menu bar.
2. Click **Windows Tutorial**.
3. Key **m** to begin the Mouse lesson. After completing the Mouse lesson, continue with the *Windows* Basics lesson.

KEYPAD DRILLS 4, 5, 6, 0, ENTER

Curve the fingers on the right hand and place them over the home keys as follows:

- first finger on 4
- second finger on 5
- third finger on 6
- fourth finger on Enter
- thumb on the 0

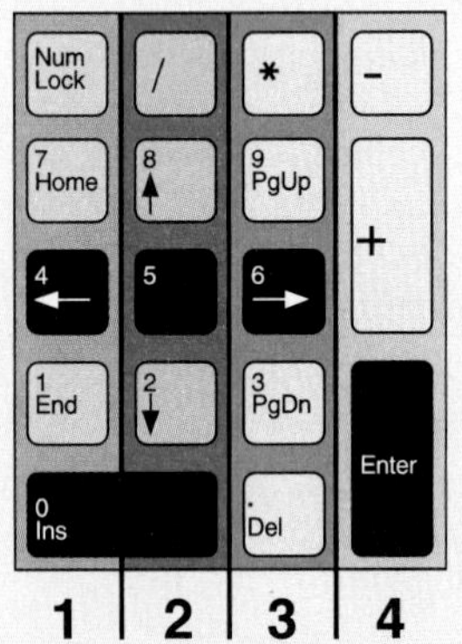

Practice zero (0) key. Keep the thumb tucked under the palm. Strike the zero key with the right thumb, using the same down-and-in motion used on the space bar.

Drill 1

a	b	c	d	e	f
46	55	56	46	55	56
45	64	45	45	64	45
66	56	64	66	56	64
56	44	65	56	44	65
54	65	45	54	65	45
65	54	44	65	54	44

Drill 2

466	445	546	654	465	665
564	654	465	545	446	645
456	464	546	545	564	456
556	544	644	466	644	646
644	455	464	654	464	554
454	546	565	554	456	656

Drill 3

400	404	505	606	500	600
404	505	606	500	600	400
500	600	400	404	505	606
650	506	404	550	440	550
506	460	605	460	604	640
406	500	640	504	460	560

Drill 4

504	640	550	440	660	406
560	450	650	450	505	550
640	504	440	640	450	660
400	600	500	500	600	400
650	505	404	606	540	560
504	404	640	404	406	606

Drill 5

460	445	546	654	465	605
564	654	460	465	545	446
605	504	546	640	604	564
540	466	664	554	405	656

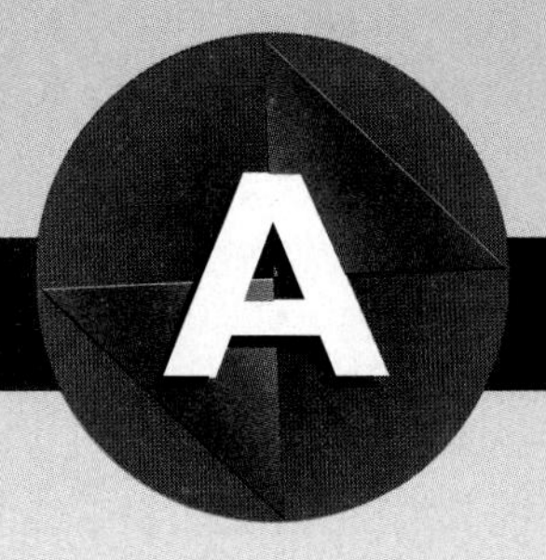

APPENDIX

WELCOME TO WINDOWS

Exploring *Windows*

Before using a *Windows*-based software, you will need to know a few basic concepts of *Windows*, which is the operating system software you are using. *Windows* controls the operation of the computer and the peripherals such as the mouse and printer. Software that runs under *Windows* has several features in common. All *Windows* application programs use similar icons, and the menus are consistent. Once you learn the basics of *Windows 3.1* or *Windows 95*, you can apply that knowledge to every *Windows* application. On the next few pages, you will start *Windows 3.1* or *Windows 95*, use the mouse, and learn a few of the basic operations.

Using the Mouse

Windows software requires the use of a mouse or other pointing device. You will use the mouse to select items, to find and move files, to execute or cancel commands, to move and size items, and to draw images. The mouse pointer changes in appearance depending on its location on the screen and the task that it is doing.

I The I-beam indicates that the mouse is located in the text area. When you pause, it blinks. As you use your software, most of the time you will see the I-beam.

The arrow selects items. It displays when the mouse is located outside the text area.

The hourglass indicates that *Windows* is processing your command. You must wait until *Windows* finishes what it is doing before keying text or entering another command.

Move the mouse on a padded, flat surface. If you run out of space, pick up the mouse and place it in another spot. With the mouse, you can perform the following actions:

Point: Move the mouse so that the pointer touches the icon or text.

Click: Point to the desired item, then press and release the left mouse button once.

Double-click: Point to the desired item and quickly press and release the left mouse button twice.

Click with the right mouse button: Press and release the right mouse button once. A shortcut menu appears *(Windows 95).*

Drag: Point to the desired item; hold down the mouse button; drag the item to a new location; then release the button.

KEYPAD DRILLS DECIMALS

Follow the directions on p. A52.

Decimal points are often included in numerical data. The decimal **(.)** key is usually located at the bottom right of the keypad. Use the third finger to reach down to strike the decimal key.

Technique tip

Strike each key with a quick, sharp stroke. Release the key quickly. Keep the fingers curved and upright, the wrist low and relaxed.

Drill 1

a	b	c	d
.28	.19	.37	.42
.51	.67	.81	.27
.64	.50	.60	.50

Drill 2

a	b	c	d
7.10	8.91	5.64	3.12
5.32	4.27	9.21	6.47
8.94	3.06	7.38	5.89

Drill 3

a	b	c	d
3.62	36.94	86.73	.60
8.06	10.31	537.34	5.21
321.04	10.55	687.52	164.84
.75	.26	10.85	627.98
687.46	357.95	159.46	85.21
20.46	220.48	6.10	3.04

Drill 4

a	b	c	d
761.64	2.82	627.25	196.25
285.46	34.60	.29	89.24
33.99	739.45	290.23	563.21
60.41	52.79	105.87	951.32
108.97	211.00	46.24	82.47
3.54	5.79	5.41	1.32

Drill 5

a	b	c	d
.05	1.19	77.54	112.96
112.54	561.34	114.85	.24
35.67	22.01	67.90	41.08
579.21	105.24	731.98	258.96
.34	1.68	.24	.87
21.87	54.89	2.34	5.89

CONTENTS

85 Measurement

Skill-Building Warmup

85a 5'

alphabet 1 Jim Zwanka expects the equitable plan to gain approval on Friday.
fig/sym 2 Wallpaper for this large room (26'10" x 38'9") cost them $247.58.
third row 3 We were worried; Trey quit to try to play polo with Torry or you.
fluency 4 Glen may work with the auditor to do the big audit for the panel.

| 1 | 2 | 3 | 4 | 5 | 6 | 7 | 8 | 9 | 10 | 11 | 12 | 13

85b 10'

SKILL BUILDING

Measure straight-copy skill

1 Key one 3' writing. Circle errors; determine *gwam*.
2 Key one 5' writing. Circle errors; determine *gwam*.

A all letters

gwam 3' | 5'

Mergers and acquisitions are very common events today. When 4 | 2 | 41
two companies join work forces, workers often suffer severe 8 | 5 | 44
stress because of fear of the unknown. The guides under which 12 | 7 | 46
they operated and the promises made to them were made by execu- 16 | 10 | 49
tives who may no longer be employed by the organization or who 21 | 12 | 51
may no longer have the power to follow through on their promises. 25 | 15 | 54
The one sure thing is that many, if not all, of the workers in- 29 | 18 | 57
volved in the merger will face drastic changes. 33 | 20 | 59

The changes that occur during a merger may be in the best 36 | 22 | 61
interests of some employees, but they may be to the detriment 41 | 24 | 63
of other employees. The fact that these employees were loyal 45 | 27 | 66
for years is of no consequence; therefore, they feel betrayed. 49 | 29 | 68
Frustration is high because they do not know whom to trust. 53 | 32 | 71
Employees must depend on their own resources. A good self- 57 | 34 | 73
concept and the ability to cope with change may be the most 61 | 37 | 76
important skills needed to survive mergers or acquisitions. 65 | 39 | 78

gwam 3' | 1 | 2 | 3 | 4 | 5 |
5' | 1 | 2 | 3 |

85c 35'

FORMATTING

Measure production: letters

Time schedule

Assemble materials .... 3'
Timed production .... 25'
Final check;
compute *n-pram* .... 7'

1 Key each document. Proofread and correct errors.
2 Address an envelope for each letter; compute *n-pram*.

Document 1
Short simplified letter (LM p. S53)

words

Current date | Mr. Toyohiko Soga, President | Instructional Technology, 14
Inc. | 284 Virginia Drive | Ogden, UT 84404-7291 | Request for Proposal 27

A request for proposal for the development of three interactive laser video- 42
discs is enclosed. Our instructional programs to be contained on the 56
videodiscs will teach employees how to use word processing, spreadsheet, 71
and database applications. 76

If you have any questions about the project, please call me. We look 90
forward to receiving your proposal. 98

Ms. Elise Conyers | Project Coordinator | xx | Enclosure 108

Document 1 (continued)

words

ranges, plains, and rivers through out the state and surround- 338
ing Twin Falls. 340

We would like to discuss with you how your talents could 352
be used to meat the challenges of transportation electronics 366
industry. Transportation Electronics, Inc. has a great deal to 379
ofer in job incentives, career development, and opportunity for 392
advancement. Our benefit package are among the very best in 404
the industry, and our salary offers to college graduates are 416
extremely competitive. Ms. Osborne, we hope you will accept 428
this invitation to visit us at our expense and talk with us 440
about career opportunities. Please use our toll free number 455
to call us to discuss arrangements for your visit. 466
Sincerely | TRANSPORTATION | Alfred G. Gammel | Technical 480
Recruiter | xx | Enclosure: Company literature | c Carolyn 491
White, Personnel Manager | Please identify yourself 501
as a UAR candidate when you call; also give us your accession 513
number. 515

Documents 2 and 3
Simplified letter with variable information
(LM pp. S49-S51)
Key the letter, inserting the following variable information:

Document 2
V1—
Ms. Ruth Wilson
53 West Silver Street
Butte, MT 59701-3874
V2—Dr. Todd Metcalf
V3—
3:45 p.m., June 7, on
Sun Flight 382
(Total words: 176)

Document 3
V1—
Mr. Phillip Dupre
3855 Waterline Road
Butte, MT 59701-6284
V2—Dr. Mary Jarvis
V3—
1:25 p.m., June 7, on
Treetop Flight 402
(Total words: 174)

Document 4
Revise the shell document at the right inserting the addressee's first name after *committee* in ¶1 and after *questions* in the last ¶. Include a comma before the name in ¶ 1 and after the name in ¶3.

Documents 2 and 3

May 15, 19--

(V1—Name and address)

TENTH ANNUAL PROFESSIONAL DEVELOPMENT SEMINAR

Thank you for accepting our invitation to serve as a member of the Local Arrangements Committee. We appreciate your willingness to accept this responsibility.

As I indicated earlier, each member of the Local Arrangements Committee will be responsible for meeting a speaker at the airport, serving as host during the speaker's visit, and taking the speaker back to the airport. You are assigned to serve as host for (V2—Name), who arrives at (V3—Time, date, flight).

Each member of the Local Arrangements Committee will be sent a seminar notebook as soon as it is complete. Biographical sketches of all speakers are included in the notebook. If you have any questions, please call me.

Rosa Longora, Seminar Coordinator | xx

Document 2
Two-page block letter
(LM p. S55)

words

Current date | OVERNIGHT | Attention Ms. Alisa 9
Nelson | Manager, Human Resources | Marion 17
Industries | Box 1769 | Marion, VA 24354- 24
1769 | Re: Customer No. 986 | Ladies and 32
Gentlemen 34

Thank you for your inquiry about our new au- 43
tomated test development and generation sys- 51
tem. This system, as you noted in your 59
inquiry, is quite different from the other prod- 69
ucts you have purchased. However, the sys- 78
tem is not a new product for us. Many clients 87
who certify employees have used previous ver- 96
sions for more than ten years. 102

Recently, we decided to upgrade our system 111
and market it as a system rather than as a 120
complete testing service provided by our staff. 129
The system automates all phases of assess- 138
ment: generating tests, taking tests, and scor- 147
ing tests. It enables an organization such as 157
yours to incorporate quality testing in the se- 166
lecting and training of employees. 173

The test generation component enables you to 182
maintain a large database of all standard types 192
of test items. Validated items stored with com- 202
plex competency identifiers, answer keys, 210
critiques of answers, and a variety of item sta- 220
tistics enable you to generate automatically a 229
test that meets high standards. 236

The test administration component enables you 245
to produce traditional tests on paper or tests 254
stored on disk for interactive testing. Tests 264
taken interactively on the computer can be 272
answered using the keyboard or a mouse. At 281
the conclusion of the tests, the results are pro- 291
duced immediately. The report can be read 299
from the screen or can be printed. 307

The scoring component enables you to scan 315
test answer sheets, score all tests, produce 324
score reports, and itemize analysis statistics. 334
These statistics can then be added to the item 343
database so that they can be used for future 352
test generation purposes. In addition to 361
individual score reports, reports for groups 370

words

and a variety of subgroups can be prepared 378
automatically. 381

The enclosed packet of material provides you 390
with detailed information about the testing sys- 400
tem, training, and costs for a site license. Our 410
sales representative, Amy Roberts, will call you 420
next week to answer questions you might have 429
about the system. 433

Sincerely | AUTOMATED ASSESSMENT SYS- 440
TEMS | Juan T. Mendez | Sales Manager | xx 447
| Enclosure | c Amy Roberts | You will be 454
amazed at how easy the system is to use. 462

Document 3
Short modified block letter—
mixed punctuation
(LM p. S57)

Current date | FACSIMILE | Mr. Ryan Yates | 8
Senior Vice President | Yates and Associates | 17
2857 Bluff Drive | Goshen, IN 46526-9017 | 24
Re: Order No. 346R938 | Dear Mr. Yates 32

Thank you very much for your order. Brenda 41
Mace requested and was granted special ap- 49
proval to ship the order today even though it 58
exceeds your current credit limit by 30 per- 68
cent. 69

Please complete and return the forms accom- 77
panying this letter so that we may consider 86
increasing your credit limit. Future orders can 96
be shipped only if they are within your credit 105
limit. 107

Sincerely | OFFICE BARGAINS | Tyler C. Rabon 115
| Credit Manager | xx | Enclosure | c Brenda 122
Mace 123

Document 4
(plain paper)

1 Revise Document 3 and format it as a shell document.
2 Convert the colored text to variables.
3 Identify the variables appropriately.
4 Delete *Facsimile* below the date.

84c 35'

FORMATTING

Build production skill

Time schedule

Assemble materials .... 3'
Timed production .... 25'
Final check;
compute *n-pram* .... 7'
(total words - penalty ÷ 25')

Document 1
Two-page letter
(LM p. S47)

1 Format the letter at the right in block format.

2 Use an appropriate second-page heading.

3 Proofread; correct errors; address an envelope.

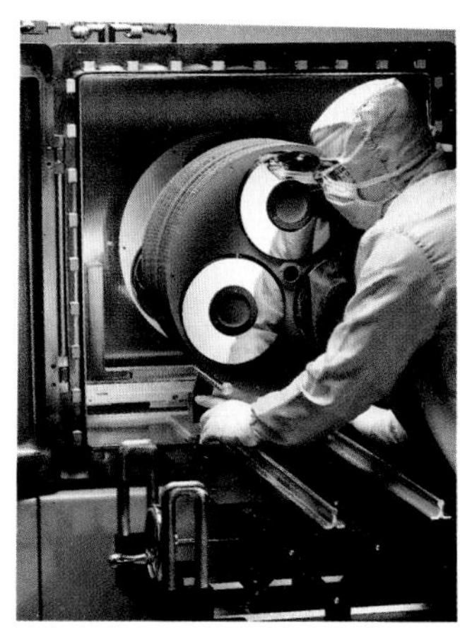

words

March 17, 19-- | OVERNIGHT MAIL | Ms. Anita C. Osborne 12
425 Bayside Village | Newport, RI 02840-3976 | Dear 22
Ms. Osborne 24

University abstracts registries has provid us with a 35
copy of your resume, and we are pleased to extend toyou 47
an invitation to visit Transportation Electronics, Inc., 58
in Twin Falls, idaho. We would like to show you our 69
facility and discuss available career oportunities. 80

The introductory literature that is enclosed will help 91
you become acquainted with our organisation. As the 101
electronics components division of Century Motor Company, 113
we are challenged with the task of developing and manufac- 125
turing all electric component used in Century transportation 137
products. These products include engine control systems, and 159
security systems, as well as many other convenience produxts 171
for ground vehicles. We also design navigational systems for 184
commercial airlines, government air craft, and vessels. 197

Transportation Electronics is one of the largest semi- 208
conductor manufacturers in the United States. In addition 220
to producing a wide variety of electronic product, we are 231
an industry leader in automated assembly and test equipment. 244
We build all of our custome microprocessors here in Twin 255
Falls. Currently, we have many microprocessor-based systems 267
in development and in variousstages of production. 278

Twin Falls, the home of Transportation Electronics, is a 289
moderate city in the southern portion of Idaho, offering you 303
a wide variety of recraetional and cultural opportunities. 315
The beauty of Idaho is seen in the diversity of mountain 326

Communication Workshop 5

Margins: 1" or 65-space line

MicroAssistant: To select Communication Workshop 5, key **C5** from the Main menu.

Drill 1
Improve capitalization skills

1 Key the sentences, correcting all capitalization errors.

2 Proofread; correct errors.

1 The group will meet at the lakeview hotel in seattle, washington.
2 the manager of the customer service department is phillip redfin.
3 robin is enrolled in accounting 101; lee is in a marketing class.
4 jan earned a bachelor of science degree at central state college.
5 vice president smith will speak at the sales meeting on thursday.
6 ginger marks, ph.d., is working to earn her cpa rating this year.
7 george is the leading sales representative in the western region.
8 we told them smart write is a registered trademark of holt, inc.
9 we will meet with the governor in the northern part of the state.
10 i like the quote on page 43 of the new book on display in room c.

Drill 2
Improve language arts skills

1 Key the sentences, correcting all grammar, punctuation, capitalization, and number-usage errors.

2 Proofread; correct errors.

11 if it rains this afternoon brenda will not play tennis with james
12 the advertising department got a fifteen % increase in the budget
13 why did the company moved there office to 1829 westside boulevard
14 do you no with who he plan to go to the game with on friday night
15 my manager douglas c westerfield got his mba from western college
16 we plan to leave at two twenty p.m. to go to a three p.m. meeting
17 the typing prize is 10 thousand dollars cash and a $21,000.00 car
18 the meeting is scheduled for march 8th at 5 o'clock in building d
19 judy and thomas is going to the mall after they finish there work
20 is the game schedule for friday march 6 or for saturday march 7th
21 beach music was popular in the 60s but it are not as popular now
22 the meeting was pastponed by the secretary because the speaker is ill
23 jimmy drove passed there new house in the driving rain last night
24 jo sanchez head of the finance department called me at 8;30 AM
25 did a sales representative sell jennifers car for it's full value
26 the highway is very slippery therefore please drive very cautious
27 a leader must encouraged their employees to assume responsibility
28 majorie should of course be invited to participate in the meeting
29 they saw 48 ducks 8 deer 6 gooses 9 cows 4 horse and 12 squirrels
30 elizabeth the best tennis play on the team injure her ankle today

84 Review

Skill-Building Warmup

84a 5'

alphabet 1 Max Weggins ordered five blazer-style jackets from a quaint shop.
figure 2 The material is from page 276, lines 21-39, and page 508, line 4.
direct reach 3 Izumi Matsumma's book on debt service is good for anyone to read.
fluency 4 Fleur's firm may profit if they handle the problems and the risk.

| 1 | 2 | 3 | 4 | 5 | 6 | 7 | 8 | 9 | 10 | 11 | 12 | 13 |

84b 10'

SKILL BUILDING

Build/measure straight-copy skill

1 Key one 3' writing. Determine *gwam*.

2 Key one 5' writing. Proofread; circle errors; determine *gwam*.

Scanner: equipment that "reads" keyed or printed pages and converts them to electronic data for computer processing.

A all letters

gwam 3' | 5'

Scanning technology has been used for some time in data- 4 | 2 | 45
entry work. Today, scanning is being used extensively for many 8 | 5 | 47
desktop and production publishing applications. One of the fac- 12 | 7 | 50
tors that must be considered is that the material to be scanned 16 | 10 | 53
is generally part of a bound document such as a report. An 20 | 12 | 55
excellent question to ask is, will the report have to be cut 25 | 15 | 57
apart before it can be scanned? The dimensions and the finish of 29 | 17 | 60
a document may be almost as important as the type of document. 33 | 20 | 63
If the sizes and types of documents are important considera- 37 | 22 | 65
tions, then a flatbed unit is necessary. This type of scanner 41 | 25 | 68
is the only one that can be used to scan bound documents without 46 | 27 | 70
cutting them apart. It can handle reports of almost any thick- 50 | 30 | 73
ness on standard-sized paper. An optional feeder can be pur- 54 | 32 | 75
chased to handle oversized paper. The finish does not matter. A 58 | 35 | 78
good scanner can handle any type of finish; therefore, a picture 63 | 38 | 80
can be scanned just as easily as text. Installing the unit is a 67 | 40 | 83
simple process, and the unit is certainly very easy to use. 71 | 43 | 85

gwam 3' | 1 | 2 | 3 | 4 | 5 |
5' | 1 | 2 | 3 |

Drill 3
Spelling

1 Key the ¶, correcting all errors as you key.
2 Proofread; correct remaining errors or rekey the ¶.

The personell in the resturant were not very accomodating. Customers who recieve poor service are not likely to patronize a resturant very long. Its not in there best interst to return to a resturant whose employes do not give appropraite service. The benefits of good service cannot be underestimated. The dineing area should be clean and orderlly, and servers should work quikly and be courteus.

Drill 4
Editing

1 Key the ¶, correcting all errors in grammar, word usage, spelling, capitalization, and punctuation.
2 Proofread; correct remaining errors or rekey the ¶.

in a economie that is base on information and technologie a good education are critical. the united states will not be competetive in world markets unless it's employes have the skills necessry too be productive. learning how to thing and how to continue learning may be the survival skill of the future. the word force of the future must by better educted then ever before in hour history.

Drill 5
Editing

Follow the directions for Drill 4.

what competencies does entry-level office workers need. surveys indecate that the most important competency are interpersonal skills communiction skills and basic office skills. a office worker with out these basic skills are not likely to be sucessful. while these skills are prerequisites for sucess, they are just the begining. office workers also need to develope technical and proceedural skills

Drill 6
Editing

Follow the directions for Drill 4.

a person needs to have a number fo specific competences to be an affective communicator. they include listining speaking reading writing and communicating nonverbaly. listining is prehaps the most important of the competences. most employes spent more time listining then they do speaking reading or writing. of all the skills employes has listining is usualy the weakest skill

83c 30'

FORMATTING

Documents with variable information

Documents 1 and 2
Block letters
(LM pp. S39-S41)

Key the (long) letters at the right, inserting the following variables:

Document 1

V1—
Dr. Anne Jones
81 East Lovell Street
Troy, MI 48098-7263
V2—Dr. Jones
V3—June 6
V4—1:30-4:30 p.m.
V5—professionalism
V6—5 and 6
(Total words: 239)

Document 2

V1—
Mr. Roger Sharpe
3200 Mayfield Street
York, PA 17402-9365
V2—Mr. Sharpe
V3—June 7
V4—8:30-11:45 a.m.
V5—time management
V6—6 and 7
(Total words: 239)

Documents 3 and 4
Simplified letters
(LM pp. S43-S45)

Key the (average-length) letters, inserting the following variables:

Document 3

V1—
Mr. George Reynolds
542 South Belmont Street
Dover, PA 17403-9286
V2—afternoon
V3—6
V4—Dr. Anne Jones
(Total words: 157)

Document 4

V1—
Ms. Lucy Bennett
2694 Chestnut Road
York, PA 17404-6158
V2—morning
V3—7
V4—Mr. Roger Sharpe
(Total words: 155)

Documents 1 and 2

March 21, 19--

(V1)

Dear (V2)

Thank you for accepting our invitation to participate in our Tenth Annual Professional Development Seminar, which will be held at Pat's Island Club on Isle of Palms, June 5-9. We are delighted that you will be a participant in the program, and we know that you will make an outstanding contribution to the seminar.

The program schedule has been set. Your session will be presented on (V3) from (V4) in the Island Club Grand Salon. The general topic area we agreed upon is (V5).

Please send us within the next week or two the exact title you would like to have appear in the program. The standard meeting room arrangement is schoolroom-style with a lectern, lavaliere microphone, flip chart, overhead projector, and slide projector. Please let us know if you prefer changes in the room arrangement or if you need any additional equipment.

An oceanside villa has been reserved for you on June (V6). We know you will enjoy the luxurious facilities of this beautiful island resort. We look forward to working with you.

Sincerely | Ms. Rosa C. Longora | Seminar Coordinator | xx

Documents 3 and 4

April 6, 19--

(V1)

TENTH ANNUAL PROFESSIONAL DEVELOPMENT SEMINAR

You have been selected by the Program Committee to preside at the (V2) session of our Professional Development Seminar on June (V3). The speaker at your session will be (V4).

Your primary responsibilities are to see that the meeting room is arranged appropriately for the speaker with all the equipment requested, distribute handout materials, introduce the speaker, and make a few remarks to close the session. A biographical sketch of the speaker, the room arrangement and equipment request, and a copy of the program are attached.

Please let us know if you will accept this responsibility.

Rosa Longora, Seminar Coordinator | xx | Attachments

Formatting Workshop 2

MicroAssistant: To select Formatting Workshop 2, key **F2** from the Main menu.

Document 1 Standard Memo words

TO: Interactive Videodisc Enthusiasts | **FROM:** 9
Elise Conyers | **DATE:** April 4, 19-- | **SUB-** 16
JECT: Laser Videodisc Seminar 22
(¶1) The program for the Laser Videodisc Semi- 31
nar on April 24 has been finalized, and we are 40
excited about the caliber of speakers we have 49
been able to attract. 54

(¶2) The seminar will be held in the audito- 62
rium. Lunch will be provided in the Atrium. 71
Please return the attached reservation form by 80
April 15 so that appropriate arrangements can 89
be made. 91

(¶3) Please make every effort to participate in 100
the excellent program. 105

xx | Attachments 108

Document 2 Standard Memo

TO: Merri C. Jones | **FROM:** Cliff R. Heath | 8
DATE: Current | **SUBJECT:** CSU Field Studies 16
(¶1) Today, I received the enclosed brochure from 25
Central State University describing their sum- 34
mer field studies. The program is interesting 44
and could be of benefit to us. 50

(¶2) I called several of the major companies who 59
worked with CSU last summer, and they all 67
reported excellent results from the teams who 77
worked with them. The most frequent com- 85
ment was that CSU provided quality consult- 93
ing work at a nominal charge. 100

(¶3) Please review the brochure and let me know 108
what you think. If you agree that this is a 117
good idea, I will ask the Planning Committee 126
to develop the proposal and submit it to CSU. 136

xx | Attachment 138

Document 3 Two-page simplified memo

Current date | Planning Committee | PROPOSAL 9
FOR CSU FIELD STUDY 13

(¶1) Central State University recently sent us a 21
brochure describing their summer field study 30
opportunities for industry. Merri Jones and I 40

words
investigated the program and were very 48
pleasantly surprised to find that many major 57
companies compete to be selected for a field 66
study project. We called six companies that 75
sponsored field studies last summer, and they 84
reported excellent results. All six plan to sub- 94
mit proposals again this summer. 100

(¶2) The field study team consists of five MBA 109
students who have completed the first year of 118
the two-year program and a faculty member 126
who directs the project. In addition, a commu- 136
nication consultant works with all of the field 145
study teams to ensure that the formal report 154
and the oral presentation to management are 163
effective. 166

(¶3) Each team works full-time on a project for 174
approximately eight weeks. The work is done 183
both in company facilities and at CSU. The 192
sponsoring organization pays all costs associ- 201
ated with the project. However, no charges are 211
assessed for the time of either the faculty mem- 220
bers or the students. 225

(¶4) CSU has conducted about a hundred field 233
studies over the past three years. A brief de- 242
scription of a sample of 25 of the projects is 252
attached. Six or eight of the projects are the 261
type that would be very beneficial to us. The 271
ones that particularly attracted our attention 280
were the projects that involved a competitive 289
analysis and the development of a strategic 298
marketing plan. 302

(¶5) The glass industry has become very com- 309
petitive in the last three years, and an analysis 319
of the industry and a strategic marketing plan 329
would be extremely valuable to us. Further, 338
we believe that a team of university research- 347
ers could get far better access to competitive 356
data than we could. 361

(¶6) Please do the following: 1. Review the at- 369
tached sample projects and the proposal guides. 379
2. Determine exactly what we want to have the 391
project team do. 3. Decide which managers will 401
be assigned to work with the various components 411
of the project. 4. Prepare the proposal according 421
to the specifications that CSU provided. 429

Cliff R. Heath | xx | Attachments 435

83 Form Letters With Variables

Skill-Building Warmup

83a 5'

alphabet	1	Corwin Czajka quit a very good team because of a schedule mix-up.
fig/sym	2	The new note ($24,375 @ 8%) replaces the old note ($40,615 @ 9%).
adjacent reach	3	Luisa opted to wear a topcoat over her sweater to the polo match.
fluency	4	Kent did go with my neighbor to the ancient chapel on the island.

1 | 2 | 3 | 4 | 5 | 6 | 7 | 8 | 9 | 10 | 11 | 12 | 13

83b 15'

FORMATTING

Preapplication drill: merge variable information

(LM pp. S35-S37)

1 Study the information at the right carefully.
2 Create the form document in Figure 1 below; use simplified letter format.
3 Prepare the letter (Figure 2) by merging the variable information.

Merging variables in a form document

One easy way to create form documents is to prepare a shell document and then insert the variable information at designated points. The examples below show how a shell or form document for making hotel reservations can be created and how variable information can be added to it. The way a form document is created depends on whether word processing software or a typewriter is being used.

If you are using word processing, refer to the procedures in your user's manual for merging variable information.

If you are using a typewriter, prepare and save a form document, indicating the point at which variable information must be inserted. Then key each document, inserting the variable information. Each document must be keyed individually, unless your equipment can save the form document electronically.

Price Associates
829 Kirk Lane
Troy, MI 48044-7536
313-555-9221

(V1—Current date)

(V2—Hotel name and address)

REQUEST FOR RESERVATIONS

Please reserve a single room with a king-size bed for me for arrival on (V3—Arrival date). I will depart on (V4—Departure date). I prefer a nonsmoking room.

Please guarantee the room for late arrival and confirm this reservation.

Lee Price, President

xx

Figure 1: Form document

Price Associates
829 Kirk Lane
Troy, MI 48044-7536
313-555-9221

March 8, 19--

Seaside Inn
2439 Ocean Drive
Myrtle Beach, SC 29577-3847

REQUEST FOR RESERVATIONS

Please reserve a single room with a king-size bed for me for arrival on May 28. I will depart on June 9. I prefer a nonsmoking room.

Please guarantee the room for late arrival and confirm this reservation.

Lee Price, President

xx

Figure 2: Final letter with merged variables

Use current date on all letters, add a salutation, complimentary close, and other necessary letter parts. Follow other directions in italics.

words

Document 4
Modified block letter with indented paragraphs
(LM p. S59)

Mrs. Lelia Ramirez
2836 Foster Road
Portland, OR 97206-3185

opening lines 19

Your request to have the credit limit on your Royal Bank Card increased 33
to $5,000 has been reviewed carefully. 41

Two months ago, your credit application was reviewed and approved for 55
a $3,000 credit limit. The $3,000 credit limit was the maximum for which 70
you qualified at the time. Although you have maintained your account 84
properly for two months, your credit limit cannot be increased until you 99
have maintained your account for at least six months. 110

If your financial position has improved significantly in the past two months, 125
please send us the new information; and we will be happy to reconsider 140
your request. 145

Charles T. Rawls | Credit Manager | xx total 152

Document 5
Block letter
(LM p. S61)

Ms. Elise Conyers
Project Coordinator
Hoosier Industries, Inc.
362 East Inglefield Road
Evansville, IN 47711-9508

Add Overnight Mail Notation | Add subject line: Response to Request for Proposal

opening lines 34

The proposal for developing three interactive laser videodiscs for Hoosier 49
Industries, Inc., is enclosed. The proposal meets and exceeds all of the 64
specifications in your Request for Proposal. 73

We are delighted that you requested all vendors to provide information 87
about previous experience in developing laser videodiscs for microcom- 101
puter applications. This area is one of our specialties, and we believe our 117
experience in developing many instructional modules for word processing, 131
spreadsheet, and database applications will be very valuable to you. 145

Please let me know if you have any questions about the proposal. We 159
hope to have the opportunity to work with you. 169

INSTRUCTIONAL TECHNOLOGY, INC. | Toyohiko Soga | President | c Victor 188
Flores, Production Chief total 193

Document 6
Simplified block letter
(LM p. S63)

Cellular Telephones, Inc.
28 Hillside Avenue
Dover, NJ 07801-5362

Add Subject Line: Cellular Telephone Service

opening lines 22

Your advertisement in the morning paper attracted my attention. In fact, 36
you described my work style perfectly. I spend a significant amount of 51
my work time in my automobile. Please send me a copy of the brochure 65
on how to turn my driving time into productive work time. 77

The price information in your advertisement indicates that cellular tele- 91
phone technology is now affordable. The bulk of my driving time is spent 106
within twenty miles of Newark. Please send price information on a cel- 120
lular telephone for this range. 127

I look forward to learning more about the cellular telephone service you 142
offer. I would be happy to speak with your sales representative if you 156
have one who covers this area. 162

Robert T. Anderson | Sales Coordinator total 170

82b (continued)

Documents 1-3
(LM pp. S29-S33)

1 Store each ¶ as a separate file, using the name given. If you cannot store ¶s, go to Step 2.

2 Prepare a block letter (average length) for each work request (page 198).

3 Supply the salutation and complimentary close.

Document 4
Betty Darcus is the new Beach Cove Conference coordinator. Rex Findlay now serves as Fairway Clubhouse Conference coordinator. Modify ¶L82C-C2 to reflect Rex's new title. Create a new ¶L82C-C3 for Betty with her title. Print a copy of the ¶s.

L82C-B1
Pat's Island Club is delighted to host your conference. Our state-of-the-art meeting and banquet rooms, luxurious beach villas, and unsurpassed recreational facilities combine to provide a superb setting for your meeting. The Oceanview Conference Center is ideal for groups of one hundred to five hundred.

L82C-B2
Pat's Island Club is delighted to host your conference. Our state-of-the-art meeting and banquet rooms, luxurious beach villas, and unsurpassed recreational facilities combine to provide a superb setting for your meeting. The Fairway Clubhouse is ideal for groups of fewer than a hundred.

L82C-B3
Pat's Island Club is delighted to host your conference. Our state-of-the-art meeting and banquet rooms, luxurious beach villas, and unsurpassed recreational facilities combine to provide a superb setting for your meeting. The Beach Cove is ideal for groups of fewer than fifty.

L82C-M1
All of the villas in the Island House have been blocked for your conference attendees. Every villa in the Island House has a full ocean view and is beautifully appointed. The Meeting Planners Guide that is enclosed contains a worksheet giving the size and rental rate for each villa.

L82C-M2
A group of near-beach villas has been blocked for your conference attendees. The beautifully appointed villas are located near the meeting facilities and are a very short walking distance from the beach. The Meeting Planners Guide that is enclosed contains a worksheet giving the size and rental rate for each villa.

L82C-M3
A group of oceanside villas in the Atlantic Club has been blocked for your conference attendees. Every villa in the Atlantic Club has a panoramic ocean view and is beautifully appointed. The Meeting Planners Guide that is enclosed contains a worksheet giving the size and rental rate for each villa.

L82C-C1
Emi Asano, our Oceanview Conference Center manager, will serve as your conference coordinator. She will contact you within the week and will work with you to finalize plans for a truly outstanding conference at Pat's Island Club.

L82C-C2
Rex Findlay, our conference specialist, will serve as your conference coordinator. He will contact you within the week and will work with you to finalize plans for a truly outstanding conference at Pat's Island Club.

Document 7 Simplified memo with table words

Current date | Proposal Evaluation Team | RE- 9
SPONSES TO OUR REQUEST FOR PROPOSAL 16

The final submission date for proposals for our 25
laser videodisc project was yesterday, and we 35
have received six proposals that meet the speci- 44
fications we provided. Two other proposals were 54
rejected because they violate a key provision in 64
the specifications. Namely, they involve third- 73
party contracts. 77

The prices quoted varied significantly. The out- 87
lined procedures, product design, and time frame 96
also have interesting variations. The following 106
information about the proposals will be of inter- 116
est: 117

Vendor	Cost	Time	
			123
Instructional Technology	$296,985	6 months	131
Videodisc Productions	328,500	12 weeks	139
Videodisc Courseware	290,975	18 weeks	147
High-Tech Productions	340,000	6 months	155
Interactive Learning	310,385	8 months	162
Instructional Media	349,975	24 weeks	170

Our staff is preparing a preliminary analysis 179
and will have it ready in time for the meeting we 189
have scheduled next Tuesday. I hope we can 198
complete the review on Tuesday, but this may 207
not be possible as major issues have yet to be 216
resolved. 218

Elise Conyers | xx 222

Document 8 Standard memo with table

TO: Steering Committee | **FROM:** Lynn Rob- 8
erts, Seminar Coordinator | **DATE:** Current | 17
SUBJECT: Housing for Seminar Participants 26

Finding appropriate accommodations for semi- 35
nar participants is becoming a serious problem. 45
Currently, all rooms blocked for the seminar at 54
the Shoreline Hotel have been assigned; and 63
more than fifty people have yet to be accommo- 72
dated. 74

The announced deadline for housing accommo- 82
dations is one week from today, and a signifi- 92
cant number of reservations may still be needed. 101
Comparable rooms located a reasonable dis- 110
tance from the convention center are available. 120

words

Several hotels in the area are willing to block 129
rooms for a two-week period. The following table 139
shows the number of rooms, the type of rooms, 148
and the flat rate that the hotels have quoted for 158
the rooms blocked for our group: 165

Hotel	Regular/Rate	King/Rate	
			177
Seabrook	14 at $109	12 at $123	183
Tradewind	10 at $112	10 at $129	189
Tide	25 at $115	14 at $132	195

The situation will be monitored carefully, and a 204
follow-up report will be provided to the Steering 214
Committee next week. | xx 219

Documents 9-12 Form letters (LM pp. S65-S71)

Document 9
V1—
Mr. Kent Beaver
Beaver Office Systems
9275 Cherokee Street
Naples, FL 33962-4826
V2—Mr. Beaver
V3—Eastern
V4—Charleston
(Total words: 104)

Document 10
V1—
Mr. Rex Marks, Manager
Marks Office Equipment
382 Dove Avenue
Rigby, ID 83442-5837
V2—Mr. Marks
V3—Western
V4—San Jose
(Total words: 104)

Document 11
V1—
Ms. Sherry Meade, President
Meade Software, Inc.
3945 Fifth Avenue
Seattle, WA 98101-5837
V2—Ms. Meade
V3—Western
V4—San Jose
(Total words: 105)

Document 12
V1—
Ms. Laura Woods, Manager
South-Eastern Publishers
572 East Main Street
Johnson City, TN 37601-6457
V2—Ms. Woods
V3—Eastern
V4—Charleston
(Total words: 107)

Current date | (V1—Name and address) | Dear (V2—Personal title and name)

The (V3—Region) Business Exposition meets in (V4—City) on July 5-10. As a former exhibitor, you have first opportunity to reserve an exhibit booth before the booths are made available to the general public.

Please review the enclosed material about this year's Exposition and indicate your booth location preferences. This priority opportunity expires one month from today.

Sincerely | Lee Davis | xx | Enclosures

82 Letters From Form Paragraphs

82a 5'

Skill-Building Warmup

alphabet 1 Jacque amazed them by fixing all five broken wicker porch chairs.
fig/sym 2 The meat for 37 cost us $146.58 (20# @ $6.98 = $139.60 x 5% tax).
space bar 3 Pam and I may go to see if we can buy a new car for the big trip.
fluency 4 Angie may pay me if the city pays for work she did on the panels.

1	2	3	4	5	6	7	8	9	10	11	12	13

82b 45'

FORMATTING

Learn to use form documents

Read the information at the right; then format the documents on page 199.

Form documents

Using forms to create documents saves a tremendous amount of time and effort when more than one document containing similar information must be prepared. Information that is the same in each document is contained in one document often called the *form* or *shell*. Information that differs in each document is called *variable information.*

Different methods can be used to prepare form documents, depending upon the hardware and software used. One method of preparing form documents is to store blocks of text (form paragraphs) that can be retrieved and combined to form documents. In Lesson 74 (pages 179-180), you learned to prepare memos from form paragraphs. In this lesson, you will prepare letters using form paragraphs.

Remember: Form messages save time even when documents are prepared on a typewriter. It takes far less time to compose one good form letter and key it 50 times than it does to compose and key 50 individual letters. When word processing software is used, additional time is saved because the documents do not have to be rekeyed or proofread. Once stored information has been proofread, it does not have to be proofread again unless changes are made.

WORK REQUEST
Form Letters with Variable Information

Date: Current
Address: Ms. Gail Stitt, President
Stitt Auto Parts, Inc.
139 Dove Avenue
Rigby, ID 83442-1224
Paragraphs: L82C-B3, L82C-M2, L82C-C2
Signature: Mark Brady
Title: Sales Manager
Copies to: Rex Findlay

Document 1 (Total words: 194)

WORK REQUEST
Form Letters with Variable Information

Date: Current
Address: Mr. Reed Collins, Manager
Wexford Industries
P.O. Box 6952
Tulsa, OK 74101-6952
Paragraphs: L82C-B1, L82C-M1, L82C-C1
Signature: Mark Brady
Title: Sales Manager
Copies to: Emi Asano

Document 2 (Total words: 196)

WORK REQUEST
Form Letters with Variable Information

Date: Current
Address: Ms. Ellen G. Weston
Weston and Weston, Inc.
2963 River Road
Lynn, MA 01852-6927
Paragraphs: L82C-B2, L82C-M3, L82C-C2
Signature: Mark Brady
Title: Sales Manager
Copies to: Rex Findlay

Document 3 (Total words: 193)

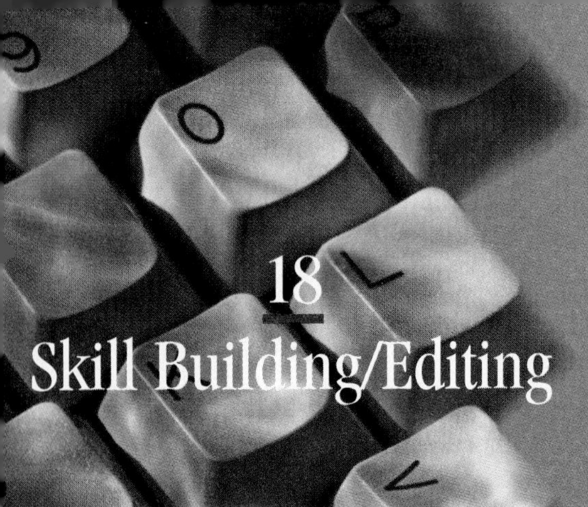

18 Skill Building/Editing

Learning goals:
1 To improve keyboarding techniques.
2 To improve basic skill on straight, statistical, script, and rough-draft copy.

Formatting guides:
1 Margins: 1" or 65-space line for drills, ¶ writings, and documents.
2 Single-space drills and documents, unless otherwise directed; double-space writings.
3 5-space ¶ indention.

86a 5'

Skill-building warmup

each line 3 times (slowly, faster, slowly); DS between 3-line groups; repeat selected lines if time permits
(Use these directions for all skill-building warmups in Lessons 86-88.)

alphabet 1 Vasquez wrote the chilling poem about the jinx of five dark days.
fig/sym 2 I need one box (25" x 40" x 8") and a small box (19" x 37" x 6").
adjacent reach 3 Sam and Guy said we were going to the polo match with ten people.
fluency 4 Claudia may fix the problem with the turn signals on the bicycle.
| 1 | 2 | 3 | 4 | 5 | 6 | 7 | 8 | 9 | 10 | 11 | 12 | 13 |

86b 15'

SKILL BUILDING

Build/measure script-copy skill

1 Key two 1' writings on each ¶.
2 Key one 5' writing. Proofread; circle errors; determine *gwam*.

A all letters

	gwam 1'	5'	
Each of us desires to influence the behavior of others at	12	2	42
some time. The individual we wish to influence might	22	4	44
be our supervisor, one of our fellow workers, or it just as	34	7	47
well might be a family member or a friend. However, we	46	9	49
must recognize that we cannot control others; we can	56	11	51
only influence others. Four approaches or techniques can	68	14	53
be used to influence the behavior of others. The same	79	16	56
techniques can be used to influence individuals on	89	18	58
the job and in our personal lives.	96	19	59
The first way to influence behavior is to be assertive.	11	22	61
To assert yourself means to tell others openly and honestly	23	24	64
how you feel about an issue. The second way to influence	35	26	66
others is through power. Power is the ability to act or	46	29	68
to move others to act. Leadership is the third way to	57	31	71
influence others. Leadership is the ability to get others	69	33	73
to follow you. The fourth way to influence others is	80	35	75
through our beliefs or expectations. What we believe	91	37	77
and expect often influences our behavior as well as others.	103	40	80

Document 2 Two-page simplified letter
(LM p. S27)

words

March 8, 19-- | FACSIMILE | Attention Program 8
Coordinator | Quality Training Associates | 28 17
Ravina Drive | Atlanta, GA 30346-9105 | Excel- 26
lence in Customer Service Seminar 32

(¶1) Six of our employees attended the Excel- 40
lence in Customer Service Seminar you offered 50
in Washington, D.C., on Monday of this week. 59
The feedback reports from all six employees 68
indicated that the program was outstanding. 77
Our customer service manager, Juan Fernandez, 86
was particularly impressed with your seminar 95
leader, Dr. Rhett P. Lauver. Juan felt that the 105
program would be extremely valuable for all of 114
our employees who have contact with cus- 123
tomers. We have targeted approximately two hun- 131
dred employees for the training program. The 141
job categories of these employees include cus- 150
tomer service representatives, outside sales 159
representatives, inside sales representatives, 168
secretaries, receptionists, order-entry clerks, 178
and credit clerks. 182

(¶2) Would you be willing to customize the 190
program for our organization and train our 199
employees? We want to limit the number of 208
participants in each session to approximately 218
thirty. Employee involvement in the program is 227
a high priority, and we believe that the small- 236
group atmosphere will encourage all of the 245
employees to participate more freely. 252

(¶3) Our training facility is ideal for the type of 261
program you offer. State-of-the-art equipment 270
is available. We have a wide range of video 279
equipment, which will allow for varied types of 289
visual displays. Slide and film projectors as well 299
as overhead projectors will be available for Dr. 308
Lauver. In addition, the facility can be config- 318
ured to suit the needs and desires of the trainer. 329
The facility consists of one large room, which 338
can be broken down with room dividers into 347
smaller or larger arrangements of two to ten 356
rooms. This versatility allows for more effective 366
small-group interaction, focus groups, and role- 375
play exercises, according to the agenda of the 385
trainer. 387

(¶4) Every effort will be made to provide an at- 395
mosphere that is conducive to effective learn- 405
ing. Employees participating in the training 414
program will not be interrupted except in the 423
case of an emergency. 427

(¶5) Our schedule is somewhat flexible. We would 436
like to have all employees trained within three 446
or four months. The training program can be 455
scheduled on consecutive days, or it can be 463
spread over time to accommodate Dr. Lauver's 473
schedule. However, you should be aware of a 482
few potential conflicts. We will be closed for the 492
holidays on Friday, April 1, and Monday, May 501
30; also, Friday, June 10, for a company pic- 510
nic. We operate on a flextime schedule with 519
core hours between 9:30 and 3:30; the semi- 528
nars should be held during these core hours. 537

(¶6) Please let us know if you are interested in 546
providing this training for our employees. If you 556
are, please send us a cost proposal for the total 566
training package. 569

Martha G. Carson, Program Coordinator | 577
xx | Juan Fernandez would be happy to meet 585
with you to help tailor the program to our needs. 595

86c 15'

SKILL BUILDING

Improve keyboarding technique

each set of lines 3 times; DS between 9-line groups; key one-hand words letter by letter; key balanced-hand words as units

one hand

5 were link trees jump create milk free plump extra plum crave hunk
6 Phillip, in my opinion, deserved a better test grade as a reward.
7 Bev, as you are aware, debated in a few cases after you deferred.

balanced hand

8 turn sick pant blame shame prism burns jam lap men girls lame fit
9 Jane, a neighbor, may sue for the title to the lake and the land.
10 Andy may bid for the ancient workbox; it is an authentic antique.

combination

11 into turn within pansies statement sick inform windy severe bowls
12 Fred spent some time with us on the island my neighbor, Ty, owns.
13 Why did he lend you my authentic ornament for the tree this year?

| 1 | 2 | 3 | 4 | 5 | 6 | 7 | 8 | 9 | 10 | 11 | 12 | 13 |

86d 15'

SKILL BUILDING

Build straight-copy skill

1 Key three 1' writings on each ¶. Strive for a higher *gwam* on each writing.

2 Key one 5' or two 3' writings. Proofread; circle errors; determine *gwam*.

A all letters

	gwam 3'	5'	
Most people have good intentions, but they rarely find time	4	2	46
to convert those good intentions into action. They wonder how	8	5	49
some very busy individuals frequently can find adequate time to	12	7	51
do extra little things for others who are not as fortunate as	17	10	54
they are. The answer is quite simple; those individuals care	21	12	56
enough to make helping others a major priority in their sched-	25	15	59
ules. Relatively few people are so organized that they have time	29	18	61
to do everything that they might like to do. Most people, how-	34	20	64
ever, manage to find time to do the things they truly want to do.	38	23	67
What factors distinguish those individuals who are able to	42	25	69
turn their good intentions into actions from those who simply	46	27	71
have good intentions? Some people believe that growing up in a	50	30	74
family that has a tradition of helping others is a major factor.	54	33	77
Yet, key differences in attitude exist among children who grew up	59	35	79
in the same family. Perhaps the only factor that is different is	63	38	82
that some people think helping others is a nice thing to do,	67	40	84
while others find that they get more joy when they give to others	72	43	87
than when they receive.	73	44	88

gwam 3' | 1 | 2 | 3 | 4 | 5 |
5' | 1 | 2 | 3 |

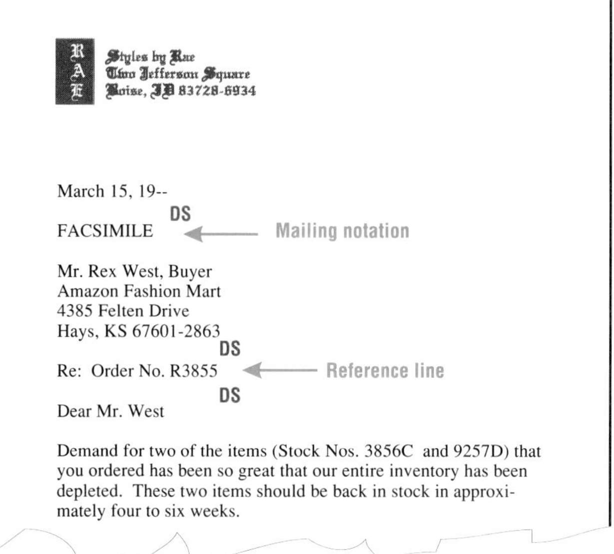

Styles by Rae
Two Jefferson Square
Boise, ID 83728-6934

March 15, 19--

FACSIMILE

Mr. Rex West, Buyer
Amazon Fashion Mart
4385 Felten Drive
Hays, KS 67601-2863

Re: Order No. R3855

Dear Mr. West

Demand for two of the items (Stock Nos. 3856C and 9257D) that you ordered has been so great that our entire inventory has been depleted. These two items should be back in stock in approximately four to six weeks.

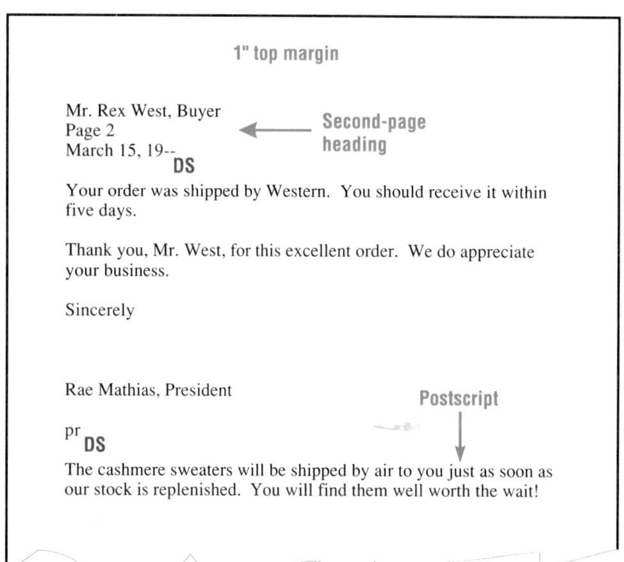

Mr. Rex West, Buyer
Page 2
March 15, 19--

Your order was shipped by Western. You should receive it within five days.

Thank you, Mr. West, for this excellent order. We do appreciate your business.

Sincerely

Rae Mathias, President

pr

The cashmere sweaters will be shipped by air to you just as soon as our stock is replenished. You will find them well worth the wait!

81d 30'

FORMATTING

Two-page letters with special notations

Document 1 Two-page block letter

Include a second-page heading.
(LM p. S25)

words

Current date | OVERNIGHT | Mr. Roger Ames, 8
President | The Block C Company | 1893 Cen- 16
tury 21 Drive | Jacksonville, FL 32216-8427 | 24
Re: Account USC9307GB | Dear Mr. Ames 31

(¶1) Thank you for selecting Gator Distributors 40
to serve as the official marketers and distribu- 50
tors for all Block C products for the Citrus Bowl. 60
We are certain that this unique partnership 69
will prove to be very profitable for both of us 78
and will enhance fan support at the game. 87

(¶2) The sample package of Block C sweatshirts, 95
jerseys, sweaters, jackets, sun visors, caps, 105
cups, mugs, rain ponchos, and bumper stick- 114
ers arrived yesterday. Our marketing staff 122
is doing some spot tests with each of the items 131
to determine which ones are likely to be the 140
best sellers and to forecast the inventory needs 150
for the game. Initial results indicate that 159
sweatshirts, jerseys, and mugs are the most 168
popular items. 171

(¶3) In accordance with our agreement, the De- 179
sign Department is customizing a number of 188
your stock items with the bowl logos. A number 197
of design sketches are enclosed for your approval. 208
Please note in particular the "spirit rag" design. 219

(¶4) The Varsity Club has contracted with us to 227
provide 40,000 spirit rags, which they plan to 237
give to the first 40,000 fans who enter the 245
stadium. Normally, spirit rags sell for $2.50. 255
Because of the volume ordered by the Varsity 264
Club, we were able to give them a contract price 274
of $30,000. In addition, we plan to stock 10,000 284
spirit rags for sale at $2.50. 290

(¶5) Our market tests indicate a great deal of 298
interest in a tailgating package. The cost for a 308
box lunch for four is $15. The lunch will include 319
chicken, potato salad, coleslaw, and rolls. We 328
could add Block C napkins, plates, plastic uten- 338
sils, and souvenir mugs and sell the package for 348
$25. 349

(¶6) Please review our preliminary design sketches. 358
We will contact you in a few days for your reac- 368
tion to the design samples. By then, we should 378
have the final results of our marketing tests. 387

Sincerely | GATOR DISTRIBUTORS | Anne Jones, 395
Manager | xx | This game will be a bright spot 404
for your team and your financial standing. 412

87 Skill Building

Skill-Building Warmup

87a 5'

alphabet 1 Jeffery quickly packed a dozen boxes of goods and gave them away.
figure 2 We will meet in Building 870, Room 69, at 12:45 p.m. on March 30.
direct reach 3 Brecken hunted in many places for those recent surveys on hunger.
fluency 4 Did the six big bowls, six mementos, and eight maps fit in a box?

1	2	3	4	5	6	7	8	9	10	11	12	13

87b 15'

SKILL BUILDING

Build/measure rough-draft copy skill

1 Key two 1' writings on each ¶.
2 Key two 3' writings at your "control" rate.
3 Proofread; circle errors; determine *gwam.*

A all letters

	gwam 1'	3'	
Most Many people in the early stage s of a career	9	3	55
think of advancing to high er positions within the	19	6	59
organization. a small number of Fewer and fewer positions stet are	28	9	62
available at the higher levels to handle the large	38	13	65
number of people wanting to move up. Therefore,	48	16	68
not all employees can moveup at a steady rate.	58	19	72
Periods exist in which a n employee stays atthe same	68	23	75
level. Reaching a level and not being able to	78	26	78
move upward is called "plateauing."	<u>85</u>	28	81
Quite often, plateauing is the product of the	9	31	84
way an organization is structured. tr College teach-	19	35	87
ers for example, who attain a full Professorate	29	38	90
reach a plateau. They are at the highest top level and	39	41	94
can not be promoted unless they change careers.	49	45	97
An individual can also reach a plateau by mas-	58	48	100
tering the content of a job so well good that it no	67	51	103
longer is a challenge.	<u>72</u>	52	104

81 Special Features

81a 5'

Skill-Building Warmup

alphabet 1	Buzz quickly gave them an explanation justifying your withdrawal.
figure 2	I read pages 135-183 of Chapter 4 and pages 267-290 of Chapter 6.
shift key 3	Don G. Lamb lives near A. Hay on S. Park Road in La Paz, Bolivia.
fluency 4	Jane may pay for the sorority emblems and for the enamel emblems.

1 | 2 | 3 | 4 | 5 | 6 | 7 | 8 | 9 | 10 | 11 | 12 | 13

81b 10'

SKILL BUILDING

Build straight-copy skill

1 Key three 1' writings striving for a new *gwam* rate.

2 Key one 3' writing at a controlled rate.

3 Proofread; circle errors; determine *gwam.*

A all letters

	gwam 3'	
Does the notion of being able to shop, to bank, and to	4	37
schedule a flight from your home or your office appeal to you?	8	41
To many individuals, the thought of conducting business at home	12	45
usually brings to mind the stack of merchandise catalogs that	16	49
frequently arrive in the mail. Today, the scope of business	20	53
activities that can be conducted at your home or your office	24	57
through a two-way information service called videotex is just	29	62
amazing. Conducting business at home is now a very simple task.	33	66

gwam 3' | 1 | 2 | 3 | 4 | 5 |

81c 5'

FORMATTING

Letters with special features

Study the information at the right and the illustrations on page 196.

Facsimile (FAX): electronic mail that uses scanning and telephone technology to transfer text over telephone lines. Delivery takes only a few minutes.

Overnight: a courier service that delivers within 24 hrs.

These mailing notations provide a record of when a document should have been received.

Mailing notations

In a letter, a notation such as FACSIMILE, OVERNIGHT, CERTIFIED, SPECIAL DELIVERY, or REGISTERED provides a record of how the letter was sent. Other notations such as CONFIDENTIAL or PERSONAL indicate how the letter should be treated by the recipient.

Key special notations in ALL CAPS at the left margin a double space below the dateline. On an envelope, key mailing notations that affect postage below the stamp (about line 8). Key notations that pertain to the recipient a double space below the return address.

Reference line

A reference line such as *Re: Policy No. R34286* directs the reader to source documents or files. Key the reference line a double space below the letter address.

Subject line

A subject line indicates the main topic of the letter. Key the subject line a double space below the salutation. Subject lines are optional except on simplified block letters.

Second-page heading

The second and succeeding pages of a letter should contain a heading consisting of the name of the person to whom the letter is addressed, the page number, and the date. The heading is keyed on plain paper of the same quality as the letterhead 1" from the top edge. It is followed by a double space.

Postscript

Key a postscript a double space below the last notation on a letter. The postscript is generally used to emphasize information.

87c 15'

SKILL BUILDING

Improve skill transfer

1 Key two 1' writings on each line.

2 Compare speed on various lines.

Note: Count each complete line as 13 words; estimate for partial lines.

5 Learning to key rapidly from different types of copy is critical.

6 Try to key the remaining lines as quickly as you keyed this line.

7 *Script, statistical, and rough-draft copy are common in industry.*

8 *The average number size increased by seven digits in a few years.*

9 You cansave time by useing Proofreader's mark to edit a document.

10 use proof readers' marks to editt that print copy of you reports.

11 Her 1952 telephone number was 3756; in 1992, it was 803-555-4683.

12 He keyed 50 wpm on lines 1 and 2 and 48 wpm on lines 3, 6, and 7.

87d 15'

SKILL BUILDING

Build straight-copy skill

1 Key three 1' writings on each ¶. Strive for a higher *gwam* on each writing.

2 Key one 5' or two 3' writings.

A all letters

	gwam 3'	5'	
Most people tend to resist change. Yet, one thing that is	4	2	41
definite is that change will occur. Why do people have the	8	5	43
tendency to resist change? The explanation is that people fear	12	7	46
that a change may produce results that are not in their best	16	10	48
interest. Worrying about the consequences of change is natural	21	12	51
and can be expected. Thus, the way change is introduced is	25	15	53
critical. Change must be introduced very gradually, and people	29	17	56
who are going to be affected by the change should be asked for	33	20	58
input about the change.	35	21	59
Technology is bringing about many changes in offices. Smart	39	23	62
managers recognize that not only will the technology be new, but	43	26	64
also the way work is done will be changed. These managers in-	47	28	67
volve all workers in the planning of the changes. They offer to	51	31	69
train those who need it, and they let all workers know what the	56	33	72
impact of the technology will be on their jobs. Smart managers	60	36	75
help workers to be change agents, rather than change resisters.	64	39	78

gwam 3' | 1 | 2 | 3 | 4 | 5

5' | 1 | 2 | 3

IMAGE MAKERS
5131 Moss Springs Road
Columbia, SC 29209-4768
(803) 555-0127

words

Dateline October 28, 19-- line 14 3
QS

Letter address Ms. Vera M. Hayes, President 9
Vera's Word Processing Services 16
4927 Stuart Avenue 19
Baton Rouge, LA 70808-3519 DS 25

> **Subject Line:** Indicates the main topic of the letter. It may be keyed in all capital letters or main words capitalized.

Subject line Simplified Block Letter Format DS 31

Body
The format of this letter is called simplified block letter 43
format. This letter style is similar to block format in that all 56
lines are positioned at the left margin. However, the simplified 69
block format does not contain a salutation or a complimentary 82
close. A subject line is required with this style. As the label 95
implies, a subject line indicates the main topic of the letter. 108
The key words contained in a subject line help office personnel 121
to sort and route incoming mail and to code documents for storage 134
and retrieval. DS 137

1" side margins
The simplified block format is especially useful when the name or 150
title of the receiver of the letter is unknown. For example, a 163
person writing for hotel reservations likely would not know the 176
name of the reservation clerk. With simplified block style, the 189
letter can be addressed to the hotel, and the subject line should 202
indicate that the letter is a request for reservations. 214

In some simplified letter styles, the subject line is preceded 226
and followed by a triple space. Please note that a double 238
space precedes and follows the subject line in this letter. We 251
have eliminated the use of triple spacing in document formats to 264
simplify the processing of documents. As you will note, the sim- 277
plified block letter format is one of the recommended formats in 290
the enclosed Image Makers Format Guide. QS 298

Sender's name Patrick R. Ray 301
Communication Consultant DS 306

Reference initials xx 306
DS

Enclosure notation Enclosure 308

> **Note:** If an enclosure is mentioned in the body of a letter, include an enclosure notation—without being instructed to do so. Also, add your reference initials without being instructed to do so.

88 Skill Building

Skill-Building Warmup

88a 5'

alphabet	1	Jeff made Buzzy walk six hours to visit a quaint shopping center.
fig/sym	2	I paid $51.79 to ship the large executive desk (86" x 42" x 30").
one hand	3	Barbara, as you are aware, gave Jim Millin a bad grade on a test.
fluency	4	Pamela's goal is to bid for the ancient oak chapel on the island.

1	2	3	4	5	6	7	8	9	10	11	12	13

88b 5'

SKILL BUILDING

Build straight-copy skill

1 Key two 1' writings at your top rate.

2 Key a 1' writing at your "control" rate.

A all letters

Most men and women in executive positions accept travel as a part of corporate life. At the same time, executives try to keep time spent on the road to a minimum. Top management usually supports the efforts to reduce travel time as long as effectiveness is not jeopardized. One of the reasons for support is that it is quite expensive for executives to travel. Other reasons are that traveling can be tiring and frequently causes stress.

88c 15'

SKILL BUILDING

Build/measure statistical copy skill

1 Key two 1' writings on each ¶ at your top rate.

2 Key two 3' writings at your "control" rate.

3 Proofread; circle errors; determine *gwam*.

all letters

gwam	1'	3'	
Even though investments in real estate do not have the same	12	4	54
tax advantage that they had some years ago, they still can be	24	8	58
sound investments. An example would be a 12-unit apartment	36	12	63
building that costs $485,625. Assume that $450,000 was financed	49	16	67
at 9.75% interest. Amortized over 30 years, the debt service	62	21	71
would be $3,865. Other outlays would be about $1,235 for a	74	25	75
combined monthly outlay of $5,065.	81	27	77
If the 12 units rented for $475 per month each or a total	12	31	81
rent of $5,700, the apartments would have a positive cash flow at	25	35	86
just 90% occupancy. The apartments would appreciate quickly, and	38	40	90
the initial outlay of $35,625 would be worth a great deal plus	51	44	94
the tax benefits. Of course, the risks must be considered	62	48	98
carefully before you invest your money.	70	50	101

gwam 1'	1	2	3	4	5	6	7	8	9	10	11	12	13
3'	1		2			3			4		5		

80 Simplified Block Format

Skill-Building Warmup

80a 5'

alphabet 1 Jim Winnifred, the proud quarterback, got criticized excessively.
fig/sym 2 Pat paid $85.90 each ($171.80) for 2 tickets in Row #34 on May 6.
double letters 3 Will the committee have access to all the books at noon tomorrow?
fluency 4 Jake, their neighbor, paid for the right to fish on the big dock.

| 1 | 2 | 3 | 4 | 5 | 6 | 7 | 8 | 9 | 10 | 11 | 12 | 13 |

80b 10'

SKILL BUILDING

Improve skill transfer

1 Take a 1' writing on line 5.
2 Take two 1' writings on each of the remaining lines. Try to match or exceed your *gwam* on line 5.

5 All of your customers expect and deserve good, courteous service.
6 Providing quality service helps to ensure a strong customer base.
7 The 9,430 calls on June 1 broke the July 1 record of 8,765 calls.
8 ~~Keeping~~ Retaining good customers is ~~cheaper~~ less expensive than finding ~~all~~ new ~~customers~~ ones.

| 1 | 2 | 3 | 4 | 5 | 6 | 7 | 8 | 9 | 10 | 11 | 12 | 13 |

80c 35'

FORMATTING

Format simplified block letters

Document 1 (LM p. S21)
1 Read the letter on page 194.
2 Key the (long) letter in simplified block format.
3 Proofread and make needed corrections.
4 Address an envelope.

Document 2 (LM p. S23)
1 Key the average-length letter at the right in simplified block format.
2 Proofread; correct errors.
3 Address an envelope.

Document 3 (plain sheet)
1 Take a 5' writing on the letter on page 194.
2 Proofread; circle errors.
3 Determine *gwam* by dividing total words keyed by 5.

words

Current date / Mr. Dale Ott / Ott and Associates / 9
P.O. Box 6891 / Irmo, SC 29063-6891 / Scanner 18
Recommendations 21

(¶1) Your assessment, Mr. Ott, is right on target. 30
The payback period for a scanner would be about 40
six months. We are pleased to provide you with 49
our recommendations. 53
(¶2) Your test generation software handles both 62
text and graphics; therefore, an intelligent OCR 72
should be purchased. The enclosed analysis 81
provides specifications, price information, and 91
our recommendations for both the scanner and 100
the software. Please call us if you have any 109
questions about the analysis or our recom- 117
mendations. 120

Saeed Sharma / Technical Manager / xx / bc Lisa Webb, 129
Account Manager 132

88d 10'

COMMUNICATION

Build composing/editing skills

1 Format using 1.5" top margin; DS; 1" side margins.

2 Compose a 4- or 5-sentence ¶ to supplement the copy presented.

3 Proofread; mark the 5 errors in the copy shown and any errors in copy you composed.

4 Edit the ¶, correcting errors in copy and adding the title **COMMUNICATING WITH POWER** centered in all caps and bold. QS below the title.

Leigh West write in her book, <u>Power Communications</u>, that interview decisions are ofen made in less than 5 minutes. She suggests that nonverbal communications are critical in make a good first impression.

During the interview, you can make a good first impression by using the following affective nonverbal communication techniques:

88e 15'

SKILL BUILDING

Build straight-copy skill

1 Key two 3' writings. Strive for a higher *gwam* on the second writing.

2 Key one 5' writing.

  all letters

	gwam 3'	5'	
Telecommuting refers to workers who work at home and trans-	4	2	31
mit the work to the office by electronic means. Telecommuting	8	5	34
has a number of good points. Travel time is saved, and business	12	7	36
attire is not needed. For some workers, this option is a solu-	17	10	39
tion to many complex dilemmas. For example, people with children	21	13	42
or relatives in need of care can also have a job.	24	15	44
Some people who work at home are amazed at how much they	28	17	46
depend upon the social interaction that usually occurs in an	32	19	48
office. In fact, a job that can be performed in isolation may	37	22	51
be quite limited. Supervising an employee in a remote location	41	24	53
also can be a big problem. In other words, not all jobs nor all	45	27	56
workers are good candidates for telecommuting.	48	29	58

gwam 3' | 1 | 2 | 3 | 4 | 5 |
5' | 1 | 2 | 3 |

Documents 1 and 2
(LM pp. S15-S17)
Format the average-length letters using block format.

Note: Use standard 1" side margins for all letters, unless directed otherwise by your instructor.

words

Current date | Attention Ms. Donna Wollett | Keith Computers | 254 Kirk 14
Lane | Troy, MI 48084-7291 | Ladies and Gentlemen 23

The new Keith 486-333P computer arrived today and was configured 36
exactly as we ordered. All of the software was loaded at the factory, 50
and the computer was ready to boot up as you promised. 61

The sales representative who confirmed our order suggested that we 75
substitute the Keith mouse for the one we ordered, and we approved 88
that change. However, we did not approve any change in the communica- 102
tion software. The software that was loaded on the computer is 115
QuickCom software rather than QuickCom Plus which we ordered. 128

Please provide us with QuickCom Plus and the manuals to accompany it. 142
We look forward to receiving this software soon. 152

Sincerely | MCBRIDE ASSOCIATES | Lindsey McBride | Finance Director | xx 165

Current date | Ms. Lindsey McBride | Finance Director | McBride Associates 14
| P.O. Box 4395 | Laurel, MS 39441-4395 | Dear Ms. McBride 27

Your QuickCom Plus software was shipped to you this morning 39
by second-day air service. We are sorry that the incorrect software 52
was installed on your new Keith 486-333P computer. We are 64
pleased, however, that everything else met your specifications. 77

Easy-to-follow instructions for installing the new software over the 91
current software are enclosed. You will also note on your copy of the in- 106
voice that you were billed originally for the QuickCom software. The 120
QuickCom Plus software is $69 more; however, we are pleased to pro- 133
vide it at no extra cost to you. 140

Please let us know if we can be of further service to you. 152

Sincerely | KEITH COMPUTERS | Ms. Donna Wollett | Customer Service 164
Manager | xx | Enclosure | bc Randy Willis, Sales Manager 175

Document 3
(LM p. S19)
Format the short letter in block format.

Current date | Wheat Street Properties | Attention Ms. 15
Tiffany Demars, Manager | 7538 Wheat Street | Columbia, 21
SC 2905-6137 | Ladies and Gentlemen 28

Lee Marcus whom you sent to clean the carpets in our of- 47
fice spill carpet cleaner on a expensive piece of silk that 61
was left table waiting to be framed. The owner indicate 79
to us that he would have the silk refinished or re placed if 91
it could be salvaged 97

We felt that your should be aware of the damage in case 108
your agents does follow through as promise We will keep 120
you informed abuot the situation. 127

Sincerely | TAR SYSTEM | Jay Thompson | President | xx 136

19 Skill/Production Measurement

Learning goals:

1 To measure basic skill on straight copy.

2 To measure skill in producing business documents taught in Level Three.

Formatting guides:

1 Margins: 1" or 65-space line for ¶ writings and documents.

2 SS documents, unless otherwise directed; DS ¶ writings.

3 5-space ¶ indention.

89a 5'

Skill-building warmup

each line 3 times (slowly, faster, slowly); DS between 3-line groups

(Use these directions for all skill-building warmups in Lessons 89 and 90.)

alphabet 1 Vasquez managed to fix a flat tire for Peggy with my broken jack.

fig/sym 2 Order 1,275, 5 1/4" disks (#39C) and 2,800, 3 1/2" disks (#76C1).

double letter 3 Lynne called a committee meeting about the swimming pool terrace.

fluency 4 Leigh Dirkens, a neighbor, may visit the downtown chapel with us.

| 1 | 2 | 3 | 4 | 5 | 6 | 7 | 8 | 9 | 10 | 11 | 12 | 13 |

89b 12'

SKILL BUILDING

Measure straight-copy skill

1 Key one 3' writing. Circle errors; determine *gwam*.

2 Key one 5' writing. Circle errors; determine *gwam*.

A all letters

	gwam 3'	5'	
How are letters and other documents produced in the modern	4	2	52
office? They are prepared in a number of ways. Just a few years	8	5	54
ago, with rare exceptions, a document was composed by a manager	13	8	57
who either wrote it in longhand or dictated it. Then, one of the	17	10	60
office staff typed it in final form. Today, the situation is	21	13	62
quite different. Office staff may compose and produce various	25	15	65
documents, or they may finalize documents that were keyed by	29	18	67
managers. In some cases, managers like to produce some or all of	34	20	70
their documents in final form.	36	22	71
Many people question how this dramatic change in the way	40	24	73
documents are prepared came about. Two factors can be cited as	44	26	76
the major reasons for the change. The primary factor is the	48	29	78
extensive use of computers in offices today. A manager who uses	52	31	81
a computer for a variety of tasks may find it just as simple to	57	34	83
key documents at the computer as it would be to prepare them for	61	37	86
office personnel to produce. The other factor is the increase in	65	39	89
the ratio of office personnel to managers. Today, one secretary	70	42	91
is very likely to support as many as six or eight managers.	74	44	94
Managers who share office staff find that they get much quicker	78	47	96
results by finalizing their own documents when they compose them.	82	49	99

gwam 3' | 1 | 2 | 3 | 4 | 5 |

5' | 1 | 2 | 3 |

79 Attention Line; Company Name

Skill-Building Warmup

79a 5'

alphabet	1	Zack Javis quietly left the big X-ray room and went to play golf.
figure	2	The shelter fed 64 men, 59 women, and 78 children at 12:30 today.
adjacent reach	3	Wendy Depuy was pointing to a new polo field where we were going.
fluency	4	Diana, a neighbor, may tutor the girl if the usual tutor is sick.

| 1 | 2 | 3 | 4 | 5 | 6 | 7 | 8 | 9 | 10 | 11 | 12 | 13 |

79b 10'

SKILL BUILDING

Improve keyboarding technique

each set of lines 3 times; DS between 9-line groups; work at a controlled rate

balanced hand

5 pair slam their cork pay men cut burn turn jam worn lent pan slap
6 Diana may pay for the bush the men cut down if they fix the sign.
7 Elana and a neighbor may go to the island to cut the bush for us.

one hand

8 were plum freeze junk crave hunk zebra lump grave loop trace milk
9 Kim Pummo saw my bad grades; we agreed I deserved a better grade.
10 Johnny badgered my mom after I faced a great defeat in my career.

combination

11 zebra polo their clay goals slap traces link face mane plum tight
12 Fred fears the high tax rate may decrease the profit of the firm.
13 Dave may sit on the raft and read a book; we may go to dig clams.

| 1 | 2 | 3 | 4 | 5 | 6 | 7 | 8 | 9 | 10 | 11 | 12 | 13 |

79c 35'

FORMATTING

Letters with special features

Read the information at the right; then study the illustrations before formatting the letters on page 192.

Attention line

The attention line directs a letter to a specific person or position within the company to which the letter is addressed. Key the attention line as the first line of the letter address. Disregard the attention line when supplying a salutation. The letter is for the organization, not exclusively for the person or position named in the attention line.

Company name

The company name, an optional letter part, is keyed in ALL CAPS a double space below the complimentary close; a quadruple space separates the company name and keyed signature. Some companies use the company name when a letter is in the nature of a contract or when plain paper, rather than letterhead, is used.

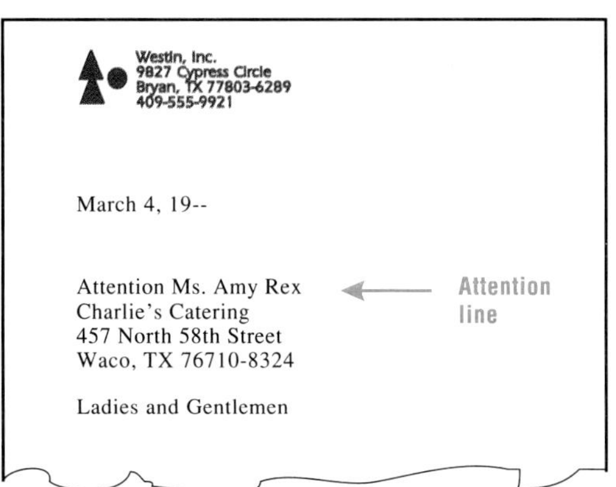

Westin, Inc.
9827 Cypress Circle
Bryan, TX 77803-6289
409-555-9921

March 4, 19--

Attention Ms. Amy Rex ← Attention line
Charlie's Catering
457 North 58th Street
Waco, TX 76710-8324

Ladies and Gentlemen

Attention line

Please call us if we can be of further service. We look forward to working with you.

Sincerely
DS
WESTIN, INC. ← Company name
QS
Ms. Ellen Turnquist
General Manager

rt

Enclosure

Company name

89c 33'

FORMATTING

Measure production

Time schedule

Assemble materials . . . . 3'
Timed production . . . . . 25'
Final check;
compute *n-pram* . . . . 5'

1 Organize your supplies (plain sheets).

2 When directed to begin, key each document. Proofread; correct errors. Work for 25'.

3 Proofread carefully; correct errors; compute *n-pram*; (total words keyed minus penalty) ÷ 25'.

Document 1
Simplified memo

words

May 28, 19-- | School Reform Task Force | BUSINESS LEADER SURVEY 12

The first phase of the survey of leaders in the business community is 26
nearing completion. All of the returns have been tabulated, and the 40
preliminary analysis has been conducted according to the procedures 53
agreed upon by the task force. A copy of the preliminary report is 67
enclosed for your review. 72

The task force needs to meet with our consultants to complete the 86
analysis and make recommendations to the board of education. The 99
meeting has been scheduled for June 14, at 2:30 p.m., in the board 112
room. Please call us and let us know whether you will be able to 125
attend the meeting. 129

Please let us know if you have any questions about the preliminary 143
report. We look forward to seeing you at the task force meeting. 156

Susan T. Miller | Superintendent | xx | Enclosure 165

Document 2
Simplified memo

June 16, 19-- | School Reform Task Force | BOARD RECOMMENDATIONS 12

Our staff finalized the report that we agreed to send to the board 26
of education. A draft copy is enclosed for your review. Please mark 39
any correction that you feel should be made and return the draft to 53
us within three days. 58

The report must be delivered to each board member no later than 70
Friday in order to be placed on the agenda of the next board of 83
education meeting. If we do not hear from you within three days, we 97
will assume that you approved the draft as submitted. 108

James J. Leonard | Assistant Superintendent | xx | Enclosure 119

Document 3
Standard memo report

Note: Three side headings are included in the report.

TO: Career Education Teachers | **FROM:** William Causby, Career 12
Education Coordinator | **DATE:** June 18, 19-- | **SUBJECT:** Report 23
on Proposed Curricula for the Technologies 32

The task force approved all core competencies and is now ready to 45
address the skills applications. The task force agreed that all career 60
education instruction should be organized under three umbrella programs. 74

<u>Information Technologies</u> | The business educators proposed a 91
foundation course based on competencies relating to work ethics and 104
information systems. This course would be a prerequisite for all 118
work in this area. 122

<u>Physical Technologies</u> | The educators representing the physical 138
technologies proposed three options without a required foundation course. 153
The task force recommends that the foundation course proposed by the 167
business educators be considered as a foundation course for this area. 181

<u>Biotechnologies</u> | The educators representing the biotechnologies 197
proposed only a health-care option initially. Other options would be 211
explored after the analysis of community jobs has been completed. 224
The task force recommends that the information technologies foundation 238
course be considered for this area as well. | xx 248

78c 10'

SKILL BUILDING

Improve keyboarding techniques

each set of lines 3 times; DS between 9-line groups; work at a controlled rate

1/2 fingers

5 run try tin find very three fun dumb cut kick jet much brunt gone
6 Can Rhett or Jim get a free pack of the best hot dogs every week?
7 Fredie hurt a knee by jumping over a barrel on the ice and cried.

3/4 fingers

8 quiz saw polo tax walk quizzes lap laws sap paws explain zeal zoo
9 We saw Maxwell quickly swim past Pablo and Polly at the zoo pool.
10 Maxine's quilt was in a show at the Dallas Plaza and won a prize.

all fingers

11 quip were mend travel zone fresh play grab taxes them jail jacket
12 Jewel packed big quilt boxes carefully and drove them to Zone 50.
13 Jack and Maxwell quibble with zeal about several types of things.

78d 25'

SKILL BUILDING

Build straight-copy skill

1 Key three 1' writings on each ¶ to explore higher speeds.

2 Key two 5' writings at a controlled rate.

3 Proofread; circle errors; determine *gwam.*

  **all letters** *gwam* 5'

Today, knowing why and how data is transmitted electroni- 2 40
cally is essential. Information can be sent through the mail 5 43
services, but it may take days to reach its destination. Data 7 45
sent electronically arrives in a few minutes rather than a few 10 48
days and does not have to be converted to paper. Data sent by 12 50
mail must be produced as hard copy; that is, printed on paper. 15 53
Analyze if speed is crucial and if so, remember that electronic 17 55
communication is the quickest way to transmit documents. 20 58

Learning how data is sent is more difficult than learning 22 60
why data is sent electronically. Three things are needed to send 25 62
data from one point to another. Both the sending and receiving 27 65
units or terminals must have software that supports data com- 30 67
munications; each unit requires a modem to convert the data so 32 70
that it can be sent over telephone lines; and a communication 35 72
link must exist. The link may be a cable, a satellite, or just 37 75
a telephone line. 38 76

gwam 5' | 1 | 2 | 3 |

90 Letter Measurment

Skill-Building Warmup

90a 5'

alphabet 1	Jack maximized his lead over us before I quit playing water polo.
figure 2	I baked 973 cookies, 48 cakes, 60 cream pies, and 125 fruit bars.
space bar 3	If we can get the car, we may try to go to the big lake with Lee.
fluency 4	They may fish at the dock and then go to the land of enchantment.

1	2	3	4	5	6	7	8	9	10	11	12	13

90b 12'

SKILL BUILDING

Measure straight-copy skill

1 Key one 3' writing. Circle errors; determine *gwam*.

2 Key one 5' writing. Circle errors; determine *gwam*.

A all letters

	gwam 3'	5'	
Who needs to understand and be able to use information	4	2	57
systems today? The obvious answer is that most office work is	8	5	59
quite dependent on access to information; thus, anyone who ex-	12	7	62
pects to work in an office definitely needs to understand and to	16	10	64
be able to use information systems. However, office staff are	21	12	67
just one of many groups of workers whose jobs are very dependent	25	15	69
on information systems. In fact, if you analyze the jobs of	29	17	72
blue-collar workers, you will find that many of the jobs require	33	20	74
quick access to information. Computer systems are often used to	38	23	77
manage and control access to the information used in blue-collar	42	25	80
jobs.	42	25	80
One outstanding example of a blue-collar worker who is now	46	28	82
required to use information in a database is a mechanic who has	50	30	85
the responsibility of repairing cars that have computers. The	55	33	87
diagnostic work on most of the later model automobiles is handled	59	35	90
by computers. The mechanic who has to fix one of these auto-	63	38	92
mobiles must first check the computer on board the automobile to	67	40	95
determine the cause of the problem and then check an on-line data-	72	43	98
base to find out how to repair the problem. The manufacturers	76	46	100
now store the technical manuals for new automobiles in a database	80	48	103
because of frequent changes that are required. Making changes in	85	51	105
a manual that is in print is more difficult than making changes	89	53	108
in one that is on-line.	91	54	109

gwam 3'	1	2	3	4	5
5'	1	2	3		

Learning goals:
1 To improve keyboarding techniques.
2 To learn/review letter formats.

Formatting guides:
1 Margins: 1" or 65-space line for drills and ¶ writings.
2 Use standard 1" side margins and open punctuation unless directed otherwise for letters.
3 Single-space drills; double-space writings.

78a 5'

Skill-building warmup

each line 3 times (slowly, faster, slowly); DS between 3-line groups; repeat selected lines if time permits
(Use these directions for all skill-building warmups.)

alphabet 1 Chris Zweig quickly examined the job analysis forms we developed.
fig/sym 2 The trip cost $545.68 (1,859 miles at $.22 + $136.70 for a room).
double letter 3 Ann called a committee meeting at noon to discuss several issues.
fluency 4 Claudia and my neighbor got fishbowls by the docks on the island.
| 1 | 2 | 3 | 4 | 5 | 6 | 7 | 8 | 9 | 10 | 11 | 12 | 13 |

78b 10'

COMMUNICATION

Improve composition skills

1 Use 1.5" top margin; DS; center and bold title.
2 Use hanging indent for enumerated items.
3 Proofread; correct the 9 errors in the copy and complete the two ¶s that have been started.
4 Proofread your work.

IMPROVING DOCUMENT PRODUCTIVITY

My plan for improve my productivite in producting documents is to focus on time managment and on work organization. If I can improve both of this factors, my overall productivite will be significant higher.

Time management is important because, at my current rate, each second represents an additional word of the document. I can manage my time better when I am producing documents by doing the following:

1. *(Add three or four numbered items to complete the previous sentence.)*

Work organisation is important in producing documents because organization not only saves time but also lets me focus attention on accurate work. I can improve my work organisation by doing the following:

1. *(Add three or four numbered items to complete the previous sentence.)*

90c 33'

FORMATTING

Measure production

Time schedule

Assemble materials . . . 3'
Timed production . . . . 25'
Final check;
compute *n-pram* . . . 5'

1 Organize your supplies.
2 When directed to begin, work for 25'.
3 Format and key each document.
4 Address an envelope for each letter. Proofread carefully; correct errors; compute *n-pram* (total words keyed – penalty) ÷ 25'.

Document 1
Block letter
(average length)
(LM p. S73)

words

July 8, 19-- | FACSIMILE | Dr. Lynn Appleby, Director | Institute for Educational Leadership | 1540 Mahan Avenue | Richland, WA 99352-5875 | Re: Contract No. PSCR4592 | Dear Dr. Appleby 13 26 35

Considerable progress has been made since you worked with us in finalizing the report that was submitted to the board of education. The members of the board reviewed all of the concepts that were proposed by the task force and approved all of them in principle. As you will note on the enclosed letter, several items need clarification in our next report to the board. 47 61 76 90 105 109

The curriculum changes that you suggested have been approved by the teachers. All of the material will be sent to you within a day or two so that your staff can finalize the course catalog. Please send us camera-copy at least three days prior to the next meeting so that the material will be available for all participants. 121 136 150 164 174

The next task force meeting is scheduled for July 26. This date is one of the two dates that you tentatively reserved for us. Jim Leonard will handle all of your travel arrangements. 189 202 212

Sincerely | CIMARRON SCHOOLS | Susan T. Miller, Ph.D. | Superintendent | xx | Enclosure | c James Leonard 224 230

Document 2
Simplified letter with variable information
(LM p. S75)
Insert the variable information from the work request in this short letter.
(Total words 182)

WORK REQUEST

Form Letters with Variable Information

Date: *July 9*

Address: *Ms. Anita Bennett*
Vail View High School
P.O. Box 6739
Sitka, AK 99835-6739

V1: *assessment*

V2: *afternoon*

V3: *July 14, 16, or 18*

Signature: *James Leonard*

Title: *Assistant Superintendent*

Copies to: *Dr. Lynn Appleby*
Dr. Susan Miller

ASSIGNMENTS FOR TASK FORCE MEETING

The next task force meeting is scheduled for July 26. The meeting will focus on scheduling alternatives, instructional strategies, and assessment. Your group will be responsible for the (V1) component of the meeting.

Each group is being asked to schedule a planning session at least one week prior to the task force meeting. I hope to be able to participate in each planning session. I have tentatively reserved the (V2) of (V3) for your group. Please let me know if any of these dates are acceptable.

Dr. Appleby has sent us the preliminary material that should be reviewed at the planning session. Please call my office and indicate the date you prefer for the meeting.

Drill 4
Improve word usage skills

1 Key the ¶ DS, selecting the correct word from the choices given in parentheses.
2 Proofread; correct errors or rekey the ¶.

Before she went to the meeting of the County (Council/Counsel), the (principle/principal) asked for our (advice/advise) on the best (cite/site/sight) for the new school. The (principal/principle) reason she (excepted/accepted) our (advice/advise) was that I (cited/sited/sighted) evidence documenting the support of the key constituent groups.

Drill 5
Improve word usage skills

1 Key the ¶, correcting errors as you key.
2 Proofread carefully; correct errors or rekey the ¶.

Joe earned $50 for the work he done on Saturday. He hoped to work near every Saturday so he could saves enough money to pay for his tuition. He certain were ambitious to work while his friends was playing football. There parent's payed for there tuition.

Drill 6
Improve word usage skills

Key the two ¶s, correcing errors as you key. Proofread using proofreaders' marks to indicate any errrors. Correct errors or rekey the ¶s.

Powerfull work processing softwear makes editting a document easy. If the document is in hard copy, read the document first and use proofreader's marks to indicate all corrections to be make. Then make the edits bye inserting, deleting, or replacing all text that needds to be corrected. If the document is on-line, use spelling an grammar verification software to locate erros. However, You must still proofread the document.

First impressions does count, and you never get a second chance to made a good first impresion. This statement applys too both documents and people. The minute you walk in to a room you are judged by you appearance, your facial expressions, and the way you present your self. As soon asa document is opened, it is judged by it's appearence and the way it is presented. First impressions are ofen lasting impressions; theerefore, you should strive to make s positive firxt impression for yourself and for the documents your prepare. Learn to manage your image and the image of you documents bye starting with a good first impression.

Document 3
Two-page block letter
(LM p. S77)
add an appropriate second-page heading

words

July 15, 19-- | OVERNIGHT MAIL | Dr. Susan T. Miller | Superinten- 12
dent | Cimarron Schools | P.O. Box 8547 | Sitka, AK 99835-8547 | 23
Dear Dr. Miller 27

Thank you for confirming the task force meeting on July 26. The 40
camera-ready copy of the course catalog that you requested is en- 53
closed. You may wish to consider putting the material in a loose-leaf 67
binder rather than using a spiral binding as was used on the previ- 80
ous documents. The loose-leaf binder would facilitate updating the 94
material. 96

After our telephone conversation last week, I gave a lot of thought to 110
the assessment component of the new program. The key point 122
that we need to emphasize to the members of the task force and to 135
all of the educators participating in the meeting is that the curricula 150
must drive the assessment component rather than having the 161
assessment dictate curricula. The primary reason for moving to 174
outcome-based curricula is to avoid having assessment as the 187
ultimate goal with instruction being designed simply to ensure that 201
students pass the tests. 205

I am enclosing a draft of a plan that emphasizes assessment as a 218
developmental tool that will enable teachers to be sure that their 232
students are making satisfactory progress toward achieving the 244
outcomes that are being mandated by your board of education. 257
Self-assessment is a key part of any assessment program that focuses 271
on development. 274

Developmental assessment works best when a computer delivery 286
system is utilized effectively. Good computer-based assessment 299
software is difficult to find. The best software that I have been able 313
to locate is produced by a firm in Columbia, South Carolina. The 327
system automates all three phases of assessment: item banking and 340
test creation, test administration, and test scoring and reporting. 354

The developers have worked with me to implement effective assess- 367
ment in several projects. You may want to consider having them 379
work with us on this project. Information about both the software 393
and the developers is enclosed. Please let me know if you would 406
like me to contact them. 411

Please call me after you have had an opportunity to review all of 424
the materials. I look forward to hearing from you. 435

Sincerely | INSTITUTE FOR EDUCATIONAL LEADERSHIP | Lynn Appleby, 447
Ph.D. | Director | xx | Enclosures | The draft of the staff develop- 459
ment plan is almost complete. I will bring it with me to the meeting 473
on July 26. 475

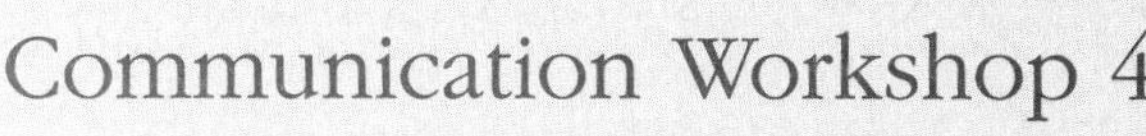

Communication Workshop 4

MicroAssistant: To select Communication Workshop 4, key **C4** from the Main menu.

Margins: 1" or 65-space line

Drill 1
Improve grammar skills

1 Correct all grammar errors.
2 Proofread; correct errors.

1 Their new office located on the corner of Devine and Main Street.
2 Did Clifford handles registration for the meeting all by hisself?
3 Its important to she to sell that house for more than it's value.
4 I hire Ann because they always do their work very quick and neat.
5 We divide the lunch between the six of us it were very delicious.
6 With who do you plans to go to the next championship soccer game?
7 The trainer past out manuals to each participants in the seminar.
8 Rob told Mary that he be going to the game on Saturday afternoon.
9 She always make nasty remarks about the people with who she work.
10 Manager should make sure that their employees are payed fairly.

Drill 2
Improve punctuation skills

1 Correct all punctuation errors.
2 Proofread; correct errors.

11 Pat went to Atlanta Georgia he bought a suit shirts tie and shoes
12 Betsy Arntson treasurer took minutes for Betsy Matthews secretary
13 The convention in Dallas Texas begins I think on Friday October 9
14 Christopher Jeansonne the well-known golf pro lives in Amana Iowa
15 Margaret will of course ask him about his famous hole-in-one shot
16 If it rains on Saturday the game will be played we will stay home
17 Josephs new job is very challenging but it requires a lot of work
18 Professors who teach computer applications effectively are needed
19 I know what I want to eat but Alan has not decided what he wants
20 Steve coaches Lisa Joe and Lynn but Mark coaches Jeff Sue and Tom

Drill 3
Improve number usage skills

1 Correct all errors in number usage.
2 Proofread; correct errors.

21 Eric and Kate bought 6 notebooks. Each notebook holds 350 pages.
22 200 people plan to attend the technology conference on March 6th.
23 Justiz will arrive either at 8 o'clock or at 11 o'clock tomorrow.
24 The college had a ten % budget cut that amounted to $375,396.
25 Caroline paid fifty dollars for 8 tickets on the 14 of September.
26 Technology of the 60's is quite different than that of the 1990s.
27 The meeting is scheduled to begin at seven p.m. and last 3 hours.
28 The chef prepared dinner for 38 women, 27 men, and eight children.
29 His office is located at 3856 Avery Boulevard, Suite one hundred.
30 30 people paid $15.00 each for a 2-pound lobster at the dock today.

Level Four
Formatting Reports, Tables, and Administrative Documents

OBJECTIVES

KEYBOARDING SKILLS

To key approximately 55 wam with good accuracy.

FORMATTING SKILLS

To format business reports, tables, forms, and administrative documents efficiently.

COMMUNICATION SKILLS

To produce error-free documents and apply language arts skills.

Document 2
Standard memo with table

Center, bold, and underscore column heads of the table.

words

TO: All Employees | **FROM:** Alexis Ierardo, Personnel Manager | **DATE:** 13
November 14, 19-- | **SUBJECT:** Holidays Announced 22

The Senior Management Committee met last week to review the 34
new holiday schedule recommended by the Employee Involvement 46
Council. Two of the three new holidays requested were approved. Twelve 61
holidays will be provided to employees next year: 71

<u>Holiday</u>	**<u>Dates</u>**	76
New Year's Day	January 1 and 2	83
Spring Holiday	April 6	87
Memorial Day	May 30	91
Independence Day	July 4	96
Labor Day	September 7	100
Thanksgiving Day	November 23 and 24	108
Winter Holidays	December 25 and 26	115
Floating days (2)	Selected by employee	122

Substitution of holidays for religious or other purposes must be 135
approved by your immediate supervisor and the Personnel Office. 148

xx 149

Document 3 Simplified Memo

words

December 3, 19-- | Cary Cohen | EVALUA- 7
TION OF PROPERTY FOR APARTMENT 13
PROJECT 15

The evaluation of the building site for the 24
proposed apartment complex has been 32
completed. The contractor reported that the 41
property is suitable for building a small apart- 50
ment complex. The land requires little prepa- 59
ration for building. 64

<u>Zoning</u> 66

The property is zoned RG-2, which is a high- 75
density general residential zoning. The lot is 85
100 feet by 300 feet and qualifies for a maxi- 94
mum of 11 rental units. 99

<u>Configuration</u> 104

A combination of two-story garden apartments 113
and townhouse units is ideal. Three build- 122
ings fit well on the lot. Adequate parking is 131
available for 25 automobiles. 137

<u>Conclusion</u> 142

All concerns have been settled. The contin- 150
gencies on the contract are not needed. 158

Dawn Roxborough | xx 162

Document 4 Simplified Memo

words

Current date 3

Shannon Murphy 6

WOMEN HELPING WOMEN SEMINAR 11

Thank you for your interest in the Commu- 19
nity Support Agency, Women Helping 26
Women. A representative will talk with us 35
next Thursday about the agency's services 43
and provide information on volunteer in- 51
volvement. 54

Bring your lunch and join us to learn more 62
about this worthwhile community organization. 72

WHEN: *Thursday, March 2* 77
TIME: *Noon - 1 p.m.* 81
WHERE: *Special Events Dining Room* 87

Chris Brown 90

xx 90

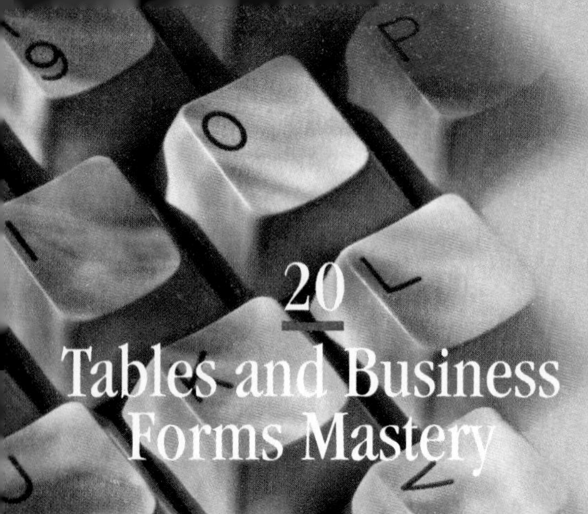

20 Tables and Business Forms Mastery

Learning goals:
1 To improve keyboarding skill.
2 To learn to format tables and forms.

Formatting guides:
1 Margins: 1" or 65-space line for drills and ¶ writings.
2 Single-space drills; double-space writings; SS documents unless otherwise directed.
3 Indentions: 5-spaces or default tabs for ¶ writings.

91a 5'

Skill-building warmup

each line 3 times (slowly, faster, slowly); DS between 3-line groups; repeat selected lines if time permits

(Use these directions for all skill-building warmups in Lessons 91-98.)

alphabet 1 David quickly won six big money prizes as the jockey of the year.
fig/sym 2 Please bill me for the supplies ($2,871.50) and fees ($1,394.65).
double letter 3 Lynn will call Tommy before the committee meets tomorrow at noon.
fluency 4 Pamela may be the auditor for the endowment of the island chapel.

| 1 | 2 | 3 | 4 | 5 | 6 | 7 | 8 | 9 | 10 | 11 | 12 | 13 |

91b 8'

SKILL BUILDING

Build straight-copy skill

1 Key two 1' writings at your top rate.
2 Key one 3' writing at your "control" rate.

 all letters

	gwam 1'	3'	
The technology used in offices today requires employees to	12	4	58
be flexible and to be willing to learn new ways to accomplish the	25	8	62
work that they do. Too often workers try to adapt the new tech-	38	13	66
nology to the old procedures rather than modify the way they do		17	70
work to maximize the advantages of the technology. Although most	64	21	75
people think they can adapt to change very easily, the truth is	77	25	79
that change is very frustrating for most people. The majority of	90	30	83
the changes in offices caused by technology are difficult to make	103	34	88
because many things have to change at the same time. A change in	116	39	92
hardware or software requires changes in the way work is done as	129	43	97
well as learning to use the new software or hardware. These	141	47	101
changes might be easier to implement if they could be made gradu-	154	51	105
ally rather than simultaneously.	161	54	107

gwam 1' | 1 | 2 | 3 | 4 | 5 | 6 | 7 | 8 | 9 | 10 | 11 | 12 | 13 |
3' | 1 | 2 | 3 | 4 | 5 |

77 Measurement

Skill-Building Warmup

77a 5'

alphabet	1	Jack won five or six pan pizzas after the racquetball game today.
fig/sym	2	My $5,406 of stock (102 shares at $53/share) is now worth $7,489.
adjacent reach	3	Klaus and Opal were going to try hard to prepare the guide today.
fluency	4	Alan, a neighbor, may fix a clam or lamb dish for us at the lake.

1 | 2 | 3 | 4 | 5 | 6 | 7 | 8 | 9 | 10 | 11 | 12 | 13

77b 12'

SKILL BUILDING

Measure straight-copy skill

1 Key one 3' writing.
2 Key one 5' writing.

A all letters

	gwam 3'	5'	
An important goal of most companies is to create stakeholder	4	2	42
value. Who are the stakeholders, and what is meant by this new	8	5	45
concept? A stakeholder is one who has a stake or claim in the	13	8	47
success of a company. A stakeholder might be a customer, a cli-	17	10	50
ent, an investor, an employee, or perhaps the community in which	21	13	52
the firm is located. Value is created by increasing the return	25	15	55
on the investment of each stakeholder.	28	17	57
A person who invests money expects a good return on equity.	32	19	59
A person who invests time and effort expects a rewarding job and	36	22	62
fair wages. A customer or client who buys products or services	41	24	64
expects high quality, good service, and fair prices. A community	45	27	67
wants a good corporate citizen. The needs of one group of stake-	49	30	69
holders may conflict with the needs of one of the other groups.	54	32	72
For example, can workers be paid higher wages without affecting	58	35	75
the prices customers will have to pay? The groups must be will-	62	37	77
ing to accept trade-offs in order for everyone to be winners.	66	40	80

gwam 3' | 1 | 2 | 3 | 4 | 5
5' | 1 | 2 | 3

77c 33'

FORMATTING

Measure production: memos

Time schedule

Assemble materials .... 3'
Timed production .... 25'
Final check;
compute *n-pram* .... 5'

Proofread carefully; correct errors; compute *n-pram*: (total words keyed - penalty ÷ 25').

Document 1 Standard memo

	words
TO: All Employees | **FROM:** Anita Suko | **DATE:** January 26, 19-- |	12
SUBJECT: Building Security	17
Effective today, a new security system has been installed. The	30
system protects you, as well as the company's property.	41
The security procedures for the regular working day that have been	55
in effect for the past two years remain the same. Please adhere to	68
the attached procedures for night security.	77
xx | Attachment	80

91c 7'

SKILL BUILDING

Tabs

1 SS body; 8 spaces between columns.

2 Set tabs to align Columns 2 and 3 at the right.

3 Set tabs to align Columns 4 and 5 at the decimal point.

System	MHz	MB	Floppy	Quote 4/6	words
					11
386SX	16	40	5.25	$ 999.95	17
386SX	25	80	5.25	1,495.99	22
386DX	33	120	3.5	1,695.99	25
486DX	33	200	3.5	2,295.99	30
486DX2	50	230	3.5	2,899.95	36

91d 10'

FORMATTING

Preapplication drill: leaders

Read the information at the right and complete the drill.

1 Use default or 1" margins; DS.

2 Key the second column to end flush right.

Electronic typewriters: Use the right flush function; then key Number.

Electric typewriters: Backspace from right margin six times; key **Number**.

3 Insert leaders.

wp **Flush right:** Text aligns against the right margin.

Leaders

Leaders (periods alternated with spaces) are used to improve the readability of tabulated documents. The dots serve to **lead** the eye to the appropriate row in the next column. Some electronic typewriters and word processing software insert leaders automatically when a leader tab is set.

Keying leaders

1 Space once after the first item in Column 1. Alternate periods and spaces to a point 2 or 3 spaces short of the next column.

2 Note on the line-of-writing scale whether the first period was keyed on an odd or even number. Begin periods on all subsequent lines accordingly.

Player and Position	Number
Nathaniel Hartwell--Small Forward	20
Cedric McCoy--Power Forward	24
Robert Marschink--Center	18
Joseph Manning--Point Guard	14
Barry English--Shooting Guard	30

91e 20'

FORMATTING

Documents with leaders

Document 1
Table of contents

Format the Table of Contents on page 226 as though it were part of a leftbound report.

Document 2
Standard memo

1 Format memo, positioning the table flush with left and right margins; insert leaders.

2 DS above and below table.

Document 2

words

TO: Marc L. Howard | **FROM:** Judith R. Baysmith | **DATE:** Current | **SUB-** 12
JECT: Reprints of Training Manuals 19

Our supply of training manuals is low. Please reprint the following manuals 35
in the quantities indicated. 41

Positive Customer/Client Service	5,000	49
Communicating with Power	300	54
Teamwork--The Key to Productivity and Job Satisfaction	1,875	67
Career Strategies for Women in Management	750	76

We are totally out of the Executive Secretary Program manuals. However, we 91
want to update the manual before it is reprinted. We will get the new copy to 107
you within a few days. 112

xx 112

76d 27'

FORMATTING

Build production skill

Time schedule

Assemble materials .... 3'
Timed production .... 20'
Final check; compute *n-pram* .... 4'

1 Arrange supplies for easy handling. Use plain sheets.

2 As you key, correct errors. Proofread documents as they are completed and make needed corrections.

3 Compute net production rate a minute (*n-pram*). (Total words keyed - penalty ÷ 20'.) Penalty = 15 words for each uncorrected error.

Document 1 Simplified Memo

words

Current date | All Employees | OFFICE AUTOMATION INSTALLATION 12

All of the office automation equipment was installed last week. The final 27
testing will be completed within the next day or two. Training is scheduled 42
to begin next Monday. Schedules will be posted in each department. 56

The Corporate Communications Department was asked to revise our report 70
format to conform to the default standards of our new equipment. You will 85
receive the new standards shortly. 92

Alicia Roberts | xx 96

Document 2 Standard Memo

TO: All Credit Department Employees | **FROM:** Charles T. Rawls, Credit 13
Manager | **DATE:** Current | **SUBJECT:** Revision of Form Letters 26

All form letters have been reviewed, revised, and approved for general use. 41
You will receive a new copy of the correspondence manual within a few days. 56

Special thanks are due each of you for your help on this important and 70
exciting project. The consultants were most complimentary of the excellent 85
cooperation they received and of the quality of your suggestions for 99
improving the letters. 104

xx 104

Document 3 Standard Memo

TO: All Design Employees **FROM:** Lester Ray **DATE:** Current 11
SUBJECT: Installation of Electronic Publishing System 22

The new electronic publixhing sytem will be installed next week. 36
Each of you will recieve a new workstation with tremendous capa- 48
bilities. All of our froms design work can be done right at you 62
work stations. The system can handle virtual any type of text, 75
structured and freehand graphics, scientific notation, and sev- 87
eral foeign languages.Mor than 25 fonts families are availabe 100
in point sizes ranging from 6-point type to 36-point type. In 113
adddition any form can be printed in landscape or portrait 125
layout on letter-or legal-size paper. Train on the styem si 138
scheduled for thursday or FRiday of next week. Because laerning 151
the wen system is important to everyone, all employees must 163
participate inthe two-day training porgram. 172

Document 4
Simplified memo

Reformat Document 3 as a simplified memo.

1.5" top margin → **TABLE OF CONTENTS**

Flush right

1.5" left margin →

← 1" right margin

iii

Table of contents with leaders

76 Review

Skill-Building Warmup

76a 5'

alphabet 1 Meg explained that Suzy left town quickly to interview for a job.
fig/sym 2 Carolyn bought 34 lobsters (1.5 to 2# @ $7.90 per #) for $486.75.
direct reach 3 Jimmy swerved around a bunch of junk; Cecil broke his left thumb.
fluency 4 A girl cut down a big bush at the end of the lane to hang a sign.

| 1 | 2 | 3 | 4 | 5 | 6 | 7 | 8 | 9 | 10 | 11 | 12 | 13 |

76b 8'

SKILL BUILDING

Improve keyboarding technique

1 Key each set of lines 3 times; DS between 9-line groups.
2 Key one-hand words letter by letter.
3 Key balanced-hand words as units.

one hand

5 pool was junk draft lump zebra look free jump card hunk crave tax
6 Jo, in my opinion, deserves a better grade on a test as a reward.
7 Kim, as you are aware, debated in a few cases after you deferred.

balanced hand

8 duck bush slam ham tuck sick work queue bud pale girl pen six sit
9 Nancy may sue the city for the title to the lake and to the land.
10 Jane may bid for the ancient oak box; it is an authentic antique.

combination

11 flame snap zebra handy land clap slap into inform shall statement
12 They tasted the tea from the cafe and had the fish and crab dish.
13 A mangy dog ran past a cat to jump in my lap and nap by the pool.

| 1 | 2 | 3 | 4 | 5 | 6 | 7 | 8 | 9 | 10 | 11 | 12 | 13 |

76c 10'

SKILL BUILDING

Measure straight-copy skill

1 Key one 3' writing.
2 Key one 5' writing.

A all letters

	gwam 3'	5'	
A new type of software, called an expert system, is cur-	4	2	30
rently available. This unique software is designed to analyze	8	5	32
data and apply decision rules that have been built into the	12	7	35
system. It can then provide answers to questions that normally	16	10	37
would be answered by an expert in a specified field. A large	20	12	40
base of information is stored by the system.	23	14	41
Some people call expert systems artificial intelligence	27	16	44
because the systems can make decisions. It should be noted,	31	19	46
however, that the types of decisions that can be made are very	35	21	49
limited. The system does not think in the way that people think;	40	24	51
it just applies rules that have been given to it. Even so, the	44	26	54
software is very useful.	46	27	55

gwam 3' | 1 | 2 | 3 | 4 | 5 |
5' | 1 | 2 | 3 |

92 Table Review

Skill-Building Warmup

92a 5'

alphabet	1	Zacke was an example of a very quiet but charming and fair judge.
fig/sym	2	Jay paid Invoice #2846 ($3,017.35) and Invoice #7925 ($8,409.16).
adjacent reach	3	Where were Mario, Guy, and Luis going after the water polo class?
fluency	4	Helene may suspend the formal audit if their firm pays a penalty.

92b 8'

SKILL BUILDING

Proofread numbers

1 Clear tabs; set 6 tabs 10 spaces apart or use default tabs; key drill.

2 Proofread your copy carefully. Circle errors.

Note: To proofread numbers, you must compare each digit to the original copy.

29485	58395	32017	31058	84560	48321	21901
75038	05837	20486	28457	01938	13145	07975
27564	02948	62636	19438	02030	37219	13953
18475	22749	94859	10203	54925	18562	73716

92c 7'

SKILL BUILDING

Improve keyboarding technique

each pair of lines 3 times; work at a controlled rate

right hand

5 kill ploy milk junk pin monk my limp joy jump kimono mill holy in
6 mill ply moon hulk imply ink poll link loop lymph mink yolk polio

left hand

7 web garage wax zest zebra treat serve brew test debate decree red
8 rest were draw crave great extra craze excess draft weed rage red

combination

9 Kaye and Freddy received an activity guide prior to leaving home.
10 Wendy and Kris paid dearly to ship the overweight box I received.

92d 30'

Read the material at the right; then format the documents on page 228.

Note: Tables on page 229 are optional.

Table Format Review

Review the general guides for formatting tables and for centering column heads on pages 162-163.

- ✓ Use a plain full sheet for each table.
- ✓ Use standard 1.5" top margin unless directed to center the table vertically.
- ✓ Key the main heading in ALL CAPS.
- ✓ If bold is an option on your equipment, bold the main and secondary headings and the column headings.
- ✓ Underline all column heads.

75b (continued)

Memo reports

Informal business reports are often prepared in memo format, especially reports sent to others within an organization. Reports are informal primarily because of their format rather than their content. Memo reports are often used for reports up to five pages.

Use standard memo format for the heading and body (margins: 1.5" top; 1" side). Should the memo report be a multipage document, include a heading (Reference page 177). Side and paragraph headings are formatted as they are in a report.

words

TO: All Managers 3
FROM: Ginger Bouvain, Training Director 11
DATE: November 6, 19-- 16
SUBJECT: Interactive Videodisk Training Pro- 25
grams 26

A project team has been assembled to assist 35
in the development of interactive videodisk 43
training programs for all divisions of the 52
company. The team consists of an instruc- 60
tional design specialist, a specially trained 70
programmer/analyst, a graphic arts special- 78
ist, a technical writer, and a video production 88
director. 90

A content specialist will work with each 98
project team. The content specialist may 107
be a consultant hired for the project or a 115
representative of the department request- 123
ing the training module. 129

Project Approval 135

A separate proposal is required for each 143
videodisk training module. Each module is 152
divided into 30-minute segments. The maxi- 160
mum training time for each module is six 168
hours. A proposal must be approved by 176
the department head, division manager, and 185
training director. 189

Budget implications. One-half of the cost 201
of developing each training module is shared 210
by the requesting division and the Training 219
and Development Department. The remain- 227
ing cost is covered by the Special Projects 236
Fund. The training director will assist in 244
preparing a cost estimate of each project. 253

Quality control. The initial quality check 265
is made by the project team and the 272
content specialist. An evaluation special- 280
ist reviews the program after it has been 289
pilot tested and refined; only then is the 298
program transferred to a disk. 304

Time Required for Development 316

The time required for each project depends 324
upon the complexity of the project and the 333
length of the training module. An estimate 342
of the time required to prepare a six-hour 350
training module follows: 356

Development Phase	Approximate Time	words
		369
Draft design script	3 to 4 days	376
Review of design script	1 to 2 days	383
Screen display document	1 to 2 days	390
Programming	12 to 15 days	395
Videotaping	10 to 12 days	401
Pilot testing	1 to 3 days	406
Final evaluation	1 to 2 days	412
Transfer to videodisk	10 to 15 days	419

A considerable amount of overlap exists in 427
the time for programming and the time for 436
videotaping. Much of the work can be done 444
concurrently. The time allowed for the trans- 454
fer to videodisk varies with the schedule of 463
the videodisk pressing company used. 470

Documentation 476

Training manuals are prepared to accom- 483
pany each module. A technical writer works 492
with the instructional designer and the con- 501
tent specialist to develop the manuals. 509
Usually, the manuals are developed con- 517
currently with the videodisk. 523

Technology 527

Constant Angular Velocity videodisks are 536
used. Each disk holds a 30-minute seg- 543
ment of video motion or well over a billion 552
bytes of digital information. 558

xx 559

words

Document 1
average-width table; DS; center column headings

EMPLOYEE DIRECTORY 4

Personnel Department 8

Employee Name	Street Address	City/State/ZIP Code	
Pam C. Anderson	5437 Main Street	Columbia, SC 29201	38
Liz C. Massey	8532 Wheat Street	Columbia, SC 29205	50
Alonzo C. Romero	3856 Blossom Street	Columbia, SC 29205	61
Hisako H. Yoko	3845 Saluda Avenue	Columbia, SC 29205	72
Jackie R. Mavis	1356 Woodwind Court	Columbia, SC 29212	83

(Column headings line: 27)

Document 2
wide table; DS; center column headings

CLASS SCHEDULE 3

Class	Teacher	Location	Time	14
Algebra	Dr. Yamaguchi	Lee Hall 232	9:30-10:45 TR	24
English	Dr. Roswell	Humanities 385	12:30-1:45 TR	34
Keyboarding	Dr. Dougherty	Business 487	9:00-9:50 MWF	45
Computer App.	Dr. Kalinowski	Business 245	1:00-1:50 MWF	56

Document 3
wide table; DS; center column headings

TOP SALES PERFORMANCE 4

Central Region 7

Employee Name	Employee I.D.	Hardware Sales	Software Sales	Total Sales	16 / 30
Alexander	R492	$1,295,345	$ 573,208	$1,868,553	39
Courtenay	R856	894,625	735,285	1,629,910	48
Holsonback	C845	451,930	801,583	1,253,513	56
Lowenstein	J396	210,583	1,028,462	1,239,045	65
McPherson	B284	1,364,293	352,693	1,399,556	73

74d

SKILL BUILDING

Timed writing (optional)

Key this writing as a 3' or 5' timing.

all letters

	gwam 3'	5'	
If you wish to advance in your career, you must learn how to	4	2	37
make good decisions. You can develop decision-making skills by	8	5	39
learning to follow six basic steps. The first three steps help	13	8	42
you to see the problem. They are identifying the problem, ana-	17	10	44
lyzing the problem to find causes and consequences, and making	21	13	47
sure you define the goals that your solution must meet.	25	15	49
Now, you are ready to solve the problem with the last three	29	17	52
steps. They include finding alternative solutions to the prob-	33	20	54
lem, analyzing each of the alternatives carefully to locate the	37	22	57
best solution, and putting the best solution into action. Once	41	25	59
you have implemented a plan of action, check to make sure that	46	27	62
it meets all of your objectives. If it does not, then determine	50	30	64
if the problem is with the solution or with the way it is being	54	33	67
implemented. Always keep all options open.	57	34	69

gwam 3' | 1 | 2 | 3 | 4 | 5 |
5' | 1 | 2 | 3 |

75 Memo Report With Table

Skill-Building Warmup

75a 5'

alphabet 1 Patrick Jimenez waxed eloquently about visiting the famous group.
fig/sym 2 Our invoice #R2837 was for $26,514.80 ($25,495 x 4% = $1,019.80).
double letters 3 Lynn will meet me to sell the drill at noon tomorrow at the pool.
fluency 4 I may risk half of the profit we make downtown on the island bid.

1 | 2 | 3 | 4 | 5 | 6 | 7 | 8 | 9 | 10 | 11 | 12 | 13

75b 45'

FORMATTING

Memo reports with table

Read "Memo reports" on page 182. Then key Documents 1 and 2.

Document 1

1 Format the memo report on page 182; insert second- and third-page headings.

2 Bold and underline all headings within the body.

3 Center the table horizontally; DS above and below table; center column heads; SS table.

Document 2

If time permits, reformat Document 1, making the following changes:

1 Remove the table from the report and place it on a separate page with the title: **APPENDIX** centered in bold and all caps; 1.5" top margin.

2 Change the last sentence prior to the table to indicate that the time estimate is in the Appendix. Add enclosure notation.

Note: To maintain a bottom margin of 1" to 2", you may divide a table (about) equally between two pages. If the table in this problem must be divided, for example, the page break should occur after "Programming, 12 to 15 days." Try to avoid dividing a table. Also, always check to see that a heading is not left alone at the bottom of a page.

words

92e
Optional table documents

Document 1
center the average-width table horizontally and vertically; DS; center column heads

			words
DESKTOP PUBLISHING SOFTWARE CONTENTS			7
Ten-Unit License Fee			12
Product Code	**Description**	**License Fee**	26
8650 XMP 20	MasterPak Software Option	$1,280.75	36
8650 XMP 20A	Document editor		42
8650 XMP 20B	Network communications		49
8650 XMP 20C	Font selection (25)		55
8650 XMP 40	MasterPak Software Option	$2,495.99	65
8650 XMP 40A	PC emulation		70
8650 XMP 40B	Data-driven graphics		77
8650 XMP 40C	Spreadsheet/file conversion		85
8650 XMP 60	MasterPak Software Option	$2,795.95	95
8650 XMP 60A	Free-hand drawing		101
8650 XMP 60B	List manager		106
8650 XMP 60C	Data capture		111

Document 2
center the average-width table horizontally and vertically; DS; center column heads

			words
LUDWIG INTERIOR DESIGN AND ARCHITECTURE GROUP			9
Rate Schedule			12
Responsibility Level	Hourly Rate	Daily Rate	29
Principal	$ 75	$ 450	33
Project manager	60	400	38
Certified interior designer	55	325	45
Senior draftsperson	40	285	50
Draftsperson	35	200	54
Technical assistant	25	150	60

Document 3
1 Center the table horizontally; block column heads.
2 DS above and below the table.
3 SS the body of table.
Note: Generally the table has the same spacing as the document.

TO: Jane Greenbaum | **FROM:** Angela Atwater | **DATE:** May 2, 19-- | 12
SUBJECT: Installation of Equipment 19

The workstations have arrived and will be installed in a few days. The 33
tentative schedule for delivery is shown below. 43

Employee	Location	Date	Time	words
				54
R. Judy	Annex 3B	5/8	9:00	59
C. Flores	RC 280	5/8	1:00	65
B. Lott	Annex 3C	5/11	9:00	70
M. Rogers	RC 282	5/11	1:00	75

Please call me immediately if this schedule is not satisfactory. We have very 91
limited flexibility, but we will try to accommodate any changes needed. 106

xx 106

74c 30'

FORMATTING

Standard memos using form paragraphs

(plain sheets)

1 If you are using word processing software or an electronic typewriter with adequate memory, key the seven ¶s at the right. Store each ¶ as a separate file, using the name given at the top of each ¶. If you cannot store the ¶s, go to step 2.

2 Follow the instructions given for Documents 1 and 2 to create two memos using these form ¶s.

L74C-B1

The task force assigned the responsibility for developing form paragraphs to use in key departments of our company plans to work in your department beginning two weeks from today. Please assign two representatives from your department to coordinate the work with us.

L74C-B2

The task force for developing form paragraphs needs to have a large sample of documents that are most commonly used in your department. We would like to review the documents in detail before we schedule an appointment with your staff.

L74C-B3

The task force for developing form paragraphs has completed the first draft of form paragraphs for your area. Please have your staff review the enclosed material and give us feedback on the material using the guidelines that are included with the paragraphs.

L74C-M1

The procedure that the Executive Committee asked us to follow is to collect samples of typical correspondence, meet with departmental representatives to collect additional information, and then to prepare a draft of the form paragraphs for review. After we receive your feedback on the draft copy, we will schedule a meeting to finalize the paragraphs.

L74C-M2

The meeting with your representatives is designed to help us identify situations that have created problems in the past and that need special attention. We also look for solutions that have worked especially well.

L74C-E1

Matthew Redfern has been assigned as the task force coordinator for your department. Please direct all communications about the project to him.

L74C-E2

Madge Pearman has been assigned as the task force coordinator for your department. Please direct all communications about the project to her.

Document 1
Memo from form ¶s
(Total words: 170)

TO: Martin Adamson | **FROM:** Form Paragraph Task Force | **DATE:** Current | **SUBJECT:** Initial Meetings with Task Force

Retrieve or key ¶s L74C-B2, L74C-M1, and L74C-E2 for the body of the memo. Add your reference initials.

Document 2
Memo from form ¶s
(Total words: 203)

TO: Distribution List | **FROM:** Form Paragraph Task Force | **DATE:** Current | **SUBJECT:** Initial Meetings with Task Force

Retrieve or key ¶s L74C-B1, L74C-M1, and L74C-E1 for the body of the memo. Add your reference initials and the distribution list below.

Roberta Layman, Underwriting | Nestor Garcia, Claims | Rosa Romero, Agency Services | Diana Wang, Business Services

93 Tables in Unarranged Format

Skill-Building Warmup

93a 5'

alphabet 1 Jennifer quickly packed a dozen boxes of food and gave them away.
figure 2 Ted bought 240 shares of stock at 89.75 and sold them for 136.25.
direct reach 3 Bryce found a brown bag of junk and dumped much of it on my desk.
fluency 4 Claudia did pay for eight antique bowls and also for six emblems.

| 1 | 2 | 3 | 4 | 5 | 6 | 7 | 8 | 9 | 10 | 11 | 12 | 13 |

93b 15'

SKILL BUILDING

Build/measure straight-copy skill

1 Key two 1' writings on each ¶. Strive to increase your speed on the second writing.
2 Key one 3' writing at your control rate. Proofread; circle errors.
3 Key one 5' writing at your control rate. Proofread; circle errors.

A all letters

	gwam 3'	5'	
Much has been written about leadership, but very little has	4	2	49
been written about the art of subordinateship. Just who is a	8	5	51
good subordinate? What we do know is that some subordinates are	12	7	54
sought after by leaders and others are avoided. The way a worker	17	10	56
performs is not the only measure of success as a subordinate.	21	13	59
Producing good results in work performed alone may not be as	25	15	61
essential as being an effective member of the team. Results	29	17	64
produced by the entire team will always be more crucial than the	33	20	66
results produced by one worker.	36	21	68
An effective subordinate must possess both competence and	39	24	70
confidence. In addition to these qualities, he or she must be	44	26	73
able to visualize the job of her or his supervisor and should be	48	29	75
able to adapt to the work style of the supervisor. Understanding	52	31	78
what a supervisor expects and being able to meet those expecta-	57	34	80
tions are important. A good employee should not have to be told	61	37	83
what to do all of the time. An effective worker knows her or his	65	39	86
responsibilities and performs them without being told what to do.	70	42	88
A good worker must be able to communicate effectively and must be	74	45	91
able to represent the team in a positive way.	77	46	93

gwam 3' | 1 | 2 | 3 | 4 | 5 |
5' | 1 | 2 | 3 |

74 Distribution List; Form Paragraphs

Skill-Building Warmup

74a 5'

alphabet	1	Wade Jantz, our very fine quarterback, played the six good games.
figure	2	Those 1,863 bars cost $27.05 each for a total cost of $50,394.15.
shift key	3	I may go to the zoo or to see you if I do not go to the new pool.
fluency	4	The men may be busy, but they go to the lake to work on the dock.

1 | 2 | 3 | 4 | 5 | 6 | 7 | 8 | 9 | 10 | 11 | 12 | 13

74b 15'

FORMATTING

Distribution list

Drill 1

1 Read "Distribution list."

2 Set a tab stop 10 spaces from the left margin and a 1.5" top margin.

3 Key the memo at the right; your line endings will not be the same.

Distribution list

The same memo is often sent to a number of individuals. One way to handle multiple recipients of a memo is to list each person's name in the heading following the word TO:. Another way to handle multiple recipients is to key Distribution List after the word TO:, then, key the names of the individuals on the distribution list at the bottom of the memo, starting in the same position that a copy notation would be keyed. Names may be indented 5 spaces or to the first default tab.

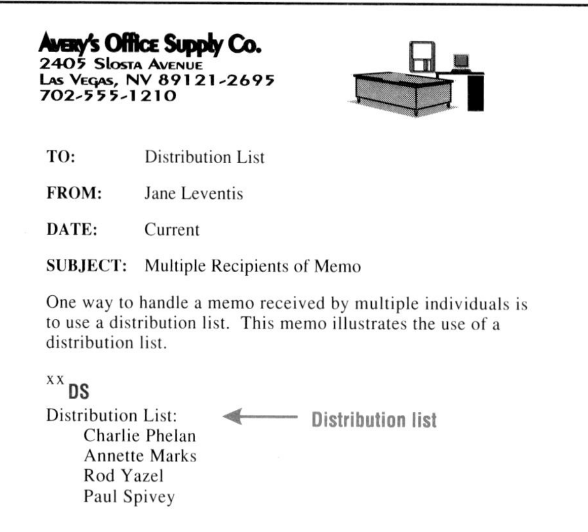

Avery's Office Supply Co.
2405 Slosta Avenue
Las Vegas, NV 89121-2695
702-555-1210

TO: Distribution List

FROM: Jane Leventis

DATE: Current

SUBJECT: Multiple Recipients of Memo

One way to handle a memo received by multiple individuals is to use a distribution list. This memo illustrates the use of a distribution list.

xx

DS

Distribution List:
Charlie Phelan
Annette Marks
Rod Yazel
Paul Spivey

Drill 2

Use form paragraphs

Study the information on form paragraphs at the right.

Form paragraphs

An effective way to create documents is to prepare a series of form paragraphs or blocks of text. Appropriate paragraphs can then be selected to fit a particular situation and merged to form a complete document.

Paragraphs should be written so that they "fit together" coherently. To ensure that paragraphs will flow smoothly, they are often labeled as beginning, middle, and closing paragraphs. A complete document would consist of a beginning paragraph, one or more middle paragraphs, and a closing paragraph.

Many different types of documents—such as memos, letters, legal documents, medical documents, reports, etc.—can be created from form paragraphs. Form paragraphs save time composing documents. More time is saved when the paragraphs are stored and retrieved.

To create a memo, key the heading. Then key or retrieve the paragraphs that have been selected for the document you are preparing. Add your reference initials and appropriate mailing notations if needed.

93c 30'

FORMATTING

Tables from computer printouts

The documents in this section require you to extract data from the computer printout.

Follow the guidelines on page 227 for formatting all five average-length tables. Use a standard 1.5" top margin and DS data.

Document 1

Prepare a table showing the six employees who have reached 40 percent or less of their sales budget.

1 Main heading: **TERRITORIES OF CONCERN.**

2 Column heads: **Employee**, **Manager**, **Total Revenue**, and **% of Budget**. Use a two-line heading for Columns 3 and 4.

Document 2

Prepare a table showing the 14 employees who have achieved more than 50 percent of their sales budget.

1 Main heading: **TOP SALES PERFORMERS**.

2 Secondary heading: **January 1 - June 30, 19--**.

3 Column heads: **Employee**, **Annual Budget**, **Total Revenue**, and **% of Budget**. Use a two-line heading for Columns 2, 3, and 4.

Documents 3, 4, and 5

Prepare a table for each of the three managers showing the overall sales performance of their sales teams.

1 Main heading: **TEAM PERFORMANCE**.

2 Secondary heading: **Manager:** (Insert name).

3 Column heads: **Employee**, **Annual Budget**, **Total Revenue**, and **% of Budget**. Use a two-line heading for Columns 2, 3, and 4.

		Annual	Revenue Generated			% of
Employee	Manager	Budget	Office Sys.	Publishing	Total	Budget
Anderson	Jackson	1,256,840	315,875	257,931	573,806	45.65
Appleton	Mendoza	1,159,225	173,894	275,962	449,856	38.81
Bagby	Jackson	1,375,500	824,975	520,875	1,345,850	97.84
Brown A.	Mendoza	1,195,550	411,835	398,752	810,587	67.80
Brown C.	Larson	975,850	285,750	195,782	481,532	49.34
Castillo	Mendoza	1,075,955	432,985	496,075	929,060	86.35
Cheng	Jackson	1,205,874	524,764	560,871	1,085,635	90.03
Davis	Larson	1,100,500	235,000	294,750	529,750	48.13
Emmons	Jackson	1,250,500	135,987	186,832	322,819	25.82
Fasio	Mendoza	1,000,000	250,000	275,000	525,000	52.50
Glenn	Larson	1,275,850	650,000	501,175	1,151,175	90.23
Hess	Jackson	1,315,000	596,450	698,532	1,294,982	98.48
Hart	Mendoza	1,015,575	135,985	140,765	276,750	27.25
Jones	Jackson	975,842	245,975	215,762	461,737	47.32
Kato	Larson	1,283,764	75,384	28,760	104,144	8.11
Lyman	Larson	1,075,325	386,974	285,985	672,959	62.58
Nozaki	Mendoza	1,300,000	275,864	236,987	512,851	39.45
Otis	Larson	1,295,845	345,985	410,245	756,230	58.36
Pulliam	Jackson	1,308,950	175,975	450,826	626,801	47.89
Quinn	Mendoza	1,234,987	498,673	536,702	1,035,375	83.84
Rogers	Larson	895,962	265,987	329,841	595,828	66.50
Schultz	Jackson	1,050,572	246,873	285,073	531,946	50.63
Stuart	Jackson	1,298,450	237,825	656,432	894,257	68.87
Taylor	Mendoza	1,275,000	453,987	532,109	986,096	77.34
Thomas	Larson	1,249,085	82,150	25,075	107,225	8.58

73d 35'

FORMATTING

Two-page memos

Documents 1 and 2
(plain sheets)
1 Top margin: 1.5" on first page; 1" on second page.
2 Block enumerated items. (See page 175 for reference.)

Documents 3 and 4
Rekey Documents 1 and 2 following the same directions, except use hanging indent for the enumerated items. (See page 154 for reference.)

Document 1

words

Current date | Marketing Staff | STATUS OF 8
INTERACTIVE TESTING SYSTEM 13

The new version of our interactive testing sys- 23
tem is in the final stages of Beta testing. 32
Technical documentation has been written and 41
edited. The user manuals should be completed 50
in approximately six weeks. 56

The new version consists of three modules that 65
can be marketed separately or as a package: 74
1. The first module automatically generates 83
tests that are printed on paper. 2. The second 93
module automatically generates tests that 101
can be taken interactively on the computer. 110
3. The third module automatically scores both 120
interactive and printed tests. 126

The attached summary presents the following 135
features that need to be explained to our sales 144
force and to be emphasized in all sales and 154
promotional materials: 1. Test items may be 164
keyed using macros or may be scanned from 173
printed copy. 2. Word processing features are 181
fully integrated with attributes such as bold, 190
underline, large fonts, superscripts, and 198
subscripts. 3. The system has graphics 206
capabilities that enable users to scan, create, 216
maintain, and modify high-resolution graphic 225
images. 4. The system associates those 233
images with items both for printing test items 243
and presenting items for interactive testing. 252
5. A current default record allows the test ad- 261
ministrator to set system parameters for the 271
test, reducing the data test takers must enter. 280
6. The system allows users to enter param- 289
eters to produce scaled scores, percent-correct 298
scores, and percentiles. 7. The scoring 307
module provides industry standard statistical 316
analyses. 8. The system has a complete score 326
reporting mechanism. 330

The first marketing preview is scheduled on 339
Friday afternoon. Please plan to attend. 347

Rex Boykin | xx | Attachment 352

Document 2

words

Current date | Robin Pratt | SYSTEM DESIGN 8

Thank you for the feedback you have given me 17
on the features of the new version of our inter- 26
active testing system. We appreciate your 35
taking time to compare the features of the 44
current system with the new version. Your 52
analysis will be very helpful to all of our sales 62
staff. 64

I spent several hours with the system design 73
team trying to determine which aspects of the 82
design should be featured in the materials. A 91
copy of my notes is enclosed. Lee Jordan, one 101
of the designers, briefed me on the features 110
described in this memo. The system has the 119
following features: 1. A comprehensive secu- 128
rity system that limits access on a need-to- 137
know basis. 2. Easy-to-use menus for all pro- 146
gram execution and on-line, interactive help 155
support. 3. Effective utility programs to import 165
and export data and to maintain the database. 175
4. A sophisticated word processing component 184
integrated into the system. 5. Table-driven 193
printer support. 6. The ability to provide 202
scoring keys to and accept item statistics from 212
both batch and interactive test scoring sys- 220
tems. 7. A mechanism for acquiring, storing, 230
and integrating graphics material with test items. 240
8. A report generation capability for data 249
structures such as classification data. 257

Perhaps the most important technical change 266
in the design of the system is the ease with 275
which the system can be customized to meet 284
the needs of the specific user. The database 293
administrator can access a work screen to 301
modify the titles given to many of the data 311
structures. 313

I will call you as soon as I can set up a meet- 322
ing with the creative development team. Hope- 331
fully, it will be one day next week. 339

Lynn R. Brewer | xx | Enclosure 344

94 Ruled Tables

Skill-Building Warmup

94a 5'

alphabet 1 Maxwell jeopardized most of his savings by acquiring risky stock.
figure 2 Be sure to read pages 185-263 and 409-578 of the 1,895 page book.
space bar 3 Jo saw one of the new cars, and she may buy a red one if she can.
fluency 4 Ty may sign the form and handle the work on the dock at the lake.

| 1 | 2 | 3 | 4 | 5 | 6 | 7 | 8 | 9 | 10 | 11 | 12 | 13 |

94b 10'

SKILL BUILDING

Improve techniques

1 Key the drill 3 times; DS between 9-line groups.
2 Work at a controlled rate.

1/2 fingers
5 dirt nut fun drum try buy been curt very hunt bunt rent cent jump
6 We think Julio may give Ruth a ring Sunday if she will accept it.
7 My name is Geoffrey, but I very much prefer Jeff on the name tag.

3/4 fingers
8 was pill look zoom loop west low loose quiz walk saw wax box zeal
9 Paul Velasquez was at a popular plaza quilt shop when he saw Sal.
10 Sal was at a Palawan zoo; he was also at Wuxi Plaza for six days.

all fingers
11 frequent zebra yogurt magazine luxury jacket wave fished politics
12 Jan Zink performed very well as quarterback for the mixed league.
13 Jacques Weitzel may pay for six black shirts for the diving team.

94c 10'

FORMATTING

Preapplication drill: tables with rules

1 Study the information at the right; then format the narrow table.
2 Use a 2" top margin; center column heads.
3 Set spacing for SS to simplify the keying of rules. To DS the body of a ruled table, return twice after each entry in the body of the table.
Tip: Column headings are never underlined in ruled tables. Bold may be used.

Horizontal rulings
The table below shows the correct vertical spacing within a ruled table. **Note:** Some electronic typewriters and most word processing programs permit you to key both lines of a double rule at the same time. With other equipment, key the first rule; then roll the platen slightly forward using the variable line spacer (or the reverse index key on some electronic typewriters) and key the second rule. If you cannot key a second rule, use a single rule.

Vertical rulings
Remove the page and use a black pen to draw a vertical rule at the midpoint between columns.

PURCHASE AGREEMENT

DS

Item No.	**Quantity**	**Price**
R38475-L	12	$84.50
C92579-T	5	29.75
X47824-L	20	98.99

(DS above headings; SS below headings; DS above body; SS after last entry)

73 Second-Page Heading

Skill-Building Warmup

73a 5'

alphabet 1 Jamie quickly apologized for submitting the complex reviews late.
figure 2 Chapters 7, 18, 19, and 23 had 65 pages; the others had 40 pages.
shift key 3 Amy, Ty, Jo, Ann, Lee, Al, and Bob may go to El Paso or San Jose.
fluency 4 Claudia and my neighbor may fix duck, lamb, and panfish for them.

1	2	3	4	5	6	7	8	9	10	11	12	13

73b 5'

SKILL BUILDING

Build straight-copy skill

Key two 1' writings at your top rate; key a 1' writing at your "control" rate.

A all letters

Too often workers learn the basic functions of software but never take time to learn the more advanced ones. They are too busy trying to meet the demands of their job rather than taking steps to increase their efficiency. To maximize productivity, workers must learn the software quickly before a new product is out. Learning how to learn new software is a critical skill for the future.

73c 5'

FORMATTING

Second-page headings

1 Study "Second-Page Headings."

2 Format the second page of the simplified memo shown at the right.

Second-page headings

1 Use standard format for the first page, maintaining about a 1" bottom margin.

2 Key a heading 1" from the top edge of the second page consisting of the addressee's name, page number, and date blocked at the left margin. A DS follows the heading.

3 Memohead stationery may be used for the first page; successive pages are keyed on plain paper of the same quality as the memohead.

4 If a paragraph must be divided between pages, key at least two lines on both pages; do not divide a word between pages.

words

Renee H. Alford 3
Page 2 5
March 8, 19-- DS 7

Please call me after you have had an opportunity to talk with our clients and to review the material we sent yesterday. We need to make a decision within a few days. QS 21 33 41

Shawn D. Halpern DS 44

xx 44

94d 25'

FORMATTING

Ruled tables

Insert vertical and horizontal rules.

Document 1

1 Use 2" top margin.

2 Align figures at the decimal point; use the decimal tab feature if it is available.

words

SEMINAR REGISTRATION 4

18

Registrant	Seminar Fee	Airport Limousine	Guest Tickets	Total	words
					23 / 31
					45
Arlene C. Rogers	$1,350.00	$ 69.00	$ 45.95	$1,464.95	56
Georgina F. Bates	1,350.00	34.50	0	1,384.50	65
Peggy M. Brewer	1,350.00	103.50	91.90	1,545.40	74
Lawrence C. Simpkin	1,350.00	138.00	137.85	1,625.85	84
Carlos T. Vasquez	1,350.00	69.00	45.95	1,464.95	94
Suzanne T. Nickels	1,350.00	0	0	1,350.00	102

116

Document 2

1 Center the (wide) ruled table horizontally; 2" top margin.

2 Center and bold main heading in CAPS; center and bold column heads.

3 Align figures at the decimal point; use the decimal tab feature if it is available.

WORKSTATION COST COMPARISON 5

Workstation	Price	Software	Peripherals	Total Cost	words
					44
X 290 C	$ 2,300.00	$ 495.95	$ 700.50	$ 3,496.45	53
X 390 D	2,600.00	525.75	795.95	3,921.70	61
X 690 D	3,500.00	795.00	1,200.95	5,495.95	69
X 890 P	4,500.95	825.95	1,400.00	6,726.90	78
X 990 P	10,200.95	1,050.00	2,600.85	13,851.80	100

Document 3

Reformat Document 1, making the deletions and additions indicated at the right.

Delete: A. Rogers registration (entire row)
Add: (at bottom of table)

Lucas R. Wellington	1,350.00	34.50	45.95	$1,430.45
Merri C. Zimmer	1,350.00	69.00	45.95	1,464.95

Document 4

Reformat Document 3 and place all registrants in alphabetical order. Be sure to move an entire row when a change is made.

Document 2

1 Use 1.5" top margin and 1" side margins.

2 Proofread; correct errors.

3 Make a copy of the memo and then add a blind copy notation (bc) to Amy Beall.

words

Current date QS 3

All Employees DS 6

Office Automation Installation DS 12

All of the office automation equipment was installed last week. The 26
final testing will be completed within the next day or two. Training is 40
scheduled to begin next Monday. Schedules will be posted in each 54
department. 56

The corporate Communications Department was asked to revise our 68
report format to conform to the default standards of our new equipment. 83
You will receive the new standards shortly. QS 92

Alicia Roberts 95

xx 95

Document 3

Use same directions as for Document 2; add bc notation to Lee Brunson on the second copy for Document 3.

Current date | George C. Tipton, Distribution Director | TRIP TO MID- 13
WEST CONTAINERS 17

My visit with Alex Carrington, general manager of Midwest 28
Containers, was most successful. Mr. Carrington understands the 41
shipping problems we have encountered with Midwest Containers 54
and has agreed to make the changes we requested at current contract 67
price. A new price will be negotiated when the contract expires. 81

Complete specifications should arrive in time for our staff meeting. 95
Please extend the time for my presentation to 30 minutes. 106

Carolyn Anderson, Quality Control Director | xx 115

Document 4

Prepare the memo in simplified format with blocked enumerations; add your reference initials; add a bc notation to Alyce Slagle on the second copy.

May 5, 19-- | Production Planning Committee | MAY 20 MEETING 11

The Production Planning Committee is scheduled to meet in the Board 25
Room at 10:30 a.m. on May 20. Final decisions must be made on three 39
renovation issues. 43

1. The expansion of Line 3 to accommodate the new products that have 57
been added to the current product line. 2. The complete renovation of 72
the Gilbert Plant. 3. The retooling necessary to utilize the new tech- 87
nology recommended for the Atherton Plant. 96

Please review the attached material that supplements the material you 110
already have received. 115

Phillip Trennepohl | Attachment 125

95 Purchase Orders; Invoices

Skill-Building Warmup

95a 5'

alphabet 1 Quincy Ziff worked very hard to build just six wellness programs.
figure 2 I caught 20 halibut (69.5# average) and 37 trout (4.81# average).
adjacent key 3 Trey and Guy Walker were going to join us for a very quick snack.
fluency 4 He may shape the clay bowl in a form, or he may shape it by hand.

1 | 2 | 3 | 4 | 5 | 6 | 7 | 8 | 9 | 10 | 11 | 12 | 13

95b 10'

FORMATTING

Study business forms

Read the information at the right and study the illustration below.

Invoice: a bill for merchandise sold.

Purchase order: a request to buy merchandise.

Preparing business forms

Businesses use forms extensively to collect and record data. They present data in a concise and easy-to-read format. Forms can contain handwritten or printed data generated on a computer or a typewriter.

Information on preprinted forms is often filled in using a typewriter. Care must be taken to fit the data in the space provided and to key slightly above the line rather than cutting through it.

Formatting guides

1 Set tabs to align the address block and the guide words at the right. Key the address in ALL CAPS to facilitate using window envelopes for bulk mail.

2 Set the left margin so that items in the Quantity column are approximately centered.

3 In the Description column, set a tab 2 spaces after the vertical line. Copy is generally separated from vertical lines by two spaces. However, if the line replaces a decimal in money amounts, begin one space after the vertical line.

4 Set additional tabs for aligning numbers in other columns.

5 Begin the body a DS below the horizontal rule.

6 Do not key dollar signs.

7 SS each entry; DS between entries.

8 Underline the last amount in the Total column; DS and key the total.

95c 35'

FORMATTING

Format business forms

Proofread carefully; correct errors. (LM pp. S79-S85)

Document 1
Invoice

Key the invoice on page 235.

Document 2
Purchase order

Key the purchase order on page 235.

Document 3
Invoice

Rekey Document 1; double the quantity of each item and compute totals.

Document 4
Purchase order

Rekey Document 2; reduce the quantity ordered by 50% and compute totals.

The Henderson Company
667 Farmington Avenue
West Hartford, CT 06119-7284
(203) 555-6941

INVOICE (2 spaces)

Tab

PAT'S SECRETARIAL SERVICE
461 OAKWOOD AVENUE
RALEIGH, NC 27601-6452

Date: October 18, 19--
Customer Order No.: XC917302
Our Order No.: 6PS49296
Date Shipped: 10/18/--
Shipped Via: Tarheel Delivery
Terms: 2/10, n/30

Quantity	Description/Stock No.	Unit Price		Total	
1	Formatted Tape Drive, PC1	5,795	95	5,795	95
6	Network Connections, PC26X	320	50	1,923	00
1	8065 Expert Illustrator, PC44X	1,375	75	1,375	75
1	8065 Expert Drafting/Illustrator	6,125	00	6,125	00
Approximate center	2 spaces			15,219	70

Dateline June 3, 19-- (Line 10 or 1.5") QS

Recipient's name Ms. Allison Mueller, Vice President DS

Subject line PRINTED MEMO FORMS DISCONTINUED DS

The supply of printed memo forms has been depleted, and our Office Standards Committee made the decision not to reprint the forms. Staff members who use word processing software no longer use the printed forms. They either use the simplified format illustrated in this memo or a macro to print the traditional memo heading automatically so they do not have to key it each time they prepare a memo.

Body

The simplified memo has several advantages: DS

1. It eliminates the need to rekey the heading for each memo. Some of our managers also prefer the simplified memo format because they like to sign their memos rather than initial them by their names. DS

1" side margins

2. Simplified memos may be prepared on our regular letterhead, on the internal letterhead with just our company name, or on plain paper.

3. The style is progressive, attractive, and easy to format.

As you will note from the enclosed style guide, we have agreed to use all capitals for the subject line. The use of courtesy and job titles is optional. The addendum for the Office Handbook will be printed this week. Please let me know if you have any further questions about the use of the simplified memo format. QS

Ernie Stands

Sender's name Ernie Stands, Office Manager DS

Reference initials xx DS

Enclosure notation Enclosure

Note: The subject line on simplified memos may be keyed in all caps or cap/lowercase.

Document 1

	words
The Henderson Company	
667 Farmington Avenue	
West Hartford, CT 06119-7284	
(203) 555-6941	

INVOICE

		words
Date:	March 24, 19--	3
Customer Order No.:	2945CT3	8
Our Order No.:	TC21087	17
Date Shipped:	3/24/--	19
Shipped Via:	Cajun Shipping	21
Terms:	Net 30 days	24

THE SCHULTZ COMPANY 8
129 RENA DRIVE 11
LAFAYETTE LA 70504-2853 17

Quantity	Description/Stock No.	Unit Price		Total		words
12	10-Pack Diskette Boxes, 3.5", CP2384	12	95	155	40	33
10	Diskette Trays with Locks, 3.5", CP7042	39	69	396	90	44
4	Modem, 9600FP, CP9938	1,849	99	7,399	96	52
8	Six Outlet Power Strip, ES2750	24	95	199	60	62
				8,151	86	64

Document 2

CONSOLIDATED INDUSTRIES OF AMERICA
28 Ravina Drive
Atlanta, GA 30346-9105
(404) 555-6427

PURCHASE ORDER

		words
Purchase Order No.:	395RT2394	2
Date:	11/14/--	8
Date Required:	11/30/--	18
Terms:	2/10, n/30	20
Shipped Via:	Bayou Transfers	23

ARDOIN AND ASSOCIATES 8
375 WEEKS DRIVE 11
YOUNGSVILLE LA 70592-5724 18

Quantity	Description/Stock No.	Unit Price		Total		words
12	Continuous Banner Paper, CP3853	10	75	129	00	32
6	Dart Fax Paper, TP2905	14	95	89	70	39
4	XT Rewritable Optical Disks	249	95	999	80	47
10	Dart Glare Shields	49	25	492	50	55
				1,711	00	57

72 Simplified Memorandum

Skill-Building Warmup

72a 5'

alphabet 1 Liz Page quickly found six major errors in the book she reviewed.
fig/sym 2 The pool (17'6" x 35'9" and 3'4" to 8'10" deep) held 14,290 gals.
space bar 3 Ty saw us as we got in a new car to go to the zoo; he did not go.
fluency 4 Is the problem with the ancient chapel or the chapel at the lake?

| 1 | 2 | 3 | 4 | 5 | 6 | 7 | 8 | 9 | 10 | 11 | 12 | 13 |

72b 10'

SKILL BUILDING

Improve keyboarding technique

each set of lines 3 times; DS between 9-line groups; work at a controlled pace

1/2 fingers

5 free join day five nut gain hunt mint cut tray five cry trick but
6 Much can be said about a velvet jacket Yvonne just bought for me.
7 Brady just found a very nice cut diamond that he may give to Kim.

3/4 fingers

8 was pale six zoo quip saw lap soup zone slap wrap loop well pools
9 Polly was at Warsaw Plaza at the quilt show; Wilson placed sixth.
10 Stella will sell wax for Vasquez as we open a booth to sell soup.

all fingers

11 quip zoo bay rusty plaza sixty very draft wind jackets much great
12 Javis analyzed the problem and fixed the switch quickly for Gwen.
13 Brooks gave a major quiz which caused anxiety for lots of people.

72c 5'

FORMATTING

Learn blind copy notation

Study the information at the right.

A **copy notation** indicates to the recipient of a memo or letter others who receive a copy of the document. In some cases, a copy of a document is sent to another without the recipient's knowledge. This copy is called a **blind copy** (bc). The blind copy notation is shown only on a copy of the original—not on the original document.

Morrison Crafts
1429 Plainsfield Road
Cincinnati, OH 45241-2215

May 15, 19--

Megan Jamison

BLIND COPY NOTATION

The original of this memo has no copy notation. Megan Jamison has no indication that Pamela Morrison received a copy of the memo. The blind copy notation (bc) is shown only on the copy of the memo. It is keyed after the original is produced. The enclosed guide explains blind copy notations.

Clay Jeffers

xx

Enclosure

Original document

Morrison Crafts
1429 Plainsfield Road
Cincinnati, OH 45241-2215

May 15, 19--

Megan Jamison

BLIND COPY NOTATION

The original of this memo has no copy notation. Megan Jamison has no indication that Pamela Morrison received a copy of the memo. The blind copy notation (bc) is shown only on the copy of the memo. It is keyed after the original is produced. The enclosed guide explains blind copy notations.

Clay Jeffers

xx

Enclosure

bc Pamela Morrison

Copy of document

72d 30'

FORMATTING

Format simplified memos

(plain sheet)

Document 1

Read and key the memo on page 175. Enumerated items may be blocked as illustrated or formatted using hanging indent.

96 Expense Forms

Skill-Building Warmup

96a 5'

alphabet 1	Jack Quincy will not buy frozen vegetables except wild mushrooms.
figure 2	A lot that was 268 feet deep and 396 feet wide sold for $104,750.
direct reach 3	Cec Mun left many huge debts unpaid, but a great uncle paid them.
fluency 4	Is the bowl an authentic antique, or did she make it in the form?

| 1 | 2 | 3 | 4 | 5 | 6 | 7 | 8 | 9 | 10 | 11 | 12 | 13 |

96b 10'

SKILL BUILDING

Improve skill transfer

1 Key two 1' writings on each line.

2 Try to approximate line 5 speed on other lines.

5 Mergers, acquisitions, and restructuring happen quite frequently.

6 *Restructuring usually means downsizing or reducing staff numbers.*

7 In a 5-year period, 6 companies laid off 279,348 people (10-25%).

8 few employes can handle lay offs psychologicaly mand financialy.

96c 35'

FORMATTING

Expense forms

(LM pp. S87-S91)

Document 1

1 Format the travel expense form on page 237.

2 Key copy slightly above the line, not cutting through it.

3 Position the information in the top section 2 spaces after the colon.

4 In Column 1, align copy at the left; in Columns 2-6, align copy at the decimal.

Document 2

1 Prepare a second expense form for Anita R. Meyers of the Personnel Department who went to Chicago to conduct a training seminar for Great Lakes Region employees from April 16-21, 19--. Use same I.D. and budget center no. as in Document 1.

2 Include this information:

Trav. Auth. No.: 356-49-3
Advance: $1,000
Airfare: $375
Lodging: $1,010.50
Rental car: $195.25
Audio visuals: $345.95
Meals:

4/16	$32.60	4/17	38.00
4/18	52.95	4/19	45.75
4/20	49.65	4/21	26.50

3 Compute totals and amount due.

Document 3

1 Prepare an expense form for June C. Mitchell of the Personnel Department who went to Seattle to meet with recruiters on May 6-7, 19--.

2 Include this information:

Trav. Auth. No.: 356-72-2
I.D. No.: R46
Advance: none
Budget center: HR1
Airfare: $594.00
Lodging: $165.85
Recruiter dinner: 5/6, $358.75
Taxis: $32
Meals:

5/6 $12.75 | 5/7 $36.59

3 Compute totals and amount due.

71d 10'

COMMUNICATION

Composing/editing skills

1 Format as an unbound report; DS.

2 Compose 4 or 5 sentences to supplement the copy presented.

3 Proofread; mark the 5 errors in the copy shown and any errors in copy you composed.

4 Edit ¶, correcting errors in copy and adding the title **POWER DINING** centered in all caps and bold.

In his book, entitled <u>Business and Dining</u> Ross Moore suggest that often buisness is conducted overa meal. Therefore, when employees are interviewed, it is important to assess there social skills.

If you are taken to lunch during an interview, you should observe the following good etiquette practices:

71e 20'

SKILL BUILDING

Build/measure straight-copy skill

1 Key one 1' writing on each ¶.

2 Key one 3' writing.

3 Key one 5' writing.

A all letters

	gwam 3'	5'	
Managing time usually is a very difficult task. Often, the	4	2	43
things we enjoy doing the most do not have the highest priority.	8	5	46
To be effective in managing our time, we must analyze how we are	13	8	48
spending our time and assign priorities to tasks based on their	17	10	51
importance. Then we must follow through and do the tasks in the	21	13	54
order of importance. An additional problem in managing time	25	15	56
results from the way we reward ourselves when we are efficient.	30	18	59
Often, our reward is to give ourselves more work. Additional	34	20	61
work is not an incentive to do better.	36	22	63
Software products, called calendaring or time management	40	24	65
systems, are available to help us manage our time. These elec-	44	27	68
tronic tools may be more effective in keeping track of time than	49	29	70
are manual tools, but the same problem still exists. We must	53	32	73
decide which tasks are the most important to do, and we must do	57	34	75
the tasks in the order of importance. We are often the main	61	37	78
problem. We have to question ourselves to determine if we really	66	39	80
want to manage our time effectively.	68	41	82

gwam 3' | 1 | 2 | 3 | 4 | 5 |
5' | 1 | 2 | 3 |

EXPENSE REPORT
(Trips Involving Air Travel)

Employee: Anita R. Meyers	Travel Authorization No.: 356-48-9
Department: Personnel	I.D. No.: R83
Destination: San Francisco	Budget Center: HR1
Dates: March 4-9, 19--	Advance: $1,500

Purpose of Trip:
Conduct a training seminar for Western Region employees

Date	Airfare	Lodging	Meals	Other*	Total
March 4	$455.00	$1,150.75	$40.65	$210.79	$1,857.19
March 5			56.50	24.75	81.25
March 6			38.79		38.79
March 7			46.55		46.55
March 8			51.00		51.00
March 9			24.25		24.25

*Other (List): Rental car $210.79; handout reproduction $24.75

*Note: Receipts must be attached for all expenses over $25.

Signature:	Total Expenses:	$2,099.03
Approved:	Less Cash Advance:	1,500.00
Date:	**Amount Due:**	$599.03

16 Memorandum Mastery

Learning goals:
1 To improve keyboarding techniques.
2 To learn/review memorandum formats.

Formatting guides:
1 Margins: 1" or 65-space line for drills, ¶ writings, and documents.
2 Single-space drills and documents, unless otherwise directed; double-space writings.
3 5-space ¶ indention.

71a 5'

Skill-building warmup

each line 3 times (slowly, faster, slowly); DS between 3-line groups (Use these directions for all skill-building warmups.)

alphabet 1 Maxwell paid just a quarter for a very big cookie at the new zoo.
fig/sym 2 The cost to ship a 354# box (6'10" x 9'2") 780 miles was $239.45.
3/4 fingers 3 Quin will oppose an opinion of Max about a jazzy pop show we saw.
fluency 4 Angie, the neighbor, paid to go to the island and fish for smelt.

| 1 | 2 | 3 | 4 | 5 | 6 | 7 | 8 | 9 | 10 | 11 | 12 | 13 |

71b 10'

SKILL BUILDING

Improve skill transfer

Key two 1' writings on each line; compare speed on various types of copy.

5 Excellent social skills are so important for success in business.
6 *A significant amount of business is conducted in social settings.*
7 Lunches for the 14 customers cost $77.37 ($67.28 x 15% = $10.09).
8 A candidates ~~who is~~ being interviewed maybe observe in socail settings.

| 1 | 2 | 3 | 4 | 5 | 6 | 7 | 8 | 9 | 10 | 11 | 12 | 13 |

71c 5'

SKILL BUILDING

Build straight-copy skill

Key two 1' writings at your top rate; key a 1' writing at your "control" rate.

 all letters

Entering the employment market within our society today can be quite a complex experience. Due to the number of job choices available, a very real concern facing a potential employee is to select a career that will remain in existence for a long period of time. A career should be analyzed to determine whether it matches your personality and how much satisfaction it will give to you during your work life. You should also keep in mind that four or five career changes in a life are not uncommon.

97 Designing Forms

Skill-Building Warmup

97a 5'

alphabet 1 Zack Bigg may require extra help with dinner for just five teams.
fig/sym 2 The desk (72" x 46" x 28") weighs 105 pounds and costs $3,190.75.
double letter 3 Gregg Mann will meet us at the pool before the committee meeting.
fluency 4 Jane may go with them to the authentic burial chapel at the lake.

| 1 | 2 | 3 | 4 | 5 | 6 | 7 | 8 | 9 | 10 | 11 | 12 | 13 |

97b 10'

SKILL BUILDING

Measure straight-copy skill

1 Key one 3' writing; circle errors; determine *gwam*.
2 Key one 5' writing; circle errors; determine *gwam*.

  all letters

	gwam 3'	5'	
What characterizes the life of an entrepreneur? Those who	4	2	43
have never owned their own businesses may think owning a business	8	5	46
means being your own boss, setting your own hours, and making a	13	8	48
lot of money. Those who have run their own businesses are quick	17	10	51
to report that owning a business may be exciting and challenging;	21	13	54
but it also requires hard work, long hours, and personal sacri-	26	15	56
fice. A good idea is not the only prerequisite for a successful	30	18	59
business. A little luck even helps.	32	19	60
Many small businesses are operated as businesses from the	36	22	63
initial stages. However, some small businesses that turn out to	41	24	65
be successful are just hobbies in the early stages. The entre-	45	27	68
preneur has a job and uses the income from it to support the	49	29	70
hobby. When the hobby begins to require more and more time, the	53	32	73
entrepreneur has to choose between the job and the hobby. The	57	34	75
decision is usually based on finances. If enough money can be	62	37	78
made from the hobby or can be obtained from another source, the	66	39	80
hobby is turned into a business.	68	41	82

gwam 3' | 1 | 2 | 3 | 4 | 5 |
5' | 1 | 2 | 3 |

Improve capitalization skills

Key Drills 5 and 6, inserting capital letters where appropriate as you key. Proofread; correct errors or rekey the ¶s.

Drill 5

my favorite professor, anna c. wong, taught administrative office systems I at lakeland state university. she also taught some of the information processing courses at one of the technical schools. she has an mba and a ph.d. from a large university in the midwest. she majored in the general area of administrative systems.

Drill 6

john made an appointment to meet me on tuesday, july 14, at 10:30 a.m., to discuss a research project for our finance class at central state university. we will meet in conference room c of the business administration building on south campus. ichiro watanabe, ph.d., is our professor. prior to coming to state, he was comptroller of overbrook, inc. he still serves on the board of directors of overbrook.

Improve word usage

Key Drill 7 selecting the appropriate words as you key. Proofread; correct errors or rekey the ¶.

Drill 7

Miss Alvarez was (here/hear) to speak on ethical (principals/principles) in business. She (complemented/complimented) the company for discussing the issues with (its/it's) employees and encouraged managers to discuss the (effects/affects) of any new policies or goals with workers. She (cited/sighted/sited) examples of excessively high productivity goals causing employees to cheat in order to meet those goals. (It's/Its) important that goals be realistic and that employees understand that violating ethical (principals/principles) to attain goals is unacceptable. She explained (further/farther) that management must (accept/except) responsibility for setting a good example. Managers who do not treat employees fairly should not expect employees to treat (their/there) coworkers or customers fairly.

97c 10'

COMMUNICATION

Build proofreading skill

1 Key the ¶, correcting grammar, capitalization, punctuation, spelling, number usage, and other errors as you key.

2 Check the correctness of all numbers in the ¶ by comparing them to the data in the Mail Register on page 240; circle any incorrect numbers on your copy.

3 Rekey the ¶, correcting all errors in numbers.

A total of $29752.00 were recieved, register, and deposited on february 14. 2 peaces of mail contained a money order and 2 peaces of mail contained cash. Although the amount of cash usually is relative small ($12 and $6 in this case) handling cash places an unnecessary burden on our employees. The responsibility for handling the two largest checks ($14,750.00 and $2,469.73) is far less then the responsiblity for handling the small cash Enclosures.

97d 25'

FORMATTING

Design forms

Document 1
Design mail register
(plain paper)

1 Examine the form on page 240.

2 On a blank sheet, create the form using the same procedures that you used to format ruled tables. (Refer to page 232, if necessary.)

Document 2
Complete mail register
(LM p. S93)

1 Compare the Mail Register form you created in Document 1 with the one provided in your laboratory materials. Basic forms can be created using an electronic typewriter, but more attractive forms can be created using graphics features of word processing.

2 Key the data shown on page 240 on the form provided.

Document 3
Design a class record form

1 Create a table with 3 columns and 25 rows.

2 Main heading: **CLASS RECORD**

3 Column heads: **Student**, **Major**, and **Social Security No.**

4 Format the form attractively, incorporating some of the features used in Document 1.

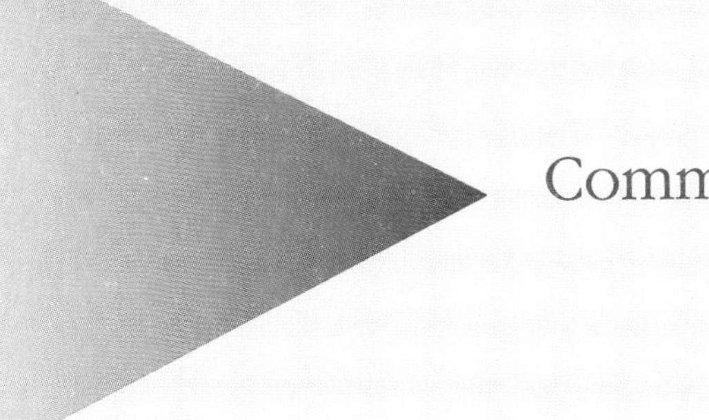

Communication Workshop 3

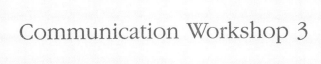

MicroAssistant: To select Communication Workshop 3, key **C3** from the Main menu.

Improve editing skill

1 Key Drills 1 and 2 correcting all errors in grammar, word usage, spelling, capitalization, and punctuation.

2 Proofread. Check to see that you located the 20 errors embedded in each ¶ and that additional errors were not added when you keyed the material.

3 Edit your copy.

Margins: 1" or 65-space line

Drill 1

what competencies does entry-level office workers need. surveys indecate that the most important competency are interpersonal skills communiction skills and basic office skills. a office worker with out these basic skills are not likely to be sucessful. while these skills are prerequisites for sucess, they are just the begining. office workers also need to develope technical and proceedural skills

Drill 2

a person needs to have a number of specific competences to by an affective communicator. they include listining, speaking, reading, writing, and communicating nonverbaly. listining may be the most important of the competences. most employees spent more time listining then they do speaking reading, or writing. of all the skills employees has, listening it usualy the weakest skill.

Improve punctuation skill

Key Drills 3 and 4 using appropriate punctuation. Proofread and edit your copy.

Drill 3

If Shelly arrives before noon please ask her to call Al Joan or me. We want her to meet Peter Marshank our new consultant before he leaves. Peter was scheduled to be with us for two days but he had to return home. However he does plan to return next Tuesday May 5.

Drill 4

Betty Bill and I plan to leave on Tuesday March 15 to go to Garden City Tennessee. We thought Frank our manager would ride with us but he is unable to do so. However he will meet us in Garden City on Wednesday March 16. If you would like to ride with us we have extra room and would enjoy your company. Please let us know if you would like to join us.

MAIL REGISTER
MONEY RECEIVED

Clerk: Jan Borkowski	Date: February 14, 19--			
Received From	**Amount**	**Cash**	**Ck.**	**M.O.**
Chiang Exporters, Ltd.	$ 1,675.50			X
The Mason Company	450.00		X	
Oscar Perez	12.00	X		
Pagan Industries	2,469.73		X	
Henderson, Inc.	875.25		X	
Burge and Burge	1,390.79		X	
Tien Lin	650.45			X
Consolidated Services	14,750.00		X	
Leslie Perkins	6.00	X		
Double D, Inc.	1,840.95		X	
Rexford, Inc.	595.25		X	
Boykin Industries	2,790.40		X	
Carlota Torres	395.62		X	
Mark Harrington	254.75		X	
Etsuko Matsumi	1,276.30		X	
Midge Porter	320.00		X	
Total Money Received	$29,752.99			
Reconciled With Deposit Yes X No ____ If no, discrepancy:	**Supervisor's Signature**			

Document 2

1 Key the report as a leftbound report; DS.

2 Use 1.5" top margin; bold main heading.

words

VOICE MAIL RECOMMENDED 5

The study of messaging and answering services 14
needed by Altman Corporation has been completed, and 24
voice mail is the alternative recommended. Voice mail was 36
selected as the ideal system for Altman's large field 49
service operation and will meet the needs of the 59
entire organization. 63
¶ Voice mail is a telephone answering and messaging 73
system. The user gains access to the system through touch 85
tone telephone service and speaks the message into the 96
telephone. The message is then converted to digital 107
signals and stored by a computer for the recipient. 117
¶ The features that will be of particular benefit to 127
Altman Corporation are broadcast and call forwarding. 138
The broadcast feature enables a user to record one 149
message and send it to a large group of people. With 159
call forwarding, telephone calls can be redirected to 170
the voice mail box, to an operator, or to paging devices 182
or beepers. These two features solve the problems 192
of getting messages to the field service employees 202
in a timely fashion. 206

Document 3

1 Rekey Document 2, inserting the ¶ at the right between ¶1 and ¶2.

2 Proofread; correct errors.

(Total words: 251)

A complete proposal is attached. The proposal includes the cost justification, the procurement alternatives, and the specifications of the system recommended. A brochure describing the system recommended is also attached.

98 Measurement

Skill-Building Warmup

98a 5'

alphabet 1 Jacqueline Katz made extra money by singing with the five groups.
figure 2 I sold 27 roses, 10 irises, 68 lilies, 54 tulips, and 39 orchids.
space bar 3 If she may go with me to a lake, I may do all of the work and go.
fluency 4 The girls got the bicycle at the land of enchantment at the lake.

| 1 | 2 | 3 | 4 | 5 | 6 | 7 | 8 | 9 | 10 | 11 | 12 | 13 |

98b 10'

SKILL BUILDING

Measure straight-copy skill

1 Key one 3' writing; circle errors; determine *gwam*.
2 Key one 5' writing; circle errors; determine *gwam*.

 A all letters

	gwam 3'	5'	
Employees who work together as a team are more effective	4	2	39
than those who work solo. This concept is known as synergy.	8	5	42
Synergy simply means that the joint action exceeds the sum of	12	7	44
individual actions. The results are not just in the quantity of	16	10	47
work; major gains in quality result when people work together as	21	12	49
a team. Teamwork is critical for success.	24	14	51
What characterizes an excellent team member? An excellent	28	17	53
team member understands the goals of the team and will place team	32	19	56
values above her or his individual objectives. An excellent team	36	22	59
member helps to determine the most effective way to reach the	40	24	61
goals that were set by the group and will help to make each	44	27	63
decision that affects the group. Above all, an excellent team	49	29	66
member will support a decision made by the team. Each member	53	32	68
must understand her or his role and respect the roles of others.	57	34	71
Every member of a team must share in both victory and defeat.	61	37	74

98c 35'

FORMATTING

Measure production

Time schedule
Assemble materials .... 5'
Timed production .... 25'
Final check;
compute *n-pram* .... 5'

1 Read the directions, especially for Document 4, to be sure you understand them.
2 Organize your supplies.
3 When directed to begin, work for 25'.
4 Proofread carefully; correct errors; compute *n-pram* (total words keyed – penalty) ÷ 25'.

Good organization enhances productivity

1 Remove appropriate stationery and forms from your laboratory materials.
2 Place laboratory materials and plain paper in a convenient place positioned in the order you will use them.
3 Clear a space in your work area to place completed documents facedown so that they will remain in the proper sequence.
4 Move quickly from one document to the next.

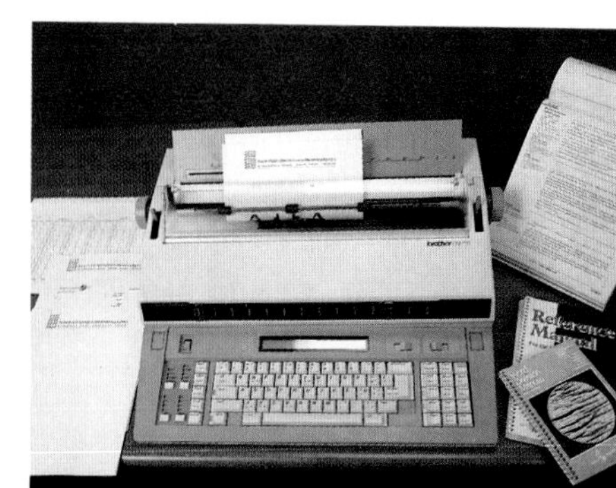

Document 1
Key the report in leftbound format. For added emphasis, add bold to main and side headings.

Note: When reports are double-spaced, paragraphs are indented 5 spaces. Extra space is not added between ¶s.

Line 10 or 1.5" → **PROFESSIONAL AFFILIATIONS**
QS

1.5" → ← 1"

A survey of our employees indicated that approximately 20 percent are members of professional associations. However, technical employees were more likely to belong to these organizations than were individuals in other occupational groups.

Senior managers expressed a strong desire to have a high percentage of all employees affiliate with professional organizations. This study focused on ways to encourage employees to join professional associations.

Side heading →

Reasons for Not Joining Associations

The primary reasons cited for not joining organizations were lack of time, cost, unawareness of associations for field, and never giving organizations much thought.

Reasons for Joining Associations

The major reasons cited for belonging to professional associations were the opportunity to network with other professionals, availability of literature addressing current issues in the field, and commitment to the profession.

Company Incentives

Employees indicated that with more company incentives they would join professional associations. Incentives desired were dues paid by company, recognition of employees who participate, and establishment of company chapters.

Leftbound report—double-spaced

words

Document 1
Table with centered column heads
Use 2" top margin and bold headings.

SOFTWARE RELEASE RECORD 4

Personal Computer Division 10

Product Code	Software	Version	Release	words
PCTP 24	QuickPublisher	4.2	September 20	32
PCCM 28	QuickCom	5.0	December 30	39
PCDP 24	QuickCalc	3.4	November 26	46
PCGD 40	QuickDraw	2.0	October 28	52
PCSC 20	QuickCapture	1.0	September 30	60

(Column heads line: 24)

Document 2
Standard memo with table
1 Use 1.5" top margin.
2 Key the table flush with left and right margins; add leaders.

TO: Angela Martinez | **FROM:** Brett Winfield | **DATE:** Current | **SUBJECT:** 10
Software Update 12

Several new versions of software are in the final stages of Beta testing, and 27
the product codes and release dates have been approved. The following 41
products you manage are on the list: 49

QuickCalc, PCDP 281, Version 4.0 .... February 28 58
QuickCapture, PCSC 204, Version 2.0 .... December 22 68
QuickCom, PCCM 282, Version 5.2..................... September 28 77
QuickPublisher, PCTP 240, Version 5.0 .... January 25 86
QuickDraw, PCGD 404, Version 2.1 .... September 30 96

Roger Sedgwick is coordinating the development of promotional materials. 110
He plans to schedule the initial meeting next month. 121

xx 122

Document 3
Purchase order
(LM p. S95)
Address order to:
WAYSIDE OFFICE EQUIPMENT
PO BOX 4938
BOONE NC 28607-4938
(Total Words: 52)

Purchase order # 4CD952570; Date Nov. 25, 19--; Date required Dec. 9, 19--; Terms 2/10, n/30; Shipped via Mountain Expresss

1	511CD	6284 Copier	$18,505.95	$18,505.95
1	151RHD	Document handler	412.75	412.75
1	115 FIN	Finisher	195.00	159.00
2	155SOR	Sorter	1,089.99	1,089.99
				$ 20,203.69

Document 4
Table with centered headings
Format and rekey Document 1 using the information from Document 2 to update the Software Release Record (Document 1).

70 Leftbound Report

Skill-Building Warmup

70a 5'

alphabet 1 Rex Czajkas quoted them a good price for a lovely brown swimsuit.
figure 2 Did 29 boys and 38 girls consume 476 cookies and 150 cold drinks?
space bar 3 Jan may go to the gym to see who is at the pool at noon each day.
fluency 4 Ty and a neighbor paid for the antique rug in the ancient chapel.

| 1 | 2 | 3 | 4 | 5 | 6 | 7 | 8 | 9 | 10 | 11 | 12 | 13 |

70b 12'

SKILL BUILDING

Improve straight-copy skill

1 Key one 3' writing.
2 Key one 5' writing.

A all letters

	gwam 3'	5'	
Subtle differences exist among role models, mentors, and	4	2	32
sponsors. A role model is a person you can emulate, or one who	8	5	35
provides a good example to follow. A mentor is one who will	12	7	37
advise, coach, or guide you when you need information about your	16	10	40
job or your organization. A sponsor is a person who will support	21	12	42
you or recommend you for a position or a new responsibility.	25	15	45
One person may fill all three roles, or several people may	30	18	48
serve as role models, mentors, or sponsors. These individuals	34	20	50
usually have higher ranks than you do, which means they will be	38	23	53
able to get information that you and your peers may not have.	42	25	55
Frequently, a mentor will share information with you that will	46	28	58
enable you to make good decisions about your career.	50	30	60

gwam 3' | 1 | 2 | 3 | 4 | 5 |
5' | 1 | 2 | 3 |

70c 33'

FORMATTING

Leftbound reports

Read the information at the right. Then, format and key the reports on pages 168-169.

Formatting leftbound reports

The binding on a report usually takes about a half inch of space; therefore, on a leftbound report, a 1.5" left margin should be used on all pages.

The center of the line of writing moves to the right about 3 spaces:

10-pitch: 15 + 75 ÷ 2 = 45
12-pitch: 18 + 90 ÷ 2 = 54

The same right-side, top, and bottom margins are used for both unbound and leftbound reports. Reports may be either single-spaced or double-spaced. Paragraphs must be indented when double spacing is used.

Communication Workshop 6

MicroAssistant: To select Communication Workshop 6, key **C6** from the Main menu.

Drills 1-4
Improve language art skills

1 Use 1.5" top margin; default or 1" side and bottom margins; DS.
2 Key the ¶s on this page, correcting all errors as you key.
3 Proofread; correct errors.

Drill 1

Spelling verification sofware helps too detect typographical errors. How ever, proofreading is still essential even it you use spelling verification soft ware. Many types of errors are not detected by spelling verification package. These erros range form errors in use of similar words, proper nouns, and numbers to errors in grammer and punctuation. spacing errors or offen missed, two. Proof read ever document carefully so that you work will be error free.

Drill 2

Typographical and spelling erors are ofen detected when copy is red form right to left. reading from right to left forces your to read each word indilvidually. this proceedure is helpful when speling verification software is not availabe. spelling verifiction software normally locates the same types of erors that are detected when copy is red form right to left. You must still read copy in in the normal fashion to detect substitution of similar words, omission of words, insertion of unnecesssary words, and other erors.

Drill 3

People are ofen judged by the way they right or they speak. good communication skills is important and they can be developed. One way to develop goods communication skills ils to have some one who is knowledgeable critique you speaking on the telephone or in a face-to-face situation and to critique letters or papers you have writen. Then you can determine the types of errors you are making and review basic guides in those areas.

Drill 4

The restuarant could not accomodate us on Wenesday night because it was all ready booked, but we were able to reschedule the event. Our committe beleived that it would be better to change the date then to move to another resturant. Since many of our members are not familar with the city and they all ready no how to get to the Carriage House, it will be for more convient form them if we do not change locations. Please mark your calandar for Tuesday of next week.

Document 2

1 Use 1.5" top margin and default or 1" side and bottom margins.

2 Review guides on page 162 for placing a table within a document, if necessary.

Note: Business reports are generally single-spaced. Block ¶s within a SS report; DS between ¶s. For added emphasis, add bold to all headings.

1.5" top margin → **REPORT WRITING SERIES** DS

Guide 6 QS

This sixth guide in the series of ten guides is designed to improve and standardize the reporting process in all divisions of Marcus Computer Services, Inc. Guide 6 has the dual objectives of enhancing readability and emphasizing key ideas effectively. Effective formatting is central to both of these objectives. DS

Readability DS

Vocabulary, sentence and paragraph length and structure, and formatting affect the readability of a document. Particular attention should be paid to these factors in preparing reports.

Vocabulary. Word length affects the difficulty level of copy; however, familiarity of words may be more important than the length of words. Multisyllable, technical, and unfamiliar words should be minimized in reports to enhance readability.

1" side margins

Sentence and paragraph length and structure. Variety may be essential, but direct order and reasonably short sentences and paragraphs enhance readability. The following guides are helpful in judging average sentence and paragraph length: DS

Units of Measure	Sentences	Paragraphs
Words (average)	18	75
Lines (average)	2	8

DS

Formatting. Effective use of white space affects readability. Appropriate line length, space between paragraphs, and vertical placement set material apart and make it easier to read.

Emphasis Techniques

Extra space and underlining were traditional emphasis techniques. Current technology makes bold and large-sized fonts (when they are available) more effective emphasis techniques. Both bold and underlining can be used when large-sized fonts are not available. Marcus standard style has been changed from using a triple space before headings for emphasis to using bold, which is a more effective emphasis technique. It is also easier to format.

Unbound report—single-spaced

Drills 5-6
Improve
language art skills

1 Use 1.5" top margin; default or 1" side and bottom margins; DS.
2 Key the first two ¶s on this page, correcting errors as you key.
3 Proofread; correct errors.

Drill 5

Many executive are concern that american industry is threatened buy a inadequately prepared entry-level word force. Many workers is hired whom cannot read write or count. Industry spend $25 billion a years on remedial training of new workers. One executive said "When business do remedail training they are doing the product recall work for the nations school."

Drill 6

Style is a matter of perception. Two question are quiet important. How are you perceived and how do you won't to be percieved? If the answers does not match, then you should try too manage you image more effective. Your dress your language and the degree of formality you exhibit are all a part of style.

Drills 7-8
Improve
composition skills

1 Use 1.5" top margin; default or 1" side and bottom margins; DS.
2 Compose a 4- or 5-sentence paragraph completing the statements in Drills 7-8.
3 Edit the ¶s; proofread; correct errors.

Drill 7

TEAMWORK

Companies are placing major emphasis on the ability of employees to work as effective members of a team. I believe I will be an effective team member because . . . ***(Give several reasons why you think you would be an effective team member.)***

Drill 8

CHARACTERISTICS OF EFFECTIVE EMPLOYEES

Many personal characteristics are important. The characteristics that I believe are the most important ones for me to develop to be successful in school are . . . ***(Select several characteristics such as punctuality, willingness to devote time to study, honesty, etc. and explain why you think they are important for your success in school.)***

69 Outline and Report Review

Skill-Building Warmup

69a 5'

alphabet	1	Mixon plays great jazz with a quintet at a club five days a week.
fig/sym	2	Errors were found on page 389 (line #17) and page 460 (line #25).
direct reach	3	Brad and Cec had a great lunch and much fun with many youngsters.
fluency	4	The city may pay for half of the maps, and Jake may pay for half.

1 | 2 | 3 | 4 | 5 | 6 | 7 | 8 | 9 | 10 | 11 | 12 | 13

69b 5'

COMMUNICATION

Proofreading

1 Key the ¶, correcting errors as you key.

2 Proofread your copy using proofreaders' marks (see Reference Guide).

3 Key the ¶ again from your marked copy, making all corrections.

error corection is an simple process whenelectronic equiptment is used. Softwear packages even help too locate erors. How ever electronic tecnology doesnot eliminate the need to proof read careful.Errors in names punctuation number and similar words are not detected by speling verifiction softwear.

69c 40'

FORMATTING

Outlines and unbound report

Document 1

1 Read "Formatting Outlines."

2 1.5" top margin and 1" side margins.

Formatting Outlines

Outlines help writers organize and structure documents and presentations. Therefore, consistent format is essential in outlines. Use these features:

1 Key first-level topics in all caps. DS above and below first-level topics.

2 Capitalize main words in second-level topics. SS items.

3 Capitalize the initial word in third-level topics. SS items.

4 Use topics only when they have two or more parts.

5 Align both Roman and Arabic numerals at the decimal.

6 Begin topics under the first word of the preceding line, rather than under the designating letter or number.

EFFECTIVE PRESENTATIONS
DS

I. PLANNING AND PREPARING PRESENTATIONS
DS
 A. Opening
  1. Gain attention
  2. Set the tone
 B. Body of the Presentation
  1. Focus on objective
  2. Organize information
  3. Prepare support materials
 C. Closing DS

II. DELIVERING PRESENTATIONS DS
 A. Delivery Techniques
  1. Engage audience
  2. Project voice effectively
  3. Control environment
 B. Visuals and Supporting Materials
  1. Ensure readability
  2. Use effectively

III. FOLLOW-UP ACTIVITIES
 A. Discussion and Questions
 B. Postpresentation Activities

THE PRINCIPLES OF DOCUMENT FORMATTING

Formatting complex business documents effectively is becoming as much an art as it is a science. Document format deserves special attention because it contributes significantly to communication effectiveness. Format is not simply a matter of appearance. Format provides structure and organization to a document. It affects the ease with which a document can be read, and it often determines which ideas are emphasized.

Historically, the typewriter offered little flexibility in formatting documents. Three features illustrated in Figure 1—space or position, capital letters, and underlining—were generally used to add structure, enhance readability, and provide emphasis.

To show the importance of the title, it was keyed in all capitals with extra space below it (emphasis by isolation). To show that side headings were less important than the main heading and more important than paragraph headings, extra space was left below them, and they were underlined. To add structure, copy was often indented. Alphanumeric characters were used to signal a list, even though sequence was not a factor in the listing. Space or position was the primary way to emphasize tabular information.

As electronic typewriters replaced electric typewriters, bold became a commonly used attribute. Now, sophisticated word processing software offers numerous features, such as italics, varied font size and type, special characters such as bullets (small circles or squares), boxes and other typographic symbols, vertical as well as horizontal lines, and imported graphics, that can be selected to create a particular effect.

The challenge today is to select features that provide the desired effect and to use the features appropriately. Using too many features can have a negative effect. For example, using both the large, bold font and a quadruple space below the title in Figure 2 would overemphasize the title and would not be an effective format.

Format also affects productivity. Operator skill often determines the format used. Many managers (with limited training) format some of their documents. They tend to use the default standards of their software without modification.

Document formatting, which is both a science and an art, is in a state of transition. New features will continue to evolve. To produce the best documents, the principles of good design should be used to create the best effect.

Figure 1

DOCUMENT FORMAT

Changing a few format features can have a dramatic impact on the design of a document. This document illustrates the traditional format that was used for many years. Several features generally available on a typewriter can be used to add structure, enhance readability, and emphasize ideas:

1. Keying copy in all capitals
2. Underlining specific text
3. Using space to isolate text

These formatting features determine the page design and the physical appearance of specific text. Standardizing the design or layout of a document helps to create a consistent image.

<u>Page Design</u>

Several formatting features affect the design of this page. The most obvious features are spacing and attributes.

<u>Spacing</u>. The effect of spacing is very evident. The title is emphasized by adding space to isolate it from the rest of the document. Enumerated items are positioned on separate lines. Space between paragraphs makes the document much easier to read. The text can be either single-spaced or double-spaced.

<u>Attributes</u>. Attributes affect the physical appearance of text. The most obvious attributes are all capitals and underlining. Both of these techniques give emphasis to specific text.

<u>Typestyle</u>

Very few alternatives for varying typestyle are available on a typewriter. Generally, the choice is limited to using either elite or pica type.

Typestyle	Horizontal Spaces	Vertical Spaces
Elite	12 spaces per inch	6 lines per inch
Pica	10 spaces per inch	6 lines per inch

Fixed spacing makes it extremely difficult to justify the right margin. Usually, a ragged right margin is used.

Figure 2

DOCUMENT FORMAT

Changing a few format features can have a dramatic impact on the design of a document. This document illustrates a few of the many formatting features that are available in word processing software. Features can be used to add structure, enhance readability, and emphasize ideas:

- Keying copy in all capitals and/or bold
- Using different font sizes
- Using space to isolate text

These formatting features determine the page design and the physical appearance of the text. Select features to enhance communication and to create a consistent image.

Page Design

Several formatting features affect the design of this page. The most obvious features are spacing and attributes.

Spacing. The effect of spacing is very evident. Enumerated items are positioned on separate lines. Space between paragraphs makes the document much easier to read. The text can be either single-spaced or double-spaced.

Attributes. Attributes affect the physical appearance of text. The most obvious attributes are bold and large font sizes. Both of these techniques give emphasis to specific text.

Typestyle

Numerous alternatives for varying typestyle are available depending on the type of printer used with word processing. Generally, the choice consists of a variety of fonts or typeface families. Scalable fonts range from very small sizes to extremely large sizes.

Typestyle	Horizontal Spaces	Vertical Spaces
Elite—variety of typefaces	12 spaces per inch	6 lines per inch
Pica—variety of typefaces	10 spaces per inch	6 lines per inch
Scalable fonts—variety	Wide range of point sizes	Varies with selection

Proportional spacing makes it very easy to justify the right margin. Usually, full justification is used for reports.

68d 25'

FORMATTING

Tables with centered column heads

Center column heads; use bold and underline for each table.

Document 1
DS data; 2" top margin; 6 intercolumn spaces.

			words
HIGH PERFORMERS FOR 19--			5
Agent	**Sales**	**Office**	12
Jacqueline C. Zahradnik	$3,869,451	Lakeshore Boulevard	23
Alonza T. Azotea	3,185,374	Center City	31
Katherine Anne Harrington	2,564,081	Lexington Heights	41
Michael T. Wang	1,975,392	Center City	49
Conchita A. Delgado	1,783,094	Lexington Heights	59

Document 2
DS data; 10 intercolumn spaces; center the table vertically.

Document 3

1 Rekey Document 2.

2 Add fourth column; 6 intercolumn spaces.

$500,000
33
38
51
61
89
138

(Total words: 39)

TERM LIFE INSURANCE			4
(Monthly Rates)			7
Age	**$100,000**	**$200,000**	15
30	12	20	17
35	14	23	19
40	17	30	21
45	22	40	22
50	28	53	24
55	42	87	26

Document 4
2" top margin; decide spacing of data based on guidelines on page 162.

HIGH PERFORMERS			3
First Quarter, 19--			7
Name	Highest Speed	Number of Errors	21
Jacqueline Lozyczenko	143	3	27
Wayne Carrington	130	2	31
Marianne Muhlankamp	127	2	36
Michael Greensides	124	4	41
Andrea Benson-Waters	121	1	47

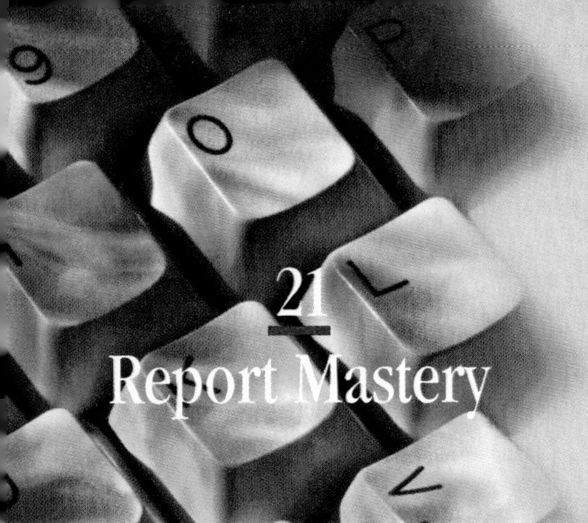

Learning goals:
1 To improve keyboarding skill.
2 To learn to format business reports.

Formatting guides:
1 Margins: 1" or 65-space line for drills and ¶ writings.
2 Single-space drills; double-space writings; SS documents unless otherwise directed.
3 Indentions: 5-spaces or default tabs for ¶ writings.

99a 5'

Skill-building warmup

each line 3 times (slowly, faster, slowly); DS between 3-line groups; repeat selected lines if time permits

(Use these directions for all skill-building warmups in Lessons 99-107.)

alphabet 1 Eve Quinn played my saxophone for a jazz group about once a week.
figure 2 I took 378 people on a 654-mile bus trip and made 19 or 20 stops.
shift key 3 Pat, Al, Jan, Ty, Rod, Pam, Quin, and Blair made the tennis team.
fluency 4 Rick may make a lamb dish, or he may fix fish for us at the lake.
| 1 | 2 | 3 | 4 | 5 | 6 | 7 | 8 | 9 | 10 | 11 | 12 | 13 |

99b 10'

FORMATTING

Preapplication: Title page

1 Read the information at the right.

2 Format the title page shown for an unbound report; use bold.

Title page

The title page usually conveys to the reader a concise title identifying the subject of the report, the name and title of the individual or organization for whom the report was prepared, the name and title of the writer, and the date the report was completed.

Center items on a title page horizontally. Remember that extra space must be provided for the binding when reports are bound. Vertical placement depends on the amount of copy contained on the title page. The information should be positioned so that it is attractive and easy to read.

2"

FORMATTING GUIDES FOR REPORTS

2"

Prepared for
(Your instructor's name)
Keyboarding Instructor
School Name

2"

Prepared by
(Your name)
Keyboarding Student
School Name

2"

Current date

68 Centered Column Headings

Skill-Building Warmup

68a 5'

alphabet 1 Frances Zwanka exited very quietly just prior to the big seminar.
figure 2 Please call 235-9167 or 294-3678 before 10:45 a.m. on January 18.
adjacent reach 3 Louis, Sadi, Art, and a few other people were going to a concert.
fluency 4 Vivian may go with a neighbor or with me to work on an amendment.

| 1 | 2 | 3 | 4 | 5 | 6 | 7 | 8 | 9 | 10 | 11 | 12 | 13 |

68b 10'

SKILL BUILDING

Improve keyboarding technique

each pair of lines 3 times; work at a controlled rate

balanced hand
5 The visitor to the island kept both mementos for a sick neighbor.
6 The auditor may handle the work for them if the city pays for it.

one hand
7 Phillip defeated Lynn in a race on a hilly street in Cedar Acres.
8 My grades in art were bad; Dave regrets my grade average was bad.

combination
9 Doris and Lilly were in debt for the cornfield on the big island.
10 My neighbor and I may fix the bicycle at the garage and trade it.

| 1 | 2 | 3 | 4 | 5 | 6 | 7 | 8 | 9 | 10 | 11 | 12 | 13 |

68c 10'

FORMATTING

Centering column heads

1 Read the information at the right.
2 Format the two drills.

Center column heads

Review the procedures on page 162 to format the columns of a table. If the column head is the longest line in the column, use it for determining horizontal placement of the table.

For heads shorter than columns:

1 From column starting point, space forward once for each two strokes for the longest line in the column. From this point, backspace once for each 2 spaces in the column heading. Ignore a leftover or odd space when backspacing.

2 Begin the column head at this point.

For heads longer than columns:

1 From the column starting point, key heading.

2 For first column entry, space forward once for each two strokes in the heading. From this point, backspace once for each 2 spaces in the longest column entry. Ignore an odd or leftover space when backspacing.

Drill 1

Player	Home	words
	DS	4
Christopher J. Mayotte	San Francisco, California	14
Renee S. Dougherty	New Orleans, Louisiana	23
Rebecca T. Bauerschmidt	Albuquerque, New Mexico	32

Drill 2

Convention City	Average Temperature	
	DS	14
Atlanta	58	16
Chicago	44	18
Toronto	36	21

99c 35'

Leftbound business report

Document 1

1 Read the information at the right as well as the report on pages 247-249.

2 SS the report; margins: left, 1.5", right, 1"; remember when centering the main heading that the line of writing moves to the right 3 spaces. Refer to pages 166-167 if necessary.

Note: If you are unable to compose the block to signal the enumeration, use lowercase letter **o** in bold.

Report Format Review

Reports with headings

Headings provide structure and make reports easier to read. A combination of capitalization, bold, position, and underscoring are used to indicate levels of importance.

Main heading: bold, CAPS, centered, quadruple-space below the heading.

Side headings: bold, underlined, double-spaced above and below the headings; capitalize main words.

Paragraph headings: bold, underlined, part of paragraph, isolated by white space; capitalize first word.

Option: Increase type sizes for all headings.

Second and succeeding pages

1 Number second and subsequent pages at the right margin 1" from the top; DS below number.

2 Avoid dividing the last word on a page.

3 Avoid carrying over a single line of a paragraph to a subsequent page or leaving a single line on a page.

4 Key references on the last page of a report only if all references can be confined to that page. Otherwise, use a separate, numbered page.

words

FORMATTING GUIDES FOR REPORTS 6

Business reports are documents that are used 15
internally and externally. Managers often 24
delegate the preparation of internal reports to 33
subordinates; therefore, most reports go up to 43
higher ranks in the organization. External 51
reports often are used to secure business or 60
to report on business that has been conducted 70
for a client. Since reports can have a signifi- 79
cant impact on an organization's business and 88
on an individual's upward career mobility, they 97
are usually prepared with a great deal of care. 107

The following factors must be considered in 116
formatting reports: 120

- Placement--spacing, margins, and pagi- 128
nation 130
- Headings--main, secondary, side, and 137
paragraph 139
- Documentation--internal citations, end- 147
notes, and references 152
- Report assembly--preliminary pages, 159
body of report, and appendices 165

<u>Placement</u> 169

Effective report design requires many decisions 179
about each of the factors just enumerated. The 188
software and the type of printer usually deter- 197
mine which features can be used to 204
enhance the format of a document. A few basic 214
guides can be applied to assist in making good 223
formatting decisions. 228

<u>Spacing</u>. Reports may be formatted using 237
either single or double spacing. Commercially 247
prepared reports are generally single-spaced 256
using many typesetting features. The desktop 265
publishing capabilities available in most word 274
processing software enable employees to 282
prepare reports similar to those prepared 291
professionally. Therefore, the trend is to single- 301
space reports, use full justification, and to in- 311
corporate desktop publishing features in the 320
report. 321

<u>Margins</u>. Reports are formatted with one-inch 332
top, side, and bottom margins. A half inch of 341
extra space is provided in the top margin (1.5") 351
for the first page of the report and for major 360
sections that begin on a new page. A half inch 370
of extra space is provided for the binding 378

67c (continued)

FORMATTING

Table with blocked headings

Read the guidelines for formatting a table.

Guidelines for formatting a table

To format a table, the following questions must be answered:

1 *Single- or double-space?* Double spacing is generally more attractive and easier to read, but may require more space than you have available. As a rule, single-space tables of more than 20 lines; double-space shorter tables. However, in single-spaced documents, single-space tables; in double-spaced documents, double-space tables.

2 *Vertical center or standard top margin?* Tables on a separate page may begin at a specified point, such as 1", 1.5", or 2" top margin, or they may be centered vertically. Using a specified top margin is more efficient, but sometimes a centered format is desirable. Tables within documents are usually placed a double space below the line of text.

3 *Intercolumn spaces?* On an electronic typewriter, automatic centering may be used to center columns between margins, or columnar tabs may be set. Word processing software may feature automatic table formatting. Use an even amount of space between columns. The amount should vary depending on the width and number of columns as shown in the guide below:

Width	Description	Intercolumn Spaces
Narrow	2 columns or 3 narrow columns	10 spaces
Average	3 columns or 4 narrow columns	6-8 spaces, depending on width of columns
Wide	4 or more columns	4-6 spaces

Documents 1 and 2

1 Format the tables (average) using 8 intercolumn spaces.

2 Use a 2" top margin.

3 Bold and underscore column heads; DS the table.

Document 1

words

REVIEW OF REPOSSESSED PROPERTY 6

Property Address	Price Listed	Recommendation	
			24
5739 Overbrook Dr.	$47,600	Bid list plus 10%	33
4928 Deerwood St.	$64,975	Bid list minus 5%	42
6837 Suber St.	$42,759	Bid not recommended	50
9356 Kilbourne Rd.	$71,450	Bid list price	59

Document 3

1 Rekey Document 2 adding a fourth column.

Yield
7.28%
7.09%
8.05%
8.33%
8.65%

2 Use 4 spaces between columns; 2" top margin; DS the table. (Total words: 60)

Document 2

BEST RATE ON HIGH-YIELD SAVINGS 6

Savings Account	Association	Best Rate	
			21
Money market	Southeastern	7.03%	27
One-month CDs	Northwestern	6.85%	34
Three-month CDs	Central	8.05%	40
Six-month CDs	Southeastern	8.00%	47
One-year CDs	Federal	8.00%	52

when a report is bound. Most reports are 387
bound at the left (1.5" left margin); a few are 396
bound at the top (1.5" top margin). 404

Pagination. The way a report is paginated 414
depends on the binding. A leftbound or an 423
unbound report usually is paginated at the 432
top, right margin. A topbound report is 440
paginated at the center, bottom margin. 448
Arabic numerals (1, 2, 3) are used for the body 458
of the report and the appendix; lowercase 466
Roman numerals (i, ii, iii) are used for the 475
prefatory (preliminary) pages. The body of the 485
report starts with page 1 even though sev- 493
eral preliminary pages precede it. The first 502
page is counted, but it is not numbered. Nor- 511
mally, the preliminary pages are prepared 520
after the report is written; therefore, they are 530
handled as a separate document and num- 537
bered with lowercase Roman numerals to avoid 546
duplicate numbers. 550

Headings 554

Topical headings or captions introduce the 562
material that follows and provide structure 571
in a report. Position, capitalization, font 580
size, and attributes, such as bold and 588
underlining, indicate levels of importance. 597
Headings also set segments of copy apart and 606
make the copy easier to read. The spacing 615
before and after headings depends on 622
the type and size of font used. With 630
regular typewritten copy, spacing (a 637
quadruple space after the main heading 645
and a double space before and after side 653
headings) is important for emphasis. If a 662
larger type size is used for the main head- 670
ing, less space is needed below it. The large 680
type commands attention; therefore, additional 689
space to set the heading apart from the 697
report is not necessary. 702

Documentation 708

Most writers give credit when they use the 716
work of others. Quotes or extensive use of 725
published material should be referenced. In 734
business, many employees feel that the 742
internal reports they use as references be- 750
long to the company; therefore, referencing 759
is not necessary. Employees should keep in 768
mind, however, that referencing also helps the 777
reader locate more complete information 785
than the report contains. Documentation can 794
be provided in several ways. 800

Endnotes. A superior number keyed at the 810
point of reference serves as an indicator that 819
the source is provided at the end of the docu- 829
ment. All sources are placed on a separate 838
page at the end of the report in numerical 846
order. The endnotes come before the bibli- 855
ography or list of complete references. The 864
page is numbered in sequence with the pre- 872
ceding page. Endnotes are single-spaced with 882
a double space between notes; the first line 891
of each entry is indented five spaces. 899

Internal citations. Internal citations pro- 909
vide the source of information within the body 919
of the report. The name(s) of the author(s), 928
publication date, and the page numbers are 936
separated by commas and enclosed in paren- 945
theses before the terminal punctuation, as 953
illustrated in this sentence (VanHuss, 1994, 962
10-12). When the author's name is used in 971
context, only the date and page numbers are 978
included in the citation. 985

References. The reference list at the end of 996
the report contains all references whether 1005
quoted or not in alphabetical order by au- 1013
thor name. The names of authors, titles of 1022
publications, the name and location of the 1031
publisher, and the publication date make up 1039
the reference. References are single-spaced 1048
with a double space between items. Book 1057
and periodical titles are generally indicated 1066
by underlining. The trend today, when the 1074
printer can accommodate it, is to use italics. 1084

Report Assembly 1090

The components of a business report vary 1098
depending on the formality of the report. 1107
Reports generally are assembled in three 1115
separate segments. Generally, the body of 1124

67 Table Review

Skill-Building Warmup

67a 5'

alphabet 1	Liz Bowhanon moved very quickly and just played exciting defense.
figure 2	I fed 285 cats, 406 dogs, 157 birds, and 39 rabbits at a shelter.
1/2 fingers 3	Jimmy or Vick sent my fur hat this summer, but I did not need it.
fluency 4	An authentic ivory tusk may be key to the ancient island rituals.

1 | 2 | 3 | 4 | 5 | 6 | 7 | 8 | 9 | 10 | 11 | 12 | 13

67b 10'

SKILL BUILDING

Build straight-copy skill

Key three 1' writings at your top rate. Key one 3' writing at a controlled rate.

A all letters

	gwam 1'	3'	
Color laser printers add a whole new dimension to the con-	12	4	34
cept of in-house publishing. Until quite recently, all the	24	8	38
printing that required color had to be sent to external sources	36	12	43
for production. Today, two-color printers can have a major	48	16	47
impact on the amount of work that has to be sent out to be	60	20	51
printed. A good professional image can be created at quite a	73	24	55
reasonable production cost for most of the documents that an	85	29	59
organization might need to produce.	92	31	62

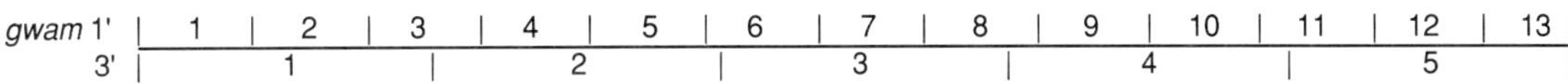

67c 35'

FORMATTING

Basic table format

Study the table and the description of its components carefully. Note that the column headings are blocked at the left.

Note: Guides for centering tables are contained in the Reference Guide. You may wish to review these guides before keying tables on page 162.

MAIN HEADING: Identifies table content. Center the title in all caps and bold.

SECONDARY HEADING: Further identifies table content. Center a double space below main heading. Use initial caps on principal words; bold.

COLUMNS: Vertical lists of information. Usually spaced equal distances apart.

ROWS: Horizontal lines of information. Usually single-spaced for long tables (20 lines or more) and double-spaced for short tables.

CELL: The intersection of a column and a row.

COLUMN HEADINGS: Identifies information in columns. Block or center headings over columns and underline. Double-space below the columnar headings. Bold may be used if desired.

INTERCOLUMNAR SPACE: Space between columns; usually 4 to 10 spaces depending on width of table. Use more intercolumn space in narrow tables than in wide tables.

EXCELLENCE IN CUSTOMER SERVICE DS

Videotape Version DS

Title of Module ← row →	Videotape Time	Cost
Image Building	24 minutes	$79
Quality Service	45 minutes	99
Problem Solving	40 minutes	89

DS (below column headings); column ↑ (first column); cell ↑ (40 minutes)

the report is prepared first; then, the mate- 1134
rial to be appended; and, finally, the front 1142
matter. 1144

Preliminary pages. A title page, letter of 1155
transmittal, table of contents, and executive 1165
summary are often placed at the beginning 1173
of a report. Other pages, such as a list of 1182
figures, may be added. 1187

The title page makes the initial impression 1196
for the report; therefore, it deserves special 1205
attention. An effective title page is format- 1215
ted attractively and contains the title of the 1224
report, who the report was prepared for, 1232
who the report was prepared by, and the 1240
date. 1242

Body of the report. The body of the 1252
report varies widely depending on the type of 1262
report. Reports frequently contain enumer- 1270
ated items, tables, charts, and graphics. Many 1280
organizations have style guides for the vari- 1289
ous types of reports commonly used in the 1297
organization. 1300

Appendices. Materials that support a re- 1310
port, such as questionnaires, biographical 1319
sketches, and large computer printout tables, 1328
are often placed at the end of the report in 1337
a section called the appendix. Often the 1346
material is segmented into several different 1355
appendices. Printed items in the appendix, 1363
such as questionnaires, usually are preceded 1372
by a page naming the appendix. 1378

Document 2

Prepare a table of contents for the **leftbound** report. Refer to pages 225-226 if necessary.

(Total words using leader tab: 50)

Document 3

Prepare a title page for the **leftbound** report, including the same information shown on the title page on page 246.

Document 4

1 Compose a short letter to your instructor transmitting your report.

2 Suggest that the report be used as a format guide for your class.

3 Position the number **ii** at the center bottom.

words

TABLE OF CONTENTS 4

<QS

add leaders and page numbers

words

Document 2
(LM p. S11)
Format the (short) letter using modified block style, indented paragraphs, mixed punctuation, and standard margins.

March 1, 19-- | Ms. Wanda Roe, President | Crafts Unlimited, 11
Inc. | 483 Long Lane | Casper, WY 82609-3714 | Dear 21
Ms. Roe: 23
Thank you for inviting us to participate again in 33
your annual craft fair, May 15-17. We are delighted 45
to participate again this year. 52
Our check and booth preference forms are enclosed. 62
We will handle all of the setup ourselves. The booth 73
should have a table and two chairs. 81
Our booth was very profitable last year, and we 90
hope to do even better this year. We have several new 101
designs to exhibit. 105
Sincerely, | Jessica Price | xx | Enclosures 113

Document 3
(LM p. S13)
Format the (short) letter using modified block style, block paragraphs, open punctuation, and standard margins.

March 18, 19-- | Ms. Jessica Price | HandPrints, Inc. | 10
53 W. Silver Street | Butte, MT 59701-4826 | Dear Ms. 20
Price 22
Booth 48 your first choice had been reserved 31
for you for the annual craft fair on May 15th- 40
17th. You booth was extreme popular last year and 50
we are very please to have you participated in the 61
fare again this year. 65
Our standard agreement from is enclosed. 74
Please sign it and return it to us by April 15th. 83
Your booths will have a large table and a minimum 93
of two chair. If you need anything else for the 103
booth please let us know prior to the opening 116
ofthe fair. 119
Sincerely | Ms. Wanda Roe | President | xx | Enclosure 128

100-101 Executive Summary; References; Contents

Skill-Building Warmup

100-101a 5'

alphabet 1	Zam injured five fingers, but he produces excellent quality work.
fig/sym 2	Robison shipped a 24# box (18" x 30" x 9") of shrimp for $176.45.
direct reach 3	Cecil Mund, my brother, broke my brush; he has too much strength.
fluency 4	Claudia did sign both forms for the auditor and paid the penalty.

| 1 | 2 | 3 | 4 | 5 | 6 | 7 | 8 | 9 | 10 | 11 | 12 | 13 |

100b 15'

SKILL BUILDING

Build straight-copy skill

1 Key three 1' writings on each ¶. (On the first two writings, strive to increase keystroking speed; then, regain control on the third writing.)

2 Key one 5' writing; proofread; circle errors; determine *gwam*.

A all letters

	gwam 1'	5'	
People come in many sizes and shapes. Thus, a workstation	12	2	44
designed for the average person will not fit all people. A	24	5	46
workstation should be designed for the person who will use it.	37	7	49
If more than one person will use it, then it must be adjustable	49	10	51
to meet the needs of each person who will use it. Ergonomics is	62	12	54
the term used to describe human factors engineering. Today,	75	15	56
desks, chairs, keyboards, and video display terminals are avail-	87	17	59
able with a number of features that can be adjusted to accommo-	100	20	61
date the person who will use the furniture or equipment.	112	22	64
Just because furniture or equipment has adjustable features	12	25	66
does not mean that the person using the furniture or equipment	24	27	69
will adjust it properly. Too often they do not. Maximum return	37	30	71
from the money spent on ergonomic furniture is dependent on how	50	32	74
the furniture is used, and comfort may not be the best guide for	63	35	76
making adjustments. Many people have habits that may cause them	76	38	79
to adjust furniture in an improper way. They need to be told and	89	40	82
taught what will work best.	95	41	83

gwam 1' | 1 | 2 | 3 | 4 | 5 | 6 | 7 | 8 | 9 | 10 | 11 | 12 | 13 |
5' | 1 | 2 | 3 |

Document 1
(LM p. S9)
Key the letter in modified block format (average length) with mixed punctuation; use standard margins. Proofread; make needed corrections.

IMAGE MAKERS
5131 Moss Springs Road
Columbia, SC 29209-4768
(803) 555-0127

Dateline — October 27, 19-- (Line 16)
QS
Horizontal center

Letter address
Ms. Vera M. Hayes, President
Vera's Word Processing Services
4927 Stuart Avenue
Baton Rouge, LA 70808-3519

Salutation
Dear Ms. Hayes:
DS

Body

The format of this letter is called modified block. Modified block format differs from block format in that the date, complimentary close, and the signature lines are positioned at the center point.
DS

Paragraphs may be blocked, as this letter illustrates, or they may be indented five spaces from the left margin. We suggest you block paragraphs when you use modified block style so that an additional tab setting is not needed. However, some people who use modified block format prefer indented paragraphs.

Although modified block format is very popular, we recommend that you use it only for those customers who request this letter style. Otherwise, we urge you to use block format, which is more efficient, as your standard style.

Both formats are illustrated in the enclosed <u>Image Makers Format Guide</u>. Please note that the block format is labeled "computer compatible."
DS

Complimentary close
Sincerely,
QS

Writer's name
Title
Patrick R. Ray
Communication Consultant

Reference initials
xx
DS

Enclosure notation
Enclosure
DS

Copy notation
c Scot Carl, Account Manager

Mixed Punctuation: Place a colon after the salutation and a comma after the complimentary close.
Copy Notation: Indicates who receives a copy of the document. The title is optional, but helpful.

Modified block letter format—mixed punctuation

100-101c 75'

FORMATTING

Business report with executive summary, internal citations, and references

Document 1

1 Format the leftbound report; SS.

2 The Executive Summary precedes the first page of the report. Position it on a separate page with a 1.5" top margin. Number it page **iv**; position the number at the center bottom.

3 Begin the first page of the report with a 1.5" top margin. Do not number the first page.

Executive Summary: Sometimes referred to as a synopsis, the executive summary briefly states the purpose of the report, the conclusions, and recommendations.

words

EXPANSION OF MEADE OUTPATIENT CENTER 7
Executive Summary 11
The demand for outpatient services at Meade Outpatient 22
Center has increased significantly over the past five years. 34
The purpose of this study was to determine if Meade Out- 46
patient Center needed to be expanded and, if expansion was 57
warranted, to develop a general business plan for the expan- 70
sion. 71
Data were collected from Meade Center records, Depart- 82
ment of Health records, interviews with area hospital admin- 96
istrators, and questionnaires sent to physicians and other 107
health care providers, and from industry literature. 118
The outpatient expansion was justified both on a needs 129
basis and on a cost basis. The project is projected to have 141
a positive cash flow in the first year. The Meade Out- 152
patient Center is critically needed and will enhance the 163
services offered to patients. The project should be imple- 175
mented as soon as necessary approvals are obtained. 185

EXPANSION OF MEADE OUTPATIENT CENTER 193
Today, doctors perform a significant segment of all 203
health-care procedures on an outpatient basis. The volume 217
at Meade increased 62% over the past five years (Snyder, 230
1993, p. 6). The Strategic Planning Committee reviewed the 241
Metro Analysis Feasibility Study (Emerson, 1993, p. 8) and 253
determined that the expansion of Meade Outpatient Center 264
could be justified. The Strategic Planning Committee then 276
directed the Outpatient Expansion task force to prepare a 287
general business plan for the expansion of Meade Outpatient 299
Center. 301

66 Modified Block Review

66a 5'

Skill-Building Warmup

alphabet 1 Jo Eizaburo will give them daily price quotations for six stocks.
fig/sym 2 That room (48' long x 35' wide with 10' ceilings) cost $6,972.50.
3/4 fingers 3 Pam was quick to zap Dex about a poor sample that was on display.
fluency 4 A neighbor may bus the six girls to the lake to fish on the dock.

66b 10'

SKILL BUILDING

Improve keyboarding technique

each pair of lines 3 times; DS between 6-line groups; work at a controlled rate

direct reaches

5 Junior received maximum respect by being humble, not by bragging.
6 Barbie browses at many music and ceramic places on Second Avenue.

adjacent reaches

7 Very popular artists read poetry to the very sad group of people.
8 A few important people were scoring points at the policy session.

double letters

9 Lynnette needs good support at the sessions at the swimming pool.
10 Jenny will keep the cherry dresser and maroon rug in the bedroom.

66c 35'

FORMATTING

Modified block letter

Read the information at the right carefully before preparing documents on pages 159 and 160.

Letter placement guides

The table at the right serves as a guide for placement of letters of various lengths. Using the table requires you to determine or judge the length of a letter. Counting words or lines provides an exact, but not an efficient, placement guide.

A short letter usually has one or two paragraphs and contains fewer than 100 words. An average letter has about three or four paragraphs and contains 100-200 words. A long letter has five or more paragraphs and contains more than 200 words.

Don't depend on your textbook to tell you the length of a letter. In an office, you will have to estimate the length of all letters you key. Try to estimate the length of each letter by counting the paragraphs and judging the amount of space it takes before you read the directions in the text.

Letter placement table

Letter Classification	Standard Side Margins	Variable Side Margins	Dateline Position
Short	1 inch	2 inches	line 18
Average	1 inch	1.5 inches	line 16
Long	1 inch	1 inch	line 14
Two-page	1 inch	1 inch	line 14

- Standard default side margins are more efficient than variable margins; therefore, use standard margins unless directed otherwise.
- In letters containing special features or tables, adjust the dateline position upward.
- When a deep letterhead prevents use of the recommended dateline position, place date a double space below the last line of the letterhead.
- When a window envelope is to be used, the appropriate dateline position is 2" or line 12.

words

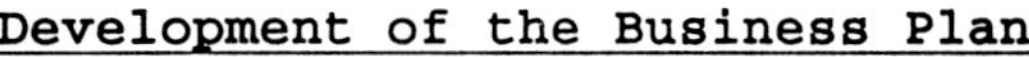

Development of the Business Plan 314

This study focused on identifying the specific 323
facilities needed, preparing the cost justification, and on 335
obtaining the certification of Need from the Department of 346
Health. Data was collected from Meade Center records, De- 358
partment of Health records, interviews with administrators 370
of area hospitals, questioaires sent to physicians and 381
other local health care providers, and from industry litera- 393
ture. 394

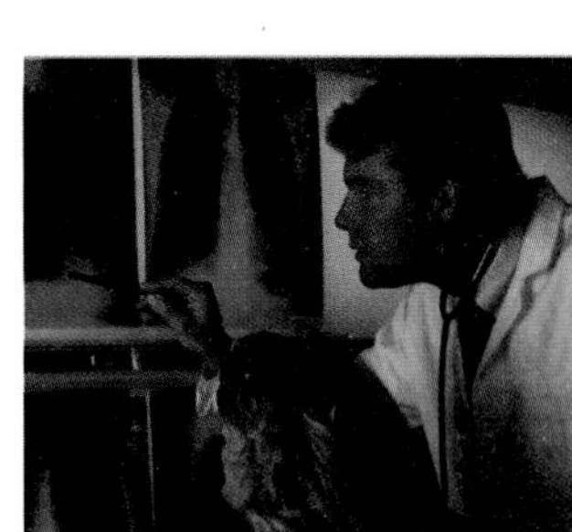

Meade Medical Center is more than double the size of 405
it's closest competitor in bed capacity, utilization, 419
Medicare utilization, and in revenue generated. Meade was 432
compared to Central Hospital, Roxy Medical Center, and to 444
Walk In Care. Walk In Care has only a two-bed capacity and 456
was dropped from the analysis because it has no impact on 467
Meade Medical Center. 472

Bed capacity and utilization. The following table 488
presents all data required for the certification of Need. 499

Capacity	Roxy	Central	Meade	words
Number of beds	165	184	385	513
Hospital utilization				518
average daily census	136	94	326	524
Medicare utilization				529
average daily census	60	53	104	535
Full-time equivalent	615	364	1,682	542

(Heading row: 508)

Meade clearly is the primary provider of medical care 553
in the regional area served. Meade also provides a large 564
number of units, including Psychiatric Service Unit, 577
Pediatric Unit, Level III Neonatal Intensive Care Unit, 588

Documents 2 and 3
(LM pp. S5-S7)
Block format; 1" or default side margins; date on line 18 (3"). Proofread; make needed corrections.

Document 2

words

Current date | Mr. Angelo Paterzo | 624 Meadville Pike | 10
Franklin, PA 16323-8574 | Dear Mr. Paterzo 19
(¶) Thank you for participating in our Executive 22
Advisory Board meeting and for agreeing to chair our 39
Public Relations Committee. The Public Relations 49
Committee is very important to our organization, 58
and we know that this committee will be active 68
and successful under your leadership. 76
(¶) Mr. Paterzo, we appreciate your strong support. 85
Please call on our staff to assist you in any 95
way we can. 97
Sincerely | Ms. Anna Maria Albertson | Executive Director | 108
xx 108

Document 3

Current date | Mr. Alex T. Carrington | General 9
Manager | Midwest Containers | 4563 N. Allen Road | 19
Peoria, IL 61614-9378 | Dear Mr. Carrington 27

Thank your for the hospitality extended during my 38
visit to your plant. The meeting with your Quality 48
Control Manager was most productive. I am very 58
pleased with the reached solution for the problems 68
with our shippping containers. The protection of 78
products from damage in shipping is, as you know 88
imperative. 90

It was a pleasure to working with you. I look 99
forward to recieving a copy of the new shipping 109
container specifications within the week. 118

Sincerely | Carolyn Anderson | Quality Control Director | 128
xx 128

Document 4
(plain paper)

1 Refer to Document 3, ¶2. The shipping container specifications referred to in ¶2 arrived.

2 Compose a short letter to Mr. Carrington indicating that the specifications arrived and Ms. Anderson is pleased with them. Use the same address, closing lines, and directions as for Document 3.

3 Prepare the draft for Ms. Anderson's approval.

words

Level II Emergency Service Unit, and floors dedicated to 602
various specialties. 606

Revenue Generated. Last year, Meade had $6,842M excess 621
of revenue over expenses. In comparison, Roxy had $2,359M 634
excess of revenue over expenses, and Central had $1,748M ex- 646
cess of revenue over expenses (Maxey, 1994, ~~page~~ 36). 656

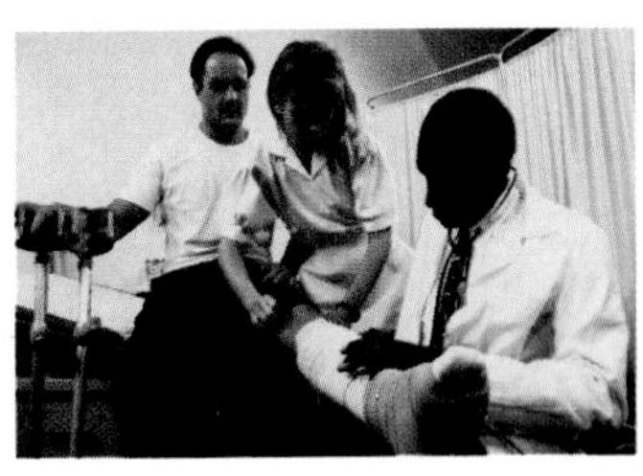

Outpatient Expansion Proposed 668

The proposed facilities have received tentative ap- 678
proval. The top priorities are to provide 30 additional 690
out patient surgery beds and a cancer clinic with a full 701
range of outpatient diagnostic and treatment services, in- 713
clude surgery, radiation oncology, and chemotherapy. 724
Specific units given tentative approval included a g.i. lab, 736
and endoscopy lab, a plastic surgery unit, a burn unit, 6 748
therapy rooms, and a large reception room. 757

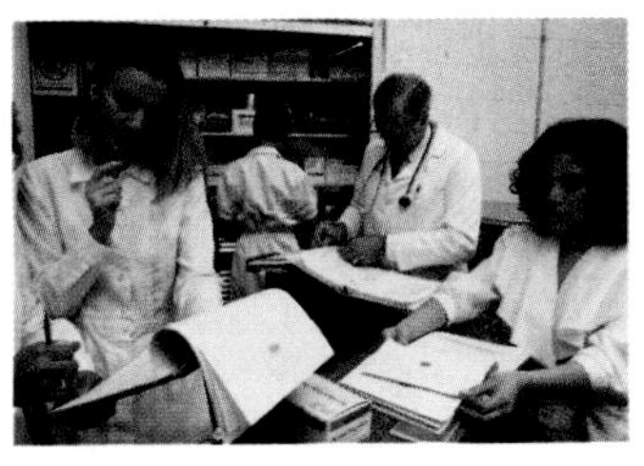

DS

Financial Evaluation 765

The complete budget is contained in Appendix A.

The project was evaluated both from a cost perspective 776
and a revenue generation perspective. A projected annual 787
budget was prepared for three years. 804

Projected Costs. The proposed cost of the 26,000 sq. 819
ft. expansion project is $2,165,960. This cost equates to 831
$83.31 per sq. ft. The bed capacity increases by 48 with a 844
resulting cost of $45,124 per bed. 851

Projected Revenue. The revenue projections were based 866
on a 75 per cent occupancy rate the first year, netting a 877
gain of $52,847. The occupancy rate the second year is 888
projected at 85 per cent, netting a gain of $78,542. The 900
occupancy rate for the third year is projected to be 95 per 912
cent, netting a gain of $143,985. 919

Timeframe ← Do not leave heading alone at bottom of page. 923

Block letter format

Document 1
(LM p. S3)
1 Study block format.
2 Use 1" side margins; date on line 16. Proofread; make needed corrections.

TRINITY TRAINING ASSOCIATES
1368 Weeks Drive
Youngsville, LA 70592-1046
(318) 555-2479

Dateline — January 24, 19-- (Line 16)
QS

Letter address — Mr. Steven P. Nations, Manager
Human Resources Department
Klienwood Manufacturing Company
1486 Bistineau Street
Ruston, LA 71270-3695
DS

Salutation — Dear Mr. Nations
DS

The details for the training program for all Klienwood associates who prepare documents have been finalized. An agenda of the program, a content outline, and the new Klienwood Style Manual are enclosed. The agenda indicates the trainer for each session.
DS

The word processing, spreadsheet, and graphics software training modules are scheduled first. All training sessions are scheduled in three-hour blocks and are offered twice on the same day.

Body — The session on image of documents that you requested for all managers and support staff is scheduled as the final session. The survey results show that many of your managers prepare some of their documents themselves. Therefore, the consistent image you desire can be achieved only if all individuals who prepare documents follow the standard formats.

Please call me if you have any questions about the program. Our trainers are anxious to conduct the program for you.
DS

Complimentary close — Sincerely
QS

Writer's name — Cherie E. LaBorde
Title — President
DS

Reference initials — xx
DS

Enclosure notation — Enclosures

Open punctuation: No punctuation follows the salutation or complimentary close.

Block letter format—open punctuation

100-101c (continued)

Document 2
Title page

1 Assume that you, as Chair of the Strategic Planning Committee, prepared the report for **Dr. Amy VanDuesen, Administrative Vice President**.

2 Use the current date.

Document 3
Letter of transmittal

1 Compose a letter to **Dr. VanDuesen** from you; indicate that the study has been completed and that you hope she will be pleased with the results. Offer to answer questions.

2 Address the letter to her at **P.O. Box 2500, your city, state, and ZIP Code**.

3 Position the number **ii** at the center bottom.

Document 4
Table of contents

1 Prepare a table of contents; include all headings.

2 Use leaders to make the document easier to read.

3 Number the page **iii** at the center, bottom margin.

4 Assemble and staple the entire report.

words

The projected timeframe is based on having the Certifi- 934
cation of Need and all other approvals within three months. 946
The estimated time is 10 months for construction of 956
facilities, two months for furnishing laboratories, and one 968
month for testing laboratory equipment. This timeframe also 981
assumes that federal funds are not involved in the project. 993

Results of Analysis 1001

The outpatient expansion was justified both on a needs 1012
basis and on a cost basis. The project is projected to have 1023
a positive cash flow in the first year. The current 1034
facilities can not accomodate the growing demand for out- 1046
patient medical service. Other hospitals in the area cannot 1058
meet the needs of the region. 1064

Action Recommended 1070

The Meade Outpatient Center is critically needed and 1080
will enhance the current services offered to patients in the 1092
region. The project should be implemented as soon as the 1104
necessary approvals are obtained. 1111

References 1113

Emerson, Frank. Metro Analysis Feasibility Study--Meade 1132
Outpatient Center. Atlanta, 1993. 1143
Maxey, Barbara J. "Outpatient Costs in the Southeast." New 1154
Orleans: Health Care News, 1994. 1165

Snyder, Jason. Hospital Growth Analysis. Atlanta, 1993. 1189

65 Block Letter Review

65a 5'

Skill-Building Warmup

alphabet 1 Jozef fixed my lovely wicker chair and my grey quilted bedspread.
fig/sym 2 The premium (Policy #8193) is $245.67 a year or $20.47 per month.
double letter 3 Ann called at noon to tell Lee she missed the meeting with Betty.
fluency 4 I pay the city for the right to cut hay in a field the city owns.

| 1 | 2 | 3 | 4 | 5 | 6 | 7 | 8 | 9 | 10 | 11 | 12 | 13 |

65b 10'

COMMUNICATION

Build composing/ editing skills

Compose a 4- or 5-sentence paragraph, completing the statement at the right. Use a 2" top margin and default or 1" side margins. Center and bold the heading **KEYBOARDING SKILLS**. Edit the ¶ and rekey it.

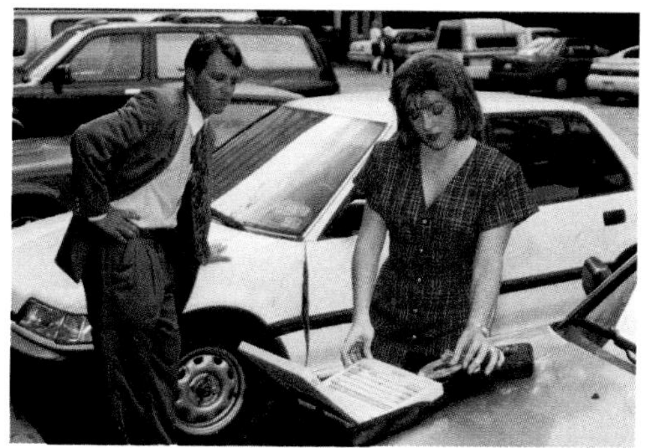

Developing keyboarding skills is important, regardless of the career I pursue because . . .

65c 35'

FORMATTING

Review letter parts

Read the information at the right before keying documents on pages 156 and 157.

LETTERHEAD: Company name and address. May include other data.

DATELINE: Current date. Usually in month, day, year order.

LETTER ADDRESS: Include personal title (for example *Mr., Ms.),* name, professional title, company, and address. Use 2-letter state abbreviation and ZIP Code.

SALUTATION: The greeting usually includes personal title and name.

BODY: Single-space text of letter; double-space between paragraphs.

COMPLIMENTARY CLOSE: An appropriate farewell such as *Sincerely.*

WRITER: Name and title. Women often include a personal title.

REFERENCE INITIALS: Identify person who keyed the document (for example, *tr*). May include identification of writer or dictator (for example, *ARB*).

ENCLOSURE NOTATION: Indicates material is enclosed. May specify what is enclosed.

Island Treats
239 Ka Drive
Kula, HI 96760-5837

March 3, 19--

Mr. Lee Woo, Manager
Island Treats
P.O. Box 3836
Hilo, HI 96720-3836

Dear Mr. Woo

All credit letters are sent over the signature of our credit manager. When you write a credit letter, please be sure to code the reference initials so that we will know who wrote the letter. Jan T. West signed this lettter, but Amy R. Best wrote it.

The enclosed format guide may be helpful to you. Please let me know if you have any questions.

Sincerely

Ms. Jan T. West
Credit Manager

ARB:tr

Enclosure: Format guide

102 103 Long Report With Appendix

Skill-Building Warmup

102-103a 5'

alphabet 1 Jack Quin refused to buy frozen vegetables except wild mushrooms.
fig/sym 2 Dave's 3 1/2' to 6' deep pool (18' x 35'7") holds 14,920 gallons.
adjacent reach 3 Mario and Teresa were going to read about the great polo players.
fluency 4 Diana's neighbor may turn the giant dish by hand to dismantle it.

| 1 | 2 | 3 | 4 | 5 | 6 | 7 | 8 | 9 | 10 | 11 | 12 | 13 |

102b 10'

SKILL BUILDING

Build straight-copy skill

1 Key two 1' writings at your top rate.
2 Key two 3' writings at your "control" rate.

A all letters

	gwam 1'	3'	
Technical, human, and conceptual skills are the three types	12	4	35
of skills all supervisors are expected to have. The skills are	25	8	40
quite different, and they vary in importance depending on the	37	12	44
level of the supervisor in an organization. Technical skills	50	16	48
refer to knowing how to do the job. Human skills relate to	62	20	52
working with people and getting them to work as a team. Concep-	74	25	56
tual skills refer to the ability to see the big picture as well	87	29	60
as how all the parts fit together.	94	31	63

gwam 1' | 1 | 2 | 3 | 4 | 5 | 6 | 7 | 8 | 9 | 10 | 11 | 12 | 13 |
3' | 1 | 2 | 3 | 4 | 5 |

102-103c 80'

FORMATTING

Long report

Document 1
Business report

1 Format as an unbound report; DS.
2 Use block indent for the enumerated items on page 256. Indent items to point of paragraph.

words

FORMS DESIGN, MANAGEMENT, AND CONTROL 8

The survey of forms used by Hess and Glenn, 16
Inc., indicates that forms are used extensively through- 28
out the organization to collect and store data. The 38
survey identified 154 forms, including continuous 48
forms (9), flat sheets (134), and unit sets (11). Nine 59
(6%) of the forms were initiated in the past three 70

Document 1

1 Read memo for content.

2 Key using hanging indent format for enumerations.

3 Proofread; correct errors.

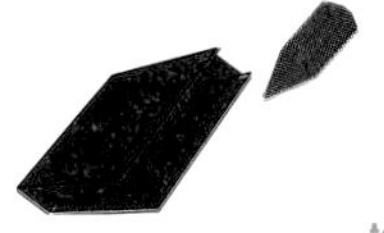

T. K. Design Studios

Interoffice Communication

tab (10 spaces from left margin)

TO: Maude M. Tassin — 1.5" top margin
DS

FROM: Patrick R. Ray

DATE: November 5, 19--

SUBJECT: Memorandum Forms for Vera's Word Processing Services
DS

Please design three memorandum forms for Vera's Word Processing Services. Ms. Hayes operates word processing services in New Orleans and Lafayette, as well as in Baton Rouge. Copies of the letterheads used in each office are on file in the Design Department.
DS

1" side margins

Ms. Hayes has requested that the forms for all three offices meet the following specifications:
DS

1. Each memo form should contain the address and telephone number of one of the three offices, and the standard printed headings should appear on all forms.
DS

2. All of the memo forms should be a full sheet.

3. The last character of the headings should be aligned vertically five picas from the left edge. Thus, the word processing specialists at Vera's can use the one-inch default margins on their system both to insert the heading information two spaces after the printed headings and to block the message flush left.

I hope you will be able to have the approval drafts ready for Ms. Hayes within a week. We made a commitment to have final forms ready in two weeks. Please let me know if this schedule presents a problem for you.
DS

xx

Note: On memos, the use of courtesy titles (i.e., Mr. or Ms.) and job titles (i.e., Communication Consultant or Sales Manager) with the sender's and receiver's names is optional.

Standard memorandum

words

months; 14 (8.8%) were revised versions of "old" 79
forms; and the remainder (85.2%) were reprints 89
of forms used in the past. Most of the forms (51%) 99
are used companywide, except the special-purpose 109
forms that are generated and used by particular 119
employees. 121

Four sources of forms have been identified: 130
1. Forms are designed and used by employees to 139
simplify particular tasks. 2. Forms are designed 150
and printed in the company print shop. 3. Forms 159
are purchased from a forms vendor. 4. Forms are 169
generated from forms software packages on the 179
computer system and printed on the laser printers. 189

<u>Current System</u> 195

No centralized forms management or control 203
system exists at present. The responsibility for 213
managing a form rests with the individual who 223
creates the form. The cost, the quality, and the 233
effectiveness of forms currently in use vary widely. 243
In fact, many forms are poorly designed and 252
simply are not cost-effective. Steps must be taken 263
to reduce the cost and increase the effectiveness of 273
all forms used by Hess and Glenn, Inc. 281

<u>New System</u> 285

The office manager has been made responsible 294
for the design, management, and control of all forms. 305
Any form that has more than 500 copies printed 315
in one year or that is used by more than one depart- 325
ment must be entered into the system. The three 335
components of the system are the analyzing of 344

64d 8'

FORMATTING

Standard memorandum

Drill 1

Memo on plain paper

Read information at the right; key the memo in Column 3.

Drill 2

Memo on printed form

(LM p. S1)

1 Use a printed form to prepare the same memo you prepared in Drill 1.

2 Set a tab to align items after the printed heading, leaving two blank spaces between printed headings and the variable information.

Memorandums

For written communications within most business organizations, an interoffice memorandum (often called a memo) is used. Memohead stationery, plain paper, or printed forms may be used.

The heading generally used with a standard memorandum is shown in the next column. The heading may be preprinted on forms or keyed when the memo is prepared.

Format (plain paper or memohead)

1 Use 1" side margins and 1.5" top margin.

2 DS and bold the memo headings; SS the body; DS between paragraphs.

3 Set a tab 10 spaces from the left margin for positioning the variable information in heading.

tab (10 spaces from left margin)

TO: Christopher White

FROM: Mike Jeansonne

DATE: September 12, 19--

SUBJECT: Macros

A **macro** is used in word processing to record the keystrokes for repetitive information such as a memo heading and to play them out automatically. Using a macro eliminates the need for printed memo forms and keying the heading when plain paper is used. Macros save time and effort.

xx

64e 25'

FORMATTING

Review standard memorandum

Document 1

(plain paper)

See directions on page 154.

Documents 2 and 3

(plain paper)

Format and key both memos shown at the right. Correct errors.

Document 2 words

TO: All Employees | **FROM:** Rebecca P. Glenn | **DATE:** May 2, 19-- | 12
SUBJECT: CAR System 16

Mr. Chi Wang of Automated Records, Inc., will present the CAR System to 30
all employees on May 8 at nine o'clock in the auditorium. As you know, a 45
final decision was made to centralize all our records and install the 59
computer-assisted retrieval system. 67

Mr. Wang will explain the installation procedures, the impact on each 81
department, the system capabilities, and the training schedule. Please 95
attend this meeting. 100

xx 100

Document 3

TO: All Employees | **FROM:** Rebecca P. Glenn | **DATE:** May 5, 19-- | 12
SUBJECT: Meeting Canceled 17

Mr. Chi Wang of Automated Records, Inc., was scheduled to present the 31
CAR System to all employees on May 8 at nine o'clock in the auditorium. 46
Unfortunately, Mr. Wang and two of his associates were in an automobile 60
accident yesterday. Therefore, the meeting has been canceled. 73

You will be notified as soon as the meeting can be rescheduled. Mr. Wang 88
expects to be able to return to work in two or three weeks. 100

xx 100

102-103c (continued)

words

current forms, the designing of new forms, and the 355
inventorying of forms. 359
Analyzing current forms. The current stock 373
of all forms should be used until it is depleted. 383
However, before a form is reprinted, it must be 393
analyzed for effectiveness. A copy of the checklist 403
used to evaluate each form is attached to this report. 414
Forms that do not meet the criteria will be redesigned 425
or replaced with a new form designed and substi- 434
tuted for the current form. Every effort will be made 445
to consolidate forms and to minimize the number 455
of forms. 457
Designing new forms. Two alternatives are 470
available for designing new forms. The first 479
alternative allows the department in need of the 489
forms to design and submit the proposed forms for 499
approval prior to printing. The second alternative 509
allows a forms designer on the staff of the office 519
manager to design the forms. Requests for assistance 530
should be directed to the office manager. 539
Inventorying forms. All current and new 550
forms must be entered into the perpetual forms 560
inventory system. The system will be used to main- 570
tain an adequate supply of forms, to minimize 579
storage costs, to enable the printing department to 590
reprint or purchase forms at the most economical 599
costs, and to eliminate obsolete forms. 607
System Implementation 616
The Senior Management Committee approved 624
the system for immediate implementation. Questions 634
about the system should be directed to the office 644
manager. 646

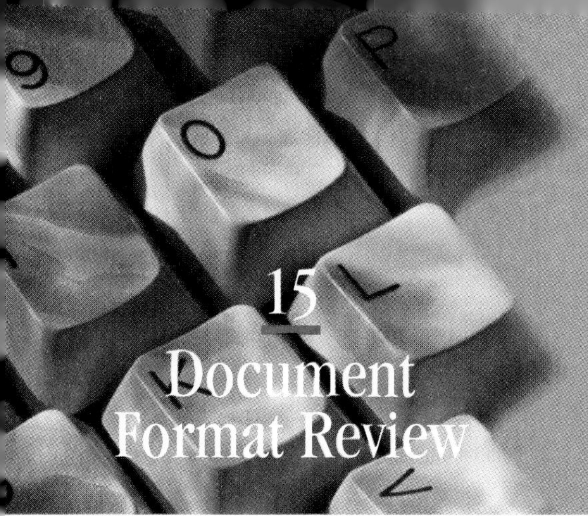

15 Document Format Review

Learning goals:
1 To improve keyboarding techniques.
2 To improve basic keyboarding skill.
3 To learn/review basic document formats.

Formatting guides:
1 Margins: Default or 1" (65-space line) for drills and ¶ writings.
2 Single-space drills; double-space writings.
3 5-space ¶ indention.

64a 5'

Skill-building warmup

each line 3 times (slowly, faster, slowly); DS between 3-line groups; repeat selected lines if time permits

(Use these directions for all skill-building warmups.)

alphabet 1 Mickey bought six lavender azaleas and quite a few nice junipers.
fig/sym 2 We gave a 15% discount on 3 invoices (#28574, #6973, and #12095).
shift key 3 Li, Jan, Al, and Carl went with Rod, Kay, and Oki to see Big Sky.
fluency 4 Jan and six girls may go to the lake to sit on the dock and fish.

| 1 | 2 | 3 | 4 | 5 | 6 | 7 | 8 | 9 | 10 | 11 | 12 | 13 |

64b 5'

SKILL BUILDING

Build straight-copy skill

Key two 1' writings at your top rate; key a 1' writing at your "control" rate.

 all letters

The format of a document is quite important to organizations because it affects image. An effective format does not have to be complex. It just has to look professional and be easy to read. To have a consistent image, always use a standard format.

| 1 | 2 | 3 | 4 | 5 | 6 | 7 | 8 | 9 | 10 | 11 | 12 | 13 |

64c 7'

FORMATTING

Indenting

Read and then key the information at the right. Use a 1.5" top margin, 1" or default side margins, and 5-space indentions or default tabs. DS between numbered items.

wp **Indent:** Indents text to the point of first tab; successive lines wrap to the tab.

Block indent from left margin:

> The block indent refers to blocking an entire paragraph five spaces from the left margin. To block indent copy, reset the left margin five spaces from the left margin. Block indent may be used to emphasize copy or to indicate a quote.

Hanging indent:

1. Hanging indent refers to aligning the second and succeeding lines of a paragraph flush with the first word, not the number.
2. To format the copy for hanging indent, reset the left margin 4 spaces to the right.
3. Then, operate the left margin release and backspace 4 times to the left margin.
4. After keying the text, reset the left margin to the original setting.

102-103c (continued)

words

Document 2
Appendix for report

1 Key the checklist to be included in the appendix of the report.

2 Use 1" side margins. If necessary, modify format so that the checklist will fit on one page.

3 Do not assign a page number to the checklist.

4 Prepare a sheet that will precede the checklist. Use 1.5" top margin; center **APPENDIX**; DS and center the title of the checklist in bold and ALL CAPS. Number this page.

Document 3
Title page

Assume that you, as a Forms Design Consultant, prepared the report for Hess and Glenn, Inc.

Document 4
Transmittal memo

1 Compose a short memo to all employees of Hess and Glenn, Inc., assuming each person will receive a copy of the report.

2 Thank them for being so cooperative in helping you to complete your analysis.

3 Add an attachment notation.

4 Edit your memo carefully.

Document 5
Table of contents

1 Prepare a table of contents for your report. Include all headings and the appendix.

2 Assemble the report after you have completed all documents.

<u>CHECKLIST FOR EVALUATING PROPOSED FORMS</u> 8

left < DS here to fit on page

Checkmark "Yes" or "No" at ~~right~~ in response to each item 20
below. DS 21

<u>Yes</u> <u>No</u> <u>Need for the Form</u> DS & bold 31

___ ___ 1. Does the expected use of the from justify 42
the cost of designing and producing it? 50

___ ___ 2. Does the form contain information col- 60
lected on other forms? sp. out 65

___ ___ 3. Can the info. on the proposed form be com- 77
bined with or replaced by an existing 85
form? 86

___ ___ 4. Has the form been authorized? 95

<u>Content of the Form</u> 102

___ ___ 5. Is all information contained onthe form 113
necessary? 115

___ ___ 6. Does the form request all necessary in- 126
formation? 128

___ ___ 7. Are related items grouped together 137

___ ___ 8. Is information sequenced to facilitate 148
work flow? 150

___ ___ 9. Is the vocabulary appropriate for users 160
of the form, and is the form easy to un- 168
derstand? 171

___ ___ <u>Design of the Form</u> 178

___ ___ 10. Is the form designed and constructed work 189
well with the equipment that is used to 197
complete it? 200

___ ___ 11. Are the instructions provided adequate 211
concise, and positioned conveniently? 219

___ ___ 12. Is the space provided on the form ade- 229
quate, 230

___ ___ 13. Can the form be printed on standard sized 241
paper? 243

___ ___ 14. Is the number of multiple copies ap- 252
propriate? 255

___ ___ 15. Does the format facilitate completion of 265
the form? 267

___ ___ 16. Is the design attractive and professional 278
looking? 280

___ ___ <u>Overall Effectiveness</u> 289

___ ___ 17. Does the form do what it was designed to 299
do? 300

___ ___ 18. Can the objective of the form be accom- 311
plished in a better way? 316

SS each item; but DS between items

63d 12'

COMMUNICATION

Improve composition skills

1 Use 1.5" top margin; 1" side margins; DS.
2 Center the title in all caps and bold. QS below the title.
3 Proofread; correct the 5 unmarked errors in the copy and complete the two ¶s that have been started.
4 Proofread and edit your work.

APPEARANCE INFLUENCES FIRST IMPRESSIONS

First impressions are usually made in the initial seconds of contact. Even though first impressions are made very quick, they tend to be long-lasting impressions. Appearence is a key factor that influence first impressions; therefore, a good appearance is very important. This principal should be applied to both the appearance of a person and of an document.

I can enhance my personal appearance by . . . . *(Add three or four sentences.)*

I can enhance the appearance of documents I prepare by . . . . *(Add three or four sentences.)*

63e 15'

SKILL BUILDING

Measure straight-copy skill

1 Key two 3' writings.
2 Key one 5' writing.

all letters

	gwam 3'	5'	
Individuals who conduct interviews often make snap judg-	4	2	41
ments. In fact, the decision to hire or not to hire an applicant	8	5	43
is usually made in the first five minutes of the interview. The	12	7	46
rest of the time is used to verify that the decision made was the	17	10	49
correct one. The wisdom of making a decision so early should be	21	13	51
questioned. When a quickly made decision is analyzed, generally	25	15	54
the result is that the decision is influenced heavily by the	30	18	56
first impression the person makes.	32	19	58
You can learn to make a good first impression in an inter-	36	21	60
view; all you have to do is be on time, dress appropriately,	40	24	62
shake hands firmly, establish eye contact, relax, smile, and show	44	26	65
that you have excellent communication skills. Doing all of this	48	29	68
may seem very difficult, but it really is not. Making a good	53	32	70
impression requires careful planning and many hours of practice.	57	34	73
Practice gives you the confidence you need to be able to do the	61	37	75
things that make an excellent impression.	64	38	77

gwam 3' | 1 | 2 | 3 | 4 | 5 |
5' | 1 | 2 | 3 |

104 Report With Table

Skill-Building Warmup

104a 5'

alphabet 1 Vicky quizzed us about the way we plan on adjusting the tax form.
figure 2 He said that 129 people made $36,750 or higher; 138 made $49,000.
double letters 3 Emma will see three moose deep in weeds by the narrow Mill Creek.
fluency 4 Pamela may fix lamb, and she may go to the lake with the auditor.

| 1 | 2 | 3 | 4 | 5 | 6 | 7 | 8 | 9 | 10 | 11 | 12 | 13 |

104b 10'

SKILL BUILDING

Build straight-copy skill

1 Key two 1' writings.
2 Key two 3' writings at your "control rate."

A all letters

	gwam 1'	3'	
Many workers are quite concerned about being able to provide	12	4	37
care for parents who are ill or elderly. For years women stayed	25	8	42
home and took care of both children and elderly parents. Today	38	13	46
as more women enter the work force, companies recognize that	50	17	50
efforts to aid workers who have to care for senior citizens may	63	21	54
be a key factor in being able to recruit and retain excellent	75	25	58
workers. Thus, they place major efforts on designing programs	88	29	63
that give them a competitive edge in hiring the best workers.	100	33	67

gwam 1' | 1 | 2 | 3 | 4 | 5 | 6 | 7 | 8 | 9 | 10 | 11 | 12 | 13 |
3' | 1 | 2 | 3 | 4 | 5 |

104c 35'

FORMATTING

Report with table

Document 1
Report with table

1 Format the unbound report SS.
2 Center the narrow table.

words

BOSA MARKETING ANALYSIS 5

The preliminary marketing analysis for the 13
new Basic Office Skills Assessment (BOSA) 22
program has been completed. This summary 30
contains the highlights of the complete report 40
presented to the Executive Committee. 47

Product Analysis 54

BOSA is a spin-off product from the Compre- 63
hensive Skills Assessment Program (CSAP). The 72
product is far less sophisticated than other 81
products in the line and is offered at a much 90

63 Skill Building/Composing

Skill-Building Warmup

63a 5'

alphabet 1 Jack Meyer analyzed the data by answering five complex questions.
fig/sym 2 On May 15, my ZIP Code will change from 23989-4016 to 23643-8705.
1/2 fingers 3 June Hunter may try to give Trudy a new multicolored kite to fly.
fluency 4 Dickey may risk half of the profit they make to bid on an island.

| 1 | 2 | 3 | 4 | 5 | 6 | 7 | 8 | 9 | 10 | 11 | 12 | 13 |

63b 10'

SKILL BUILDING

Improve keyboarding technique

each pair of lines 3 times; DS between 6-line groups; key at a controlled rate

home row
5 Dallas Klass had a dish of salad; Sal Lad also had a large salad.
6 Daggard Fallak was a sad lad; all Dag had was a large salad dish.

third row
7 Two or three witty reporters who tried to write quips were there.
8 Trey or Roy wrote two reports that were quite proper for a paper.

first row
9 Zam Benjamin came back to visit six vacant zinc mines and a cave.
10 Benjamin Zinc, a very excited man, made money on six new banners.

| 1 | 2 | 3 | 4 | 5 | 6 | 7 | 8 | 9 | 10 | 11 | 12 | 13 |

63c 8'

SKILL BUILDING

Build straight-copy skill

Key two 1' writings and one 3' writing at your "control" rate.

A all letters

gwam 3'

One of the most important skills needed for success on the job is listening. However, this is a skill that takes hours of practice. You can maximize your effectiveness by learning and using techniques for effective listening. People can listen two or three times faster than they can talk. Use the difference between the rate at which a person speaks and the rate at which you can listen to review what the person has said and to identify the main ideas communicated. This active style of listening helps you avoid the tendency to tune in and out of a conversation.

Line ends	gwam 3'	
...success on the	4	42
...takes hours of	8	46
...by learning and	12	50
...can listen two	17	55
...the difference be-	21	59
...rate at which you	25	63
...to identify the	30	68
...of listening helps	34	72
...of a conversation.	38	76

gwam 3' | 1 | 2 | 3 | 4 | 5 |

104c (continued) words

lower cost than any of the other software 99
products. 101

<u>BOSA/CSAP comparison</u>. BOSA was de- 112
signed after numerous demonstrations of 120
CSAP to users and potential users who liked 129
the system, but who indicated a strong prefer- 138
ence to have a shorter assessment tool. 146
BOSA contains three modules that can be 154
administered in less than an hour compared 163
to six hours required to administer CSAP. 171
Individual modules require less than a half hour. 181

<u>Pricing</u>. BOSA is priced very competitively 192
to stimulate widespread usage. BOSA is 200
priced at $79 per module or $195 for the 208
three module package. Discounts for multiple 217
orders and site licenses are available. 225

<u>Market Analysis</u> 232

BOSA was originally designed to appeal to 240
small businesses that hire a limited number of 249
entry-level workers. However, market data 258
show that BOSA could be marketed suc- 265
cessfully to three different markets. 273

<u>Small businesses</u>. The primary market is 285
still the small business market which includes 294
numerous small temporary help agencies that 303
screen a large number of potential workers. 312
Using a fully automated assessment program would 321
save staff time and would enable them to 330
make better selection decisions. 336

62d 10'

COMMUNICATION

Build editing skills

1 Use 1.5" top margin; 1" or default side margins; DS.

2 Key the ¶, correcting errors as you key. (There are 5 unmarked errors.) Center the heading in all caps and bold. QS below the title.

3 Proofread and edit your copy.

MY WEEKEND PROJECT

My supervisor ask me to carefully read the book, Creating a Very Good Impression, and to summarise the key points in each chapter. She want to use some ideas form it in a training program entitled Excellance in Customer Service. Since my dead line is next friday, I plan to spent some time read the book this week end.

62e 20'

SKILL BUILDING

Inventory/build straight-copy skill

1 Key two 1' writings on each ¶.

2 Key one 3' writing.

3 Key one 5' writing.

Option: Practice as a guided writing.

1/4'	1/2'	3/4'	1'
8	16	24	32
9	18	27	36
10	20	30	40
11	22	33	44
12	24	36	48
13	26	39	52

A all letters

	gwam 3'	5'	
Who is a professional? The word can be defined in many	4	2	32
ways. Some may think of a professional as someone who is in an	8	5	35
exempt job category in an organization. To others the word can	12	7	37
denote something quite different; being a professional denotes an	17	10	40
attitude that requires thinking of your position as a career, not	21	13	43
just a job. A professional exerts influence over her or his job	25	15	45
and takes pride in the work accomplished.	28	17	47
Many individuals who remain in the same positions for a long	32	19	49
time characterize themselves as being in dead-end positions.	36	22	52
Others who remain in positions for a long time consider them-	40	24	54
selves to be in a profession. A profession is a career to which	45	27	57
you are willing to devote a lifetime. How you view your pro-	49	29	59
fession is up to you.	50	30	60

gwam 3' | 1 | 2 | 3 | 4 | 5

5' | 1 | 2 | 3

words

Major corporations. The data show that 348
large organizations are also very interested in 358
using assessment tools such as BOSA both for 367
selection and for testing associated with 375
training programs. This market was much 383
stronger than anticipated. 389

Schools. BOSA was not designed for use 398
in schools. However, educators who have 406
seen the program have expressed interest 415
in using it as a tool to prepare students 423
for employment testing. 428

Recommendations 431

Table 1. Budget Recommendations 494

Brochure mailings	$16,000	499
Trade show exhibits	8,000	504
Advertisements	6,000	509
Total	$30,000	513

An initial marketing budget of $30,000 439
was approved. Generally, commissions to 447
distributors consume the major portion of the 456
marketing budget. With this product, however, 467
a direct marketing campaign using the budget 475
allocations shown in Table 1 should prove 483
to be more effective. 488

A complete plan for evaluating the 520
results has been developed. The evaluation 529
will determine how future marketing alloca- 537
tions will be made. 542

Document 2
Title page
Assume you prepared the report for **Ms. Townes Werner**, BOSA Product Manager. Use current date.

Document 3
Transmittal memo
1 Compose a memo to Townes Werner sending her the report.
2 Indicate that her manager, Jan Braden, who is a member of the Executive Committee, has a copy of the complete report, if she would like detailed information.
3 Indicate you enjoyed working on the project and that you will be happy to answer her questions.

Document 4
Table of contents
1 Prepare an appropriate table of contents.
2 Use all headings; include leaders and number page appropriately.

62 Skill Building/Editing

62a 5'

Skill-Building Warmup

alphabet 1 Jacky was given a bronze plaque for the extra work he did for me.

fig/sym 2 Order 12 pairs of #43 skis at $76.59 each for a total of $919.08.

3/4 fingers 3 Zane, Sally, and Max quit polo to swim six laps and work puzzles.

fluency 4 Claudia and I do handiwork at both the downtown and lake chapels.

| 1 | 2 | 3 | 4 | 5 | 6 | 7 | 8 | 9 | 10 | 11 | 12 | 13 |

62b 10'

SKILL BUILDING

Improve response patterns

Lines 5-16 once; DS between 4-line groups; work at a controlled rate; repeat drill.

direct reaches: reaches with the same finger; keep hands quiet

5 brand much cent numb cease bright music brief jump special carved

6 create mumps zany mystic curve annul any checks brag brunch nerve

7 Bradley broke his left thumb after lunch on a great hunting trip.

8 June is humble, but Brad and I brag about her great music talent.

adjacent reaches: keep fingers curved and upright

9 were junior sad yuletide trees polo very join safe property tweed

10 tree trio trickle tripod quit excess was free easy million option

11 Gwen and Sumio are going to be quite popular at the Western Club.

12 Fred said we were going to join the guys for polo this afternoon.

double letters: strike keys rapidly

13 dill seem pool attic miss carry dragged kidded layoff lapped buzz

14 commend accuse inner rubber cheer commission football jazz popper

15 Tammy called to see if she can borrow my accounting book at noon.

16 Lynnette will meet with the bookseller soon to discuss the issue.

| 1 | 2 | 3 | 4 | 5 | 6 | 7 | 8 | 9 | 10 | 11 | 12 | 13 |

62c 5'

SKILL BUILDING

Inventory straight-copy skill

Key two 1' writings to improve speed. Proofread; circle errors; determine *gwam*.

A **all letters**

. 4 . 8 . 12

Products are protected by patents and trademarks, but often

. 16 . 20 . 24

cheap imitations of the products exist on the market. The con-

. 28 . 32 . 36

sumer may pay for the quality of the brand name but unknowingly

. 40 . 44 . 48

may receive a product of inferior quality. If the price of a

. 52 . 56 . 60 .

product seems too good to be true, analyze the product carefully.

64 . 68

It may just be a fake.

105–106 Long Report With Endnotes

Skill-Building Warmup

105-106a 5'

alphabet 1 Jack and I analyzed the data by answering five complex questions.
figure 2 The invoice (#3968R240) is for $715.06; the terms are 2/10, n/30.
direct reach 3 Joycelyn is that young nurse in that funny brown checked uniform.
fluency 4 Rowland may fix a ham and corn dish, or he may fix lamb for them.

1 | 2 | 3 | 4 | 5 | 6 | 7 | 8 | 9 | 10 | 11 | 12 | 13

105-106b 90'

FORMATTING

Long report with endnotes

Document 1

1 Format the leftbound report SS; use a combination of bold and underscoring for headings.

2 Use superscripts (superior numbers, i.e., numbers printed above the line of writing) to indicate endnotes.

3 Key endnotes on a new page using the same margins as for page 1. Number the endnote page in sequence. SS endnotes with a DS between each. Number each endnote and indent the first line of each entry 5 spaces.

4 QS and key references.

5 Correct all marked errors and the 14 errors that are not marked.

words

GUIDES FOR PREPARING MEETING DOCUMENTATION 9
The procedures used to prepare support documents for 19
meetings in the Moss Springs Company were review during the 31
productivity analysis that was completed. The type of sup- 45
port documents used and the way in which they were prepared 57
varied widely through out the company. The primary document 69
used were meeting notices, agendas, handouts, visual aids, 81
and minutes. Format was not consistant for any of the docu- 93
ments with in or among departments. The following guides 104
were compiled on the basis of the productivity review. 115

Annual Meeting 121

The following quote from the Moss Spring Company 131
Policy Manual contains the policy for the documentation of 142
the Annual Meeting: 146

The annual Meeting of the Moss Springs Company shall be held 158
within 3 months of the end of the fiscal year. The Corpo- 171
rate Secretary shall mail to all who are eligble to attend 183
the meeting a notice and agenda thirty days prior to the 193
meeting. The Corporate Secretary shall prepare a verbatum 205
record of the meeting and provide each member of the Board 219
of Directors with a copy of the minutes within two weeks of 231
the meeting. The minutes shall be a part of the permanent 243
records of the Moss Springs Company. 250

61d 14'

COMMUNICATION

Build composing/ editing skills

1 Use 1.5" top margin; DS; 1" or default side margins.

2 Compose a 4- or 5-sentence paragraph to complete the statement at the right.

3 Edit the ¶, correcting all errors and adding the following title, centered in all caps and bold. QS below the title.

PREPARING FOR MY CAREER

4 Proofread: Mark errors.

5 Edit: Make corrections.

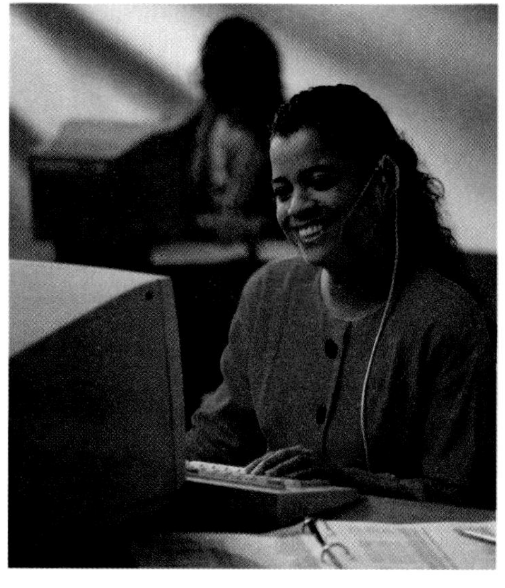

Computer skills are critical in most business jobs today. Therefore, I will prepare for my career by . . .

61e 16'

SKILL BUILDING

Improve Speed

1 Key two 1' writings on each ¶.

2 Key one 3' writing.

3 Key one 5' writing.

Option: Practice both ¶s as a guided writing. (See inside back cover for directions.)

Goal: 4 *gwam* increase

¼'	½'	¾'	1'
8	16	24	32
9	18	27	36
10	20	30	40
11	22	33	44
12	24	36	48
13	26	39	52

A all letters

	gwam 3'	5'	
Ethics is a complex topic to deal with in business. Nor-	4	2	37
mally, recognizing things that are legally wrong is not very	8	5	39
hard. The answers to ethical questions, however, are not always	12	7	42
obvious. Many people do not think it is unethical to use the	16	10	44
copier that belongs to the company to make a personal copy, but	21	12	47
most people do think it is unethical to make a thousand personal	25	15	49
copies on the copy machine. In truth, the principle is the same.	29	18	52
The difference is in the degree or extent of the abuse.	33	20	54
An equally perplexing issue relates to others with whom you	37	22	56
work. Should you blow the whistle when you know someone else is	41	25	59
doing something wrong? Reporting the actions of others may be	45	27	62
the right thing to do, but it involves a major amount of risk.	50	30	64
You may not have judged the situation accurately. Even if you	54	32	67
are correct, the person may attack you personally.	57	34	69

gwam 3' | 1 | 2 | 3 | 4 | 5
5' | 1 | 2 | 3

words

Other Meetings 256

Meetings ~~other than the annual meeting~~ will be held at 267
the discretion of the Board of Directors and the appropriate 279
company managers. Regular meeting of the Board of Directors 292
~~is~~ scheduled on the first wednesday of each month. Special 304
meeting may be called as needed. Documentation for regular 316
and called meetings of the Board ~~as~~ described in the follow- 329
ing paragraphs. 332

Support Documents 339

The Senior Management Committee required that an 349
agenda be distributed prior to all formal meetings of com- 361
mittees and of staff at the departmental level or higher. 372
Minutes must be prepare and distributed to all participants 385
after the meeting. Support documents for in formal meetings 397
and work units are left to the individuals conducting the 412
meet. 414

Minutes 471

The Administrative Manager, I responsible for determin- 481
ing the appropriate documentation of meetings, developed the 494
following procedures to ~~to~~ implement the policy on maintain- 505
ing ~~appropriate~~ minutes. These procedures have been ap- 514
proved for immediate implementation. 528
by the Senior Management committee.

Agenda 417

The agenda should contain the date time and place of 428
the meeting. It also should contain a listing of all topcis 440
to be discussed during the meeting. Distribution of the 452
agenda should allow adequate time for participants to prep 464
ofr the meeting. 468

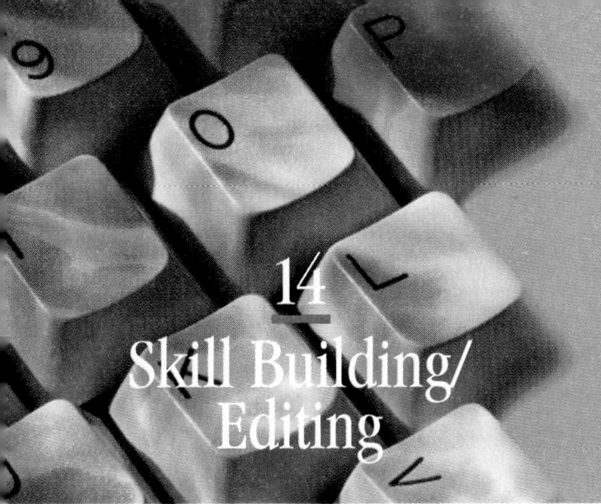

14 Skill Building/Editing

Learning goals:
1 To improve keyboarding techniques.
2 To improve basic keyboarding skill.
3 To improve editing skills.

Formatting guides:
1 Margins: Default or 1" (65-space line) for drills and ¶ writings.
2 Single-space drills; double-space writings.
3 5-space ¶ indention.

61a 5'

Skill-building warmup

each line 3 times (slowly, faster, slowly); DS between 3-line groups; repeat selected lines if time permits
(Use these directions for all skill-building warmups.)

alphabet 1 Benji Vazquez was prepared for the very difficult marketing exam.
fig/sym 2 About 25% of my team (8,460) earned the average salary ($19,637).
adjacent reach 3 Ty was the guy people wanted in government; he responded quickly.
fluency 4 My neighbor may tutor the eight girls on the theory and problems.

| 1 | 2 | 3 | 4 | 5 | 6 | 7 | 8 | 9 | 10 | 11 | 12 | 13 |

61b 10'

SKILL BUILDING

Improve keyboarding technique

each pair of lines 3 times; DS between 6-line groups

balanced hand: think and key words as units

5 The auditor may suspend work for a neighbor if the city pays him.
6 The rich widow paid for the chapel and the dock down by the lake.

one hand: key words letter by letter at a steady rate

7 In my opinion, I deserved better grades on my tests on abstracts.
8 We saw Jimmy West trade sweaters at a great craft bazaar at noon.

combination

9 The girls tasted the tea from the cafe and had the fish and crab.
10 Their dog ran past the cat to jump in my lap and nap by the pool.

| 1 | 2 | 3 | 4 | 5 | 6 | 7 | 8 | 9 | 10 | 11 | 12 | 13 |

61c 5'

SKILL BUILDING

Build straight-copy skill

Key two 1' writings at your top rate; key a 1' writing at your "control" rate.

Copy difficulty
All timings from this point on in the text will be labeled average. Average difficulty reflects these controls: 1.5 syllables, 5.7 characters per word, and 80% familiar words.

A all letters

Image is very important to success on the job. Packaging does make a difference. A messy letter or report, a disorganized office, or a poorly groomed employee all make a bad impression. The quickest way to make a good impression is to present a professional image. You can be a good example for others to follow.

| 1 | 2 | 3 | 4 | 5 | 6 | 7 | 8 | 9 | 10 | 11 | 12 | 13 |

105-106b (continued)

words

Verbatum minuets. The Annual Meeting will be recorded 542
and a verbatim transcript of the meeting will be prepared by 554
the Corporate Secretary. The preparation of verbatim 565
minutes is time/consuming and costly; there fore, verbatim 576
minutes will be used only for the annual meeting. 587

Detailed minutes. A detailed record will be 599
maintained of the regular monthly meeting and of all special 611
meetings of the Board of Directors. The minutes shouls pro- 623
vide identifying information and a comprehensive, summmary of 635
the discussion and action taken on all agenda items. 646
Detailed minutes may be used for other meetings if the 657
leader believes that the importance 664
of the meeting justifies detailed minutes. Managers are 675
cautioned not to over use detailed minutes. 684

Action minutes. Action minutes consist of identifying 698
information, a brief summary of all decisions made, and the 710
key views expressed. The emphasis in action minutes is on 722
decisions, assignment of responsability, and action planned 734
for the future. Action minutes can be quickly prepared and 746
easily; therefore, action minutes are recommended for most 758
meetings.[3] 760

MOVE A (See next page)

A **Visual aids**. Visual aids can be used to heighten in- 845
terest, to present information quickly, and to enhance 856
participants' understanding. The use of visual aids is en- 867
couraged atall meetings. Guides for preparing and using ef- 879
fectively aids, such as charts, transparencies, and 889
videotapes, are contained in the procedures mnual and should 902
be consulted as needed. 907

Level Three
Formatting Business Correspondence

OBJECTIVES

FORMATTING SKILLS

To review basic business communications and to format letters and memorandums efficiently.

KEYBOARDING SKILLS

To key approximately 50 wam with good accuracy.

COMMUNICATION SKILLS

To produce error-free documents and apply language arts skills.

105-106b (continued)

words

Handouts. The need for handouts vary widely. Hand- 772
outs should be prepared when it will enhance understanding 785
at a maating or when participants need a file copy of in- 796
formation presented during a meeting. The cost of producing 808
a hand out should always be considered, and handouts should 820
be produced only when the information justifies the cost. 832

Responsibility for Preparing Support Documents 925

The Corporate Secretary is responsible for preparing 936
support documents for the Annaul Meeting. The presiding 947
manageris responsible for the preparation of support docu- 959
ments for any meeting others than the Annual Meeting. 970
Normally, this responsibility is delegated to the adminis- 982
trative staff. 985

Standardization of Support Documents 1000

The primary goal of the Moss Springs Company are to 1010
improve productivity, achieve excelence, and reduce costs. 1023
The standardization of support documents through the use of 1035
standard formats and of forms will help to achieve each of 1046
these 3 objectives. 1051

Standardized format. A standard format for an agenda has 1067
been developed and included in the proceedures manual. The 1079
Annual Meeting Minutes Books contains copies of minutes of 1096
previous Annual Meetings; the same format is to be used for 1108
the minutes of each Annual Meeting. The form for detailed 1120
minutes and for action minutes have been revised, and the 1132
new formats are illustrated in the procedures manual. 1143

Forms. The preparation of support documents can be 1154
simplified with the use of forms. Froms for preparing 1165
agendas and for recording action minutes are available. 1176

Drill 3

Improve speed/accuracy on statistical copy

1' and 2' writings; figure *gwam*; circle errors

A all letters/figures — *gwam* 2'

For the period that began January of last year, the revenue 6
for common stock was $197 million, a rise of 23.3% over the same 13
interval last year. With a yield of 8.78% in average shares out- 19
standing, revenues per share rose an extra 10.7%, from $1.61 for 26
the period just over in January this year to $1.84 in an earlier 32
period. The primary reason for an increment this size is due to 39
a 5.21% increment in area quotas, many of which were met on time. 45

gwam 2' | 1 | 2 | 3 | 4 | 5 | 6 | 7 |

Drill 4

Measure skill: statistical copy

3' or 5' writings

A all figures and letters — *gwam* 3' | 5'

The Barak & Rinezi folio for the end of the year (Memo #98) 4 | 2
says that its last-quarter income was "26% above the historic 8 | 5
revenues of last year." The folio also says that the increase was 13 | 8
due to an upsurge in net sales of "just over 4 1/3%." 16 | 10

The increase is the seventh consecutive quarter in which 20 | 12
Barak & Rinezi have shown a profit; and the chief executive of 24 | 15
this old firm--Paul Rinezi--has told one industrial group that he 29 | 17
is slated to ask his board for an "increase of almost $1.50 a 33 | 20
common share" as its dividend for this financial year. 36 | 22

The company for the past 24 years has had its primary office 41 | 24
at 400 Big Ruby Road; the main plant is in Abilene at 17 Autumn 45 | 27
Avenue. The company employs about 350 area people, and yearly 49 | 29
sales will total about $3.5 million. Paul Rinezi has acted as 53 | 32
company CEO for 11 years; he took over the post after his uncle 57 | 34
had been the head for over 22 years. 60 | 36

gwam 3' | 1 | 2 | 3 | 4 | 5 |
5' | 1 | 2 | 3 |

105-106b (continued)

words

Both of these forms can be requisitioned form the supply 1188

room. The agenda form can be used a an source document from 1200

which the agenda is prepared, or the form itself can be used 1212

as an agenda. The action minute form can be used in the 1224

same manner; it can be used as a source document, or the 1235

minutes of the meeting can be recorded direct on the form. 1248

New Page →

ENDNOTES 1250

[1] Anil Wasu, Enhancing Productivity: The 1263

Moss Springs Company, 1994, p. 24. 1275

[2] Moss Springs Company Policy 1286

Manual, 1994, p. 42. 1292

[3] Mary Anderson, Effective Meetings, 1299

1993, pp. 74-86. 1302

REFERENCES 1305

Anderson, Mary. Effective Meetings. 1316

Boston: Bay Publishing Co., 1993. 1323

Moss Springs Company Policy Manual. 1337

Chicago: 1994. 1340

Wasu, Anil. Enhancing Productivity: 1348

The Moss Springs Company. 1358

Chicago: Productivity Consultants, 1365

Inc., 1994. 1368

Document 2
Table of contents

Prepare a table of contents; include all headings and the endnotes and references.

Document 3
Title page

The report was prepared for **Mr. Justin Markland, Executive Vice President**. Use your name and the title, **Administrative Manager**, and the current date.

Document 4
Transmittal memo

Compose a transmittal memo to **Mr. Justin Markland** sending the report you prepared. Ask if he wishes to have changes made before it is sent to all employees. Include the report as an attachment.

Drill 2

Guided writing: improve speed/accuracy

Key as 1' guided writings, working for either speed or control.

Optional: Key as a 3' writing.

To access writings on MicroPace Plus, key **W** and the timing number. For example, key **W14** for Writing 14.

Writing 14

gwam 3'

Anyone who expects some day to find an excellent job should 4 | 34
begin now to learn the value of accuracy. To be worth anything, 8 | 38
completed work must be correct, without question. Naturally, we 13 | 43
realize that the human aspect of the work equation always raises 17 | 47
the prospect of errors; but we should understand that those same 20 | 51
errors can be found and fixed. Every completed job should carry 26 | 56
at least one stamp; the stamp of pride in work that is exemplary. 30 | 60

Writing 15

No question about it: Many personal problems we face today 4 | 34
arise from the fact that we earthlings have never been very wise 8 | 38
consumers. We haven't consumed our natural resources well; as a 13 | 43
result, we have jeopardized much of our environment. We excused 17 | 47
our behavior because we thought that our stock of most resources 20 | 51
had no limit. So, finally, we are beginning to realize just how 26 | 56
indiscreet we were; and we are taking steps to rebuild our world. 30 | 60

Writing 16

When I see people in top jobs, I know I'm seeing people who 4 | 34
sell. I'm not just referring to employees who labor in a retail 8 | 38
outlet; I mean those people who put extra effort into convincing 13 | 43
others to recognize their best qualities. They, themselves, are 17 | 47
the commodity they sell; and their optimum tools are appearance, 20 | 51
language, and personality. They look great, they talk and write 26 | 56
well; and, with candid self-confidence, they meet you eye to eye. 30 | 60

gwam 3' | 1 | 2 | 3 | 4 | 5 |

107 Measurement

Skill-Building Warmup

107a 5'

alphabet 1	Buzz McGuy worked at a very quaint shop just six miles from here.
fig/sym 2	Is that 1240- x 1375-foot lot 26 miles out on Highway 689 or 793?
adjacent reach 3	Porter and Guy were quite sad; we quickly tried to cheer them up.
fluency 4	Chan may go to the land of enchantment on the island by the lake.

1 | 2 | 3 | 4 | 5 | 6 | 7 | 8 | 9 | 10 | 11 | 12 | 13

107b 12'

SKILL BUILDING

Measure straight-copy skill

1 Key one 3' writing; proofread; circle errors; determine *gwam*.

2 Key one 5' writing; proofread; circle errors; determine *gwam*.

A all letters

	gwam 3'	5'	
Automation and the downsizing of most large companies have	4	2	49
brought about major role shifts in many jobs. No job has changed	8	5	51
more in the past ten years than that of the secretary. In the	12	7	54
past, excellent typing, shorthand, and language arts skills were	17	10	56
the key to success for any secretary. Those skills are no longer	21	13	59
adequate to ensure success in the office today. In addition to	25	15	61
the basic skills, the secretary must be able to use many computer	30	18	64
applications to do the work in most offices.	33	20	66
Decision support software packages were designed to be used	37	22	68
by managers, but some of these packages are now being used by	41	25	71
office workers. Word processing was designed for office staff,	45	27	73
but often managers use it. In fact, managers use the computer	50	30	76
for a number of clerical tasks. In turn, secretaries use the	54	32	78
computer to do a number of managerial tasks. These changes in	58	35	81
the roles of both support staff and managers do cause a great	62	37	83
deal of stress and confusion, but they also open up many new	66	40	86
opportunities for all employees to work together as a unit. A	70	42	88
local area network just may provide the link needed to enable all	75	45	91
workers to be active team members.	77	46	92

gwam 3' | 1 | 2 | 3 | 4 | 5 |
5' | 1 | 2 | 3 |

107c 33'

FORMATTING

Measurement: reports

Time schedule

Assemble materials .... 3'
Timed production .... 25'
Final check;
compute *n-pram* .... 5'

Document 1
Leftbound report with endnotes

1 Format the report SS.

2 Key endnotes on a separate sheet, numbered in sequence.

Document 2
Table of contents

Prepare a table of contents; include all headings.

Document 3
Title page

1 Prepare a title page.

2 The report was prepared for **Ms. Virginia Covington**.

3 Use the current date, your name, and the title, **Project Director**.

Skill-Building Workshop 3

MicroAssistant: To access Skill-Building Workshop 3, key **S3** from the Main menu.

Drill 1
Variable rhythm patterns

each line twice SS; DS between 2-line groups; rekey difficult lines

Fluency (key phrases and words, not letter by letter)

1 it is | it is he | to us | am due | by the man | an end | by the body | go with
2 cut the firm | due to the | go to the end | did pay us | form a half firm
3 they wish us to go | kept the man down | held the box down | cut the ox

4 Did the busy men dismantle the shamrock ornament for the visitor?
5 The key to the eighth problem is to spell rogue and theory right.
6 When Jane and I go to the city, we may visit the chapel and mall.

7 The auditor had problems with the theory to make a profit for us.
8 Diane did rush the lapdog to the city when it bit their neighbor.
9 If the altos are on key, they may enrich the chant in the ritual.

| 1 | 2 | 3 | 4 | 5 | 6 | 7 | 8 | 9 | 10 | 11 | 12 | 13 |

Control (key at a steady but not fast pace)

10 we saw | ad in | as my | we are | on him | ate up | we act ill | add gas to oil
11 age was | you are only | jump on art | my faded nylon | red yolk | few were
12 best care | you read | tax base | after we oil | saw data | agreed rate was

13 Water and garbage rates fell after my rebates were added in July.
14 Acres of wet grass and poppy seeds were tested for zebras to eat.
15 Jo ate the lumpy beets and sweet tarts but craved a stewed onion.

16 Jimmy saw a cab in my garage; I was awarded it in an estate case.
17 Dad feared we'd pay extra estate taxes after debts were assessed.
18 Rebates on oil, added to decreases in taxes, affect oil reserves.

| 1 | 2 | 3 | 4 | 5 | 6 | 7 | 8 | 9 | 10 | 11 | 12 | 13 |

Variable-rhythm sentences (vary pace with difficulty of words)

19 Dad attested to the fact that the barbers paid the auditor's tax.
20 Giant oaks and sassafras trees edged the east lane of the street.
21 Holly may join us by the pool to meet the eight big team members.

22 Did you get sufficient green material to make the eight sweaters?
23 All crates of cabbages were saved after I agreed to make payment.
24 Both visitors were totally enchanted as they watched the regatta.

| 1 | 2 | 3 | 4 | 5 | 6 | 7 | 8 | 9 | 10 | 11 | 12 | 13 |

words

BENEFITS--A MATTER OF CHOICE 6

The best benefits package depends on the needs 15
of each employee. Employees who have 23
dependents have different needs than those 31
who do not have dependents. To realize 39
the greatest return on investment in benefits, 49
Zeigler Productions, Inc., must allow employees 58
to participate in the decision-making process. 68
Good decisions, however, can be made only 77
when employees have adequate information 85
about each of the options available to them.[1] 94

Benefits Available to Employees 107

Zeigler offers two types of benefits to all full- 117
time, salaried employees. Final decisions have 126
been made on the specific types of benefits 135
that will be available to all employees. These 145
benefits will go into effect during the Janu- 154
ary enrollment period. 158

Fixed benefits. Several benefits constitute 170
the standard package and are provided to all 179
employees. Industry experts recommend that 188
disability insurance, retirement plans, profit- 197
sharing plans, and stock-ownership plans be 206
part of the fixed benefits.[2] 212

Flexible benefits. Each employee is pro- 224
vided with a benefits allowance. Employees 233
pay for benefits selected that exceed the 241
allowance provided. Employees can allocate 250
the benefit allowance in the following areas: 259
medical, dental, vision care, life insurance, 269
and salary redirection. 274

Process of Making Informed Choices 287

To help employees select benefits wisely, new 297
materials are proposed to provide informa- 305
tion about each benefit offered, its costs, 314
tax considerations, and eligibility require- 323
ments. Materials proposed include a com- 331
prehensive workbook, a videotape, and a 339
decision worksheet. A special telephone 347
help desk to answer questions during the 355
enrollment period is also proposed. 363

Enrollment Procedure 371

Enrollment will be handled via a touch-tone 380
telephone. Employees must have completed 388
the decision worksheet prior to enrolling. 397
Employees will be grouped with a two-week 405
specified enrollment period to facilitate the 414
handling of 20,000 calls. Each employee will 424
be sent a written confirmation to verify the 433
benefits selected. 437

Costs of the New Program 446

A complete projection of all costs was pre- 455
pared by the benefits specialists and is avail- 464
able in the Human Resources Department. 473
A summary of the projected costs per em- 481
ployee follows: 484

Component	Cost per Employee	490
Print materials	$ 2.50	494
Videotape	3.75	497
Help desk	1.95	500
Enrollment process	2.25	507
Total	$10.45	509

The costs compare very favorably to the costs 518
incurred four years ago when major changes 527
were made in benefits. The cost at that time 536
was $9.75 per employee. 541

ENDNOTES 543

[1]Lynn Adams, Managing Benefits Effec- 555
tively, 1994, p. 26. 561

[2]Jan Marks, Benefit Allocations, 1993, pp. 573
65-74. 574

Tabulated reports

Center each document horizontally and vertically.
Reference: pages 114, 116

Document 10
Key title in bold.
Reference: pages 81, 114

		words
THE SPRINGARN MEDAL AWARD		5
Selected Winners		9
1974	Henry (Hank) Aaron	13
1978	Rosa L. Parks	17
1982	Lena Horne	20
1984	Bill Cosby	24
1988	Jesse Jackson	27
1989	L. Douglas Wilder	32
1990	Colin L. Powell	36

Document 11

COLUMBUS KIDS BASEBALL LEAGUE			6
Coaches of the Year			10
1987	Mike LaRue	Giants	15
1988	Dan McKee	Bears	19
1989	Millie Day	Cougars	24
1990	Betsy Lahr	Colts	28
1991	Rich O'Hare	Eagles	31
1992	Jane Ruiz	Bears	36
1993	Mike LaRue	Giants	40

Document 12
Reference: pages 119, 123

ANNUAL MUNICIPAL WASTE GENERATION			7
In Millions of Tons			11
Waste	Tons	Percent	18
Paper	117.8	39.87	22
Food	13.2	7.85	25
Yard	31.6	17.59	28
Metals	15.3	8.52	31
Glass	12.5	6.96	35
Plastic	14.4	8.02	38
Other	9.8	11.58	41
			45
Source: National Municipal Assn.			51

Communication Workshop 7

MicroAssistant: To select Communication Workshop 7, key **C7** from the Main menu.

Drills 1-2 Improve word usage

1 Use 1.5" top margin; default or 1" side and bottom margins; DS.
2 Key the ¶s, selecting the appropriate words.
3 Proofread; correct errors.

Drill 1

Since the (principal/principle) color in the skirt was (blue/blew), Sue wore navy shoes to (complement/compliment) the outfit. The skirt was made from a (coarse/course) -weave cotton fabric with a lot of (find/fine) detail work. She bought the skirt this (passed/past/pass) summer on (sale/sell) while they were on (their/there) vacation. John did not (know/no) until later that she bought the outfit, but he liked everything about it (accept/except) the scarf. I liked it better (than/then) he did.

Drill 2

I do not (know/no) what (affect/effect) my telephone call had on the selection of the best (cite/site/sight) for the conference. The (principal/principle) reason I called was because I was concerned about safety of our members. My (advice/advise) was not to go to a city with a high crime rate.

Drills 3-4 Improve number usage

1 Use 1.5" top margin; default or 1" side and bottom margins; DS.
2 Key the ¶s, selecting the appropriate style to express numbers.
3 Proofread; correct errors.

Drill 3

Approximately (1,000/one thousand) people attended the fund-raising dinner at (seven-thirty/7:30 p.m.) on May (7/7th). Each person was asked to donate (one/1) percent of her or his salary or a minimum of (one hundred dollars/$100.00/$100). (Fifteen/15) people volunteered to chair committees to help raise funds. Each committee will have (eight/8) or (ten/10) members. Each member is asked to devote (twelve/12) hours per month to fund raising during the campaign. The goal is to raise (five hundred thousand dollars/$500 thousand/$500,000).

Drill 4

We will receive a (10/ten) percent discount on the ($550/$550.00) bill if we pay it by the (7/7th) of the month. We will pay the bill by March (10/10th) because ($55/fifty-five dollars) is a major savings. (12/Twelve) additional reams of paper can be purchased with the money saved.

Two-page unbound report

References: pages 98,100

Document 9

Add the title, **THE GIFT OF LOUIS BRAILLE**, in bold.

words

Thanks to the dedicated work of special groups, funds, gifts, and the 19
boundless efforts of the sightless themselves, people without sight can enjoy 35
the printed word. Actually, they have had this "miracle" gift of reading for 50
more than 165 years, made possible by braille printing--the wonderful gift of 66
Louis Braille (1809-1852). "The introduction of the braille system of printing 82
probably accomplished more for a greater number of people than any 95
innovation of the early nineteenth century, truly a marvel of ingenuity" 110
(Sung, 1991, 57). 114

The Innovator 119

Louis Braille, who lost his own sight at age three, enrolled in the 133
National Institute for the Blind in Paris when he was ten. A very good 147
student, he excelled in music and science; and following graduation, he 162
stayed on at the Institute as a teacher. In this capacity, "probably by 176
adapting a dot-dash system then in use by the French military for night 191
signaling," he developed in 1829 the system of printing that carries his name 206
(Tippett, 1991, 12). 211

The Innovation 216

Young Louis believed that a series of small, raised (embossed) dots on 231
paper could be interpreted, or "read," by sensitive fingertips. Arranged in a 246
six-dot configuration called a "cell," 63 possible combinations could form 261
letters, figures, punctuation marks, etc. With practice, such printing, he 277
conjectured, could be comprehended rapidly and accurately. He was right, 291
of course; and braille has since widened personal and professional avenues 305
for millions of sight-diminished people. 314

Today, easing its use, a number of shortcuts and abbreviations have 327
been introduced into the braille system. Still, despite its obvious merits, 343
braille remains cumbersome; because of its larger "print," braille copy 357
requires more space than other kinds of copy. 366

> Picture if you will an ordinary set of encyclopedias of, say, 15 379
> volumes. Such a set printed in braille likely would involve about 150 394
> volumes, weigh about 700 pounds, and fill about 45 feet of shelf 407
> space (Dunn, 1992, 78). 412

Braille may be keyed on a special braillewriter, on which the keyboard 426
consists of six striking keys, each capable of establishing an embossed dot in 442
a certain location, and three directional keys. With such a keyboard, a writer 458
is able to communicate in print with braille readers--all in all, a fine gift 473
indeed from Louis Braille. 479

REFERENCES 481

Dunn, Sondra B. Bits and Pieces. Atlanta: Montberry Press, 1992. 497

Sung, Charles Kye. "Little Steps, Big Strides." American Science and 515
History, October 1991. 521

Tippett, Wilson A. "Braille: A Short History." Paragon Monthly, August 539
1991. 540

Drill 5
Improve editing skills

1 Use 1.5" top margin; default or 1" side and bottom margins; DS.
2 Correct all errors in the draft of the speech as you key.
3 Proofread carefully; correct errors.

BENEFITS--NEW OPTIONS

Most of you has recieved the report prepared by our Human Resources Department outlining our new benefits program. i thank the staff for giving me the opportunity to add a few opening comment to the videotape that was prepared to help you made a wise choice on you benefits package. I also commend the staff on design a program that is tailored to meet the specific needs of each employee.

Most companies are concern about both the rising costs of benefits and the need to provide adequate protection for all of our employees. The fixed and flexable benefits combine to offer you the most comprehensive package of benefits that Zeigler has ever be able to offer. The disability insurance and retirement plans are a key part of your future security. The profit-sharing and stock-ownership plans give you a stake in the future of Zeiger Productions, inc.

Since many family have access to benefits from more than one source, we have made it possible for you too select the benefits that best meet your needs. This flexible approach enables your to avoid duplicate coverage and to determine which benefits is of most value to you.

Benefit contracts are becoming extreme technical and complicated. Our staff has done an out standing job of putting together a package of materials that is easy to understand and that provides comprehensive information I urge you to reed the information careful to watch this video, and to call the help desk if you or members of your family has any questions about any of the benefits described. The decisions you make may be some of the most important important decisions you will ever make.

Interoffice memorandums

(plain sheets)
Proofread and correct errors.
Reference: page 82

words

Document 6

TO: Lonny Ashmyer | **FROM:** Breton S. Vreede | **DATE:** January 11, 19-- | 13
SUBJECT: Wheelchair Access 19

Recently I explained to you my efforts on a variety of projects to facilitate 35
wheelchair entry into public buildings. I may have found a solution to one 50
problem, Lonny; that is, how does someone open a large public door from a 65
wheelchair. 67

The answer may lie in the installation of an electrical signal (similar to a 83
garage door opener) that can be activated from the chair. All signals would 98
be identical, of course, permitting universal application. 110

Can you provide me with a rough estimate of the costs for these items: 124

1. Conducting the necessary preliminary research. 135
2. Equipping a wheelchair. 140
3. Tooling our factory to manufacture this item. | xx 151

Document 7

TO: Katrin Beaster
FROM: J. J. Bouhm
DATE: Current
SUBJECT: May Seminar

I have invited Lynda A. Brewer, Ph.D., Earlham 25
College, Richmond, Indiana, to be our seminar 34
leader on Friday afternoon, May 10. 41
Dr. Brewer, a well-known psychologist who has 50
spent a lot of time researching and writing in the new 61
field of ergonomics, will address "Stress Management." 73
Please make arrangements for rooms, speaker 82
accommodations, staff notification, and refreshments. 93
I will send you Dr. Brewer's vita for use in 102
preparing news releases. 107

Document 8

```
TO:      J. Ezra Bayh                                    4
FROM:    Greta Sangtree                   ) DS           8
DATE:    August 14,  19--                               13
SUBJECT: Letter-Mailing Standards                       20
                                        , because of
                    chk sp               the delay,
Recently the post office delivered late a letter that caused   36
us some embarassment.  To avoid reoccurrence, please ensure    48
that all administrative assistants and mail personnel follow   60
postal service guidlines.                                      67
U.S.                  e

Perhaps a refresher seminar on correspondence guidelines is    79
in in order.  Thanks or you help.  for your                    85
```

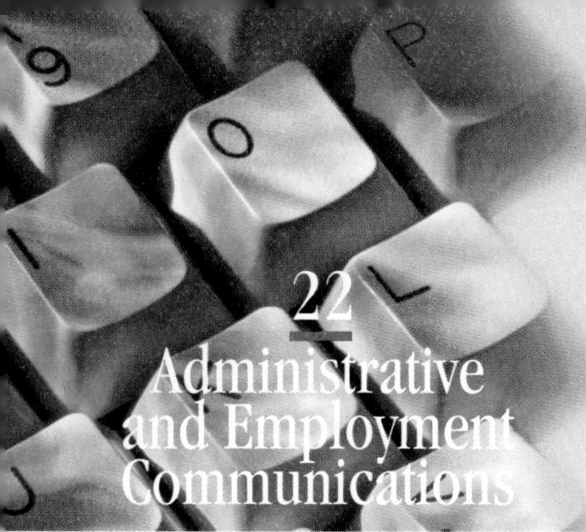

22 Administrative and Employment Communications

Learning goals:
1 To improve keyboarding skill.
2 To learn to format administrative communications.

Formatting guides:
1 Margins: 1" or 65-space line for drills and ¶ writings.
2 Single-space drills; double-space writings; SS documents.
3 Indentions: 5-spaces or default tabs for ¶ writings.

108a 5'

Skill-building warmup

each line 3 times (slowly, faster, slowly); repeat selected lines if time permits
(Use these directions for all skill-building warmups in Lessons 108-115.)

alphabet 1 Jacque Zwanka gave us very good explanations of both experiments.
figure 2 My farm had 297 cows, 80 sheep, 31 horses, 475 ducks, and 6 dogs.
double letter 3 Ann said that the committee needs to meet in the summer and fall.
fluency 4 The auditor paid both of them to work for the firm on the island.
| 1 | 2 | 3 | 4 | 5 | 6 | 7 | 8 | 9 | 10 | 11 | 12 | 13 |

108b 15'

SKILL BUILDING

Build straight-copy skill

1 Key two 3' writings (strive to increase speed).
2 Key one 5' writing at your "control" rate.

all letters

	gwam 3'	5'	
Rightsizing is a word that brings fear to many people be-	4	2	54
cause it is frequently associated with layoffs. Just a few	8	5	56
years ago, companies added layers of management. Today, the	12	7	59
trend is quite different; companies are getting rid of layers of	16	10	61
management. They often describe themselves as becoming "lean and	21	12	64
mean." Two extremely complex issues must be addressed. One key	25	15	67
issue is the number of employees who must cope with job loss.	29	17	69
The other key issue is managing a company with a new structure	33	20	72
and with employees who fear that they may be in the next group of	38	23	74
workers on the list to be eliminated.	40	24	76
Coping with job loss is never easy. Usually it damages an	44	27	78
employee's self-concept. Some people respond to the situation by	49	29	81
becoming very angry. Often those who survived the layoff have	53	32	83
similar problems. Many feel guilty that they still have a job,	57	34	86
and they no longer trust the company. These reactions are very	61	37	88
normal, but they do not solve the problem. Both those employees	66	39	91
who have lost their jobs and those who remain in the company must	70	42	94
focus their efforts on the future rather than bemoan the past.	74	45	96
One lesson they should learn is that their careers are too valu-	79	47	99
able to entrust to the company to manage. Each person must	83	50	101
be responsible for managing his or her own career.	86	52	103

gwam 3' | 1 | 2 | 3 | 4 | 5 |
5' | 1 | 2 | 3 |

Letters in modified-block format

(plain sheets)

1 Estimate letter length.

2 Supply letter address from the business cards. Use current date; add an appropriate salutation.

3 Correct errors; prepare envelopes.

Reference: pages 70, 77-78

Document 3

Estancia Imports
Ramon Figueroa, Prop.
192 Las Palamas
San Juan, PR 00911-9110
Telephone (809) 555-3546

Document 4

Baxter, Varnum, & Wertz
Patti Baxter, President
2200 Uhle Street, South
Arlington, VA 22206-0662
Telephone (304) 555-7657
Fax (304) 555-9864

Document 5

Miss June Boehm
5450 Signal Hill Road
Springfield, OH 45504-5440

Document 3

words

This afternoon we marked your statement "PAID IN FULL." We appreci- 35
ate the prompt manner with which you have always handled your 48
account here, and we sincerely hope we will have an opportunity to serve 62
you again soon. 66

We take this opportunity to introduce our new GINO swim wear line to 80
you. The enclosed sketches illustrate the beauty of the line; and I will 95
ask Eri Rigby, coordinator of the line, to send you a catalog as soon as it 110
comes from the press. 114

Please accept our good wishes for a prosperous spring season. 127

Cordially | Alvin Twodeer | Sales Manager | xx | Enclosure | c Eri Rigby 139

Document 4

As a sales associate for Real Estate Enterprises, Inc., I have had many 41
unique opportunities to analyze and interpret the real estate market. Com- 56
mercial and investment properties, including apartment income buildings, 70
commercial realty, office space, and vacant land, are my specialties. 85

You may take advantage of my expertise in corporate real estate marketing, 100
including selling, buying, and leasing commercial and investment realty. A 115
copy of the recent newsletter published by Real Estate Enterprises is 129
enclosed for your review. 134

Please keep the enclosed business card in a convenient place, and call me 149
when I can be of assistance. Real Estate Enterprises stresses professional- 164
ism and adheres to the code of American Realtors. 175

Sincerely | Wilma Lopez | Sales Associate | xx | Enclosures: Newsletter | 188
Business card 190

Document 5

Our head teller Guy Raberger tells me that you have 30
closed your account with us. You have been a customer valued 42
by us for years, and we are sorry to lose you business. 52

Our business policy dictates that we provide our 58
customers with prompt, accurate, courteous service at all 69
times. If we in some way failed to follow this policy, we 78
want to know how and why; if not, you have our genuine 96
appreciation for allowing us to care for your account.
The staff of this bank is commited to serving you however 107
we can. 109

Very truly yours | Cicely A. Murgraff | President | xx 119

108c 30'

FORMATTING

Agenda and action minutes

Study the illustrations at the right. Then key Documents 1-4.

Summary-type documents, such as agendas, minutes, and itineraries may be formatted as tabulated documents (DS below the heading) or as reports (QS below the heading). When large fonts are used, a DS is preferred. The date may be shown as a subpart of the main heading for emphasis; it may also be included as part of the document. Items on an agenda may be numbered. The margins for agendas, minutes, and itineraries are as follows: top 1" or 1.5"; side 1"; bottom 1".

1.5"

SALES KICK-OFF MEETING
January 4, 19--
DS

Agenda
QS

Goal Attainment . . . . Mark Rex
Assessment of past year by region
President's Club Award
DS

1" Strategic Plan . . . . Jan Long 1"
Company directions
Market strategy

Compensation Plan . . . . Lynn Ray
Commission changes
Benefit changes

Sales Team Meeting . . . . Sales Managers

Flush right

1.5"

SALES KICK-OFF MEETING
January 4, 19--
DS

Action Minutes
QS

Presiding: President Mark Rex
DS

Participants: All Marketing and Sales Staff

1" President Rex summarized the results for the year and commended Region 3 for attaining its goals. He presented 146 President's Club awards (list attached). 1"

Jan Long, national sales manager, presented the new directions and the marketing strategies to attain the goals set. A 15 percent increase in overall sales is the target for the year.

Lynn Ray, vice president of human resources, presented the new compensation plans and announced that dental coverage is now provided.

Sales teams met individually.

Documents 1 and 2

Format the agendas using a 1.5" top margin.

Document 1

DOCUMENTS STANDARD COMMITTEE
May 25, 19--

Agenda

Report from Senior Management
Committee . . . . Mary E. Albergetti

Standard Format . . . . Jill Brown
Action minutes
Traditional minutes

Distribution Plan . . . . Roger Perez
Employee notification
Illustrations for manual

(Total words: 66)

Document 2

BENEFITS COMMITTEE
March 3, 19--

Agenda

Cost Containment . . . . *Jim Bass*
Current costs
Projected costs

Options Review . . . . *Joan Nye*
Fixed benefits
Flexible benefits

Wellness Project . . . . *Kirk Ott*

(Total words: 60)

Formatting Workshop 1

Letters in block format

Use current date; add an appropriate salutation; correct errors; prepare envelopes.

Reference: pages 70-72, 75 (LM pp. S37-S39)

MicroAssistant: To access Formatting Workshop 1, key **F1** from the Main menu.

Document 1
Short letter

words

Miss Vera Grant | 1121 Hunter Avenue | Brooklyn, NY 11214-1124 12

Springtime holds the promise of things to come. That's when the swal- 26
lows come back to Capistrano, the buzzards return to Hinckley, and the 40
ants and spiders set up housekeeping on your back patio. 51

Part of the promise of spring, though, involves telephoning The Garrison 66
and having those little intruders sent scurrying. 76

Make your patio or deck YOUR patio or deck. If it isn't yours now, call 91
The Garrison; and we will take it back for you pronto. Our enclosed 105
brochure has full details. 110

Cordially yours | Ted Estevez | Chief Hunter | xx | Enclosure 121

Document 2
Average-length letter
Use hanging indent for the enumerated items.

Mr. Lance H. Brinks, President | All Grain Shippers, Inc. | 8500 Exeter 14
Street | Duluth, MN 55806-0086 19

This letter serves to notify you of cancellation of the contract between our 35
company and All Grain Shippers to carry our cargo in your ships between 49
Duluth and other ports. Official documents will arrive from our attorneys 64
within a few days. 68

Good and legal cause exists to abnegate this agreement. 80

1. Your ships have delivered late every shipment we have made during the 94
   past four months. 98

2. The cargo bins are unacceptable for carrying grain; damage has 112
   occurred in two shipments. 117

Payment of our balance with your company has been made. Please direct 132
any questions or comments to the attention of our Legal Department. 145

Very truly yours | Grace J. Beebe | President |xx | c Legal Department 158

Document 3 words

DOCUMENT STANDARDS COMMITTEE 6
May 25, 19-- 8
DS

Action Minutes 11
QS

Presiding: Mary Ellen Albergetti 18
DS

Participants: Jill Brown, Oki Nagai, Carl 27
Lamonz, Angela Metts, Roger Perez, Lynn Sims, 36
and Leslie Waters 39

The standard formats for minutes of meet- 48
ings were approved by the Senior Manage- 56
ment Committee, and the procedures to be 64
used in implementing these formats were set 73
by the Document Standards Committee. 80

The Committee decided to send a memo to 88
all employees notifying them that action 96
minutes will be the standard minutes for all 105
meetings with the exception of meetings of 114
the Board of Directors and formal meetings 123
so designated by the Senior Management Com- 131
mittee. Angela Metts and Roger Perez will 140
prepare and send the memo by June 1. 147

The action minutes will contain the heading 156
illustrated in this document, a summary of 165
each agenda item with the decision made or 173
action taken, the person responsible for the 182
item, and the date due if applicable. Action 192
minutes should be limited to one page when 200
possible. 202

Jill Brown and Carl Lamonz will prepare and 211
distribute the illustrations of the standard for- 221
mat for both action and traditional minutes 230
for the <u>Document Standards Manual</u> by 241
June 4. 243

Document 4 words

BENEFITS COMMITTEE 4
March 3, 19-- 7

Action Minutes 10

Presiding: 14

Participants: Jim Bass, Sabrina 20
Burge, Leslie Coker, Joan Nye, 29
Bridget Perkins, and Clay Tassin 36

Joan Nye presented an analysis of 42
the current costs of benefits show- 49
ing that costs have risen 21 percent 57
over last year. Benefits costs are 64
projected to increase 15 percent 70
this year; therefore, action must be 78
taken. 83

Joan Nye reviewed the benefits that 90
are currently offered and matched 97
the individual benefits to the costs 104
provided by Jim Bass. The 110
Committtee agreed that the fixed 116
benefits should remain the same. 123
Several alternatives for reducing 130
costs of the flexible benefits were 137
considered. The alternative that 144
appears to be most desirable is to 151
shift part of the benefit costs to 158
employees. Sabrina Burge was asked 166
to prepare analyze the strategies 173
taken by other companies in the in- 180
dustry. She will report back to the 188
Committee at the next meeting on 194
March 26. 196

Kirk Ott presented an update on the 203
Wellness project. Preliminary data 211
indicate that the program would have 218
a positive effect on the costs of 225
benefits. Kirk agreed to have a 233
proposal ready for the March 26 239
meeting. 241

60c 33'

FORMATTING

Measurement: tables and topic outline

(4 plain sheets)

Time schedule

Assemble materials .... 2'
Timed production .... 25'
(Key problems in order; proofread and correct errors as you work.)
Final check .... 6'
(Proofread and circle any remaining errors. Calculate *g-pram*—total words keyed divided by 25'.)

Document 1
2-column table

Key the table, centering it horizontally and vertically.

Document 2
Topic outline

Key the topic outline; use 3" top margin; add appropriate spacing and capitalization.

Document 3
3-column table

Key the table, centering it horizontally and vertically.

Document 4

If you finish before time is called, repeat Document 1. Alphabetize the entries.

		words
NORTH HOLLYWOOD JUNIOR COLLEGE		6
School Records		9
High Jump	*6 ft. 4.5 in.*	14
Long Jump	*22 ft. 5.0 in.*	19
Triple Jump	*50 ft. 9.1 in.*	24
Discus Throw	*222 ft. 3.7 in.*	30
Javelin Throw	*210 ft. 8.4 in.*	36
Shot-Put	*56 ft. 9.3 in.*	41

THE POWER OF WORDS 4
I. purpose of words 8
A. inform 10
B. convince 13
C. impress 15
D. entertain 18
II. increase word power 23
A. why 25
1. to be clearly understood 30
2. to be specific as required 37
3. to know/use proper terminology whenever appropriate 48
B. how 49
1. listen 52
2. read 53
III. learn grammar 57
IV. learn construction 62
A. punctuation 65
1. "read signs" 69
2. helps with inflection 74
3. takes the place of facial expression 82
B. structuring and phrasing 88

NORTH HOLLYWOOD JUNIOR COLLEGE			6
Gifts from Other Countries			12
Country	Coordinator	Total Gifts	24
Canada	Wilma E. King	$12,300.35	31
Denmark	H. A. Bjoerma	1,250.68	37
France	Andre V. Tori	150.89	42
Germany	Johann Boehme	700.46	48
Honduras	Hector Garza	1,450.93	54
Italy	Maria A. Toma	5,225.14	60
Japan	Io Maneki	870.90	65
Mexico	Jose H. Ortiz	750.68	70

109 Itinerary

Skill-Building Warmup

109a 5'

alphabet 1	Quincy Jaworski is moving six of those azalea plants to that bed.
fig/sym 2	Fred, Inc. (a firm with 26 people) had sales of $704,835 in 1992.
space bar 3	Ty and I may go to see you swim if we can get a ride to the pool.
fluency 4	The panel may blame us for the toxic odor problems on the island.

| 1 | 2 | 3 | 4 | 5 | 6 | 7 | 8 | 9 | 10 | 11 | 12 | 13 |

109b 45'

FORMATTING

Itinerary

1 Study the illustration and explanation at the right.

2 Format Documents 1-3 on plain paper. Use 1.5" top margin.

Itineraries are prepared to assist travelers; therefore, the format and the information contained in an itinerary may vary, depending on the preferences of the individual traveler. Some travelers prefer a separate schedule of appointments. Others prefer appointments combined with travel information.

Itineraries that are concise, complete, and easy to read are most helpful to travelers. Always use good design principles in formatting documents.

The margins for itineraries are: top 1" or 1.5"; side and bottom, 1". The second column of the itinerary is indented 1.5" from the left margin. Times should align at the colons.

1" or 1.5"

ITINERARY FOR CARL BATES
April 2-3, 19--
QS

1" (left margin) · 1" (right margin)

Monday, April 2	**Atlanta to Denver**
	DS
10:05 a.m.	Leave Atlanta, MCC Flight 286; breakfast; arrive Dallas at 11:15 a.m.
11:53 a.m.	Leave Dallas, MCC Flight 32; arrive Denver at 1:10 p.m.; met by Jane Covington; reservations at the Mountainview Hotel (Confirmation #295864).
3:30 p.m.	Meet with Jane Covington and Mark Hanson, Snowbank Room of the Mountainview.
7:30 p.m.	Dinner with Jeff and Annette Greenwald at the Cliffhanger.
	DS
Tuesday, April 3	**Denver to Atlanta**
	DS
8:30 a.m.	Breakfast with Jane Covington and Mark Hanson in the Coffee Shop, then meet in Snowbank Room until 2:30 p.m. Lunch served at 12:15 p.m.
3:30 p.m.	Leave Denver, MCC Flight 365 to Atlanta; dinner, 7:00 p. m.; arrive 8:30 p.m.

Document 1

words

ITINERARY FOR ROBIN COHN 5
October 10-11, 19-- 9
QS

		words
Tuesday, October 10	**Chicago to Seattle**	17
	DS	
8:05 a.m.	Leave Chicago, National Flight 485; breakfast; arrive Salt Lake City at 10:13 a.m.	26 32 35
10:50 a.m.	Leave Salt Lake City, National Flight 832; lunch; arrive Seattle 12:45 p.m.; Bay Area Limo; Bay Inn (Confirmation #856357).	45 52 58 63
2:00 p.m.	Meeting with managers.	70
	DS	
Wednesday, October 11	**Seattle to Chicago**	78
8:30 a.m.	Meeting with sales staff.	86
4:30 p.m.	Leave Seattle, National Flight 552; arrive Salt Lake City at 7:10 p.m.	95 102
8:45 p.m.	Leave Salt Lake City, National Flight 46; dinner; arrive Chicago 11:54 p.m.	112 118 119

60 Table Measurement

Skill-Building Warmup

60a 6'

each line 3 times SS; DS between 3-line groups

alphabet 1 Dubuque's next track meet will have prizes given by forty judges.

fig/sym 2 Interest in 1985 climbed $346 (as the rates rose from 7% to 20%).

double letters 3 Ann and Buzz will carry my bookkeeping supplies to Judd's office.

easy 4 The auditor may laugh, but the penalty for chaotic work is rigid.

| 1 | 2 | 3 | 4 | 5 | 6 | 7 | 8 | 9 | 10 | 11 | 12 | 13 |

60b 11'

SKILL BUILDING

Measure skill growth: rough-draft copy

Key a 3' and a 5' writing; proofread and circle errors; determine *gwam* on both writings.

A all letters

	gwam 3'	5'	
The Search for Success assures a more serious aspect when	4	2	43
we study the factors that measure it. After all, if Success is	8	5	45
the end of a carefe road upon which we have embarked, then we	12	7	48
certainly should know when we have finally arrived there. How	16	10	50
can we recognize success? Where will we ultimately find this	20	12	53
phenomenon we call success?	21	13	54
How about a fine job and a large apartment for starters? Ad	26	15	56
a shiney new auto, a lake front home and a boat too. But wait	30	18	58
a minute. These things show quantity, but not necessarily	34	20	61
quatity. If, for instance a job is truly to identify Success,	38	23	63
then how much pecking order it should have? How many square	42	25	66
feet measure a success apartment?	45	27	67
Success is more readily found when we view our goals in	48	29	69
terms of personal ideals in stead of social achievements.	52	31	72
Success has no precise measuring stick, so each and everyperson	56	34	74
has to manufacture one. If we think of success in terms of	60	36	77
personal satisfaction, term of each of us can recognize and	64	39	79
enjoy, our search for success can be a success.	67	40	81

Document 2

ITINERARY FOR RITA L. EICHELBERGER 7
October 14-15, 19-- 11

Monday, October 14   Baton Rouge to New York 20
10:12 a.m. Leave Baton Rouge Airport, CEA Flight 286; 30
breakfast; arrive Hartsfield Airport, Atlanta at 11:21 42

11:35 a.m. Leave Atlanta, CEA Flight 998; arrive 52
LaGuardia Airport, 12:45 p.m.; met by Exec Limo Service; 64
reservations at Bel Monde Hotel (confirmation #295784). 75

4:30 p.m. Meet Jerry Walker in hotel lobby. 84

8:15 p.m. Dinner with J. Walker, Li-Ming Han, Lynn Brown 100

Tuesday, October 15   New York to Baton Rouge 109
10:15 a.m. Meet J. Walker and group, Conference Room 6. 121

2:45 p.m. Exec Limo Service pick-up from Bel Monde lobby. 132

4:15 p.m. Depart, CEA Flight 904; arrive Atlanta 5:35 p.m. 148

6:15 p.m. Depart Atlanta, arrive Baton Rouge at 7:25 p.m. 163

NEWS *on . . .* the Mobile Office

The "mobile" office refers to a work environment other than the traditional office to which employees report to perform work on a daily basis. Sometimes the mobile office is described as work anywhere, anytime.

The concept of telecommuting or working in the mobile office has been around for many years, but it is usually applied to employees such as sales representatives who work out of their cars or homes. Today, technology makes it very feasible for many different types of employees to work away from the traditional office.

The equipment typically required includes a computer with appropriate software, a modem, a laser printer, a fax machine, a separate telephone line, electronic mail, and voice mail. Companies often furnish the equipment to employees, which generally costs far less than providing office facilities for employees.

Working in a mobile office requires employees to work without direct supervision, coordinate their own activities, assume responsibility for their own work, and be self-starters. The benefits include flexibility, commute time saved, and savings on business attire.

59c 32'

FORMATTING

Measurement: reports

(4 plain sheets)

Time schedule

Assemble materials .... 2'
Timed production .... 25'
(Key problems in order; proofread and correct errors as you work.)
Final check .... 5'
(Proofread and circle any remaining errors. Calculate *g-pram*—total words divided by 25'.)

Document 1
Unbound report

Format and key the unbound report at the right.

Document 2

Rekey Document 1, omitting side headings.

words

THE PROFESSIONAL TOUCH 5

Although its contents are of ultimate importance, a finished report's 19
looks are of almost equal importance. If it is to achieve the goal for which it 35
was written, every report, whether it serves a business or academic purpose, 50
should be acceptable from every point of view. 60

<u>Citations, for Example</u> 69

No matter which format is used for citations, a good writer knows 82
they are inserted for the reader's benefit; therefore, anything the writer 97
does to ease their use will be appreciated and will work on the writer's 111
behalf. Standard procedures, such as those stated below, make readers 126
comfortable. 128

> Underline titles of complete publications; use quotation marks 141
> with parts of publications. Thus, the name of a magazine is under- 154
> lined, but the title of an article within the magazine is placed in 168
> quotation marks. Months and certain locational words used in the 181
> citations may be abbreviated if necessary (Mayr, 1994, 13). 193

<u>And the Final Report</u> 202

The final report should have an attractive, easy-to-read look. 214

The report should meet the criteria for spacing, citations, and binding 223
that have been established for its preparation. "Such criteria are set up by 244
institutional decree, by generally accepted standards, or by subject de- 259
mands" (Chung, 1994, 27). A writer should discover limits within which he 274
or she must write and observe those limits with care. 285

The final number of copies needed should be determined in advance 297
and made available upon presentation. We are reminded by one author that 313
"preparing too many copies is better than asking readers to double up" (Hull, 328
1994, 93). Also, the report should be presented on time. A lot of good 343
information loses value with age. 350

<u>In Conclusion</u> 355

Giving the report a professional appearance calls for skill and patience 370
from a writer. First impressions count when preparing reports. Poorly 384
presented materials are not read, or at least not read with an agreeable 399
attitude. 401

REFERENCES 403

Chung, Olin. <u>Reports and Formats</u>. Cedar Rapids: Gar Press, Inc., 1994. 421

Hull, Brenda, and Muriel Myers. <u>Writing Reports and Dissertations</u>. 5th 443
ed. New York: Benjamin Lakey Press, 1994. 452

Mayr, Polly. "Styles/Formats/Computers." <u>Business Weekly</u>, June 1994. 469

110 News Release

Skill-Building Warmup

110a 5'

alphabet 1 My objectives were analyzed very quickly during that proxy fight.
figure 2 We need 240 orchids, 1,396 roses, 287 carnations, and 510 tulips.
shift key 3 Pat, Ty, Max, Al, and Rod took the test; Ben, Jan, and I did not.
fluency 4 If the firm pays for it, the auditor may handle the six problems.

| 1 | 2 | 3 | 4 | 5 | 6 | 7 | 8 | 9 | 10 | 11 | 12 | 13 |

110b 45'

FORMATTING

News release
(LM pp. S97-S103)

1 Read the information about a news release and study the illustration at the right.

2 Format the news releases in Documents 1-4. Note the special instructions for Document 4.

3 Use the stationery provided or key the heading shown.

News release

A news release contains information that an organization wishes to publicize. Usually, a public relations department prepares releases on special forms, but letterhead or plain stationery may be used. The company name, address, and telephone number should be keyed if it is not printed. A heading or title is often suggested, even though a newspaper may write its own heading.

Providing the name of a contact person is helpful in case the publisher must verify the information to be released. The more important news should be presented first, in case part of the news is cut off or not used. On a multipage release, "--more--" is usually keyed after the last line on each page. After the last line of a release, "###" is usually keyed to indicate the end of the information.

1"

METZ OFFICE SERVICES
1843 Main Street
Columbia, SC 29201-3846 DS

Personnel Department
(803) 555-4927
QS

For Release: Immediately DS

Contact Person: John Manning DS

Columbia, South Carolina, October 6, 19--. Metz Office Services announced today that it acquired Palmetto Printing Services. Claire Metz, president, indicated that Frank Ross, president of Palmetto, will serve as vice president of Metz Office Services. All Palmetto employees will transfer to Metz.

The acquisition makes Metz the largest office services firm in the state. Metz now offers complete desktop publishing and printing services as well as a full range of office services. DS

###

Document 1

ODC
OVERBROOK DEVELOPMENT CORPORATION
520 State Street Natchez, MS 39120-8476

Public Relations Department
(601) 555-9473

words

For Release: Immediately | **Contact Person:** 8
Susan T. Hernandez 12
Natchez, Mississippi, August 15, 19--. The 21
Overbrook Development Corporation announced 30
today that it is consolidating its statewide of- 39
fices and moving its headquarters to Natchez. 49
The company has leased space in the Magnolia 58
Building until its Riverview Tower can be built. 68
Overbrook employs 645 people. Of the 78
645 employees, 210 are expected to transfer to 85
Natchez. During the next 15 months, Overbrook 94
expects to hire 435 employees in the sales, sec- 104
retarial, accounting, engineering, architectural, 114
and management areas. 118
Overbrook develops a variety of projects 127
throughout the South. Its primary focus is on 136
commercial real estate development. Overbrook 145
has already developed 3 shopping centers in the 154
Natchez area and 20 in the state. 162
163

59 Report Measurement

Skill-Building Warmup

59a 6'

each line 3 times SS; DS between 3-line groups

alphabet	1	Jack Voxall was amazed by the quiet response of the big audience.
fig/sym	2	Our #3865 clocks will cost K & B $12.97 each (less 40% discount).
shift	3	In May, Lynn, Sonia, and Jason left for Italy, Spain, and Turkey.
easy	4	It is the duty of a civic auditor to aid a city to make a profit.

1 | 2 | 3 | 4 | 5 | 6 | 7 | 8 | 9 | 10 | 11 | 12 | 13

59b 12'

SKILL BUILDING

Measure skill growth: straight copy

Key a 3' and a 5' writing; proofread and circle errors; determine *gwam* for both writings.

all letters

	gwam 3'	5'	
At a recent June graduation ceremony, several graduates were	4	2	43
heard discussing the fact that they had spent what they thought	8	5	46
was a major part of their lives in school classrooms. They esti-	13	8	48
mated the amount of time they had been in elementary school, in	17	10	51
high school, in college, and in graduate school had to be about	21	13	54
nineteen or twenty years.	23	14	55
Indeed, two decades is a significant span of time. Even if	27	16	57
little additional effort is used seeking education, about a	31	19	59
quarter of a person's life will have been spent on learning ac-	35	21	62
tivities. Graduation is a time for looking at the past and the	39	24	65
present and analyzing how they can be merged to form a future.	44	26	67
And thus begins The Search.	45	27	68
The Search begins with introspection--attempting to sort out	50	30	71
and pinpoint all that has gone before, to identify purpose behind	54	32	73
the years of effort and expense, to focus it all on some goal.	58	35	76
If encouraged to name the goal, we call it, probably for lack of	63	38	78
a more definitive name, Success. We desire to be successful.	67	40	81
But what is "success"?	68	41	82

gwam 3' | 1 | 2 | 3 | 4 | 5 |
5' | 1 | 2 | 3 |

Document 2

O D C

OVERBROOK DEVELOPMENT CORPORATION
520 State Street Natchez, MS 39120-8476
Public Relations Department
(601) 555-9473

words

For Release: Immediately | **Contact Person:** 9
Susan T. Hernandez 12
Natchez, Mississippi, March 15, 19--. The 21
Overbrook Development Corporation announced 30
today that it named Rachael White as its new 39
president. White joined the firm eight years ago 49
and served in a number of positions, including 58
executive vice president. She replaces the late 68
William Anderson. 72
White has a degree in engineering from 80
Northwestern University and an MBA from Cen- 88
tral University. Prior to joining Overbrook, she 98
owned her own consulting firm. White is mar- 107
ried to Alex Johnson, and they have two sons 116
and a daughter. 120
White was in charge of the project to con- 128
solidate the statewide offices of Overbrook and 138
move its headquarters to Natchez. She also 147
directed the Riverview Tower construction work. 156
157

Document 3

CENTRAL COUNSELING SERVICES
Central State University
P.O. Box 340 • Omaha, NE 68132-7826
Public Relations Department
(402) 555-1280

words

For Release: Immediately | **Contact Person:** 8
Karen LeDeau 11
Omaha, Nebraska, May 4, 19--. Central 19
Counseling Services of Central State University 28
opened today and will provide free counseling to 38
the public. The new facility was established 48
under a grant from the Martin Foundation. 56
Central Counseling Services is staffed by 65
doctoral students who are enrolled in a practicum 75
during their final semester in the counseling 84
degree program at Central State University. The 94
doctoral students are supervised by four 102
full-time professors who have as their sole 111
responsibility the management of Community 119
Counseling Services. Specific assignments 128
will be made according to students' areas of 137
specialty in counseling. 142
For additional information about the pro- 150
gram or to schedule an appointment, call 555- 159
1283. 160
161

NEWS

on. . . Diversity

Today's workforce is very different from that of just a few years ago. Forecasts are that by the turn of the century at least 80 percent of those entering the workforce will be women, minorities, or immigrants. Cultural diversity mandates that we *value* the differences in people, not just *tolerate* these differences. Ethnic background, gender, life-style preference, or religion cannot be an issue. All individuals must have an opportunity to progress in their careers in direct correlation to their abilities to contribute to the objectives of the company.

To meet these high goals, top management must be absolutely committed to a culture of inclusiveness. Companies are instituting various programs and practices to implement inclusiveness: training programs for employees, recruitment policies, and mentoring of new employees. Because there will be situations where harassment or discrimination occur, clear channels must be available to hear complaints.

58c 33'

FORMATTING

Measurement: letters and memo

Time schedule

Assemble materials .... 2'
Timed production .... 25'
(Key the problems in order; proofread and correct errors as you work.)
Final check .... 6'
(Proofread and circle any remaining errors. Calculate *g-pram*—total words keyed divided by 25'.)

Document 1
Letter in block format
(LM p. S31)
Key this average-length letter in block format; prepare an envelope.

words

Current date | Mrs. Cluny Baer | 1651 Poplar Street | Erie, PA 16502-5112 | Dear 15
Mrs. Baer 17

Welcome to Erie. I hope that your move from Tulsa has not been overly 31
disruptive and that you are beginning to feel at home here. 43

I apologize for keeping your husband away from home during the past 57
two weeks while he has attended the seminar at our home office. These 71
seminars are very important to us, for we are eager that our representa- 85
tives thoroughly understand our company philosophy, product line, and 99
methods of operation. 104

Enclosed you will find a voucher good for two theater tickets at the Schubert 120
Theater at a time and for a performance of your choice. This is our way of 135
welcoming you to our company family, Mrs. Baer, and of apologizing for 149
spiriting your husband away. 155

Sincerely | J. Dake Hunter | President | xx | Enclosure 164
envelope 178

Document 2
Letter in modified block format
(LM p. S33)
Key this average length-letter in modified block format; prepare an envelope.

Current date | Mr. Guy Berger | 544 Duquesne Avenue | Dayton, OH 45431- 13
1334 | Dear Mr. Berger 17

When was the last time you had your roof checked? I don't mean just 31
casting a glance upward at it; I mean really checked. 42

We expect a lot of a roof--protection from heat, wind, and rain in the 56
summer; cold and snow in the winter--and a good roof asks little of us in 71
return. But the elements take a toll on even the best roof, and in time it 86
gives out. 89

That's why we suggest that you have our experts take a look at your roof. 104
For a flat fee of $25, we will come to your home, thoroughly examine your 118
roof to look for potential problems, and prepare a written report for you. 134

Call us today if we can include you on our schedule. 144

Sincerely | Kin-Lo Rigby | Sales Director | xx 152
envelope 166

Document 3
Interoffice memorandum

TO: Eunice A. Bates | **FROM:** Edward Baxter | **DATE:** Current | **SUBJECT:** 13
Car Assignments 17

After the two new representatives in the West Coast District are assigned, we 32
shall need to supply them with automobiles. One vehicle will be assigned to 48
Lynn Brewer, District #3, and the other to Myrle Ortega, District #5. I 62
suggest that we obtain authorizations to buy these two automobiles. 76

Each authorization should cover the purchase price of a light van. The 90
representatives may choose the exact make, color, etc. If a van is not the 106
vehicle of choice, an appropriate substitution may be requested. 119

xx 119

Document 4
Letter in block format
(LM p. S35)
Repeat Document 2, but change "roof" to "chimney" whenever it appears in the letter.

111 Resume

111a 5'

Skill-Building Warmup

alphabet	1	Hazel J. Quincy played in sixteen movies before working on stage.
fig/sym	2	The room (60'3" x 45'7") took 128 days to build and cost $76,985.
shift key	3	June and Guy may meet us for lunch or after work at five o'clock.
fluency	4	Kent and Clay may both go to work for the big firm on the island.

1	2	3	4	5	6	7	8	9	10	11	12	13

111b 45'

FORMATTING

Resumes

Read the information in "Guidelines for resumes" and study the resume illustrated on page 279.

Document 1

1 Format the resume illustrated on page 279 using a 1" top margin and 1" side or default margins.

2 Analyze the document to determine if the same format would be effective for preparing your own resume.

3 Decide what changes you would make if you were doing your own resume.

Document 2

1 Prepare a resume using your own data.

2 Adjust margins or format, if necessary, to fit copy on one page.

Document 3

1 Analyze your resume to determine if it emphasizes your strengths.

2 Experiment with formats to determine if a different organization or if emphasizing different items by use of position, bold, CAPS, or underline would enhance your resume.

Guidelines for resumes

A **resume** (sometimes called a data sheet or vita) is a summary of facts about you. Prior to preparing a resume, you should analyze yourself carefully to determine what you want to do and what you have to offer an employer. Your resume should be an outgrowth of the self-analysis process and should present your strengths in the most effective way.

The way you organize your resume may depend on how much job experience you have had. Individuals with job experience usually emphasize the results they have attained in their careers. They generally integrate information about special skills and qualifications in their job experience. The job experience section usually requires more space than other segments of the resume.

Individuals with little or no work experience usually emphasize skills and abilities. If they have some college education or a degree, they also emphasize their education. More space is devoted to these segments than to other segments of the resume.

Most resumes contain some or all of the following information:

Identifying Information: Include your name, telephone number, and address. Students may need to include both a temporary and a permanent address.

Career Objective: Specify the type of position you are seeking. Let the employer know how you want to apply your educational background.

Qualifications and Special Skills: Summarize what you believe are your most important qualifications. Emphasize special skills, such as foreign languages, computer skills, or special job skills.

Education: List diplomas or degrees earned, schools attended, and dates. Include information such as majors and grade point averages when it is to your advantage to do so.

Experience: Provide job titles, employer, dates, and a brief description of positions held. Emphasize results rather than activities.

Honors and Activities: Demonstrate leadership potential and commitment.

References: Indicate how to obtain references.

Measurement goals:

1. To demonstrate basic skill on average difficulty paragraphs in straight, rough-draft, and statistical copy.
2. To demonstrate ability to key letters, tables, reports, and outlines in proper format from semiarranged copy according to directions.

Formatting guides:

1. Default margins or a 65-space line.
2. Single-space drills; double-space paragraphs.
3. Indentions: 5-space ¶ indentions.

58a 6'

Skill-building warmup

each line 3 times SS; DS between 3-line groups

alphabet	1	Jayne promised to bring the portable vacuum for next week's quiz.
figures	2	Our main store is at 6304 Grand; others, at 725 Mayo and 198 Rio.
1st fingers	3	After lunch, Brent taught us to try to put the gun by the target.
easy	4	He may make a profit on corn, yams, and hay if he works the land.

| 1 | 2 | 3 | 4 | 5 | 6 | 7 | 8 | 9 | 10 | 11 | 12 | 13 |

58b 11'

SKILL BUILDING

Measure skill growth: statistical copy

Key a 3' and a 5' writing; circle errors; determine *gwam*.

A all letters/figures

	gwam 3'	5'	
Now and then the operation of some company deserves a closer	4	2	41
look by investors. For example, Zerotech Limited, the food, oil,	8	5	44
and chemical company, says in its monthly letter that it will be	13	8	46
raising its second-quarter dividend to 85 cents a share, up from	17	10	49
79 3/4 cents a share, and that a dividend will be paid July 12.	21	13	51
This fine old area firm is erecting an enviable history of	25	15	54
dividend payment, but its last hike in outlays came back in 1987,	30	18	56
when it said a share could go above 65 cents. Zerotech has, how-	34	21	59
ever, never failed to pay a dividend since it was founded in	38	23	61
1937. The recent increase extends the annual amount paid to	42	25	64
$5.40 a share.	43	26	65
In this monthly letter, the firm also cited its earnings for	47	28	67
the second quarter and for the first half of this year. The net	52	31	70
revenue for the second quarter was a record $1.9 billion, up 24.2	56	34	72
percent from a typical period just a year ago. Zerotech has its	61	36	75
main company offices at 9987 Nicholas Drive in Albany.	64	38	77

gwam 3' | 1 | 2 | 3 | 4 | 5 |
5' | 1 | 2 | 3 |

1" top margin → **KATRINA W. CASSIDY**

Flush right

Temporary Address (May 30, 1994)
763 East Hillside Drive
Bloomington, IN 47401-3692
(812) 555-6862

Permanent Address
3467 Senate Lane
Kokomo, IN 46902-1835
(317) 555-6065

Career Objective

A graphic design position with an opportunity to advance to a management position.

Qualifications and Special Skills

Desktop Publishing Skills. Key at 70 words per minute. In-depth knowledge and experience using several leading desktop publishing, word processing, and graphic software packages.

Computer Skills. Basic knowledge of major computer operating systems and database and spreadsheet software.

Communication/Interpersonal Skills. Superior interpersonal, speaking, writing, editing, and design layout skills.

1" left margin → **Education** ← 1" right margin

Central University, Bloomington, Indiana, Candidate for Bachelor of Business Administration Degree, May, 1994. Majored in administrative management (3.2 grade point average). Serve as president of Professional Women on Campus.

Kokomo Junior College, Kokomo, Indiana, Associate Degree, 1992. Majored in administrative systems (3.6 grade point average). Served as editor of the Kokomo Reporter.

Southside High School, Kokomo, Indiana, diploma, 1990. Graduated in top 10 percent of class; served as junior class vice president and senior class president.

Experience

Central University Alumni Office, Bloomington, Indiana. Assistant editor and producer of the Central Alumni News, 1993 to present time. Worked 25 hours per week. Responsible for editing six features and for the layout and production. Met every publishing deadline and won a design award.

Production manager of the Central Alumni News, 1992-93. Worked 25 hours per week. Managed layout and production and supervised all desktop publishing activities.

References

Request portfolio from Central University Placement Office.

Resume

1"

DALE E. BROWN
404 San Andres Avenue, NW
Albuquerque, New Mexico 97110-1170
(505) 555-0550

1" **Career Objective** 1"

Eager to bring education and sales training experience in advertising/retailing to a management trainee position with potential for advancement.

Education

Santa Fe Community College, Santa Fe, New Mexico.
A.S. Degree in Business Management June 19--. Major area of study in advertising with a specialty in art; 3.25 GPA.

Courses relevant to an advertising/retailing position include Retail Marketing I and II, Work Study I and II, behavioral psychology, Marketing Art I and II, economics, information systems.

Albuquerque Senior High School graduate, 1990.

Honors and Activities

President of Marketing Careers Club, current year.
Phi Beta Lambda business organization, 1991-1993.
Summer study (6 weeks) with economic seminar group, sponsored by Albuquerque Junior Chamber of Commerce.
National Honor Society in high school.

Experience

Advertising artist. Rendall's, Santa Fe, New Mexico. Assisted in advertising layout and design for two major campaigns. January 1993 to present.

Work-study.
La Paloma Travel Guides, Santa Fe; advertising campaign; winter 1992.

Simmons Sporting Goods, Albuquerque; sales; fall 1992.

El Senor Men's Shop, Albuquerque; assisted in buying, display, and sales; winter 1991.

Yordi's Appliances, Albuquerque; customer service; fall 1991.

References

Will be furnished upon request.

112 Application Letters

112a 5'

Skill-Building Warmup

alphabet 1 Jimmy Kloontz required extra help with lunch for five big groups.
figure 2 Flight 1975 was due at 10:53; it arrived at Gate 28 at 12:46 p.m.
3/4 finger 3 Alan was quite glad that Max told Sal about the six jazz players.
fluency 4 Did he fish with Pamela by the island or in the lake by the dock?

| 1 | 2 | 3 | 4 | 5 | 6 | 7 | 8 | 9 | 10 | 11 | 12 | 13 |

112b 45'

FORMATTING

Application letters

Read the information at the right and application letters shown as Documents 1 and 2.

Documents 1 and 2
(plain sheets)
1 Format the letters in block style.
2 Center and bold the name and address to create a personal letterhead.

Guidelines for application letters

The main purpose of an application letter is to obtain an interview. The focus should be on convincing the employer to give you the opportunity to demonstrate in person why you should be hired.

Application letters vary depending on how you learned of the position. Always try to show that your skills match the position requirements. A good strategy for writing an application letter is to:

- ✓ Establish a point of contact.
- ✓ Specify the type of job you are seeking.
- ✓ Highlight your major qualifications.
- ✓ Request an interview.

Plain paper or personal stationery–never an employer's letterhead–may be used for an application letter. You can create your own letterhead using bold and centered copy (shown at the right) or use the personal business letter format, keying your address immediately above the date. Block, modified block, or simplified format may be used.

Katrina W. Cassidy
763 East Hillside Drive
Bloomington, IN 47401-3692
(812) 555-6862

Current date

Mr. Paige Bass, Editor
Financial News
2413 West Maple Avenue
Flint, MI 48507-2754

Dear Mr. Bass

Your advertisement in the Desktop Report indicates a production management position available for someone with graphic design experience and knowledge. I have both knowledge and experience in graphic design; therefore, please consider me for the position.

Desktop publishing training and experience as assistant editor and producer of the Central Alumni News enabled me to develop the skills you desire. The enclosed resume presents additional information showing you why I am qualified for the position.

May I come in and tell you about the project for which I won a design award? Please let me know the time and date that would be most convenient.

Sincerely

Katrina W. Cassidy

Enclosure

Document 1

words

Katrina W. Cassidy | 763 East Hillside Drive 9
| Bloomington, IN 47401-3692 | (812) 555- 16
6862 17

Current date | Mr. Paige Bass, Editor | Financial 28
News | 2413 West Maple Avenue | Flint, MI 37
48507-2754 | Dear Mr. Bass 42

Your advertisement in the Desktop Report 53
indicates a production management position 61
available for someone with graphic design expe- 71
rience and knowledge. I have both knowledge 80
and experience in graphic design; therefore, please 91
consider me for the position. 97

Desktop publishing training and experience as 106
assistant editor and producer of the Central 116
Alumni News enabled me to develop the skills 128
you desire. The enclosed resume presents ad- 137
ditional information showing you why I am quali- 146
fied for the position. 157

May I come in and tell you about the project for 161
which I won a design award? Please let me 169
know the time and date that would be most 178
convenient. 180

Sincerely | Katrina W. Cassidy | Enclosure 188

57 Resume

57a 6'

each line 3 times SS; DS between 3-line groups

Skill-Building Warmup

alphabet 1 Our unexpected freezing weather quickly killed Jo's mauve shrubs.
figures 2 Paul has moved from 195 East 26th Street to 730 West 48th Street.
double letters 3 Betty fooled Annabell by hitting a ball across the narrow valley.
easy 4 I fish for a quantity of smelt and may wish for aid to land them.

1	2	3	4	5	6	7	8	9	10	11	12	13

57b 14'

COMMUNICATION

Compose at the keyboard

2" top margin

The questions at the right are similar to those sometimes asked in job interviews. Select ten of the questions and answer each of them in a brief SS paragraph. Use complete sentences in answering, as you might if you were being interviewed.

1. Why do you want this particular job?
2. What is the hardest work you have ever done?
3. Why did you leave your last position?
4. How would you feel about an employee who was late or absent once or twice a month?
5. Do you think you would rather work alone or with a group?
6. How do you think group leadership is established?
7. What is the one hobby you enjoy most?
8. What salary do you expect to earn?
9. Describe the "perfect boss."
10. Professionally, where do you plan to be ten years from now?
11. What are your future academic plans?
12. What nonacademic book have you recently read?

57c 30'

FORMATTING

A resume

1" top and side margins

1 Read "Preparing a resume" at the right.

2 Study and key the resume on page 130.

Preparing a resume

A resume is used by a job applicant to present her or his qualifications to a prospective employer. The purpose of sending a resume is to obtain a job interview. Note the following guidelines:

1 Use top, side, and bottom margins that are nearly equal; confine the resume to one page—two at most.

2 Provide headings (centered or flush left) for the information listed.

3 Emphasize important information with capitals, bold type, underlines, etc.

4 Use specific action words (such as *coordinated, increased, organized, prepared*); maintain parallel construction (use phrases or complete sentences, not both).

5 Space evenly within and between sections of the resume.

Document 2 words

Peter C. Bonn 3
2216 Felten Drive 6
Hays, KS 67601-3859 10
(316) 555-2044 13

Current date | Ms. Claire Chong | Vice President, 23
Marketing | RCT Systems, Inc. | 354 Garden Road 32
| Ames, IA 50010-9364 | Dear Ms. Chong 39

Your Chief Executive Officer, Barrios Mendez, 48
wrote in this year's Annual Report that RCT Sys- 57
tems, Inc., is assured of long-term success because 67
of its quality products, outstanding employees, 77
and commitment to excellence in customer service. 87
I share those ideals and would like to be one of 97
those outstanding employees helping Mr. Mendez 106
achieve his goals. Please consider me for a sales 117
management position if you have one available. 126

My sales and customer service experience in the 136
systems area helped me develop leadership skills 146
that are essential for managers in a technical 155
environment. I attribute my sales success to tech- 165
nical competence as well as the ability to commu- 175
nicate technical information to non- 182
technical users. The enclosed resume presents 192
additional information showing why I would be 201
an excellent sales manager for RCT Systems. 210

May I come in and tell you about the plan I used to 220
turn a sales territory that was below budget for 230
three years into a territory that met President 240
Club's requirements in one year? I can be available 250
for an interview at your convenience. 258

Sincerely | Peter C. Bonn | Enclosure 265

Document 3

1 Compose a letter applying for one of the four positions described.

2 Create your own personal letterhead.

3 Format the letter in an appropriate style.

4 Edit and proofread carefully; correct errors.

Option A

Your instructor told you that Mr. Robert Yazel of Yazel Interiors is looking for an assistant for the summer. He needs an intelligent individual with keyboarding skills, good communication skills, and a good work ethic. The person will assist him with a number of projects. No special skills or experience is required. Yazel Interiors is located at 2457 Main Street, your city, state, and ZIP Code. Write a letter of application; enclose the resume you prepared in Lesson 111.

Option B

Your instructor told you that Ms. Sandy Fowler of Fowler and Associates is looking for an office assistant for the summer. She needs an intelligent individual with good keyboarding and communication skills. She especially wants someone who has initiative and can work without supervision. Some telemarketing is involved in the position, and she is willing to train the person. Fowler and Associates is located at 3457 Main Street, your city, state, and ZIP Code. Write a letter of application; enclose the resume you prepared in Lesson 111.

Option C

MANAGEMENT TRAINEE

Excellent opportunity for an intelligent person with limited or no experience. Six-month training program leading to management position. Must have good communication skills, good interpersonal skills, and good work ethic. Business background desirable but not required. Send letter and resume to Jill C. Watson, Personnel Manager, Whit, Inc., 843 Main Street, your city, state, and ZIP Code.

Option D

SALES TRAINEE

Leading office technology firm looking for a confident, aggressive sales trainee who enjoys talking and working with people. Computer knowledge is preferred but not required. Base salary plus commission. Opportunity for high earnings. Send letter and resume to June Adams, Sales Manager, DocuSystems, Inc., 739 Main Street, your city, state, and ZIP Code.

Return address 404 San Andres Avenue, NW
Albuquerque, NM 97110-1170
April 13, 19--
QS

Mr. Michael S. Brewer
Personnel Manager
Hunter's Department Store
3500 Santa Clara Avenue, SE
Albuquerque, NM 97196-1769
DS

Dear Mr. Brewer
DS

Are you looking for a creative and enthusiastic new employee to join the staff of Hunter's Department Store? If so, please consider my application for employment with you.

I will graduate in June from Santa Fe Community College with an associate of science degree in business management. My goal is to obtain a position as a marketing trainee in a progressive and forward-looking company such as yours. Dr. Ken Davis, professor of marketing, suggested that I contact you.

As you will see from my enclosed resume, advertising is my major area of academic study, with a specialty in art. You will be interested, I know, in noting that my involvement with a work-study program allowed me to gain marketing experience with four diverse retail stores. Also, part of one year was spent studying with an economic seminar group in Albuquerque.

After you have had a chance to read my resume, may I have an opportunity to discuss my qualifications? You may reach me at 555-0550 or at the address shown above.
DS

Sincerely yours
QS

Dale E. Brown
DS

Enclosure

113 Application Forms

Skill-Building Warmup

113a 5'

alphabet 1 Mavis quickly fixed her car so we could go play jazz with a band.
figure 2 Jayne asked 492 men, 180 women, and 376 children 1,925 questions.
one hand 3 I gave him my opinion on a great estate tax case we read at noon.
fluency 4 Did a man sign a form and pay for the right to fish on the docks?

| 1 | 2 | 3 | 4 | 5 | 6 | 7 | 8 | 9 | 10 | 11 | 12 | 13 |

113b 45'

FORMATTING

Application forms
(LM pp. S105-S107)

Document 1

1 Format the application form at the right and continued on page 283.

2 Abbreviate, if necessary, to fit the information in the space provided.

PALMETTO INDUSTRIES
Application for Employment

Name Katrina W. Cassidy **Telephone** 812-555-6862

Address 763 East Hillside Drive, Bloomington, IN 47401-3692

Position Desired Graphic Designer

Education (List in reverse chronological order.) **Social Security No.** 467-32-8542

School	*Location*	*Degree/Diploma*	*Dates*
Central University	Bloomington, Indiana	BBA	May, 1994
Kokomo Junior College	Kokomo, Indiana	AS	1992
Southside High School	Kokomo, Indiana	Diploma	1990

Work Experience (Give organization, location, dates, position, and major duties.)

Central University Alumni Office, Bloomington, Indiana:

Assistant editor and producer of Central Alumni News, 1993-present. Responsible for editing six features for layout and production. Met every deadline; won design award.

Production manager, 1992-1993. Managed layout and production; supervised desktop publishing. (25 hours per week)

Specific Job Qualifications

Keyboard 70 wpm. Know two desktop publishing, four word processing, and two graphic software application packages.

56c 10'

FORMATTING

Topical outline

1.5" top margin; key the topical outline.

words

FINDING THE JOB 4

I. ANALYZE THE JOB MARKET 9

A. Locate Employment Opportunities 16

1 A. Read Newspapers and Professional Journals 26

a 1. Check help wanted ads 31

b 2. Watch for news items 36

2 B. Ask Knowledgeable Friends and Associates 45

3 C. Use School Placement Services 52

4 D. Consider Commercial Placement Services 60

B. Research Specific Companies 67

II. MAKE APPLICATION 71

Human Resources

A. Acquire Information from ~~Personnel Office~~, if Necessary 83

B. Send Letter and Resume to Appropriate Supervisor 93

III. INTERVIEW FOR THE POSITION 100

A. Prepare for Interview Investigate the 105

1. ~~Learn about~~ position and the company 114

2. Know job requirements; have salary range in mind 125

3. Anticipate questions/prepare answers 133

B. Dress Appropriately 138

1. Wear conservative clothing 144

2. Use accessories sparingly; groom neatly 153

C. Participate Intelligently 159

1. Arrive early 162

2. Have pen, small note pad, extra resume available 173

3. Answer questions briefly but fully 180

4. Listen actively; Ask questions that show your interest and potential 195

5. Observe interviewer's body language 203

56d 22'

FORMATTING

Personal/business letters

Document 1

1 Read "Personal/business letters" and "Letter of application" at the right.

2 Key the personal/business letter on page 128 in modified block format; use plain sheet.

Document 2

1 Compose a letter of application that might work well for you. Use as many actual facts as you can. Key in format of your choosing.

2 Edit the first draft; revise as necessary.

Personal/business letters

Personal letters of a business nature may be keyed on plain stationery or personal letterhead. If plain stationery is used, the letter must include the sender's return address. Personal business letters should never be prepared on a company's letterhead stationery.

Personal business letters also contain the other regular parts of a business letter. Either block or modified block format may be used.

Letter of application

A letter of application must accompany a resume. It is formatted as a personal/business letter. The purposes of the letter are to attract attention to the resume and to obtain an interview. Follow these guides:

1 Keep the letter error free. It should appear to have been written especially for the recipient.

2 Address the letter to a specific person.

3 Avoid overuse of *I* and *me*.

4 Keep it brief.

5 Stimulate the reader's interest in your resume; refer indirectly to it in the letter.

6 Indicate the position for which you are applying if you are pursuing a specific job.

7 Mention how you learned of the opening. Mentioning a name always helps, but first have permission to do so.

8 Ask for an interview.

113b (continued)

Document 2

1 Format an application form using your own data. The form is for the position you applied for in Document 3 of 112c on page 281.

2 Use your resume to help you organize the information.

Other Qualifications

Computer skills: Know major operating systems, database, and spreadsheet software.

Excellent communication and interpersonal skills.

Professional Organizations and Activities

Central University-- Professional Women on Campus--President

Kokomo Junior College-- Editor of Kokomo Reporter

Southside High School-- Senior Class President
Junior Class Vice President

State Why You Believe You Should Be Hired

I should be hired because I have the technical skills required to be an excellent graphic designer. I work well as a member of a team, and I have a good work ethic. I demonstrated my abilities by winning a design award. My goal is to continue learning and growing in my profession. I am convinced I can contribute to the success of Palmetto Industries.

References

Complete portfolio available from Central University Placement Office. The portfolio includes references from:

Dr. Maria Diaz, Professor of Administrative Systems, Central University

Ms. Donna Chan, Editor, Central Alumni News

Ms. Chris Keebler, Desktop Publishing Instructor, Kokomo Junior College.

Signature ______________________ **Date** ______________________

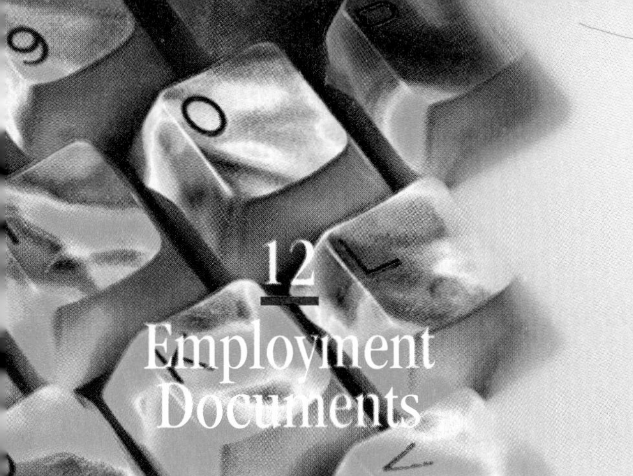

Learning goals:

1. To format a transmittal letter.
2. To format a personal resume.
3. To review topical outlines.
4. To review modified block letter format.

Formatting guides:

1. Default margins or a 65-space line.
2. Single-space drills; double-space paragraphs.
3. Indentions: 5-space ¶ indent.

56a 6'

Skill-building warmup

each line 3 times SS; DS between 3-line groups; work for error-free lines

alphabet 1 Pam Beck recognized the excellent quality of this silver jewelry.
figures 2 On May 28, 15 men and 30 women drove 476 miles to Ohio in 9 vans.
3d row 3 We were there when Terrie tried on her pretty new oyster sweater.
easy 4 Due to the rigor of the quake, the city may dismantle the chapel.

| 1 | 2 | 3 | 4 | 5 | 6 | 7 | 8 | 9 | 10 | 11 | 12 | 13 |

56b 12'

SKILL BUILDING

Check straight copy

Take three 3' writings; compute *gwam* and number of errors.

all letters

	gwam 3'	
Many of us are always in a hurry. We scramble about, trying	4	51
quickly and desperately to do dozens of things, but we never have	8	56
an adequate amount of time, it seems, to finish any one of them.	13	60
As a result, emergencies, not reason, directly affect many of our	17	65
decisions; and too many tasks, not done correctly the first time,	22	69
keep reappearing in our schedules. On the other hand, though, we	26	74
can always look as examples to those capable people who somehow	30	78
manage to get jobs done in the same amount of time available to	35	82
us. They pace themselves, budget time, and set priorities. They	39	86
rarely put off until tomorrow what they can do today, and when	43	91
they are done, they are, believe it or not, done. Remarkable!	47	95

gwam 3' | 1 | 2 | 3 | 4 | 5 |

114 Review

Skill-Building Warmup

114a 5'

alphabet 1 Max Jordan was quickly convicted of embezzling the company funds.
fig/sym 2 I paid only $432.10 ($2.98 each) for 145 of the 76-page booklets.
adjacent reach 3 Guy and Trey Dupuy were going to play polo with my older brother.
fluency 4 Vivian may go with them to town to dismantle the antique bicycle.
| 1 | 2 | 3 | 4 | 5 | 6 | 7 | 8 | 9 | 10 | 11 | 12 | 13 |

114b 15'

SKILL BUILDING

Build/measure straight-copy skill

1 Key one 3' writing on each ¶; strive to increase your keystroking rate.
2 Key one 5' writing at your "control" rate. Proofread; circle errors; determine *gwam*.

 all letters

	gwam 3'	5'	
Should volunteer work be listed on a job resume? This ques-	4	2	39
tion is often asked. Most employers would like to know if a job	8	5	42
applicant does volunteer work. Businesses like to be thought of	13	8	44
as good corporate citizens; therefore, they usually value a	17	10	47
worker who is a good citizen and who is willing to make a major	21	13	49
commitment of time to his or her community. Many employers feel	25	15	52
that workers who do volunteer jobs gain skills and also demon-	29	18	54
strate a willingness to do more than is expected.	33	20	56
People who do volunteer work gain more than favorable atten-	37	22	59
tion from employers. Usually people who do unpaid jobs gain	41	24	61
valuable job skills or make very good contacts that help to en-	45	27	64
rich their lives. The most rewarding thing they gain, however,	49	30	66
is the feeling that results from knowing they made a difference	54	32	69
in the lives of others who may not be able to help themselves.	58	35	71
That super feeling makes it all worth the effort.	61	37	73

gwam 3' | 1 | 2 | 3 | 4 | 5 |
5' | 1 | 2 | 3 |

114c 30'

FORMATTING

Administrative communications

Document 1
Action minutes

words

BUDGET COMMITTEE | November 14, 19-- | Action Minutes | Presiding: Fred Brewster | **Participants**: Betty Chambers, Lilly Davis, Ann Kaminski, Daniel Pressley, Shirley Widener, and Norma Zoller 11 27 37

The Budget Committee reviewed the process used to determine the budget for the current year and agreed that the same process should be used to prepare next year's budget. Norma Zoller agreed to have the data collection forms ready for the meeting next Thursday. 52 66 81 90

Ann Kaminski and Daniel Pressley agreed to write the memo to each department requesting the necessary information and to enclose the data collection forms. The draft of the memo will be reviewed at the meeting next Thursday and mailed with the forms on Friday. 105 120 135 143

Betty Chambers, Lilly Davis, and Shirley Widener will summarize the information returned on the data collection forms. They estimate that the process will take approximately two weeks. 158 173 181

55c 34'

FORMATTING

Measurement: tables

(3 plain sheets)

Time schedule:

Assembling materials .... 3'
Timed production .... 25'
Final check; proofread;
compute *g-pram* .... 6'

g-pram = total words keyed / time (25')

Directions:

Center each table horizontally and vertically; determine intercolumn spacing.

Document 1

		words
SINGLE-FAMILY DWELLINGS		5
1990 Median Prices		9
Baltimore	$105,900	13
Cleveland	80,600	16
Detroit	76,700	19
Honolulu	325,000	22
Las Vegas	93,000	26
Los Angeles	212,000	30
Milwaukee	84,400	33
Phoenix	84,000	36
Seattle	142,000	39
____________________		42
Source: U. S. Realty Group		48

Document 2

		words
AVON SCHOOL OF CULINARY ARTS		6
Metric Conversions		10
Metric Measure	Liquid Measure	21
1 milliliter	.2 teaspoon	26
5 milliliters	1.0 teaspoon	32
34 milliliters	1.0 tablespoon	38
100 milliliters	3.4 fluid ounces	44
240 milliliters	1.0 cup	49
1 liter	34.0 fluid ounces	54
1 liter	4.2 cups	58
1 liter	2.1 pints	61

Document 3

			words
COUNTRIES SELDOM IN THE NEWS			6
World's Smallest Nations			11
Country	Capital	Location	21
Andorra	Andorra la Vella	Europe	27
Djibouti	Djibouti	Africa	32
Kiribati	Tarawa	Mid Pacific	38
Nauru	Yaren	W Pacific	42
San Marino	San Marino	Europe	49
Tonga	Nuku'alofa	S Pacific	53
Tuvalu	Funafuti	SW Pacific	59

114c (continued) words

Document 2
Itinerary

Itinerary for Michael Walters, March 12-16, 19-- 10

Wednesday, March 12, Atlanta to Anchorage 18

9:15 a.m. Leave Atlanta on Northern Flight 8394; 28

lunch; arrive Anchorage at 2:35 p.m.; reservations at 39

Snow Bird (Confirmation #385202). 46

7:30 p.m. Banquet in McKinley Ballroom. 54

Thursday and Friday, March 13-14 61

9:15 a.m.-4:15 p.m. Convention activities. 70

Saturday, March 15 74

Free for sight-seeing. 78

Sunday, March 16 Anchorage to Atlanta 86

9:12 a.m. Leave Anchorage on Northern Flight 95

3692; arrive Atlanta at 6:45 p.m.; brunch 103

and dinner served. 107

Document 3
News release
(LM p. S109)

PIEDMONT DENTAL CLINIC

3954 Devine Street **Columbia, SC 29205-3482** **803-555-3856**

For Release: ~~Immediately~~ *March 20, 19--* 3

Contact Person: Judy Farb 5

March 15, 19--.

Columbia, South Carolina, Thomas Farley, DMD and Lynn 19

DMD,

Leppard, announced today that the Piedmont Dental Clinic is 32

new

moving form its Five Points location to the Shandon Medical 45

Street

Complex located at 3954 Devine. The Piedmont Dental Clinic 58

a.m. *p.m.,* *Friday*

is open from 8:30 to 5:30 Monday through ~~Saturday~~. Drs. 71

Dr. *dentistry*

Farley and Leppard specialize in family and are now 84

accepting new patients. 89

All patients are invited to attend the Shandon Medical 100

Complex grand opening at 4:30 p.m. on March 28, 19--. 111

112

55 Measurement

Skill-Building Warmup

55a 6'

each line 2 times SS; DS between 2-line groups; 1' writings on line 4 (work for accuracy)

alphabet 1 Jimmy Bond quickly realized we could fix the poor girl's vehicle.
figures 2 On April 12, send me Files 34 and 76; my official number is 5890.
adjacent reaches 3 Last autumn, Guy and Isadore loitered here as they walked to Rio.
easy 4 Eight neighbor girls and I wish to work in the cornfield by dusk.

| 1 | 2 | 3 | 4 | 5 | 6 | 7 | 8 | 9 | 10 | 11 | 12 | 13 |

55b 10'

SKILL BUILDING

Measure straight-copy skill

Take one 3' and one 5' writing; determine *gwam*; proofread and circle errors.

 all letters

	gwam 3'	5'	
Whether any company can succeed depends on how well it fits	4	2	44
into the economic system. Success rests on certain key factors	8	5	47
that are put in line by a management team that has set goals for	13	8	49
the company and has enough good judgment to recognize how best to	17	10	52
reach those goals. Because of competition, only the best orga-	21	13	55
nized companies get to the top.	23	14	56
A commercial enterprise is formed for a specific purpose;	27	16	58
that purpose is usually to equip others, or consumers, with	31	19	61
whatever they cannot equip themselves. Unless there is only one	36	21	63
provider, a consumer will search for a company that returns the	40	24	66
most value in terms of price; and a relationship with such a com-	44	27	68
pany, once set up, can endure for many years.	47	28	70
Thus our system assures that the businesses that manage to	51	31	73
survive are those that have been able to combine successfully an	56	33	75
excellent product with a low price and the best service--all in a	60	36	78
place that is convenient for the buyers. With no intrusion from	64	39	80
outside forces, the buyer and the seller benefit both themselves	69	41	83
and each other.	70	42	84

gwam 3' | 1 | 2 | 3 | 4 | 5 |
5' | 1 | 2 | 3 |

115 Measurement

Skill-Building Warmup

115a 5'

alphabet 1 Lex Jacks bought a very nice quartz pendant watch for his mother.
figure 2 The 12 units ranging from 986 to 1,543 square feet cost $472,800.
direct reach 3 Kunio Enumi doubts that many bright, young aces make good grades.
fluency 4 Claudia paid for a rug and the enamel bowl in the ancient chapel.

1	2	3	4	5	6	7	8	9	10	11	12	13

115b 12'

SKILL BUILDING

Measure straight-copy skill

1 Key one 3' writing. Circle errors; determine *gwam.*
2 Key one 5' writing. Circle errors; determine *gwam.*

A all letters

	gwam 3'	5'	
An effective job search requires very careful planning and a	4	2	42
lot of hard work. Major decisions must be made about the type of	8	5	45
job, the size and the type of business, and the geographic area.	13	8	48
Once all of these basic decisions have been made, then the com-	17	10	50
plex task of locating the ideal job can begin. Some jobs are	21	13	53
listed in what is known as the open job market. These positions	25	15	55
are listed with placement offices of schools, placement agencies,	30	18	58
and they are advertised in newspapers or journals.	33	20	60
The open market is not the only source of jobs, however.	37	22	62
Some experts believe that almost two-thirds of all jobs are in	41	25	65
what is sometimes called the hidden job market. Networking is	46	27	67
the primary way to learn about jobs in the hidden job market.	50	30	70
Employees of a company, instructors, and members of professional	54	32	72
associations are some of the best contacts to tap the hidden job	58	35	75
market. Much time and effort is required to tap these sources,	63	38	77
but the hidden market often produces the best results.	66	40	80

gwam 3' | 1 | 2 | 3 | 4 | 5 |
5' | 1 | 2 | 3 |

115c 33'

FORMATTING

Measure production

Time schedule
Assemble materials........ 3'
Timed production .... 25'
Final check; compute *n-pram* .... 5'

1 Organize your supplies.
2 When directed to begin, key the four documents on page 287 for 25'.
3 Proofread carefully; correct errors; compute *n-pram* (total words keyed – penalty ÷ 25').

54c 30'

FORMATTING

Tables

Document 1
Long table

Calculate appropriate horizontal and vertical placement and key this wide, long table. Margins will need adjustment.

Reference: page 114.

words

OFFICIAL BIRDS AND FLOWERS 5

For Selected States 9

State	Official Bird	Official Flower	24
Alaska	willow ptarmigan	forget-me-not	31
Arkansas	mockingbird	apple blossom	38
California	California valley quail	golden poppy	48
Connecticut	American robin	mountain laurel	56
Delaware	blue hen chicken	peach blossom	64
Georgia	brown thrasher	Cherokee rose	72
Idaho	mountain bluebird	syringa	78
Illinois	cardinal	native violet	84
Louisiana	eastern brown pelican	magnolia	93
Maryland	Baltimore oriole	black-eyed Susan	101
Massachusetts	chickadee	mayflower	108
Nebraska	western meadowlark	goldenrod	116
New Jersey	eastern goldfinch	purple violet	124
New Mexico	roadrunner	yucca	130
North Carolina	cardinal	dogwood	136
Pennsylvania	ruffed grouse	mountain laurel	145
Rhode Island	Rhode Island red chicken	violet	154
South Dakota	ringnecked pheasant	pasque flower	163
Tennessee	mockingbird	iris	168
Texas	mockingbird	bluebonnet	174
Washington	goldfinch	western rhododendron	183
Wyoming	meadowlark	Indian paintbrush	190

Document 2
Table with source note

1 Format and key the table. Align the colons in Column 3.

2 To place the source note, DS after the last line of the table, key an underline of about 1.5"; then DS and key the source note.

SQUARE ISLAND MARINA RACE RESULTS 7

Official Placements and Times 13

Contestant Boat	Place	Off. Time	25
Challenger A	Fourth	7:18:02	31
Dayswift	Sixth	8:22:32	36
Furious	First	5:31:56	40
Harlen's Dream	Ninth	15:20:25	46
Justabote	Fifth	7:19:03	51
Red Menace	Tenth	15:34:09	56
Rollin' Stone	Second	7:56:44	62
Stalwart	Eighth	9:26:01	67
Swingalong	Third	7:33:48	72

DS
____________________ 75

DS
Source: New York Maritime Association 82

Document 1— Itinerary words

ITINERARY FOR SHIRLEY LABORDE 6
May 2-4, 19-- 9

Monday, May 2, 19-- | Denver to New Or- 16
leans | 6:05 a.m. Leave Denver on Gulf Flight 25
274; arrive New Orleans 10:55 a.m.; breakfast; 34
Acadian Rental Car (Confirmation #324756); 43
Saints Hotel (Confirmation #583754). | 1:30 p.m. 52
Lloyd Desselle of Desselle Catfish and Crawfish 62
Packing, Inc., 2845 St. Charles. Dinner guest 71
of Desselle. 74

Tuesday, May 3, 19-- | 7:00 a.m. Drive to 82
Marksville (4 hours). | 12:00 Lunch at Old River 92
Inn with Eric Baudin, of Baudin Catfish Ponds. 101
| 2:30 p.m. Drive to Breaux Bridge (2 hours). 110
Bayou de Glaise Inn (Confirmation #5398). 119
Crawfish Festival. 123

Wednesday, May 4, 19-- | New Orleans to 131
Denver | 9:30 a.m. Crawfish Festival | 2:00 139
p.m. Drive to New Orleans (3 hours). | 6:00 147
p.m. Leave New Orleans on Gulf Flight 4958; 156
arrive Denver at 9:15 p.m.; dinner served on 165
flight. 166

Document 2—Agenda
Format names flush right.

SYSTEMS FOR EMPLOYMENT TRAINING | 6
November 3, 19-- | Agenda 11

Overview of Conference . . . . . Mark Brown 24
Welcome 26
Role of Systems Training, Inc. 32
Role of participants 36

Workplace Needs . . . . Helen Lee 50
Types of jobs available 54
Types of workers' needs 59
Specific skills required 64

Programs for Success . . . . Jon Mills 77
Computer-based programs 82
Alternative learning sites 89

Document 3—Action minutes

SYSTEMS FOR EMPLOYMENT TRAINING | 6
November 3, 19-- | Action Minutes 13

Presiding: Tomas Diaz | **Participants:** Toni 22
Clamp, Delta Dowis, Helen Lee, Lynn Miles, 30
Jon Mills, Wesley Ross, and Leslie Tate 38

Tomas Diaz welcomed the group and indicated 47
that, in addition to hosting the meeting, Sys- 56
tems Training, Inc., would like to use the group 66
as consultants for the development of computer- 75
based training systems. 80

Helen Lee presented a summary of her work- 89
place analysis. A copy is attached. She sum- 98
marized that the primary jobs that were being 107
targeted were entry-level workers in the 115
medical, clerical, and basic services area. The 125
skills required were placed in broad categories 135
of technical job skills, communication skills, 144
interpersonal skills, and workplace dynamics. 154

Jon Mills reported on three pilot programs 162
and indicated that all three showed initial 171
promise. The computer-based programs were 180
far more successful than the traditional pro- 189
grams. A comprehensive report will be com- 197
pleted in two weeks, and Jon will mail a copy 206
to all participants. | Attachment 213

Document 4—Application letter
Center and bold the address to create a personal letterhead; use block format.

Bart C. Mataloni | 8 Crestwood Road | Milford, 9
CT 04640-2580 | 203-555-3674 | October 15, 16
19-- | Ms. Lisa Waskowicz, Director | ElderCare, 25
Inc. | 427 Cedar Hollow Drive | Rocky Hill, CT 34
06067-3483 | Dear Ms. Waskowicz 40

My word processing instructor, Mr. Lee Tetsch, 49
told me about the part-time position you have 59
available for an office manager. Please con- 68
sider me an applicant. 72

Mr. Tetsch indicated that the position requires 82
good communication skills and the ability to 91
organize, schedule, and coordinate office work. 101
I am a business major and have excelled in 109
the areas of communications and office 117
systems. My strengths include initiative, good 127
organizational skills, and the ability to work 136
with little supervision. The enclosed resume 145
provides additional information about my busi- 155
ness background and work experience. 162

Please give me an opportunity to talk with 171
you about the position of office manager for 180
ElderCare, Inc. 183

Sincerely | Bart C. Mataloni | Enclosure 190

Document 2

Center the table vertically and horizontally. Block and underline column heads. Remember to set the decimal tab after keying columnar heads.

			words
BANCHESTER STATE UNIVERSITY			6
Departmental Growth			10
Department/College	Number	Rate	22
Arts and Sciences	218	2.5%	27
Business	1,405	11.3%	31
Education	906	3.9%	35
Engineering	315	10.4%	40
Health/Human Services	85	5.6%	46
Technology	927	8.7%	49

Document 3

Rekey 51c, Document 3, page 118, aligning the names in Column 2 at the right edge of the column.

54 Tables With Source Notes

Skill-Building Warmup

54a 6'

each line 3 times SS; DS between 3-line groups

alphabet 1 Frank expected to solve a jigsaw puzzle more quickly than before.
figures 2 Of 290 pens, Ito stored 9 in Bin 13, 5 in Bin 46, and 7 in Bin 8.
colon 3 Key this: To: Earl Jorin; From: Kay Pohn; Subject: Tax Rates.
easy 4 When did the city auditor pay the proficient firm for a big sign?

| 1 | 2 | 3 | 4 | 5 | 6 | 7 | 8 | 9 | 10 | 11 | 12 | 13 |

54b 14'

SKILL BUILDING

Improve tab control

1 Set five tabs 10 spaces apart with Column 2 beginning 10 spaces from the left margin.

2 Key three 1' writings on lines 5-7. Work to eliminate pauses.

3 Key three 1' writings on lines 8-10. Emphasize smooth, continuous movements.

4 Key two 3' writings on all lines.

Goal: 18 *gwam* on 3' writings (each line = 6 words)

							gwam 1'	3'	
5	Kent	Nels	Clem	Glen	Maya	Lana	6	2	14
6	Dick	Iris	Ruby	Tory	Jane	Ivie	12	4	16
7	Buck	Lark	Yale	Jaye	Quan	Tico	18	6	18
8	1828	2039	3758	4920	5718	6304	6	8	20
9	8191	9465	6307	2016	7395	2048	12	10	22
10	2630	8195	2637	8405	1947	6263	18	12	24

23 Skill Building

Learning goals:
1 To improve keyboarding techniques.
2 To improve keyboarding skill.

Formatting guides:
1 Margins: 1" or 65-space line for drills and ¶ writings.
2 Single-space drills; double-space writings.
3 Indentions: 5-spaces or default tabs for ¶ writings.

116a 5'

Skill-building warmup

each line 3 times (slowly, faster, slowly); DS between 3-line groups; repeat selected lines if time permits

(Use these directions for all skill-building warmups in Lessons 116-118.)

alphabet 1 Jacqueline and Li played with five or six big, bulky zoo animals.
figure 2 Sales were $68,235,078 in 1984; in 1994, sales were $129,306,715.
double letter 3 Rebecca will keep three kittens and will sell three in Tennessee.
fluency 4 A neighbor and I may visit with them and fuel the flame for them.
| 1 | 2 | 3 | 4 | 5 | 6 | 7 | 8 | 9 | 10 | 11 | 12 | 13 |

116b 15'

SKILL BUILDING

Build script-copy skill

1 Key two 1' writings on each ¶. Strive for a higher *gwam* on the second writing.

2 Key two 3' writings. Proofread; circle errors; determine *gwam*.

A all letters

	gwam 1'	3'	
Graphs and charts can be used to enhance documents	10	3	54
and make them easier to read. The software available on	22	7	58
the market today makes providing graphics in a document	33	11	62
a relatively simple process. Until just recently, the only	45	15	66
colors that could be produced by the office employee were	56	19	70
black and white. When color graphics were used, they	69	23	74
had to be prepared in a special department; or they had	80	27	78
to be sent out to a professional printer.	89	30	81
Now, office equipment that can print a variety of colors	11	33	84
can be purchased. Good graphics can be prepared by the	23	37	88
same worker who keys a document. The use of color printers	35	41	92
and copy machines is expected to increase because most	46	45	96
people recognize that color is a very good communication	57	49	100
tool if effective use is made of it.	64	51	102

53b 14'

SKILL BUILDING

Improve accuracy

Key a 2' writing; count errors. Key three more 2' writings. Try to reduce errors with each writing.

A all letters used

gwam 2'

Little things do contribute a lot to success in keying. 6
Take our work attitude, for example. It's a little thing; yet, 12
it can make quite a lot of difference. Demonstrating patience 18
with a job or a problem, rather than pressing much too hard for a 25
desired payoff, often brings better results than we expected. 31
Other "little things," such as wrist and finger position, how we 38
sit, size and location of copy, and lights, have meaning for 44
any person who wants to key well. 47

gwam 2' | 1 | 2 | 3 | 4 | 5 | 6 | 7 |

53c 30'

FORMATTING

Right align columns

Read "Aligning numbers in columns" at right; then key the drill and Documents 1, 2, and 3.

wp Word processors use a **right align tab** to align numbers or words at the right edge of a column.

Aligning numbers in columns: Numbers within columns align at the first position at the right of the column. Set a tab to accommodate the most frequently appearing number of digits in a column, then space forward or backward for the others.

A decimal tab may also be used to align a column without decimals. Note the position of the decimal tabs below.

Decimal tab	Decimal tab	Decimal tab
$110,000.75	1,423	Rob
760.10	690	Sarah

Drill

Lemon Valley		MO		25
Halford		LA		217
Balsley		MA		1,423
Lake Juno		NV		528
Edelton		RI		690
Lemon Valley	10	MO	10	1,423

Document 1

Center the table vertically and horizontally.

			words
SCHUMANN MANUFACTURING CO.			5
Prize-Winning Suggestions for 19--			12
Prize Winner	Department	Prize	24
Helen Grose	Sales	$1,200	29
John Holtz	Maintenance	200	35
Pedro Lopez	Advertising	550	40
Ernesto Mye	Accounting	75	45
Nyna Paige	Purchasing	550	51
Erica Ortiz	Art	525	55
Rose Ervine	Security	1,200	60
Albert Suoka	Marketing	550	65
Dino Litti	Research	75	70

116c 15'

SKILL BUILDING

Improve keyboarding technique

each set of lines 3 times; DS between 9-line groups; key one-hand words letter-by-letter; key balanced-hand words as units

one hand

5 was milk trace plum greet pony gave junk vast jump cast ploy west
6 Teresa saw Barbara start a debate on a minimum tax on a monopoly.
7 Rebecca gave Phillip a great award after we gave him a brass bed.

balanced hand

8 pant wisp turn sick pact quantity make spend wish visit when lend
9 Henry and Pamela may go to the big city to visit with a sick man.
10 Did Pamela pay for the ornament they got for the man in the city?

combination

11 bugle curl faster hymn corn faze lake robot jump title problem ax
12 Did Jan taste the water and make the statement after their visit?
13 That mangy dog grabbed the fish and jumped into the lake with it.

| 1 | 2 | 3 | 4 | 5 | 6 | 7 | 8 | 9 | 10 | 11 | 12 | 13 |

116d 15'

SKILL BUILDING

Build straight-copy skill

1 Key two 1' writings on each ¶. Strive for a higher *gwam* on the second writing.

2 Key two 3' writings. Proofread; circle errors; determine *gwam*.

A all letters

	gwam 3'	5'	
Perception is often referred to as "what you see is what you	4	2	49
get." A better definition is "becoming aware through our senses	8	5	52
or our ability to understand." How we perceive situations is a	13	8	54
product of numerous factors, and our perceptions are often in-	17	10	57
accurate. The perception others have of us may not be accurate	21	13	59
either. Part of the problem is that one person rarely sees the	25	15	62
whole picture. Just as the six blind men each felt a different	30	18	64
part of an elephant and got quite a different perception of what	34	20	67
an elephant looks like, so we base our views on limited informa-	38	23	70
tion that may not give us an accurate perception.	42	25	72
Empathizing with others helps to improve your perception of	45	27	74
them. Empathy is more than just mentally putting yourself in the	50	30	77
position of another person. Empathizing requires that we under-	54	32	79
stand why a person did something and the emotions the person felt	59	35	82
at the time. Empathizing is not easy because it requires us to	63	38	84
have an open mind and to be willing to put aside our thoughts as	67	40	87
we focus on the other person. The results of using empathy,	71	43	89
however, are worth the effort we must exert. Empathy is one of	75	45	92
the keys to good human relations.	78	47	94

gwam 3' | 1 | 2 | 3 | 4 | 5 |
5' | 1 | 2 | 3 |

Document 2

Center the table vertically and horizontally. Align numbers at the decimal points. Indent *Total* 5 spaces from the left margin.

Dollar sign: Consider a $ as part of the column. Place a $ before the first amount to accommodate the number with the most digits and before the total if one is included. Indicate a total with a line under the columnn. DS above the total figure.

SCHUMANN MANUFACTURING CO.

Group B Hourly Salaries

John E. Sheard	$ 9.12
Laurel D. Bedore	10.47
Betsy A. Yorke	8.03
Esther Ferrier	9.12
Alan M. Woods	10.47
Louise Ybarra	9.12
Rita A. Montgomery	8.03
Roger E. Osuma	8.03
Orin Swauger	9.12
Total	$81.51

Document 3

Three-column tables: Determine vertical placement as with any other table. For horizontal placement, include all three columns and two intercolumns in key line.

			words
SHERWOOD SCHOOL			3
Computer Lab			6
Code	Description	Unit Cost	16
E4-TC152	Workstation	$189.95	22
S2-90097	3 1/2" Diskettes	13.30	29
S2-90098	5 1/4" Diskettes	8.85	35
T1-0642A	Computer data tabs	.59	41
TA-8R023	Locking disk tray	26.95	51
Total		$244.85	53

53 Three-Column Tables

Skill-Building Warmup

53a 6'

each line 3 times SS; DS between 3-line groups

alphabet 1 Dixie Vaughn acquired that prize job with a firm just like yours.

figures 2 My May 15 note read: Call Ext. 390; order 472 clips and 68 pens.

easy/figures 3 The 29 girls kept 38 bushels of corn and 59 bushels of rich yams.

easy 4 The men paid half of the aid endowment, and their firm paid half.

| 1 | 2 | 3 | 4 | 5 | 6 | 7 | 8 | 9 | 10 | 11 | 12 | 13 |

117 Skill Building

117a 5'

Skill-Building Warmup

alphabet 1 Alex Czajka quit swimming because his team performed very poorly.
fig/sym 2 We paid $1,459.87 ($830 for the flight and $629.87 for expenses).
space bar 3 Li, Jo, and I got in the car to go to the pool to lie in the sun.
fluency 4 Jake and a neighbor own the island with the big dock in the lake.

| 1 | 2 | 3 | 4 | 5 | 6 | 7 | 8 | 9 | 10 | 11 | 12 | 13 |

117b 15'

SKILL BUILDING

Build rough-draft copy skill

1 Key two 1' writings on each ¶. Strive for a higher *gwam* on the second writing.
2 Key two 3' writings.

A all letters

	gwam 1'	3'	
Workers at times will need to find data on a	13	4	67
certain topic. If the information is not found in	23	8	70
references that are maintained in the office, the	33	11	74
worker may goto a public library to ~~search for~~ the	43	14	77
data. Today, an electronic library can be used as	54	18	80
key reference source. A on-line library is called	64	21	84
information utility. This service is provided to	75	25	87
client for a fee.	79	26	89
A subscriber with a questions concerning a	8	29	91
specific topic ~~and~~ electronically search for the	18	32	95
answers. Some services provide just a listing of	28	36	98
the references ~~but~~ others furnish an abstract of	39	39	101
the article. Some services even provide complete	49	42	105
test of an article. The user can print the	57	45	108
article and read it ~~and~~ have the service mail it	67	48	111
to her or him. Most users ~~like~~ to have the ser-	77	52	114
vice mail a copy of the article to them rather	86	55	117
than print it on-line. Those users who have	95	58	120
analized the cost have learned that ~~is~~ approach	105	61	124
save them money.	109	62	125

52 Tables With Decimals

Skill-Building Warmup

52a 6'

each line 3 times SS; DS between 3-line groups

alphabet 1	Jimmy Favorita realized that we must quit playing by six o'clock.
figures 2	Joell, in her 1987 truck, put 25 boxes in an annex at 3460 Marks.
double letters 3	Merriann was puzzled by a letter that followed a free book offer.
easy 4	Ana's sorority works with vigor for the goals of the civic corps.

1 | 2 | 3 | 4 | 5 | 6 | 7 | 8 | 9 | 10 | 11 | 12 | 13

52b 14'

FORMATTING

Align decimals

Read "Aligning decimals"; then follow the directions to key the drill.

Aligning decimals

Numbers with decimals must align at the decimal point. Electronic typewriters and word processing software use a **decimal tab** to align numbers with decimals.

To set a decimal tab, move the carrier or cursor to the decimal point position and set the tab. (See equipment manual for more specific directions.)

On equipment without a decimal tab feature (electric typewriters and Micro-Assistant), set a tab to accommodate the most frequently appearing number of digits in a column; then space forward or backward to align the other digits.

	Beef		3.29
	Cheese		1.07
	Chicken		.99
	Franks		.68
	Pork		2.45
Key line	Chicken	10	3.29

Set decimal tab here

52c 30'

FORMATTING

Tables with decimals

Document 1

Center the table horizontally and vertically. Align numbers at the decimal points.

		words
SCHUMANN MANUFACTURING CO.		5
Group A Salary Factors		10
William Talbot	.87	14
Beatrice Guided	.86	18
Natalie Dress	1.02	21
Otto E. Forrest	.79	26
Melanie Dougherty	1.01	30
Patricia Armstrong	1.10	35
Christine Lorenz	.98	39
Charles Chang	.90	43

117c 10'

SKILL BUILDING

Improve keyboarding technique

each set of lines 3 times; DS between 9-line groups; work at a controlled rate

direct reaches

5 cent dumb curved many brave young record hunt my jump great lunch
6 June and Brent fixed a great brunch and served it with much care.
7 Cecil and Junior broke the curved glass hunting for a decent gun.

adjacent reaches

8 sad pony tree quiet were polka ask poker action quit western yule
9 Guy Klien is a great polo player, but steroids ruined his health.
10 Lois and Trent said they were going to try to take polka lessons.

home row

11 fad lad has lass dusk lush slash glass ask gas glad flash jag mad
12 Sam has fast sleds; Jake clocked his speed last night after dark.
13 Gladys had a great sale last week; she slashed all marked prices.

| 1 | 2 | 3 | 4 | 5 | 6 | 7 | 8 | 9 | 10 | 11 | 12 | 13 |

117d 20'

SKILL BUILDING

Build straight-copy skill

1 Key two 1' writings on each ¶. Strive for a higher *gwam* on the second writing.
2 Key one 3' writing.
3 Key one 5' writing.

all letters

	gwam 3'	5'	
One of the key problems of owning a small business with	4	2	42
partners is that often you must depend on others to get the job	8	5	44
done. The only way that clients of small businesses get good	12	7	47
service automatically is for employees of those businesses to	16	10	49
give each other good service. Getting a job done is much easier	21	12	52
when everyone cooperates and synergy results. The case is quite	25	15	55
different when people cannot be depended upon to honor the com-	29	17	57
mitments they make to external or internal clients.	33	20	59
A good question to consider is, what can you do once you	36	22	62
recognize that a partner cannot be depended upon to honor com-	41	24	64
mitments? The simple answer is either to get the partner to	45	27	66
change the way he or she operates or to change partners. Neither	49	29	69
of these options is easy to accomplish. Therefore, the real	53	32	72
solution lies in learning more about an individual and the way he	57	34	74
or she conducts business before getting involved in a partnership	62	37	77
with that person. Problems are easier to prevent than to cure.	66	40	79

gwam 3' | 1 | 2 | 3 | 4 | 5 |
5' | 1 | 2 | 3 |

51c 30'

FORMATTING

Tables with special headings

Document 1

Read "Special headings." Then, center the table horizontally and vertically (the longest line in each column is shaded). Decide all spacing.

Special headings

Secondary headings follow the main heading; they are centered and all important words are capitalized.

Column headings identify the information within the column. Blocked column headings begin at the tab. Important words are capitalized, and the heading is underlined.

If a column heading is the longest item in the column, use it for determining the key line. Leave one blank line (DS) above and below all headings, regardless of table spacing.

			words
	WORD POWER		2
Secondary heading	Commonly Used Foreign Terms		8
Blocked column heads	Term	Literal Translation	18
	ad infinitum	to infinity	23
	bona fide	in good faith	27
	bon mot	clever saying	32
	de facto	in reality	36
	fait accompli	deed accomplished	42
	faux pas	social blunder	47
	flagrante delicto	caught in the act	54
	hoi polloi	general populace	60
	non sequitur	does not follow logically	68

Document 2

Center the table horizontally and vertically. Decide all spacing.

DELEMORE CLINIC		3
Staff		4
Physician	Specialty	12
Johnny J. Bowers	Cardiovascular Disease	20
H. Myles Bynum	Dermatology	25
Violet A. Geddes	Gastroenterology	32
Julio S. Diaz	Geriatrics	37
Walter T. McWerther	Heart	42

Document 3

Use 1" top and side margins. Make all changes marked.

```
FROM:      T. Richard Wynn                                      4
TO:        Martha L. Trent                                      9
DATE:      March 15, 19--                                      13
SUBJECT:   Dinner Program (Order #577-A)                       21

Please include the following as the only information on page 3   34
of the March 3 porgram you are printing (Order #577-A).           42

  Preliminary remarks           Drew Bargas                     49
  Introductions                 Herbert Blackmun                55
  Address                       Viola Mannes Garrett            61
  Commentary                    Myrle Ortega                    66
  Closing remarks               Drew Bargas                     71

We espect the programs will be finished by Firday of thisweek.   84
xx                                                              84
```

118 Skill Building

Skill-Building Warmup

118a 5'

alphabet 1	Jax Zwanka and my friends plan to go back to that quaint village.
fig/sym 2	I paid $59.75 ($5.69 a yard) for 10 1/2 yds. of #34 cotton (80%).
shift key 3	Don, Jan, Sue, Tim, Lee, Ty, and I will go to see Tien and Chien.
fluency 4	Kent and Clay may fix fish or lamb for the neighbors at the lake.

1 | 2 | 3 | 4 | 5 | 6 | 7 | 8 | 9 | 10 | 11 | 12 | 13

118b 15'

SKILL BUILDING

Build statistical-copy skill

1 Key two 1' writings on each ¶. Strive for a higher *gwam* on the second writing.

2 Key two 3' writings. Proofread carefully; circle errors; determine *gwam*.

A all letters

	gwam 3'	5'	
Significant changes are occurring in the labor force cur-	4	2	39
rently. The greatly publicized baby boom generation is aging.	8	5	42
In 1975, roughly 25% of the labor force was in the 16- to 24-	12	7	44
year-old age group. By the year 2000, an estimated 16% to 18% of	17	10	47
the labor force will be between 16 and 24 years of age; and the	21	12	49
largest group will be those 35 to 50 years old. Approximately,	25	15	52
25% of the force will consist of new entrants.	28	17	54
Another key change is in the number of women entering the	32	19	56
labor force. By 2000, nearly 50% of the work force will be	36	22	59
female. The number of women professionals has doubled since	40	24	61
1974. Of all the professionals in the labor force, 51% are women	45	27	64
and 49% are men. The types of jobs women seek have also changed	49	29	66
drastically. Many women actively seek positions that were for-	53	32	69
merly male-dominated positions. One thing is quite clear: The	57	34	71
work force of 2000 will be very different from that of 1985.	61	37	74

gwam 3' | 1 | 2 | 3 | 4 | 5 |

5' | 1 | 2 | 3 |

Document 2

Calculate horizontal and vertical placement of the table, then key it.

For intercolumn: Is the table wide, average, or narrow?

For single- or double-spacing: Does the table contain more or fewer than 20 lines?

FAMOUS COMPOSERS AND THEIR NATIONS		words
		7
Bela Bartok	Hungary	11
Alban Berg	Austria	15
Leonard Bernstein	United States	21
Benjamin Britten	Great Britain	27
Dietrich Buxtehude	Denmark	33
Frederic Chopin	Poland	37
Aaron Copland	United States	43
Antonin Dvorak	Czechoslovakia	49
Manuel de Falla	Spain	53
George Gershwin	United States	59
Christoph W. Gluck	Germany	65
Arthur Honegger	Switzerland	70
Aram Khachaturian	Armenia	76
Franz Liszt	Hungary	80
Maurice Ravel	France	84
Dimitri Shostakovich	Russia	90
Jan Sibelius	Finland	94
Ralph Vaughan Williams	Great Britain	101
Giuseppe Verdi	Italy	105
Heitor Villa-Lobos	Brazil	111
Richard Wagner	Germany	115

51 Tables With Column Headings

Skill-Building Warmup

51a 6'

each line 3 times SS; DS between 3-line groups

alphabet 1	Loquacious, breezy Hank forgot to jump over the waxed hall floor.
figures 2	Invoices 675 and 348, dated June 29 and August 10, were not paid.
one hand 3	Polk traded Case #789--24 sets of rare carved beads--as rare art.
easy 4	They may dismantle the eight authentic antique autos in the town.

1 | 2 | 3 | 4 | 5 | 6 | 7 | 8 | 9 | 10 | 11 | 12 | 13

51b 14'

SKILL BUILDING

Build speed

Take two 1' writings, two 2' writings, and two 3' writings.

Begin the first writing slowly and allow speed to develop with each subsequent writing.

A all letters

	gwam	2'	3'
A functional vocabulary can be difficult to establish; thus	6	4	30
everybody should realize how very important it is that we choose	13	8	34
with care words we include even in our daily conversations. Not	19	13	38
only will such a routine expedite building a larger and possibly	26	17	43
more stimulating stock of words, it will also require us to stop	32	21	47
and think just a bit before we speak, not a bad habit to develop.	38	26	51

gwam 2' | 1 | 2 | 3 | 4 | 5 | 6 | 7 |
3' | 1 | 2 | 3 | 4 | 5 |

118c 10'

SKILL BUILDING

Improve keyboarding technique

each set of lines 3 times; DS between 9-line groups; work at a controlled rate

1/2 fingers

5 junk feet cent give jive truck funny deer hug much bunt tiny very
6 Hunt and Kent, my friends, might buy the bicycle if they find it.
7 Judd might buy the gun for Jennifer if they decide to hunt ducks.

3/4 fingers

8 saw please low zap plow sap exist quip zero plop was warp swallow
9 Quin saw Paxton as well as Lois at the zoo; Polly was there, too.
10 Does Paul always relax and explore "zany" ideas with Quin or Max?

all fingers

11 quick mixed please walk juice believe haze very young figure tram
12 Quincy and Maxy saw just five zebras on their big trip last week.
13 Zam and Jake required five big boys to explore that aquatic show.

| 1 | 2 | 3 | 4 | 5 | 6 | 7 | 8 | 9 | 10 | 11 | 12 | 13 |

118d 20'

SKILL BUILDING

Build straight-copy skill

1 Key two 1' writings on each ¶. Strive to improve *gwam* on the second writing.
2 Key one 3' writing.
3 Key one 5' writing.

A all letters

	gwam 1'	3'	5'
The job market today is quite different than it was a few	12	4	2
years ago. The fast track to management no longer exists.	24	8	5
Entry-level managers find that it is much more difficult to	36	12	7
obtain a promotion to a higher-level position in management than	49	16	10
it was just a few years ago. People who are in the market for	61	20	12
new jobs find very few management positions available. In fact,	74	25	15
many managers at all levels have a difficult time keeping their	87	29	17
current management positions. Two factors seem to contribute	99	33	20
heavily to the problem. The first factor is the trend toward	112	37	22
self-managed teams. The second factor is that as companies	124	41	25
downsize they often remove entire layers of management or an	136	45	27
entire division.	140	46	28
Layoffs are not new; but, what is new is that layoffs are	12	50	30
affecting white-collar workers as well as blue-collar workers.	24	55	33
Coping with job loss is a new and frustrating experience for many	38	59	35
managers. A person who has just lost a job will have concerns	50	63	38
about personal security and welfare, and the concerns are com-	63	67	40
pounded when families are involved. The problem, however, is	75	71	43
more than just an economic one. Job loss often damages an in-	87	76	45
dividual's sense of self-worth. An individual who does not	99	80	48
have a good self-concept will have a very hard time selling	111	84	50
himself or herself to a potential employer.	120	86	52

gwam 1' | 1 | 2 | 3 | 4 | 5 | 6 | 7 | 8 | 9 | 10 | 11 | 12 | 13 |
3' | 1 | 2 | 3 | 4 | 5 |

50b 14'

COMMUNICATION

Compose at the keyboard

1 Read the ¶ at the right.

2 Compose a second 5- or 6-line ¶ to express your ideas about success. Begin with the words shown.

3 Proofread and correct your ¶; then key both ¶s. Center a title (ALL CAPS) over the ¶s.

Four philosophers sat in a semicircle around a small, fragrant fire. A stranger, Pilgrim by name, stood at one end of the circle. The philosophers had granted him one question, and he posed it: When could one know that she or he had achieved success? One by one the philosophers spoke. "When one has achieved power," said the first. "When one has found wealth," claimed the second. The third added, "One must find many friends."

The fourth, seemingly wiser than the others, said (compose the remainder of the second paragraph)

50c 30'

FORMATTING

Center tables vertically

Document 1

1 Read "Centering vertically" at right.

2 Calculate vertical placement of the table. Check your calculations as follows:

Lines available	66
Less lines in table	-25
Lines remaining	41
First line (41 ÷ 2 + 1)	= 21

3 Calculate horizontal placement: For intercolumn space, decide if the table is wide (4 spaces); average (6-8 spaces); or narrow (10 spaces).

Document 2 is on page 117.

Centering vertically

Text that is centered vertically has equal, or near equal, top and bottom margins. To center text vertically, follow these steps:

1 Count the lines within the table, including the title and blank lines.

2 Subtract the lines in the table from the total lines available on paper (full sheet, 66 lines).

3 Divide the remaining lines by 2 to determine the top margin. Ignore fractions.

4 Add 1 line; this is the line on which to begin.

wp The **center page** feature automatically centers copy vertically between the top and bottom margins.

SELECTED STATE NICKNAMES

Arizona	Grand Canyon State
Florida	Sunshine State
Indiana	Hoosier State
Kansas	Sunflower State
Mississippi	Magnolia State
Montana	Treasure State
New Hampshire	Granite State
New York	Empire State
Oklahoma	Sooner State
South Carolina	Palmetto State
Vermont	Green Mountain State
Wisconsin	Badger State

Learning goals:
1 To measure basic skill on straight copy.
2 To measure skill in producing business documents taught in Level Four.

Formatting guides:
1 Margins: 1" or 65-space line for ¶ writings and documents.
2 SS documents, unless otherwise directed; DS ¶ writings.
3 5-space ¶ indention.

119a 5'

Skill-building warmup

each line 3 times (slowly, faster, slowly); DS between 3-line groups

(Use these directions for all skill-building warmups in Lessons 119 and 120.)

alphabet 1 Zack Q. Davis just left a very brief message with six nice poems.
figure 2 Jan bought 27 toys at $3.98 each, a total of $107.46 plus 5% tax.
adjacent reach 3 We are going to build a store on a very quiet point west of here.
fluency 4 Tod and I may visit the ancient chapel and then go to the island.

| 1 | 2 | 3 | 4 | 5 | 6 | 7 | 8 | 9 | 10 | 11 | 12 | 13 |

119b 12'

SKILL BUILDING

Measure straight-copy skill

1 Key one 3' writing. Circle errors; determine *gwam*.
2 Key one 5' writing. Circle errors; determine *gwam*.

A all letters

	gwam 3'	5'	
A successful organization tries to put the right employee in	4	2	51
the right job. The process of selecting employees raises many	8	5	54
questions that frequently are very perplexing. A key issue	12	7	56
that must be balanced deals with the rights of the individual	16	10	59
who is seeking a position and the rights of the organization that	21	12	61
is hiring a person to fill a position. Laws specify the types of	25	15	64
information that can be asked in the hiring process to ensure	29	18	66
that bias is not a factor in hiring. However, most firms do	33	20	69
strive to be fair in the hiring process. The issue that many	37	22	71
employers struggle with is how to determine who will be the	41	25	73
right employee for a particular job that is available.	45	27	76
The ability to predict an individual's performance on the	49	29	78
job is very important. Assessing an individual in the hiring	53	32	80
process to determine how he or she will perform on the job,	57	34	83
however, is a very difficult task. Most techniques measure the	61	37	85
potential or the way that a person can perform, but the way a	66	39	88
person can perform may differ drastically from the way the person	70	42	91
will perform when he or she is hired. Past performance on a job	74	45	93
may be the best measure of future performance, which is why firms	78	47	96
seek individuals with experience.	81	49	98

gwam 3' | 1 | 2 | 3 | 4 | 5 |
5' | 1 | 2 | 3 |

Document 2
2" top margin
Center the narrow table horizontally. Use 10 intercolumn spaces as shown in the key line.

COMMITTEE LEADERS		words
		4
Marilee Blazer	Food	8
Braun Stevens	Site	11
Louise Treweser	Games	16
Spike Wing	Programs	20
Chico Alvarez	Tickets	24
Toni Osuka	Parking	28

Key line: Louise Treweser **10** Programs

Document 3
2" top margin
Determine the longest line and intercolumn spaces for this narrow table to construct a key line; center the table horizontally; DS.

TEAMS/STADIUMS VISITED IN JULY		
		6
California Angels	Anaheim Stadium	13
Chicago Cubs	Wrigley Field	18
Cincinnati Reds	Riverfront Stadium	25
Detroit Tigers	Tiger Stadium	31
New York Yankees	Yankee Stadium	38
Houston Astros	Astrodome	43
Philadelphia Phillies	Veterans Stadium	50
San Diego Padres	Jack Murphy Stadium	58

50 Vertical Centering

Skill-Building Warmup

50a 6'
each line 3 times SS; DS between 3-line groups

alphabet 1 Zak Jurex worked to improve the basic quality of his paging jobs.
figures 2 I live at 149 East 56th Street; Ben, at 270 Hier; Li, at 38 Lark.
direct reaches 3 My brother served as an umpire on that bright June day, no doubt.
easy 4 If they sign an entitlement, the town land is to go to the girls.

| 1 | 2 | 3 | 4 | 5 | 6 | 7 | 8 | 9 | 10 | 11 | 12 | 13 |

119c 33'

FORMATTING

Measure production

Time schedule
Assemble materials .... 3'
Timed production .... 25'
Final check;
compute *n-pram* .... 5'

1 Organize your supplies.
2 When directed to begin, key each document. Proofread; correct errors. Work for 25'.
3 Address an envelope.
4 Compute *n-pram* (total words keyed – penalty) ÷ 25'.

Document 1
Block letter
(LM p. S111)

Note: Key foreign country in ALL CAPS on separate line in letter address.

words

June 5, 19-- | FACSIMILE | Mr. M. Ljupco Kralev | RCP Dexion Trading 12
| Boulevard Avnoj 75-2-22 | 91000 Skopje, MACEDONIA | Dear Mr. Kralev 25

Hopefully, you had a pleasant trip back to Macedonia. We enjoyed meeting 40
you, and we look forward to working with you. Our schedules will be 54
finalized this week, and we will fax that information to you. 66

Our understanding is that our first visit will be for the purpose of going 81
with you to various companies to determine needs for management devel- 95
opment and training. We would then use that information to develop an 109
appropriate program that you could implement in your Human Resource 123
Development Center. We would also work out arrangements to provide 137
faculty to teach the program that we design. 146

We are excited about the ideas you proposed, and we believe we can help 160
you develop and staff an excellent program that will be very successful. We 176
look forward to hearing from you soon. 184

Sincerely | Peggy Coker | xx | c Ralph Manz 191

Document 2 Standard memo words

TO: Ralph Manz | **FROM:** Peggy Coker | **DATE:** 8
June 6, 19-- | **SUBJECT:** Communication 15
Difficulties 18

Yesterday, we had difficulty trying to transmit 28
the letter to Mr. Kralev. He did not send us 37
the usual confirmation letter so we do not know 46
if he actually received our fax. Therefore, I am 56
following up with an airmail letter to ensure 66
that Mr. Kralev has the information he needs. 75

My tentative schedule is ready so I plan to 84
include it with the letter I send. As you will 93
note from the enclosed copy, the schedule fol- 103
lows the plan we discussed in some depth. I 112
did not include the cost proposal, however. I 121
think we need to get together and talk about 130
it in more detail before we send it. Please let 140
my secretary know if your schedule will be 148
ready by tomorrow. If so, we can include it 157
with the materials we are sending. 165

Susie is working on the list of seminar leaders 174
that we can use to staff the first program. Of 184
course, the three of us will take the lead roles. 194

xx | Enclosure 197

Document 3 News release (LM p. S113) words

For Release: Immediately | **Contact Person:** 9
Peggy Coker 11

Charlotte, North Carolina, July 8, 19--. Coker 21
Consulting announced today that it has en- 29
tered a joint venture with RCP Dexion Trading 38
of Skopje, Macedonia, to establish Human Re- 47
source Development Programs for managers 55
and executives of leading firms throughout 64
Macedonia. 66

Coker Consulting will be responsible for 74
conducting needs analyses in a variety of 83
industries throughout the country and for 91
developing and staffing the entire program. 100
Coker has set up a cooperative arrangement 109
with the College of Business Administration at 118
Central University to use leading faculty as 127
consultants in the program. Dr. Winona Marks, 137
dean of the College of Business Administra- 145
tion, indicated that the Skopje program was a 154
wonderful opportunity to give faculty more 163
international experience. 168

The program will be designed so that company 177
executives spend two weeks of each quarter at 187
the Human Resources Development Conference 195
Center. The program will be modeled after 204
executive MBA programs in the United States. 213

214

49c 34'

FORMATTING

Center tables horizontally

1 Study "Tables" carefully at the right.

2 Format and key Documents 1, 2, and 3; correct errors.

Tables

Main heading: Center and key in ALL CAPS; DS below heading. Bold also may be used.

Columns: Vertical lists of information. Center horizontally. Generally, double-space; single-space long tables of 20 or more lines. When a table appears within a document, use the same spacing as the document.

Intercolumn space: Space between columns will vary, depending on the number of columns and their width. Use an even number of spaces:

Narrow	10 spaces
Average	6-8 spaces
Wide	4 spaces

Key line: Used for centering columns horizontally on page, a key line consists of the longest item in each column and the spaces between columns (intercolumn space).

wp The key line is centered using the **automatic centering feature**. A **left tab** (the default) is used to align columns at the left.

To format a table

1 Move margins to the left and right edges of the scale; clear all tabs.

2 Determine the **key line** (longest item in each column and the intercolumn spaces).

3 Center the key line. (Note specific directions for various equipment below.)

4 Set the left margin at Column 1 and a tab for Column 2.

5 Center the heading and key the table.

To center the key line

Electronic typewriters and **MicroAssistant:**

1 Press the center key (MicroAssistant **Alt + C**).

2 Type the key line; strike return. Set the left margin and tab according to the printout or display.

3 Delete the key line.

Electric typewriters

1 From the center of the page, backspace once for every two characters in the key line. Ignore a leftover stroke. Set left margin.

2 Space forward once for each character in Column 1 and the intercolumn spaces. Set tab for Column 2.

Document 1

2" top margin

Main heading FARLEIGH SCHOOL BOARD OF REGENTS

DS

	Kathryn Brece McCall	President
	V. Brett Badger	Vice President
	Gregory E. Becker	Secretary
	D. L. Merriwether	Treasurer
	Julio A. Esposito	Member
	John Y. Baer	Member
	B. A. Beebe	Member
Key line	Kathryn Brece McCall 10	Vice President

Column — Intercolumn space

119c (continued)

Document 4
Simplified memo

Document 5
Simplified block letter
(LM p. S115)
Rekey Document 1 in simplified block format to the address below. Delete the fax notation; add the subject line **FUTURE VISITS**. Send letter to:
Mr. James Townsen
Sentinel Electronics Inc.
2026 Eastway Drive
Charlotte, NC 28205-2736

words

Current date | Distribution List | JOINT VENTURE AGREEMENT | 11
As you ~~may be~~ are aware, Coker Consulting is involved in a joint 23
ventures with RCP Dexion Trading of Skipje, Macdedonia. The 34
purpose of the venture will be to establish Human Resource Pro- 47
grams for managers and executives of leading firms through out 59
Macedonia. 62

~~You can be assured that~~ we will continue to use part time research 70
assistants in the same manner that we always have and under the 83
same terms and conditions. The major impact that the merge will 96
have on ~~you~~ research assistants is ~~that~~ there will be ~~more~~ opporutnities for work. 111
Peggy Coker | Distribution List: Nancy Johnson, Brad Davis 123

120 Report/Table Measurement

120a 5'

Skill-Building Warmup

alphabet 1 Kralev quizzed them to find out why six big players were ejected.
fig/sym 2 Please order Item #54893 (12#) and Item #71680 (20#) for $45,996.
direct reach 3 Brad, my brother, found many funny items in junk and craft shops.
fluency 4 Did their neighbor hang the signs in the cornfield on the island?

| 1 | 2 | 3 | 4 | 5 | 6 | 7 | 8 | 9 | 10 | 11 | 12 | 13 |

120b 12'

SKILL BUILDING

Measure straight-copy skill

Key a 3' and 5' timing from 119b, page 294.

120c 33'

FORMATTING

Measure production

Time schedule
Assemble materials .... 3'
Timed production .... 25'
Final check;
compute *n-pram* .... 5'

Follow the same directions as in 119c.

Document 1
Unbound report with table
SS the report.

Bold all heads.

words

NUTRITION AND HEALTH 4
Good health is a high priority for most people. Yet, many indi- 17
viduals know relatively little about nutrition and make dietary 30
choices that are detrimental to their health. Studies show that 43
at least one-third of all cancer and heart attack deaths are 55
directly related to diet. (Anders, 1993, 12). 64
Diet Guides for Good Health 75
Diet consists of both the foods and the beverages consumed 87
daily. The foods and beverages that are consumed should be 99
selected carefully to ensure good nutrition. 108
Guides for eating. A wide variety of foods should be eaten each 125
day since no one food contains all of the nutrients needed. 137
Foods that are rich in vitamins and high in dietary fiber should 150

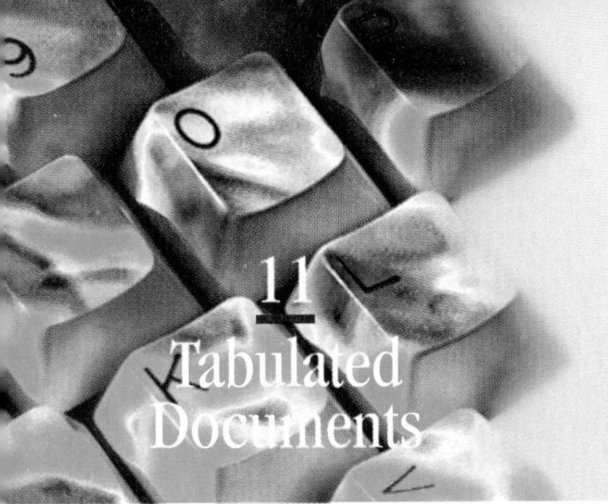

11 Tabulated Documents

Learning goals:

1. To format tables with main and secondary headings and blocked column headings.
2. To recall horizontal centering.
3. To center data vertically.
4. To arrange data in columns.

Formatting guides:

1. Default margins or a 65-space line.
2. Single-space drills; double-space paragraphs.
3. Indentions: 5-space ¶ indent.

49a 6'

Skill-building warmup

each line 3 times SS; DS between 3-line groups

alphabet 1 Jim Ryan was able to liquify frozen oxygen; he kept it very cold.
figures 2 Flight 259 left here at 8:36 p.m., arriving in Reno at 10:47 p.m.
adjacent reaches 3 We condemn her notion that we can buy safe behavior with rewards.
easy 4 If I burn the signs, the odor of enamel may make a toxic problem.

| 1 | 2 | 3 | 4 | 5 | 6 | 7 | 8 | 9 | 10 | 11 | 12 | 13 |

49b 10'

SKILL BUILDING

Improve control

Key two 1' writings on each ¶ at a steady, but unhurried pace; then key two 3' writings on all ¶s.

Goal: Fewer than 3 errors a minute.

A all letters

	gwam 1'	3'	
Chuck is a supervisor in a large department of an eastern	12	4	63
company. His department recently won a coveted company award for	25	8	67
excellence. Ask him what is so special about his department, and	38	13	72
he will tell you the credit goes to an excellent crew that works	51	17	76
together and gets things done.	57	19	78
Zadine was recently voted the outstanding employee in the	12	23	82
home office by the people with whom she works. Ask her why she	24	27	86
was chosen, and she will say that she was puzzled by the award;	37	32	91
she just likes her work and her co-workers and quietly does her	50	36	95
daily assignment without attracting much attention.	61	39	98
Success is frequently intertwined with one's ability to get	12	43	102
along with people, to lead them without offending their dignity,	25	48	107
to work beside them in a team spirit, and to support them fully	38	52	111
when assistance is needed. Cooperation is just another way of	50	56	115
saying, "I need you as much as you need me."	59	59	118

gwam 1' | 1 | 2 | 3 | 4 | 5 | 6 | 7 | 8 | 9 | 10 | 11 | 12 | 13 |
3' | 1 | 2 | 3 | 4 | 5 |

words

be eaten daily. Fruits, vegetables, and 158
whole-grain breads and cereals are par- 166
ticularly good sources of vitamins and 174
fiber. 175

A good diet also avoids harmful foods. 183
~~Too much~~ sodium, sugar, saturated fat, 190
high-fat dairy products, salt, and sugar 198
should be eaten in moderation. 204

Guides for ~~D~~rinking. The body needs a 216
significant amount of fluids. Drinking 224
water is particularly important. If 231
alcoholic beverages are consumed, they 239
should be consumed in moderation. Alco- 247
holic beverages are high in calories and 255
low in food value. In addition, exces- 263
sive drinking can lead to major health 271
problems. (Thomas, 1993, 28) 277

General Diet Guides 284

Selecting the proper foods and bever- 292
ages is only one part of a healthy 299
diet. The quantity consumed and the 306
way foods are prepared are equally 314
important. 316

Weight. A person's diet should be 324
planned carefully to maintain a desir- 331
able weight for the body size. Obesity 339
increases the risk of many diseases. 347
Being under weight can also create 354
problems. 356

A person's body frame helps to deter- 363
mine the desirable weight for that 370
person. Desirable weight for a person 378
with a small frame is less than that 386
for a person with an average or large 393
frame. The following table shows 400
desirable weights for both men and 407
women based on body frame size: 414
Insert A 468

Food ~~P~~reparation. Foods should be 478
prepared in a manner that does not add 486
fat to the food. Baking, steaming, 493
poaching, roasting, and cooking in a 500
microwave are the best ways to prepare 508
foods. 510

REFERENCES Center 512

Anders, Alana P. Diet and Health. 522
Bethesda, Maryland: Health Center 529
Publishers, 1993. 533

Thomas, Lynn G. Alcohol and Health. 543
Bethesda, Maryland: Health Center 551
Publishers, 1993. 554

(A) **Desirable Weight Levels** ← Caps

Height	Men Small	Men Aver.	Men Large	Women Small	Women Aver.	Women Large
60-62"	122	132	142	110	118	128
63-65"	134	146	158	120	130	138
66-68"	150	162	178	136	148	160
69-71"	156	165	185	140	154	165
72-75"	165	180	195	145	158	170

Document 2 Title page

Prepare a title page. The report was prepared for **Mr. Julian Reyes, President of Reeves Industries by Amy Osaka, Health Center Director on December 15, 19--**.

Document 3 Table of contents

Prepare a table of contents including all headings; add page numbers.

Document 4 Letter of transmittal

(LM p. S117)

Address for Reeves: **3259 Swift Boulevard, Richland, WA 99352-5867**. Use an appropriate salutation and closing.

words

opening lines 25

The report you asked me to prepare 32
for all employees is attached. The 39
length of the report is designed so 45
that it can also be published 51
in the monthly newsletter that 57
goes to all our plants and 61
selected customers. 67

Please let me know if you have 74
any questions about the report. I 83
enjoyed working on this project with you. 92

Drill 3
Review confusing words

1 Use 1"top margin; 1" side or default margins.

2 Indent example lines 5 spaces.

3 Use bold for the confusing words and the title.

CONFUSING WORDS

accept (v) to take or receive willingly.
except (v) to exclude, omit.
     They all can **accept** the invitation **except** Bjorn, who is ill.

addition (n) the result of adding.
edition (n) a version in which a text is published.
     This fifth **edition** is an excellent **addition** to our texts.

advice (n) opinion as to what to do; helpful counsel.
advise (v) to recommend; to give information.
     I **advise** you never to listen to bad **advice**.

already (adv) previously; prior to a specified time.
all ready (adj) completely ready.
     It was **already** too late by the time dinner was **all ready**.

any one (n) any singular person in a group.
anyone (pron) any person at all.
     Anyone could tell the hat did not belong to **any one** of us.

assistance (n) the act of helping; help supplied.
assistants (n) those who help.
     We hired the **assistants** to give us **assistance** at five o'clock.

further (adv) to a greater degree (time or quantity).
farther (adv) at a greater distance (space).
     Look **further** into the future; rockets will travel **farther**.

it's contraction of "it is" or "it has."
its (adj) possessive form for the pronoun "it."
     It's a long time since the lion had **its** last meal.

lay (v) to put down; to place.
lie (v) to rest; to be situated.
     Lay a blanket on the bed; I want to **lie** down for awhile.

passed (v) moved along; transferred.
past (adj, adv, prep) gone by; (n) time gone by.
     It was **past** five o'clock when the parade **passed** by.

sale (n) act of exchanging something for money.
sell (v) to exchange property for money.
     We must **sell** these lamps; plan a **sale** for next week.

setting (v) to place.
sitting (v) to rest in place.
     I am **setting** this fruit here; it was **sitting** in the sun.

your (adj) belonging to you.
you're contraction of "you are."
     If **you're** not careful, you will be late for **your** meeting.

Formatting Workshop 3

Document 1
Standard memo

words

TO: Terry Meister | **FROM:** Joyce Smeltz | **DATE:** May 6, 19-- | **SUB-** 14
JECT: Research Proposal 17

A copy of the proposal that Ernie and I prepared for Marktex is enclosed. 32
We talked with Julio Fuentes, and he indicated that the general pricing 46
structure was appropriate. However, he felt that it was imperative that 61
the overall bid be very competitive. 69

Research opportunities in Eastern Europe and in South America appeal 82
to many people; thus, the competition is expected to be strong. The 96
message that Julio is trying to give us, in my opinion, is that he may try 111
to negotiate a lower price. 116

The basic issue for us will be to determine if we are willing to do the job at 132
a lower price to get the in-country experience in three additional coun- 147
tries in Eastern Europe and one in South America. I will call you as soon 166
as I hear from Julio. 167

xx | Enclosure 169

Document 2
Simplified memo

April 30, 19-- | Doctoral Students | PROPOSED RESEARCH OPPORTUNITIES 13

Csiszar Associates is bidding on a subcontract from Marktex to do 26
market research in the textile industry in several countries in Eastern 41
Europe and in South America. Since the work on our current subcontract 55
with Marktex in Poland and Hungary is producing such good results, 69
we are very optimistic about winning the award for this new project. 83

If we are successful in obtaining the subcontract, we will need to hire 97
several research assistants on a part-time basis to help collect data. We 112
would like to include in the proposal biographical sketches of indi- 126
viduals who would be working with us. 133

A meeting has been scheduled on May 4 at ten o'clock in Conference 147
Room A to provide information to individuals interested in being consid- 161
ered for the research assistant positions. A copy of the agenda is 163
attached. Doctoral students interested in the project should bring a one- 190
page biographical sketch to the meeting. The award for the subcontract 204
should be made by May 30. 209

Pat C. Walker | xx | Attachment 215

Communication Workshop 2

MicroAssistant: To select Communication Workshop 2, key **C2** from the Main menu.

Drill 1
Review use of the apostrophe
1.5" top margin; 1" or default side margins; use bold and hanging indent format as shown; center the title

USING AN APOSTROPHE TO SHOW POSSESSION

1. Add **'s** to a singular noun not ending in **s**.

2. Add **'s** to a singular noun ending in **s** or **z** sound if the ending **s** is pronounced as a syllable; as, Sis's lunch, Russ's car, Buzz's average.

3. Add **'** only if the ending **s** or **z** is awkward to pronounce; as, series' outcome, ladies' shoes, Delibes' music, Cortez' quest.

4. Add **'s** to a plural noun that does not end in **s**; as, men's notions, children's toys, mice's tracks.

5. Add only **'** after a plural noun ending in **s**; as, horses' hoofs, lamps' shades.

6. Add **'s** after the last noun in a series to show joint possession of two or more people; as, Jack and Judy's house; Peter, Paul, and Mary's song.

7. Add **'s** to each noun to show individual possession of two or more persons; as, Li's and Ted's tools, Jill's and Ed's races.

Drill 2
Review use of quotation marks
1.5" top margin; 1" or default side margins; indent examples 5 spaces

SPACING WITH QUOTATION MARKS

Use quotation marks:

after a comma or a period; as,
     "I bought," she said, "more paper."

before a semicolon; as,
     She said, "I have little money"; she had, in fact, none.

before a colon; as,
     He called these items "fresh": beans, peas, and carrots.

after a question mark if the quotation itself is a question; as,
     "Why did you do that?" he asked.

before a question mark if the quotation is not a question; as,
     Why did he say, "I will not run"?

Document 3
Agenda
Date the agenda for **Csiszar Associates, May 4, 19--**. Add an appropriate heading. Format names flush right.

		words
	words in headings	9
Update on Poland/Hungary Management		16
Training Project	Pat Walker	30
Briefing on Research Proposal	Joyce Smeltz	45
Role and Compensation of Research		52
Assistants	Ernie LeGuere	66

Document 4
Block letter
(LM p. S119)
Send letter to the attention of **Julio Fuentes**; add a facsimile notation. Address envelope.

May 6, 19-- | Marktex Corporation | 1856 N. Fort Myer Drive, Suite 13
820 | Arlington, VA 22209-4864 19

The proposal for market research in the textile industry that 31
you requested is enclosed. We analyzed the costs carefully, and 37
per minimum
$50,000 / country is the cost for doing the research and satisfying
all of the specifications outlined in the scope of work. The pro- 38
posal covers the entire scope of work provided in the Rfp however it 52
is very brief. The short time frame just did not permit a more in 66
depth proposal. Hope-fully, our expereince in this area will be 78
evident. Move 80

Ideally, it would be better to spend more time in each coun- 127
try, but doing so would increase the cost substantially. The analy- 140
sis is based on the 4 counties you suggested. The 2 countries that 155
we are most eager to work with are Czecheslavakia and check spelling 166
Argentina . However, any of the countries are acceptible. 178

Please let us know if you need any additional information. 190
We hope to have the oppertunity to work with you on this project. 203
Sincerely | Joyce Smeltz, Ph.D. | Research Coordinator | Enclosure 215

Document 5
Table
Add double underscore under total line if software permits.

Proposed Budget		3
(Per Country)		6
Senior research associates	$20,000	13
Research assistants	8,500	18
Travel expenses	16,000	23
Telephone, FAX, duplication	4,000	29
Administrative costs	1,500	36
Total	Supply	39

48c 10'

COMMUNICATION

Key from edited copy

1 Key the ¶ as if it were the beginning of the first page of an unbound report.

2 Compose a title.

3 Make all marked changes and correct errors.

words

There is no question about it. many of the problems we face 12
now stem from the fact that over years we have been not very 25
wise Consumers. We have not used our natural resources well 38
and we have jeopardized much of our environment. We have these 52
actions of ten in the belief that our supply of mostresources has 65
no limits? Now we are beginning to realize how wrong we were and 79
we are takeing steps to re-build our world. 87

48d 10'

SKILL BUILDING

Improve control of manipulative parts

Key each group three times.

Goal:

Lines 10-14: Eyes on copy.

Lines 15-16: Easy, fluid stroking and correct capitalization.

Lines 17-18: Proper spacing between words and punctuation.

10 When eyes are on the copy,
11 body straight, wrists low,
12 fingers curved, elbows in,
13 maybe just a slight smile,
14 then success can be yours.

15 Do Dr. and Mrs. J. D. Mumm take the DENVER POST or the NEWS MAIL?
16 Both Jose and Joy have read MY AFRICA; Tryna Zahn has read UHURU.

17 If you and I can do all of the jobs now, then we all can go home.
18 Watch out; the lamp is lit. See it? I do. I, too, may be seen.

48e 13'

SKILL BUILDING

Reach for new goals

1 Key four 1' guided writings; determine *gwam*.

2 Take two 2' writings; try to maintain your best 1' rate.

3 Take a 3' writing. Use your *gwam* in Step 1 as your goal.

A all letters

	gwam 2'	3'
If you believe that office management is a viable objective	6	4
on your horizon, maybe you envision how essential it is that you	13	8
learn to work with others. As a leader, for example, you should	19	13
quickly become part of the company team. You will learn much by	26	17
working closely with your fellow workers; at first, you actually	32	21
depend on them to give you a better idea of how everyone fits in	39	26
the overall picture and how best to improve on office efficiency.	45	30

gwam 2' | 1 | 2 | 3 | 4 | 5 | 6 | 7 |
3' | 1 | 2 | 3 | 4 | 5 |

Documents 6-9 Form letters, block format(LM pp. S121-S127)

Document 6

V1—
Ms. Alexis Mayes
3923 Wheat Street
Columbia, SC 29205-1267
V2—Alexis
V3—Czechoslovakia
V4—15
V5—$18
(Total words: 145)

Document 8

V1—
Ms. June Lee
2948 Bull Street
Columbia, SC 29201-3475
V2—June
V3—Argentina
V4—12
V5—$20
(Total words: 141)

Document 7

V1—
Ms. Amy Norris
5839 Leesburg Road
Columbia, SC 29209-3475
V2—Amy
V3—East Germany
V4—12
V5—$18
(Total words: 142)

Document 9

V1—
Mr. Lee Chung
2938 Harden Street
Columbia, SC 29205-4563
V2—Lee
V3—Hungary
V4—15
V5—$20
(Total words: 141)

June 4, 19-- | (V1—Name and address) | Dear (V2—First name)

The proposal Csiszar Associates submitted to Marktex for market research in the textile industry was selected for funding. The project is scheduled to begin in three weeks.

You have been selected as one of the research assistants for (V3—Country). This position will require approximately (V4—Number) hours per week. The rate of pay will be (V5—Amount) per hour. The project is targeted for completion in approximately four to six weeks.

Please plan to visit our offices one day next week to talk about the plan of work. If you cannot accept this position, please call me immediately.

Sincerely | Joyce Smeltz, Ph.D. | Research Coordinator | xx

Document 10 Form

Prepare form on plain sheet; 1" side margins; insert 12 lines.

WEEKLY PROJECT ACTIVITY LOG

Name ______________________

Date	**Activity/Tasks**	**Hours**

Total Hours ______________

Documents 11-12 Form letters, modified block with mixed punctuation
(LM pp. S129-S131)

Document 11

June 4, 19--
Mr. Rex Mason
Meade Industries
24 Osceola Road
Wayne, NJ 07470-4344
Use paragraphs:
Merger-1.beg;
Merger-2.mid;
Merger-1.end
Sender: P.R. Csiszar
President
(Total words: 197)

Document 12

June 4, 19--
Ms. Alison Cone
Cone Fashions
343 Chestnut Road
York, PA 15009-3857
Use paragraphs:
Merger-1.beg;
Merger-1.mid;
Merger-2.end
Sender: P.R. Csiszar
President
(Total words: 173)

Merger-1.beg On July 1, 19--, Csiszar Associates will merge with ComTech Corporation. We have been involved in many successful joint ventures with ComTech during the past five years, and now we are combining resources to meet the needs of our clients more effectively.

Merger-1.mid The research contract that we have with you will not be affected in any way. The same research associates and assistants will be handling your project.

Merger-2.mid The research project that we are conducting for you will be completed using the same high standards we have always met. We will be able to utilize some of our resources in ComTech in your project. The enclosed plan of work explains all changes.

Merger-1.end One of our associates will be visiting with you within the next three weeks to answer any questions that you might have about the changes in our organizational structure. Please be assured that you will continue to be an important client; and our high-quality standards will be enhanced, rather than compromised, by this merger.

Merger-2.end One of our associates will call you within the next three weeks to answer any questions that you might have about the changes in our organizational structure. Please be assured that you will continue to be an important client; and our high-quality standards will be enhanced, rather than compromised, by this merger.

47c 13'

SKILL BUILDING

Strengthen finger reaches

Keep wrists low, fingers curved, elbows in. Key the lines; practice troublesome lines until you can key them fluently.

1st finger

5 My group says that a huge gray monster lunged at the five braves.
6 They truly thought that the tugboat might brave the foul weather.
7 I trust none of you hunt tigers in the jungle of northern Africa.

2d finger

8 Kerrie says these kind, decent acts decidedly reduced skepticism.
9 Di conceded that kicking a cedar stick at Ike was a bad decision.
10 His reed kite descended quickly; lack of wind killed its chances.

3d/4th fingers

11 Was it Polly or was it Sam who saw Sally swallow a sour lollipop?
12 Wallis was appalled at the low slope of that excavation at Aswan.
13 Who applies wax to old autos? It wastes a load of costly polish.

47d 15'

SKILL BUILDING

Statistical copy

1 Key ¶ for orientation.
2 Take four 2' writings. Try for a higher *gwam* with each successive writing. Ignore errors temporarily.

A **all letters/figures**

	gwam 2'	
Fully inspired only 11 weeks before, I decided to start on	6	44
this project; now I kept telling myself that my residence at 569	12	50
Azalea Avenue would be done well before the 30th. My contractor	19	57
and a swarm of 48 "quality experts" had promised it would be. I	25	63
needed this house quickly--in precisely 17 days, to be exact. My	32	70
24-month lease was expiring, and I needed a place to live.	38	76

gwam 2' | 1 | 2 | 3 | 4 | 5 | 6 | 7 |

48 Skill Building

Skill-Building Warmup

48a 7'

each line 3 times; DS between 3-line groups

alphabet 1 Jayne Cox puzzled over workbooks that were required for geometry.
figures 2 Edit pages 308 and 415 in Book A; pages 17, 29, and 60 in Book B.
one hand 3 Plum trees on a hilly acre, in my opinion, create no vast estate.
easy 4 Did the foal buck? and did it cut the right elbow of the cowhand?

| 1 | 2 | 3 | 4 | 5 | 6 | 7 | 8 | 9 | 10 | 11 | 12 | 13 |

48b 10'

SKILL BUILDING

Build accuracy

Key each line twice at a slow but steady pace. DS between 2-line groups. Rekey twice lines having more than one error.

5 A plump, aged monk served a few million beggars a milky beverage.
6 Few beavers, as far as I'm aware, feast on cedar trees in Kokomo.
7 Johnny, after a few stewed eggs, ate a plump, pink onion at noon.
8 In regard to desert oil wastes, Jill referred only minimum cases.
9 Link agrees you'll get a reward only as you join nonunion racers.

words
words in heading 9

Document 13
Unbound business report (SS)
Use the following title:
Technology and Communications Joint Venture
Make decisions where the originator has used a question mark. Check closely for errors that may have been overlooked. Use hanging indent style for enumerated items.

ComTech Corp. notified the Corporate Communications Institute 23
today that its Board of Directors approved the proposal for a commu- 36
nications research joint venture. Under the contract, ComTech Corp. 54
has agreed to provide hardware, software, and services worth over 67
$1,000,000 to the CCI. The CCI, in turn, has agreed to provide 93
staff and support resources. 104

The Project 108

The research is focused on two primary areas: using the com- 121
puter as a tool to enhance the communications process and as a tool 140
for teaching communication skills. These two areas were selected as 153
the result of both need and opportunity. Previous research shows 167
virtually all organizations view communication as an area that is 181
critical to the success of the organization. General consensus is 194
that many employees need to improve communication skills. 209

WP, desktop publishing, graphics, and numerous other software 225
applications have tremendous potential for enhancing the quality of 238
communications. In addition, the computer may be an ideal training 251
tool. The opportunity to conduct research that is both process and 265
product-oriented is exciting. The process phase of the research 278
focuses on teaching employees how to communicate more effectively. 292
The product phase focuses on the improvement of documents and pre- 304
sentations. 306

The System 310

The system provided by ComTech consists of both general and 322
special purpose hardware and software. ComTech maintains all hard- 336
ware and provides technical support services. Software upgrades 349
will be provided as new software is released. 358

Hardware. The system consists of 30 training workstations, 370
20 staff workstations, and a variety of special purpose hardware 383
units in a network configuration. The training work stations and 396
special purpose hardware are configured in one network and the staff 410
workstations are configured in a separate network. However, the 421
training and staff networks are connected by a bridge; and they also 436
have a gateway to the mainframe computer and to external networks. 450
Each training and staff workstation has a Model 6D computer with a 463
70 megabyte fixed disk, a high resolution color display, a mouse, 476
and a printer. 483

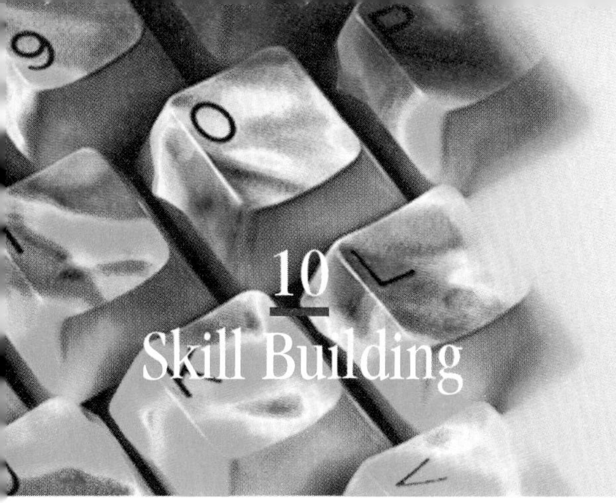

10 Skill Building

Learning goals:

1. To improve keying techniques.
2. To improve concentration.
3. To improve ability to key straight, statistical, and rough-draft copy.

Formatting guides:

1. Default margins or 65-space line.
2. Single-space drills; double-space paragraphs.

47a 7'

Skill-building warmup

each line 3 times (work for fewer than 3 errors per group)

alphabet 1 Jacky Few's strange, quiet behavior amazed and perplexed even us.
figures 2 Dial Extension 148 or 276 for a copy of the 30-page 95-cent book.
double letters 3 Ann will see that Edd accepts an assignment in the school office.
easy 4 Did a cow, six foals, six turkeys, and a duck amble to the field?

| 1 | 2 | 3 | 4 | 5 | 6 | 7 | 8 | 9 | 10 | 11 | 12 | 13 |

47b 15'

SKILL BUILDING

Improve concentration

1 Key a copy of the ¶ DS. Where a blank occurs, insert either the word **that** or **and**.

2 Proofread and make a final corrected copy.

3 Use your final copy for 3' writings as time permits.

A all letters

gwam 3'

It has been said ________ human intelligence is the ability to 4 42
acquire and retain knowledge ________ will permit a person, based on 8 46
her or his past experience, to respond quickly ________ with success 13 50
to new ________ different occasions and situations. And that's right. 17 55
But intelligence is also the ability to use mental power ________ good 21 59
judgment--what some people call plain common sense--to recognize 26 64
problems and work to find proper solutions for them. It is, in 30 68
other words, the exciting force ________ moves our minds and bodies 34 72
from place to place, sometimes like game-board pieces. 38 76

gwam 3' | 1 | 2 | 3 | 4 | 5 |

The special purpose hardware consists of two desktop publish- 495
ing systems with laser printers, a scanner, a color plotter, an 80 508
megabyte file server, a laser page printer, an ink jet printer, a 522
Model 8D workstation with a touch-sensitive display screen, and a 535
videodisc player. The special purpose hardware is physically lo- 548
cated in the training facility, but the network is bridged to the 561
staff network. Change to a side heading 564

Training. Special sessions have been scheduled to acquaint 722
all team members and support staff with the new system hardware and 735
software. More in-depth sessions have also been scheduled for those 747
team members who indicated they would need additional training. 760

Software. The software has been grouped into two categories: 577
core and optional software. The core software consists of those 590
packages that are installed on all workstations. The core software 619
installed on all training workstations includes the oprating sytem, 633
word processing, spreadsheet, graphics, hard disk organizer, network 647
software, statistical applications, desktop publshing, database, 660
window applications, and mouse software. Move 669
No ¶ Optional software is installed on a limited number of staff
workstations. Optional software includes thought organizers, cre- 679
ativity enhancement software, Ⓐ 708

Project Management 768

The project team consists of the 20 staff members who have 777
been provided with the staff workstations. A list of all project 779
team members was included with the copy of the proposal sent to all 792
employees several weeks ago. The entire project team is responsible 804
for the overall direction and success of the project. A project 817
steering committee has been established to handle the day to day 830
management of the project and coordinate all project activities. 844
The membership will be announced this week. of the Project Steering Committee 859

Requests for additional software modifications to the or resources 873
present system, resources and project changes must be directed to 884
the project steering comittee. Weekly meetings for the project 897
steering committee and monthly meetings for the entire project team 910
has been established. Team members are expected to participate 923
fully and make the project there top priority. 934

Ⓐ group decision-support software, financial applications, and application and expert software for several fields.

Document 14
Table of contents
Prepare a table of contents including all headings; center bottom page number **ii**.

Document 15
Title page
Prepare a title page; use the current date; the report was prepared for ComTech Corporation and Corporate Communications Institute by **Lynn Marks** the Project Director.

46c (continued)

words

TIME, TECHNOLOGY, AND TEMPERAMENT 7

"Time marches on." These words were once used to conclude a popular 21
movie series that highlighted current events. The words were meant to 35
indicate to the viewing audience that changes were taking place constantly. 50
The thoughtful listeners, however, sometimes pictured Time as not only 65
marching on, but marching very rapidly--maybe too rapidly. 77

> Every human generation is a segment of history unto itself. It 89
> has its own customs; dances; taboos; technologies; fashions; and, 103
> yes, even its own language. While generational changes are subtle 116
> and occur slowly, they are definite. Each generation has always 129
> insisted upon its own identification (Ruiz, 1993, 90). 140

Technological changes tend to enhance differences between 152
generations, sometimes very sharply. The First Bank of Rockford, for 166
example, reporting on the popularity of its automated banking facilities, 180
found that users of this service were primarily members of the "younger 195
generation" and that older bank customers much preferred the tradi- 209
tional teller service. "We know that we will not be employing tellers in the 225
forseeable future; but we know, too, that such changes will not happen in 239
just a week's time" (Carver, 1994, 3). 247

Much of the movement for technological change today centers on 260
efficiency, saving time and energy. "Precious metals have tended to 274
fluctuate in value over the years--sometimes up, sometimes down; time, 288
viewed as a commodity, has only become more valuable" (Nyles, 1994, 301
72). 302

Sociologists say that society does not adopt new technology until 316
conditions, always changing, make it ready to do so; then it assimilates 330
change very rapidly. The automobile, for example, was invented years 344
before its acceptance as a popular method of transportation. Society 358
seems to need pioneers with foresight who will continue to "create tech- 373
nological changes with no assurance of immediate, or even ultimate, 386
acceptance" (Su, 1994, 38). 392

Certain "agents of change," often not identifiable, work to prepare 405
developing generations to accept change; to support it financially; and, 420
above all, to use it. Maybe the greatest challenge involving technology is 435
not to create change but to learn how to live with it. 446

REFERENCES 448

Carver, Myrnah L. "'First' to Go Hi-Tech." <u>The Rockford Ledger</u>, January 466
11, 1993. 469

Nyles, Carolyn Lee. <u>The Magic Time Machine</u>. Montgomery: Brevard 487
Publishing Company, 1994. 492

Ruiz, Jorge A. "History, Technology, and the Fortune Teller." <u>Computer</u> 508
<u>News</u>, April 1993. 513

Su, Debra M. <u>Time as a Lineal</u>. Savannah: Amyte Press, Inc., 1994. 529

Level Five
Office Concierge Simulation

OBJECTIVES

FORMATTING SKILLS

To review all business document formats and apply decision-making skills.

KEYBOARDING SKILLS

To key approximately 55 wam with good accuracy.

COMMUNICATION SKILLS

To produce error-free documents and apply language arts skills.

46 Measurement

Skill-Building Warmup

46a 7'

each line 3 times SS; DS between 3-line groups

alphabet 1 Dave Cagney alphabetized items for next week's quarterly journal.
figures 2 Close Rooms 4, 18, and 20 from 3 until 9 on July 7; open Room 56.
upward reaches 3 Toy & Wurt's note for $635 (see our page 78) was paid October 29.
easy 4 The auditor is due by eight, and he may lend a hand to the panel.

1	2	3	4	5	6	7	8	9	10	11	12	13

46b 12'

SKILL BUILDING

Measure straight-copy skill

Key three 3' writings; proofread and circle errors; determine *gwam*.

LA all letters used

	gwam 1'	3'	
In a recent show, a young skater gave a great performance.	12	4	69
Her leaps were beautiful, her spins were impossible to believe,	25	8	74
and she was a study in grace itself. But she had slipped during	38	13	78
a jump and had gone down briefly on the ice. Because of the high	51	17	82
quality of her act, however, she was given a third-place medal.	64	21	87
Her coach, talking later to a reporter, stated his pleasure	12	25	91
with her part of the show. When asked about the fall, he said	25	30	95
that emphasis should be placed on the good qualities of the per-	37	34	99
formance and not on one single blemish. He ended by saying that	50	38	104
as long as his students did the best they could, he would be	63	42	108
satisfied.	65	43	108
What is "best"? When asked, the young skater explained she	12	47	112
was pleased to have won the bronze medal. In fact, this perfor-	25	51	117
mance was a personal best for her; she was confident the gold	37	55	121
would come later if she worked hard enough. It appears she knew	50	60	125
the way to a better medal lay in beating not other people, but her	64	64	130
own personal best.	67	65	131

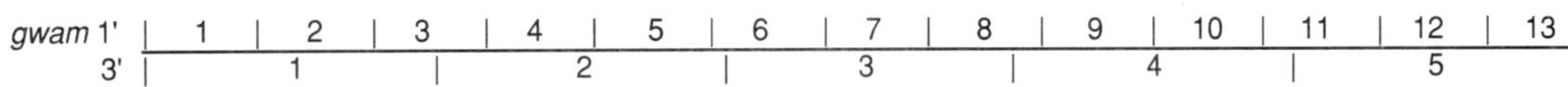

46c 31'

FORMATTING

Measurement: two-page unbound report with references

Time schedule

Assemble materials .... 1'
Timed production .... 25'
Final check; compute *g-pram* .... 5'

Format the report on page 107 as an unbound report DS. Begin again if you have finished and time has not been called. Proofread; circle errors, calculate *g-pram*.

g-pram = total words keyed / time (25')

Office Concierge Simulation

Procedures Manual, Part 1

Business Correspondence (Letters and Memos)
(Lessons 121-130)

Daily plan

Skill-building workshop/
paragraph writings .... 5'-15'
Simulation .... 35'-45'
OR
Simulation .... 50'

Work assignment

You have just been hired as an administrative assistant for OFFICE CONCIERGE, a new office automation firm that will be opening in Irvine, California. Office Concierge (pronounced kon se erzh') is located in a high-tech community with large business complexes housing many Fortune 500 companies and multinational corporations.

Office Concierge provides support to clients in word processing, transcription, Fax services, desktop publishing, and production keying of projects such as proposals, academic reports, and manuals.

Christopher Raleigh, the owner, has asked you to prepare a procedures manual that will be used as a reference guide by the newly hired office personnel. The company's success depends on quality standards and uniform styling. To assure that all word processing employees provide this high level of quality and present a good company image, you begin your task today.

The manual provides illustrations and directions for formatting the documents most often requested by clients. Most of the documents are in rough-draft format. All documents should be proofread for errors in spelling, punctuation, word usage, and so forth that may have been overlooked. Proofread, key, label, and mark each document with the necessary directions for keying it.

The manual will consist of three parts:

Part 1: Business Correspondence (letters and memos)
Part 2: Outlines, Reports, and Tables
Part 3: Administrative Documents

Each part will have a divider page, and the complete manual will have a title page and table of contents. You will create these pages when all other pages are completed.

Follow these steps to produce each document in the manual:

1 Use stationery that Mr. Raleigh has provided you.

2 Key the document in proper format. Use the Reference Guide to COLLEGE KEYBOARDING to review format when necessary.

3 Label the parts of the document and the spacing between document parts if directed. Use a black pen and write neatly. Documents 2 and 3 have been labeled as examples.

4 When more than one variation of a document is included, label only the parts/spacing that differ in consecutive documents.

5 Key the name of the document at the left margin and the page number flush right .5" from the bottom of the page. If your equipment permits, use a larger type font and bold for this footer.

6 Number the pages 1.1, 1.2, 1.3, 2.1, 2.2, and so on. The decimal system of numbering makes it easy to update the manual when inserting pages. The first number refers to the manual part; the second number refers to the sequence of the document within the part.

1.2
Manual part ┘ └ Page number within part

wp If available, utilize the time-saving features of the word processing function referenced by the icon.

Document 2
Unbound 2-page report
Reference: pages 98, 100, 102.

words

UNTAPPED RESOURCES 4

We directors of company personnel have important responsibilities, 17
among the most important being the acquisition of dedicated, conscien- 31
tious workers to carry out the daily functions of our businesses. 44

Staff Resources 51

Generally, we each have developed our own sources, which range 62
from local educational institutions, through employment offices, news- 76
papers, and on down to walk-ins, from which we find new employees. 90
But we always welcome new sources. 97

One supply often overlooked--though not by the more ingenious of 110
us--is the pool of available workers who have one or more noticeable or 124
definable "disabilities" or "handicaps." Occasionally, a supply of these 139
potential workers will go untapped in an area for a long period of time; 154
when discovered, they become a genuine treasure trove for a wide variety 168
of jobs. 170

Performance Level 177

Studies have shown that disabled workers, while perhaps 189
restricted to the exact jobs they can do, perform well above the minimum 203
requirements on jobs not beyond their capabilities. Limitations vary 217
with individuals; but once reasonable accommodations are made, these 231
workers become uniquely qualified employees. 240

Abrahms, writing of the reluctance of some employers to hire 252
handicapped workers, says that "workers with handicaps have high 265
rates of production, often higher than those achieved by other workers" 280
(Abrahms, 1994, 61). Munoz goes one step further by reminding us that 294
disabled workers "have high work-safety histories with low job-changing 308
and absentee records" (Munoz, 1994, 37). 317

From a practical as well as a personal point of view, then, hiring 330
workers who are physically or mentally handicapped can provide a 343
positive occupational impact for a company as well as a very rewarding 357
experience for its personnel director. One such director says: 370

> Recently, I told a potential employee who was sitting in my 382
> office in her wheelchair of our success with handicapped workers. 396
> "That's great," she said. "You know, most of us rarely think about 409
> things we can't do. There are too many things we can do and can 422
> do well." I hired her (Moky, 1994, 78). 431

And so say all of us who sit in the employer's chair. 442

REFERENCES 444

Abrahms, Hollin C. "Searching for Employees." The Human Services 461
Monthly, January 1994. 467

Moky, Latanya R. An Investment in Social Action: The Caseville Study. 491
Macon: Meadowbrook Press, 1994. 498

Munoz, Hector. "Changing Aspects of the American Workforce at the Close 512
of the Twentieth Century." National Vo-Tech News, May 1994. 529

Document 3
Composition (Optional)

1 Prepare a rough-draft 4- or 5-line ¶ summarizing the content of the report. Use a title.

2 Key a final copy of the ¶ with errors corrected.

Document 1
Unbound report

1 Read and key the report from your procedures manual. Indent and block enumerations as shown.

2 Add a footer .5" from the bottom of each page: **LETTER TIPS**. Number the pages **1.1**, **1.2**, and **1.3**.

Proofreader's Tip: Always verify the correct sequence of enumerated items. When edits are added, errors can "slip in" easily.

TIPS FOR FORMATTING LETTERS (bold)

Insert A.

Letters are keyed in block, modified block, or simplified ~~style~~ format as directed by the client. Use block format with open punctuation if the client does not specify a format. With modified block format, use blocked paragraphs and open punctuation unless indented paragraphs and mixed punctuation are requested.

Letter Placement

~~To~~ Formatting a letter attractively requires judging its length. A short letter contains one to three short paragraphs or about 100 words; an average letter, three or four paragraphs, and 100-200 words; and a long letter, more than four paragraphs ~~and~~ or more than 200 words. Length is also affected by ~~number of~~ including words, number of paragraphs, or special features such as a table or enumerated items, ~~and special features such as~~ enclosures and mailing notations. When formatting letters, follow these guidelines:

1. Use 1" or default standard margins unless variable placement is requested.

2. If variable placement is requested, use 2", 1.5", or 1" margins for short, average, and long letters, respectively.

3. Use the "floating dateline" with both standard and variable placement.

4. Raise the dateline one line Insert B if it for each two special features. 5. Consider a letter ~~that~~ includes a table or several enumerated items to be long.

Salutation

The salutation ~~should~~ contains the personal title and last name of the person to whom the letter is addressed. Do not use the first name in the salutation unless requested by the

(B)

Short letter	line 18
Average letter	line 16
Long letter	line 14

(continued on next page)

45 Enumerations and Review

Skill-Building Warmup

45a 7'

each line 3 times SS; DS between 3-line groups

alphabet 1 Max Biqua watched jet planes flying in the azure sky over a cove.
figures 2 Send 105 No. 4 nails and 67 No. 8 brads for my home at 329 Annet.
3d row 3 We two were ready to type a report for our quiet trio of workers.
easy 4 Pamela owns a big bicycle; and, with it, she may visit the docks.

1 | 2 | 3 | 4 | 5 | 6 | 7 | 8 | 9 | 10 | 11 | 12 | 13

45b 43'

FORMATTING

Review document formats

Document 1
Memorandum

Use bold for the headings. Correct errors.

Reference: pages 81-82.

MicroAssistant: Use indent to format the enumerations in hanging indent format.

1 Key the number 1 and period.

2 Turn on indent (**Alt + I**). The second and successive lines will wrap to the first tab.

3 Turn off indent after the last indented enumeration.

words

TO: Andrew Anhut 3

FROM: Marge Oxward 7

DATE: October 5, 19-- 12

SUBJECT: Enumerated Items 17

This memo illustrates both the hanging indent format and the block 31
format for numbered items in documents. The hanging indent format 44
provides maximum emphasis, but the block format is more efficient. The 58
purpose of the document should guide the writer in choosing the appro- 72
priate format. Unless specified otherwise, use hanging indent format. 81

<u>Hanging Indent Format</u> 87

1. The numbered items are single-spaced with a double space between 101
   items. 103

2. Indent second and succeeding lines four spaces (or to the position of 118
   the first tab, depending on the software used). 127

<u>Blocked Enumerations</u> 136

1\. The numbered items are single-spaced with a double space between 150
items. 151

2\. The second and succeeding lines of numbered items are blocked 164
immediately under the number. 171

When enumerations appear within a <u>report</u>, they should be indented and 185
blocked five spaces from the left margin. The block format is recom- 298
mended, since the items receive emphasis by being single-spaced and 212
indented. 214

xx 215

Document 1 (continued)

client. Abbreviate the titles Mr., Mrs., Ms., Messrs., and Dr. Spell out other abbreviations such as Professor.

Use the salutation "Ladies and Gentlemen" when the letter is addressed to a firm or when an attention line is used.

Writer's Identification

The format of the writer's name and title vary, depending on the length of the writer's title.

Style 1. When the name and title are both short, key them on the same line with a comma separating them.

John Smith, Manager

Style 2. When either the name and/or title is long, key the title below the name.

Charlene Beckenridge
Vice President

Style 3. When the name, title, and department are all part of the closing, key the name and title on the same line with a comma separating them. Key the department on the line below.

Robert Wong, Manager
Advertising Department

Punctuation Styles

Letters are keyed with either open or mixed punctuation. The punctuation style refers to the punctuation following the salutation and the complimentary closing.

Open Punctuation:	Dear Mr. Brown	Sincerely
Mixed Punctuation:	Dear Mr. Brown:	Sincererly,

All business letters are prepared on company letterhead stationery, which includes the company name, address, telephone number, and logo. Always prepare an envelope or a label for each letter, whichever is appropriate.

44b (continued)

words

THE IMPORTANCE OF BUSINESS 5
COMMUNICATION 8
QS

Probably no successful enterprise 15
exists that does not rely for its success upon 24
the ability of its members to communicate 33
with each other and with third 39
parties. The role that effective communica- 48
tion plays in business success cannot be 56
stressed too strongly; it is essential that 65
strict attention be paid to the application, 74
implementation, and administration of 81
communication within a business venture. 90

> Effective communication results 96
> when information is transmitted from 104
> a sender to a receiver, and the 110
> message is understood. It is not nec- 118
> essary that the message result in any 125
> specific outcome, only that it be sent, 133
> received, and understood (Estevez, 140
> 1994, 12). 143

Business communication falls into two 150
main categories, written and verbal. More 159
time is spent by most business firms 166
studying and perfecting their written com- 175
munications. It is verbal communication, 183
however, that makes up a major portion of 192
all communication and deserves more 200
attention than is typically the case. "Suc- 208
cessful businesses have long known the 217
importance of good verbal communication, 225
yet many of them still give written com- 234
munication greater emphasis" (Hunter, 242
1993, 29). 244

Written communication confirms facts 252
and intentions, and any important verbal 260
conversation should be confirmed in 267
writing. Written communication also 275
constitutes proof; a letter signature can have 284
the same effect as a contract signature. Fur- 293
ther, written communications can be retained 302
for later reference, affirmation being as close as 312
the filing cabinet. Written communication avoids 322
some of the natural barriers of verbal communi- 332
cation. Shyness, speech problems, and other 341
distractions are not found in a letter. 349

Since verbal communication often involves 357
encounters on a one-on-one basis, it can bring 367
quicker results. Misunderstandings are avoided; 377
questions are answered. It is usually less 385
formal and friendlier; moods, attitudes, and 394
emotions are more easily handled. Verbal com- 404
munication is augmented with facial expressions 413
and gestures, assuring greater clarity of the mes- 423
sage. Words and phrases can be given special 432
emphasis not possible in a written message, 441
where emphasis is given by the receiver, not the 451
sender. 453

Murphy points out the importance of 460
communication: 463

> Make no mistake; both written and 470
> verbal communication are the stuff upon 478
> which success is built. Both forms de- 485
> serve careful study by any business that 494
> wants to grow. Successful businesspeople 502
> must read, write, speak, and listen with 511
> skill (Murphy, 1994, 57). 516

QS

REFERENCES 518

QS

Estevez, Ted. "The Art of Communicating in 527
Business." New Age Magazine, July 1994. 538

DS

Hunter, Dake R. Business Communications 550
Today. Fort Worth: Big Bend Publishers, 560
Inc., 1993. 562

Murphy, Grace. "Sharp Management Tools." 571
Modern Business, May 1994. 579

Document 2
Block letter, open punctuation

(LM p. S1)

1 Add a footer .5" from the bottom edge: **BLOCK LETTER, OPEN PUNCTUATION** and the page number **1.4**.

2 Neatly label the letter parts and spacing between the parts.

Note: Use standard placement for all letters.

Dateline — Current date

QS

Letter address — Mrs. Lucia Fuentes
Office Manager
Lorenson Equipment Company
17 Hobbs Road
Long Beach, CA 90840-0792

DS

Salutation — Dear Mrs. Fuentes

DS

Body — Thank you for calling about our bid to produce your company 's procedures manual. As I mentioned to you on the phone, the project will be starting by the end of this week.

DS

Ms. Carla Price will be coordinating the project and will be your contact should questions arise during the project. Please direct all questions to her.

DS

Drafts of the completed sections will be provided for you to proofread. Of course, you and your staff are welcome to visit our office at any time to discuss the project or to use our facilities for proofreading.

DS

We look forward to working with you.

DS

Complimentary close — Sincerely yours

QS

Writer's name and Title — *Student's Name*
Administrative Assistant

DS

Reference initials — xx

44 Unbound Report

Skill-Building Warmup

44a 7'

each line 3 times SS (work for fewer than 3 errors per group); DS between 3-line groups

alphabet 1 Joyce Wexford left my squad after giving back the disputed prize.
figures 2 Reply to Items 4, 5, and 6 on page 39 and 1, 7, and 8 on page 20.
double letters 3 A committee supplied food and coffee for the Mississippi meeting.
easy 4 In Dubuque, they may work the field for the profit paid for corn.

1 | 2 | 3 | 4 | 5 | 6 | 7 | 8 | 9 | 10 | 11 | 12 | 13

44b 43'

FORMATTING

Two-page report with direct quotations

Read "Moving to a second page" and "Direct quotations" at the right. Then key the 2-page report on page 103 DS. Use appropriate format.

Moving to a second page

1 Number second and subsequent pages at the right margin 1" from the top; DS below number.

2 Try to leave at least a 1" margin at the foot of a previous page.

3 Avoid dividing the last word on a page.

4 Avoid carrying over a single line of a paragraph to a subsequent page or leaving a single line on a page.

5 Key references on the last page of a report only if all references can be confined to that page. Otherwise, use a separate, numbered page.

Direct quotations

Word-for-word quotations from published works of other authors must be acknowledged with an internal citation.

Short quotations: Short quotations are simply enclosed in quotation marks followed (or preceded) by an internal citation.

```
and deserves more attention than is typically the case.  "Suc-

cessful businesses have long known the importance of good verbal

communication, yet many of them still give written communication

greater emphasis" (Hunter, 1993, 29).
```

Long quotations: A quotation that runs to four or more lines of text should be set off in single spacing and indented 5 spaces (10 spaces for the first line of the paragraph) from the left report margin. No quotation marks are used.

wp The **indent** feature, also known as a temporary margin, is used when more than one line needs to be indented from the left margin. Text is indented to the first tab stop.

MicroAssistant: Use indent to format the long quotation.

1 Set SS,

2 Turn on indent (**Alt + I**) at the left margin on the line beginning the long quotation; cursor indents to the first tab.

3 Strike Tab to indent the first line.

4 Turn indent off after keying the long quotations; set DS.

```
application, implementation, and administration of communi-

cation within a business venture.

          Effective communication results when information
     is transmitted from a sender to a receiver, and the
     message is understood.  It is not necessary that the
     message result in any specific outcome, only that it
     be sent, received, and understood (Estevez, 1994, 12).

     Business communication falls into two main categories,

verbal and written.  More time is spent in most organizations
```

Document 3
Block letter with special features

(LM p. S3)

1 Move the dateline up about 1 line for each 2 special features and use 1" side margins. (Do not position the date higher than line 14.)

2 Add footer: **LETTER WITH SPECIAL FEATURES,** page **1.5**.

3 Neatly label the letter parts and spacing between the parts.

Dateline	Current date DS
Special notation	OVERNIGHT MAIL DS
Attention line	Attention Ms. Stephanie Reynoza Washington Industrial Insurance Department of Labor and Industries General Administration Building Olympia, WA 99504-4401 DS
Reference line	Re: P 864812 DS Ladies and Gentlemen DS
Subject line	PSYCHOTHERAPY TREATMENT FOR ROGER M. BROWN DS Mr. Roger M. Brown has been under my care during the past three months. Therapy has proved to be a very stabilizing influence for him. DS The far-reaching effects of his industrial injury coupled with his emotional instability require that he continue outpatient therapy for an additional two months. DS I am enclosing a copy of his charts for your files. Please let me know if authorization for further psychotherapy will be provided for Mr. Brown. DS Sincerely DS
Company name	HOLISTIC PSYCHOLOGICAL CLINIC QS
Writer's name and Title	Samuel Ibrahim, Psy.D. Licensed Psychologist DS xx DS
Enclosure notation	Enclosure: Charts DS
Copy notation	c Dr. Austin Palachik, M.D. DS
Postscript	A quick response to this matter will be appreciated so that Mr. Brown can continue receiving therapy on a regularly scheduled basis.

DS

and thus oxygen becomes a crucial part of any aquatic ecosystem. Dissolved oxygen is derived from the atmosphere as well as from the photosynthetic processes of aquatic plants. Oxygen, in turn, is consumed through the life activities of most aquatic animals and plants (Bruce, 1994, 129). When dissolved oxygen reaches very low levels in the aquatic environment, unfavorable conditions for fish and other aquatic life can develop.

Conclusion

The absence of dissolved oxygen may give rise to unpleasant odors produced through anaerobic (no oxygen) decomposition. On the other hand, an adequate supply of oxygen helps maintain a healthy environment for fish and other aquatic life and may help prevent the development of unacceptable conditions that are caused by the decomposition of municipal and industrial waste (Ryn, 1993, 29).

QS

REFERENCES

QS

Book reference Beard, Fred F. The Fulford County Dilemma. Niagara Falls: Dawn General Press, 1992.

DS

Periodical reference Bruce, Lois L. "Hazardous Waste Management: A History." State of Idaho Bulletin No. 7312. Boise: State of Idaho Press, 1994.

DS

Periodical reference Ryn, Jewel Scott. "But Please Don't Drink the Water." Journal of Environmental Science, Winter 1993.

Document 4
Block letter with FAX notation

(LM p. S5)

1 Add **FACSIMILE** as a mailing notation.

2 Add FAX phone number a DS below the reference initials:

FAX (505) 555-1007

3 Add subject line: **CHANGES IN CONTRACT 68-MK**

4 Add footer: **BLOCK LETTER WITH FAX NOTATION,** page **1.6**.

5 Label the FAX notations.

Mr. Leon Underwood
Hoffmeyer & Marco Industries
38 Alameda Road, Suite 101
Albuquerque, NM 87114-9355

This letter is to confirm ~~our~~ *this morning's* telephone conversation ~~of this morning regading~~ *about* the June through August date changes for services ~~on~~ *in* contract 68-MK. We have changed the schedule to provide you with *all-day* teleconferencing ~~line~~ servics *e* on June 1~~3~~ *2*, July 16, and August 20, 19--. The remaining *nine* dates and the original contract cost of $5,690 for each day Ⓐ remain the same.

Please let me know ~~when~~ *as soon as* your plans ~~have~~ *s* materialized *s* for the conference you plan *this fall* between Las Cruces and your European affiliates in London. We will prepare a bid ~~quote~~ for you at any time for our services. Thank~~s~~ *you* for your *continued* business. Yours truly, Marcia Stevens, Customer Service Representative

Ⓐ *we provide services*

Document 5
Modified block letter, mixed punctuation

(LM p. S7)

Add the footer **MODIFIED BLOCK LETTER, MIXED PUNCTUATION,** page **1.7**.

Label the beginning point for the dateline and complimentary close.

Mr. Jackson Richards
Richards and Baker Waterworks
1805 Bradford Place
San Antonio, TX 78216-6200

Welcome, Richardsand Baker Waterworks, to the select group of stores that market Spas of the World spa shells and portables. We are confident you will be proud to market Spas of the World items to your clientele because these products are of the finest craftsmanship.

I enjoyed visiting with you in your San Antonio show-room last week and meeting some of your employees. As men-tioned then, our new South Pacific spa (also available as a portable) will be ready in two weeks. This "family" model holds 600 gallons of water and seats ten to twelve people comfortably.

Again, Mr. Richards, welcome to the circle of dealers who handle Spas of the World products. You will, we believe, have tremendous sales success with these hot-water products. Please call if we can assist you in any way. Cordially yours, Ms. Monica Castillo, Marketing Manager

43 Unbound Report

Skill-Building Warmup

43a 7'

each line 3 times SS; DS between 3-line groups; work for fewer than 3 errors per group

alphabet 1 Jacki might analyze the data by answering five complex questions.

figures 2 Memo 67 asks if the report on Bill 35-48 is due the 19th or 20th.

double letters 3 Aaron took accounting lessons at a community college last summer.

easy 4 Hand Bob a bit of cocoa, a pan of cod, an apricot, and six clams.

| 1 | 2 | 3 | 4 | 5 | 6 | 7 | 8 | 9 | 10 | 11 | 12 | 13 |

43b 13'

COMMUNICATION

Compose at the keyboard

Construct an outline that could have been used in the composition of the report on page 99. Use the same main heading as was used for the report.

43c 30'

FORMATTING

Unbound report: second page with references

1 Read "Report documentation" at the right.

2 Study the model showing the second page of a report. Note especially the top margin and page number position.

3 Key the last page of a report shown on page 101. (Your lines might not match those in the copy.)

MicroAssistant: Indent sets a temporary left margin at the first tab. Press **Alt + I** to toggle indent off and on. To format the references:

1 After keying the first word (or at any point beyond the first tab in line 1 of the first bibliography entry), turn on indent.

2 Strike Enter twice between enumerations.

3 Turn off indent after the last enumeration.

Report documentation

Documentation shows sources of quotations or other information cited in a report.

Internal citations are an easy and practical method of documentation. The last name of the author(s), the publication date, and the page number(s) of the cited material are shown in parentheses within the body of the report; as, **(Bruce, 1994, 129)**. This information cues a reader to the name Bruce in the references listed at the end of the report.

References cited in the report are listed in alphabetical order by authors' last names at the end of the report. The list may be titled **REFERENCES** or **BIBLIOGRAPHY**.

References are keyed single-spaced in "hang indent" style; that is, with the first line flush left and each additional line indented 5 spaces. DS between references.

A book reference includes the name of the work (underlined), city of publication, publisher, and copyright date. A magazine reference shows the name of the article (in quotation marks), magazine title (underlined), and time of publication.

2

and thus oxygen becomes a crucial part of any aquatic ecosystem. Dissolved oxygen is derived from the atmosphere as well as from the photosynthetic processes of aquatic plants. Oxygen, in turn, is consumed through the life activities of most aquatic animals and plants (Bruce, 1994, 129). When dissolved oxygen reaches very low levels in the aquatic environment, unfavorable conditions for fish and other aquatic life can develop.

Conclusion

The absence of dissolved oxygen may give rise to unpleasant odors produced through anaerobic (no oxygen) decomposition. On the other hand, an adequate supply of oxygen helps maintain a healthy environment for fish and other aquatic life and may help prevent the development of unacceptable conditions that are caused by the decomposition of municipal and industrial waste (Ryn, 1993, 29).

REFERENCES

Beard, Fred F. The Fulford County Dilemma. Niagara Falls: Dawn General Press, 1992.

Bruce, Lois L. "Hazardous Waste Management: A History." State of Idaho Bulletin No. 7312. Boise: State of Idaho Press, 1994.

Ryn, Jewel Scott. "But Please Don't Drink the Water." Journal of Environmental Science, Winter 1993.

Document 6
Two-page letter, modified block

(LM p. S9)

1 Proofread document for errors that may have been missed.

2 Replace **L.A.** with **Los Angeles**.

3 Key the footer and page number on both pages of the letter: **TWO-PAGE LETTER, MODIFIED BLOCK,** pages **1.8** and **1.9**.

wp Use the header, search and replace, and move functions.

Mr. Harold Hernandez
34 Crescent Lane
Buena Park, CA 90620-7690

Mr. Harold Hernandez
Page 2
Current date

To help you in your p
available from Carlen
ment. The kits can b
toilets at home.

Presently California is experiencing

As most of you are aware, we are currently in the longest drought that Claifornia has experienced in decades. We are having entering ed the 5th SP year of below-normal snowfall in the Sierra snow pack watersheds and less than normal rainfall in the L.A. basin. Growing concern about our diminishing water supply has prompted Californians to reevaluate the ways we use water.

MOVE

Although A

We are facing a severe water problem. The good news is that we can find ways to cut back our water use. age Some will be simple and inexpensive, others more complicated and costly. Remember, each of us can make a difference; together we can solve the problem. Simple actions like reporting steam and water leaks can make a significant difference.

A mandatory water conservation program has been approved by L. A. and the surrounding countries and Benjamin Franklin Power and Water. This program that requires all residential and commercial customers to reduce water usage 10% SP below 1993 levels effective March 1st and to 15% SP below 1993 levels effective May 1st. We will may be required to cut our water usage by one-half before this drought ends.

A local newspaper recently published an artical le identifying Ethyl Petroleum as being the largest industrial water user in the L. A. area--a dubious honor, --and one that we must pass on to someone else. Water conservation in the refinery must become a natural part of how we do ing business, not a practice pursue d only during droughts or summer months.

A committee consisting of 3 SP engineers and a representative from Benjamin Franklin Power and Water has been formed to evaluate water usage conservation at our refinery. This committee will also research alternative processes of refining crude oil that require less water.

Insert A

1.5" top margin

BASIC STEPS IN REPORT WRITING

QS

1" side margin The effective writer makes certain that reports that leave her or his desk are technically correct in style, usable in content, and attractive in format. 1" side margin

DS

Side headings <u>The First Step</u>

DS

Information is gathered about the subject; the effective writer takes time to outline the data to be used in the report. This approach allows the writer to establish the organization of the report. When a topic outline is used, order of presentation, important points, and even various headings can be determined and followed easily when writing begins.

<u>The Correct Style</u>

The purpose of the report often determines its style. Most academic reports (term papers, for example) are double-spaced with indented paragraphs. Most business reports, however, are single-spaced; and paragraphs are blocked. When a style is not stipulated, general usage may be followed.

<u>The Finished Product</u>

The most capable writer will refrain from making a report deliberately <u>impressive</u>, especially if doing so makes it less <u>expressive</u>. The writer does, however, follow the outline carefully as a first draft is written. Obvious errors are ignored momentarily. Refinement comes later, after all the preliminary work is done. The finished document will then be read and reread to ensure it is clear, concise, correct, and complete.

Document 6 (continued)

To help you in you personal efforts, free water-saving kits are available from Carlene Cooper, Room 225, ~~in the~~ Human Resources Department. The kits can be installed in your faucets, showers, and toilets at home.
Sincerely, Thomas Ducaynce, Vice President, Public Relations and Human Resources c George Scott

Reprints of the article "101 Ways to Conserve Water" from the Los Angeles Herald are also available from Human Resources.

Document 7
Modified block letter, indented paragraphs
(LM p. S11)

1 Replace each occurrence of **LCC** with **Lincoln Community College.** Check copy for errors.

2 Add footer: **MODIFIED BLOCK LETTER, INDENTED PARAGRAPHS,** page **1.10**.

Ms. Janice Black
1663 Ridge Road
Mill Spring, MO 63952-1594

Thank you for your ~~the~~ letter of March 2~~nd~~ requesting an updated transcript showing your final Spanish II grade. Please excuse our delay in getting ~~making~~ the grade change to you.

Prof. Jose Guerra, who ~~as you know, only has~~ resently returned from a sabbatical leave, just ~~gave~~ provided us with your current grade. Please note on the enclosed transcript that your incomplete Spanish II (238) grade for ~~last~~ spring quarter has been changed from an "I" to an "A".

LCC charges ~~three dollars~~ $3 for each transcript issued. Please send us a check for this amount. Sincerely
Alexander McCloresky, Dean
Records and Admissions

42b 13'

FORMATTING

The underline

Read the information at the right and then key Drills 1 and 2.

See the Reference Guide for rules for using underline.

Electric typewriter

1 Find the underline key in the upper right of the keyboard.

2 To underline a word, backspace to its first letter and strike the underline key once for each character to be underlined.

MicroAssistant

Strike **Alt + U** to turn underline on and off.

Word processing/electronic typewriter

1 Turn on the underline feature by striking the underline key or combination of keys.

2 Key the text.

3 Turn off the underline feature by striking the same keys used to turn it on.

WP Word processors may underline text that has already been keyed. Often this is done by blocking existing text and then keying the underline command.

Drill 1

Key the line as shown.

I saw the movie once; they saw it three times.

Drill 2

Titles of books may be shown either underlined or in ALL CAPS. Key the paragraph once DS; as you key, change the book titles from ALL CAPS to underlined with main words capitalized. Correct errors.

When Daniels wrote his popular book, REASONING WITH THE UNREASONABLE, he was fulfilling a desire of some years standing. When he was younger, he had read Traczewsky's MINDS UNLIMITED and Grbak's NO ROOM FOR ARGUMENT; and these books had created in his mind the necessity for a rebuttal based on his own theories. His earlier book, THE IMMATURITY CRISIS, would indeed prove to be a worthy prelude to REASONING WITH THE UNREASONABLE.

42c 30'

FORMATTING

Unbound report with main and side headings

Read carefully "Unbound reports" at right. Follow these guidelines as you key the report on page 99. (Your lines may not end as shown in the illustration.)

Unbound reports

Reports are often prepared without covers or binders. Reports longer than one page are usually attached with a staple or paper clip in the upper left corner. Such reports are called **unbound reports**. Follow these formatting guidelines for unbound reports:

1 Top margins: 1.5" for the first page; 1" for second and succeeding pages.

2 Side margins: 1" on all pages.

3 Bottom margins: At least 1" and not more than 2" on all pages but the last one, which might be deeper.

4 Spacing: Double-space educational reports and indent paragraphs 5 spaces. Business reports are usually single-spaced; paragraphs are blocked with a double space between them.

5 Page numbers: Number the second and subsequent pages 1" from top edge. DS below page number to the first line of the body. The first page is not numbered.

6 Main headings: Center in ALL CAPS; follow with a QS (3 blank lines).

7 Side headings: Begin at left margin and underline; capitalize first letters of main words; DS above and below.

BASIC STEPS IN REPORT WRITING

The effective writer makes certain that reports that leave her or his desk are technically correct in style, usable in content, and attractive in format.

The First Step

Information is gathered about the subject; the effective writer takes time to outline the data to be used in the report. This approach allows the writer to establish the organization of the report. When a topic outline is used, order of presentation, important points, and even various headings can be determined and followed easily when writing begins.

The Correct Style

The purpose of the report often determines its style. Most academic reports (term papers, for example) are double-spaced with indented paragraphs. Most business reports, however, are single-spaced; and paragraphs are blocked. When a style is not stipulated, general usage may be followed.

The Finished Product

The most capable writer will refrain from making a report deliberately impressive, especially if doing so makes it less expressive. The writer does, however, follow the outline carefully as a first draft is written. Obvious errors are ignored momentarily. Refinement comes later, after all the preliminary work is done. The finished document will then be read and reread to ensure it is clear, concise, correct, and complete.

Document 8
Simplified block letter

(LM p. S13)

1 Key an appropriate subject line in ALL CAPS and the enumerations in block format.

2 Replace **FOSC** with **Franklin Office Systems Consultants'** and **LNBC** with **Lakeview National Bank of Casper**.

3 Add footer: **SIMPLIFIED BLOCK LETTER,** page **1.11**.

Ms. Claudia Jean Whitehead
Senior Vice President
Lakeview National Bank of Casper
P.O. Box 301
Casper, WY 82602-3944

Thank you for considering FOSC assistance in implementing your customer service improvement plan in the loan Department. The enclosed proposal covers our consulting services listed below: 1. Consult with employees and determine areas for ~~in-depth~~ evaluation. 2. Evaluate the current loan-processing system. 3. Assess the efficiency and effectiveness of employees. 4. Prepare a report of findings and recommendations.

Each of the phases also will be conducted with the feedback of LNBC ~~Man~~ management in order to reflect accurately the goals and philosophy of your organization in the final report.

I look forward to meeting with you next Thursday, (insert correct date), to discuss our proposal. If you have any further inquiries, please call me. Guy Simon, Manager

Document 9
Envelope

1 Address a large envelope (No. 10) as shown.

2 On a plain sheet of paper, key the footer **ENVELOPE**, page **1.12**.

3 Mount the envelope on the sheet so that it can be placed in the manual.

4 Label the envelope as shown.

line 2 ↓
HAZELYN J TREDSHAW
657 CARSWELL STREET
OMAHA NE 68123-1880
DS
↑ PERSONAL (notation for addressee)
3 spaces

(line 8-9) SPECIAL DELIVERY

about .5" left of center →

MS BUUNA WERTZ PRESIDENT (line 14)
PRIME MOVERS INCORPORATED
3467 SUNNYSIDE AVENUE S
SOUTH BEND IN 46615-9333

Document 2

Use 1" side margins and a 2" top margin. Roman numerals I and II must be placed appropriately so the periods will align with III.

```
                PLANTING GRASS SEED

Space forward
twice ──────► I.  PREPARING THE SOIL FOR SEEDING
from margin
                  A.  Breaking Up and Pulverizing Soil
                      1.  Spade, rake, hoe
                      2.  Power tiller
                          a.  Purchase
                          b.  Rent
                  B.  Soaking Area to Be Planted
                  C.  Adding Nutrients

Space forward
once ──────► II.  SMOOTHING OUT/PREPARING THE SEEDBED FOR PLANTING
from margin
                  A.  Leveling the Soil
                  B.  Eliminating High Spots
                      1.  "Homemade" drag
                      2.  Weighted roller
                      3.  Rake

            III.  SEEDING AND SUBSEQUENTLY PROTECTING THE PLANTED
                  AREA AGAINST EROSION

                  A.  Manual Seeding
                  B.  Mechanical Seeding
                  C.  Adding Protective Cover
                      1.  Straw
                      2.  Cloth
                  D.  Sprinkling to Set Seed
```

41c 13'

COMMUNICATION

Compose at the keyboard

Compose a short outline on a subject of your choice; for example, MY CURRENT CLASSES, in which you show the class name, instructor, location, etc., on appropriate levels. Other possible subjects include RECENT BOOKS READ or PLANS FOR THE MONTH.

42 Unbound Report

Skill-Building Warmup

42a 7'

each line 3 times SS (work for fewer than 2 errors per group); DS between 3-line groups

alphabet 1 Di quickly won several junior prizes at the Foxburgh swim trials.
figures 2 From July 13 to 20, the extension numbers will be 45, 67, and 89.
shift/lock 3 Ms. Ing keyed the notations REGISTERED and CERTIFIED in ALL CAPS.
easy 4 Did he visit a city to handle the authentic enamel dish and bowl?

| 1 | 2 | 3 | 4 | 5 | 6 | 7 | 8 | 9 | 10 | 11 | 12 | 13 |

Document 10
Memorandum tips

Prepare these tips as a single-spaced business report. Use hanging indent for enumerations.

Formatting instructions

Continue to add a footer to each document in the procedures manual. Use the document title to name the footer. Number all pages consecutively, beginning with page **1.13**. You will no longer be reminded of this step.

(A) Regardless of the format selected,

(B) memo heading is

MEMORANDUM FORMAT

Correspondence within an organization is prepared as an interoffice memorandum. Individuals who have access to E-Mail send many of their routine messages via their computers. ¶Printed memos may be formatted in one of the three ways described below. (A) The body of the memo is single-spaced, and a double space is left between paragraphs. Reference initials and other special notations may be added at the end of the memo.

1. Standard Format. Beginning 1.5" from the top, key the headings **TO:, FROM:, DATE:,** and **SUBJECT:** at the left margin and double-spaced. Set a tab 10 spaces from the margin for the data to be keyed after these headings. Begin the body a double space below the last heading line. If you are using a word processing to prepare the memo, record the headings as a macro so that it can be reused each time the a memo is prepared. stet

2. Preprinted Form. Preprinted memo forms are (B) formatted similar to the standard format, except that the words TO:, FROM, DATE, and SUBJECT are already printed on the form. If the form is designed well, these headings will be preprinted in the left margin. efficient

3. Simplified Format. The Simplified format memos save the operator's time of keying the traditional memo heads. They may be printed on either plain or memohead stationery. Simplified memos

(A) Personal as well as professional titles are may be optional, depending on the writer's choice. ~~Include titles.~~

(A) Prepare a plain envelope for each memo. Include the receiver's name and department. Key COMPANY MAIL in the usual stamp position.

Figure A and Figure B illustrate two kinds of interoffice envelopes. They are usually colored to distinguish them from outgoing mail.

COMPANY MAIL

JUNE BOSWELL
PERSONNEL DEPARTMENT

Figure A

INTER-DEPARTMENTAL CORRESPONDENCE
DELIVER TO LAST PERSON NAMED

NAME	PLANT OR DEPT	NAME	PLANT OR DEPT

Figure B

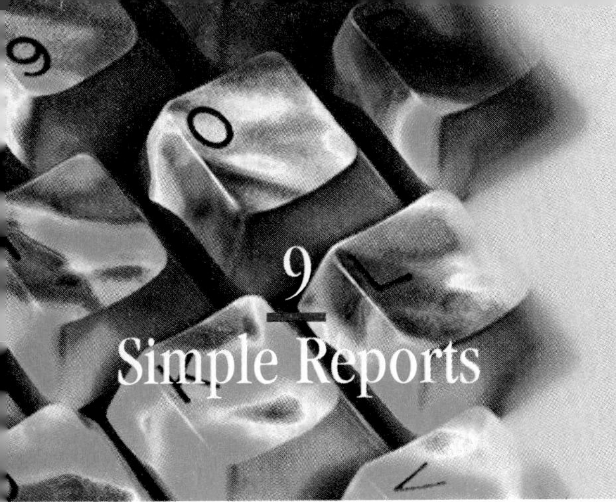

Learning goals:

1 To format topical outlines.
2 To format unbound reports with side headings, internal citations, and reference lists.
3 To concentrate on data as you key.
4 To compose at the keyboard.

Formatting guides:

1 Default margins or a 65-space line.
2 Single-space drills; double-space paragraphs.

41a 7'

Skill-building warmup

each line 3 times SS (concentrate on copy to avoid errors); DS between 3-line groups

alphabet 1 Jakob will save the money required for your next big cash prizes.
fig/sym 2 I saw Vera buy 16 7/8 yards of #240 cotton denim at $3.95 a yard.
3d/4th fingers 3 Zone 12 is impassable; quickly rope it off. Did you wax Zone 90?
easy 4 Did an auditor handle the formal audit of the firms for a profit?

| 1 | 2 | 3 | 4 | 5 | 6 | 7 | 8 | 9 | 10 | 11 | 12 | 13 |

41b 30'

FORMATTING

Outlines

Study "Preparing outlines"; then study the example below.

Document 1

1 Format the outline below with 2" side margins and a 1.5" top margin.

2 Set 3 tab stops—4 spaces, 8 spaces, and 12 spaces—from the Roman numeral I.

Preparing outlines

Outlining is a critical first step in the process of organizing data, especially for reports. Making an outline clarifies a writer's thinking and helps her or him give ideas appropriate emphasis. A good outline has the following format features:

1 Capitalize topics as follows: first level, ALL CAPS; second level, main words; third level, first word only.

2 Single-space outlines; double-space above and below first-level topics.

3 Include at least two parts within each level.

4 Align all numbers, Roman and Arabic, at the period.

5 Indent each successive level four spaces under the previous level.

6 If a level has a second line, begin it under the first word of the line above, not under the number or letter.

7 Use 1" margins unless an outline is narrow and a shorter line length is more appropriate.

TOPICAL OUTLINE FORMAT

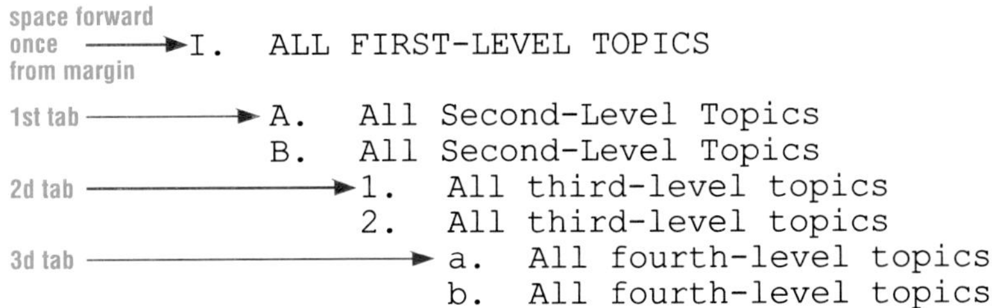


```
 I.  ALL FIRST-LEVEL TOPICS

     A.  All Second-Level Topics
     B.  All Second-Level Topics
         1.  All third-level topics
         2.  All third-level topics
             a.  All fourth-level topics
             b.  All fourth-level topics

II.  ALL FIRST-LEVEL TOPICS

     A.  All Second-Level Topics
         1.  All third-level topics
         2.  All third-level topics
     B.  All Second-Level Topics
```

Document 11
Standard memo
Label the spacing between memo parts.

Prepare the memo heading as a macro. Use the macro to prepare this memo.

Document 12
Memo on printed form
(LM p. S15)
Key Document 11 as a memo on a printed form. Begin the heading information two spaces after the colons; do not label any parts of this document.

Document 13
Simplified memo
Key Document 11 as a simplified memo; Use ALL CAP format for subject line. Label memo parts and spacing between parts.

TO: June Boswell, Personnel Manager

FROM: Breanda R. Oliver, SEnior Vice President

DATE: Current date

SUBJECT: Employee Evaluations

All employee evaluation forms musst be completed by the midle of April. Please duplicate copy the attached form; each evaluation muts be cmpleted on this form.

Return this evaluations and add a summary for each depart-ment to me on or before the following dates:

Sales	Tuesday, March 22
Production	Tuesday, March 29
Accounting	Monday, April 5 Tuesday

Evaluations from other departments are due **Friday, April 15.**

xx

Attachment

Document 14
Two-page standard memo
Label the second-page heading.

Use the stored macro for the memo heading.

TO: Distributors of Parkinson Parts and Products / **FROM:** Warranty Registration Departmen*t* / Parkinson Manufacturing Company / **DATE:** Current / **SUBJECT:** Ten-Year Warranty

Parkinson Manufacturing Company offers the following ten-year warranty to all original purchaser s (not non transfer-able to any other individual) of on the PMC product s* that listed below. This warranty applies to are manufactured and sold by them against defects in materials and craftsmanship arising under normal usage

Drill 8
Develop/measure skill growth

Key 3' and 5' writings.

 all letters

Writing 11: **Straight copy**

gwam 3' | 5'

Even the experienced authors know when they write that their 4 | 2 25
original copy often is not the best copy. Of course, the first 8 | 5 27
try will be readable; but there usually are a few areas that will 13 | 8 30
need polishing. An excellent method for you as a creative writer 17 | 10 33
is to sit down at your keyboard and place your ideas on paper as 21 | 13 35
quickly as possible, then reorganize as needed. Read your paper 26 | 15 38
aloud; if it sounds good to you, chances are it will sound just 30 | 18 40
as good to a reader. Time will not allow you to be overly fussy. 35 | 21 43
Learn when to polish--and when to finish. 37 | 22 45

Writing 12: **Statistical copy**

One stormy night last winter, just 29 days before Christmas, 4 | 2 28
I was driving my little Bentley automobile to South Ionia, a town 8 | 5 31
about 75 miles away. I had been invited by Major Bill Jellison, 13 | 8 34
just mustered out of the U. S. Marines, where I too had served 10 17 | 10 36
years as a captain, to see a new English play in the City Center. 22 | 13 39
The night was quite dark; snow had started lazily to fall. After 26 | 16 42
going about 38 miles, I remembered that Bill had said to me: "Be 30 | 18 44
sure to turn east at the corner of Level and South Essex roads. 35 | 21 47
Do not take a chance and turn west"; or, at least I thought that 39 | 23 49
was what he said. So, I turned east on Level Road, Route 46. 43 | 26 52

Writing 13: **Rough-draft copy**

According to studies done at a State University, one quick ~~method~~ 4 | 2 25
way to get rid of physical ~~tiredness~~ weariness, given ~~the~~ an opportunity, is to 8 | 5 28
jump into a cold shower. while we still don't exactly know ~~which~~ why 13 | 8 30
this has the affect that it does, it seems to do the trick. The 17 | 10 33
researchers have discovered also the that average person can work 21 | 13 36
both ~~harder~~ better and ~~harder~~ longer if she or she takes short, frequent rests. 26 | 15 38
They have found also that ~~some~~ good music, any kind from classical to 30 | 18 41
jazz, usually have some affect on the amount and quality of work 34 | 21 43
completed, as well as upon the well being of the workers. 38 | 23 46

gwam 3' | 1 | 2 | 3 | 4 | 5
5' | 1 | 2 | 3

Document 14 (continued)

and care from the date of original sale providing a valid, completed Warranty Registration CArd is submitted to PMC withing one month of the original date of purchase.

Insert Table 1

PMC warrants its electronic system to be free from defects for a period of twenty four months. This limited warranty does not apply to any of the following parts:

Insert Table 2

Written notification of any defects related to product within the warranty period must be sent to PMC with the following information: serial number, date of purchase, model name, copy of bil of sale, and retailers current, complete full address and telephone number. The warranty is contingent upon full payment of the original purchase price. Purchaser signature on the warranty card signifies acceptance of the conditions of the limited warranty.

Distributors of Pa
Page 2
Current date

Company with the fo
of purchase; model n
current, complete ad
contingent upon full
chaser's signature
the conditions of t

Bold and underline Column headings

Table 1

Description	Model Number
CPU Module	C983-2745
Tone Generator Module	H293-3348
SDDI Digital Tuner	M204-5893
HydroBath Cleaning Unit	P394-4772
Blackplane Receiver	B937-1928
E & M Card--8 port	E612-0644
Digital Line Card--16 port	W893-2054
Analog Line Card--16 port	X957-2833
Auto-Reverse Cassette Deck	T283-0132

Table 2

Description	Part Number
Fan Cooling Unit	FCU08-4386
Housing Assembly	HA387-0021
Remote Alarm Unit	RAU92-7153
Power Supply	PS100-4397
100-Watt Power Amplifier	JC187-4211
2-Way Mobile Speaker	JCL16-3857
Chassis Frame	CFX08-4276

Drill 7

Measure skill growth: straight copy

1 Key 1' writings on each ¶ of a timing. Note that ¶s within a timing increase by 2 words. **Goal:** to complete each ¶.

2 Key a 3' timing on the entire writing; DS.

To access writings on *MicroPace Plus*, key **W** and the timing number. For example, key **W8** for Writing 8.

Writing 8: **34, 36, 38 *gwam***

	gwam 1'	3'
Any of us whose target is to achieve success in our professional	13	4
lives will understand that we must learn how to work in harmony	26	8
with others whose paths may cross ours daily.	35	12
We will, unquestionably, work for, with, and beside people, just	13	16
as they will work for, with, and beside us. We will judge them,	26	20
as most certainly they are going to be judging us.	38	24
A lot of people realize the need for solid working relations and	13	28
have a rule that treats others as they, themselves, expect to be	26	33
treated. This seems to be a sound, practical idea for them.	40	37

Writing 9: **36, 38, 40 *gwam*** 

	1'	3'
I spoke with one company visitor recently; and she was very much	13	4
impressed, she said, with the large amount of work she had noted	26	9
being finished by one of our front office workers.	36	12
I told her how we had just last week recognized this very person	13	16
for what he had done, for output, naturally, but also because of	26	21
its excellence. We know this person has that "magic touch."	38	25
This "magic touch" is the ability to do a fair amount of work in	13	29
a fair amount of time. It involves a desire to become ever more	26	34
efficient without losing quality--the "touch" all workers should	39	38
have.	40	38

Writing 10: **38, 40, 42 gwam**

	1'	3'
Isn't it great just to untangle and relax after you have keyed a	13	4
completed document? Complete, or just done? No document is	25	8
quite complete until it has left you and passed to the next step.	38	13
There are desirable things that must happen to a document before	13	17
you surrender it. It must be read carefully, first of all, for	26	22
meaning to find words that look right but aren't. Read word for	39	26
word.	40	26
Check all figures and exact data, like a date or time, with your	13	31
principal copy. Make sure format details are right. Only then,	26	35
print or remove the work and scrutinize to see how it might look	39	39
to a recipient.	42	40

gwam 1' | 1 | 2 | 3 | 4 | 5 |
3' | 1 | 2 | 3 |

Document 15
Form letter
(plain paper)

Create the form document in block format, identifying the variables. Add necessary letter parts. Use hanging indent style for enumerated items.

MicroAssistant: Key the variable markers as they are shown.

wp Merge combines data from two sources into one document. Insert the appropriate codes for your software at each variable position.

Form Document Review

Form documents with variables

Form documents are often prepared when the same document is sent to many persons. The message is basically the same for all persons, but the document is personalized by adding *variables* such as an address, name, or amount. The portion of the document that does not change for each person is called the *standard text.*

Procedures for processing form documents depends on whether you are using a typewriter or word processing software.

Current date
(V1- Letter address)
Dear (V2- First name)

Congratulations on your (V3- Semester, year) Graduation from Lexus University. Your educational experience has provided you with opportunities for gaining new insights both personally and professionally.

Your university experiences can continue by joining the Lexus Alumni Association. Alumni meetings and socials provide the following opportunities for you:

1. Networking--see former classmates and discuss ideas.

2. Enriching both your Personal and professional ~~enrichment~~ life--attend special interest seminars.

3. Contributing to Lexus' future--assist in recruitment of new students, participate in fundraising drives, and make suggestions to the President's Advisory Council.

Don't be left out, (V2- first name)! Complete and return the enclosed form to receive additional information about becoming a Lexus Alumni member.

Sincerely yours
Yolanda Durand, President
Lexus Alumni Association

Drill 4
Build production skill

1 Key 1' writings (18 *gwam*) on the letter parts, arranging each line in correct format. Ignore top margin requirements.

2 Return 5 times between drills.

Reference: pages 72 and 78.

1 May 15, 19-- | Mr. Brad Babbett | 811 Wier Avenue, W. | Phoenix, AZ 83018-8183 | Dear Mr. Babbett

2 May 3, 19-- | Miss Lois J. Bruce | 913 Torch Hill Road | Columbus, GA 31904-4133 | Dear Miss Bruce

3 Sincerely yours | George S. Murger | Assistant Manager | xx | Enclosures: Warranty Deed | Invoice

4 Very cordially yours | Marvin J. Cecchetti, Jr. | Assistant to the Comptroller | xx | Enclosures

Drill 5
Reach for new goals

1 From the second or third column at the right, choose a goal 2-3 *gwam* higher than your best rate on either straight or statistical copy.

2 Take 1' writings on that sentence; try to finish it the number of times shown at the top of the goal list.

3 If you reach your goal, take 1' writings on the next line. If you don't reach your goal, use the preceding line.

	words	1' timing 6 times *gwam*	1' timing 5 times *gwam*
Did Dixie go to the city?	5	30	25
I paid $7 for 3 big maps.	5	30	25
Do they blame me for the goal?	6	36	30
The 2 men may enamel 17 oboes.	6	36	30
The auditor may handle the problem.	7	42	35
Did the 4 chaps focus the #75 lens?	7	42	35
She did vow to fight for the right name.	8	48	40
He paid 10 men to fix a pen for 3 ducks.	8	48	40
The girl may cycle down to the dormant field.	9	54	45
The 27 girls paid their $9 to go to the lake.	9	54	45
The ensign works with vigor to dismantle the auto.	10	60	50
Bob may work Problems 8 and 9; Sid did Problem 40.	10	60	50
The form may entitle a visitor to pay for such a kayak.	11	66	55
They kept 7 panels and 48 ivory emblems for 29 chapels.	11	66	55

| 1 | 2 | 3 | 4 | 5 | 6 | 7 | 8 | 9 | 10 | 11 |

Drill 6
Build accuracy with figures

Choose a line (they get progressively more difficult) and key that line for one minute. The number of correct groups is approximately your correct *gwam.*

1849 3729 4016 4039 1616 2758 4820 3736 5656 4910 2838 5057

2393 3562 7050 9047 4293 5461 7856 6719 1504 3582 8037 9618

1518 6965 1420 6892 5247 7682 4310 8073 4349 7982 5317 9063

4132 8709 5143 6708 5132 9067 8690 4132 7087 4235 8086 1452

Document 16
Reference copy of standard paragraphs

1 Center the company name **DATA SERVICES UNLIMITED** 1" from top.

2 Key the paragraphs at the right SS; key the filenames above each paragraph.

MicroAssistant: Follow the directions above.

wp If your software can combine stored files on the screen:

1 Key each paragraph separately and save it using the filename given.

2 Create the reference copy by keying the title and then retrieving each file. Above each paragraph, key the appropriate filename.

Form Document Review

Documents built from form paragraphs

Form letters or memos may also be built from a group of frequently used paragraphs. Appropriate paragraphs can then be selected and merged to construct a complete document. A reference copy of the standard paragraphs is prepared for the originator(s) of form letters and memos. Form paragraphs may also contain variables (see P5 below).

To create a document from form paragraphs, the operator keys the paragraphs that have been selected or retrieves them if they have been saved. Reference initials and other appropriate document parts are added.

P1

Thank you for inquiring about the services that Data Services Unlimited offers your business. Data Services is an information processing service that can help you with almost any project requiring data entry and processing or media conversion.

P2

Our competent, well-trained staff of data-entry and data processing specialists uses state-of-the-art automated equipment, assuring you both top-quality output and minimum turnarounds. On your one-time projects, we would first conduct a "key test." Thus, you would see a sample of the product we would deliver. Also, you could decide whether the expected turnaround and estimated cost, determined on the basis of the test, would be satisfactory. A price list for "standard" or repeat projects is enclosed.

P3

The conversion capabilities available to you go well beyond keying or scanning hard copy to disk or tape. If you need to convert from tape to tape, tape to disk, or disk to disk, Data Services can do it. In addition, your 5 1/4" floppies can be converted to 3 1/2" disks; and disks configured for the most common operating systems can be reconfigured for the other systems. We would do a test conversion of your media, enabling us to assess quality and estimate costs of the conversion.

P4

All preliminary tests (for data-entry and media conversion projects) are performed without charge, and we urge you to take advantage of this free service. Later you likely will agree that the preproject tests are the key to your satisfaction with our products and prices.

P5

We would be happy to discuss your next project with you, *(addressee's title and last name)*. Call me at 304-555-DATA or send a sample of your work for a free test and estimate.

Skill-Building Workshop 2

MicroAssistant: To access Skill-Building Workshop 2, key **S2** from the Main menu.

Default margins or 65-space line

Drill 1

Compare skill sentences

1 Take a 1' writing on line 1; determine *gwam* and use this score for your goal as you take two 1' writings each on lines 2 and 3.

2 Take a 1' writing on line 4; determine *gwam* and use this score for your goal as you take two 1' writings each on lines 5 and 6.

1 Did the visitor on the bicycle signal and turn to the right?
2 The 17 girls kept 30 bushels of kale and 29 bushels of yams.
3 *The hen and a lamb roam down the field of rocks to the corn.*
4 The penalty she had to pay for the bogus audit is a problem.
5 Do 10 ducks, 46 fish, and 38 hams for the big island ritual.
6 *We got the usual quantity of shamrocks for Pamela to handle.*

| 1 | 2 | 3 | 4 | 5 | 6 | 7 | 8 | 9 | 10 | 11 | 12 |

Drill 2

Review number and symbol reaches

each line twice SS; DS between 2-line groups; repeat difficult lines

1 The inn opened at 6789 Brentt; rooms are $45 (May 12 to July 30).
2 I paid $1.56 for 2% milk and $97 for 48 rolls of film on June 30.
3 Order #4567-0 (dated 2/18) was shipped on May 30 to Spah & Erven.
4 Send Check #3589 for $1,460--dated the 27th--to O'Neil & Company.
5 Ann's 7% note (dated May 13) was just paid with a check for $285.
6 Send to The Maxi-Tech Co., 3489 D Drive, our Bill #10 for $25.67.
7 I wrote "Serial #1830/27"; I should have written "Serial #246/9."

| 1 | 2 | 3 | 4 | 5 | 6 | 7 | 8 | 9 | 10 | 11 | 12 | 13 |

Drill 3

Improve keying techniques

concentrate on each word as you key it; key each group twice; DS between 3-line groups

direct reaches

1 runny cedar carver brunt numbs humps dunce mummy arbor sects hymn
2 Irvyn jumped over a clump of green grass; he broke my brown pump.
3 My uncle Cedric carved a number of brown cedar mules in December.

adjacent reaches

4 trios where alert point buyer spore milk sands sagas treads ports
5 There were three points in Porter's talk on the ports of Denmark.
6 Has Bert Welker prepared loin of pork as her dinner on Wednesday?

double letters

7 glass sells adder offer room sleek upper errors inner pretty ebbs
8 The committee soon agreed that Bess's green wool dress looks odd.
9 Three sweet little moppets stood happily on a green grassy knoll.

| 1 | 2 | 3 | 4 | 5 | 6 | 7 | 8 | 9 | 10 | 11 | 12 | 13 |

Office Concierge Simulation (continued)

Procedures Manual, Part 2

Outlines, Reports, and Tables
(Lessons 131-136)

Document 17
Outline

1 Key the outline according to the guidelines; use standard top margin; bold main heading.

2 Label the spacing between outline parts.

3 Number pages in Section 26 beginning with page **2.1**.

Use the automatic outline feature.

```
                 GUIDELINES FOR KEYING OUTLINES
                                               DS
  I.  PLACEMENT
          DS
      A.  Standard Top Margin of 1.5" or Centered Vertically
      B.  Default 1" Side Margins or Set Margins to Accommo-
          date Average Line Length
                                  DS
 II.  DIVISION LEVELS
              DS
      A.  First-Level Topics
          1.  Labeled with Roman numerals
          2.  Keyed in all capitals
      B.  Second-Level Topics
          1.  Labeled with capital letters
          2.  Capitalize first letter in main words
      C.  Third- and Subsequent-Level Topics
          1.  Labeled with Arabic numerals
          2.  Capitalize first letter in the first word
                                                      DS
III.  LINE SPACING
            DS
      A.  Double-Space Below Title
      B.  Double-Space Above and Below First-Level Topics
      C.  Single-Space Second- and Subsequent-Level Topics
```

Document 18
Outline using Arabic numerals

1 Follow the guidelines given in Document 17, except use Arabic numerals for the first-level topics and lowercase letters for second-level topics.

2 Apply correct capitalization within the entries.

3 Label the spacing between outline parts.

ORDER PROCESSING PROCEDURES

1. NEW ORDERS
   a. Check to see that order is filled immediately
   b. Verify account number with address
   c. Verify credit screen
      i. Verify credit region
      ii. Verify credit status
   d. Review shipping method
   e. Verify price

2. CHANGE ORDERS
   a. Verify what is being changed
   b. Verify that form is filled out completely

3. ADD-ON ORDERS
   a. Order must be filled as a new order
   b. Mark line item for additional quantity

Drill 3

Review capitalization rules

1 Follow general format guides on page 90.

2 Set a tab 39 spaces from left margin for examples.

3 Study each line and its example from your printed copy.

CAPITALIZATION GUIDES

Capitalize

Specific persons or places:	She lives in Tudor Hall.
First words of sentences:	He had some good news.
Weekdays, months, holidays:	Friday, May 1, is May Day.
First words of direct quotes:	Dan shouted, "He's home."
Titles preceding personal names:	Dr. Iki phoned Lt. Moe.
Adjectives drawn from proper nouns:	Don likes Italian sausage.
Political/military organizations:	A Democrat has a Navy map.
Nouns followed by numbers:	Pack Order 7 in Bin 9.

Do not capitalize

Titles following a name:	Jan is our secretary.
Plurals of geographic designations:	I saw Ice and Swan lakes.
Compass points not part of a name:	Ride west to North Dakota.
Common nouns such as page or line followed by a number:	Copy the words on page 7.
Seasons (unless personified):	Next is fall, then spring.
Generic names of products:	He likes Flavorite coffee.
Commonly accepted derivatives:	I ordered french toast.

Drill 4

Apply capitalization rules

Provide capitalization as you key. Check your copy with Writing 12 on page 95 when you finish.

one stormy night last winter, just 29 days before christmas, I was driving my little bentley automobile to south ionia, a town about 75 miles away. i had been invited by major bill jellison, just mustered out of the u. s. marines, where i too had served 10 years as a captain, to see a new english play in the city center. the night was quite dark; snow had started lazily to fall. after going about 38 miles, i remembered that bill had said to me: "be sure to turn east at the corner of level and south essex roads. do not take a chance and turn west"; or, at least i thought that was what he said. so, I turned east on level road, route 46.

Document 19
Unbound business report with internal citations

1 Apply business report format: SS; block ¶s; DS between ¶s.

2 Bold headings; bold and underline side headings; DS above and below side headings.

3 Label the side headings and references and mark the spacing.

Spell out FTCS throughout

FAST-TRACK COMMUNICATIONS SYSTEM

Point-of-Sale Terminal

Introduction

DS The FTCS provides an interface to a computer host allowing for the centralized maintenance of the point-of-sales system files. There are 2 basic variants of the system: one is for use in a Systems Network Architecture (SNA) environment and the other is for use in a non-SNA environment using the Binary Synchronous Communications (BSC) protocol. "Both systems are intended to interface with the Basic Host Communications Software (BHCS) running on the host computer" (Cramer 1993, 25).

The first FTCS for use in the non-SNA environment was designed to use the AT bus based terminal controller board.

Major Components

The FTCS consists of three major components: the driver, the control task, and the Application Program.

The Driver is responsible for handling the Fast-Track protocol sequences. Statically defined mailboxes are used to pass message data between the Driver and Control Task, which is permanently resident in memory. The Control Task provides a queued interface to the application layer, therefore allowing the code to be placed in bank memory. The Application Program Interface module enables communications by sending data.

Communication Workshop 1

Format guides

1 1" side margins; 1.5" top margin.

2 Center title; DS; use bold as shown.

3 Proofread carefully; correct errors.

Drill 1
Review spacing skills

1 Set a tab 36 spaces from the left margin for the examples.

2 Key a spacing guide beginning at the left margin; tab; key the example.

3 Study each line and its example from your printed copy.

PUNCTUATION SPACING GUIDES

Space twice after	
A sentence period:	Jo ran. Peter walked alone.
A question mark:	Who is it? Someone called.
A colon (except in time):	The way to win: go, go, go.
An exclamation point:	Oh! It can't be!
Space once after	
An abbreviation period:	Mr. Coe met Adm. A. T. Brum.
A semicolon:	Meg met us; she visits daily.
A comma (except in numbers):	Rae, Lu, and I joined a team.
Do not space before or after	
A hyphen:	We saw a first-rate ballet.
A dash:	He--I mean Bo--left early.
A comma in large numbers:	Key $1,000,000 or $1 million.
A colon in time figures:	We closed at 5:30 p.m.
A period within an abbreviation:	At 3 p.m. the meeting begins.

Drill 2
Improve spelling skills

1 Set tabs 25 and 50 spaces from left margin.

2 Center the title.

3 Key the first word at the left margin; tab and key the word again; then tab and key it a third time without looking at the word.

4 Study the words that you often misspell.

FREQUENTLY MISSPELLED WORDS

installation	installation	installation
committee		
corporate		
employees		
immediately		
interest		
necessary		
opportunity		
personnel		
received		
services		

Document 19 (continued)

Communication Capabilities

The FTCS provides the communications support necessary to allow the transfer of messages between the Application Layer and the CBR host computer. "A point-to-point protocol is used for these communications, with the FTCS assuming initially the slave station role" (Hitch, 1994, 3).

The transparent text mode of operation is used enabling the transmission of binary data (Prescott 1994, 107). The FTCS uses the synchronous RS232-C port of the IBM Multi-protocol Adapter and an appropriate external synchronous modem to communicate at speeds up to 4800 bps. bits per second

REFERENCES

Cramer, Scott A. Communicating with the Host Computer. Madison, Wisconsin: University Press, 1993.

Hitch, Roberta L. "Installing Point-of-Sale Terminals." The Superstore Manager, January 11, 1994.

Prescott, David O. Linking the PS/2. Local Area Networks Atlanta, Georgoa: Occidental Press, Inc., 1994.

Document 20
Leftbound business report with endnotes

1 If your equipment does not permit keying a superscript above the line of writing, key it on the line of writing preceded and followed by a diagonal line.
. . . and distribution.[1]
. . . and distribution. /1/

2 Adjust the spacing below the main headings so that the entire report will fit on one page.
MicroAssistant: Key the reference numbers between diagonal lines.

The endnote feature formats reference numbers and corresponding endnotes.

ROUTING OF WORK ORDERS

Work order forms in "quad-packs" are used to process work orders. The four copies of work orders are each color coded for ease of distribution and filing.

A QUAD-PACK is a carbonless snap-out work order form in quadruplicate. It is color coded in white, yellow, blue, and pink for ease of processing and distribution.[1]

Distribution of copies among the departments of the organization is as follows:

Sales Department. Initiates the work order and routes all four copies to Scheduling Group. According to the company handbook, "A work order form must

(continued on next page)

40b 15'

COMMUNICATION

Key edited copy

Key as shown; make marked changes.

Time is money. In fact, I talked with a person last week to whom this is an heart-felt sentiment. She explained to me that if her salary were $10 an hour, waiting in line in a grocery store could theoretically add $2.50 to her grocery bill. She looses that much she says waiting at stoplights on her way to work and tardy friends cost her she figures $10 a week. Waiting in her doctors office cost her a fortune. To her, punctuality is a genuine virtue.

40c 13'

SKILL BUILDING

Compare skill sentences

1 Take a 1' writing on line 5 DS; determine *gwam* and use this score for your goal as you take two 1' writings on line 6 and then on line 7.

2 Repeat Step 1 for lines 8-10.

5 A cozy island Jan and Pamela visit is a land of enchantment.

6 A man got 62 of the fish, 26 cod and 36 sockeye, at Dock 10.

7 *An auditor may handle the fuel problems of the ancient city.*

8 Blame me for their penchant for the antique chair and panel.

9 The 20 girls kept 38 bushels of corn and 59 bushels of yams.

10 *It is a shame to make such emblems of authentic whale ivory.*

| 1 | 2 | 3 | 4 | 5 | 6 | 7 | 8 | 9 | 10 | 11 | 12 |

40d 15'

SKILL BUILDING

Build staying power

Take two 1' writings on each ¶, then two 3' writings on all ¶s; avoid pauses.

all letters/figures

	gwam 1'	3'	
Julia had a garden near her house at 4728 Western. She gave	12	4	35
it expert care--not one single plant ever went without its water	25	8	39
or fertilizer. And due to all this attention, nature was kind; a	38	12	43
bit of new growth became evident each day.	47	15	46
Now, Julia knew that she had several tomatoes here, 9 squash	12	19	50
over there, and 36 limas on down the line. What she did not know	25	23	54
was that two small beady eyes were also looking over her garden;	38	27	58
and at 5:10 that evening, some brown fur sat down to dinner.	50	31	62

gwam 1' | 1 | 2 | 3 | 4 | 5 | 6 | 7 | 8 | 9 | 10 | 11 | 12 | 13 |
3' | 1 | 2 | 3 | 4 | 5 |

Document 20 (continued)

accompany all requests for work. Work received without the work order form must be returned to the Sales Department."[2]

Scheduling Group. Logs in the work order and routes white and pink copies to Production Department, yellow copy to Shipping Department, and blue copy to Accounting Department.

Production Department. Receives white and pink copies of work order from Scheduling Group; signs white copy after final product inspection and routes white copy to Shipping Department with the invoice and bill of lading; attaches pink copy of work order to product and routes to Quality Assurance Group.

Shipping Department. Receives yellow copy of work order from Scheduling Group and sets shipping date(s) for listed products; routes yellow copy to the Quality Assurance Group.

Accounting Department. Receives blue copy of work order from Scheduling Group, white and yellow copies from Shipping, and pink copy from Production; reassembles QUAD-PACK and sends work order with "paid" invoice to IPD File.

ENDNOTES

[1] Frank C. Eastman, Managing the Automated Office Environment (Topeka: Boswell Press, Inc.), p. 36.

[2] Procedures Manual and Employee Handbook. Data Services Unlimited (January 1993), p. 19.

39d 8'

COMMUNICATION

Edit as you key

DS; correct as marked

Someone has said, "you are what you eat." the speaker did not mean to imply that fast food make fast people, or that a hearty meal makes a person heart, or even that good food manes a perso good. On the other hand, though, a health full diet does indeed make person healthier; and good health is one of the most often over looked treasures within human existance.

39e 15'

SKILL BUILDING

Reach for new goals

1 Key a 1' timing; note *gwam*.

2 Add 4 *gwam* to this rate. Mark your ½' and 1' goals in the copy.

3 Take three 1' timings; try to reach your goals as your instructor calls ½' guides.

4 Take two 3' timings. Use Step 1 *gwam* as your goal.

LA all letters

	gwam 3'	
. 4 . 8 . 12		
So now you are operating a keyboard. And don't you find it	4	38
. 16 . 20 . 24		
amazing that your fingers, working with very little visual help,	8	43
. 28 . 32 . 36 .		
move easily and quickly from one key to the next, helping you to	13	47
40 . 44 . 48 .		
change words into ideas and sentences. You just decide what you	17	51
52 . 56 . 60 . 64		
want to say and the format in which you want to say it, and your	21	56
. 68 . 72 . 76		
keyboard will carry out your order exactly as you enter it. One	26	60
. 80 . 84 . 88 .		
operator said lately that she sometimes wonders just who is most	30	64
92 . 96 . 100 .		
responsible for the completed product--the person or the machine.	34	69

gwam 3' | 1 | 2 | 3 | 4 | 5 |

40 Skill Building

Skill-Building Warmup

40a 7'

each line 2 times SS; repeat as time permits

alphabet 1 When Jorg moves away, quickly place five-dozen gloves in the box.

figures 2 Flight 372 leaves at 10:46 a.m. and arrives in Omaha at 9:58 p.m.

direct reaches 3 I obtain unusual services from a number of celebrated decorators.

easy 4 She may sign an authentic name and title to amend this endowment.

| 1 | 2 | 3 | 4 | 5 | 6 | 7 | 8 | 9 | 10 | 11 | 12 | 13 |

Document 21
Preapplication drill

Read "Footnotes." Then apply the steps for keying footnotes in the drill, "Organizational Subsystems." This document will not be placed in the Procedures Manual. Do not add a footer.

wp The footnote function formats footnotes automatically.

Footnotes

Footnotes are often used in academic reports to document sources that have been quoted or closely paraphrased. A reference number, keyed immediately after the quoted material, directs the reader to the corresponding footnote at the bottom of the same page.

Separate the text from the footnote by a DS and a 1.5" divider line. If the footnote is on a partially filled page, place the footnote at the bottom of the page. DS below the divider line. Indent the first line of the footnote 5 spaces; SS the footnote; DS between footnotes.

Footnote placement tips

1 Place a pencil mark 1" above the bottom edge of the paper to indicate the bottom margin.

2 As you key the report, save 3 lines for each footnote by placing another pencil mark .5" above the previous mark each time you key a reference number.

3 Continue keying until you reach the first pencil mark (or if the page is short, strike Return until the pencil mark is displayed).

ORGANIZATIONAL SUBSYSTEMS

What are the boundaries within which an administrative reform is to be confined ? This question has many ramifications because public administration is a complex system; it is actually a subsystem of a larger system such as a political system and the societal system as a whole.

Ricter stresses the importance of realizing that all organizations are subsystems of a larger system.[1] Rholm seems to support this theory in his statement: "Educational changes engage all subsystems that together comprise complex educational organizations."[2]

---

[1]Joel Ricter, "Policies for Reform," Changing with Society (New York: New Press, 1992), 43.

[2]Laurel Rholm, Educational Reform (Seattle: Bay Press, 1991), 57.

ORGANIZATIONAL SUBSYSTEMS

What are the boundaries within which an administrative reform is to be confined? This question has many ramifications because public administration is a complex system; it is actually a subsystem of a larger system such as a political system and the societal system as a whole.

Ricter stresses the importance of realizing that all organizations are subsystems of a larger system.[1] Rholm seeems to support this theory in his statement: "Educational changes engage all subsystems that together comprise complex educational organizations."[2]

[1]Joel Ricter, "Policies for Reform," Changing with Society (New York: New Press, 1992), 43.

[2]Laurel Rholm, Educational Reform (Seattle: Bay Press, 1991), 57.

Learning goals:
1 To improve keystroking.
2 To gain skill in keying numbers and symbols.
3 To improve ability to work with script and rough-draft copy.

Formatting guides:
1 Default or 65 space line.
2 Single-space drills; double-space ¶ writings.
3 5-space ¶ indention for writings and all DS copy.

39a 7'

Skill-building warmup

each line 2 times SS; DS between 2-line groups; take a 1' writing on line 4 as time permits

alphabet 1 Which oval jet-black onyx ring blazed on the queen's prim finger?
figures 2 Cy will be 19 on May 4; Jo, 27 on May 6 or 8; Mike, 30 on June 5.
adjacent reaches 3 We acquire few rewards for walking short treks to Union Terminal.
easy 4 To augment and enrich the visual signal, I turn the right handle.

| 1 | 2 | 3 | 4 | 5 | 6 | 7 | 8 | 9 | 10 | 11 | 12 | 13 |

39b 10'

SKILL BUILDING

Improve keystroking technique

fingers curved, hands quiet; each line twice as shown

1st finger
5 My 456 heavy brown jugs have nothing in them; fill them by May 7.
6 The 57 bins are numbered 1 to 57; Bins 5, 6, 45, and 57 are full.

2d finger
7 Ed decided to crate 38 pieces of cedar decking from the old dock.
8 Mike, who was 38 in December, likes a piece of ice in cold cider.

3d/4th finger
9 Polly made 29 points on the quiz; Wex, 10 points. Did they pass?
10 Sally saw Ezra pass 200 pizza pans to Sean, who fixed 10 of them.

| 1 | 2 | 3 | 4 | 5 | 6 | 7 | 8 | 9 | 10 | 11 | 12 | 13 |

39c 10'

SKILL BUILDING

Practice figures and symbols

each line 2 times SS, then DS; work for smooth, fluid keying

" %
11 Use "percent," not "%," for most writing. Use "%" to save space.
\# /
12 On 7/3, fill Hoppers #10/1, #3/7, and #19/9 each with #27 gravel.
$ -
13 My son-in-law gets up-to-date $35-value lamps for $27, saving $8.
\# $
14 Policies #7301 and #8448 for $50,000 and $20,000 run for 4 years.
% -
15 She--Ms. Borek--said we lost "9%, 7%, 5%, and 3%" on those deals.
& /
16 Bort & Lee sold 2 tons on 6/9 and 6/13; J & J sold 9 tons on 7/5.
$ ( )
17 Serial #15 (40) marks his (Ron's) motor (this is not Model #206).
\# /
18 See reference to Invoice #14/910; the date, 8/27; the file, #359.

| 1 | 2 | 3 | 4 | 5 | 6 | 7 | 8 | 9 | 10 | 11 | 12 | 13 |

Document 22
Unbound report with footnotes

1 DS; indent ¶s. Check for errors that may have been overlooked.
2 Replace each occurrence of **Techne-100** with **Carnegie**.
3 Number the footer starting with page **2.6**.

Use the footnote feature.

Consumer Information Services
in Techne-100 Library

Business and Economic students and staff, last year expressed a need for a Business school library that was equipped with on-line computer research capabilities as well as personal enrichment readings. The administration allocated money for building the Techne-100 Library according to recommendations made by the Irving Report: ". . . erection of a business school library with on-line research capabilities is greatly needed for a college of this size."[1]

Student and Staff Survey

In recent months the library staff at Techne-100 has surveyed students and staff to determine preferences and patterns in their use of various public sources of information. The results of the survey then were used to expand and update the list of consumer publications and data services to which the school library subscribes.

The results of our survey are consistent with those conducted on a nationwide basis Schmidt Research Institute recently published their findings as follows:

In times of a recession or a sluggish economy, readers switch from purchasing hobby and travel publications to purchasing publications that offer cosumer purchasing tips and management advice.[2]

Not surprisingly respondents made frequent use of magazines that rate products (e.g. Consumer Digest) or offer money management advice (e.g INVESTOR'S AGE). The SHOPPER'S INFORMATION REPORT, containing a list of booklets issued (often free) by thirty government agencies, is also regarded by the survey participants as an excellent source of valid information. All of the free booklets listed in the catalog will be on file in the school library.

On-Line Computer Resources

Lists of 200 consumer information sources and nearly 75 health and safety information sources are now available for student and staff use in the Techne-100 Library. Methods for alerting students and staff of these sources and helping them use them should be planned by library staff.

---

[1] Theresa L. Schrauth, "Performance Study Report" (Laguna Hills, California: Irving Consultants and Associates, June 1993), 28.

[2] David C. Schmidt, "Readers Reflect the Times," Consumer Reseach Quarterly (February 1994), 69.

Document 1
Business letter
block format (average length); envelope

words

Current date | AMASTA Company, Inc. | 902 Greenridge Drive | Reno, NV 13
69505-5552 | Ladies and Gentlemen 19

We sell your video cassettes and have since you introduced them. Follow- 33
ing instructions in your recent flyer, we tell customers who buy your Super 48
D video cassettes to return to you the coupon we give them; and you will 63
refund $1 for each cassette. 69

Several of our customers now tell us they are unable to follow the direc- 83
tions on the coupon. They explain, and we further corroborate, that there 98
is no company logo on the box to return to you as requested. We are not 113
sure how to handle our unhappy customers. 121

What steps should we take? A copy of the coupon is enclosed, as is a 135
Super D container. Please read the coupon, examine the box, and then let 150
me know your plans for extricating us from this problem. 161

Sincerely | John J. Long | Sales Manager | xx | Enc. 2 170

Document 2
Business letter
modified block format (average length); envelope

Current date | Mr. John J. Long | Sales Manager | The Record Store | 12
9822 Trevor Avenue | Anaheim, CA 92805-5885 | Dear Mr. Long 23

With your letter came our turn to be perplexed, and we apologize. When 37
we had our refund coupons printed, we had just completed a total 50
redesign program for our product boxes. We had detachable logos put on 64
the outside of boxes, from which each could be peeled and placed on a 78
coupon. 80

We had not anticipated that our distributors would use back inventories 94
with our promotion. The cassettes you sold were not packaged in our 108
new boxes; therefore, there were no logos on them. 118

I'm sorry you or your customers were inconvenienced. In the future, 132
simply ask your customers to send us their sales slips; and we will honor 147
them with refunds until your supply of older containers is depleted. 161

Sincerely yours | Bruna Wertz | Sales and Promotions Dept. | BW:xx 173

Document 3
Interoffice memo
plain paper; bold headings

TO: Brenda Hull | **FROM:** Bruna Wertz | **DATE:** Current | **SUBJECT:** 13
Current Promotion 16

We have a problem, Brenda. I have learned that some of our distributors 31
are using older stock with our latest promotion. As you know, our older 46
boxes have no logos; but our refund plan asks for them. 57

Nothing can be done now to rectify the situation. I believe you will agree, 72
however, that we must honor those coupons that arrive without logos. 86
There should not be many of them. Please alert your staff. 98

xx 98

Document 23
Table with blocked column heads

1 Center the table horizontally and vertically.

2 Neatly label the table parts and spacing between the parts.

 Use the table feature.

Table Format Review

Review formatting guides for tables.
- ✓ Bold main heading.
- ✓ Bold and underline column headings.
- ✓ DS table data unless the table is long (20 or more total lines).
- ✓ Suggested intercolumn spaces:
  2-columns: 10 spaces
  3-columns: 6-8 spaces
  4-columns: 4 spaces
- ✓ Center tables vertically or use a standard top margin (1.5").

Televideo Equipment, Inc. - all caps and center

19-- Sales Staff - initial caps and center

Area	Representative	Sales
North East	Solara, Thomas	87,000
East	Quinlan, Linda	178,000
Mid-west	Rebecca Rolands	92,000
South	Ashmere, Grayson	125,00
Plain	Tyrell, Nicole	66,000
North West	Sequoia, ~~Lin~~ Lynn	94,000
West	Simpson, Roger	249,000

Document 24
Table with centered column heads

Refer to Reference Guide for help in centering column heads.

1 Center table horizontally and vertically.

2 Determine the total enrollment for the various schools in Column 4. Determine final total for Columns 2, 3, and 4.

PACIFIC COAST UNIVERSITY
Graduating Class of 19--

School	Male Graduates	Female Graduates	Total
Business	428	320	748
Communications	31	46	✓
Engineering	179	86	✓
Agriculture	17	12	✓
Total	✓	✓	✓

DS

______ DS

Schools with fewer than ten graduates are not listed.

38 Measurement

Skill-Building Warmup

38a 7'

each line 2 times SS; DS between 2-line groups

alphabet 1	Two exit signs jut quietly above the beams of a razed skyscraper.
figures 2	At 7 a.m., I open Rooms 18, 29, and 30; I lock Rooms 4, 5, and 6.
direct reaches 3	I obtain many junk pieces dumped by Marvyn at my service centers.
easy 4	The town may blame Keith for the auditory problems in the chapel.

1 | 2 | 3 | 4 | 5 | 6 | 7 | 8 | 9 | 10 | 11 | 12 | 13

38b 10'

SKILL BUILDING

Measure straight-copy skill

Take two 3' writings; key fluently, confidently; determine *gwam*; proofread; count errors.

LA all letters

	gwam 3'	
Whether or not a new company will be a success will depend	4	62
on how well it fits into our economic system. Due to the demands	8	66
of competition, only a company that is organized to survive will	13	71
likely ever get to be among the best. Financial success, the	17	75
reason why most companies exist, rests on some unique ideas that	21	79
are put in place by a management team that has stated goals in	25	83
mind and the good judgment to recognize how those goals can best	30	88
be reached.	31	89
It is in this way that our business system tries to assure	34	92
us that, if a business is to survive, it must serve people in the	39	97
way they want to be served. Such a company will have managed to	43	101
combine some admirable product with a low price and the best ser-	47	106
vice--all in a place that is convenient for buyers. With no	52	110
intrusion from outside forces, the buyer and the seller benefit	56	114
both themselves and the economy.	58	116

gwam 3' | 1 | 2 | 3 | 4 | 5 |

38c 33'

FORMATTING

Measurement: basic business correspondence

(LM pp. S27-S29) or 4 plain sheets

Time schedule

Planning time	3'
Timed production	25'
Final check; proofread; determine *g-pram*	5'

1 Organize your supplies.

2 On the signal to begin, key the documents in sequence; use the current date and your reference initials.

3 Repeat Document 1 if time allows.

4 Proofread all documents; count errors; determine *g-pram*.

$g\text{-}pram = \frac{\text{total words keyed}}{25'}$

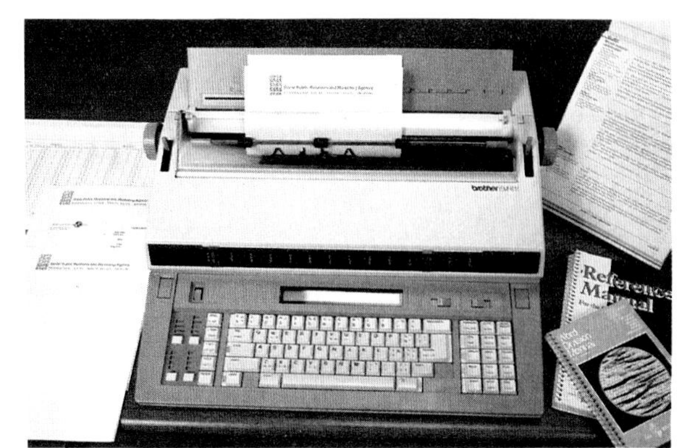

Document 25
Ruled table

1 Use standard top margin. Center column heads.

2 Neatly label the spacing between the table parts.

PRINCETON STORES

Extended Review Function

Description	Number	Location	Support
Scan Override Number	90	3863	487
Discounts Exemption Tax	8432	36	923
Void Transaction	17	2754	N/A
Print Messages	54	4216	18

Document 26
Table with leaders

1 Standard top margin; 1" side margins; leave 4 spaces between Columns 2 and 3 because they are closely related.

2 Neatly label the spacing between the table parts.

Use leader tabs and double underscore features.

KEY STONE REAL ESTATE INVESTORS FUND
CONSOLIDATED STATEMENTS OF OPERATIONS

For the Year Ended September 30, 1994 and the Period From December 4, 1992 (commencement of operations to September 30, 1993)

	1994	1993
Revenue:		
Rents	$16,402	$4,965
reimbursements	2,008	385
Interest	2,005	2,764
Parking	817	171
TOTAL	$21,232	$8,285
OPERATE EXPENSES:		
Interest	8,684	2,695
Real property taxs	2,032	584
Direct services	1,776	571
Property management	1,187	365
General and administrative	637	373
Janitorial services and supplies . . .	630	229
Insurance	519	85
Repairs & maintenance	453	125
Computer services	78	74
Depresheation and amortization . . .	7,702	2,484
TOTAL OPERATING EXPENSES . . .	26,185	8,461
NET LOSS	(4,953)	(176)

More about formats

When memos are sent to more than one person, list their names after **TO:** in alphabetical order or in order of rank. If there are more than three names, list them vertically at the end of the memo under Distribution list.

37c 22'

FORMATTING

Interoffice memorandums

Document 1

Key the memo; bold headings; correct errors.

		words
TO:	John J. Lo DS	3
FROM:	Rosetta Kunzel	7
DATE:	Current	11
SUBJECT:	ZIP Code Information DS	17

Please stress information about ZIP Code use 26
when you meet with our office staff next Fri- 35
day: The ZIP Code follows the city and state 45
on the same line one space after the approved 54
two-letter state abbreviation. Encourage full 63
use of 9-digit ZIP Codes on our mail. 71

Also, be sure everyone has a copy of the 81
approved two-letter state abbreviations and the 91
USPS booklet ADDRESSING FOR AUTOMATION. 99
DS

xx 99

Document 2

Key the three *TO* names on one line. Correct errors.

		words
TO:	Hollis Carver, Maxine Findlay, and	8
	Dorcas Washington	12
FROM:	T. R. McRaimond	16
DATE:	Current	20
SUBJECT:	Gym Benefits	24

As part of a special contract with the propri- 33
etors of HEALTH GLOW, Inc., our employees 41
can now use without charge the HEALTH GLOW 50
gym facilities at 27 Boone Drive each Tuesday 59
and Thursday afternoon after 4 p.m. 66

This privilege is an extension of the better- 75
health policy this company adopted last Janu- 84
ary. You will receive more information as it 93
becomes available. 97

xx 97

37d 11'

COMMUNI

Compose as you key

(plain sheet)

Refer to Document 2 above. Assume you are Hollis Carver or Maxine Findlay. Compose a memo to T. R. McRaimond. State in one or two paragraphs how you think your department members will react to the HEALTH GLOW program.

Office Concierge Simulation (continued)

Procedures Manual, Part 3

Administrative Documents
(Lessons 137-141)

Document 27
Minutes in traditional format

1 Use 1" top and side (or default) margins; SS.

2 Bold side headings and underline paragraph headings.

3 Begin the page numbering for documents in this part with **3.1**.

MINUTES OF THE LAKEVIEW COMMUNITY COLLEGE
ACADEMIC SENATE MEETING

November 7, 19--

Check spelling & number expression carefully.

QS

Time and Place

The 6th meeting of the Lakeview Community College Academic Senate was called to order by President Pat Gardner at 3:00 p.m. in the Wilson Conference Room.

Approval of Minutes

~~It was moved and seconded to~~ were approve the minutes of the October 4, 19-- meeting as amended to include the Senate's meeting dates for this school year.

Insert (A)

Committee Reports

The Faculty Affairs Committee presented recommendations ~~and suggestions on possible~~ for policy changes and preventive measures that need to be enforced to ensure faculty and staff safety. The Senators will review the written materials and discuss the issues ~~presented~~ with there divisions. ~~Further discussion~~ This topic will be on the agenda for our next meeting.

Old Business

Instructional Quality Assessment. The Instructional Quality Assessment (IQA) will be an on-going process in which each program will be reviewed ~~for~~ every four years to ~~support and maintain~~ assure quality educational programs. The Senate vote unamiously to support the goals and ~~urge active~~ participation in the process of IQA.

MINUTES OF THE LAKEVIEW COMMUNITY COLLEGE
ACADEMIC SENATE MEETING
November 7, 19--

Time and Place

The sixth meeting of the Lakeview Community College Academic Senate was called to order by President Pat Gardner at 3 p.m. in the Wilson Conference Room.

Approval of Minutes

The minutes of the October 4, 19-- meeting were approved as amended to include the Senate's meeting dates for this school year.

President's Report

Pat Gardner reported that Michael Tanaka has been appointed chair of the Campus Safety Committee.

Committee Reports

The Faculty Affairs Committee presented recommendations for policy changes and preventive measures that need to be enforced to ensure faculty and staff safety. The senators will review the written materials and discuss the issues with their divisions. This topic will be on the agenda for our next meeting.

Old Business

Instructional Quality Assessment. The Instructional Quality Assessment (IQA) will be an on-going process in which each program will be reviewed every four years to assure quality educational programs. The Senate voted unanimously to support the goals and participate in the process of IQA.

Ronald Taylor resolution. A resolution was presented to honor Dr. Ronald Taylor for 27 years of service to the district.

New Business

Interdisciplinary dining area. Dee Williams presented the idea of a dining area to be shared by all faculty members. She felt that such an area would promote communication among faculty and job satisfaction.

The Senators suggested that the college's Culinary Arts dining area might serve this purpose. Robert Inowe recommended that the

MINUTES IN TRADITIONAL FORMAT 3.1

Document 2
Key the memorandum, using bold mode for headings; proofread and correct errors.

words

TO: Tyrone A. Bledsoe, Production 6
DS
FROM: Kim Bressuyt, Human Resources 12

DATE: Current 15

SUBJECT: Vacation Time and Pay 19
DS
When an employee's vacation coincides with a national holiday, the 32
employee will receive one additional day added to the scheduled vaca- 46
tion time. The maximum number of employees who may schedule a 59
vacation during a particular holiday period will be based upon the 72
production schedule set for the period. 80

Employees may pick up vacation pay on the last payday before the 93
scheduled vacation time. Any other adjustment to an employee's sched- 107
uled vacation must be approved by the department manager at least one 121
month prior to the month in which the vacation falls. 132

xx 132

37 Review Standard Memo

Skill-Building Warmup

37a 7'
each line 2 times SS; DS between 2-line groups

alphabet 1 The explorer questioned Jack's amazing story about the lava flow.

fig/sym 2 I cashed Cartek & Bunter's $2,679 check (Check #3480) on June 15.

adjacent reaches 3 As Louis said, few questioned the points asserted by the porters.

easy 4 The eighty firms may pay for a formal audit of their field works.

1 | 2 | 3 | 4 | 5 | 6 | 7 | 8 | 9 | 10 | 11 | 12 | 13

37b 10'

SKILL BUILDING

Build staying power
Take two 3' writings.

all letters

	gwam 1'	3'	
When you write, how does the result portray you? Some of us	12	4	38
seem to take on some unique personality when we write. We forget	25	8	42
writing is just another way of talking, and what we write may	38	13	47
project an image that is not natural. Some writers, on the other	51	17	51
hand, try to humanize what they write so that it extends genuine	64	22	56
warmth and makes one want to read it. Apparently, correct format	77	26	60
and language, common sense, and some idea that a writer is still	90	30	64
among the living can add up to be very fine writing.	101	34	68

gwam 1' | 1 | 2 | 3 | 4 | 5 | 6 | 7 | 8 | 9 | 10 | 11 | 12 | 13 |
3' | 1 | 2 | 3 | 4 | 5 |

Document 27 (continued)

Ronald Taylor Resolution. A ~~Senate~~ resolution was presented to honor Dr. Ronald Taylor for 27 years of service to the district. ~~was presented to the Senators. It was moved and seconded to present the resolution of appreciation and recognition to Ronald Taylor.~~

New Business

Interdisciplinary Dining Area. Dee Williams presented the idea of a dining area to be shared by all faculty members. She felt that such an area would promote communication among faculty ~~growth~~ and job satisfaction.

The senators suggested that the college's Culinary Arts Dining Area might serve this purpose. Robert Inowe ~~It has been suggested~~ recommended that the Senate begin the process by inviting faculty to an open forum for lunch. Mr. ~~Robert~~ Inowe will ~~offered to~~ chair a committee for implementing the first luncheon.

President's Report (A)

Pat Gardner reported ~~reprts~~ that Michael Tanaka has been appointed chair of the Campus Safety Committee.

Adjournment

The meeting was adjourned at 5:15 p.m.

Center point

QS > Respectfully submitted

Roger McKraig

Gender Equity Statement

Ross Nortin suggested that the college catalog and other appropriate publications contain a gender equity statement. This suggestion will be researched before the next meeting.

Document 28
Action minutes

1 Generate action minutes using the paragraphs under "President's Report," "Committee Reports," and "Gender Equity Statement" in Document 27. Do not include the headings for these paragraphs.

2 Key the heading

LAKEVIEW COMMUNITY COLLEGE
ACADEMIC SENATE MEETING
November 7, 19--
DS
Action Minutes
QS

3 Add the following:

Presiding: Pat Gardner
DS
Participants: Carla Alburto, Keena Cory, Robert Inowe, Roger McKraig, Dee Williams, and Paul Yee

wp Use the copy feature to duplicate paragraphs from Document 27 to Document 28.

LAKEVIEW COMMUNITY COLLEGE
ACADEMIC SENATE MEETING
November 7, 19--

Action Minutes
QS

Presiding: Pat Gardner

Participants: Carla Alburto, Keena Cory, Robert Inowe, Roger McKraig, Dee Williams, and Paul Yee

Pat Gardner reported that Michael Tanaka has been appointed chair of the Campus Safety Committee.

The Faculty Affairs Committee presented recommendations for policy changes and preventive measures that need to be enforced to ensure faculty and staff safety. The senators will review the written materials and discuss the issues with their divisions. This topic will be on the agenda for our next meeting.

Ross Nortin suggested that the college catalog and other appropriate publications contain a gender equity statement. This suggestion will be researched before the next meeting.

ACTION MINUTES 3.3

36d 23'

FORMATTING

Interoffice memos

Document 1

1 Read "Interoffice memos"; then study the memorandum below.

2 Key the memo, using bold mode for form headings.

3 Take three 1' writings on opening lines and ¶1. Do not use the bold mode for timings.

Document 2 is on the next page.

Interoffice memos

Not all business correspondence is "outside mail." Mail is often sent between offices within an organization in the form of interoffice memorandums.

In this section, you will learn one acceptable memo format. See the Reference Guide for an example of a simplified memo format.

Memos are sent in plain envelopes or in interoffice envelopes, which can be reused several times. The receiver's name and department are included on the outside of the envelope. "Confidential" tabs may be attached to seal the envelope when appropriate.

Format: Interoffice memos may be formatted on memohead, plain paper, or printed forms. Follow these guides when using plain paper or memohead stationery:

1 Use 1" side margins and 1.5" top margin (or begin a DS below the memohead).

2 Set a tab 10 spaces from the left margin to accommodate the longest line in the headings (**SUBJECT:** plus two spaces).

3 Key the form headings in bold. The recipient's and sender's personal and/or official titles are optional.

4 DS headings and between ¶s; SS body.

5 Include reference initials and enclosure notations when appropriate.

Set tab 10 spaces from margin

gwam 1'

TO: Manuel E. Muni **1.5" (line 10)** 3

DS

FROM: Brett Luxward 6

DATE: February 9, 19-- 9

SUBJECT: Company Newspaper 13

DS

1" This fall, the Human Resources Department begins a monthly news- 1" 26
paper that will report company announcements and activities 38
directly to each employee, bypassing much bulletin-board and 51
word-of-mouth communications. 56

The paper will contain personal news about employees, also. 65
Sports achievements, volunteer work, prizes won, and other news- 78
worthy activities will be included. 85

Please give this project some thought. Then report to me within 98
the next ten days the name of a person in your area willing (and 111
able) to accept responsibility for reporting such news to Denise 124
Byung, Human Resources Department, who will edit the paper. 136

DS

xx 136

Document 29
News release
(LM p. S17)

1 Use 1.5" top and 1" side margins; DS.

2 Edit copy for errors that may have been missed.

Formatting tips: Center # # # a DS below the last line of the news release to indicate the end.

For Release: Immediately
Contact Person: Brian Leonard

Vallejo, California, April 24, 19--:

Tele Transcom, a licensed satellite data-transfer company, is ~~pleased to announce the~~ addition ing ~~of~~ several new products and services to ~~the~~ its current line. ¶ Tele Transcom now provides image telephones that send and receive high resolution still pictures such as graphs and blue-prints to multiple receptor sites.

Now ~~you~~ customers can enhance their reports and presentations with state-of-the-art visual representations with several new Tele Transcom custom-design computer graphics systems.

Physicians and other health care personnel can now save crucial minutes and steps by using the newest medical image transfer services. Images are scanned and send to computers for display or storage.

For additional information, contact Carol Steves, Tele Transcom Broadcast (Assoc.) sp, (415) 555-0908 or Telex # 29574 TTC MK.

# # #

36 Standard Memo; Bold

Skill-Building Warmup

36a 7'

each line 2 times SS; DS between 2-line groups

alphabet 1 Perhaps Max realized jet flights can quickly whisk us to Bolivia.
fig/sym 2 Send 24 Solex Cubes, Catalog #95-0, price $6.78, before April 31.
1st finger 3 The boy of just 6 or 7 years of age ran through the mango groves.
easy 4 The auditor did sign the form and name me to chair a small panel.

| 1 | 2 | 3 | 4 | 5 | 6 | 7 | 8 | 9 | 10 | 11 | 12 | 13 |

36b 10'

SKILL BUILDING

Build staying power

Take a 1' writing on each ¶, then a 3' writing on all ¶s.

LA all letters

	gwam 1'	3'	
All of us can be impressed by stacks of completed work; yet,	12	4	39
we should recognize that quality is worth just as much praise, or	25	8	44
maybe even more, than the quantity of work done.	35	12	47
Logically, people expect a fair amount of work will be fin-	12	16	47
ished in a fair amount of time; still, common sense tells us a	24	20	55
bucket of right is better than two wagonloads of wrong.	35	24	59
The logic of the situation seems lucid enough: Do the job	12	27	63
once and do it right. If we plan with care and execute with	24	32	67
confidence, our work will have the quality it deserves.	35	35	70

gwam 1' | 1 | 2 | 3 | 4 | 5 | 6 | 7 | 8 | 9 | 10 | 11 | 12 | 13 |
3' | 1 | 2 | 3 | 4 | 5 |

36c 10'

FORMATTING

Bold mode

1 Set 1" margins; set a tab 10 spaces from left margin; DS.

2 Do Drill 1; if your equipment will bold existing text, do Drill 2 also.

Bold mode

The bold mode emphasizes text by printing characters darker than normal print. To key copy in bold:

Computers or electronic typewriters

1 Turn on the bold feature by striking the bold key or combination of keys.

2 Key the text.

3 Turn off the bold feature by striking the same key(s) used to turn it on.

MicroAssistant: Strike **Alt + B** to turn bold on and off.

Word processing programs also enable bold to be added to text that is already keyed. This is often done by blocking the existing text and then keying the bold command.

The proofreaders' mark for bold is a wavy underline (~~~~~).

Drill 1

1 Turn on bold; key **TO:**; turn off bold.

2 Tab and key the information at the tab stop. Repeat for each line of the heading.

TO: Arthur Abt

FROM: Bette Ashmyer

DATE: January 23, 19--

SUBJECT: Sick Leave Policy

Drill 2

1 Key text as shown:

No other vendor keeps you "in the know" like FIRST SOLUTIONS.

2 Revise the text as shown.

No other vendor keeps you "in the know" like FIRST SOLUTIONS.

Document 30
Itinerary

1" top and 1" side margins.

Formatting tips:

✓ SS entries; DS between entries.

✓ Space approximately five times after the dates and times.

✓ Bold each day, date, and destination to make it stand out.

ITINERARY FOR THOMAS STEVENS
October 22-25, 19--

Wednesday, October 22 Orange County to Detroit

1:30 p.m. Leave Orange County Airport, Central Airlines, Flight 710; dinner. Arrive O' Hare International Airport, Chicago, at 8:34 p.m.

9:15 p.m. Leave Chicago, Central Airlines, Flight 326; arrive Detroit Metropolitan Airport, Detroit, at 10:05 p.m. Mid-size car reserved at A-1 Car Rental (confirmation #5610). Reservations at Fairlane Cadillac Hotel (confirmation #71325) 900 Michigan Avenue, Dearborn, MI (313) 555-9711.

Thursday, October 23 Studebaker Motor Headquarters
710 Michigan Avenue
Dearborn, MI 48126-0710

9:00 a.m. Meeting with Mr. Walter Dodd, Manager, Process Engineering, regarding commitment to new model requirements.

10:00 a.m. Meet with Ms. Susana Lee, Head Engineer, Front-end Electrical, regarding wiring requirements.

11:30 a.m. Lunch with Joseph Mucholli, Project Coordinator.

2:00 p.m. Meet with all Coordinators on Ralleigh Project.

7:00 p.m. Dinner with Ms. Laura Mays, Vice President of Automotive Assembly Division.

Friday, October 24 Flint Assembly Plant, 42 Roland Avenue
Flint, MI 48532-0042 (313) 555-4325

9:00 a.m. Drive to Flint Assembly plant.

11:00 a.m. Lunch with Mr. Russ Nguyen, Plant Manager.

1:00 p.m. Plant tour.

2:30 p.m. Meet with Mr. Jon Tallaski, Plant Facilities Engineer, regarding retooling.

3:30 p.m. Meet with Ms. Janice Schmidt, Quality Control Specialist, about testing requirements for meeting federal environmental regulations.

Saturday, October 25 **Detroit to Orange County**

9:00 a.m. Leave Detroit Metropolitan Airport, Central Airlines, Flight 318; breakfast. Arrive Orange County Airport at 10:08 a.m.

Document 2

1 Key the letter at right (average) in modified block format. Add closing notations. Correct errors. If necessary, review proofreaders' marks on page 61.

2 Address an envelope with this return address:

METAL ENGINEERING INC
198 SANTA YNEZ DRIVE
LAS VEGAS NV 89105-9808

Document 3

Key Document 2 again with these changes:

1 Address the letter to:

Mr. Charles B. Onehawk
139 Via Cordoniz
Santa Barbara, CA 93105-0319

2 Use an appropriate salutation.

3 Omit the final paragraph.

words

Current date 3

Mr. Herbert Brackmun 7
747 Myrtle Street 11
Evansville, IN 47710-3277 16

Dear Mr. Brackmun 20

Your recent letter has us more than a little entrigued. 31

In it, you describe a back yard squirrel feeder you 41
have built, one that keeps out birds. This is certainly 52
a the turnaround from the usual winter animal feeding bird- 62
situation, and we believe it may have some apeal for 73
many of our customers. We are interested. 82

We are interested enough, in matter of fact, to 90
invite you to send or bring to our office plans for your 101
new feeder. If it can be built at a reasonable cost, we 112
want to talk with you about representation in the market 123
place. 124

We have a several agency plans that we used have with 134
success in representing clients like you for a number of 145
years. We shall be happy to explain them to you. 155

A copy of our recent catalog is enclosed. 163

Very truly yours 166

Miss Debra Stewert 170
Sales manager 176

VIEWS on . . . Protocol in Addresses

Specific protocol is demanded by letter writers as they compose appropriate letter addresses and salutations. Use a courtesy title before the recipient's name or a professional title after the name. Do not use both.

Ms. Rachel Lindsey	not	Rachel Lindsey
Dr. William Jones or William Jones, M.D.	not	Dr. William Jones, M.D.
Dr. Susan Chain or Susan Chain, Ph.D.	not	Dr. Susan Chain, Ph.D.
The Honorable Steven Combs	not	Mr. Steven Combs

The women's movement challenges us to ask why we distinguish between married and single women when we don't make the distinction in men. As a result, the use of *Miss* and *Mrs.* has decreased. Just as we use *Mr.* for men, *Ms.* is becoming the preferred title by many women. However, if you know that a woman has a different preference, use it.

Document 31
Agenda

1.5" top margin and 1" side margins; names flush right; adjust leaders as necessary

LA MESA UNIVERSITY--PSYCHOLOGY DEPARTMENT

June 1, 19--

Aagenda

QS

1.	Call to Order	Patricia McCall
2.	Reading of Minutes of Last Meeeting	Harry Tuggle
3.	Special Reports	
	Psy intern program	Kyle Standifer
	State baord review and exam . .	Melinda Davis
	Graduation	Joe Henderson
4.	Spring Activities	Alison Milans
5.	New requirments for graduation . .	Matthew Chochran
6.	Ajournment	Patricia McCall

Document 32
Balance sheet

1 Insert leaders in each row containing figures. DS below rules.

2 Leave 2 spaces between columns representing subtotals and totals.

3 Center the following heading on the financial statement DS; use 1.5" top margin:

GREENWOOD GENERAL FUND
Balance Sheet
June 30, 19--

ASSETS DS

Cash		$74,360.12
Taxes Receivable--Delinquent	18,640.34	
Less Allowance for Uncollectible Taxes .	8,750.00	9,890.34
Interest Receivable DS	2,940.78	
Less Allowance for Uncollectible Interest	588.00	2,352.78
Inventory of Supplies DS		3,120.00
Total Assets		$89,723.24

DS LIABILITIES AND FUND EQUITY

Liabilities: DS		
Accounts Payable		$36,125.34
Fund Equity: DS		
Unreserved Fund Balance	47,837.90	
Reserve for Encumbrances--Prior Year	2,640.00	
Reserve for Inventory of Supplies . .	3,120.00	
Total Fund Equity DS		53,597.90
Total Liabilities and Fund Equity		$89,723.24

35 Review Modified Block

Skill-Building Warmup

35a 7'

each line 2 times SS; DS between 2-line groups

alphabet	1	Melva Bragg required exactly a dozen jackets for the winter trip.	
figures	2	The 1903 copy of my book had 5 parts, 48 chapters, and 672 pages.	
shift/lock	3	THE LAKES TODAY, published in Akron, Ohio, comes in June or July.	
easy	4	Did he vow to fight for the right to work as the Orlando auditor?	

1 | 2 | 3 | 4 | 5 | 6 | 7 | 8 | 9 | 10 | 11 | 12 | 13

35b 10'

SKILL BUILDING

Build production skill

1 Key 1' writings on the letter parts, arranging each drill line in correct letter format.

2 Use 1" or default top and side margins; return 5 times between drills. Use your reference initials.

		gwam 1'
5	May 28, 19--	3
	QS	
	Ms. Dora Lynn	6
	128 Avon Lane	9
	Macon, GA 31228	11
	DS	
	Dear Ms. Lynn	13

		gwam 1'
6	Cordially	2
	QS	
	Rebecca Dexter	5
	Engineer	7
	DS	
	xx	8
	DS	
	Enclosures: Draft 251	13
	Area maps	15

7 February 4, 19-- | Mr. Bill Bargas | 3945 Park Avenue | Racine, WI 53404-3822 14

8 Miss Lois Bruce | 8764 Gold Plaza | Lansing, MI 48933-8121 | Dear Miss Bruce 14

9 Sincerely yours | Manuel Garcia | Council President | MG:xx | c Ron N. Nesbit 14

10 Yours truly | Ms. Loren Lakes | Secretary General | xx | Enclosure | c Libby Uhl 14

35c 33'

FORMATTING

Business letters: modified block

(LM pp. S21-S25)

Document 1

1 Key the (short) letter in modified block format. Correct errors.

2 Address an envelope with this return address:

GREATER BIRMINGHAM INC
163 UNION DRIVE
BIRMINGHAM AL 16303-3636

words

Current date | Dr. Burtram M. Decker | 800 Barbour 9
Avenue | Birmingham, AL *35208-5333 | Dear Dr. Decker* 19

The Community Growth Committee offers you its sincere 30
thanks for taking an active part in the sixth annual Youth 42
Fair. We especially appreciate your help in judging the 53
Youth of Birmingham Speaks portion of the Fair and of 64
contributing to the prize bank. 70

Participation of community leaders such as you makes this 82
event the annual success it has become. We sincerely hope 94
we can seek your help again next year. 102

Cordially | Grace Beebe Hunt | Secretary | GBH:*xx* 111

Document 33
Section dividers

Create section dividers for each of the three sections (see Contents in Document 35). The footer will contain only the page number at the right. Two ideas for section dividers are shown.

Select fonts.

Document 34
Title page

Create a title page for the Procedures Manual to include your name and title, Administrative Assistant.

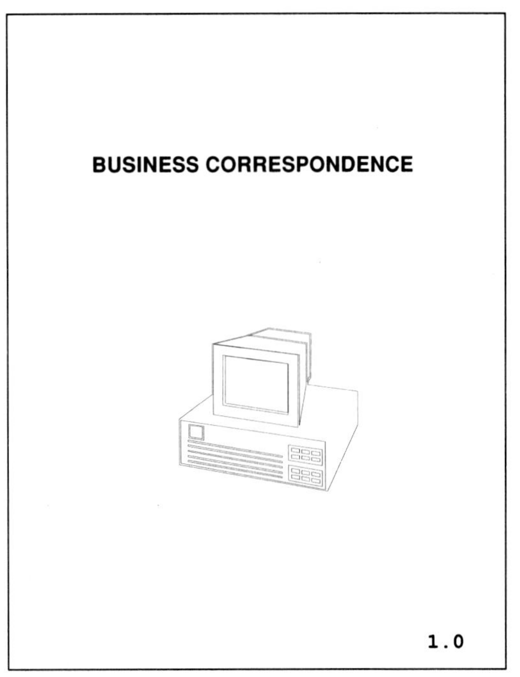

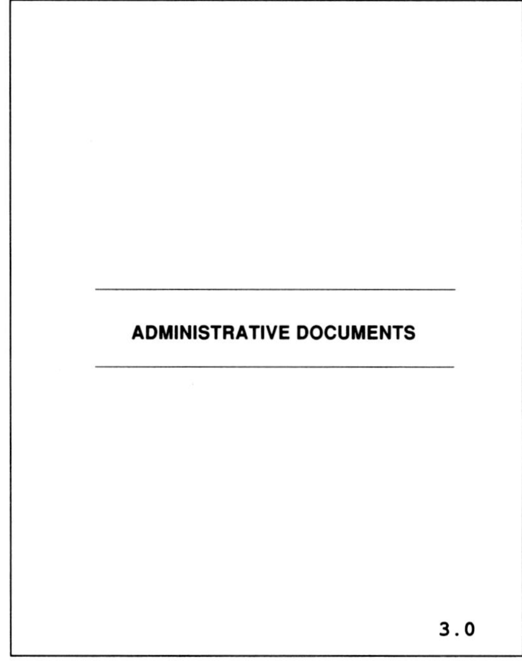

Document 35
Table of contents

Create a contents page with leaders similar to the one illustrated. Page numbers should correspond to your manual. Center the page number **ii**.

Use leader tab and flush right.

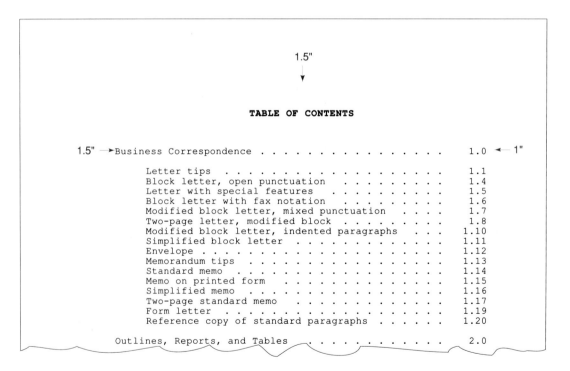

1.5"

TABLE OF CONTENTS

1.5" →		1"
Business Correspondence	1.0	← 1"
Letter tips	1.1	
Block letter, open punctuation	1.4	
Letter with special features	1.5	
Block letter with fax notation	1.6	
Modified block letter, mixed punctuation	1.7	
Two-page letter, modified block	1.8	
Modified block letter, indented paragraphs . . .	1.10	
Simplified block letter	1.11	
Envelope	1.12	
Memorandum tips	1.13	
Standard memo	1.14	
Memo on printed form	1.15	
Simplified memo	1.16	
Two-page standard memo	1.17	
Form letter	1.19	
Reference copy of standard paragraphs	1.20	
Outlines, Reports, and Tables	2.0	

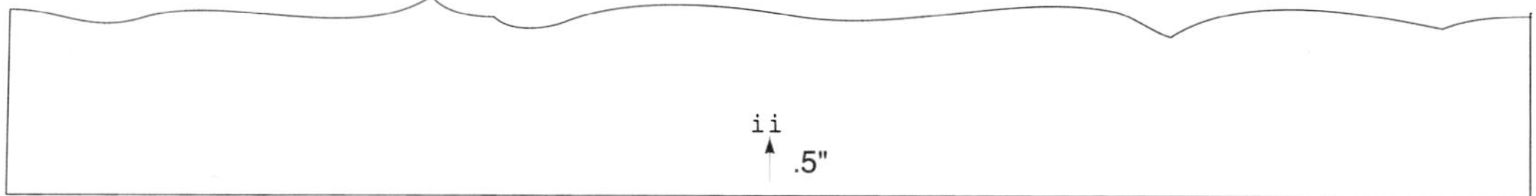

ctagon Club
3851 Farmington Avenue
Flint, MI 48521-9109

Dateline November 27, 19--
QS

Letter address Mr. Jose E. Morales, Director
Flint Business Association
584 Brabyn Avenue
Flint, MI 48508-5548
DS

Salutation Dear Mr. Morales
DS

Body The Octagon Club is concerned about Baker House.

As you know, Baker House was built on Calumet Road in 1797 by Zaccaria Baker; he and his family lived there for many years. It was home for various other families until 1938, when it became an attractive law and real estate office. Flint residents somehow assumed that Baker House was a permanent part of Flint. It wasn't.

Baker House was torn down last week to make room for a new mall. It's too late to save Baker House. But what about other Flint landmarks. Shall we lose them, too? Shopping malls may indicate that a community is growing, but need growth destroy our heritage?

We ask for your help. Will you and Mr. Wilkes include 20 minutes on your January meeting agenda for Myrna Targlif, president of the Flint Octagon Club, to present our views on this problem? She has information that I guarantee you will find interesting; a brief outline is enclosed.
DS

Complimentary close Sincerely yours
QS

Writer's name Barbara Brahms
Title Secretary, Octagon Club
DS

Reference initials BB:xx
DS

Enclosure notation Enclosure
DS

Copy notation c Andrew Wilkes

On the Job at Office Concierge

On the Job

(Lessons 142-147)

Business is overwhelming; assignments are already coming in for you. Use your procedures manual as a reference when preparing these documents.

Document 36
Form letters

(LM pp. S19-S27)

Prepare the form letter created in Document 15, page 316, for each work request. Supply an appropriate salutation and closing.

 Use merge.

Request for **FORM LETTER** Doc. 15

Variables

1. Mr. Mario Garcia
   59 Jefferson Road
   Mesa, AZ 85203-7236
2. Mario
3. Fall, 19--

Requested by Y. Durand

Organization Lexus Alumni Association

Request for **FORM LETTER** Doc. 15

Variables

1. Ms. Sharon Schmidt
   2025 Lochmoor
   Grosse Pointe, MI 48236-9011
2. Sharon
3. Spring, 19--

Requested by Y. Durand

Organization Lexus Alumni Association

Request for **FORM LETTER** Doc. 15

Variables

1. Mr. Roger Palms
   3561 Primrose Circle
   Seal Beach, CA 90740-4751
2. Roger
3. Fall, 19--

Requested by Y. Durand

Organization Lexus Alumni Association

Request for **FORM LETTER** Doc. 15

Variables

1. Ms. Carolyn Holtz
   4386 Pine Road
   Alberta, T8V 3C4
   Canada
2. Carolyn
3. Spring, 19--

Requested by Y. Durand

Organization Lexus Alumni Association

Request for **FORM LETTER** Doc. 15

Variables

1. Mr. Richard McKnight
   2215 Wisteria Avenue
   Bonsall, CA 92003-2461
2. Richard
3. Spring, 19--

Requested by Y. Durand

Organization Lexus Alumni Association

34 Modified Block With Notations

Skill-Building Warmup

34a 7'

each line 2 times SS; DS between 2-line groups

alphabet 1 Johnny Willcox printed five dozen banquet tickets for my meeting.

fig/sym 2 Check #3589 for $1,460--dated the 27th--was sent to O'Neill & Co.

1st finger 3 It is true Greg acted bravely during the severe storm that night.

easy 4 In the land of enchantment, the fox and the lamb lie by the bush.

| 1 | 2 | 3 | 4 | 5 | 6 | 7 | 8 | 9 | 10 | 11 | 12 | 13 |

34b 10'

COMMUNICATION

Compose at the keyboard

1 Compose an answer to each question in one or two sentences. Join the sentences into 3 paragraphs (as shown). Center the title **MY CAREER** over the paragraphs. Divide words if necessary.

2 Proofread; identify errors with proofreaders' marks; rekey in final form.

¶1
1 What is your present career goal?
2 Why do you think you will enjoy this career?

¶2
3 Where do you think you would most like to pursue your career?
4 Why do you think you would enjoy living and working in that area?

¶3
5 What civic, political, or volunteer activities might you enjoy?
6 What other careers may lie ahead for you?

34c 33'

FORMATTING

Business letters: modified block format

(LM pp. S17-S19)

Read the information at the right; then study the letter on page 78.

Document 1

Key the letter (average) on page 78; address an envelope. Proofread; correct errors.

Document 2

Rekey Document 1 on page 71 in modified block format.

Modified block format

The modified block format is a variation of the block format. It is "modified" by moving the dateline and the closing lines from the left margin to the center point of the page. Paragraphs may be indented, but it is more efficient not to indent them. Do not indent paragraphs in Section 7.

Reference initials: If the writer's initials are included with those of the keyboard operator, the writer's initials are listed first in ALL CAPS followed by a colon:

BB:xx

Enclosure notation: If an item is included with a letter, an enclosure notation is keyed a DS below the reference initials. Acceptable variations include:

Enclosure
Enclosures: Check #8331
Order form
Enc. 2

Copy notation: A copy notation *c* indicates that a copy of the document has been sent to person(s) named. Key it a DS below reference initials (or enclosure notation):

c Andrew Wilkes

Express Rapid Delivery
8000 Iliff Avenue
Denver, CO 80237-4512

October 19, 19--

Miss Latanya Denny
208 Humboldt Street
Denver, CO 80218-8828

Dear Miss Denny

Today our delivery service tried unsuccessfully a second time to deliver at the above address the merchandise you ordered. The merchandise is now at our general warehouse at 8000 Iliff Avenue.

We regret that no further attempts at delivery can be made. You may claim your merchandise at the warehouse if you will show a copy of your order (a duplicate is enclosed) to John Kimbrough at the warehouse.

We shall hold your merchandise for 30 days. After that time, it will be transferred to our main warehouse at 218 Harvard Avenue, East; unfortunately, we must charge a rental fee for each day the goods are stored there.

Yours very truly

Elizabeth A. LeMoyne
Dispatcher

BB:xx

Enclosure

c John Kimbrough

Document 37
Document assembly

(LM p. S29)

Using Document 16, page 317, and the information in the work request at the right, create a simplified letter.

REQUEST FOR LETTER FROM STANDARD PARAGRAPHS Doc. 16

Date: Current

Address: Ms. Rebecca Pham
2201 Arthur Avenue
Mission Viejo, CA 92692-3175

Subject: Conversion Services

Paragraphs: 1, 3, 4, and 5

Signature: Colin Murphy

Title: CIS Manager

Copies: ____________

Document 38
Graph

Generate a horizontal bar graph for Pacific Coast University to illustrate the total number of graduates from each school. The data are found in Document 24, page 324. A copy of **last year's** graph is attached to give you an idea how this graph might look.

```
                     PACIFIC COAST UNIVERSITY

                     Graduating Class of 1992


Business        | XXXXXXXXXXXXXXXXXXXXXXXXXXXXXXXXXX (659)

Communications  | XXX (53)

Engineering     | XXXXXXXXXXXX (225)

Medicine        | XXXXXXXX (165)
                |_____________________________________________
                  0    1    2    3    4    5    6    7    8

                                Hundreds
```

33c 21'

FORMATTING

Business letters and envelopes

(LM pp. S13-S15)

Personal titles

Personal titles (for example, Mr. or Ms.) should be included in the letter address unless a professional title (Dr.) is appropriate.

1 Use Mr. when the recipient's first name is obviously masculine.

2 Use Ms. when the recipient's first name is obviously feminine and no other title (Mrs., Miss) is indicated.

3 A short job title may follow the name; key a long job title as the second line of the address.

words

Document 1

Key the (short) letter in block format; proofread and correct errors; address an envelope.

Current date | Mr. Trace L. Brecken | 4487 Ingram Street | Corpus Christi, 14
TX 78409-8907 | Dear Mr. Brecken 20

We have received the package you sent us in which you returned goods 34
from a recent order you gave us. Your refund check, plus return postage, 49
will be mailed to you in a few days. 56

We are sorry, of course, that you did not find this merchandise personally 71
satisfactory. It is our goal to please all of our customers, and we are 86
always disappointed if we fail. 92

Please give us an opportunity to try again. We stand behind our mer- 106
chandise, and that is our guarantee of good service. 117

Cordially yours | Margret Bredewig | Customer Service Department | xx 129

Document 2

Use directions in Document 1 for this average letter.

Current date | Mrs. Rose Shikamuru | 55 Lawrence Street | Topeka, KS 13
66607-6657 | Dear Mrs. Shikamuru 19

Thank you for your recent letter asking about employment opportunities 33
with our company. We are happy to inform you that Mr. Edward Ybarra, 47
our recruiting representative, will be on your campus on April 23, 24, 25, 62
and 26 to interview students who are interested in our company. 75

We suggest you talk soon with your student placement office, as all 89
appointments with Mr. Ybarra will be made through that office. Please 103
bring with you the application questionnaire they provide. 115

Within a few days, we will send you a company brochure and more 128
information about our offices; plant; salary, bonus, and retirement plans; 143
and the beautiful community in which we are located. We believe a close 158
study of this information will convince you, as it has many others, that 173
our company builds futures as well as small motors. 183

If there is any other way we can help you, please write to me again. 197

Yours very truly | Miss Myrle K. Bragg | Human Services Director | xx 210

33d 10'

COMMUNICATION

Compose at the keyboard

2" top margin; 1" side margins; 5-space indention; DS

1 Center your name horizontally; then QS.

2 Key a complete sentence to answer each question. Avoid beginning all answers with "I" or "My." Then combine sentences into a paragraph.

3 Proofread; make pencil corrections; rekey the ¶.

1. What is your birth date?
2. What do you enjoy doing during the summer?
3. What are your favorite winter activities?
4. What is your favorite food?
5. What sports activities do you like to watch or play?
6. What is your favorite shopping trip?

The next four assignments are from Harold D. Long & Son, Inc., a general construction business. Check copy carefully for overlooked errors.

Document 39
Memo composition with table

(LM p. S31)

Compose a response to the memo of March 4 at the right. Follow Mr. Long's annotations on the memo.

HAROLD D. LONG & SON, INC.
8175 Macarthur Boulevard, Irvine, CA 92711-4328 **(714) 555-8967**

Interoffice Communication

TO: Harold Long

FROM: Lorna Lee Patchet

DATE: March 4, 19--

SUBJECT: Lewiston Project Expenses

According to records, the expenses to date for the months of January, February, and March include, respectively: wages, $12,374, $13,529, $930; benefits: $3,917, $4,280, $297; materials: $5,609, $17,394, $284.

Let me know if you have further questions.

jlr

Please compose a memo to Rick Stonecipher, supervisor of the Lewiston Project. Ask for the final job expense estimate and the projected completion date. Include a table showing by month (January-March) the total payroll (sum of wages and benefits) plus materials costs per month (use figures from Lorna Lee Patchet's memo). We will need this report by Friday of next week.
Harold

Document 40
Modified block letter

(LM p. S33)

Key this letter to John Berthelson to accompany the change order (Document 41, page 335). Add subject line: **El Prado Street Project**.

John Berthelson, Engineer
County Engineer's Office
1628 Civic Center Plaza
Santa Ana, CA 92701-4122

In response to your inspection of ~~the Project~~ [our El Prado Street] No. 38219 [transpose: 38291] for the City of Orange, we have ~~drawn up~~ [prepared] the ~~attached~~ [enclosed] change order. This form ~~reflects the use of~~ [documents your request to use] 5/8" ~~pea gravel~~ [rock] to bed the storm drains instead of [the] prevous bedding. Compaction tests [stet] will continu[e] as in the [original] contract. Test results will be avalable for [on-site] inspection.

Please ~~feel free to~~ contact me or David [transpose: David or me] ~~about~~ [regarding] any other particulars on this project. Sincerly

Harold D. Long, General Contractor

33 Block Format and Envelopes

Skill-Building Warmup

33a 7'

each line 2 times SS; DS between 2-line groups

alphabet 1 Jim Daley gave us in that box the prize he won for his quick car.

figures 2 Send 346 of the 789 sets now; send the others on April 10 and 25.

one hand 3 I deserve, in my opinion, a reward after I started a faster race.

easy 4 Enrique may fish for cod by the dock; he also may risk a penalty.

1 | 2 | 3 | 4 | 5 | 6 | 7 | 8 | 9 | 10 | 11 | 12 | 13

33b 12'

FORMATTING

Address large envelopes/ insert letters

(LM pp. S9-S11) or 3 large envelopes

1 Read placement information at the right.

2 Address a business envelope to each addressee listed below; proofread; correct errors.

3 Fold three sheets correctly and insert them into the envelopes.

Envelope address: Set a tab about .5" left of center. Space down to about line 14 from the top edge of the envelope and begin keying at the tab. Learn to visualize this position so that you can address envelopes quickly.

Use ALL CAPS, block format, and no punctuation. Leave one space between the state and ZIP Code.

Return address: When a return address is printed on the envelope, the writer's name may be keyed above the company address. If the return address is not printed, key it in ALL CAPS on line 2, beginning about 3 spaces from the left edge.

Special notations: Key special notations for the addressee (as PLEASE FORWARD, HOLD FOR ARRIVAL, PERSONAL) in ALL CAPS a DS below the return address. Key mailing notations for postal authorities (as SPECIAL DELIVERY and REGISTERED) in ALL CAPS a DS below the stamp position on line 8 or 9.

DALLAS D O'HARGAN
717 GERVAIS CREEK ROAD
ST PAUL MN 55117-5115
DS
PERSONAL

DS
SPECIAL DELIVERY

(line 14)

about .5" left of center

MR SAMUEL MONTGOMERY
TELEMAX COMPUTERS
339 EDISON HIGHWAY
BAKERSFIELD CA 93305-5035

Envelope 1

From T L LEWIS | 1594 EASY STREET | MOUNTAIN VIEW CA 90756-8765 to MS GERTRUDE SCHUYLER | 633 SLEEPY HOLLOW AVENUE | TAMPA FL 33617-6711

Envelope 2

From (supply your own return address) to MR ALBERT CHUNG | 254 SHERBORN DRIVE | CINCINNATI OH 45231-5112. Include the special notation CONFIDENTIAL.

Envelope 3

Assume the company address of the writer is printed on the envelope. From C VOLTZ to MISS CELIA PEREZ | 399 RED BRIDGE ROAD E | KANSAS CITY MO 64114-2344. Include the mailing notation SPECIAL DELIVERY.

Folding and inserting letters into large envelopes

Step 1
With letter face up, fold slightly less than 1/3 of sheet up toward top.

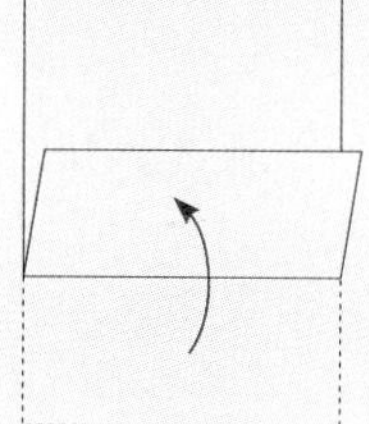

Step 2
Fold down top of sheet to within 1/2 inch of bottom fold.

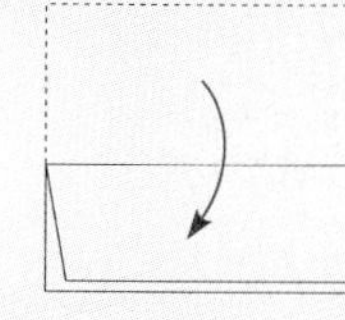

Step 3
Insert letter into envelope with last crease toward bottom of envelope.

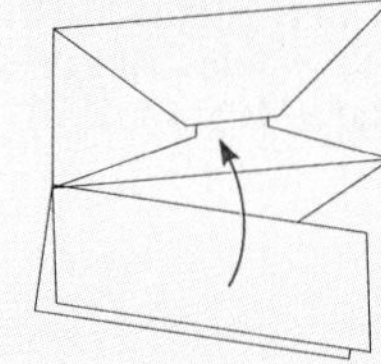

Document 41
Change order
(LM p. S35)
Key this change order regarding the El Prado contract.

CONTRACTOR'S CHANGE ORDER

To: City of Orange

The owners of the property herein described authorize Harold D. Long & Son, Inc., to make the following changes in plans and specifications as originally set forth under contract.

Work being performed on the following described real property in the County of Orange, Lot --, Block --, Tract --, Project No. L-38291, commonly known as El Prado St. Project, City of Orange, State of California.

Description of change Per engineer's request regarding storm drains between southwest corner of 600 block of El Prado St. at the Olive St. intersection, change specified rock fill to bed pipe with 5/8" rock per DOT, State of California, at an additional cost of $2.10 a lineal foot.

An addition/~~deduction~~ of $9,346.12 is made to/~~from~~ the contract price of the aforementioned changes.

Signed ____________ Harold D. Long, Inc. Date ________

Signed ____________ City of Orange Date ________

Document 42
Purchase order
(LM p. S37)
Key **PO #16** to:
GOSSMAN'S PRODUCT CENTER
6329 FARNSWORTH LANE
HUNTINGTON BEACH CA 92646-9741
Materials needed: 2 weeks from today (you determine date).
Shipper: **Ely's Express**
Terms: **Net/60 days**
Replace question marks with numbers on the attached note.
Calculate totals.

Items & Unit Prices
1) Tape, #48-9209, $5/roll
2) Tarps, #69-1735, $138 roll
3) Glue, 385-42DD, $32 box
4) Sealer, #57-385B, $65 drum

3 dozen No.? Reinforced Ceiling Tape
1 dozen No.? 15' x 30' Canvas Tarps
5 boxes No.? 16 oz. Wood Glue-All Refills
2 drums No.? Resin Sealer, 50-Gallon Drum
Harold D. Long, General Contractor

32c 12'

SKILL BUILDING

Practice letter parts

1 Key the letter parts, spacing correctly between each. Use 1" or default top and side margins. Return 5 times between exercises. Do not correct errors.

2 Take a 2' writing on 1 and 2, then 1' writings on 3 and 4, following the directions above.

gwam 2'

1 April 15, 19-- 2

QS

Miss Joyce Bohn, Treasurer 4
Stapex Stamping Co. 6
118 Lehigh Parkway 8
Allentown, PA 18103-8181 11

DS

Dear Miss Bohn 12

2 March 21, 19-- 14

Parkway Construction Company 17
2188 Hawthorne Place, E. 19
Niagara Falls, NY 80206-2006 22

Ladies and Gentlemen 24

gwam 1'

3 Very sincerely yours 2

QS

Marianne R. Robert 4
District Attorney 6

DS

xx 6

4 Thank you for your help. 9

Sincerely 10

F. E. Dravis 11
President 12

xx 12

32d 18'

FORMATTING

Business letters: block format

(LM pp. S5-S7)

Document 1

Key the (short) letter; proofread carefully; correct errors.

words

Current date 3

QS

Mr. Grady Atgood 6
Personnel Director 10
Letter Beams, Inc. 14
2112 Smythe Road, N. 19
Arlington, VA 22201-1201 23

DS

Dear Mr. Atgood 26

DS

Miss Carolyn Carvere, an employee of Letter 35
Beams, Inc., from 1990 to 1993, has applied 44
for a position with our company as a com- 52
puter analyst. She has given us your name 60
and her permission to ask you about her work 69
history with Letter Beams, Inc. 76

Will you, therefore, please verify Carolyn 84
Carvere's employment with you and respond 93
as you desire about her performance with your 102
organization. Thank you, Mr. Atgood. 109

DS

Sincerely yours 113

QS

A. Alonzo Cruz, Director 118
Personnel Services 121

DS

xx 122

Document 2

Follow directions in Document 1 for this average-length letter.

words

Current date 3

Dr. Myron Moilion 7
690 Edward Place 10
Stamford, CT 06905-5069 15

Dear Dr. Moilion 18

Thank you for your letter regarding the 26
mislabeled tree. We are certainly embarrassed 35
that one of the "white birch" we planted for 44
you two years ago has matured into a wild 52
cherry tree. While birch and cherry trees look 62
quite similar when they are immature, there is 71
a remarkable difference as they grow older. 80

We will be happy to replace the wild cherry 89
tree with a similarly matured white birch at 98
your convenience. Call us to set a date for the 108
planting. We will also, if you desire, remove 117
the cherry tree at that time. 123

We appreciate your patience. 129

Very truly yours 132

Ms. Lynn Harley, President 137

xx 137

Document 43
Topbound report with references

Place the header for the second page on line 10: **SPRING SEMESTER ENROLLMENTS, 1994** at left margin and page number at right margin. Replace each occurrence of **LCC** with **Lincoln Community College**.

Check for unmarked errors.

Top margin of a topbound report is 2" on page 1 and 1.5" on all continuing pages.

REPORT OF LCC ENROLLMENTS] Center

SPRING SEMESTER, 1994

Data reflecting Spring Semester, 1994, enrollments at LCC are presented in the following report. Our enrollment pattern parallells the trends reported by schools comparable throughout the nation. The data contained in this report donot include students who have withdrawn from classes either before or after the final drop date.

A total of 1,574 students were enrolled at LCC during the Spring Semester, 1994. The current enrollments represent 1,181 full-time equivalents (FTE) for Spring Semester, 1994, ~~This~~ which represents an increase of 2% over the past year.

Female students continue to outnumber male students. The ratio of female to male students, however, is similar to institutions of our size and purpose.

> Enrollment of female students in community colleges will trend outnumber male students throughout the nineties. This can be attributed to the increasing number of women returning to the workforce and the decline in the male population (Palms, 1993, 74).

A breakdown of enrollments by gender is listed in Table 1.

Table 1] Center

Female/Male Enrollments] Center, all caps

1993-1994] Center

center	1993 Female	1993 Male	1994 Female	1994 Male
Freshman	866	821	937	862
Sophomore	913	844	955	871
Junior	847	808	826	801
Senior	820	794	844	818

(continued on next page)

32 Block Format and Error Correction

Skill-Building Warmup

32a 7'

each line 2 times SS; DS between 2-line groups

alphabet 1 I quickly explained to two managers the grave hazards of the job.
figures 2 All channels--16, 25, 30, and 74--reported the score was 19 to 8.
shift keys 3 Maxi and Kay Pascal expect to be in breezy South Mexico in April.
easy 4 Did the man fight a duel, or did he go to a chapel to sign a vow?

| 1 | 2 | 3 | 4 | 5 | 6 | 7 | 8 | 9 | 10 | 11 | 12 | 13 |

32b 13'

FORMATTING

Error correction procedures

Study the information at the right. Do the drill below.

Proofread: Before documents are complete, they must be carefully proofread and all errors must be corrected. Error-free documents send the message that you are detailed-oriented and capable.

Proofreading tips

- ✓ Never assume work is error free.
- ✓ Read each line carefully for keying errors.
- ✓ Check for misused words; repair faulty sentence structure.
- ✓ Read the document once for meaning/ content.
- ✓ Check documents for format errors.
- ✓ Compare the printed copy to the original, checking for omissions.

Computers: Correct errors using either the backspace key or the delete key. Strike the backspace key to delete characters to the left of the cursor. Striking the delete key erases characters at the cursor. Correct on-screen errors before the document is printed.

Typewriters: Most typewriters have a correction key located at the right of the keyboard coded with an *x*. Backspacing to the error and depressing this key activates a tape or ribbon that "lifts off" incorrect characters.

Drill

1.5" top and side margins; DS; divide words appropriately; correct errors; proofread

Work that contains careless errors almost always has exactly the opposite effect from the one intended by a writer. So, for example, if what we key is meant to earn a top grade, to gain a job interview, or to impress someone important in our lives, it must be error free. When we write on behalf of someone else, such as a business, our letter at once becomes representative of that company; and our responsibility for error detection is compounded.

The statistics also indicate an 8 % increase in minority students and an 6 % increase in English as a Second Language (ESL) students. The demographics cited by national reports shows the minority population growing in portions of the United States.

> Minorities will constitute forty percent of the population in the United States. The heaviest minority population will be in the southern, southeastern, and southwestern portions of the country (Cook, 1992, 114).

Table 2

Ethnic Population

Data From 1994 Census

Semester	Asian	Black	Hispanic	White	Other
Fall	13	7	12	66	2
Spring	14	8	13	61	4

Statistical reports reflecting the breakdown of this data as well as enrollments by major classes and status of students are being available upon request.

REFERENCES

Cook, Paul A. "Managing the Diversified Classroom." Education In the Year 2000. Seattle, Washington: Lexicon Press, 1992.

Palms, Cheryl R. The Workforce of the Nineties. Ann Arbor, Michigan: Zierath Publishing Co., 1993.

The Henderson Company

6677 Farmington Avenue
West Hartford, CT 06119-7284
(203) 555-6941

Dateline May 6, 19-- (Line 16)

QS

Letter address Ms. Sara Arbecki, Editor
Alpha Communications
676 Hundley Drive
St. Joseph, MO 64506-6766

DS

Salutation Dear Ms. Arbecki

DS

Body Your article "Efficient Correspondence" described the block format letter as "effective, economical, and easy to read." I can see from the illustration that the block format is efficient.

DS

Your article made me aware of the parts of a business letter and the importance of arranging the parts in a particular order. The examples you gave helped me realize that attractive letter placement is a "hidden message" in every letter I send.

I have attempted to follow all of your directions in formatting my letter in block style. In your article, you offered to answer readers' questions about block format letters. My question: How did I do?

Personal business and civic responsibilities require me to write letters quite often. I shall appreciate any advice you can give me to improve my communications.

DS

Complimentary close Sincerely yours

QS

Writer's name Miss Muriel Werter
Title Administrative Assistant

DS

Reference initials jrm

Document 44
Letter

(LM p. S39)

Modified block, mixed punctuation; add company name, **TRANSCRIBER CORPORATION**, in the closing lines; list multiple enclosures. Replace *revolutionary* (where circled) with another appropriate word(s) from a thesaurus. Check for unmarked errors. Keep letter until enclosure in next job is completed.

Use thesaurus.

Kelly Court Reporting Services
33 City Drive
Santa Ana, CA 92706-6721

TRANSCRIBER unveiled 2 new revolutionary products last week at the National Court Reporting Convention. We challenges you to be a leader in the court reporting field by trying one of the new revolutionary products: TransCAT and StenoScribe writers. The StenoScribe is a manuel machine designed for notetakers who's ability to communicate with a computer. The TransCAT interfaces with industry standard word processing packages includes ram memory.

Our writer priceing is extremely competitive and is reflected on the enclosed price list. As an added incentive, Transcriber is offering a trade in credit on your existing writers against the purchase of either the TransCAT or StenoScribe writers.

Please take the time to examine the attached fact scheets describing the features and benefits of these revolutionary products. Then compare what TRANSCRIBER has to offer, both in featuares and pricing, with that of the competitors. Switch to TRANSCRIBER, the company that has superior writers, time real translation, sensible pricing, and a trade-in on your exiting writrs. Your reporters will thank you. call our tele marketing department at 1-800-555-7641 for more information.

Document 1

(LM p. S1) LM page references refer to the Laboratory Materials, Lessons 1-60.

Format and key the letter on page 72 (average length); proofread; circle errors.

Document 2

(LM p. S3)

Format and key the short letter at the bottom of this page; proofread; circle errors.

Parts of a business letter

Business letters contain a variety of parts that serve very specific purposes. Listed below are basic parts of a typical business letter:

Dateline: The letter is dated the day it is mailed.

Letter address: The address of the person who will receive the letter begins a quadruple space (QS) below the dateline. Include a personal title (for example, Mr. or Ms.) unless a professional title (Dr.) is appropriate.

Salutation: Key the salutation, or greeting, a double space (DS) below the letter address. The salutation should correspond to the first line of the letter address. Use Ladies and Gentlemen when the first line of the address is a company name.

Body: The body is the message of the letter. Begin the body a double space (DS) below the salutation. Single-space the body and double-space between paragraphs.

Complimentary close: The complimentary close, which is the formal closing of the letter, begins a double space below the body.

Writer's name and title: Leave three blank lines (QS) for the writer's signature, keying the name on the fourth line. Women generally include a personal title with their names. If the writer's title is short, it may follow the name; if the title is long, key it on the next line.

Reference initials: When business letters are keyed by someone other than the writer, the keyboard operator's initials are keyed in lowercase a double space below the writer's keyed name and/or title. Initials are not included when the writer keys the letter.

Colbran's
Consumer Affairs Department
P.O. Box 3058
Natchez, MS 39120-8476
1-800-555-9473

March 6, 19-- **line 14**

Ms. Brenda A. O'Flynn
468 Heumann Drive
Lincoln, NE 68504-5046

Dear Ms. O'Flynn

1" Let me introduce myself. My name is Jorge Lund; and since last August I have served as marketing manager for Colbran's Market, a Midwest chain of retail grocery stores. **1"**

Since its advent, the purpose and philosophy of "grocery store" operation has rested on providing for the needs, particularly in the kitchen, of the American home. Part of my "mission," as it has evolved here at Colbran's, encompasses exploring new concepts in the field of food retailing.

History shows that the grocery store has progressed through a number of stages, from the small corner shop to the modern supermarket. Colbran's is now ready to take the next step; to extend store services beyond simply selling food items. We are gearing up now to be a total food center, introducing nutritional and cooking services. We intend to become your local headquarters for food selection, preparation, and consumption.

Edward Kinlo, of our Lincoln office, tells me that you might be interested in serving as one of our planning consultants for this new endeavor. Hours would not be demanding, and remuneration and privileges accompany the appointment. If, as we hope, you have some interest in working with a progressive group dedicated to improving consumer service, please contact me for details.

Sincerely yours

Jorge L. Lund
Marketing Manager

xx

Long letter

Document 2 | words

	words
May 1, 19--	2
QS	
Mr. John M. Browert	6
1403 Poplar Lane	10
Annapolis, MD 21403-0314	15
DS	
Dear Mr. Browert	18
DS	
Please stop at your convenience to pick up	28
your travel tickets. You are scheduled to sail	38
for one week on the SS CONTESSA, leaving	48
Pier 40, Miami, May 21, at 2 p.m. We under-	57
stand you have made your own arrangements	66
for travel to and from Annapolis.	70
Thanks very much for allowing us to serve	77
you.	78
DS	
Ship ahoy!	80
QS	
Frances Westburg	83
General Agent	86
DS	
xx	86

Document 45
Ruled table

Use standard top margin and center column heads. Enclose table with Document 44.

TRANSCRIBER CORPORATION
19-- Price List

Item	Retail	Your Price
StenoScribe Writer	$695	$595
TransCAT Writer	995	765
Hardcase	99	84
Tripod	89	79
128K memory module	495	425
Ribbon cartridge	30	27

Document 46
Form letter

(LM pp. S41-S47)

1 Prepare a form letter, identifying the variables. Use block format and plain paper.

2 Calculate the total fee as indicated for each firm based upon $35 per hour for services.

3 Finally, prepare a letter for each firm listed on letterhead paper, inserting the variables.

Reference: page 316

MR WES CRANSTON
GENERAL MANAGER
RONSTADT AND CRANSTON
ONE TREMONE AVENUE
AVALON NJ 08202-2078
7 HRS

MS DENISE LAKE
BURLINGTON SUPPLY CO
128 WINDSOR STREET
HARTFORD CT 06120-2002
12 HRS

MS JEAN SIMPSON
HALL REAL ESTATE
6414 CONNECTICUT PLAZA
AUGUSTA ME 04330-7802
17 HRS

MRS SUE THAM
ROBERTS MEDICAL CORP
P O BOX 78
ABINGTON PA 19001-5209
9 HRS

Yesterday we received your request for lables, and today we ~~We received you address labels yesterday and understanding your firm's need for the labels, I am happy~~ are pleased to present ~~give~~ you with the following bid~~; we are ready to beign as soon as you notify us to do so~~.

Since our scanners were unable to "read" the print on your labels, a keying test was completed to estimate ~~run and check~~ the time involved in transferring the lables to disk for your database.

A projected ______ hours are needed to complete ~~finish~~ the labels. Our charge for keying and editing is $35 per hour.

Therefore, the total cost for keying the labels is $______, payable by check or money order. You will receive two data disks and one printout (sent COD by Midland Express) within three days of your notification for us to do ~~begin~~ this project.

Your business is greatly appreciated. Please call us again when we can be of service.

Cordially, Deana Shu
Office Manager

31c 6'

COMMUNICATION

Compose at the keyboard

1" top and side margins; DS

1 Key the ¶, inserting the missing information. Do not correct errors.

2 Remove the paper and make pencil corrections. Rekey the ¶ from the marked copy. Proofread; circle errors.

My name is (your name). I am now a (class level) student at (name of your school) in (city and state) where I am majoring in (major area of study). I was graduated from (name of your high school) in (name of town) in (year), where my favorite subject was (name of subject). My hobby is (name of hobby). In my free time, I like to (name a free-time activity you enjoy). I operate a keyboard at approximately (state the *gwam* rate in figures).

31d 30'

FORMATTING

Business letters in block format

Study carefully the information about business letter placement on this page and about letter parts on the next page. Then key Documents 1 and 2 as directed on page 71.

Business letters

Business letters are prepared on letterhead stationery, which has the company name, address, telephone number, and logo (the company trademark or symbol) printed at the top of the page. Most letterheads are between 1" and 2" deep. If a letter is sent on plain stationery, a return address must be keyed immediately above the date.

Letter placement: Placing a letter attractively on the page requires learning to judge its length. An average-length letter has at least three paragraphs and about 100 to 200 words. A short letter, however, may have one or two paragraphs and fewer than 100 words. A long letter has four or more paragraphs and more than 200 words.

Margins and dateline: The letter placement table serves as a guide for placement of letters of varying lengths. Using standard (default) side margins is efficient, but variable side margins often provide better placement. Variable side margins will be used for letters in Section 7.

Letter Placement Table

Letter length	Variable side margins	Standard side margins	Dateline
Short	2"	1"	line 18
Average	1.5"	1"	line 16
Long	1"	1"	line 14

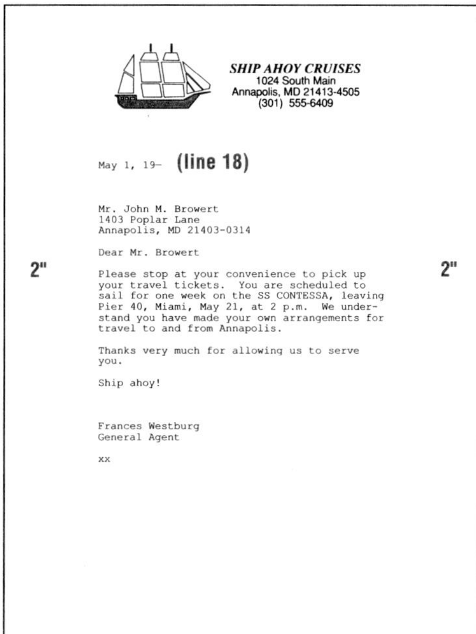

SHIP AHOY CRUISES
1024 South Main
Annapolis, MD 21413-4505
(301) 555-6409

May 1, 19– **(line 18)**

Mr. John M. Browert
1403 Poplar Lane
Annapolis, MD 21403-0314

Dear Mr. Browert

2" Please stop at your convenience to pick up your travel tickets. You are scheduled to sail for one week on the SS CONTESSA, leaving Pier 40, Miami, May 21, at 2 p.m. We understand you have made your own arrangements for travel to and from Annapolis. **2"**

Thanks very much for allowing us to serve you.

Ship ahoy!

Frances Westburg
General Agent

xx

Short letter

The Henderson Company
6677 Farmington Avenue
West Hartford, CT 06119-7284
(203) 555-6941

May 6, 19-- **line 16**

Ms. Sara Arbecki, Editor
Alpha Communications
676 Hundley Drive
St. Joseph, MO 64506-6766

Dear Ms. Arbecki

1.5" Your article "Efficient Correspondence" described the block format letter as "effective, economical, and easy to read." I can see from the illustration that the block format is efficient. **1.5"**

Your article made me aware of the parts of a business letter and the importance of arranging the parts in a particular order. The examples you gave helped me realize that attractive letter placement is a "hidden message" in every letter I send.

I have attempted to follow all of your directions in formatting my letter in block style. In your article, you offered to answer readers' questions about block format letters. My question: How did I do?

Personal business and civic responsibilities require me to write letters quite often. I shall appreciate any advice you can give me to improve my communications.

Sincerely yours

Miss Muriel Werter
Administrative Assistant

jrm

Average-length letter

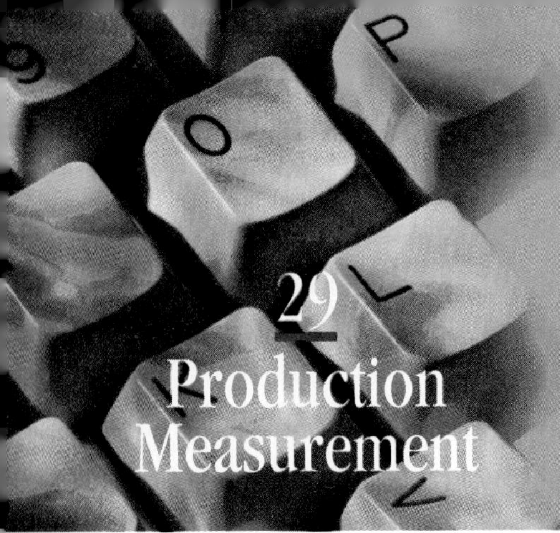

29 Production Measurement

Measurement goal
To demonstrate speed and accuracy of document production (keying, formatting, proofreading, and handling materials applied to various business documents).

Machine adjustments
1 Margins: as appropriate for documents.
2 Line spacing: as appropriate for documents.

148a 5'

Skill-building warmup

Key each line as many times as time permits. Use this warmup for Lessons 149 and 150 also.

alphabet 1 Zack vacuumed, waxed, and quickly polished Jeff's new Bronco GTO.
fig/sym 2 O'Connor & O'Shannon placed 178 orders for #36 cable on 10/25/94.
first row 3 Zelda needs more vitamin B and C to give her extra vigor and vim.
fluency 4 The neighbor may handle the problem of the torn gown and mend it.
| 1 | 2 | 3 | 4 | 5 | 6 | 7 | 8 | 9 | 10 | 11 | 12 | 13 |

148b 10'

Production measurement procedures

Follow the procedures at the right for Lessons 148-150.

1 Arrange laboratory materials (LM), plain paper, reference sources, etc., in your work area (3').

2 When instructed to begin, follow directions for each job; proofread carefully; make corrections before going on to the next job. Some jobs may contain unmarked errors. You are expected to supply all necessary parts to documents, such as dates, enclosure notations, etc. Complete as much work as you can in the time allotted.

3 When time is called, proofread and circle all errors in the jobs you completed and the last job on which you were working.

4 Compute *n-pram* (net production rate a minute). Penalty is 15 words for each uncorrected error (Steps 3-4: 7').

148c 35'

Production measurement

Document 1
Two-page letter
(LM p. S49)

Key the letter in block format to the address listed below. Use the date **January 15, 19--**. Add subject line **A SPECIAL INVITATION TO OUR OPEN HOUSE.**
Identify the enclosure.

Ms. Margarita Gonzalez
2190 Crescent Lane
Seal Beach, CA 90740-7312

words

inquiring
Thank you for your letter about furthering your education at 14
Lakeview Community College
LCC. We believe that LCC provides excellent educational 34
standards and, with a faculty-student ratio of 1:5, the 46
school offers each student personalized attention. The en- 57
college of study
closed catalogue has specific information regarding programs, 73
admission, tuition and fees, financial aid and scholarships, 85
housing, and student ~~life and~~ services. Insert A 91

A high school transcript and college transcript(s), if 102
college work has been completed, must be sent to the 113
Registrar's Office by individual institutions; official Act 125
and/or Sat scores are likewise required. Freshman admission 137

7 Business Correspondence

Learning goals:

1. To format business letters in block and modified block format on letterhead stationery.
2. To address business envelopes.
3. To format standard inter-office memorandums.
4. To correct keyboarding errors.
5. To develop composing skills.

Formatting guides:

1. Margins: Default or 1" (65 spaces).
2. Single-space drills; double-space ¶ writings.
3. 5-space ¶ indention for writings and all DS copy.

31a 7'

Skill-building warmup

each line twice SS; DS between 2-line groups

alphabet 1 Buddy Jackson is saving the door prize money for wax and lacquer.
figures 2 I have fed 47 hens, 25 geese, 10 ducks, 39 lambs, and 68 kittens.
one hand 3 You imply Jon Case exaggerated my opinion on a decrease in rates.
easy 4 I shall make hand signals to the widow with the auditory problem.

| 1 | 2 | 3 | 4 | 5 | 6 | 7 | 8 | 9 | 10 | 11 | 12 | 13 |

31b 7'

SKILL BUILDING

Straight copy

Key two 1' writings on each ¶. Each ¶ contains 2 more words than the previous one. Try to complete each ¶ within 1'. **Optional:** Take 2' and 3' timings to build staying power.

LA all letters used

	gwam 2'	3'
Have you thought about time? Time is a perplexing commod-	6	4
ity. Frequently we don't have adequate time to do the things we	12	8
must, yet we all have just the same amount of time.	17	12
We seldom refer to the quantity of time; to a great extent,	24	16
we cannot control it. We can try to set time aside, to plan,	30	20
and therefore, to control portions of this valuable asset.	36	24
We should make an extra effort to fill each minute and hour	42	28
with as much quality activity as possible. Time, the most pre-	47	32
cious thing a person can spend, can never be realized once it	54	36
is lost.	55	36

gwam 2' | 1 | 2 | 3 | 4 | 5 | 6 | 7 |
3' | 1 | 2 | 3 | 4 | 5 |

Document 1 (continued)

is based on high school performance and college test scores. 149
Students transferring from other colleges will be mostly 159
admitted on the basis of previous college-level work. 172
In the back of the catalog is information as well as the 182
application form you will need for admission into your pro- 193
gram if study. Complete the appropriate from and return it 205
to the registrar's office along with (2) letters of recommenda- 218
tion by the dead line. 222

We invite you to come to the (LCC) Open House on February 238
18, 199--. Tours of the campus will be conducted. Academic 249
deans and advisors will be available for questions. Repre- 262
sentatives from campus clubs will present to provide you with 275
information on student activities. A tentative schedule for 288
the afternoon is as follows: 294

(LCC) OPEN HOUSE 301

February 18, 19-- 305

11:00 - 1:00 A lunch by the pond can be purchased. 315
Clubs will feature ethnic foods. 322
Entertainment provided. 327
1:15 - 2:00 Guided tours of the campus. 335

2:45 - 3:15 General assembly in auditorium. 344

3:30 - 5:00 Deans, academic advisors, and club repre- 355
sentatives will be available to answer 363
questions. 365

Sincerely, Dr. J. Nakahara, Vice President, Student Services 412
As you can see, we have an informative and fun-filled 374
afternoon scheduled for you on February 18. We hope 384
that you can join us. Please contact us if you 392
have any questions. 400

Level Two
Formatting Basic Business Documents

OBJECTIVES

KEYBOARDING

To key approximately 40 wam with good accuracy.

FORMATTING SKILLS

To format basic letters, memorandums, reports, and tables.

COMMUNICATION SKILLS

To proofread and correct errors; to apply capitalization and other basic language arts skills.

Document 2
Letter with variables: simplified block format
(LM p. S51)
Prepare the collection message at the right, using the variable information provided. Use **May 9, 19--** on both letters. Use the account number as the reference in the simplified block format letters. The letters will be signed by **Mrs. Nancy Kramer, Collection Department.**

Last month, ___1___ , we reminded you of the amount now due on your credit account. Your last payment was for ___2___ for the ___3___ you purchased on ___4___ . Your account is now more than 60 days past due.

So that you may keep your account privileges, please send your check for ___5___ by return mail. We will try to work out an arrangement for bringing your account up to date if need be.

Please pay the ___5___ at once or call ___6___ at 555-2424.

Mr. Donald L. Fisher	Ms. K. Paula Bobst
7023 Concho	966 Bellfontaine Avenue
Arvada, CO 80001-4738	Arvada, CO 80002-4827
Account No. 203-91-725	Account No. 102-80-614
1 Mr. Fisher	1 Ms. Bobst
2 $75.64	2 $86.32
3 software and book	3 paper and video games
4 January 21, 19--	4 January 26, 19--
5 $225.53	5 $365.35
6 Ram Mitra	6 Nancy Collins
Total words: 123	Total words: 126

Document 3
Standard memo
Key this memo regarding overtime from Harold D. Long to the BOC Framing Crew.

words

BOC Framing Crew / Overtime (Supply date and month) 5
Beginning next Monday, ~~all~~ overtime will 15
be limited to ~~an~~ emergency ~~basis~~ work only. 23
Supervisors ~~or foremen~~ will give you as much 29
advance notice as possible when overtime is 40
needed. Time cards should be turned in to your super- 50
visor no later than ~~usual~~ 6 p.m. ~~everyday~~ Friday. 57
Supervisors will total hours to be the nearest 67
quarter hour ~~each~~ daily and weekly. 73

words

Document 1
Center lines
2" top margin; DS; center each line horizontally

The 1
City of 2
Los Portales 5
Mencken Public Library 10
New Books for July and August 16
LIFE IN ARGENTINA TODAY (Carmody) 22
ACHILLES AND THE DARDANELLES (Dodds) 30
BODY BUILDING: FOR EVERYBODY? (Szakely) 38
MARYE, THE WILL-O'-THE-WISP (O'Hargan) 46
LOST ON THE LOST ISLAND (Loupoin) 53
Hours: 54
10-10 55
Daily 56

Document 2
Key paragraph from script
1.5" top and side margins; DS; 5-space ¶ indention; center title; divide words appropriately

COMMUNICATION SKILLS = EARNING POWER 7

The story in the newspaper emphasized one fact: 17
Ability to communicate is vital. An area survey reveals 29
that young people recently hired to staff jobs in local 40
offices have more chances for promotion and wage in- 50
creases if they have better-than-average ability to 61
communicate. Apparently, language and grammar are 71
still important for one reason: They earn money! 82

Document 3
Key paragraph from rough draft
2" top and side margins; SS; 5-space ¶ indention; center title; divide words appropriately

A MODERN FABLE 3

There was once a rich man ~~who was not very happy.~~ He had 13
spend large sums of for fancy clothes, a ~~beautiful~~ home, 25
luxurious cars --even his own plans --but none of it brought 37
him happiness. his psychiatrist, after weeks oftherapy 48
finally explained that happiness can't be bought; it must be 60
found. And--you guessed it--the unhappy man paid for these 72
words of wisdom with ~~another~~ large sum. 80

149a-b 15'

Skill-building warmup

Use the warmup and production measurement procedures on page 340.

149c 35'

Production measurement

Document 1
Unbound business report with references

words

CLIMBING THE CAREER LADDER] Center 5

The metaphor of climbing a straight career ladder ~~is of~~ no 16
longer exists ~~the past~~. Workers now live in an era ~~of~~ with a turbulent economy 30
and frequent restructuring of workplaces. Corporate ~~M~~mergers, acquisi- 44
tions, and layoffs take place daily. 51

Today, the average worker will experience three career 62
changes before retirement (Robinson, 1993, 75). This fact 74
requires that ~~the~~ workers ~~be more~~ have diverse ~~in their~~ abilities 83
and skills. ~~They~~ Workers will need to update and sharpen their 95
skills constantly. 98

Gain ~~some~~ Technical Expertise 108

Computers have become an ~~vital~~ integral part of every job. 119
Learning how to use the popular computer software packages on 131
the market ~~, such as WordPerfect and Lotus,~~ will give workers 137
an edge over their competitors. Gain ~~some~~ working knowledge on the 151
following software packages: 157

FREQUENTLY USED APPLICATION ~~SOFTWARE~~ PROGRAMS 162

Application	Software Package	
Word processing	WordPerfect	179
Spreadsheet	Lotus	183
Database	dBASE	186
Desktop publishing	PageMaker	192

(Application / Software Package: 174) Center table

~~Classes on using computer~~ Software courses are offered at 198
community colleges, adult education programs, and ~~private~~ career 210
~~business schools~~ colleges. Large corporations often offer computer 220
classes during the workday ~~to~~ for their employees. 229

30 Measurement

Skill-Building Warmup

30a 7'

each line twice SS; DS between 2-line groups; 1' writings on line 4 as time permits

alphabet 1 Jewel quickly explained to me the big fire hazards involved.
symbols 2 Her $300 note (dated May 3) was paid (Check #1343 for $385).
- (hyphen) 3 Pam has an up-to-the-minute plan to lower out-of-town costs.
easy 4 Did the girl make the ornament with fur, duck down, or hair?

| 1 | 2 | 3 | 4 | 5 | 6 | 7 | 8 | 9 | 10 | 11 | 12 |

30b 10'

SKILL BUILDING

Measure skill growth: straight copy

Key with controlled speed two 3' writings DS.
Goals: 3', 19-27 *gwam*

all letters

	gwam 1'	3'
I have a story or two or three that will carry you away	11	4
to foreign places, to meet people you have never known, to	23	8
see things you have never seen, to feast on foods available	35	12
only to a few. I will help you to learn new skills you want	47	16
and need; I will inspire you, excite you, instruct you, and	59	20
interest you. I am able, you understand, to make time fly.	71	24
I answer difficult questions for you. I work with you	11	27
to realize a talent, to express a thought, and to determine	23	31
just who and what you are and want to be. I help you to	35	35
know words, to write, and to read. I help you to comprehend	47	40
the mysteries of the past and the secrets of the future. I	59	44
am your local library. We ought to get together often.	70	47

gwam 1' | 1 | 2 | 3 | 4 | 5 | 6 | 7 | 8 | 9 | 10 | 11 | 12 |
3' | 1 | 2 | 3 | 4 |

30c 33'

FORMATTING

Measure formatting skills

3 full sheets

Time schedule

Assemble materials; check marked references .... 2'
Timed production .... 25'
Final check: Proofread; mark any format errors you see .... 6'

1 Organize your supplies.
2 When the signal to begin is given, insert paper (if using a typewriter) and begin keying Document 1. Key the documents in sequence until the signal to stop is given. Repeat Document 1 if you have time after completing Document 3.
3 Scan for format errors and mark any that you find.

Do the best, not the most, you can do; and you will have better results.

Document 1 (continued)

Continue with Formal Education 241

Obtaining a graduate degree is still a good way to make 253
jump from one job level to another. The average Masters of 269
Business Administration (MBA) student doubles his/her earn- 280
ings within 5 years of graduating (Brown, 1992, 41). 292

Check to see whether the employer provides a tuition 302
reimbursement program. If they do, take advantage of this; 315
it is an investment in the future. 322

Develop a Network 329

Relationships with others can be a workers most valu- 341
able asset. "Networking," says John Pale, "has been, is now, 353
and always will be your greatest asset" (Pale, 1992, 15). 365

Interdisciplinary networks. Networks should be expaned 429
to include people in other industries. If jobs are elimi- 440
nated in the employees' industry, contacts will have been 452
established in others. 456

Internal networks. Develop networks with people within 381
the company. Friendships should not be limited to the imme- 393
diate department or job level; attempt to befriend as many 404
corporate encounters as possible. 411

Bibliography 458

Brown, Raleigh. "Job Hopping--Normal and Expected." Career Magazine. New York: Golden Press, December, 1992. 471 483

Pale, John A. Survival for Today's Job Market. Hayden Lake, Idaho: Corona Press, 1992. 502 508

Robinson, Hilda. The Workplace in the Year 2000. Arlington, Virginia: U.S. Department of Labor Press, 1993. 527 537

29d 13'

SKILL BUILDING

Measure figure skill

Key with controlled speed three 3' writings.

Goals: 3', 16-24 *gwam*

all letters/figures

	gwam 3'	
Do I read the stock market pages in the news? Yes; and	4	35
at about 9 or 10 a.m. each morning, I know lots of excited	8	39
people are quick to join me. In fact, many of us zip right	12	43
to the 3d or 4th part of the paper to see if the prices of	16	47
our stocks have gone up or down. Now, those of us who are	19	51
"speculators" like to "buy at 52 and sell at 60"; while the	23	55
"investors" among us are more interested in a dividend we	27	59
may get, say 7 or 8 percent, than in the price of a stock.	31	62

gwam 3' | 1 | 2 | 3 | 4 |

29e 13'

COMMUNICATION

Key edited copy

1.5" top and side margins; DS

Make corrections as indicated by proofreaders' marks; divide words as appropriate or as directed.

	words
First Impressions	4
take time to evaluate your completed work. Look	13
caefully at what you haved done. Would be you impressed	25
with it ifyou wre a reader? Is it attractive in form and	37
acccurate in content? Does it look like something you wou	49
pick up becaese it looks interesting? Does the title	60
attract you. Do the first couple of lines catch your	70
attention? Personal appraisal of your own work is very	82
important. For If it does not impress you,	91
it will not impress any one else.	96

Document 2
Business report
Key the report SS.

words

TAKAKI COMPONENT PRODUCTS 5
QUOTE SYSTEM 8

The most important function of a sales force is to 18
secure or book business. It is crucial that members of the 31
sales force understand the quote system. The purpose of the 43
quote system is to provide the customer with price and deliv- 55
ery information in a timely manner, to provide a follow-up on 68
each quote to ascertain status, and to book the business. 80

Quote Procedure 86

Three levels of quote have been established. Quotes must be made 101
within the set parameters for each level of sales employees. 113

Sales representative. A sales representative may quote any 129
price equal to or greater than district expense without 140
obtaining approval. 144

Area manager. An area manager may quote any price equal to 158
or greater than the established Area Manager Minimum with- 170
out obtaining prior approval. 175

Headquarter manager. A headquarter manager must quote all 191
price(s) below the established Area Manager Minimum. 202

Upon receipt of a Request For Quote from a customer, the 215
representative will determine if his or her pricing authority 227
is adequate to secure the order. If not, the representative 239
will submit to the appropriate area office a completed Semi- 257
conductor Quote Request Form.

Quote Log 261

Every quote issued will be entered in the Quote Log. Each 273
quote will be given an eight-digit quote number. The area 285
office will fax a version of the log at the end of each week 300
to headquarters. 303

6 Review/Measurement

Learning goals:
1. To achieve smoother, more continuous keying.
2. To key script and rough-draft copy smoothly.
3. To measure ability to key production, straight copy, and copy with figures.

Formatting guides:
1. Default margins or 60-space line.
2. Single space drills; double-space paragraphs.
3. Indent paragraphs 5 spaces.

29a 7'

Skill-building warmup

each line twice SS; DS between 2-line groups; 1' writings on line 4 as time permits

alphabet 1 My wife helped fix a frozen lock on Jacque's vegetable bins.
figures 2 Sherm moved from 823 West 150th Street to 9472--67th Street.
double letters 3 Will Scott attempt to sell his bookkeeping books to Elliott?
easy 4 It is a shame he used the endowment for a visit to the city.

| 1 | 2 | 3 | 4 | 5 | 6 | 7 | 8 | 9 | 10 | 11 | 12 |

29b 10'

SKILL BUILDING

Practice figure and symbol keyreaches

Work for fluency; key each line twice SS; DS between 2-line groups; repeat lines that seemed difficult.

$
5 He spent $25 for gifts, $31 for dinner, and $7 for cab fare.

/
6 As of 6/28, my code number is 1/k; Mona's, 2/k; John's, 3/k.

#
7 Bill #773 charged us for 4# of #33 brads and 6# of #8 nails.

%
8 He deducted 12% instead of 6%, a clear saving of 6%, not 7%.

( )
9 All of us (including Vera) went to the game (and it rained).

29c 7'

SKILL BUILDING

Improve keying techniques

Concentrate on quiet hands, curved fingers; key each line twice SS; DS between 2-line groups.

first row
10 Mr. Caz, an excited man, visits a monument to the brave men.

home row
11 Hal had a glass of soda; Jas had half a dish of fresh salad.

third row
12 You were to key quietly three erudite reports that were due.

top row
13 On April 2, Flight 89 left at 1:30 with 47 men and 65 women.

| 1 | 2 | 3 | 4 | 5 | 6 | 7 | 8 | 9 | 10 | 11 | 12 |

Document 3
Outline

Organize and key this outline; title it **ITC SEMINAR**; use the secondary heading:

Tuesday, (Date)
1 p.m., Red Conference Room

words

I. Overview of Company 5
A. Satellite Service 1. World-wide Links 13
2. Transmission and Reception B. Earth Stations 22
II. Services 25
B. Portable Up/Downlink 30
A. Individual and Group needs: 1. Education 38
2. Business 3. Industry 4. Government 5. Comercial 49
C. Encryption 52
D. Methods: 1. Telephone Lines 2. Cable/Fiber 61
3. Microwave 4. Other Analog/Digital 68
E. Modes: 1. Audio/~~Visual~~ Video 3. Stereo 75
2. Mono 4. Full-Motion 5. Compressed 82
IV. Discussion 85
III. Facility Tour 89

150a-b 15'

Skill-building warmup

Use the warmup and production measurement procedures on page 340.

150c 35'

Production measurement

Document 1
Table

Key the table DS; center column heads; center vertically.

TELETRANSCOM VIDEOCONFERENCE SERVICES AND EQUIPMENT 10

Prices Effective Through June 30, 19-- 18

(center & bold)

Service/Equipment	Time Unit	Cost Per Unit	
			35
Up link	Day	$5,100	38
Down link	Day/Site	850	43
Projector (5'x8' Screen)	Day	1,100	50
Television Monitor	Day	90	55
Public Address System	Day/site	~~250~~ 225	62
Satellite Time	Hour	550	67
Production	Day	5,600	72
Total*		$13,515	75
			79

*Total assumes one site each for downlink and public address system. 91 92

28c 10'

SKILL BUILDING

Troublesome reaches

Key smoothly, unrushed; avoid pauses, and allow your fingers to work. Repeat difficult lines.

n/m

19 Call a woman or a man who will manage Minerva Manor in Nome.

q/?

20 When did Marq Quin go? Did Quentin or Quincy Quin go? Why?

v/b

21 Barb Abver saw a vibrant version of her brave venture on TV.

w/q

22 We were quick to squirt a quantity of water at Quin and Wes.

4/5

23 On July 5, 54 of us had only 45 horses; 4 of them were lame.

9/0

24 Back in '90, Car 009 traveled 90 miles, getting 9 to 10 mpg.

28d 7'

COMMUNICATION

Edit as you key

Read carefully and key each line twice at a controlled pace; edit as indicated by proofreaders' marks; compare your completed lines with those of 26e, page 59.

25 Ask Group 1 to read Chater 6 of Book 11 (Shelf 19, Room 5).

26 All 6 of us live at One Bay road, not at 126--56th Street.

27 AT 9 a.m. the owners decided to close form 12 noon to 1 p.m.

28 Ms. Vik leaves June 9; she r eturns the 14 or 15 of July.

29 The 16 per cent discount saves 115. A stamp costs 35 cents.

30 Elin gave ~~$300,000,000~~; our gift was only 75 cents.

28e 12'

SKILL BUILDING

Build staying power

Keep eyes on copy, wrists low. Key a 1' writing on each ¶; then key two 3' writings on both ¶s.

E all letters

gwam 3'

Why don't we like change very much? Do you think that 4 26
just maybe we want to be lazy; to dodge things new; and, as 8 30
much as possible, not to make hard decisions? 11 33

We know change can and does extend new areas for us to 15 37
enjoy, areas we might never have known existed; and to stay 18 41
away from all change could curtail our quality of life. 22 44

gwam 3' | 1 | 2 | 3 | 4 |

Document 2
Ruled table
Block column headings; center vertically.

					words
Balboa College Enrollment) Bold					5
Spring Semester, 1991-1994)					11
					30
Class	1991	1992	1993	1994	35
					44
Freshman	1,521	1,516	1,531	1,503	51
Sophomore	1,340	1,343	1,350	1,351	58
Junior	1,298	1,302	1,275	1,309	64
Senior	850	935	926	917	68
					78

Document 3
Balance sheet
Key this 3-column balance sheet; insert leaders in each row containing figures.

			words
HALL GENERAL FUND			
Balance Sheet			4
			6
June 30, 19--			9
ASSETS _ DS			11
Cash		$93,420.12	25
Taxes Receivable--Delinquent	16,240.34		40
Less Allowance for Uncollectible Taxes . .	7,294.00	8,946.34	55
Interest Receivable . . . . DS>	2,344.00		67
Less Allowance for Uncollectible Interest	325.00	2,019.00	80
Inventory of Supplies } DS		3,995.00	93
Total Assets		$108,380.46	109
LIABILITIES AND FUND EQUITY — center DS			114
Liabilities:			117
Accounts Payable _ DS		$45,125.30	128
Fund Equity:			130
Unreserved Fund Balance	56,451.16		141
Reserve for Encumbrances--Prior Year	2,942.00		152
Reserve for Inventory of Supplies	3,862.00		165
Total Fund Equity _ DS		63,255.16	177
Total Liabilities and Fund Equity		$108,380.46	193

28 Other Symbols

Skill-Building Warmup

28a 7'

each line twice SS; DS between 2-line groups; 30" writings on line 4 (try to complete the line)

alphabet 1 Pfc. Jim Kings covered each of the lazy boxers with a quilt.
figures 2 Do Problems 6 to 29 on page 175 before class at 8:30, May 4.
" 3 They read the poems "September Rain" and "The Lower Branch."
easy 4 When did the busy girls fix the tight cowl of the ruby gown?

1 | 2 | 3 | 4 | 5 | 6 | 7 | 8 | 9 | 10 | 11 | 12

28b 14' OS

Note location of <, >, [,], @, *, +, =, and !

each pair of lines twice SS; DS between 2-line groups

These keys are less commonly used, but they are needed in special circumstances. Unless your instructor tells you otherwise, you may key these reaches with visual help.

- * = asterisk, star
- + = "plus sign" (use a hyphen for "minus"; x for "times")
- @ = "at sign"
- = = "equals sign"
- < = "less than"
- > = "more than"
- [= "left bracket"
-] = "right bracket"
- ! = exclamation point

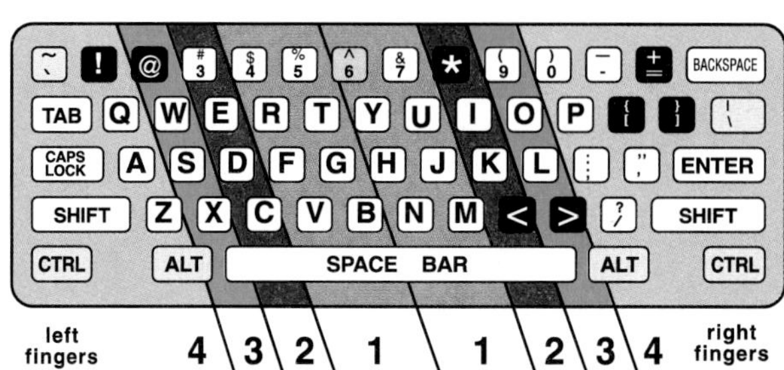

* Shift; reach up with right second finger to *.

5 * *k k8* * *; aurelis*; May 7*; both sides*; 250 km.**; aka*
6 Note each *; one * refers to page 29; ** refers to page 307.

\+ Shift; reach up with right little finger to +.

7 + ;+ +; + + +; 2 + 2; A+ or B+; 70+ F. degrees; +xy over +y;
8 The question was 8 + 7 + 51; it should have been 8 + 7 + 15.

@ Shift; reach up with left third finger to @.

9 @ @s s@ @ @; 24 @ .15; 22 @ .35; sold 2 @ .87; were 12 @ .95
10 Ship 560 lbs. @ .36, 93 lbs. @ .14, and 3 lbs. @ .07 per lb.

= Reach up with right little finger to =.

11 = =; ;= = =; = 4; If 14x = 28, x = 2; if 8 = 16, then 1 = 2.
12 Change this solution (where it says "= by") to = bx or = BX.

< Shift; reach down with right second finger to <. > Shift; reach down with right third finger to >.

13 Can you prove "a > b"? If 28 > 5, then 5a < x. Is a < > b?
14 Is your answer < > .05? Computer programs use < and > keys.

[ ] Reach up with right little finger to [and].

15 Mr. Wing was named. [That's John J. Wing, ex-senator. Ed.]
16 Mr. Lanz said in his note, "I am moving to Filly [sic] now."

! Shift, reach up with left little finger to !.

17 Yes! My new clubs are in! Just watch my score go down now!
18 I got the job! With Ross & Myer! Please call Lonal for me!

words

Document 4
Agenda
Insert leaders between columns. Key second column flush right.

TENTH ANNUAL ONCOLOGY CONGRESS 6

Concurent Session No. 4 11

Center

Tuesday, November 3, 19-- 1:00-5:00p.m. 20 31

Session Topic: Regulation of Cell Growth 39

50

No.	Topic	Presenter	
			58
4A	Radiation-Induced Genetic Mutations	Dr. Wade Bilello	69
4B	Hybridization of Onconogenes	Dr. Sherry Fitz	79
4C	Soft Tissue Tumors	Dr. Michael Chong	87
4D	Myelomas and Radiation Therpay	Ms. Sue Brooks	97
4E	Regulation of Cell Defferentiation	Dr. Plam Nguyen	108

119

Moderator: Dr. Julie Bishop Recorder: Dr. David Perez 130

Document 5
Action minutes
Center title appropriately:
MEDICINE COMMITTEE
August 12, 19--
Action Minutes

Presiding: Paul Bidell, M.D. 6

Participants: Arthur De La Rosa, M.D.; Susan Burke, M.D.; 18
Timothy Lim, M.D.; Susan Otto, R.N.; Regina Rajan, M.D.; and 30
Laura Weiss, Medical Records Director 38

Dr. Burke presented the Quality Assessment Reporting Form 49
covering the months of April through July. The Emergency 61
Room (ER) Charts were reviewed. It was recommended that the 73
number of charts reviewed be limited to ten per month. The 85
chief ER physician is responsible for notifying physicians 97
who have noncompliant charts and for assisting them with mak- 109
ing corrections. 113

Dr. Rajan gave a brief update on the Psychiatry Department. 125
The department's Quality Monitoring Evaluation Plan was ten- 137
tatively approved. 141

Dr. De La Rosa reviewed the Blood Transfusion Report for the 153
months of June and July; no additional recommendations were 165
needed. 167

The Medical Mortality Report was deferred until the next 178
meeting. 180

Writing 42 all letters

	gwam 3'	5'	
One significant way a person can improve her or his ability	4	2	63
to be effective when communicating thoughts is to concentrate on	8	5	65
improving speaking and listening skills. Much can be said for a	13	8	68
person who is able to present a message that is comprehended and	17	10	71
used by another. Much can be said, also, for a person who lis-	21	13	73
tens to an idea and interprets the speaker's meaning. Engaging	25	15	76
in an exchange of ideas is a great way of adding to an informa-	30	18	78
tion base as well as broadening the mind.	33	20	80
A free exchange of thought is based on the premise that each	37	22	82
person should be able to add to and gain some benefit from a con-	41	25	85
versation. This simple rule of thumb is why it is vitally impor-	45	27	87
tant not only to express oneself but also to have extremely good	50	30	90
listening skills. A dull conversation usually is the unfortunate	54	32	93
outcome of one individual doing most of the talking. Such a	58	35	95
person is not mindful of the needs and interests of others.	62	37	98
Everyone should just realize that a key to good conversation is	66	40	100
meeting the interests of all involved.	69	42	102
Skills in exchanging ideas are sharpened when good con-	73	44	104
versation techniques are learned. That is, a person needs to	77	46	106
know when to ask a question, when to debate an issue, when to	81	49	109
voice an opinion, and when to listen to others. When all people	85	51	111
involved are able to be a part of the conversation and each per-	89	54	114
son is able to listen to others and also contribute ideas, unique	94	56	117
and broad insights into a situation can be gained, resulting in	98	59	121
a productive exchange of information.	101	60	121

gwam 3' | 1 | 2 | 3 | 4 | 5 |
5' | 1 | 2 | 3 |

Document 12
Align text flush right
Word: From the Tab dialog box, set a right leader tab at 6.0".
WordPerfect: Key the text at the left margin and press ALT + **F7** twice.

Pitcher . . . . Matthew Daniel
First base . . . . John D. Forde
Second base . . . . Jeff Watson
Third base . . . . Miquel Sanchez
Shortstop . . . . Patrick Johnson

Page Numbers

Use the **Page Numbers** function to automatically number the pages as you want them. Generally, position page numbers at the top of the page at the right margin. To avoid printing the page number on page 1 of the document, suppress the page number on page 1. Suppress is the default in *Word*, so it is not necessary to turn on this command.

To insert page numbers:

Word:

1. Choose *Page Numbers* from the Insert menu.
2. Select *Top of Page (Header)* in the position box.
3. Select *Right* in the Alignment box. A check mark should not appear in the Show Number on First Page box.
4. Choose *Page Layout* from the View menu to view the page numbers.

WordPerfect:

1. Choose *Page Numbering* from the Format menu, then *Select.*
2. From the Position drop-down list, select *Top Right.*
3. From the Page Numbering Format box, click **1** to select it.
4. To turn on Suppress, choose *Format, Page,* and *Suppress.* Click the Page Numbering box to place an "x" in the box.

Widow/Orphan

Widow/Orphan prevents a single line of a paragraph from printing at the bottom or top of a page. Widow/Orphan is the default in *Word.* In *WordPerfect,* choose *Page* from the Format menu, then *Keep Text Together.* Click the **Widow/Orphan** box and **OK** to activate Widow/Orphan.

Document 13
Create page numbers

1. In a new document, turn on the page numbering command; choose the option for printing just the page number in the upper right corner of the page. Suppress the page number so it doesn't print on the first page. Then key the following text.

   This is page 1 of my document. I have inserted the command for page numbering at the top of the document and suppressed the page number so it does not print on page 1.

2. Insert a hard page break a DS below the text.
3. Key the following text. This is page two of my document.
4. Insert a second hard page break. Key: This is page 3 of my document.
5. Preview your document on screen. Check that the page number does not show on page 1; and that page numbers 2 and 3 display.

Headers and Footers

The **Header** function places information at the top of each page. Footers place information at the bottom. In *Word* a header or footer is placed 0.5" from the top or bottom of the page; the default for *WordPerfect* is 1". Page numbers, graphic lines, and the date can be added to a header or footer automatically. Headers may be suppressed on the first page.

Progressive goal writings

all letters

Writing 40: **85 *gwam***

	gwam 1'	3'	
Business letters can be defined by their goals; for example,	12	4	60
a letter of inquiry, a reply letter, a promotion letter, a credit	25	8	65
letter, or other specialized letter. While you learn to compose	38	13	69
these letters, just keep each letter's individual goals always in	52	17	74
front of you. If you fix in your mind a theme, pattern, and	64	21	78
ideal for your writing, composing good business letters may	75	25	82
emerge as one of the best tricks in your bag.	85	28	85
Competent business writers know what they want to say--and	12	32	89
they say it with simplicity and clarity. Words are the utensils	25	37	93
they use to convey ideas or to convince others to accomplish some	38	41	98
action. The simple word and the short sentence usually are more	51	45	102
effective than the big word and the involved sentence. But don't	64	50	106
be afraid of the long or unusual word if it means exactly what	77	54	111
you intend to say in your business letter.	85	57	113

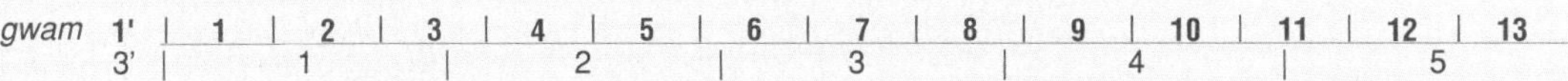

Writing 41: **90 *gwam***

	gwam 1'	3'	
Although many of us are basically comfortable with sameness	12	4	64
and appear to dislike change, we actually prize variation. We	24	8	68
believe that we are each unique individuals, yet we know that we	38	12	72
are really only a little different; and we struggle to find	50	16	76
"sense of self" in how we think and act. Our cars, too, built	62	21	81
on assembly lines are basically identical; yet when we purchase	75	25	85
one, we choose model, color, size, and style which suits us	87	29	89
individually.	90	30	90
Also many people expect to find security by buying things	12	34	94
that are in keeping with society's "image" and "status." But	24	38	98
what we think of as "status" always changes. The wise buyer will	37	42	102
buy those items that give most in utility, comfort, and satisfac-	50	47	106
tion. Status should just be a thing we create in ourselves, not	63	51	111
a thing created for us. Common sense should guide us in making	76	55	115
good decisions--and if our "status" is increased thereby, well,	89	59	119
why not?	90	60	120

gwam 1' | 1 | 2 | 3 | 4 | 5 | 6 | 7 | 8 | 9 | 10 | 11 | 12 | 13 |
3' | 1 | 2 | 3 | 4 | 5 |

Document 14
Add multi-page commands

1. Open any two-page document such as a report that you have previously prepared.
2. Delete any existing page numbers or hard returns.
3. Add the following information to create a header on page 1:

   Your name
   Page #
   Today's date
4. Suppress the header on page 1. Turn on Widow/Orphan protection on page 1.
5. Save and print.

Lines and Borders

Lines and borders are two common names that describe lines placed around text to make it more attractive. Lines may either be horizontal or vertical. Borders enclose text within a box. Borders may be applied to paragraphs or an entire page. The thickness and style of lines may vary. Line thickness is measured in points—the larger the point size, the thicker the line.

The default for horizontal lines is the distance between the left and right margins. You can create lines that are shorter or that begin at a point other than the left margin.

WordPerfect: From the Graphics menu, choose *Custom line.* Set the horizontal or vertical starting position and then set the line length.

Word: Drag the left indent triangle on the ruler to the starting position of the line; drag the right indent triangle for the end position.

________________ 3/4 pt.

________________ 1 1/2 pt.

Lines

Student Name

Your Course Name

Borders

Fill or Shading

Shading or Fill emphasizes text. When shading is added to text within a border, be sure that text can be read easily. Generally shading of 10-20% is readable. Photocopy machines tend to darken shading; therefore, use caution. Shading or Fill is applied from the Paragraph Border/Fill dialog box (*WordPerfect*) or from the Borders toolbar (*Word 6/7*).

Document 15
Lines, Borders, Shading
Follow the steps at the right.

1. Center the heading in 20-point font.
2. Add a graphic line on the line above the title. DS below the heading and add another horizontal line.

Crown Lake Connection

---

3. Center the heading again in 20-point bold font. Add a paragraph border around the heading.

Crown Lake Connection

Document 16
More lines and borders
Practice creating lines and borders similar to the four examples shown preceding Document 15.

4. Copy and paste the title created in Step 3. Add a 20% fill to the box.

Crown Lake Connection

Progressive goal writings

all letters

Writing 38: **75 *gwam***

	gwam 1'	3'	
Getting a job interview is certainly a triumph for the job	12	4	54
seeker. Yet anxiety quickly sets in as the applicant becomes	24	8	58
aware of the competition. The same attention to details that was	37	12	62
used in writing the successful resume will also be needed for the	51	17	67
interview. Experts often say that the first four minutes are the	64	21	71
most crucial in making a strong impact on the interviewer.	75	25	75
First, people focus on what they see. Posture, eye contact,	12	29	79
facial expression, and gestures make up over half of the message.	26	33	84
Next, people focus on what they hear; enthusiasm, delivery, pace,	39	38	88
volume, and clarity are as vital as what is said. Finally,	51	42	92
people get to the actual words that are said. You can make a	63	49	96
good impression. But, realize, you have just four minutes.	75	50	100

Writing 39: **80 *gwam***

	gwam 1'	3'	
Would a pitcher go to the mound without warming up? Would a	12	4	57
speaker go to the podium without practice? Of course not! These	25	8	62
experts have spent many long hours striving to do their best.	38	13	66
Similarly, the performance of business employees is rated. The	51	17	70
manager's evaluation will include a record of actual performance	64	21	75
and a list of new goals. A good mark in these areas will demand	77	26	79
much hard work.	80	27	80
Many work factors can be practiced to help one succeed on	12	30	84
the job. Class attendance and punctuality can be perfected by	24	35	88
students. Because work is expected to be correct, managers do	37	39	92
not assign zeros. Thus, students must learn to proofread their	49	43	96
work. A project must also be completed quickly. Students can	62	47	101
learn to organize work and time well and to find ways to do their	75	52	105
work smarter and faster.	80	53	107

gwam														
1'	1	2	3	4	5	6	7	8	9	10	11	12	13	
3'		1		2		3		4			5			

Columns

Columns provide an easy way to format newsletters in an attractive, easy-to-read format. Similar to a newspaper, text is read down one column and up the next. By default, text is formatted in two columns of equal widths. Options are available in the Columns dialog box for changing the number of columns and their widths. The Columns feature is often available on the Format menu; it may also be available on the toolbar. When text formatted in newspaper columns is less than a page long, the columns are balanced—that is, the text is divided about equally among the columns. Generally, columns have a **banner heading**—that is, a heading that spans or is centered over all columns.

Document 17
Two-column newsletter

1. Set 1" side margins. Use 20-point font for the banner. Add a paragraph border, 100% shading, and change the font to white for the banner.
2. Using Columns, format the newsletter with two equal 3" columns with 0.5" between columns.
3. DS above and below each heading.

Crown Lake News and Views

New Development Project

Crown Lake won the bid to develop and construct the new multimillion dollar Business Center adjacent to Metro Airport. Connie McClure, one of the three senior project managers, has been named as the Business Center project manager. The project will take more than two years to complete.

Approximately fifty new permanent employees will be hired to work on this project. The recruiting referral program is in effect for all jobs. You can earn a $100 bonus for each individual you recommend who is hired and remains with Crown Lake for at least six months.

Blood Drive Reminder

The Crown Lake quarterly blood drive is set for Friday, April 4, in the Wellness Center. The Community Blood Bank needs all types of blood to replace the supplies sent to the islands during the recent disaster caused by Hurricane Lana. The top priority is for Type O blood this quarter.

Lee Daye Honored

The Community Foundation honored Lee Daye with the Eagle Award for outstanding service this year. The Community Foundation recognized Lee for his work with underprivileged children. Congratulations, Lee, for making a difference in the lives of many citizens in our community.

New Training Program

The pilot test of the new Team Effectiveness training program was completed last month, and the results were excellent. Thanks to all of you who participated in the development and testing of the program.

Students Function as Consultants

In late spring, President John Marcus notified us that a team of international MBA students from the Business School at State University would be working with us to develop an export strategy for Crown Lake and asked us to cooperate fully with the team. Most of us felt that we were being asked to take on a project that was essentially a "public service" contribution to the University.

Were we ever wrong!!! It only took us one day to realize that these five graduate students would function as a highly effective, results-oriented consulting team.

This past week the team presented the final results of their field consulting project to our division management team. The bottom line is that we now have an export strategy for three of our product lines and a viable implementation plan to begin exporting to Canada and Mexico early next year. Partnering with the University was truly a win-win situation!

—Roberta C. West

Newsletter Staff
Eric Burge
Editor
Christopher Hess
Anne Reynolds
Associate Editors

March 25, 19--

Crown Lake News and Views

New Development Project

Crown Lake won the bid to develop and construct the new multimillion dollar Business Center adjacent to Metro Airport. Connie McClure, one of the three senior project managers, has been named as the Business Center project manager. The project will take more than two years to complete.

Approximately fifty new permanent employees will be hired to work on this project. The recruiting referral program is in effect for all jobs. You can earn a $100 bonus for each individual you recommend who is hired and remains with Crown Lake for at least six months.

Blood Drive Reminder

The Crown Lake quarterly blood drive is set for Friday, April 4, in the Wellness Center. The Community Blood Bank needs all types of blood to replace the supplies sent to the islands during the recent disaster caused by Hurricane Lana. The top priority is for Type O blood this quarter.

Lee Daye Honored

The Community Foundation honored Lee Daye with the Eagle Award for outstanding service this year. The Community Foundation recognized Lee for his work with underprivileged children. Congratulations, Lee, for making a difference in the lives of many citizens in our community.

New Training Program

The pilot test of the new Team Effectiveness training program was completed last month, and the results were excellent. Thanks to all of you who participated in the development and testing of the program.

Students Function as Consultants

In late spring, President John Marcus notified us that a team of international MBA students from the Business School at State University would be working with us to develop an export strategy for Crown Lake and asked us to cooperate fully with the team. Most of us felt that we were being asked to take on a project that was essentially a "public service" contribution to the University.

Were we ever wrong!!! It only took us one day to realize that these five graduate students would function as a highly effective, results-oriented consulting team.

This past week the team presented the final results of their field consulting project to our division management team. The bottom line is that we now have an export strategy for three of our product lines and a viable implementation plan to begin exporting to Canada and Mexico early next year. Partnering with the University was truly a win-win situation!

—Roberta C. West

Newsletter Staff
Eric Burge
Editor
Christopher Hess
Anne Reynolds
Associate Editors

March 25, 19--

Progressive goal writings

all letters

Writing 36: **65 *gwam***

	gwam 1'	3'	
Humor is very important in our professional and our personal	12	4	47
lives. Fortunately, we realize that many things can and do go	25	8	52
wrong. If we can learn to laugh at ourselves and with other	37	12	56
people, we will get through the terrible times. Adding a little	50	17	60
extra laughter can help put the situation in proper perspective	63	21	64
much quicker.	65	22	65
Maintaining our sense of humor lets us enjoy our positions	12	26	69
to a greater degree. No one is perfect, and we cannot expect	24	30	73
perfection from ourselves. However, the quality of our perfor-	37	34	77
mance is greater when we do the things we like. We realize our	50	38	82
prime time is devoted to work. Thus, it is important that we	62	42	86
enjoy this time.	65	43	87

Writing 37: **70 *gwam***

	gwam 1'	3'	
Foreign study and travel take extra time and effort, but	11	4	50
these two activities quickly help us to understand people. Much	24	8	55
can be learned from other cultures. Today, business must think	37	12	59
globally. Learning about the culture of others is not a luxury.	50	17	63
Even the owner of a small business realizes that he or she cannot	64	21	68
just focus on the domestic scene.	70	23	70
Many examples can be used to show how a local business may	11	27	74
be influenced by global competition. A hair stylist may be re-	24	31	78
quired to learn European styles because customers may want to try	38	36	83
a style just like they saw on their travels. Or salons may want	51	40	87
to offer other services such as facials that people have tried	63	44	91
while they were traveling abroad.	70	47	93

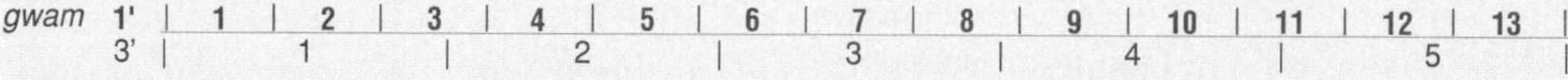

Clipart

Clipart is a collection of images that are ready to be inserted in your document from your software. Once clipart is added, it can be sized or moved. To size an image, click to select it. Handles (small squares) will appear. Position the pointer on one of the corners. When the arrow changes, drag the double-pointing arrow to size the image. To move an image, first select it. When the pointer becomes a four-way pointing arrow, hold down the left mouse button and drag the image to its new location. In *Word 6*, insert the image in a frame (Insert menu, Frame) and then click, hold down the left mouse button and move it.

Document 18
Announcement with graphic

1. Insert a graphic image of your choice. (Choose Insert menu, Object, *Microsoft Clipart Gallery*, and OK.)
2. Size image to about 50% of its original size.
3. Select and center the image.
4. Format the text as marked.

Jazz Band Concert

DS

Thursday, June 11, 19--

SS

8 p.m.

Student Center Auditorium

Arial 36 pt.

QS

Come join the Jazz Band as it plays favorites from the 60s, 70s, and 80s. Listen to the bands smooth sounds playing selections from the John Tesch Project, Manhattan Transfer, Chicago, and Windham Hill.

Arial 18 pt.

Document 19
Announcement with image and lines

1. Key heading at margin; use bold, 20 pt., and SMALL CAPS (font dialog box).
2. Add a horizontal line below the heading.
3. Insert an image from the *Microsoft Clipart Gallery*. Position to the right of the heading; make it about 2.5" wide.
4. Format "Market Trends" as marked. Add a border to the heading and shade.
5. Add second image where marked.
6. Key the last line as a footer.

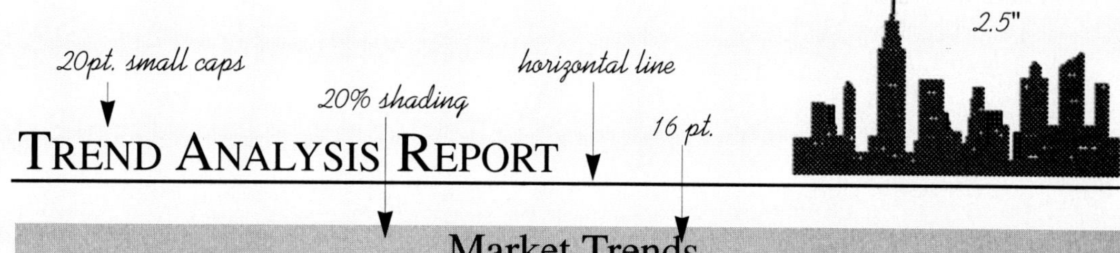

- The population in the metropolitan area is growing both in the college's service area and in the demographic segments that represent the greatest market enrollment penetration.
- The metropolitan area continues to add employment opportunities at a growth rate of 22 percent, but the area economy suffers from insecurities about the future.
- Information technology is creating more customer potential and new demands for the delivery of course work.
- The pace of change is forcing people at all levels of the economy to learn new skills at the same time people are being asked to work harder--and sometimes hold more than one job.

add 2d image

Understanding our community to prepare for our future

Progressive goal writings

all letters

Writing 34: **55 *gwam***

	gwam 1'	3'	
A crucial life skill is the ability to put things in proper	12	4	41
perspective. Individuals often fail to realize that many things	25	8	45
are just not worth fighting about. A quick way to know whether	38	13	50
an issue is worth fighting for is to look at the situation from a	51	17	54
long-term perspective.	55	18	55
If you will care five or six years from now that you de-	11	22	59
fended an issue, it is a principle worth defending. If you will	24	26	63
not even remember, the situation does not justify the effort	36	31	67
required for defending it. The odds of winning are also impor-	49	35	72
tant. Why fight a losing battle?	55	37	74

gwam 1' | 1 | 2 | 3 | 4 | 5 | 6 | 7 | 8 | 9 | 10 | 11 | 12 | 13 |
3' | 1 | 2 | 3 | 4 | 5 |

Writing 35: **60 *gwam***

	gwam 1'	3'	
Why do we remember some things and forget others? Often,	12	4	44
we associate loss of memory with aging or an illness such as	24	8	48
Alzheimer's disease. However, the crux of the matter is that we	37	12	52
all forget various things that we prefer to remember. We tend to	50	17	57
remember things that mean something special to us.	60	20	60
For many people, recalling dates is a difficult task; yet	12	24	64
they manage to remember dates of special occasions, such as anni-	25	28	68
versaries. Processing requires one not only to hear but to	37	33	72
ponder and to understand what has just been said. We recall	49	37	77
things that we say and do longer than things we hear and see.	60	40	80

gwam 1' | 1 | 2 | 3 | 4 | 5 | 6 | 7 | 8 | 9 | 10 | 11 | 12 | 13 |
3' | 1 | 2 | 3 | 4 | 5 |

APPENDIX

SELKIRK COMMUNICATIONS, PROJECT 1

For use after Lesson 60.
Project objectives:
1. Apply your keyboarding, formatting, and word processing skills.
2. Work with few specific directions.

Selkirk Communications is a training company that is relocating its office from Spokane, Washington, to Nelson, Canada. As an administrative assistant, you will prepare a number of documents using many of the formatting skills you have previously learned. Selkirk Communications uses the block letter format and unbound report style.

Document 1 Invitation

Format this document attractively. Use bold for the main heading and callouts (PLACE, TIME, etc.). DS between listed items; position the document attractively on the page.

WP Vary font sizes. Use bullets for the listed items.

words

OPEN HOUSE 2

PLACE: Selkirk Communications 8
1003 Baker St. 11
Nelson BC V1L 5N7 15

TIME: 1:00-4:00 p.m. 20

DATE: Saturday and Sunday, April 27 and 28 29

Selkirk Communications is excited to open its tenth international com- 43
munications office in downtown Nelson. Please plan to attend the Open 57
House. 58

Come in and meet our friendly staff. Learn how we can help meet your 72
training needs. 76

Selkirk Communications specializes in: 84

* Instructor-Led Training in Our Classroom or Your Facility 96

* Newsletters Designed to Meet Your Needs 104

* Authorized Training Center for *Microsoft Office* and *Corel Suite 7* 118

* Oral and Written Communication Refresher Courses 128

Progressive goal writings

1' and 3' writings (pp. A41-A45)

Strive for speed and control separately at each speed by:

1. Completing each ¶ in 1'.
2. Completing each ¶ with no more than 1 error per minute.

Each set of paragraphs progresses by 5 words. Try to maintain your skill for 3'.

 all letters

Writings 31-41 are available on MicroPace Plus software. To access writings on MicroPace Plus, key W and the writing number. For example, key **W31**.

Writing 31: **40 *gwam***

	gwam 1'	3'	
"An ounce of prevention is worth a pound of cure" is really	12	4	31
based on fact; still, many people comprehend this statement more	25	8	35
for its quality as literature than as a practical, common-sense	38	12	39
philosophy.	40	13	40
Just take health, for example. We agonize over stiff costs	12	17	44
we pay to recover from illnesses; but, on the other hand, we give	25	22	48
little or no attention to health requirements for diet, exercise,	38	26	53
and sleep.	40	27	53

Writing 32: **45 *gwam***

	gwam 1'	3'	
Problems with our environment show an odd lack of foresight.	12	4	34
We just expect that whatever we may need to support life will be	25	8	38
available. We rarely question our comforts, even though they may	39	13	43
abuse our earth, water, and air.	45	15	45
Optimism is an excellent virtue. It is comforting to think	12	19	49
that eventually anything can be fixed. So why should we worry?	25	23	53
A better idea, certainly, is to realize that we don't have to fix	38	28	58
anything we have not yet broken.	45	30	60

Writing 33: **50 *gwam***

	gwam 1'	3'	
Recently, a friend of mine grumbled about how quickly papers	12	4	37
accumulated on her desk; she never seemed able to reduce them to	25	8	42
zero. She said some law seemed to be working that expanded the	38	13	46
stack today by precisely the amount she reduced it yesterday.	50	17	50
She should organize her papers and tend to them daily. Any	12	21	54
paper that needs a look, a decision, and speedy, final action	24	25	58
gets just that; any that needs closer attention is subject to a	37	29	62
fixed completion schedule. Self-discipline is the key to order.	50	33	67

gwam 1'	1	2	3	4	5	6	7	8	9	10	11	12	13
3'	1			2			3			4		5	

words

Document 2
Block letter

This letter includes the company name. Key it a DS below the complimentary closing in ALL CAPS. QS to the writer's name.

February 8, 19-- | Chamber of Commerce | 225 Hall St. | Nelson BC V1L 13
5X4 | CANADA 15

Selkirk Communications will be relocating its headquarters from 32
Spokane, Washington, to downtown Nelson on April 1. We are an inter- 46
national communications company, offering the following services: 59

1. Written and oral communications refresher workshops 70
2. Customized training on-site or in our training center 82
3. Mail-order newsletters 87
4. Computer training on popular business software 97
5. Individualized or group training sessions 106

I would like to attend the Nelson Chamber of Commerce meeting in 119
March to share some of the exciting ways we can help Chamber members 133
meet their training needs. Is there time available for us on your March 147
agenda? Please contact Anthony Baker, public relations coordinator, at 162
our Nelson office at (604) 555-1093. 169

Selkirk Communications will be holding an open house during the month 183
of April, and we will be inviting you and the Nelson community to attend. 198
We look forward to becoming actively involved with the business com- 212
munity of Nelson. 216

Yours truly | SELKIRK COMMUNICATIONS | Richard R. Holmes, President 229

Document 3
Memorandum

TO: Marilyn Smith, Public Relations Media Assistant | **FROM:** Anthony 14
Baker, Public Relations Coordinator | **DATE:** February 16, 19-- | 26
SUBJECT: Electronic Presentation 33

Richard Holmes has been invited to introduce our company at the March 47
15 meeting of the Nelson Chamber of Commerce. Please prepare a 20- 60
minute electronic presentation for this meeting by extracting the key 74
points from Richard's speech, which is attached. 84

As you prepare the presentation, remember these key points: 96

1. Write phrases, not sentences, so that listeners focus on the key points. 111
2. Use parallel structure and limit wraparound lines of text. 124
3. Create *builds* to keep the audience alert. 133
4. Add transitions between slides (suggest fade in and out). 145
5. Add graphics and humor--we want them to remember us. 156

Please have the presentation ready for Richard to review by February 24. 171
After he has made his revisions and the presentation is final, print the 186
presentation as a handout. | xx | Attachment 194

Drill 15
Response patterns

Key: each set of lines twice.

Tip: Combination response drills contain both word- and letter-response sequences. Use top speed for easy words and lower speed for words that are harder to key.

Combination Response Drills

1 it to the us me you so go now we my he two in can her by of do no
2 it is | it is the | is it | is it you | he can | can he | he can go | can he go
3 who is | who is it | is it you | you can go | can you go | you can go to it

4 car mail two you may just can lake ask sail sign his form her who
5 who can sail | you can sail | you may sign | can you sign | sign his form
6 sign the form | mail the form | sign and mail | sign and mail that form

7 look back ahead spend time carve beef play songs happy times sing
8 look back | look ahead | spend time | sing songs | happy times | carve beef
9 sing happy songs | look back | carve that beef | spend happy time ahead

Phrases

10 it was | was it so | she can go to | can he go to the | can she go to the
11 she can | she may not | she may not go | can you go to the | so we may go
12 sign the | sign the form | they may sign that | they may sign that form
13 find the | find the lake | find the lake soon | did they find that lake
14 cut the | cut the cake | they cut the cake | can they cut that cake now
15 they work | they may work | did they work here | she may soon work here
16 sign the | sign the form | sign the form to | sign the form to work now
17 they left | they left when | when can they move | so they can move soon

Variable Rhythm

18 Sue and Bob may go to the zoo, and he or she may pay for the bid.
19 Jim was sad; Ted saw him as we sat on my bed; we saw him get gas.
20 Les may go to see Pam, and we may try to go see her if we can go.
21 Lee is ill; Ann is ill, too; but Ann can pay the fee for the tee.

22 She can call Jake and Hale; Jane paid them for the work they did.
23 Jimmy gave Fred fast car after fast car; Ted gave Fred extra gas.
24 Dave only paid for the room and gas; Lynn paid for the meal cost.
25 Ann will drop that book off for Lynn; add all fees Buzz will pay.

26 Eight firms turn down city work; they said risks shape city work.
27 Jimmy saved vast cedar trees; extra water rates only defer waste.
28 The data from the firm audit show the city faces risk from debts.
29 Jeff will cook eggs from noon until Lee Ann feeds that huge mass.

1' | 1 | 2 | 3 | 4 | 5 | 6 | 7 | 8 | 9 | 10 | 11 | 12 | 13 |

Note: Word counts for missing parts have been added to appropriate lines.

Document 4
Table

1. Format the purchase order as a 4-column table. Center the table vertically and horizontally.
2. Calculate all totals.

WP Use table formatting options to add lines and shading.

words

PURCHASE ORDER 3

(Current date) 7

Quantity	Description	Unit Price	Total Price	words
				15
2	Ergonomic Comfort computer chairs	$455.00		26
2	Slide-out keyboard shelf	54.00		33
36	3 1/2" high-density/double-sided formatted disks	1.99		46
1	10-ream carton laser printer paper (20 lb.)	54.25		57
3	HP LaserJet Series 4 toner cartridge #92298A	145.89		69
2	Address labels 1" x 2 5/8", white, #5160	24.95		80
	Total			83

Document 5
Block letter

1. Key the Document 4 table again as part of this order letter.
2. Make the letter fit on one page.
3. Use the current date.
4. Add an appropriate salutation.
5. Format the company name in closing lines in ALL CAPS.

WP Copy Document 4 and place in letter.

WP You can adjust vertical placement of a document after it is keyed.

West Coast Office Supplies 9
3245 Granville St. 12
Vancouver BC V6B 5H8 17

Please ship the following items, which are listed in 32
your current office supplies catalog. 39

Insert the table here (Document 4)

Please bill this to our account number 4056278. This 50
order is urgent; therefore, ship it overnight by Loomis. 62

Yours truly 64
Selkirk Communications 69

Allan Burgess, Purchasing Agent 75

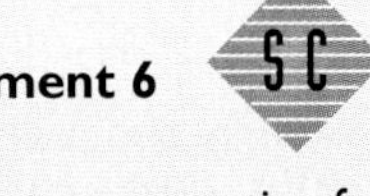

Document 6
Table

1. Select an attractive format for the table.
2. Add at least 2 words that you frequently misspell.
3. Supply the correct spellings in the right-hand column.

Frequently Misspelled Words 6

Misspelled	Correct Spelling	words
		11
recieve		14
accomodate		19
convience		23
similiar		27
to (meaning also)		31
congradulations		38
envelop		41
inclosure		45

Drill 13
Improve speed

Key: each 3-line group as a 1' writing.

Goal: to increase your speed with each successive writing.

Tip: Key easy, balanced-hand words and phrases as a unit.

2- and 3-stroke words and phrases

1 ox aid us rut am pan do and go ant is rub by ape do he if is
2 I am | did do | or own | he got | aid us | and so | to pay | it may | an end
3 by and by | it may go | to sow it | go and do | am to dig | his to fit

4 it age me jay of pen big or bit so man to bob us box rug owl
5 the bus | big jay | of age | may rub | to lay | is due | may dig | big bow
6 to fit it | is to sit | if it cut | and to rub | and fix it | it is so

3- and 4-stroke words and phrases

7 bug airy bus also but rich bye auto cob cog wit cot the elan
8 make jam | sit down | six keys | big rut | did wish | sue them | cut hay
9 bid and pay | own the dog | box and bow | hem the gown | fix the ham

10 cub does six hale rot bowl cur fish chap land gush bush bury
11 kept ham | auto key | rich men | fur pelt | cut fir | oak box | did fish
12 dish and cod | dub the cue | ant and bug | cut the ivy | eye for eye

4- and 5-stroke words and phrases

13 keys these visit flap usual dish world tutor idle make shake
14 wiry chap | clay bowl | auto body | rich heir | rush down | work audit
15 make them laugh | they kept busy | turn worn disk | lend them fuel

16 down spend rotor hand prism fury laugh panel half oboe slang
17 roan foal | risk duty | lake fish | idle land | such pans | ivory tusk
18 soak lake fish furl airy flag fish with kayak rush the disks

1' | 1 | 2 | 3 | 4 | 5 | 6 | 7 | 8 | 9 | 10 | 11 | 12 |

Drill 14
Improve accuracy

Key: each line for 30".

Goal: no more than one error in 30".

Tip: Concentrate on finger control.

2- and 3-stroke words and phrases

1 ad bag at oil be zed ere in tea lop oh ace poi up era bet as
2 in no | on up | at tea | few are | in bed | are no | I'm in | no oil | by my
3 up to bat | in my car | no red ink | as you sat | bad tea bag | in awe

3- and 4-stroke words and phrases

4 bed card egg data few fact lip gear ply noon tar vat was yon
5 bad bet | cab fee | get set | tax free | set hook | face east | are oily
6 see yon bat | was set far | saw you act | car was fast | add raw wax

4- and 5-stroke words and phrases

7 brag crest inky milk taste union wear bread daze hilly nylon
8 after date | base data | feed deer | fade fast | aged junk | brew cafe
9 serve rare beef | area base rate | fact upon fact | ease vast debt

1' | 1 | 2 | 3 | 4 | 5 | 6 | 7 | 8 | 9 | 10 | 11 | 12 |

Document 7
Standard memo with table

1. DS heading lines.
2. Alphabetize the list before keying the table.
3. Format the table attractively. Center it horizontally.

words

TO: All Staff, Spokane Branch 6
FROM: Marilyn Josephson, Office Manager 14
DATE: Current 19
SUBJECT: American versus Canadian Spelling 28

All correspondence addressed to our Canadian office should now include 42
Canadian spelling. Some of the differences are shown in the following 56
table. We'll need to get a list of other words that differ as well. 70

U.S. Spelling	**Canadian Spelling**	77
counseling	counselling	81
honor	honour	84
endeavor	endeavour	88
defense	defence	91
center	centre	94
check (meaning money)	cheque	99
color	colour	102
marvelous	marvellous	106
z	"zed"	107

Document 8
Multiple-page report with table and appendix

1. Format the report as a DS unbound report. Proofread carefully; not all errors are marked.
2. Include the agenda as an appendix in the report. (See the directions, p. A21.)
3. Prepare a title page. Assume that the report was prepared for **Nelson Chamber of Commerce** by **Richard R. Holmes, President**. Date the report **March 15**.

WP Use the spelling feature to help you proof your document.

PROPOSAL FOR COMMUNITY GOALS CONFERENCE 8

The Steering Committee for the chamber of commerce com- 19
munity enhancement proposes the sponsorship of a goals con- 31
ference for all citizens of Nelson. This recommendation is 43
based on research data compiled from conferences sponsored 55
in other cities similar to Nelson. Also, the recommendation 66
is supported by the committee's combined experience in work- 79
ing with varied groups of citizens and commitment to 90
progress. The reports presents a proposed outline for a 101
goals conference. 105

Purpose of Conference 109

The purposes of this conference are (1) to improve educa- 121
tion, economic development, youth services, and recreation and 133
(2) to reduce crime in the Nelson and district. All members 145
of the community will be invited to attend this conference and 157

Drill 10
Numbers and symbols

Key: each 2-line group twice; key without pauses.

Tip: Keep fingers lightly touching home row; reach with fingers, not hands.

1/8

1 line 8; Book 1; No. 88; Seat 11; June 18; Cart 81; date 1881
2 Note on line 8, "11 No. 8 mowers; Invoice 881; ship May 18."

2/7

3 take 2; July 7; buy 22; sell 77; mark 27; adds 72; Memo 2772
4 Mark the 7th source: Book 2, Chapter 27, page 772, line 72.

3/8

5 feed 3; bats 8; age 33; Ext. 88; File 38; 83 bags; band 3883
6 Take the figure 383; add 83; subtract 38; now divide by 383.

4/0

7 set 0; push 4; Car 00; score 44; jot 04; age 40; Billet 4004
8 Set at 04, not 40, and run 404 to 440 lines of Invoice 4040.

5/9

9 scan 5; size 9; drive 55; set 99; at 59; Bin 95; Flavor 9559
10 Of the 5, I am 59; Lou is 5; Bo is 9; Ty is 5; and Pops, 95.

6/7

11 April 6; lock 7; set 66; fill 77; hit 67; pick 76; adds 7667
12 Either 6 or 7 of the 67 workers worked 67 to 76 added hours.

1' | 1 | 2 | 3 | 4 | 5 | 6 | 7 | 8 | 9 | 10 | 11 | 12 |

Drill 11
Numbers and tabulation

Format: 1.5" top margin, 10-space intercolumn; DS.

Tip: Keep eyes on copy as you key.

INSTALLATION SCHEDULE

Date	Address	Model
March 17	75 Crowell, City	6421
March 22	398 Borner, Leeton	7825
March 26	5639 Fig, City	7825
March 29	4474 Trubell, Summit	3900
April 01	135 Plaza, City	3900
April 07	6 Mount Ross, City	6241
April 08	868 Ferrier, Summit	7825
April 10	3459 Fox Court, City	6421

Drill 12
Number timing

Key: 1' timing; the last number keyed times 2 equals your approximate *gwam*.

Goal: to improve with each writing.

1 and the 2 and the 3 and the 4 and the 5 and the 6 and the 7 and the 8 and the 9 and the 10 and the 11 and the 12 and the 13 and the 14 and the 15 and the 16 and the 17 and the 18 and the 19 and the 20 and the 21 and the 22 and the 23 and the 24 and the 25 and . . .

words

contribute the the achievement of these goals. Publicity com- 170
mittee will be resonsible for informing the community. 181

Goals Conference Format 186

The Steering Committee recommends that the confence be 197
held at Canadian International College (CIC) on March 18, 211
19--, from 9:30 a.m. to 4:00 p.m. Facilities can be 222
reserved by calling Patzy Frazier at 606-555-3789. 233

The conference would begin with an opening session and 244
should inlcude introductions of key leaders in the community 256
as well as Chamber of Commerce officers. The keynote 267
should be a prominent state leader who has vision for 279
quality communities. 284

Following the opening sessions, participants will 294
choose from one of the following five breakout groups: edu- 306
cation, youth services, education, economic development, 317
youth services, recreation and crime. Breakout sessions 323
will be directed by facilitators trained in working with 335
diverse groups. Lunch will follow and be served in the 345
Banquet Room of the college. The afternoon sessions will be 355
a repeat of the workshops so that participants may attend 366
different sessions. 368

Recommended facilitators include: 381

Team	Team Leaders	Facilitators	
			387
Education	Dale Coppage, Nelson BC	Ellen Obert, Spokane WA	399
Youth Services	Lawrence Riveria, Portland, OR	Jack Jones, Vancouver BC	413
Recreation	Bradley Greger, Nelson BC	Carolos Pena, Calgary AB	425
Economic Development	Jon Guyton, Nelson BC	Harvey Lewis,	439
Crime	Monica Brigham, Toronto ON	Shawn McNullan, NC	450

Drill 8
Alphabetic sentences

Key: each line once slowly, but with rhythm.

Tip: Keep fingers curved and upright over home row; reach with fingers.

1 Judge McQuoy will have prizes for their next big track meet.
2 Jack may provide some extra quiz problems for the new group.
3 Gary Quazet mended six copies of books and journals we have.
4 Jack quibbled with a garrulous expert on Zoave family names.
5 Jake will study sixty chapters on vitamins for the big quiz.
6 Max asked Quin to provide a jewel box for the glossy zircon.
7 This judge may quiz the Iowa clerks about extensive profits.
8 Meg Keys packed and flew to Venezia to acquire her next job.

1' | 1 | 2 | 3 | 4 | 5 | 6 | 7 | 8 | 9 | 10 | 11 | 12 |

Drill 9
Opposite-hand combinations

Key: each line once; proofread; repeat 4-line groups with 6 or more errors.

Tip: Key fluently, without rushing.

i/e

1 icing icicle iris picnic iliac ibis idiom limit idiot skiing
2 ever ewer levee eyes cede even fete gene mete cere here mere
3 lien leis bier pies ties mien diet hies lies seine tier view
4 Neither Micki nor Lennie is dieting; they fed me raisin pie.

o/w

5 solo oboe bolo odor coho dodo oleo Ohio loco folio lobo polo
6 way waw wigwam walkway Warsaw whew wigwag windrow waterworks
7 wow crow widow work willow down wallow woke winnow owes woes
8 Working down among the willows, Lowe saw an old wolf wallow.

d/k

9 died dado dads dodo dada dead deed did dyed dido dodged dude
10 kick kirks kulak kirk kink skink kaka kayak knack knock kook
11 deck kudo dirk dark desk dank dinky disk dock duke duck dunk
12 Did Dick Kirk indeed knock on a door on the dark, dank deck?

r/u

13 roar rare rear rural prior crier dryer rip friar riper armor
14 unjust undue usury ump umlaut tutu unused uncus uncut unduly
15 turn burn true cure tour dour rut mourn rust hurt curt Uhuru
16 True, Rory must turn around their burned, rusted church bus.

s/l

17 says uses sets asps sons asks spas isms sums oasis sags sows
18 lapel lilt level lily leal legal lilac lilt ladle label lily
19 silt also slots gels lobs salt sole ales lips alms lose elks
20 Nelly said Elsa looks as if she will also slip off to sleep.

g/h

21 gags gauge grog gorge gag gouge agog going gig gigs gage gag
22 harsh shah hath heath huh health hash hush hitch hatch hutch
23 gash high ghee hug gush hugs hag ghat huge hog hogs hag hags
24 Greg forgot he had gone higher than Hugh to hunt eagle eggs.

b/n

25 kabob blab bub bibs blurb bob bribe bobs barb baby babe bulb
26 inane nun noun none nee nine neon ninth nonce noon nylon nun
27 nibs bean nab bins nib buns neb ban numb band bans bone nobs
28 The baby saw nine tiny bunnies in a bin behind Bobb's Store.

1' | 1 | 2 | 3 | 4 | 5 | 6 | 7 | 8 | 9 | 10 | 11 | 12 | 13 |

words

After the first breakout sessions, participants will join 462
for lunch in the H. L. Calvert Union Building. The Steering 474
Committee recommends that Mayor Alton johnson address the 486
topic of meeting educational challenges of the next century. 498
A reapat of the morning breakout sessions will begin at 1:30. 512
This repeat will allow participants to contirube to antoher 524
topic. In the closing session breakout facilitators will 536
present the goals and plans to the audience. 546

Sponsors 547

The Steerting Committee has discussed the sponsorhsip of 559
a goals conference with a number of partners in the Nelson 570
area. The following organizations have agreed to serve as 582
sponsors: Nelson Economic Development Foundation, Bank of 594
Canada, Northeast Bottling Company, and Bank of Nelson, and 605
Farthington's Clothiers. 610

Summary 612

The Steering Committee strongly recommends this goals 623
conference. The committee will be avilable at the Camber 635
of commerce meeting to answer any questions. 644

Document 9
Agenda

1. Prepare a sheet that will precede the agenda. Use 1.5" top margin; center-align APPENDIX; DS and center the title of the agenda. Number this page in sequence.
2. DS between items of the agenda.

Goals Conference Agenda 5

9:30 a.m.-9:45 a.m. Welcome 11

9:45 a.m.-10:15 a.m. Opening Remarks 19
Overview of Community Quality Initiative 25 27
Purpose of Goals Conference 33
Process 34
Introduction of Community Leaders and Chamber Officers 41 45

10:15 a.m.-10:35 a.m. Refreshment Break 54
10:35 a.m.-12 noon Breakout Sessions: 62
12 noon-1:00 p.m. Lunch 79
Speaker on Educational Challenges of the 21st Century 86 90

1:00 p.m.-2:30 p.m. Goals Setting Workshops 98
2:30 p.m.-2:45 p.m. Refreshment Break 106
2:45 p.m.-4:00 p.m. Presentation of Goals 115

Drill 5
Outside reaches

Key: each line once.

Goal: to complete each line with no more than one error.

Tip: Outside reaches often cause omissions—concentrate.

a/p

1 tapioca actual against casual areas facial equally aware parallel
2 empower purpose people opposed compute pimple papyrus pope puppet
3 Perhaps part of the chapter page openers can appear on red paper.

s/w

4 class sash steps essential skills business discuss desks insisted
5 wow wayworn away awkward wrong awaits wildwood waterworks wayward
6 The snow white swan swayed as the waves swept the swelling shore.

z/l

7 hazard zip zero zeolite freezer zoom zealous z-axis zodiac sizing
8 likely indelibly laurel finally leaflet regularly eloquently lily
9 A New Zealand zoologist was amazed as a zebra guzzled the zinias.

x/?

10 fax oxford exert excite examples xylan exercise oxygen exact taxi
11 When? Where? Which? For her? How much? What color? To whom?
12 After examining the x-rays, why did Dr. Ax exempt an exploratory?

1' | 1 | 2 | 3 | 4 | 5 | 6 | 7 | 8 | 9 | 10 | 11 | 12 | 13 |

Drill 6
Transpositions

Key: each group once; repeat.

Goal: to key with a maximum of one error per line.

r/t

1 boardroom operator forward regard recourse armor interrupt grater
2 stratus motto that gutter student title thought myth tight throat
3 precept regiment control rejected merriment overtop stretch other

m/n

4 mammal simmer memo minimax sometimes memory dimmer immediate mama
5 none anything concord understanding concentrate painting pantheon
6 important incumbent element minimum impression minute inform mana

q/o

7 quit inquire quail esquire qualm earthquake quaver quencher query
8 hoof knockabout forgot offertory omission zoology toehold conform
9 quotations quorum questions equipoise quarto consequences bouquet

b/v

10 baby bareback butter beans fiberboard bobby bib babble ribbon tab
11 Pavlov involved savvy vetiver velvet viva vivacious novice vivify
12 Bev everybody believe behavior bivalent vestibule beehive bolivar

1' | 1 | 2 | 3 | 4 | 5 | 6 | 7 | 8 | 9 | 10 | 11 | 12 | 13 |

Drill 7
Long words

Key: each line once for control.

1 Telecommunication and hypermedia will be demonstrated next month.
2 The gubernatorial candidate mustered minimal support by December.

3 Convention participants can explore over two hundred exhibitions.
4 Gratification is achieved by one's deep commitment to excellence.

1' | 1 | 2 | 3 | 4 | 5 | 6 | 7 | 8 | 9 | 10 | 11 | 12 | 13 |

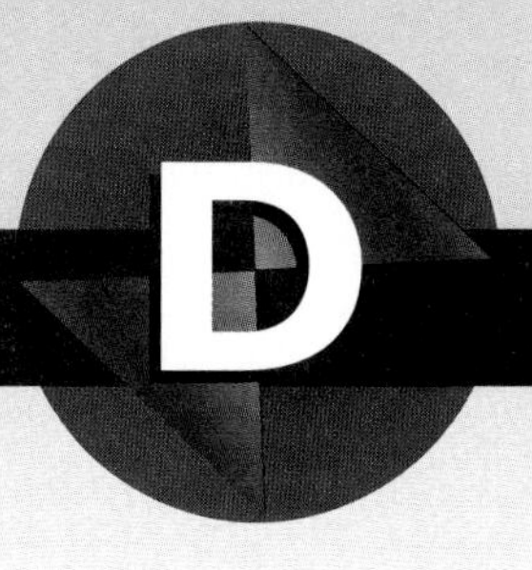

POMMERY AIR SERVICE, INC., PROJECT 2

For use after Lesson 107.
Project objective:
Integrate formatting and word processing skills.

Project Scenario

As the Senior Staff Assistant, you have been asked to finalize the business plan that the Executive Committee has been working on for several weeks (pp. A23-A28). Key it in final format following these guidelines.

1. **Report format:** SS; leftbound; justified. Option: **Font size** (optional): Title and centered headings: 16 point; side headings: 12 point; report body: 11 point. Bold all headings.

2. **Paging:** Create a new page for each Appendix. **Page numbering:** Use Arabic numbers for report pages. Use lowercase Roman numerals for preliminary pages.

3. **Tables:** Format the tables in an attractive format of your choice. Use 10-point font, if necessary, to fit information in a table. Spell out names and abbreviated titles, if necessary (obtain information from the Appendix).

4. **Preliminary pages:** Create a title page, letter of transmittal, table of contents, and executive summary.

5. **Headers:** Insert a graphic line on all pages except the title page.

6. **Footers:** Insert a graphic line. Beneath the line, key **Pommery Air Service, Inc.** at the left margin and the page number at the right margin on ALL pages except the title page. Example:

Pommery Air Service, Inc. ii

Drill 3
Specific finger

Key: each group once; repeat lines that are more difficult.

Goal: to complete each line with one error or less.

Tip: Do not twist your wrists on reaches using the outside fingers (lines 5-8).

1st

1 fun gray vent guy hunt brunt buy brunch much gun huge humor vying
2 buy them brunch; a hunting gun; Guy hunts for fun; try it for fun

2d

3 cite decide kick cider creed kidded keen keep kit idea ice icicle
4 keen idea; kick it back; ice breaker; decide the issue; sip cider

3d

5 low slow lax solo wax sold swell swollen wood wool load logs doll
6 wooden dolls; wax the floor; a slow boat; saw logs; pull the wool

4th

7 quip zap Zane zip pepper pay quiz zipper quizzes pad map nap jazz
8 zip the zipper; jazz at the plaza; Zane quipped; La Paz jazz band

1st and 2d

9 Jimmy urged them not to buy my big hunting gun, but Ty bought it.
10 Fred might give them free gifts, but I think they might buy them.
11 Rebecca might buy brunch for us if my friend comes here to visit.

3d and 4th

12 Paul and Quinn play polo at the plaza one week and jazz the next.
13 Pat said Maxwell always expects to pass his quizzes, and he does.
14 Paxton Lopez quietly explored the cold slope with only a sweater.

1' | 1 | 2 | 3 | 4 | 5 | 6 | 7 | 8 | 9 | 10 | 11 | 12 | 13 |

Drill 4
Direct reaches

Key: each set once; repeat difficult reaches.

Tip: Long direct reaches made with the same finger (lines 1-10) are made without moving the hands forward or downward.

br/rb

1 break barb brawn orbit brain carbon brakes barbecue brazen barber
2 Barbara Brady brought us a new brand of barbecue to eat at break.

ce/ec

3 cease decide cent collect cell direct cedar check center peck ice
4 Cecil recently received a check for his special barbecue recipes.

mu/um

5 mull dumb must human mud lumber mulch lump mumps slump music fume
6 Bum Muse must have dumped too much muddy mulch on the bumpy lawn.

nu/un

7 nut sun fun nurse gun sinus number punch nuzzle pound lunch until
8 Uncle Gunta, a nurse, was uneasy about numerous units unionizing.

gr/rg

9 grade merge grand purge great large grab organ green margins gray
10 Margo, our great grandmother, regrets merging those large groups.

ny/yn

11 Wayne any shyness many agony balcony Jayne lynx penny larynx myna
12 Wayne and Jayne fed many skinny myna birds on that sunny balcony.

1' | 1 | 2 | 3 | 4 | 5 | 6 | 7 | 8 | 9 | 10 | 11 | 12 | 13 |

EXECUTIVE SUMMARY

Pommery Air Service, Inc. is a charter air service headquartered in Hopkins, South Carolina. Pommery's mission is:

- To provide its charter customers with safe, reliable jet transportation, quality service, outstanding value, and low costs.
- To provide an environment for its employees that fosters teamwork and customer focus and rewards integrity and productivity.
- To deliver superior value to its shareholders.

The Company

Pommery Air Service, Inc., a Delaware corporation founded in January, 1995, currently has a fleet of four 737 jet aircraft. Pommery provides air service to almost 60,000 passengers per month. The mix is almost equally divided among business trips, athletic functions, and leisure travel.

An experienced, highly competent management team leads Pommery Air Service, Inc. Management emphasizes teamwork, empowerment, and productivity. Employee stock options provide incentives to employees to focus on quality and profitability.

Pommery Air Service, Inc. became profitable in its tenth month of existence and continues to be profitable. The company operates as a lean, efficient organization. Costs per available seat mile (ASM) have dropped from 14 cents to 10 cents. Yield per revenue passenger mile (RPM) increased from 12 cents to 16 cents.

The Market

Pommery Air Service, Inc. provides charter flights to destinations throughout the United States. The primary market, however, is defined by origination point rather than destination point. Approximately 65 percent of all flights originate in the Southeast. The secondary market by origination point is the Northeast.

The Services

Pommery Air Service, Inc. provides two types of charter services: event charter flights and contract charter flights. Event charter flights range from one-time events, to seasonal events, to regularly scheduled events. Charter flights are contracted by an individual, company, or organization. Contract charter flights provide service to one location or may be a key component of a travel package.

Both event and contract charter flights include an array of services depending on the needs of the customer. Supplementary services available with both charter and event flights include: meal and beverage services; local transportation; event tickets; side trips; conference facilities, including logistical support; and a host of special activities.

The Strategy

Pommery Air Service, Inc. strives to become the dominant air charter service in the eastern United States. Pommery's core competencies involve providing safe, high-quality jet air services that are cost-effective. All other services provided are designed to facilitate and enhance the continual development of the core competencies.

To implement this strategy, Pommery Air Service, Inc. must expand. Expansion requires the addition of two jet aircraft within 18 months. Expansion is contingent upon obtaining $4.5 million in additional capital.

POMMERY AIR SERVICE, INC.

Business Plan

Pommery Air Service, Inc. (Pommery), since it was founded as a Delaware corporation in January, 1995, has operated as a niche player in the charter air segment of the airline industry.

Industry

Three distinct segments comprise the charter air service industry:

- Small, local charter operations designed to provide point-to-point transportation for groups of fewer than 20 people in turboprop aircraft.
- Occasional charter flights provided by major passenger airlines.
- Small niche markets that target specific types of clientele.

Pommery operates exclusively in the third segment of the industry, offering contract charter flights and event charter flights. The overall charter air service industry is highly competitive. The most intensive competition exists in the other two segments of the charter air service. Pommery's board of directors and management agree that

APPENDIX

SKILL-BUILDING WORKSHOP 5

1" margins or 65-space line

Format guides

1" side margins; SS; DS between sets of lines.

MicroAssistant: From the Main menu, key **S5** to access Skill-Building Workshop 5.

Drill 1
Specific rows

Key: each set three times.

Tip: Reach to the first and third rows with a minimum of hand movement; maintain fluency with quiet hands.

Rows 3, 2, 1

1 you we quip try pot peer your wire put quit wet trip power toy to
2 salad fad glad lass lag has gall lash gas lad had shall flag half
3 comb zone exam man carve bun oxen bank came next vent zoo van cab

Rows 3, 2, 1

4 we try to; you were; put up your; put it there; you quit; wipe it
5 Gail asked Sissy; what was said; had Jake left; Darla sold a flag
6 Zam came back; can Max fix my van? a brave man, Ben came in a cab

Rows 3, 2, 1

7 Peter or I will try to wire our popular reports to Porter or you.
8 Ada Glass said she is glad she had half a kale salad with Dallas.
9 Zack drove a van to minimize expenses; Ben and Max came in a cab.

1' | 1 | 2 | 3 | 4 | 5 | 6 | 7 | 8 | 9 | 10 | 11 | 12 | 13 |

Drill 2
Adjacent keys

Key: each set three times.

Goal: to eliminate persistent errors on side-by-side strokes.

Tip: Keep fingers upright (not slanted) over the keys.

as/sa

1 has sale fast salt was saw vast essay easy say past vast mast sap
2 We saw Sam; Sal was sad; Susan has a cast; as Sam said; as I said

er/re

3 were there tree deer great three other her free red here pert are
4 we were there; here we are; there were three; here are three deer

io/oi

5 point axiom prior choir lion boil toil billion soil action adjoin
6 join a choir; prior to that action; millions in a nation rejoiced

op/po

7 polo drop loop post hope pole port rope slope power top pony stop
8 rope the pony; drop the pole; power at the top; hope for the poor

rt/tr

9 trail alert train hurt tree shirt trap smart trim start tray dirt
10 trim the tree; start the train; dirt on the shirt; alert the trio

ew/we

11 few we stew were pew went dew web sew wept crew wear brew wet new
12 we were weak; few were weeping; the crew went west; we knew a few

gh/ui

13 sight quit laugh suit might ruin ghost guide ghastly guilt ghetto
14 a ghastly suit; quit laughing; recruit the ghost; might be guilty

1' | 1 | 2 | 3 | 4 | 5 | 6 | 7 | 8 | 9 | 10 | 11 | 12 | 13 |

Pommery cannot and should not try to compete with the major passenger airlines for numerous reasons. They also agree that Pommery cannot compete with the small, local charter services because of the cost structure involved in providing jet air service exclusively.

The Service

Pommery provides event charter flights and contract charter flights throughout the United States. About 85 percent of the flights originate east of the Mississippi River, and almost 65 percent of flights originate in the Southeast.

Event charter flights. These flights are called event charters because they exist to transport passengers to attend specific events that are occurring. The range of events spans from those that occur one time or once in a significant period of time to regularly scheduled events. Examples of one-time events include charters to attend Olympic events, Mardi Gras, or a world-class art exhibition or musical production.

Seasonal events are those that occur regularly during a specified period of time. Athletic events comprise a high percentage of seasonal events. Charter flights to a ski resort or to a nearby city on weekends during the season to watch professional football, basketball, or baseball games would be an example. The flight is made available to a number of participating travel agency partners who reserve a number of seats on these charter flights for their clientele.

Regularly scheduled charters include special packages (usually weekends) to fixed destinations such as Las Vegas, a Gulf Coast casino and resort, or a country music/golf weekend in Myrtle Beach. These events are generally marketed through participating travel agency partners.

Contract charter flights. Contract charter flights often overlap with event charter flights. The primary difference is that the contract charter flights are with specific organizations or individuals. For example, a contract may be issued with an athletic department to take its football team and band to a game. The contract is with that athletic department. On the other hand, an event charter flight may go to the same football game with passengers from several travel agency partners and an alumni group.

Companies also use charter flights to take groups to conventions, meetings, and other business activities. Travel agencies often contract for charter flights between destinations on vacation packages.

Supplementary services. Meal and beverage services are frequently contracted, in addition to the transportation package. For example, box meals and cold drinks on the return flight after the game are usually a part of athletic charter flight packages. Equipment handling is also a part of the package. Tickets, convention packages, and other services provided usually are arranged through travel partners when they are part of a charter flight contract.

Market Analysis

The Southeast market was targeted first because of limited jet charter service available in the geographic area. Another determining factor was the intense interest in and support of athletics, particularly college football in the Southeast. Successful charters to games at other institutions created demand from those institutions for their travel schedule. The most profitable section of the market stems from the athletic connections.

Emerging markets. An emerging market is being created by women's athletic programs. This market is fueled by the current gender equity emphasis in college athletics. Court decisions and athletic regulations focus on equal treatment of men's and women's sports. Other emerging markets are the resort (particularly tennis, golf, beach, and ski resorts) and casino charters that are arranged by the resorts to bring in customers at a relatively low cost.

Competition. Only one other charter air service in the Southeast competes in the same niche market in which Pommery competes with all jet service. Several smaller charter air service companies try to compete with relatively large turboprop aircraft. The market clearly demands jet service. Pommery's market share is conservatively estimated to be 65 percent of the market in the Southeast.

Market expansion. The real challenge is to increase the size of this niche market through promotional activities and strategic alliances with travel partners. Pilot projects have produced

Drill 5 **Move three consecutive files**

1. *Windows 95:* Click on **3 1/2" Floppy** (a:).

   Windows 3.1: Click on **a:** to display the contents.
2. Click on the first **WordPerfect** file in the Contents pane/content list area. Hold down the SHIFT key and click on the third file below it. Three files are now highlighted.
3. Place the mouse pointer anywhere in the group of selected files.
   a. *Windows 95:* Hold down the left mouse button and drag the group of files to the Documents folder in the All Folders pane. Make sure the mouse pointer points to the correct folder before releasing the mouse button.
   b. *Windows 3.1:* Hold down the left mouse button and drag the files to the Documents folder.
4. Click the **Documents folder** to verify that the group of files was moved. Return to displaying the contents of a:.
5. *Windows 95*: From the Edit menu, click **Undo Move.** The files have moved back to their original location.

Drill 6 **Move files that are not consecutive**

1. Hold down the **CTRL** key and click on any three files that are not in consecutive order in the Contents pane/content list area.
2. Point to any one of the files selected, hold down the left mouse button, and drag the files to the Documents folder.
3. Verify that the files were moved. Return to the Contents pane of your disk.
4. *Windows 95:* From the Edit menu, click **Undo Move** to return the files to their original location.

Delete Folders and Files

Folders and files can be deleted by selecting the folder or file and pressing DELETE.

Windows 95: Delete folders and files in the Explorer window. When a folder is deleted, all the contents within the folder will also be deleted.

Windows 3.1: Delete directories and files from the Directory window. You must first delete the files in the directory before removing the directory.

Drill 7 **Delete folders**

1. Create a new folder on your disk called **Temp**. (*Windows 95:* You may need to double-click on the **Temp folder** to move it to the All Folders pane.)
2. Copy four files from your disk to the Temp folder/directory.
3. Display the contents of the Temp folder/directory.
4. Select the first file in the Contents pane/content list area.
5. Press **DELETE**. Confirm the deletion. *Windows 3.1:* Continue to delete the remainder of the files in the Temp directory.
6. *Windows 95:* Click the **Temp folder** in the All Folders pane; confirm the deletion. The folder and its contents are deleted.

   Windows 3.1: Click the **Temp folder**; confirm the deletion. Another dialog box displays asking you to confirm the deletion; click **Yes**.

promising results and are being evaluated as part of the growth strategy.

Operating Plan

Pommery is headquartered in Hopkins, South Carolina, with its corporate offices and principal operations located in a new office building at One Pommery Lane. A second facility that houses ground and flight operations is located in the Southside Airport Complex.

Facilities and equipment. Present facilities meet the operational needs of Pommery currently and for the projected growth over the next three years. Computer equipment is minimally adequate. The Technology Task Force has studied the issues pertaining to the updating of computer equipment. The Task Force makes its final recommendations for upgrading computer equipment at the next board meeting. The board supported the preliminary recommendations, and the implementation plan is expected to be approved at the next board meeting.

Operational efficiency. Airline performance frequently is judged by four major statistics:

- Load factor—percentage of seats filled on a flight
- ASM—cost per available seat mile
- Yield—available seat miles flown divided into revenues
- On-time performance

Some analysts indicate that these airline industry statistics do not translate directly to charter air service. They prefer to use cost per seat block hour. The stage length of flights and the number of passengers significantly affect the price negotiated on charter flights; therefore, either of the standards used provides a reasonable measure of efficiency. Obviously, statistics for charter service are not comparable to those of scheduled airline passenger service. However, they provide a relatively stable measure of efficiency when compared to other charter air service operations.

Competitive cost analysis. Pommery compares favorably to the charter air service industry on a national scale when traditional measures of efficiency are applied (Table 1).

(Insert Table 1 from p. A27 here.)

Operational certification. Pommery is fully certified and meets all regulatory requirements. Certificates of airworthiness are maintained for all aircraft. The company is committed to safety and high standards of maintenance.

Board of Directors and Key Personnel

The board of directors consists of seven members: Cyndi Jeansonne—Chair and Chief Executive Officer; Michael White—President and Chief Operating Officer; Natalie Bass—Airline Consultant, RTA and Associates; Herman Davis—Chief Financial Officer, Financial Securities, Inc.; Britt Burge—President, Associated Travel Services; Joseph Wayne Perkins—Senior Vice President, River Industries; and Kimberly Hess—Professor of Business Administration, Central University. Brief biographical sketches are contained in Appendix 1.

Key company officers are listed in Table 2 along with their titles, compensation, and number of stock option shares.

(Insert Table 2 from p. A27 here.)

Workforce

Pommery employs 126 full-time employees and a variable number of part-time and contract workers. Significant training has been provided, and all employees participate in an ongoing training and quality development program.

Financial Plan

Pommery's fiscal year coincides with the calendar year. Pommery earned its first profit in October 1995—a profit of $28,500. The 1995 and 1996 audit statements are provided as a supplement to the business plan. In 1995 the average cost per seat block hour was $25. In 1996 this figure improved to an average cost per seat block hour of $22.50.

Seasonality. Charter air service business parallels the seasonality of passenger airline service to some degree. Charter air service business peaks in March as does the entire airline industry. Event charter service helps to combat the weak fourth quarter that is prevalent in the

Drill 3 Move files

In this exercise, you will copy and move files from Drive a or b to the folder you created called *Documents* on Drive a or b.

1. In Windows Explorer or File Manager, click on **3 1/2" Floppy** (**a:**) to display the contents of your disk.
2. Point to a file in the Contents pane/content list area that was created in *WordPerfect.*

   Windows 95
   Hold down the left mouse button. Drag the file to the Documents folder in the Contents pane.

   Windows 3.1
   a. Hold down the left mouse button. Drag the file to the Documents folder in the directory tree. Confirm moving the file.
   b. Double-click on **Documents** folder. The Contents pane should now display the file that you moved.
3. Click on **3 1/2" Floppy** (**a:**) to display the contents of your disk.

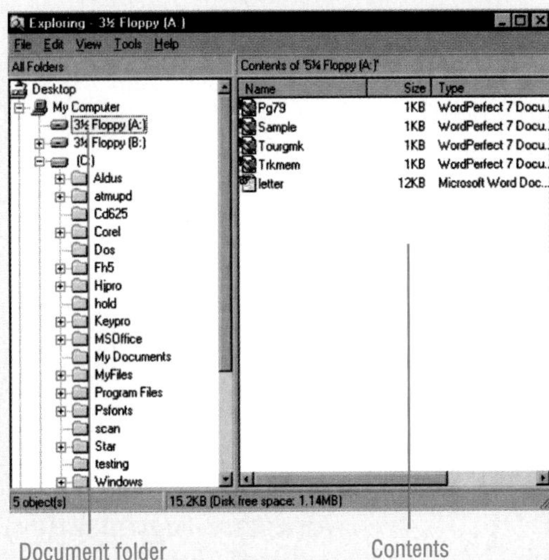

Document folder   Contents

Windows 95

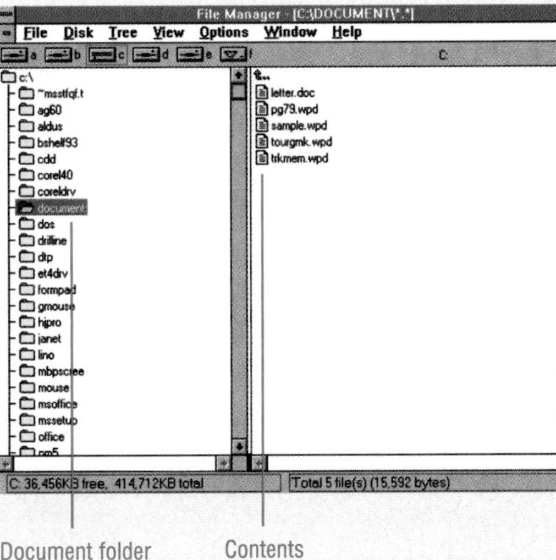

Document folder   Contents

Windows 3.1

Drill 4 Copy a file

1. *Windows 95:* Click on **3 1/2" Floppy** (**a:**). The Document folder displays in the All Folders pane under 3 1/2" Floppy (a:).

   Windows 3.1: Click on **a:** to display the contents of the drive.
2. Hold down the CTRL key and point to another file in the Contents pane/content list area. Drag the file into the Document folder. (In *Windows 3.1*, a box displays asking you to confirm the copy; click **Yes.**) Notice that the file still remains in the Contents pane/content list area.
3. Double-click the **Document folder**. Your copied file should be listed in the content list area.

airline industry. The emphasis on football events has created a special niche that contributes significantly to the load factor and, in turn, reduces costs.

Insurance. Aircraft insurance rates have increased significantly over the past year for the entire industry. The average increase for the industry was 15 percent. Pommery lowered its insurance rates from $32,750 per month to $27,875 per month. These savings were obtained by changing the mix of underwriters and by reducing the amount of business handled by underwriters in the United States and transferring that business to quality, lower-cost underwriters in Europe.

Pro-Formas—1997-1999

Pro-formas for 1997, 1998, and 1999 are based on the addition of two jet aircraft within the next 18 months. Revenue and expenses are in current dollars.

(Insert Pro-Forma Statement of Income from the next page. Label the pro-formas Table 3.)

Ownership

Five million common shares have been authorized. Of the authorized shares, 2,802,654 shares have been issued. Common stock ownership is diverse as noted in the following groupings (Table 4).

(Insert Table 4 from p. A28 here.)

Capital Requirements

Pommery is actively seeking $4.5 million in additional capital in the form of equity financing. The additional capital is required for expansion, acquiring two jet aircraft, retiring debt, and improving the information technology system.

APPENDIX 1

Board of Directors

All members of the board of directors have served in that capacity since Pommery Air Service, Inc. was founded in January 1995.

Cyndi Jeansonne, Chair and CEO—Founder of the company. Previously served as Executive Vice President with responsibility for marketing for Oklahoma Charter Service.

Michael White, President and COO—Co-founder of the company. Previous experience as Vice President of Airline Operations with Southern Airways and Manager of Flight Operations with Texas Charter Service.

Natalie Bass, Airline Consultant, RTA and Associates—Senior partner of RTA and Associates for ten years; held position of Chief Pilot of Federated Package Service for six years.

Herman Davis, Chief Financial Officer, Financial Securities, Inc.—CFO for seven years; former investment analyst specializing in the airline industry.

Britt Burge, President, Associated Travel Services—Two years as President of ATS; former owner of a chain of 14 travel agencies.

Joseph Wayne Perkins, Senior Vice President, River Industries—Former Executive Vice President of Bank Services, Inc.; director on several company and civic organization boards.

Kimberly Hess, Professor, Business Administration, Central University—Prolific author and known widely for work in economic development; director on several company and civic organization boards.

APPENDIX 2

Key Personnel

All of the senior officers have served as senior officers since Pommery Air Service, Inc. was founded in January 1995.

(Copy Jeansonne and White information from Appendix 1)

Charles Walker, Vice President, Operations—Twenty years of experience in airline operations and flight operations at four airlines.

Leslie Coker, Vice President, Marketing—Six years as a brand manager for Westfield Imports and four years in Event Management for WorldWide Travel, Inc.

Patrick Ray, Chief Financial Officer—Co-founder. Previous experience includes seven years as Managing Partner of Ray and Associates, Inc.

4. Some of the folders contain + and - symbols. (If you do not see any + or - symbols, click on **Tree**, then **Indicate Expandable Branches**.) A plus sign (+) in a directory folder indicates that there are more subdirectories that are not shown. A minus symbol (-) indicates that all of its subdirectories are displayed.
5. Click **a:** or **b:** in the directory tree area. Files on Drives a or b are listed in the content list area.

Drill 2 **Create a directory**

1. From the File menu, click **Create Directory**.
2. Enter **documents** in the Name text box. Click **OK**. *Documents* is now a directory underneath the root directory in Drive a.

Select Folders/ Directories and Files

Discussion and drills from this point forward apply to either *Windows 95* or *Windows 3.1*.

Only one folder/directory can be selected at a time in the left pane. Multiple files or folders can be selected in the right pane. To select multiple files or folders listed in consecutive order, click on the first object to be selected, hold down the SHIFT key, and click the last object to be selected. The entire group of folders or files is now highlighted.

To select files or folders that are scattered throughout the Contents pane/content list area, hold down the CTRL key while you click each of the desired objects.

Move and Copy Files

As you create more files, you will probably need to create additional folders or directories and then rearrange existing files by moving or copying them into the new folders/directories. When a file is copied, the original file remains in place, and another copy of the file is placed at the destination. When a file is moved, the original file is removed from its original location and placed at the destination.

- Folders and files are moved by dragging the object from the Contents pane to its destination. If you drag a folder on the same disk, it will be moved. If you drag a file to another disk (from a to c), it will be copied.
- To copy a file/folder, use the CTRL key while dragging the file.
- To move a file/folder, use the SHIFT key.

The file or folder that is to be copied is referred to as the **source copy**, and the location where the copy is to be moved is called the **destination**. Folders and files that are moved or copied by mistake can be restored to their original location by using Undo in the Edit menu.

Project, *continued*

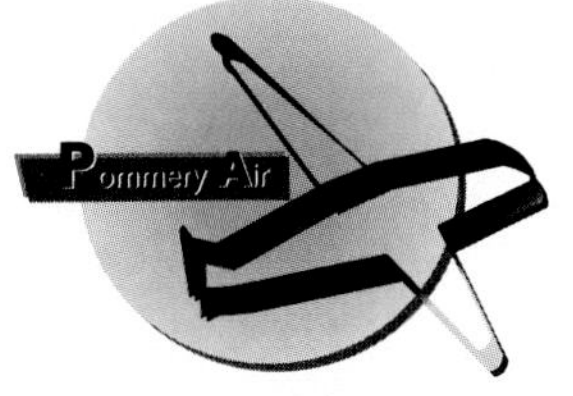

Table 1. Efficiency of Pommery Air Service

Efficiency Measure	Pommery	National Average
Load factor	62%	58%
ASM	10¢	14¢
Yield	16¢	12¢
On-time performance	88%	94%

Table 2. Key Personnel *

Officer	Position	Compensation	Stock Options
C. Jeansonne	CEO	$124,000	90,000 shares
M. White	President and COO	106,500	75,000 shares
C. Walker	V.P. Operations	85,000	50,000 shares
L. Coker	V.P. Marketing	85,000	50,000 shares
P. Ray	CFO	85,000	50,000 shares

*Refer to Appendix 2 for biographical sketches.

Table 3. 1997, 1998, and 1999 Pro-Forma Statement of Income

	1997	1998	1999
Operating Revenue	$44,438,400	$61,466,400	$78,874,400
Operating Expense	41,144,600	53,190,000	68,898,400
Operating Profit/(Loss)	3,293,800	8,276,400	9,976,000
Non-Operating Expense	(671,200)	(709,800)	(1,673,600)
Net Income/(Loss)	$2,622,600	$7,566,600	$8,302,400
Cost Per ASM	.1019	.0721	.0868
Yield	.1647	.1621	.1575
Operating Margin	7.4%	13.5%	12.6%

Table 4 on next page

Drill 1 Using Windows Explorer

1. Insert your data disk into Drive a or b.
2. Click on **Start.** Highlight *Programs.* Click on **Windows Explorer.**
3. Maximize the Explorer window.
4. If Desktop is not the top object in the All Folders pane, click on the Up scroll arrow until it is displayed.
5. If a plus sign (+) displays beside the My Computer icon, click the **+** to extend its sublevels.
6. Click on **3 1/2" Floppy** (generally a:).
7. From the View menu, click **List** to display the contents of the folder in numerical and alphabetical order.

Drill 2 Create a folder

1. From the File menu, choose *New,* then *Folder.* A new folder icon labeled "New Folder" displays in the Contents pane.
2. Enter the folder name and press ENTER. In this drill, enter **Documents.** A new folder named *Documents* has been created on your disk.

Windows 3.1

File Manager is the program in *Windows 3.1* that allows you to organize and manipulate files.

Drill 1 Using File Manager

1. At the DOS prompt, key **win** and press ENTER. Program Manager displays.
2. Double-click on the **Main** group icon, then double-click on the **File Manager** icon to display the File Manager window.
3. The Directory window displays inside the File Manager window. The title bar for this window displays the current drive and path *Windows* is using (C:\WINDOWS*.*). The second line of the window displays the disk-drive icons. The left pane contains the *directory tree,* which is a graphic representation of the disk in the current disk drive. The right pane is the *content list area,* which displays all the files, in alphabetical order, in the current directory.

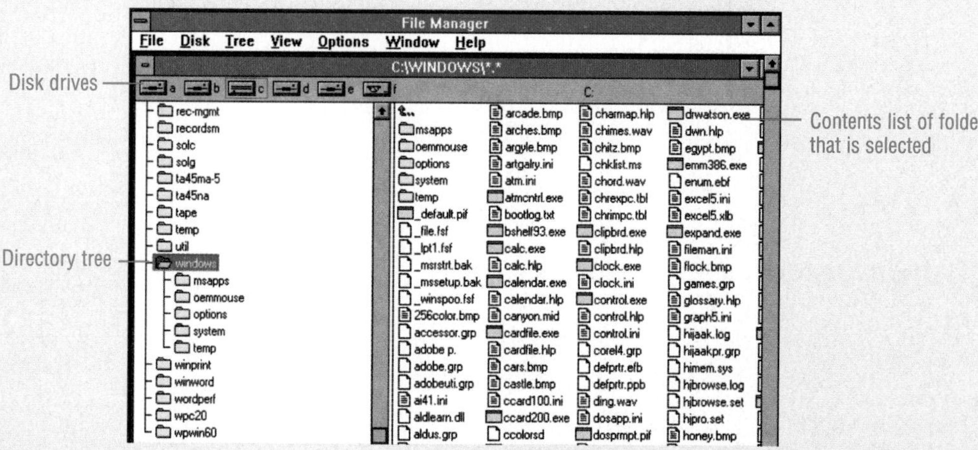

Project, *continued*

Letter of transmittal

The letter will be bound as part of the report; number it ***ii***. Prepare an individual letter for each member of the board of directors. Use name and title from report and the following addresses:

Jeansonne and White
Pommery Air Service, Inc.
P.O. Box 8473
Hopkins, SC 29061-8473

Bass
3829 Quincy Ave.
Denver, CO 80237-2756

Davis
3979 El Mundo
Houston, TX 64506-2877

Burge
3958 Highland Dr.
Sterling, CO 80751-1211

Perkins
7463 St. Andrews
Dallas, TX 75205-2746

Hess
3744 Main St.
Oakdale, LA 71463-5811

WP Only one letter will be paged with the report. Therefore, each of the other letters can be in a separate file or all of the letters can be in one file.

Number each letter as page **ii**; use the same header and footer used in the report. ■

Table 4. Stock Ownership

Group	Shares	% of Stock Issued
Employees	586,268	20.9
Senior officers	353,146	12.6
Outside directors	651,700	23.3
Business community	640,000	22.8
Founders	571,540	20.4
Total	2,802,654	100.0

Dear

The Pommery Air Service Business Plan is attached. Please review the plan carefully and be ready to vote on final approval at the board meeting next Friday. Note that this item appears on the agenda sent to you last week.

If you have any questions prior to the meeting, please call me. All of the changes recommended by the board at the last meeting have been implemented in the plan.

Sincerely

Your name
Senior Staff Assistant

Attachment

Table of contents

Include all headings and page numbers.

Title page

Format an attractive title page. Be creative with the design as long as the title page is in good taste. Use current date. Omit the Prepared for/Prepared by sections. If available, use clipart to insert a jet airplane from the Travel or Transportation category.

APPENDIX

FILE MANAGEMENT

Create Folders and Directories

The documents you create are organized and stored as files on a disk. Since you will be generating numerous files, you may want to place the files in **folders** (*Windows 95*) or **directories** (*Windows 3.1*). Similar files are stored in the same folder or directory much like documents are stored in folders within a filing cabinet. For example, you could create a folder or directory labeled "Keyboarding" for all the files you create for your keyboarding class. You could put all files for Appendix D in a *subfolder* or *subdirectory* called *Appendix D* within the larger Keyboarding folder.

An easy way to work with folders in *Windows 95* is to use the program Windows Explorer. In *Windows 3.1*, File Manager is the program for working with files.

Windows 95

Windows Explorer provides an easy way to create folders and to rename, delete, move, and copy files. To open Windows Explorer, select it from the Program menu. The Explorer window is split into two sides. The left side shows how the folders, subfolders, and files are organized in a hierarchical or "tree" view.

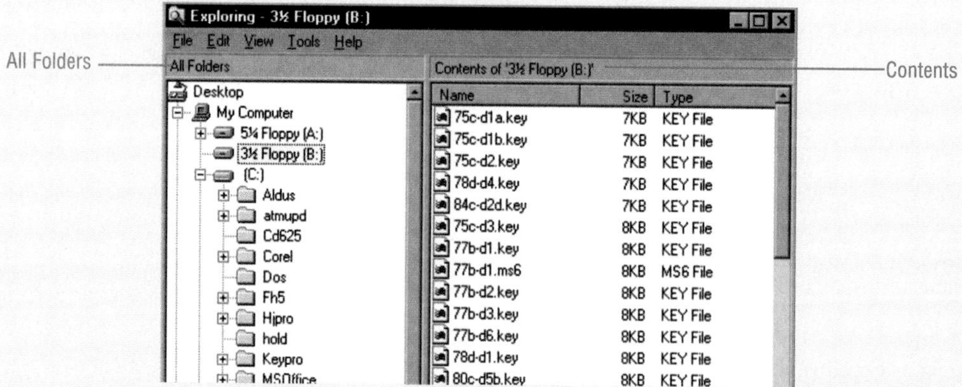

When you select a folder, the right pane displays the contents of the folder or file. The folders are arranged in a hierarchy or tree. The top-level folder on the disk is the main folder. On the hard drive (Drive C), the main folder is Desktop. On the floppy disk, the main folder is represented by the drive icon. This folder was created when your disk was formatted. All folders branch from the main folder.

Small boxes containing plus (+) or minus (-) symbols display to the left of some icons. Boxes containing a plus sign indicate folders have sublevels not currently displayed. If a box contains a minus sign, the folder is already expanded.

REFERENCE GUIDE

Abbreviations

1. If the reader may not be familiar with an abbreviation, spell it out the first time it is used and place the abbreviation in parentheses.
   computer-aided design (CAD)
   Certified Public Accountant (CPA)
2. One space follows a period used after an abbreviation and no space follows a period within an abbreviation.
   Mr. Jones p.m.
3. Spell out street names; exceptions are designators such as NW.
   Mill Avenue Bay Street 123 Rolling Hills SE
4. Use two-letter state abbreviations only with ZIP Codes.
   Cincinnati, OH 45241-3421
5. Do not abbreviate the name of a city, state, or country except when space is a problem. ("Saint" is usually abbreviated as St. in the United States.)
   Fort Worth Mount Rainier Wisconsin
   St. Louis Port Arthur United Kingdom
6. Abbreviate names of government and private agencies, organizations, radio and television stations.
   SBA ABC IBM
7. Company names often contain abbreviations such as Bros., Co., Corp., Inc., Ltd., and &. Check the letterhead for proper style.
8. Abbreviate titles used with full names or last names only.
   Mr. Messrs. (plural of Mr.) Mrs. Mmes.
9. Abbreviate titles, academic degrees, and professional titles following names.
   Steven Frey, Esq.
   Charles Forde, Ph.D.
   George Hays, Jr.
10. Business expressions, days and months, and measurements may be abbreviated in technical documents, lists, business forms, in some routine documents, or when space is a problem. Check a dictionary if in doubt about whether the abbreviation is correct.

acct.	accounting	Mon.	Monday
amt.	amount	Jan.	January
FYI	for your information	in. or in	inches

Capitalization

Capitalize:

1. First word of a sentence and of a direct quotation.
   She put the car in storage.
   He said, "Here is my book."
2. First word after a colon if it begins a complete sentence.
   Warning: The floors are slippery when wet.
3. Names of specific persons or places and their derivatives; do not capitalize commonly accepted derivatives.
   The New River passes by Price State University.
   The French fashions were displayed; french toast was served on fine china.
4. Distinctive title or personal title that precedes a name and a title in an address or signature line. Do not capitalize titles following names, unless in an address or signature line.
   Dr. Sun called Senator Dobbs.
   Ms. Jane Holmes, Advertising Director
   Kay is a vice president.
5. Specific course titles or courses derived from a proper noun; do not capitalize general courses.
   American History Keyboarding 1 word processing
6. First and main words in headings or titles in books, songs, etc.; do not capitalize articles, conjunctions, and prepositions of fewer than four letters.
   I saw the photo in *Computers in the News.*
   The topic "Interview for the Position" was omitted.
7. Weekdays, months, and holidays.
   Let's meet each Monday in May except for Memorial Day.
8. Trademarks and brand names.
   I use Essex oil in my Everlasts lawn mower.
9. Specific parts of the country; do not capitalize compass points that are not part of the name.
   Midwest South north of town
10. Specific departments or groups within the writer's organization.
    The Board of Directors discussed the restructuring of our Sales Department.
11. Nouns before a figure except for some common nouns.
    Unit 1, Section 2 page 2, verse 7, line 2

Number expression

General guidelines:

1. Use words for numbers one through ten unless the numbers are in a category with related larger numbers that are expressed as figures.

   He bought 75 acres of land.
   Mail two copies of the report.
   She wrote 12 stories and 13 plays in the last 2 years.

2. Use words for approximate numbers or large round numbers that can be expressed as one or two words. Use numbers for round numbers in millions or higher with their word modifier.

   About fifty representatives attended the conference.
   We sent out about three hundred invitations.
   She contributed $3 million.

3. Use words for numbers that begin a sentence.

   Six players were cut from the 37-member team.

4. Use figures for the larger of two adjacent numbers.

   We shipped six 24-ton engines.

Times and dates:

5. Use words for numbers that precede o'clock (stated or implied).

   We shall meet from two until five o'clock.

6. Use figures for times with a.m. or p.m. and days when they follow the month.

   Her appointment is for 2:15 p.m. on July 26, 1998.
   The convention will begin October 26.

7. Use ordinals for the day when it precedes the month.

   The 10th of October is my anniversary.
   The tenth of October is my anniversary. (formal)

Money, percentages, and fractions:

8. Use figures for money amounts and percentages. Spell out *cents* and *percent* except in statistical copy.

   The 16 percent discount saved me $145; Bill, 95 cents.

9. Use a combination of words and figures for very large amounts of money.

   The acquisition will cost $3 million.

10. Use words for fractions unless the fractions appear in combination with whole numbers.

    She read just one-half of her lesson.
    5 1/2 18 3/4

Addresses:

11. Use words for street names *First* through *Tenth* and figures or ordinals for streets above *Tenth*. Use figures for house numbers other than number One.

    My friend lives at One Lytle Place.
    Monica lives at 1590 Echo Lane.
    Meet me at Second Avenue and 53rd Street.

Punctuation

Use an apostrophe:

1. To show possession: Add an apostrophe and s to a singular noun.

   dog's Doug's arm fox's den Jess's book

   Exception: If adding an additional s to a noun already ending in s makes the word difficult to pronounce, add only an apostrophe.

   series' outline Los Angeles' freeways

2. To show possession: Add an apostrophe and s to a plural noun that does not end in s.

   men's shoes women's dresses children's coats

   Add only an apostrophe after a plural noun ending in s and after a proper noun of more than one syllable ending in s or z.

   trains' schedules Hernandez' trip Delores' report

3. To show possession: Add 's after the last noun in a series to indicate joint or common possession of two or more persons; however, show separate possession of two or more persons by adding 's to each noun.

   Sylvia and Jason's trip
   Myra's and Hank's class schedules

4 To form the plural of numbers (written as figures or words) and letters. Do not use an apostrophe in market quotations.

   5's five's F's AmeriTech 4s

5. To show omission of letters or figures; as a symbol for *feet* and *minutes*. Use quotation marks for *inches* and *seconds*.

   Rob't it's fine Class of '95
   an 8' x 10' rug a 5' timing 15'6" x 10'8"

Use a colon:

To indicate that a listing or statement follows.

He bought these items: a pen, six pencils, a notebook.
He said the magic words: Class is dismissed at 2:30.

Use a comma:

1. After introductory words, phrases, or dependent clauses.

   Yes, final grades have been posted.
   If I study tonight, I can go to the game.

2. Between words or groups of words that make up a series.

   Fuji, Don, Cyd, and Rod will go to Green Bay soon.
   I swam, played ball, and ran a race while at camp.

3. To set off explanatory and interrupting words, phrases, and clauses that are not necessary to the meaning of the sentence.

   I believe, however, he knows.
   Max, their expert, set up a booth next to mine.
   The outcome, he knew, was never in doubt.
   His plan, which depends on deception, will never work.

   Exception: Do not set off clauses (restrictive) that are necessary to the meaning of the sentence.

   Any students who are late will not be seated.

4. To set off words in direct address.

   I know, Joy, that you prefer classical music.

5. To set off the date from the year and the city from the state.

   On June 5, 1992, Sam finally graduated.
   Sam arrived in Honolulu, Hawaii, on June 9.

6. To separate two or more parallel adjectives (adjectives that could be separated by the word *and* instead of a comma). Do not use commas to separate adjectives so closely related that they appear to form a single element with the noun they modify.

   The quiet, efficient worker finished on time.
   He lives in a small white house under a green oak tree.

7. To separate whole numbers into groups of three digits each. However, numbers that identify rather than enumerate are usually keyed without commas.

   My books, all 1,640 of them, are in Room 8401.

8. To set off contrasting phrases and clauses.

   Her methods, not her objectives, caused us concern.

Use a dash:

1. To show an abrupt change of thought.

   Invoice #20--it was dated 3/4--billed $17.

2. To show the source of a direct quotation and certain special purposes.

   A dash separates; a hyphen joins. --Anonymous
   Yes--well, maybe--I'll try to finish on time.

Use an exclamation point:

After emotional words, phrases, or exclamatory sentences.

Look out! Hurrah! Don't drink the water!

Use a hyphen:

1. To join a compound adjective that immediately precedes the word modified.

   first-class ticket on-time arrival heart-stopping movie

2. To join compound numbers between 21 and 99 written as words and fractions used as modifiers.

   She read just one-half of about forty-five memos.

Use parentheses:

1. To enclose explanatory, parenthetical, or nonessential material.

   Our trees (maples) were red and gold (autumn colors).

2. To enclose letters or figures in a listing or figures that follow spelled-out amounts.

   Enter (a) name, (b) address, and (c) I.D. number.
   Your initial payment is fifty dollars ($50).

Use a period:

1. After a complete declaratory sentence or a courteous request (the reader is expected to act rather than answer).

   We like snow. We are ski enthusiasts.
   Will you please send the shipment by express.

2. After an abbreviation of a word.

   Mr. Juan de Leon's birthday is Jan. 5.

3. With an abbreviation made up of more than one word; space only once after the final period.

   Ellis Kato, M.D., was granted a Ph.D. today.

4. To form an ellipsis that represents an omission of words from quoted data. (Commonly 3 periods are used, but 4 are used when an ellipsis ends a sentence. Space once between ellipsis periods.)

   Says Audrey, "The three diodes . . . are not functional."
   The lawyer who was dressed in black denied any direct responsibility. . . .

Use quotation marks: (after a comma or period; before a semicolon or colon; after a question mark if the quotation itself is a question)

1. To enclose direct quotations.

   "I am not," she said, "going."

2. To enclose titles of written works, but not book titles.

   "Aida" " The Raven" "Hurricane Strikes Gulf Coast"

3. To enclose out-of-the-ordinary words or phrases.

   The "bleed" line ran off the side of the page.

Use a semicolon: (one space follows)

1. To separate two or more independent clauses in a compound sentence when the conjunction is omitted.

   Alan asked if Nick Curl was a guest; Sue left.

2. To separate independent clauses joined by a conjunctive adverb (however, therefore, etc.).

   Our costs have increased; however, our prices have not.

3. To separate a series of items that themselves contain commas.

   Provide lines for the employee's title; department; telephone number; and, of course, name.

Use an underline:

1. With titles of complete literary works.

   <u>PC World</u> <u>Daily News</u> <u>The Sun Also Rises</u>

2. To emphasize special words or phrases.

   Do you know the meaning of <u>prestidigitation</u>?

Proofreading procedures

Proofread documents so that they are free of errors. Error-free documents send the message that you are detail-oriented and a person capable of doing business. Apply these procedures after you key a document.

1. Use a spelling checker if you are using a word processing program. If not, check spelling manually.
2. Proofread the document either on screen or in hard copy to be sure that it makes sense. Check for these types of errors:
   - Words, headings, and/or amounts omitted.
   - Extra words or lines not deleted during the editing stage.
   - Incorrect sequence of numbers in a list.
   - Incorrect figures, names, or addresses.
   - Inconsistent document formatting style.
3. If using a word processing program, make corrections and reprint. If using a typewriter, make manual corrections (see correcting methods below).

Proofreaders' marks

Mark	Meaning	Mark	Meaning
#	Add horizontal space	. . . or *stet*	Let it stand; ignore correction
||	Align	/ or *lc*	Lowercase
~~	Bold		Move left
Cap or ≡	Capitalize		Move right
⁐	Close up		Move up
	Delete		Move down
^	Insert	¶	Paragraph
	Insert quotation marks	◯ *sp*	Spell out
	Insert comma	or *tr*	Transpose
	Insert apostrophe	———	Underline or italic

Word division

With the use of proportional fonts found in current word processing packages, word division is less of an issue. Occasionally, however, you will need to make decisions on dividing words. The following list contains generally accepted guidelines for dividing words.

1. Divide words between syllables only; therefore, do not divide one-syllable words.
2. Short words: Avoid dividing short words (five letters or fewer).

   area bonus since ideal
3. Double consonants: Divide words with double consonants between the double letters unless the root word ends with the double letters. In this case, divide after the second consonant.

   mis- sion trim- ming dress- ing call- ing
4. One-letter syllables: Do not divide after a one-letter syllable at the beginning of a word or before a one- or two-letter syllable at the end of a word; divide after a one-letter syllable within a word.

   enough abroad starter friendly
   ani- mal sepa- rate regu- late
5. Two single-letter syllables: Divide between two single-letter syllables within a word.

   gradu- ation evalu- ation
6. Hyphenated words: Compound words with a hyphen may be divided only after the hyphen.

   top- secret soft- spoken self- respect
7. Figures: Avoid dividing figures presented as a unit.

   #870331 190,886 1/22/98
8. Proper nouns: Avoid dividing proper nouns. If necessary, include as much of the proper noun as possible before dividing it.

   Thomas R./Lewiston not Thomas R. Lewis/ton
   November 15,/ 2000 not November/ 15, 2000

Correcting Methods

Computers

Correct errors using the backspace key or the delete key. Use the backspace key to remove characters to the left (behind) the cursor. Use the delete key to erase characters in front of the cursor.

Typewriters

Correcting key ("lift off"):

1. Move print point to incorrect character. (On current line, use backspace key or space bar; on previous lines, use the "previous line" function—see manufacturer's booklet.)
2. Strike the correcting key. (To erase more than one character, strike the repeat key or strike the correcting key again.)
3. Key the correct character(s).
4. Move print point to the position it was in before correction. (Relocate key is available on most electronic models.)

White out

1. Select fluid the same color as the paper.
2. Move the paper up or down to make the error accessible.
3. Brush on the fluid sparingly, lightly covering the error.
4. Turn paper to position it was in before correction; key the correct character(s).

Addressing procedures

When preparing an envelope, follow the spacing guidelines below:

Small envelope. On a No. 6 3/4 envelope, place the address near the center—about 2 inches from the top and left edges. Place a return address in the upper left corner (line 2, 3 spaces from left edge).

Large envelope. On a No. 10 envelope, place the address near the center—about line 14 and .5" left of center. A return address, if not preprinted, should be keyed in the upper left corner (see small envelope).

An address must contain at least three lines; addresses of more than six lines should be avoided. The last line of an address must contain three items of information ONLY: (1) the city, (2) the state, and (3) the ZIP Code, preferably a 9-digit code.

Place mailing notations that affect postage (e.g., REGISTERED, CERTIFIED) below the stamp position (line 8); place other special notations (e.g., CONFIDENTIAL, PERSONAL) a DS below the return address.

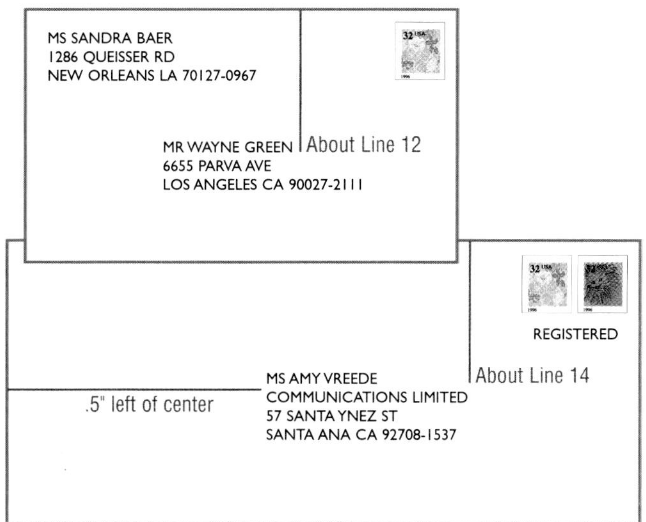

Folding and inserting procedures

Step 1 | Step 2 | Step 3

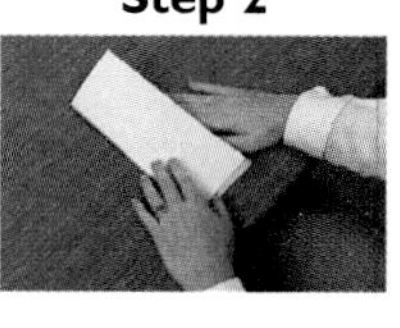

Large envelopes (No. 10, 9, 7 3/4)

Step 1: With document face up, fold slightly less than 1/3 of sheet up toward top.

Step 2: Fold down top of sheet to within 1/2" of bottom fold.

Step 3: Insert document into envelope with last crease toward bottom of envelope.

Small envelopes (No. 6 3/4, 6 1/4)

Step 1 | Step 2 | Step 3

Step 1: With document face up, fold bottom up to 1/2" from top.

Step 2: Fold right third to left.

Step 3: Fold left third to 1/2" from last crease and insert last creased edge first.

Window envelopes (full sheet)

Step 1 | Step 2 | Step 3

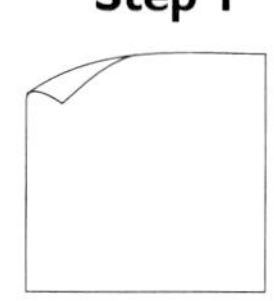
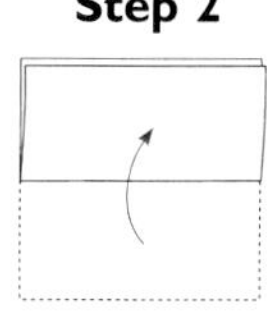

Step 1: With sheet face down, top toward you, fold upper third down.

Step 2: Fold lower third up so address is showing.

Step 3: Insert document into envelope with last crease toward bottom of envelope.

Two-letter state abbreviations

Alabama, AL
Alaska, AK
Arizona, AZ
Arkansas, AR
California, CA
Colorado, CO
Connecticut, CT
Delaware, DE
District of Columbia, DC
Florida, FL
Georgia, GA
Guam, GU
Hawaii, HI
Idaho, ID
Illinois, IL
Indiana, IN
Iowa, IA
Kansas, KS
Kentucky, KY
Louisiana, LA
Maine, ME
Maryland, MD
Massachusetts, MA
Michigan, MI
Minnesota, MN
Mississippi, MS
Missouri, MO
Montana, MT
Nebraska, NE
Nevada, NV
New Hampshire, NH
New Jersey, NJ
New Mexico, NM
New York, NY
North Carolina, NC
North Dakota, ND
Ohio, OH
Oklahoma, OK
Oregon, OR
Pennsylvania, PA
Puerto Rico, PR
Rhode Island, RI
South Carolina, SC
South Dakota, SD
Tennessee, TN
Texas, TX
Utah, UT
Vermont, VT
Virgin Islands, VI
Virginia, VA
Washington, WA
West Virginia, WV
Wisconsin, WI
Wyoming, WY

Letter parts

Letterhead. Company name and address. May include other data.

Date. Date letter is mailed. Usually in month, day, year order. Military style is an option (day/month/year: 17/1/98).

Letter address. Address of the person who will receive the letter. Include personal title (*Mr., Ms., Dr.*), name, professional title, company, and address.

Salutation. Greeting. Corresponds to the first line of the letter address. Usually includes name and courtesy title; use *Ladies and Gentlemen* if letter is addressed to a company name.

Body. Message. SS; DS between paragraphs.

Complimentary close. Farewell, such as *Sincerely.*

Writer. Name and professional title. Women may include a personal title; use Ms. if unknown.

Initials. Identifies person who keyed the document (for example, *tr*). May include identification of writer (*ARB:tri*).

Enclosure. Copy is enclosed with the document. May specify contents.

Copy notation. Indicates that a copy of the letter is being sent to person named.

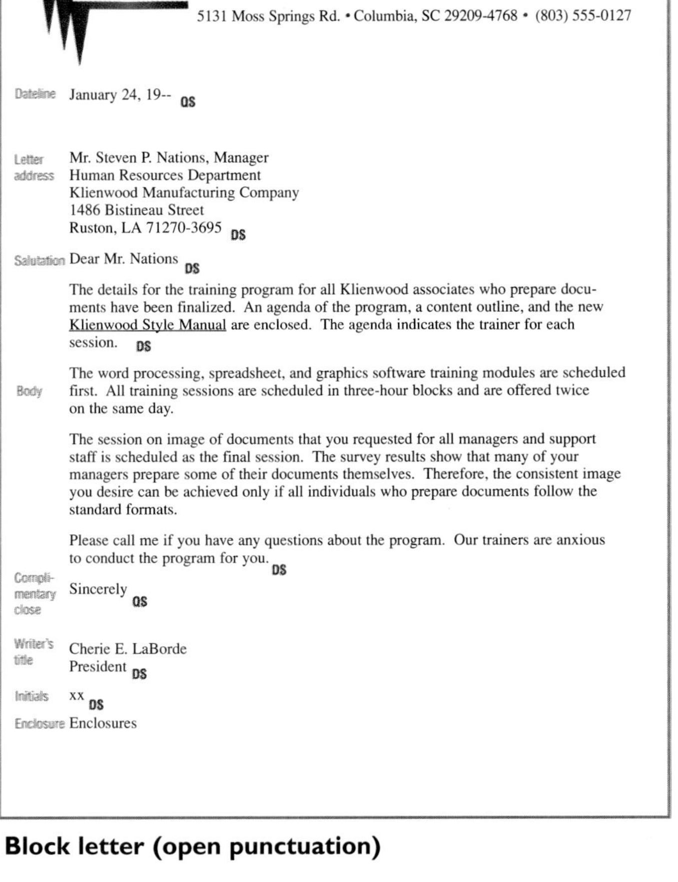
IMAGE MAKERS
5131 Moss Springs Rd. • Columbia, SC 29209-4768 • (803) 555-0127

Dateline January 24, 19-- QS

Letter address
Mr. Steven P. Nations, Manager
Human Resources Department
Klienwood Manufacturing Company
1486 Bistineau Street
Ruston, LA 71270-3695 DS

Salutation Dear Mr. Nations DS

Body
The details for the training program for all Klienwood associates who prepare documents have been finalized. An agenda of the program, a content outline, and the new Klienwood Style Manual are enclosed. The agenda indicates the trainer for each session. DS

The word processing, spreadsheet, and graphics software training modules are scheduled first. All training sessions are scheduled in three-hour blocks and are offered twice on the same day.

The session on image of documents that you requested for all managers and support staff is scheduled as the final session. The survey results show that many of your managers prepare some of their documents themselves. Therefore, the consistent image you desire can be achieved only if all individuals who prepare documents follow the standard formats.

Please call me if you have any questions about the program. Our trainers are anxious to conduct the program for you. DS

Complimentary close Sincerely QS

Writer's title
Cherie E. LaBorde
President DS

Initials xx DS

Enclosure Enclosures

Block letter (open punctuation)

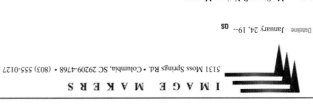

IMAGE MAKERS
5131 Moss Springs Rd. • Columbia, SC 29209-4768 • (803) 555-0127

October 27, 19-- QS

Ms. Vera M. Hayes, President
Vera's Word Processing Services
4927 Stuart Avenue
Baton Rouge, LA 70808-3519 DS

Dear Ms. Hayes: DS

The format of this letter is called modified block. Modified block format differs from block format in that the date, complimentary close, and the signature lines are positioned at the center point. DS

Paragraphs may be blocked, as this letter illustrates, or they may be indented five spaces from the left margin. We suggest you block paragraphs when you use modified block style so that an additional tab setting is not needed. However, some people who use modified block format prefer indented paragraphs.

Although modified block format is very popular, we recommend that you use it only for those customers who request this letter style. Otherwise, we urge you to use block format, which is more efficient, as your standard style.

Both formats are illustrated in the enclosed Image Makers Format Guide. Please note that the block format is labeled "computer compatible." DS

Sincerely, QS

Patrick R. Ray
Communication Consultant

xx DS

Enclosure DS

c Scot Carl, Account Manager

Modified block letter (mixed punctuation)

IMAGE MAKERS
5131 Moss Springs Rd. • Columbia, SC 29209-4768

MR STEVEN P NATIONS MANAGER
HUMAN RESOURCES DEPARTMENT
KLIENWOOD MANUFACTURING COMPANY
1486 BISTINEAU STREET
RUSTON LA 71270-3695

Envelope

Letter placement table

Letter length	Variable side margins	Standard side margins	Dateline
Short	2"	1"	line 18 (3")
Average	1.5"	1"	line 16 (2.67")
Long	1"	1"	line 14 (2.3")

- For increased efficiency, use standard placement.
- Adjust dateline up if letter contains a table or special features.
- Place dateline a DS below a deep letterhead.
- Position dateline on line 12 when a window envelope is used.

IMAGE MAKERS
5131 Moss Springs Rd. • Columbia, SC 29209-4768 • (803) 555-0127

October 28, 19-- QS

Subject Line: Indicates the main topic of the letter. It may be keyed in all capital letters or main words capitalized.

Ms. Vera M. Hayes, President
Vera's Word Processing Services
4927 Stuart Avenue
Baton Rouge, LA 70808-3519 DS

Simplified Block Letter Format DS

The format of this letter is called simplified block letter format. This letter style is similar to block format in that all lines are positioned at the left margin. However, the simplified block format does not contain a salutation or a complimentary close. A subject line is required with this style. As the label implies, a subject line indicates the main topic of the letter. The key words contained in a subject line help office personnel to sort and route incoming mail and to code documents for storage and retrieval. DS

The simplified block format is especially useful when the name or title of the receiver of the letter is unknown. For example, a person writing for hotel reservations likely would not know the name of the reservation clerk. With simplified block style, the letter can be addressed to the hotel, and the subject line should indicate that the letter is a request for reservations. DS

In some simplified letter styles, the subject line is preceded and followed by a triple space. Please note that a double space precedes and follows the subject line in this letter. We have eliminated the use of triple spacing in document formats to simplify the processing of documents. As you will note, the simplified block letter format is one of the recommended formats in the enclosed Image Makers Format Guide. QS

Patrick R. Ray
Communication Consultant DS

xx

Simplified block format

Special letter parts/features

Attention line. Directs the letter to a specific person within the company. Positioned as the first line of letter address; the salutation is *Ladies and Gentlemen*.

Company name. Company name of the sender is keyed in ALL CAPS a DS below complimentary close; may be used when plain paper rather than letterhead is used or when the document is in the nature of a contract.

Enumerations. Hanging indent format; block format may be used if paragraphs are not indented.

Mailing notation. Provides record of how the letter was sent (FACSIMILE, CERTIFIED, REGISTERED) or how the letter should be treated by the receiver (CONFIDENTIAL). DS below date.

Postscript. Used to emphasize information; DS below last line of copy.

Reference line. Directs the reader to a source document such as an invoice. DS below letter address.

Second-page heading. Addressee's name, page number, date arranged in block format about 1" from the top edge. Second sheet is plain paper of the same quality as letterhead.

Subject line. Indicates topic of the letter; DS below salutation at left margin.

MARGO'S CLOTHING
50 River Road
Lynn, MA 01852-6927
201-555-1212

March 15, 19--

Attention Fashion Buyer
Amason Fashion Mart
4385 Felten Dive
Hays, KS 67601-2863 DS

Ladies and Gentlemen DS

FALL FASHION CAMPAIGN

The demand for two of the items that were sent last week was much greater than originally expected; there-

Attention line/Subject line

Your order should be shipped via Pony Express within the next two weeks.

Thank you for your order; we appreciate your business.

Sincerely DS

STYLES BY REX QS

Ms. Ellen Turnquist
General Manager

rt

Company name

WILSON INDUSTRIES
20 Marietta Street
Atlanta, GA 30303-6280 • 404-555-1212

March 15, 19-- DS

CERTIFIED MAIL DS

Mr. John West, Buyer
Tatnal Music Center
4385 Dove Avenue
Rigby, ID 83442-1244 DS

Re: Order No. R-3855 DS

Dear Mr. West

The items that you ordered last week were sent by overnight delivery so that you could have these items by

Mailing notation/Reference line

1"

Mr. Jason Artis
Page 2
April 9, 19-- DS

You will need to perform the following steps:

1. Review the sample projects and proposed guidelines.
2. Determine the specific responsibilities of the project manager and put these in writing.

Thank you, Mr. Artis, for your cooperation. It is always a pleasure working with you.

Very truly yours

Second-page heading
Enumerated items (hanging indent format)

Turner Roofing Co.
10318 Rearview Ave.
Dayton, OH 45029-1927

CERTIFIED MAIL

MR JACK BROWN
QUALITY TRAINING ASSOCIATES
28 REVINA DRIVE
ATLANTA GA 30346-9105

Envelope with mailing notation

Sincerely QS

Ms. Rae Mathias, President DS

pr DS

The cashmere sweaters will be shipped by air to you just as soon as our stock is replenished. You will find them well worth the wait.

Postscript

Current date

(Variable 1-Name)
(Variable 2-Address)

Dear (Variable 3-Salutation)

Thank you for enrolling in the (Variable 4-Class) swimming class that runs from (Variable 5-Date). Your class will meet from (Variable 6-Time) Monday through Thursday. Fridays will be reserved for rainouts or makeups.

Our pool is open from 9 a.m. to 10 p.m. daily. You will have many opportunities to benefit from additional practice and just have fun and relaxation in the sun and pool. The enclosed brochure provides a list of other classes and recreational activities available this summer.

Please come by the recreation office before the first day of class to secure your pool pass. We look forward to having you as a part of this summer's swim classes.

Sincerely

Shane D. Randall
Recreation Director

xx

Enclosure

Form letter with variables

Current date

Mr. Brian Lipscomb
P.O. Box 3293
Starkville, MS 39759-8776

Dear Brian

Thank you for enrolling in the Beginner I swimming class that runs from June 1-10. Your class will meet from 8-8:45 p.m. Monday through Thursday. Fridays will be reserved for rainouts or makeups.

Our pool is open from 9 a.m. to 10 p.m. daily. You will have many opportunities to benefit from additional practice and just have fun and relaxation in the sun and pool. The enclosed brochure provides a list of other classes and recreational activities available this summer.

Please come by the recreation office before the first day of class to secure your pool pass. We look forward to having you as a part of this summer's swim classes.

Sincerely

Shane D. Randall
Recreation Director

xx

Enclosure

Completed form letter

Current date

{FIELD}Name~
{FIELD}Address~

Dear {FIELD}Firstname~

Thank you for enrolling in the {FIELD}Class~ swimming class that runs from {FIELD}Date~. Your class will meet from {FIELD}Time~ Monday through Thursday. Fridays will be reserved for rainouts or makeups.

Our pool is open from 9 a.m. to 10 p.m. daily. You will have many opportunities to benefit from additional practice and just have fun and relaxation in the sun and pool. The enclosed brochure provides a list of other classes and recreational activities available this summer.

Please come by the recreation office before the first day of class to secure your pool pass. We look forward to having you as a part of this summer's swim classes.

Sincerely

Shane D. Randall
Recreation Director

xx

Enclosure

Form letter with variables coded (primary document)

```
Name~Address~Firstname~Class~Date~Time~~
============================================================
Mr. Brian Lipscomb{END FIELD}
P.O. Box 3293
Starkville, MS 39759-8776{END FIELD}
Brian{END FIELD}
Beginner I{END FIELD}
June 1-10{END FIELD}
8-8:45 p.m.{END FIELD}
{END RECORD}
============================================================
Ms. Mary Miquelard{END FIELD}
88 Glenn Street
Columbus, MS 39701-8249{END FIELD}
Mary{END FIELD}
Intermediate{END FIELD}
June 14-25{END FIELD}
6-6:45 p.m.{END FIELD}
{END REPORT}
============================================================
```

Variables (secondary document)

Katrina W. Cassidy
763 East Hillside Drive
Bloomington, IN 47401-3692
(812) 555-6862

Current date

The return address may be keyed immediately above the date, or you may create a personal letterhead as shown here.

Mr. Paige Bass, Editor
Financial News
2413 West Maple Avenue
Flint, MI 48507-2754

Dear Mr. Bass

Your advertisement in the Desktop Report indicates you have a production management position available for someone with graphic design experience and knowledge. I have both knowledge and experience in graphic design; therefore, please consider me for the position.

Desktop publishing training and experience as assistant editor and producer of the Central Alumni News enabled me to develop the skills you desire. The enclosed resume presents additional information showing you why I am qualified for the position.

May I come in and tell you about the project for which I won a design award? Please let me know the time and date that would be most convenient.

Sincerely

Katrina W. Cassidy

Enclosure

Personal business letter

1" top margin

KATRINA W. CASSIDY

Temporary Address (May 30, 1994)
763 East Hillside Drive
Bloomington, IN 47401-3692
(812) 555-6862

Permanent Address
3467 Senate Lane
Kokomo, IN 46902-1835
(317) 555-6065

Career Objective

A graphic design position with an opportunity to advance to a management position.

Qualifications and Special Skills

1" side margins

Desktop Publishing Skills. Key at 70 words per minute. In-depth knowledge and experience using several leading desktop publishing, word processing, and graphics software packages.

Computer Skills. Basic knowledge of major computer operating systems and database and spreadsheet software.

Communication/Interpersonal Skills. Superior interpersonal, speaking, writing, editing, and design layout skills.

Education

Central University, Bloomington, Indiana, Candidate for Bachelor of Business Administration Degree, May, 1994. Majored in administrative management (3.2 grade point average). Serve as president of Professional Women on Campus.

Kokomo Junior College, Kokomo, Indiana, Associate Degree,1992. Majored in administrative systems (3.6 grade point average). Served as editor of the Kokomo Reporter.

Southside High School, Kokomo, Indiana, diploma, 1990. Graduated in top 10 percent of class; served as junior class vice president and senior class president.

Experience

Central University Alumni Office, Bloomington, Indiana. Assistant editor and producer of the Central Alumni News, 1993 to present time. Worked 25 hours per week. Responsible for editing six features and for the layout and production. Met every publishing deadline and won a design award. Production manager of the Central Alumni News, 1992-93. Worked 25 hours per week. Managed layout and production and supervised all desktop publishing activities.

References

Request portfolio from Central University Placement Office.

Resume

T.K. Design Studios
Interoffice Communications

tab (1" from left margin)

TO: Maude M. Tassin 1.5" or line 10
DS
FROM: Patrick R. Ray

DATE: November 5, 19--

SUBJECT: Memorandum Forms for Vera's Word Processing Services

1" side margins

Please design three memorandum forms for Vera's Word Processing Services. Ms. Hayes operates word processing services in New Orleans and Lafayette, as well as in Baton Rouge. Copies of the letterheads used in each office are on file in the Design Department.
DS

Ms. Hayes has requested that the forms for all three offices meet the following specifications: DS

1. Each memo form should contain the address and telephone number of one of the three offices, and the standard printed headings should appear on all forms. DS
2. All of the memo forms should be a full sheet.
3. The last character of the headings should be aligned vertically five picas from the left edge. Thus, the word processing specialists at Vera's can use the one-inch default margins on their systems both to insert the heading information two spaces after the printed headings and to block the message flush left.

I hope you will be able to have the approval drafts ready for Ms. Hayes within a week. We made a commitment to have final forms ready in two weeks. Please let me know if this schedule presents a problem for you.
DS

xx

Standard memo

T.K. Design Studios
300 Fourth Street
New Orleans, LA 89210-2010 • (800) 555-6522

November 5, 19-- QS 1.5" or line 10

Maude Tassin DS

Memorandum Forms for Vera's Word Processing Services

Please design three memorandum forms for Vera's Word Processing Services. Ms. Hayes operates word processing services in New Orleans and LaFayette, as well as in Baton Rouge. Copies of the letterheads used in each office are on file in the Design Department.
QS

Patrick R. Ray

xx

Simplified memo format

T.K. Design Studios
Interoffice Communications

To: Distribution List 1.5" or line 10
DS
From: Jane Leventis

Date: Current

Subject: Multiple Recipients of Memo
DS
One way to handle a memo received by multiple individuals is to use a distribution list. This memo illustrates the use of a distribution list.

lap
DS
Distribution List:
Charlie Phelan
Annette Marks
Rod Yazel

Memo on a preprinted form with distribution list

Standard unbound report and outline format

Margins. *Top* 1.5" for first page and reference page; 1" for succeeding pages; *Side* 1" or default; *bottom* 1".

Spacing. *Educational reports*: DS, paragraphs indented .5". *Business reports:* SS, paragraphs blocked with a DS between ¶s.

Page numbers. Second and subsequent pages are numbered at top right of the page. DS follows the page number.

Main headings. Centered; ALL CAPS.

Side headings. Underlined; main words capitalized; DS above and below.

Paragraph headings. Underlined; capitalize first word, followed by a period.

Note: Larger fonts may also be used for headings.

Report documentation

Internal citation. Provides source of information within report. Includes the author's surname, publication date, and page number (Bruce, 1994, 129).

Endnotes. Superior figure keyed at point of reference within report. All sources placed on a separate page at the end of the report in numerical order. Endnotes precede the bibliography or references.

Bibliography or references. List all references, whether quoted or not, in alphabetical order by authors' names. References may be formatted on the last page of the report if they all fit on the page; if not, list on a separate, numbered page.

1.5"

EFFECTIVE PRESENTATIONS DS

I. PLANNING AND PREPARING PRESENTATION DS
   A. Opening
      1. Gain attention
      2. Set the tone
   B. Body of the Presentation
      1. Focus on objective
      2. Organize information
      3. Prepare support materials
   C. Closing
DS

II. DELIVERING PRESENTATIONS DS
   A. Delivery Techniques
      1. Engage audience
      2. Project voice effectively
      3. Control environment
   B. Visuals and Supporting Materials
      1. Ensure readability
      2. Use effectively

III. FOLLOW-UP ACTIVITIES
   A. Discussion and Questions
   B. Postpresentation Activities

Outline

1.5" or line 10 BASIC STEPS IN REPORT WRITING QS

The effective writer makes certain that reports that leave her or his desk are technically correct in style, usable in content, and attractive in format. DS

Side heading — The First Step DS

Information is gathered about the subject; the effective writer takes time to outline the data to be used in the report. This approach allows the writer to establish the organization of the report. When a topic outline is used, order of presentation, important points, and even various headings can be determined and followed easily when writing begins.

The Correct Style

1" side margins — The purpose of the report often determines its style. Most academic reports (term papers, for example) are double-spaced with indented paragraphs. Most business reports, however, are single-spaced; and paragraphs are blocked. When a style is not stipulated, general usage may be followed.

The Finished Product

The most capable writer will refrain from making a report deliberately impressive, especially if doing so makes it less expressive. The writer does, however, follow the outline carefully as a first draft is written. Obvious errors are ignored momentarily. Refinement comes later, after all the preliminary work is done. The finished document will then be read and reread to ensure it is clear, concise, correct, and complete.

First page of unbound report

2 DS

and thus oxygen becomes a crucial part of any aquatic ecosystem. Dissolved oxygen is derived from the atmosphere as well as from the photosynthetic processes of aquatic plants. Oxygen, in turn, is consumed through the life activities of most aquatic animals and plants (Bruce, 1994, 129). When dissolved oxygen reaches very low levels in the aquatic environment, unfavorable conditions for fish and other aquatic life can develop.

Conclusion

The absence of dissolved oxygen may give rise to unpleasant odors produced through anaerobic (no oxygen) decomposition. On the other hand, an adequate supply of oxygen helps maintain a healthy environment for fish and other aquatic life and may help prevent the development of unacceptable conditions that are caused by the decomposition of municipal and industrial waste (Ryn, 1993, 29). QS

REFERENCES QS

Book — Beard, Fred F. The Fulford County Dilemma. Niagara Falls: Dawn General Press, 1992. DS

Periodical — Bruce, Lois L. "Hazardous Waste Management: A History." State of Idaho Bulletin No. 7312. Boise: State of Idaho Press, 1994.

Ryn, Jewel Scott. "But Please Don't Drink the Water." Journal of Environmental Science, Winter 1993.

Second page of unbound report with references

2"

GUIDES FOR PREPARING MEETING DOCUMENTATION

2"

Prepared for
Mr. Justin Markland
Executive Vice President

2"

Prepared by
(Your name)
Administrative Manager

2"

Current date

Title page—leftbound

TABLE OF CONTENTS

iii

Table of contents—leftbound

GUIDES FOR PREPARING MEETING DOCUMENTATION

The procedures used to prepare support documents for meetings in the Moss Springs Company were reviewed during the productivity analysis that was just completed.[1] The type of support documents used and the way in which they were prepared varied widely throughout the company. The primary documents used were meeting notices, agendas, handouts, visual aids, and minutes. Format was not consistent for any of the documents within or among departments. The following guides were compiled on the basis of the productivity review.

Annual Meeting

The following quote from the Moss Springs Company Policy Manual contains the policy for documentation of the Annual Meeting:[2]

> The Annual Meeting of the Moss Springs Company shall be held within three months of the end of the fiscal year. The Corporate Secretary shall mail to all who are eligible to attend the meeting a notice and agenda 30 days prior to the meeting. The Corporate Secretary shall prepare a verbatim record of the meeting and provide each member of the Board of Directors with a copy of the minutes within two weeks of the meeting. The minutes shall be a part of the permanent records of the Moss Springs Company.

Other Meetings

Meetings other than the Annual Meeting will be held at the discretion of the Board of Directors and the appropriate company managers. Regular meetings of the Board of Directors are scheduled on the first Wednesday of each month. Special meetings may be called as needed. Documentation for regular and "called" meetings of the Board are described in the following paragraphs.

Support Documents

The Senior Management Committee requires that an agenda be distributed prior to all formal meetings of committees and of staff at the departmental level or higher. Minutes must be prepared and distributed to all participants after the meeting. Support documents for informal meetings and work units are left to the discretion of the individuals conducting the meetings.

First page of leftbound report (bold headings)

1.5" 4

ENDNOTES
QS

[1]Anil Wasu, Enhancing Productivity: The Moss Springs Company, 1994, p. 24.

[2]Moss Springs Company Policy Manual, 1994, p. 42.

[3]Mary Anderson, Effective Meetings, 1993, pp. 74-86.

QS
REFERENCES
QS

Anderson, Mary. Effective Meetings. Boston: Bay Publishing Co., 1993.

Moss Springs Company Policy Manual. Chicago: 1994.

Wasu, Anil. Enhancing Productivity: The Moss Springs Company. Chicago: Productivity Consultants, Inc., 1994.

Endnotes and References

Table format

Main heading: Centered; ALL CAPS; bold is optional.

Secondary heading: Centered; main words capitalized; bold is optional.

Columns: Vertical lists of information. Generally SS long table (20 lines or more); DS short tables. Tables within a document use the same spacing as the document.

Rows: Horizontal lines of information.

Cell: Intersection of a column and a row.

Columnar headings: Blocked or centered over columns and underlined. DS above and below. Bold is optional.

Intercolumnar space: Space between columns varies depending on the width and number of columns:

Narrow	2 columns (3 if narrow)	10 spaces
Average	3 columns (4 if narrow)	6-8 spaces
Wide	4 or more columns	4-6 spaces

Vertical placement: 1.5" or 2" top margin or centered vertically on the page. Tables within documents are separated with a DS below last line of text.

Guides to tabs

Left tab: Aligns copy at the left.

Decimal tab: Aligns text at the decimal.

Right tab: Aligns copy at the right edge of a column. A decimal tab will also align copy at the right.

Decimal	**Left**	**Right**
1,200.50	Chambers	Helen
47.30	Montgomery	Rob

EXCELLENCE IN CUSTOMER SERVICE DS

Videotape Version DS

Title of Module ← row →	Videotape Time	Cost DS
Image Building	24 minutes	$ 79
Quality Service	45 minutes	99
Problem Solving	[40 minutes]	89
↑ column	↑ cell	

Table: Blocked column headings

PURCHASE AGREEMENT DS

Item No.	Quantity	Price SS
R38475-L	12	$84.50
C92579-T	5	9.75
X47824-L	20	98.99 SS

Ruled table: Centered column headings

Guidelines for formatting tables

Use the centering feature to center columns between margins. Word processing software may utilize the table feature.

1. *Electronic typewriters:* Move margins to left and right edges of scale; clear tabs. *Word processing:* Use default margins or equal margins.
2. Center the key line (longest item in each column and inter-column space); note position of each column.
3. Set the left margin at Column 1 and tabs for the remaining columns according to the printout/display.
4. Delete the key line; center heading; key table.

Guides to vertical centering

Text that is centered vertically has equal or near equal top and bottom margins. Use the **center page** feature to center text if you are using word processing software. To center text vertically, follow these steps:

1. Count lines to be centered, including blank lines.
2. Subtract lines to be centered from lines available on page (66).
3. Divide remaining lines by 2 for the top margin. Begin on the next line.

$$\text{Top margin} = \frac{\text{Lines available} - \text{Lines used}}{2}$$

1.5" or line 10 **REPORT WRITING SERIES** DS

Guide 6 QS

This sixth guide in the series of ten guides is designed to improve and standardize the reporting process in all divisions of Marcus Computer Services, Inc. Guide 6 has the dual objectives of enhancing readability and emphasizing key ideas effectively. Effective formatting is central to both of these objectives.

Readability DS

Vocabulary, sentence and paragraph length and structure, and formatting affect the readability of a document. Particular attention should be paid to these factors in preparing reports.

Vocabulary. Word length affects the difficulty level of copy; however, familiarity of words may be more important than the length of words. Multisyllable, technical, and unfamiliar words should be minimized in reports to enhance readability.

Sentence and paragraph length and structure. Variety may be essential, but direct order and reasonably short sentences and paragraphs enhance readability. The following guides are helpful in judging average sentence and paragraph length: DS

Units of Measure	Sentences	Paragraphs DS
Words (average)	18	75
Lines (average)	2	8

DS

Formatting. Effective use of white space affects readability. Appropriate line length, space between paragraphs, and vertical placement set material apart and make it easier to read.

Emphasis Techniques

Extra space and underlining were traditional emphasis techniques. Current technology makes bold and large-sized fonts (when they are available) more effective emphasis techniques. Both bold and underlining can be used when large-sized fonts are not available. Marcus standard style has been changed from using a triple space before headings for emphasis to using bold, which is a more effective emphasis technique. It is also easier to format.

Report with table

1.5"

SALES KICK-OFF MEETING

January 4, 19-- DS

Agenda DS

Goal Attainment .... Mark Rex
Assessment of Past Year by Region
President's Club Award

1" Strategic Plan .... Jan Lang 1"
Company Directions
Market Strategy

Compensation Plan .... Lynn Ray
Commission Changes
Benefit Changes

Sales Team Meeting .... Sales Managers

Agenda

1.5"

SALES KICK-OFF MEETING
January 4, 19-- DS
Action Minutes QS

Presiding: President Mark Rex

Participants: All Marketing and Sales Staff DS

1" President Rex summarized the results for the year and commended Region 3 for attaining its goals. He presented 146 President's Club Awards (list attached). 1"

Jan Lang, national sales manager, presented the new directions and the marketing strategies to attain the goals set. A 15 percent increase in overall sales is the target for the year.

Lynn Ray, vice president of human resources, presented the new compensation plans and announced that dental coverage is now provided.

Sales teams met individually.

Action minutes

1" or 1.5"

ITINERARY FOR CARL BATES
April 2-3, 19-- QS

Monday, April 2	**Atlanta to Denver** DS
10:05 a.m.	Leave Atlanta, MCC Flight 286; breakfast; arrive Dallas at 11:15 a.m.
11:53 p.m.	Leave Dallas, MCC Flight 32; arrive Denver at 1:10 p.m.; met by Jane Covington; reservations at the Mountainview Hotel (Confirmation #295864).
3:30 p.m.	Meet with Jane Covington and Mark Hansin, Snowbank Room of Mountainview.
7:30 p.m.	Dinner with Jeff and Annette Greenwald at the Cliffhanger. DS
Tuesday, April 3	**Denver to Atlanta** DS
8:30 a.m.	Breakfast with Jane Covington and Mark Hanson in the Coffee Shop, then meet in Snowbank Room until 2:30 p.m. Lunch served at 12:14 p.m.
3:30 p.m.	Leave Denver, MCC Flight 365 to Atlanta; dinner, 7:00 p.m.; arrive 8:30 p.m.

(1" left and right margins)

Itinerary

CUPERTINO ELECTRONICS 582 Elsinore Place, Cincinnati, OH 45206-3341, Tel. 800-555-1941

PURCHASE ORDER
Purchase Order No.: 395RT2394
Date: 11/14/--
Date Required: 11/30/--
Terms: 2/10, n/30
Shipped Via: Bayou Transfers

ARDOIN AND ASSOCIATES
375 WEEKS DRIVE
YOUNGSVILLE LA 70592-5724

Quantity	Description/Stock No.	Unit Price		Total	
12	Continuous Banner Paper, CP3853	10	75	129	00
6	Dart Fax Paper, TP2905	14	95	89	70
4	XT Rewritable Optical Disks	249	95	999	80
10	Dart Glare Shields	49	25	492	50
				1,711	00

CUPERTINO EONICS 582 Elsinore Place, Cincinnati, OH 45206-3341, Tel. 800-555-1941

INVOICE
Date: March 24, 19--
Customer Order No.: 2945CT3
Our Order No.: TC21087
Date Shipped: 3/24/--
Shipped Via: Cajun Shipping
Terms: Net 30 days

THE SCHULTZ COMPANY
129 RENA DRIVE
LAFAYETTE LA 70504-2853

Quantity	Description/Stock No.	Unit Price		Total	
24	10-Pack Diskette Boxes, 3.5", CP2384	12	95	310	80
20	Diskette Trays With Locks, 3.5", CP7042	39	69	793	80
8	Modem, 9600FP, CP9938	1,849	99	14,799	92
16	Six-Outlet Power Strip, ES2750	24	95	399	20
				16,303	72

Purchase order and Invoice

INDEX